PHILOSOPHY OF BEING

PHILOSOPHY OF BEING

A Reconstructive Essay in Metaphysics

Oliva Blanchette

The Catholic University of America Press
Washington, D.C.

LIBRARY OF CONGRESS CATALOGING-IN-PUBLICATION DATA

Blanchette, Oliva.

Philosophy of being : a reconstructive essay in metaphysics / by Oliva Blanchette.

p. cm.

Includes bibliographical references and index.

ISBN 0-8132-1095-X (cloth : alk. paper) — ISBN 0-8132-1096-8 (pbk.: alk. paper)

1. Ontology.   2. Title.

BD331 .B565 20002

111—dc21

2001042083

To
Nicole and Frances

Daughters
who have shown me
the goodness of difference
in the analogy of being

Contents

Contents   xi

Preface and Acknowledgments

‿≈

ETAPHYSICS has had a long and checkered career in the history of
Western philosophy. After a brilliant beginning in ancient Greek
philosophy it all but disappeared, at least in its Aristotelian form, beyond the
sands of Syria and Palestine into cultural centers like Baghdad and Teheran
following the destruction of the last great library of antiquity in the West at
Alexandria. It made a brilliant comeback in the Middle Ages by way of
North Africa and Spain thanks to Arabic, Jewish, and Christian thinkers who
brought it to new heights in their speculation about being and the divine.
Then, as a result of the challenge to everything ancient in modern philosophy, it took on a new form as abstracted from the concrete and a new name
as *ontology,* only to find itself challenged in turn by a more critical kind of
thinking bent on re-establishing contact with reality. We live in the after-
math of this challenge to modern metaphysics or ontology where the only
way to renew metaphysical inquiry may be to return to the more ancient
view of inquiry into being in the concrete.

In this respect metaphysics has to become resolutely postmodern because
the outcome of modern metaphysics has been the loss of any philosophy of
being or what Heidegger has called the total forgetfulness of being. It has to
start with a deconstruction of modern ontology, not just with a critique of
pure reason, but with a reconstruction of thought as it relates to the concrete or, as Hegel would say, to truth in the concrete. Hegel's logic was a first
attempt at such a reconstruction, but it did not go far enough to bring us
back to the concretion of being. This is why Heidegger had to continue the
task of deconstruction of what he thought of as the history of metaphysics
from Plato to Hegel. The question arises, however, did Heidegger go far
enough in deconstructing this history or did he remain too caught up in the
modern view of ontology to see that a reconstruction was called for along
another line of rational inquiry than the one he was starting from with what
he called ontological difference? Or did such a line remain hidden from him
in the ancient view of metaphysical inquiry? What Heidegger did is very

important for metaphysics, that is, returning the question of being to the forefront of philosophy. What he did not do, however, is find a way of reconstructing a philosophy of being that would meet the requirements of modern critical philosophy. Heideggerians are too complacent in their deconstruction. There is more the question of being than they have seen, namely, an implication of reconstruction as well as deconstruction.

What this book represents is an effort at critical reconstruction in the philosophy of being or metaphysics as understood in the ancient sense. Such an effort and the results that it is supposed to yield cannot be explained in a preface independently of the effort to do metaphysics itself. Strictly speaking there is no introduction to metaphysics that is not itself a part of metaphysics. Metaphysics has to introduce itself metaphysically and demonstrate its own necessity, as we try to do in Part One of this effort. In a preface we can only offer some clues as to where we begin in relation to the history of metaphysics. For us this means referring first to Heidegger, who has done more than anyone else in our time to bring the question of being back to the forefront of philosophy and to keep it as "the task for thinking at the end of philosophy" (Heidegger 1969). To be sure, his view of metaphysics will have to be questioned when he speaks only of deconstruction and not of any reconstruction. His own fundamental ontology will have to be deconstructed along with the rest of modern ontology, but in view always of a reconstruction called for by the very question of being. We cannot be satisfied with the Heideggerian conception of being or its understanding of the task for thinking at the end of philosophy. We shall have to reach back once again into the ancient approach to metaphysics in order to go forward beyond the dead end of modern ontology.

There is nothing exceptional about this resolve to begin metaphysics anew by way of a deconstruction. Every effort to do metaphysics has to begin with a deconstruction, or as a critical examination of some pre-established metaphysical construction, even if it be one's own naïve realism or idealism. Metaphysics always has to begin from scratch, so to speak, in some critical reflection. So it was for Plato and Aristotle in ancient times, and so it was also for Descartes, Wolff, Kant, and Hegel in modern times. So it remains for us in our time, given that it is a task for thinking at any time. Heidegger saw this clearly at the beginning of *Being and Time* when he was undertaking to prepare the way for pursuing this task through an analysis of *Dasein,* the one who is in a unique position to raise the question of being. We shall argue that the ancient way of raising the question of being as being does not lead to the same dead end, or to nihilism, as modern ontology does. Hence we shall conceive our task of doing metaphysics as a task of re-construction with the help of Plato, Aristotle, and Aquinas, who was the last great metaphysician in the ancient mode.

In this respect our reconstruction will be similar to Rosen's reversal of Heidegger in his recent book, *The Question of Being*. We shall attempt to show that there is more to Platonism, Aristotelianism, or Thomism, or to the ancient philosophy of being as being, than has met the eye of modern phi-losophy or Heideggerians, and that, from this "more," a way can be opened to a more positive rational discourse about being as being than has been found possible in modern metaphysics after the late Scholastic reconstruc-tion of Suarez, who framed the question in such a way that the course was set toward an abstract insoluble problem of knowledge. From the "more" of the ancients we shall try to set a new course toward a more positive rational discourse about being as being in the concrete.

Unlike Rosen, however, we shall not limit our reversal of Heidegger to a consideration of forms or to "the look" of things as they are thought of in Platonism. The French now talk of *"relooker,"* in the sense of giving the face of a structure a new look. Aristotle can be thought of as having "relooked" the Platonic structure of forms, starting with what Rosen refers to as "a step downward, out of the thin atmosphere of the floating island of Lapunta or of the balloons in which so many of our advanced thinkers are currently suspended, back into the rich air of everyday life" (Rosen x), or into what Aristotle would have referred to as the realm of the physical and the ethical. With Rosen, we agree that the attack against ancient metaphysics is as much against Aristotelianism as it is against Platonism. In Aristotelianism, however, we shall not go back only to substance or *ousia* and its properties, as Rosen does (27–28), which would bring us only to the threshold of a philosophy of being as being. We shall carry the battle into the very idea of ontological dif-ference in being, which implies something more than a formal difference among beings or between a substance and its properties, for ontological dif-ference touches on what we shall refer to as the act of being in a composi-tion with forms or with substances composed of form and matter.

In doing this we shall not leave Plato and Aristotle behind, but rather dig more deeply into what they saw of being, as Aquinas did in his time. We shall look more to the Platonic dialogues, which Rosen characterizes as less conclusive (24), but which confront the question of being more openly, as is true especially of the *Sophist*. We shall look also to the more tentative doc-trine of analogy at the beginning of book *Gamma* in Aristotle's *Metaphysics,* a doctrine of being which encompasses the doctrine of substance and its properties in a broader and more universal kind of consideration, namely, the consideration of being as being. The originality of the doctrine of analogy was recognized by Heidegger (*SZ* 4–5/22), but never exploited in relation to the doctrine of an ontological difference, as it should have been, and as it had been in fact by Aquinas in his understanding of the distinction between the act of being and essence or substance in finite being.

How all this is to be worked out can be understood only in the doing of metaphysics itself, which will consist here in holding Heidegger to the question he raised anew and not letting him run off on tangents that leave the question aside unanswered. It will consist in reconstructing an answer to the question, wherever it may lead us. To do this we shall have to come to an exercise of our own judgment, as we shall show, regarding how being presents itself in our experience. Without a proper exercise of our own judgment, there is no way of entering metaphysical inquiry. Everything hinges on one's own rational performance on the stage of the real world.

The endeavor may be thought of as a play with a beginning, a middle, and an end. The beginning consists in recognizing the necessity of raising the question of being as being. The middle, which is the act or the several acts of doing metaphysics itself in order to answer the questions that arise from the first one, flows from this beginning. It consists in the elaboration, not just of the question, but also of answers to the questions, however complex they may become. The end is that in which all this questioning culminates as an affirmation that is consistent with the beginning and that gives rise to yet another kind of questioning.

The whole play is self-contained. To understand it, one has only to follow the dialogue and let the drama unfold internally. One has to enter into the dialogue and play one's own part in it, for one does not do metaphysics except on one's own intellectual initiative even in the presence of an other. The dialogue here is between the reader and the author. One must exercise one's own critical reflection in the dialogue and so enter into the act of doing metaphysics. It is impossible to tell ahead of time, in a prologue, just what is supposed to transpire in the dialogue. That can be seen only in the performance as it unfolds through the dialogue, that is, in the reader's own response to the author.

If one wishes to have a preview of the play, which can only be from the outside looking in at this point, one can look ahead to how the book is divided into six parts, all centered on being. Each part is introduced as a distinct act in the play, requiring a certain performance of the reader as well as of the author, as it relates to the other parts as well as to the beginning and the end, or to the whole. The introduction to each part serves as a transition from one part to the next in the progression from beginning to end. Each part presupposes that one has already entered into the play with one's own performance. The most that can be said at this point is: on with the play, on with the dialogue. Let us see the performance.

It remains for me to acknowledge the debt of gratitude I owe to so many who have contributed to the writing of this book. Among these the first who come to mind are the Jesuit teachers I had in Louvain, who initiated me so well to the task of philosophy—André Hayen, Edmond LaHaye, and Gaston Isaye. The scheme for this book can be traced all the way back to their vigorous teaching.

Others have contributed to this effort as well, besides the classical authors I refer to throughout the text, but the only ones I would mention here explicitly are the students who signed up for the course over the years, never in any great number but all the more demanding in what they were looking for. Their performance in these various stagings of the play had a lot to do with the final shape this book has taken. There is no better way of learning something than by trying to teach it to students who are keen on learning and looking for answers to all their questions.

I am grateful also to Boston College for its willingness to have me teach metaphysics over the years and for a fellowship that freed me from teaching for one semester several years ago to start writing this book. Little did we know then that the project would have to go well beyond one semester and take on such large proportions. Boston College remains one of the few institutions willing to fund this kind of research, as I pointed out in my original application for the fellowship.

Finally, I am glad to acknowledge the financial support for this work I have also received from the Lynd and Harry Bradley Foundation, largely in the form of summer grants, through the Institute of Medieval Philosophy and Theology at Boston College. I should also express my gratitude to David McGonagle of The Catholic University of America Press for his willingness to take on such a large book and, more particularly the two editors, Philip Holthaus and Susan Needham, whose careful attention to the details of the text have added so much to the quality of the final version.

As always, I am grateful to my wife, Dorothy Kennedy, who professes not to understand much in all of this business of metaphysics, but who is true to her own judgment about what is good and bad, true and false in being. That is where my metaphysics begins.

Abbreviations

Listed here are works, by author, that are cited so frequently that I refer to them by abbreviated titles. I include, in parentheses after the full title, where necessary, information about the way each work is subdivided, so that the reader will be able to understand the more precise indications I give in the citations. I also include information about an English translation for the works referred to, where there is one, so that in the text I may refer to a work in both its original language and in its English translation with a slash between the first and the second. I cite other references by author's name and by year of publication, where necessary; these works are listed in the Reference List at the end of the book.

St. Thomas Aquinas

Caus   *In Librum de Causis Expositio* (Proposition, lesson, par. no.). *Commentary on the Book of Causes.* Trans. Guagliardo et al. Washington, D.C.: The Catholic University of America Press, 1996.

Ente   *De Ente et Essentia* (Chapter). *On Being and Essence.* Trans. Maurer. Toronto: Pontifical Institute of Medieval Studies, 1949.

In Metaph   *In Duodecim Libros Metaphysicorum Aristotelis Expositio* (Book, lesson, par. no.). *Commentary on the Metaphysics of Aristotle.* 2 vols. Trans. Rowan. Chicago: Regnery Press, 1964.

In Phys   *In Octo Libros Physicorun Aristotelis Exposito* (Book, lesson, par. no.). *Commentary on Aristotle's Physics.* Trans. Blackwell et al. New Haven, Conn.: Yale University Press, 1963.

Pot   *De Potentia* (Question, article). *On the Power of God.* 3 vols. Trans. English Dominican Fathers. Westminster, Md.: Newman Press, 1952.

Sent   *Scriptum super Libros Sententiarum Magistri Petri Lombardii* (Distinction, question, article). No English translation.

SpirCreat   *De Spiritualibus Creaturis* (Article). *On Spiritual Creatures.* Trans. Fitzpatrick and Wellmuth. Milwaulkee, Wis.: Marquette University Press, 1949.

SubstSep   *De Substantiis Separatis* (Chapter, par. no.). *Treatise on Separate Substances.* Trans. Lesco. West Hartford, Conn.: Saint Joseph College, 1963.

ST   *Summa Theologiae* (Part, question, article). *Summa of Theology.* Bilingual ed. in 60 vols. Trans. English Dominicans. New York: McGraw-Hill, 1964–1981.

SG   *Summa contra Gentiles* (Part, chapter, par. no.). *On the Truth of the Catholic Faith.* Trans. Pegis, Anderson, Bourke, and O'Neil. Garden City, N.Y.: Doubleday, 1955–1957.

Ver   *De Veritate* (Question, article). *On Truth.* 3 vols. Trans. Mulligan, McGlynn, and Schmidt. Chicago: Regnery Press, 1952–1954.

Aristotle

Cat   *Categories*

HA   *History of Animals*

Metaph   *Metaphysics*

NE   *Nicomachean Ethics*

PA   *Posterior Analytics*

Phys   *Physics*

Soul   *On the Soul*

Georg W. F. Hegel

(References are to German page nos. / English page nos.)

BDG *Vorlesungen über die Beweise vom Dasein Gottes.* Ed. Georg
Lasson. Hamburg: Meiner Verlag, 1966.

GW "Glauben und Wissen." In *Werke 2: Jenaer Schriften.* Frank-
furt: Suhrkamp, 287–424. *Faith and Knowledge.* Trans. W.
Cerf and H.S. Harris. Albany: State University of New York
Press, 1977.

NR "Über die wissenschaftliche Behandlungsarten des Natur-
rechtes, seine Stelle in die praktischen Philosophie und
seine Verhältnis zu den positiven Rechtswissenschaften." In
Werke 2: Jenaer Schriften. Frankfurt: Suhrkamp, 434–530.
*Natural Law: The Scientific Ways of Treating Natural Law, Its
Place in Moral Philosophy and Its Relation to the Positive
Sciences of Law.* Trans. T. M. Knox. Philadelphia: University
of Pennsylvania Press, 1975.

PhG *Phänomenologie des Geistes.* Herausgegeben von J. Hoffmeis-
ter. Hamburg: Meiner Verlag, 1952. *Phenomenology of Spirit.*
Trans. A.V. Miller. Oxford, U.K.: Clarendon Press, 1977.

PH *The Philosophy of History.* Trans. Leo Rauch. Indianapolis,
Ind.: Hackett, 1988.

WL *Wissenschaft der Logik.* Ed. Lasson. Meiner, 1971. *Science of
Logic.* Trans. A.V. Miller. Allen & Unwin, 1969.

Martin Heidegger

(References are to German page nos. / English page nos.)

Hum "Brief über den Humanismus." I *Gesamtausgabe* I, Band 9,
Wegmarken. Frankfurt: Klostermann, 1976. "Letter on
Humanism," in *Basic Writings.* Ed. David Farrell Krell. New
York: Harper & Row, 1977.

Einf *Einführung in die Metaphysik.* Gesamtausgabe II, Band 40.
Frankfurt: Klostermann, 1983. *An Introduction to Metaphysics.*
Trans. R. Mannheim. Garden City, N.Y.: Anchor Books/
Doubleday, 1963.

Ende   "Das Ende der Philosophie und die Aufgabe des Denkens," in *Zur Sache des Denkens.* Tübingen: Niemeyer, 1969. "The End of Philosophy and the Task of Thinking." In *Basic Writings.* Ed. David Farrell Krell. New York: Harper & Row, 1977.

GPP   *Die Grundprobleme der Phänomenologie.* Frankfurt am Main: Klostermann, 1975. *The Basic Problems of Phenomenology.* Trans. A. Hofstadter. Bloomington: Indiana University Press, 1982.

GBM   *Die Grundbegriffe der Metaphysik: Welt-Endlichkeit-Einsamkeit.* In *Gesamtausgabe* Abt.: *Vorlesungen 1923–1944,* Band 29/30.

KT   *Kants These uber das Sein.* In *Gesamtausgabe* I, Band 9, *Wegmarken.* Frankfurt: Klostermann, 1976.

SZ   *Sein und Zeit. Gesamtausgabe* I, Bd. 2. Frankfurt am Main: Klosterman, 1977. *Being and Time.* Trans. J. Macquarrie and E. Robinson. New York: Harper & Row, 1962.

WW   "Vom Wesen der Wahrheit," in *Gesamtausgabe* I, Band 9, *Wegmarken.* Frankfurt: Klostermann, 1976. "On the Essense of Truth." In *Basic Writings.* Ed. David Farrell Krell. New York: Harper & Row, 1977.

Immanuel Kant

KrV   *Kritik der reinen Vernunft.* 2nd ed. 1787. *Critique of Pure Reason.* Trans. N. K. Smith. London: Macmillan, 1958.

Plato

Crat   *Cratylus*

Euth   *Euthyphro*

Soph   *Sophist*

Benedict de Spinoza

Eth   *Ethics* (Proposition)

Francisco Suarez

DM   *Disputationes Metaphysicae* (Disputation, section, par. no.).
2 vols. Hildesheim: Olms, 1965.

Christian Wolff

PhRat   *Philosophia Rationalis sive Logica.* In *Gesammelte Werke,* II.
Abt. Lateinische Schriften, Band 1, herausgegeben und
bearbeitet von Jean Ecole. Hildesheim: Olms, 1983.
Preliminary Discourse on Philosophy in General. Trans. R. J.
Blackwell. Library of Liberal Arts, 1963.

Ontol   *Philosophia Prima sive Ontologia.* In *Gesammelte Werke,* II.
Abt. Lateinische Schriften, Band 3, herausgegeben und
bearbeitet von Jean Ecole. Hildesheim: Olms, 1977.

PART ONE

THE QUESTION OF BEING

Introduction: Raising the Question

❧

THIS IS A BOOK NOT *about* metaphysics, but *in* metaphysics. It is an invitation to do metaphysics for oneself as it is being done by another. But it is an invitation to do metaphysics precisely as a science of being as being, if we are to proceed according to a scientific method. In fact, the first question that we must ask in this philosophy of being as being is whether there is such a question as the question about being as being.

Many have long ignored or denied that there is such a question, and some, especially in logical positivism, have even argued that there can be no such question, because in their view the scope of questioning is totally exhausted by the range of sciences that we refer to as natural and social, none of which raises the question of being precisely as such (Ayer). If there is to be a philosophy of being, metaphysics must not only bring the question of being to the fore as a legitimate realm of rational investigation, but also open up the scope of meaningful questioning so that it transcends the realm of both the natural and the social sciences and encompasses being as a realm of inquiry precisely as being. This is not something that is easy to do, especially with someone who remains resolutely fixed in a narrow conception of science, but it is what we propose to do here as our introduction to the science of metaphysics.

To understand how this has to be done, we need only reflect on how science arises from experience through questioning according to many different forms. Different forms of questioning about the different things we know in experience give rise to different kinds of science, such as physics, biology, or economics. If we allow for different kinds of science to account for different aspects of what we know in experience, we can also ask whether any one of these particular sciences accounts for the whole of what we experience, without preempting the domain of any of the other particular sciences, or we can ask whether there does not have to be some other science, which would not be particular, like any one of the natural or social sciences, but that would account for the whole of what we experience in

3

some way that is common to all the different parts of the whole. Any attempt to account for the whole in terms of only one part's influence on another would have to be characterized as reductionist, an attempt to reduce the whole to some one of its parts by eliminating different aspects of the whole, as in physicalism or economism, which are no longer physical or economic accounts of reality, as in physics or economics, but metaphysical accounts of the whole of what is given in experience.

We should note immediately that physicalism or economism or any other such stance with regard to the whole of what we experience cannot be justified in any particular science but can only be justified in a more common science that raises questions with regard to the whole of what we know in experience. It is precisely with regard to the latter kind of questioning about everything in common that metaphysics has its beginning as a science. Needless to say, this is not the ordinary questioning we engage in in common understanding, which tends to be more oriented to practice, or in the particular sciences such as physics, biology, or economics, each of which focuses only on a particular aspect of reality. It is, nevertheless, a form of questioning that has to have its own method or way of proceeding, a method that also has to be worked out as part of the beginning of metaphysics.

Much has been said in recent times about the end of metaphysics, both by those who would proclaim its demise and by those who would defend its continuing validity. But little has been said about its beginning. In many ways the beginning of metaphysics is the most difficult part of it, especially in our antimetaphysical age. Many have declared the question *dépassée* or simply meaningless, choosing rather to restrict questioning to the realm of the physical or the social sciences. Others have admitted the question, but have found no rational way of dealing with it, and so have resorted to faith or mystical discourse to speak of being. Others still have reflected upon the long tradition of rational discourse about being and have found it wanting. These are the ones who have proclaimed "the end of metaphysics" from within metaphysics itself and who present us with the greatest difficulty as we begin in this inquiry into being.

Heidegger has had a lot to do with the way we approach this question in our time. For one thing, he has done more than anyone else to bring the question back into prominence and to keep it at the forefront of philosophy. It is the question that appears at the head of his first important work, *Being and Time,* published in 1929, and it is a question that remains for him a task of thinking at the end of philosophy or metaphysics, the task of thinking what "remains unthought in philosophy, although it is spoken about in philosophy's beginning" (*Ende* 76/388). This is what he refers to as "the opening as such as it prevails through *Sein,* through presence" (*Ende* 73/386), which somehow sends us back to the question of being in a new way, perhaps in a new beginning of metaphysics, as we shall argue here.

For Heidegger, however, metaphysics had come to its end "in the technologized sciences" (*Ende* 61–65/374–77), not in the sense that it has come to its fulfillment, but in the sense that it has come to its demise. This is why, while calling for a renewal of the question of being, he was also calling for an end of metaphysics in order to enter once again into the question of being. How are we to relate to this as we begin our own reflection on the question of being?

It would seem that Heidegger never abandoned the question of being that he raised in the "Introduction" of *Sein und Zeit.* At the end of this "Introduction," before embarking upon the analysis of *Dasein,* or human subjectivity, he outlines what was supposed to be a treatise in two parts, each with three divisions. The first part was to be the interpretation of *Dasein* on the basis of temporality and the explication of Time as the transcendental horizon of the question of being, while the second was to present the basic features of a phenomenological destruction of the history of ontology following the guidelines of the problem of temporality (*SZ* 52–53/63–64). The first part was to offer a way of gaining the "fundamental concept of 'be,'" while presumably the second part was to be an elaboration of this concept as it destructed the history of ontology, or the science of being, starting from Kant and going back to Descartes and Aristotle. Anyone interested in the question of being, or of be, however one may prefer to frame the question at this point, would surely have been interested in seeing such an ambitious project brought to term. But as is well known, it never saw the light of day, at least not as it was originally projected.

In fact, what was published as *Sein und Zeit,* more out of a certain necessity to advance a career in the German university than out of a necessity to express some truth about the question of being at that particular time, hardly got beyond the analysis of *Dasein* and left the rest of what had been proposed for part one as well as the whole of part two in the dark.

We can only regret this failure to ever get to the question of being, or of be, as it was initially proposed by Heidegger, or to bring it to any sort of conclusion. But we can also ask why he failed to take his initial project any further than he did. Was it the distraction of other university career requirements that kept him from finishing the work as initially outlined? Or was it some more compelling necessity of thought itself, like the famous *Kehre,* or "turn," which is alleged to have taken place a few years after the publication of *Sein und Zeit?* Or was it perhaps the realization that there couldn't be a second question of being, the question of be or of the be of being, after the first question, namely, the question of being as being? Whatever may have happened in the mind of Heidegger to make him turn away from the question he raised initially, we shall argue that there can be only one question of being and that the question has to be the question of being as being, not of be as be.

We shall also argue that there is not only a proper beginning for this question but also a proper way of considering it, so that there is also a middle and an end in this science of being as being that culminates in a consideration of a summit of being. This is not to say that the question of being is a simple question or that it does not allow for any further specifications of the question, such as a question about the be of being in Heidegger's ontological difference. It is rather to say that such further specifications of the question can only be understood within the single overarching question of being as being, as Heidegger himself implies when he insists that his question about the be of being can only be understood in the context of the ontological difference between be and being, a difference that must be accounted for in metaphysics only after the question of being as being has been properly raised. Our question will be whether Heidegger has properly understood what he speaks of as the "ontological difference" in the context of the question about being as being.

While Heidegger may have stopped thinking that there could be a science of being in any sense of the term, we think there is still a possibility for such a science and that this possibility appears precisely in a proper understanding of the subject matter for such an investigation, namely, being as being. Our proposal here is to attempt to do what Heidegger did not do, that is, to develop a systematic articulation of what is at issue in the question of being. In other words, it is to begin a systematic investigation into being as being that will eventually include not only Heidegger's more specific question of the be of being, but also other questions such as that of the properties of being as being or that of the causes of being as being, all the way to the final question of a summit of being.

How we shall do this and whether we succeed in this exploration will be for readers to judge for themselves. In judging, however, they will first have to come to their own understanding of the question and how such a question is to be answered. In other words, to judge of this exploration the readers will have to come to their own elaboration within an account of being as being.

As a further preliminary caution about coming to terms with this question, we should note the order in which it appears. Heidegger seems to suggest that, as a science, metaphysics came first and paved the way for the technologized sciences of our day. In one sense this could be true, and the whole process of the scientific enterprise could be blamed on Plato, or at least some interpretations of Plato. But in another more important sense it is not true. As understood by Aristotle, and most likely by Plato as well, it is not metaphysics that paves the way for the other sciences, but rather the more particular sciences that pave the way for metaphysics. At least this is the way we think the relation has to be understood here, in keeping with the understanding of the ancients.

Before the question of being can properly arise, one has to have traveled some distance along the way of questioning, which may or may not be technical at the outset, depending on where one stands in the history of questioning. Questioning does not immediately begin with being as being for human understanding. It begins with particular things or beings, how they relate to one another, and how they might serve our projects. Gradually it becomes more and more universal, theoretical as well as practical, until ultimately, if one has enough time and is diligent enough in questioning, it reaches the universality of being itself.

Aristotle gives his own thumbnail sketch of this order of questioning at the beginning of what he called "First Philosophy" and what we have since come to call his *Metaphysics* (980 a21–982 a4), a name that did not originate with Andronicus of Rhodes in his edition of Aristotle's works three hundred years after his death, as some still think (Rosen xi–xii, 30), but that rather goes back to the Peripatetic School in Aristotle's own time, as was shown some time ago by Reiner (210–37) and Chroust (601–16). It reflects the ancient view that inquiry into metaphysics, or what Aristotle would also call the science of being as being, comes only after the "physics," which encompasses the entire realm of human experience.

It is interesting to note that the idea of a late origin for the name "metaphysics" was first advanced by one Johann Gottliebe Buhle in 1788, at the height of Wolffian metaphysics, where it was understood that metaphysics had to come before any physics in accordance with the modern conception of metaphysics as "first science," meaning that it had to come before any of the empirical sciences since everything was supposed to be deduced from it *more geometrico*. Aquinas was still in tune with the ancients when he illustrated the gradual progression of questioning from the particular to the universal dimension of being in the progression of ancient philosophy itself (*ST* I, 44, 2, c; *Pot* 3, 5, c; *SubstSep* 7, 49; *In Phys* VIII, 2, §975). At first, he pointed out, philosophers gave thought only to the more gross sensible bodies. Those who saw motion in these bodies saw it as only accidental, and not as substantial, as in the case of density and rarity in some fundamental matter such as water or air, or as in the case of a congregation or a segregation of atoms, none of which changed according to their substance. Eventually philosophers came to understand that bodies were composed of substantial form and matter, which they took to be uncreated, so that change took place in bodies according to essential forms. To account for these transmutations, they posited not just particular causes but also more universal causes such as certain motions of the heavenly bodies, according to Aristotle, or separate ideas, according to Plato. Ultimately, some raised themselves to the consideration of being as being and began to inquire into causes of being, not just insofar as beings are this and that or such and such, but even insofar as they are simply beings.

Who these last philosophers were in the mind of Aquinas, if they were not Plato and Aristotle, and possibly Plotinus or the author of the *Liber de Causis,* can only be a matter of conjecture for us, but they illustrate how for him the question of being was finally raised in philosophy only after a progression from some more immediate questions even in the order of speculation or rational investigation.

Moreover, we must not think of this order only as an order of time. It is also an order of questioning itself as such or a matter of being prepared to raise higher questions. Higher questions, such as the question of being as being, which arises only after more particular questions about being have been raised, can only arise after some of these more particular questions have been dealt with. This is the only thing that makes the universal question of being as being particular in any sense. It has to relate itself to particular sciences, but only to distinguish itself from all of them as universal. One who never raises any question whatsoever about anything given in experience cannot come to understand any particular science, let alone the science of being as being. But even those who do raise particular questions about what is given in experience and so come to some scientific understanding of being, whether it be in physics, biology, or economics, must still rise to a higher form of questioning if they are to come to the question of being as being.

This is why so few ever come to the question of metaphysics. The way up to it is intellectually demanding and there are many junctions where one can branch off indefinitely in some particular science. Many do not have the leisure to raise any scientific questions whatsoever, and those who do usually find themselves totally preoccupied with the particular kinds of questions they raise. To enter into metaphysics, one must step back from every particular order of questioning and turn to a question that cannot be raised in any particular science, which is the question of being as being or being as a whole. But in order to step back in this way, one has to have something to step back *from,* that is, from questioning in some particular line of thought.

The point Heidegger makes about the task reserved for thinking at the end of metaphysics is very important for the beginning of metaphysics. It is the point where we take our stand in beginning metaphysics. Even if we do not focus only on technologized science, as Heidegger does, and take "science" to mean any kind of methodical or systematic questioning about a subject, the question of being has to mark a new beginning in questioning. Whether we call this new beginning a *beginning in thinking* or a *beginning in science* does not matter too much, as long as we have a sufficiently open understanding of science and do not keep it locked in its technologized form, as Heidegger seems to have done in rejecting the idea of a science of being as being. What does matter is that we recognize the radical newness of this beginning in questioning that gives rise to what we here call *metaphysics.*

Our aim in this beginning of our reflection, therefore, is to bring out the newness of the question we are raising, old as it may be, and to see what way can be found to explore it in its concrete fullness. To do this we shall proceed in two steps.

First, we shall try to focus on precisely what it is that the question of being is about, what we shall call the subject of consideration in metaphysics. What are we asking about when we ask the question of being? Is it about something immediately given, like something we can point to here and now or some aspect of what is immediately given, or is it about something that can be grasped only in a mediated way?

Second, having focused as clearly as possible on what it is that we are asking about in the question of being, we shall turn to the way in which an answer might be found. Having raised the question of metaphysics, we shall examine what the method of metaphysics has to be, for we shall find that the method has to follow from the question itself.

This will constitute for us the introduction into metaphysics, an introduction that is very important not only because of the intrinsic difficulty of beginning a truly metaphysical inquiry, but also because of the opposition to any such beginning on the part of so many even in philosophy, whether they be positivists, analysts, logicians, pragmatists, Marxists, phenomenologists, deconstructionists, or any other. We cannot hope to enter into contention with all of these would-be opponents here. We can only hope to show what metaphysics is, so that we may enter into it properly.

CHAPTER I

The Subject of Metaphysics

ARTICULAR SCIENCES, such as biology, always start from a certain
naiveté about being, which they take for granted. They do not ask
whether something is, but only presuppose that something is and proceed to
ask what it is or how it relates to other things. Biology, for example, does not
ask whether there are living beings, but presupposes that there are and asks
what they are or how they relate to other things. It is the science about life.
We speak of life as the subject of its inquiry. In the science where being becomes the subject of inquiry we cease taking being for granted. We become
critical about it precisely as being. We adopt a more critical attitude about
being as being, just as biology adopts a more critical attitude about living
things as living.

How is this attitude to be understood? In asking about being it would
seem that we are asking whether there is anything at all, rather than nothing.
But here we must distinguish between questioning about something as giv-
en in experience and calling its existence into doubt. Biology does not call
life as something given into doubt, but questions about it. So also metaphysics does not call being as something given in experience into doubt, but
questions about it precisely *as being*. It only makes being as such the subject
of its inquiry, something that none of the particular sciences does.

In fact, strictly speaking, it is not possible to call being, our subject of inquiry, into doubt. Even Descartes, who pushed methodical doubt to the limit, did not call being into doubt. He did not question whether there was
something, but rather what it was that he could say there was for sure. He
began from a first evidence of being, and so do we here, though Descartes
conceived of that first evidence of being differently than the way we shall
here.

Particular sciences, such as physics, biology, or economics, can in some
sense point to something in experience and say "This is what this science is

about." Biology can point to living things, for example, or psychology to thinking and feeling things. This may not be as simple as it sounds, since a science still has to determine what it wishes to investigate in what it points to. It still has to define its subject matter. But the particular sciences have at least something to point to. Even logic or methodology of science can "point," if not to something in evidence before us, at least to the activity of thinking and ordering in human beings who do science, which is something concrete at least for those who do think about and practice science. But metaphysics cannot point to anything in particular.

As the science of being as being, metaphysics has to include everything. It is about everything that is inasmuch as it is, about being as being; not being as this, or that; it is not about one kind of being or another, but about being simply as being. This is what distinguishes metaphysics from all the other sciences and makes it especially difficult to grasp in its beginning. This is why we must pay special attention to how we focus on its subject, which is all-encompassing, as we begin, for there is no other way of beginning in this science.

In the absence of anything in particular, or even of any activity such as thinking or doing science, to point to in experience on which to focus our attention in beginning metaphysics, we have only what is meant by "being" to fall back on. We can point to how the question has been raised historically to lead us into an initial understanding of the question. The question of being has arisen in many different ways in the history of science and philosophy. In fact, as Heidegger suggests, it is the question that is spoken about in philosophy's beginning and that remains a task for thinking at the end of philosophy, or at least, to put it more modestly, at the point where we now stand in philosophy. As we struggle with our own understanding of how the question of being arises, it can be helpful to look, at least briefly, at how it has been raised by others and learn from them how better to raise it for ourselves.

Before we do so, however, let us pause to reflect for a moment on how we speak about being, for in this there is already a certain perplexity in our way of speaking about "being" that is not the same in every language.

1.1   How We Speak about Being

When we begin to think of "being" as a subject of investigation, we might be inclined to think of it as very simple, in the way that Parmenides did when he spoke of it as one and unchanging. "Being" is an expression for saying what *is* and, as Parmenides saw it, what is, simply is, and what is not, simply is not. But, in fact, or more concretely, this is not the way we think of being.

In English, to begin where we stand most immediately in our discourse, the term "being" is used in different ways. It is primarily the present participial form of the verb 'to be,' or more simply of the verb 'be.' Even as a present participle, 'being' already entails some diversity of meaning, since the present participle can stand for almost any inflected form of the verb, present, past, or future, and it can express different circumstantial relations of time, space, or cause between one fact and another, as we can see when we use an expression such as "this being the case, he began to run." The same participial form, 'being,' is also used as a sort of infinitive, as when we say "being courageous is praiseworthy," which means the same as "to be courageous is praiseworthy." Moreover, it also serves as a substantive, as when we speak of the "human being" or some other particular being. 'Being,' in its present participial form, can mean "a being" as well as "to be," or simply "be," in addition to just "being" in the very wide-open sense.

We could expand on these different uses of the present participle in English at much greater length, but what is important for us here is to note the perplexity in which we find ourselves when we begin to speak of being simply as being. When we speak of being coming under questioning, in which one of these senses are we using the term? Is it as a participle, as an infinitive, or as a noun? In asking himself this question at the beginning of his metaphysics, Suarez thought of 'being' or *ens* as either a participle, *ens-participium,* or as a noun, *ens-nomen.* But he did not go with both of them. He chose rather 'being' as a noun or as a name in defining what was for him the subject or the object of metaphysics, because for him the participle only added a dimension of temporality to the question which he did not think metaphysics should have to deal with (*DM* II, 4, §3).

In starting from 'being' as a name, Suarez was shifting the meaning of the question of being from what it had been in antiquity to what it was to become in modern times, as we shall see in our historical survey of the question. For our part, at this point, we could say that being comes under questioning as all three, as a participle, as an infinitive, or as a name, since the notion seems to be the same in all three ways of using the term. But that could be to leave us still in a state of confusion as to precisely how being comes under questioning. Why do we speak of being as coming under questioning simply *as being,* and not *of be* or *of a being or beings?* It may be that we have to include a concrete temporal dimension in our understanding of the question we are raising, as Heidegger came to see in his phenomenological analysis of *Dasein,* and as Suarez had wanted to exclude in his *Disputationes Metaphysicae.* But it may also be that the different ways different languages have of presenting being for questioning can be perplexing for anyone trying to raise the question as if for the first time. Does everyone speak of being precisely as we do in English? Did the ancient Greeks speak of it at the origin of philosophy precisely as we do in modern ontological thinking?

It is interesting to note that in other languages the participial form in speaking about being is not at the center of attention as it is in English in speaking of being. In fact, in other modern European languages it is the infinitive that comes to the fore rather than the participle. The French, for example, speak of *l'être et les êtres,* both infinitives, where we would speak of *being* and *beings,* and of *l'être humain* where we speak of the *human being.* Similarly the Spaniards speak of *el ser, seres,* and *el ser humano,* all infinitive forms. In German a similar usage obtains. Where we use the participle, *being,* the Germans tend to use the infinitive, *Sein.* They speak of *das Sein,* as Hegel does at the beginning of his *Logic,* even though he later distinguishes between *Sein* (be) and *Seiende* (being). This use of the infinitive makes it difficult for Germans to speak of beings in the plural. They would have to use *Sein* in the plural. Instead they use locutions like *Dasein,* "being-there," or the participial form *Seiende.* But they do use the infinitive to express a particular kind of being, like *das menschliche Sein,* where English still uses the participle, *human being.*

It is important to note that when Heidegger speaks of the question of being he is usually thinking in terms of the infinitive, *die Frage nach dem Sein.* This is the way it would occur spontaneously to any German. But Heidegger was not just following a spontaneous inclination. He thought about how to formulate the question, knowing that the question had originally been formulated in terms of a participle, being *as being.* The question he wanted to raise was for him a second question in relation to what had been the original question of metaphysics, not the question of being as being, but the question of the be of being, *die Frage nach dem Sein des Seienden.* This is closely tied in his mind to what he thought of as the ontological difference between be and being. We shall have to look into that more carefully, once we have clarified how the question of being has to be understood in its primordial sense. But for the moment it is enough to note how a simple twist in language, from participle to infinitive, can affect the tenor of the whole question we are trying to raise. As Aristotle suggests, a small mistake in the choice of language at the beginning of a science can lead to much larger mistakes later on in the development of that science. Can there be two questions of being, or a question of be after the question of being, as Heidegger would have it, or is there only one question to be understood properly, if we are going to make any headway in our investigation (Blanchette 1991)?

It should be noted that what Heidegger is saying in German is all but impossible to render as concisely into English when we have only one term, 'being,' to serve as both infinitive and participle. Those who wish to stay with only the term "being" resort to the device of distinguishing between uppercase *Being,* for the infinitive, and lowercase *being,* for the participle. But in the process what is almost always a singular participial form in the German tends to be rendered as a plural in English. Thus, for the text we have just been referring to at the beginning of *Sein und Zeit,* we get: "Insofar as Being constitutes what is asked about, and insofar as Being means the Being of beings, beings themselves turn out to be what is interrogated" (*SZ* 9/26). In the German everything is in the singular, but in the standard translation what was singular in the German, *das Seiende,* has become plural in the English. Taken more literally, the last part of the sentence should have read: "insofar as Being means the Being of being, being itself turns out to be what is interrogated." Which of these renditions is the more correct one or what is it that Heidegger had in mind in raising the question of being as he did? If we can answer this question, we might perhaps get a better grasp on our own question of being at the beginning of metaphysics.

Another way of rendering Heidegger's approach to the question more accurately has in fact been tried by one translator, Ralph Mannheim, who has focused more on the second part of the expression, *Sein des Seienden* or "be of being," as the problem. To express this part of the Heideggerian phrase, namely, *das Seiende,* which has an odd ring in German, he coined the neologism, "essent," and has stayed with the simple expression "being" to translate *Sein.* This appears to be more in keeping with standard procedures in translating from German to English and it seems to stay closer to the German in that *Seiende* itself, used as a noun in participial form, is somewhat of a neologism in German.

In a note at the beginning of his translation Mannheim explains his strategy on the basis of a "fiction that *essens, essentis* is the present participle of *sum*" (xi), and the bastardized form only fuses the infinitive and the participle together. The only way to avoid this confusion would have been to translate *Seiende* as one would *ens,* that is, by "being," but then Mannheim would have had the problem of finding another word for *Sein* or falling back on the other ploy used by most translators, distinguishing between capital "Being" and lowercase "being" in accordance with the usage the participle has in English as both infinitive and participle.

In keeping with Mannheim's way of translating, the sentence we have just seen would go as follows: "Insofar as being constitutes what is asked about, and insofar as being means the being of essent, essent itself turns out to be what is interrogated." This version has the advantage of staying much closer to the thrust of Heidegger's thought, but it throws in a neologism that might be confusing. This, however, would not be entirely alien to Heidegger's thought, since he too seems to suggest that *Seiende* is itself a word foreign to common usage in German in a remark added to the text of *Einführung in die Metaphysik*. He speaks of *Seiendes* and *das Seiende* as words "alien to our everyday speech" (*Einf* 82/64). This would seem to justify the use of the neologism for *Seiende* in English, although the term *Seiende* in German is much more closely related to the term *Sein* than the term *essent* in English is to the terms *being* or *be*. The French had a much more felicitous way of rendering *Seiende* with *étant* or *l'étant,* which is also alien to everyday speech, but which nevertheless keeps the close relation to *être* as *Seiende* does to *Sein*. But the French had the advantage in this respect of speaking of being primarily in the infinitive, as the Germans do, whereas in English we do not.

There is a third possibility for rendering what Heidegger says in English words, if not in entirely idiomatic English, and that is by transliterating it as the "be of being," as we have already begun to do in our first approach to questioning with Heidegger. In a way, it is surprising that this one has not been tried before, since it comes almost spontaneously if we try to follow exactly how the question presents itself to Heidegger. It has the disadvantage of introducing a neologism not in word as such, but in the way of uttering the infinitive in English, and of placing the neologism in the first part of the expression, on the side of "be" rather than "being," which is the reverse of where the neologism lies in the German.

But this is a disadvantage we should be able to live with, since there is a neologism in the expression in either language. Given the difference in the way we speak primarily of being in English as a participle as compared to the way the Germans speak of it as an infinitive, there should be a reversal of the place for the neologism in going from one language to the other. Whereas for the Germans it is "being" that ends up as a neologism in the expression, for us in English it is "be" that ends up as the neologism. This is as it is bound to be, if we are to translate the expression exactly as it stands from one language into the other. Besides, it has the advantage of avoiding the necessity to introduce "beings" in the plural in order to keep lowercase "being" distinct from uppercase "Being" or, more exactly, from "be" in the infinitive. This is more in keeping with what Heidegger is saying in German and it may present some difficulty in understanding the way in which the question of being should be raised. This is the way of rendering Heidegger's locution about the be of being that we shall follow here.

What emerges from all this is the realization that the idea of being can have different inflections in different languages and that in German, as well as in French and Spanish, it has acquired a more infinitival than a participial sense. This was recognized by Heidegger himself when he began his reflection on the question of the essence of being with a reflection on infinitives and the use of the infinitive form of the verb to express the verbal noun (*Einf* 58–62, 80/45–51, 57–58). For us in English, who form our verbal nouns from the participle, and not from the infinitive, this could create some difficulty not only in translating and even interpreting the thought of a German on the question of being, especially one who insists so much on the flow of his own language in the pursuit of questions, but also in understanding the question of being itself apart from this confusion in going from a German, or a French, or a Spanish version of the question to the English version. For us now the question remains: Are we asking about being in the participial sense or in the infinitival sense or in the nominal sense? But we see how the question of being can be complexified and confused as we move from one modern language to another.

If we go back to the ancient languages of Latin and Greek and compare their way of speaking about being with these confusing differences among the modern languages, we find something quite interesting about the way the question of being was originally raised. In English we begin with a participle, whereas in German, French, or Spanish they begin with an infinitive. From either side the question can then be complexified to include the other side, but on either side we may be only overcoming a bias that is built into the question as it is framed in any of these modern languages. Ancient Greek and Latin do not seem to have had to start from this sort of bias in that they could frame the question either way, either as an infinitive, *einai* or *esse,* or as a participle, *on* or *ens,* each of which could be taken as a noun, preceded in Greek by a definite article, as in *to einai* or *to on.* In other words, the ancients seem to have begun from a more open outlook as to how the question should be framed. When we see that they settled on the participle rather than the infinitive or the nominative, as we do in English, in raising the question of being, we have to ask ourselves what difference this could make for us as well as for them and what difference it could make for the question of being as it continues to arise in modern "onto-logy" at the end of philosophy. A brief look at the history of the question and the difference between the modern way of raising the question and the ancient might help to bring us further into the question.

1.2   How the Subject of Metaphysical Inquiry Has Been Determined Historically

If we go back to the origin of philosophy, we can say with Heidegger that Parmenides "stood on the same ground as Heraclitus" (*Einf* 145/115). But we must also say that what was spoken of as a participle in Greek has a tendency to get translated as an infinitive in Heidegger's German. For, as Heidegger continues after recognizing this common beginning in both Heraclitus and Parmenides, he asks: "Where indeed would we expect these two Greek thinkers, the inaugurators of all philosophy, to stand if not in the be of being [*im Sein des Seienden*]?" Assuming that these inaugurators did stand in something, was it precisely in the be of being as Heidegger understands it or did they stand more simply in being? On what grounds does Heidegger introduce his understanding of the ontological difference into the original understanding of the question?

Heraclitus had little to say about being, or *eon,* except to insist on it as something common to many or as a certain togetherness, *xynon,* in Fragment 2, but Parmenides, as we know, dwelt on it at greater length. As a matter of fact, Parmenides speaks of being in the infinitive *(einai)* as well as in the participle *(eon).* In Fragment 3 he writes that "to think [*noein*] and to be [*einai*] is the same," in order to affirm a certain identity between two acts in knowing. But there being is not taken as that which is to be dwelt in. When Parmenides speaks of being as that in which thinking has to dwell, he speaks of it as a participle, as he writes in Fragment 4, "it is necessary that *legein* and *noein* abide in being [*eon*]," even though Heidegger immediately forces this back into his understanding of ontological difference when he translates *eon* as "being in its be [*des Seienden in dessen Sein*] for gathering [*legein*] and apprehending [*noein*]" (*Einf* 149/118).

In *The Sophist,* Plato follows from where Parmenides left off when he has the Eleatic Stranger address the question anew to Parmenides: "What do you wish to signify when you utter being [*on*]? For it is clear that you have known this of old, whereas we supposed we knew but now are in perplexity" (*Soph* 244a). Heidegger quotes this text at the beginning of *Sein und Zeit* as a way of setting the stage for his own inquiry. He speaks of "the expression 'being,'" which he renders as a participle in German, *seiend*. He goes on, however, to ask whether we today have an answer to the question of what we mean by the word *seiend*. He answers: in no way, but then he immediately changes the question into that of be rather than being. "And so it is fitting that we raise anew the question of the meaning of be [*die Frage nach dem Sinn von Sein*]," as if that were the question that the ancients had raised.

Again, it is not as if Plato could not have raised the question in terms of be, as Heidegger does. In fact, Plato speaks of being in the infinitive, *to einai*, as well as in the participle, *to on*. He even frames the question: What is this be? [*ti to einai touto*] (*Soph* 243 e).

But in doing so he is only thinking of the verb 'to be' as it is used in affirming or denying something, much as Parmenides had done before him, as when we say," not-being is according to something" and "being is not in some sense" (*Soph* 241 d). For him *einai* or be is an abstraction of speech. When he wishes to refer to being in the concrete or as that which is referred to in affirming or denying, he speaks of being, *to on*.

Aristotle goes on to insist on the same line of questioning in the first book of his work we now call *Metaphysics*, though he initially spoke of it as First Philosophy on the basis of what he thought would be the causes with which this inquiry would be concerned, namely, the first or most universal. In fact, he doubles the insistence on being when he comes to define what must be the subject of First Philosophy by speaking of it as the "science which studies being as being [*on e on*] and what pertains to it according to itself," for, as he argues, the first and most universal causes "have to be principles and causes of some nature according to itself. If therefore these principles were investigated by those who seek the elements of beings [*ton onton*], it is necessary the elements be those of being [*tou ontos*], not incidentally [*me kata sumbebekotos*], but as being [*all' e on*]. Hence we too must grasp the first causes of being as being [*tou ontos e on*]" (*Metaph* 1003a21–32).

We shall return to this argument when we come to determine the subject of metaphysics for ourselves in this inquiry. For the moment, in this historical sketching of the question, we should note that Aristotle goes on to speak immediately of being as spoken of in many ways as a way of saying that the question is by no means simple, since it depends on some analogy of being that affects how the subject of this science is to be conceived. If we lose sight of this analogy of being as being, we could end up misconstruing the original intent of the question with reference to being as it is spoken of concretely.

Aristotle's way of speaking of the subject of metaphysics became more or less the established way of determining it for the rest of antiquity and into the Middle Ages to the time of Aquinas, who, in his own introduction to the *Metaphysics,* took the pains of reconciling the three definitions of this science that Aristotle had given, namely, First Philosophy, Science of Being as Being, and Theology. For Aquinas, even as a theologian, the subject of metaphysics could only be being as being *(ens in quantum ens),* and God could not be understood as coming under that subject, even if metaphysics could ultimately arrive at some affirmation of God as First and Universal Cause of being. One could speak of metaphysics as First Philosophy or as Theology only by understanding how the idea of First and Universal Cause has to refer to being as being. In other words, there could be no question of an onto-theology such as would soon begin to emerge when a different conception of being would begin to replace Aristotle's analogous conception.

This transformation of metaphysics into some sort of onto-theology began to take place shortly after Aquinas, with Scotus, who took issue with the analogous conception of being. In denying the analogy of being, Scotus was changing the way of conceiving the subject of metaphysics so that it could include the Creator, or the Cause of being, as well as the creature. It is this transformation that culminated in Suarez's conception of the subject of metaphysics in a way that would affect the entire course of modern metaphysics, as Courtine has shown very well, by shifting attention away from being *as being* in the concrete to "being" as an abstract essence.

The *Disputationes Metaphysicae* of Suarez mark a new departure in metaphysics in many ways. For one thing, it was the first systematic work of its kind, which was to become the standard in modern metaphysics, replacing the old way of doing metaphysics by way of commentary on the *Metaphysics* of Aristotle. These disputations were conceived as a necessary preliminary for discussing supernatural theology, or as a way of elaborating necessary metaphysical truths that could be used in confirming theological truths. The second Disputation goes into a careful elaboration of what the subject of metaphysics has to be, which is now referred to as the *object* of this science.

There Suarez speaks of the formal concept of being as one and as "prescinding in reality and reason from other formal concepts of other things and objects" or as that which we have in mind when "upon hearing the name being, we experience our mind as not distracted or divided into many concepts, but rather as collected into one, as when it conceives man, animal, and similar concepts" *(DM* II, 1, §9). This is hardly in keeping with the analogy of being, though Suarez will not deny this analogy later on. What Suarez has in mind is a completely abstract concept of being, but one that has to have "an adequate and immediate objective concept of being corresponding to this formal concept which does not expressly say a substance or an accident, not God nor creature, but rather says all three in the mode of one [*per modum unius*], namely, insofar as they are similar to one another and come together in being" (*DM* II, 2, §1). By focusing on an *object,* Suarez has unwittingly created the epistemological problem of how a science reaches its object, and he solves the problem for metaphysics by saying that there has to be an objective concept of being corresponding to the adequate object of intelligence, in which the formal concept consists, and this objective concept has to include God as well as creatures from the beginning.

Suarez explicitly discusses the difference between speaking of being as a participle and speaking of it as a noun. While recognizing that being or *ens* as a participle "signifies the act of being as exercised and is the same as actually existing," he prefers to take it as a noun in order to specify the object of metaphysics, that is, as "signifying formally the essence of that thing which has or can have be [*esse*], not as exercised in act, but as potency or aptitude" (*DM* II, 4, §3). In this sense being can be conceived as objective and as real, but not as actual or anything concrete. It is taken as "something having a real essence, that is, [an essence that is] neither fictitious nor chimerical, but a true one and one apt for really existing" (*DM* II, 4, §62).

Thus, the subject of metaphysics was not only reduced to an object, which was to become problematic for modern philosophy, but the conception of being was at the same time reduced to an abstract essence, which even if it is thought of as real, is nevertheless thought of as only apt for really existing or being, in other words, as only possible, and not as actual. This is the conception of being, and consequently of metaphysics as the "science of being," that set the stage for modern ontology and which we eventually find epitomized in the systematic metaphysics of Christian Wolff, who took it as a great insight to define metaphysics as "the science of the possibles insofar as they can be" (*PhRat* §52).

This was true not only for general metaphysics, or what was now called *ontology,* but also what was thought of as particular metaphysics, whether of the soul, of the cosmos, or of God. With regard to general metaphysics, now understood as "First Philosophy," this meant that it had to do only with the possible as possible. What was meant by being was simply the possible: *quod possibile est ens est* (*Ontol* §135). Inquiry into "being" now became inquiry into what makes the possible possible, namely, into the principle of noncontradiction and its derivative principle of sufficient reason, with hardly any reference to any thing in actuality. In fact, having left actual being out of its consideration from the beginning, any attempt to say anything about being as being, rather than as merely possible, was bound to appear as dogmatic and empty of any critical or reflective sense. It is Wolff himself who claimed that philosophical method was "the order which the philosopher ought to use in treating dogmas" (*PhRat* §115).

This is the conception of metaphysics that came into question in Kant's *Critique of Pure Reason*. Kant speaks of "the celebrated Wolff, the greatest of all dogmatic philosophers" at the beginning of the *Critique* (*KrV* B xxxvi). With his strict method, Wolff would have been peculiarly well fitted to raise metaphysics to the dignity of a science, if only it had occurred to him to prepare the ground beforehand by a critique of the organ, that is, of pure reason itself, the supposed ground for the two principles governing Wolffian dogmatic metaphysics (*KrV* B xv). As we know, however, Kant's attempt to prepare this ground of pure reason proved very negative for metaphysics as "a completely isolated speculative science of reason which soars far above the teachings of experience, and in which reason is indeed meant to be its own pupil" (*KrV* B xiv).

Kant takes Wolff at his own word. He starts thinking of a science that "has to deal only with principles," but with the rider that it deals also "with the limits of their employment as determined by these principles themselves" (*KrV* B xxiv). Kant leaves aside all talk of being as such. He confines himself to a consideration of reason as it functions in experience. For him the question is "what and how much can the understanding and reason know apart from all experience" (*KrV* A xvii). By focusing on "the nature of pure speculative reason," he found a subject that contained a true structure in which everything is an organ or a part of a system that would replace the old dogmatic metaphysics as First Philosophy and set reason on its true scientific course, dealing "not with the object of reason, the variety of which is inexhaustible, but only with itself and the problems which arise entirely within itself, and which are imposed on it by its own nature, not by the nature of things which are distinct from it" (*KrV* B 23).

Without speaking of being in general, Kant did keep in mind the three realms of what Wolff had called "special metaphysics," namely, the soul, the world, and God, in order to show how each one was negatively affected by his transcendental reflection on the function of reason itself in experience. The only place in the *Critique* where Kant speaks explicitly of being or *Sein* is in connection with the ontological argument for the existence of God. What he says about it is especially telling for what has happened to the question of being in modern philosophy: be or *Sein* is "obviously not a real predicate; that is, it is not a concept of anything at all [*ein Begriff von irgend et-was*] which could be added to the concept of a thing. It is merely the positing [*Position*] of a thing, or of certain determinations in themselves [*an sich selbst*]" (*KrV* A 598; B 626). Kant is thinking not of being in the concrete as given in experience, but of be as another kind of essence than the one already expressed in our concept of a thing. To say that be adds anything essential to the concept of a thing we already have would be to call into question the very concept of the thing, for should the thing as posited contain more than the concept we have, the concept we have would not "express the whole object, and would not therefore be an adequate concept of it" (*KrV* A 599; B 627).

The famous example of the one hundred thalers illustrates this. "A hundred actual [*wirkliche*] thalers do not contain the least coin more than a hundred possible thalers." What the example also illustrates is that Kant has not moved one bit away from Suarez's conception of being as a "real essence" that is only apt for existing or Wolff's conception of being as an essence that is possible as possible. He can only think of be or *Sein* as another essence that would have to be added to the first essence and he knows that that cannot make sense. It is this essentialist conception of being that governs the negative outcome of the *Critique* and leaves it in total suspense with regard to any intelligible or noumenal content in objects of experience. Kant's philosophy is the perfect example of a philosophy that has not only forgotten the question of being, but has in effect eliminated it systematically.

This should have been the end of modern metaphysics once and for all. But it was not. It was more of a challenge that had to be met and that was met by German idealism in different ways. In Hegel's *Logic* it was met by placing be or *Sein,* pure be or *das reine Sein,* squarely as the beginning of philosophical science, thus combining logic and metaphysics into one science with a content of its own. For Hegel, there was no gap to be bridged between knowing and being or between the form and the content of knowledge, as in critical philosophy. If there was any distance between the two, it was already overcome in the concept, which entailed both form and content. If we begin with pure knowing in logic, we have to begin with what is at hand *(was vorhanden ist)* in this pure knowing, namely, its simple immediacy, which, for Hegel, can only be *das reine Sein:* pure be. "In its simple expression this simple immediacy is hence pure be . . . nothing else than be in general [*das Sein überhaupt*]: be, nothing more, without any further determination or filling" (*WL* I 54/ 69).

What Hegel has in mind in writing this is no longer the empty abstraction of the Kantian *Ding an sich* or of the Wolffian *ens in genere*. But it is not the full understanding of being in the concrete. He associates his idea of pure indeterminate be with Parmenides' idea of being, but he does not see this pure indeterminate be as a *whole,* as Parmenides did. He sees it only as one-sided or as somehow abstract, not as an essence or as a possible, but as having to be completed or taken up into its opposite, namely, pure nothing, which is not really an opposite, but only the same as pure be. Pure be is thus less than an essence or a possible. It is pure nothing, or rather it passes over into pure nothing, which in turn passes over into pure be. The two are thus understood together as becoming. "Their truth is, therefore, this movement of the immediate vanishing of the one into the other: *becoming,* a movement in which both are distinguished, but by a distinction which has precisely immediately dissolved itself" (*WL* I 67/83). In other words, it is not so much a passing over of the one into the other, but a having passed over *(nicht über-geht—sondern übergegangen ist).*

What this means is that the true beginning for Hegel is not really being or even pure be, but becoming. The full concept of being will emerge only later in the logic of *Dasein,* or finite being, which is a stabilizing of becoming, and in the logic of essence, where actuality is finally distinguished from possibility. But even there it will emerge only in the element of thought or pure knowing seen as an expression of God's own thought, "the exposition of God as he is in his eternal essence before the creation of nature and of a finite spirit" (*WL* I 31/50). In this sense the *Logic* is not only an ontology, but also an onto-theology, "the science only of divine concept," which has to sublate itself into something that once again has to be spoken of as be, not pure be any longer, but be in its immediacy all over again. "Inasmuch as the Idea posits itself as absolute unity of the pure concept and its reality [*Realität*], and thereby gathers itself into the immediacy of be, so it is as the totality of this form—Nature" (*WL* II 505/843).

From this comes Hegel's Science of Nature out of which the Idea reemerges once again as it "raises itself from externality as an existence gone into itself and completes its liberation through itself as the Science of Spirit and finds the highest concept of itself in the logical Science as in the pure concept of conceiving itself" (*WL* II 506/843–44). Having begun with the concept as the *Sache* of his consideration, Hegel can only return to this concept. Though he speaks of be as given at hand *(vorhanden)* at the beginning of the *Logic,* we can still wonder whether he raised the question of being as being in the concrete as something irreducible to the concept or to just knowing, something given and present in actuality to be thought through.

In insisting on the ontological difference between be and being and on the relation between the two, rather than on pure be in abstraction from being, Heidegger may have been more successful in coming back to this question as it was understood at the origin of philosophy. Though he wanted to raise the question of be as separate from the question of being, he was always careful to see it as relating to the question of being. Insofar as be makes up what is asked about, *das Gefragte,* and be bespeaks "be of being," it results that what is questioned *(das Befragt)* is being itself *(das Seiende selbst).* Being is, as it were, inquired of *(abgefragt)* as to its be. The question about be or the *Seinsfrage* requires, with regard to what is questioned in it, a gaining and a prior assurance of the correct access to being, even though we speak of "being" in many ways and in diverse senses (*SZ* 9/26).

One could hardly find a closer way of keeping the two sides of the ontological difference together. But to the extent that Heidegger wants to keep the question of be as a separate question from the question of being, he may be reverting back to the kind of essentialism that we found not only in Suarez and Wolff but also in Kant (Blanchette 1999). As we saw, Kant rejected the idea that be or *Sein* could be thought of as a predicate, or as a subject of questioning, because for him that meant that be would have to be some other essence over and above the essence that was already posited as a thing in the subject of a judgment, some noumenal object over and above the phenomenal object. If there were such essences or noumenal objects, we had no way of knowing them. More fundamentally still Kant would say that, if there is any real essence to be known, it is already known as the phenomenal object. This is how the question of be, or even of being, came to be eliminated or forgotten in modern philosophy. The question for us is whether it can be revived without stepping out of the essentialist conception in which it was eliminated. Was Heidegger successful in stepping out of this essentialist supposition when he affirmed the priority of the question of be as be over the question of being as being, or was he succumbing to it in a new way? Was he thinking of be as another kind of essence or was he thinking of it as an act of being in composition with an essence?

There are places where he speaks of be as of an essence. "The question about be as such is of an other essence and another origin" (*Einf* 20/15). "The 'be' has always been presupposed in all ontology up to now, but not as an available *concept,*—not as that which is the sought after" (*SZ* 10/27). Heidegger is intent on making be an available concept. But the question arises again: Can it be made available as a concept without reducing it to an essence or to what can be expressed in a concept? If not, we are still caught up in the modern essentialist conception of being, where the question of being always has to be reduced to one of particular essences or realities. If we wish to make be truly available as an act, we must go beyond the merely conceptual in knowing. To do this we must go back to a reformulation of being as being in all its scope without isolating be in any way from it. In attempting to keep the question of be as be separate from the question of being as being, Heidegger may have been not only abandoning metaphysics, but also giving up any hope of making be available as anything more than nothing, as he sometimes speaks of it, following Hegel, or some other essence than the existing thing.

This is something we shall have to come back to in speaking of the Logic of Being and the Structure of Being. For the moment it is enough to have seen how this question arises in the context of modern philosophy. Let us turn now to a more concrete reflection on how being as being comes to be understood as the proper subject for our metaphysical investigation.

1.3   How the Subject of Metaphysics Is to Be Determined for This Inquiry

We have seen several ways, ancient and modern, in which the question of being can and has been determined. Our task now is to come to our own determination about how it is to be understood as the beginning of our own metaphysical inquiry. In coming to this determination we shall proceed in three steps. First, we shall go back to the very first principle of all knowing, namely, that knowing is of being. We understand being as that which presents itself in knowing and we understand knowing as that which takes in the presence of being. Second, we shall reflect on the knowing side of this principle in order to show how there are different ways of knowing, different kinds of science, all of which, as knowing, have to do with being, and how these different kinds of knowing give rise to the idea of a first kind of knowing or, as Aristotle called it, a First Philosophy. This will lead us to our third step, which will be to ask how the subject of investigation for this first kind of knowing or this first philosophy is to be conceived. This in turn will yield a reasoned understanding of how only being taken precisely as being can be taken as the proper subject of metaphysics.

1.3.1   Knowing Is of Being

We begin with a very simple reflection on the act of knowing and on what is known in this act in their most primordial sense, prior to any distinction between common knowing and any kind of scientific knowing or prior to any specification of what is known in some acts as distinct from what is known in other acts.

In this primordial act there is contained a relation between knowing and being that is either affirmed or presupposed. Such an affirmation or presupposition underlies every claim to know anything, every epistemological stance, whether it be the "objectivist" stance of ancient philosophy or the more "subjectivist" stance of modern philosophy. In every act of knowing there is posited an identity of knowing and known. Both are one in the act and, because the unity is nevertheless one in which a distinction is to be made between the knowing and the known, we have to say that the unity is one of knowing and being, and not just one of knowing and knowing, as Hegel appears to have been saying in beginning his *Logic,* thus reducing the initial content of knowing to a pure form of knowing, as both "pure be" and "pure nothing." As the content of knowing or as what is at hand in knowing, being is not reducible to knowing as pure knowing.

Thus, being appears or presents itself in the very first act of knowing as that which is known when knowing takes place. As Aquinas put it, taking the expression from Avicenna, "That which the intellect first conceives as that which is most known [*quasi notissimum*] and into which it resolves all conceptions is being [*ens*]" (*Ver* 1, 1, c). This affirmation of the priority of being in knowing has to be understood as preceding any separation between form and content in knowing. But it must also be understood as a positive conception of being and not just as a conception of the concept. The being of this primordial act of knowing is not just the pure indeterminate be of the beginning of Hegel's *Logic;* it is as much the being known in the proper immediacy of experience itself. It does not present itself only at the end of a *Phenomenology,* in a realm of "pure knowing"; it does so from the very beginning, with sense certainty or any other form of consciousness intending an object. It is that in the presence of which knowing and conceiving begin. It is in fact the beginning of conception insofar as conception includes a content other than itself with which it becomes one in the act of knowing.

The fact that this primordial conception of being begins in experience for us does not mean, however, that "being" refers only to something material, whether it be the object or the subject of experience. It is not excluded that being as first conceived is something material, but this is not what distinguishes it as the content of knowing in its first conception. If our first conception were only of something material, it would be only of a specific kind of being, that is, some material being as opposed to immaterial being, and not simply as being or as that which is first conceived and into which both material and immaterial being are conceptually resolved. Being as first conceived is neither material nor immaterial, but simply being, including both, if the two are to be distinguished.

Being is known not just through sense impression or sense certainty, but also through intelligence, which transcends sense knowing even as it includes it. Being as it presents itself in this first act of knowing is neither just intellectual nor just sensible, but both at the same time.

Taken in this primordial conception that is the beginning of all knowing, being cannot be properly defined as things given in experience are through genus and specific difference. It is neither a specific difference that could be or not be in a genus. Nor is it a genus awaiting a specific difference as something outside of itself, as we shall see in the logic of being, for outside of being there is nothing, not even a difference. Being simply encompasses what is to be understood according to both genus and specific difference as one in its being present. It is the very first notion, with reference to which things and every other notion have to be defined.

What is meant by "being" can only be indicated by an operation such as that of knowing. It is grasped only in an act of knowing. No one who has the use of intelligence is totally deprived of such an act, not even the universal skeptic, for he too lays some claim to knowing, which in its primordial act acknowledges some presence or some representation of being. The universal skeptic is a skeptic only because he does not acknowledge this presence of being in his act of knowing, a presence he cannot deny in making any claim about knowing, even that of total denial. If he does not advert to this primordial act of knowing in his claim of universal skepticism, he cannot acknowledge any presence of being as known. But if he does advert to it in the claiming itself, he has to acknowledge some presence of being, even if it is not in any of the particular forms he wishes to deny. The presence of being we affirm in this most primordial act of knowing is one that is prior to any specific or generic determination, even though we may immediately suppose that there has to be some such determinations in being.

What we mean by "being" cannot be understood apart from the act of knowing. It can only be understood as that which is first conceived in such an act. But it should also be noted that knowing itself cannot be properly understood apart from this reference to being as a content of knowing. This primordial act on which we are reflecting is not one of knowing in itself or of pure knowing. It is a knowing *of* something, which we initially conceive only as being, when we say "it is" or "something is." Knowing is an intentional act that contemporary phenomenology has been careful to restore in its intentionality against the reductive tendencies of critical idealism or pan-logicism. Knowing takes place only as it refers to being. It cannot be understood except as an act of attaining being, or in which being is disclosed, whether it be in common sense, in empirical science, or in metaphysics.

Although this fundamental assertion about knowing as a knowing of being is not an assertion of anything properly metaphysical at this point, it has some metaphysical overtones in that it is not restricted to anything specific, like the physical. It is an assertion about any act of knowing, whether of sense or of understanding. It is also an assertion about a very first principle within any act of knowing, a principle of identity, which is present in any claim to know. In its negative form this principle takes the form of noncontradiction: I cannot claim that something is and is not at the same time and in the same respect. Here we are trying to focus on this principle in its positive form, which can be expressed by the formula "what is, is." We say that this fundamental assertion is present operatively, if not in any precise terms, in every claim to *know* anything, even in the claim that we do not know.

Because we are dealing with the very first principle of human knowing at this point, which includes a relation as well as an identity, our language tends to go around in circles. We speak first of "knowing" in order to refer to being and then of "being" in order to understand knowing, as distinct from just thinking or imagining. But the circularity is only in the words and definitions as we try to zero in on the simultaneity of an act in which the knowing and the known, knowing and being, are one.

We shall have to come back to this primordial principle of identity in any claim to know later on, when we come to work out a method for dealing with this question of being, but for the moment let us note that the claim here is not that we attain being unerringly. There are many ways of knowing being and there are even more ways of erring in the articulation of what is present to us as being. Our claim is simply that it is impossible to miss being altogether, if one knows anything, whether it be a being, many beings, or simply being as a whole. Being, as it is first conceived in the primordial act of knowing, can be any one of these, once we begin to speak of it as "what is" rather than just as "is." For, as Plato pointed out long ago in *The Sophist,* when we introduce the *what (to ti)* into the concept, then being can mean either one, two, or many (*Soph* 237d). Our point here, however, is not to think of being as either one, two, or many, but simply as the content of knowing, whatever it may be in its specifications.

The claim or the principle we are speaking of is so simple and so self-evident that we seldom advert to it in our more elaborate claims of critical thinking, science, or metaphysics. But this primordial claim underlies in some way all those other claims. We dwell on it here at the beginning of metaphysics not just for the sake of the other sciences, which are forms of knowing and therefore knowing of being, but also for the sake of metaphysics itself, which shares in the same desire to know being as other sciences do, even if it be in a different way of questioning about being.

Everyone using intelligence in some critical sense has some knowledge of being, and hence everyone can or does have some grasp in some sense of what is required to become a metaphysician as well as an empirical scientist. But not everyone has a fully articulated knowledge of being. Most of us have some knowledge of being articulated in our common knowing or in some particular science. Only a few seem to want the further articulation that comes with metaphysical questioning, over and above the questioning of common sense or of particular sciences. The way to such metaphysical questioning, however, remains open to all in that all who have the use of intelligence are somehow caught up in some knowing of being.

We should note here that, with this positive principle of identity with being in knowing, we are already well beyond the negative principle to which Wolff tried to hold himself in the beginning of his ontology or general metaphysics in saying that metaphysics has to do only with the possible as possible. When we say that knowing is of being, we do not mean that it is of possible being, but of actual being in all its amplitude. "Knowing" as we speak of it here is not just imagining or thinking about possibles. As knowers we find more meaning in the actual than in the possible. This is why we can go from the actual to the possible, by distinguishing the merely possible from the actual, but not from the merely possible to the actual, since the merely possible as distinct from the actual is only an abstraction and no longer includes all that is contained in the actual. Thus, in settling only on the possible as the subject of his general metaphysics, Wolff was not only leaving out something already included in the primordial act of knowing. He was also closing his ontology up in something particular or one-sided, an abstract possible from which he could not escape except by a dogmatic fiat to get back to the full intelligibility of actual being. He had lost sight of the being from which he was actually beginning and "discovering" that the possible as possible was no substitute for what was being ignored, namely, actual being.

Initially, in the primordial act of knowing, no distinction is made between the actual and the possible. The actual is taken to be possible because it is known to be already. What is already clearly can be. But once the distinction of what is merely possible is made from the actual, it is an error, from the standpoint of knowing, to give priority to possibility over actuality. In the act of knowing, it is the actual that has priority, and not the merely possible, which in any case is not properly *known* as being but only as abstracted from some actual knowing.

To think as if we began only with the possible in metaphysical knowing is to pass over being in the concrete in favor of an abstraction. It is typical of the particular sciences to abstract some aspect of being from other aspects of being in determining the subject of their consideration. Physics, for example, abstracts from life, which is the subject for another particular science, namely, biology. There is nothing wrong with this sort of abstraction, as long as sufficient allowance is made for other particular sciences to study other aspects of being. But it is an error for metaphysics to abstract from actual being in the determination of its subject, since there is no other human science to restore actual being to knowing once it has been overlooked at the beginning. The actual is not something we have to import into metaphysics or any other science to lead us back to being, as if by a second principle of sufficient reason outside the possible. Actual being is that from which we begin in any concrete act of knowing and in any science. As actual in the concrete, being is much richer in content than any abstract possibility.

This is the reason why it is better to speak of this content of the primordial act of knowing as "being" in the participial form rather than in its nominal form. The participial form expresses more of this actuality that we associate with being in the concrete than the nominal form does, precisely the act that Suarez was trying to exclude from his conception of the object of metaphysics. In its nominal form or as *ens in genere*, "being" stands for the most abstract of possibilities, as Wolff eventually brought out, the possible simply as possible. The same might be said also of the infinitival form, which simply abstracts from all particular forms of the verb. We can see here why the insistence on the participle, *eon*, at the origin of philosophy with Parmenides and Heraclitus was much more felicitous from the standpoint of our primordial act of knowing. In this simplest of participles was expressed an insight into the collected presence of being itself as one and whole, where knowing is a gathering and apprehending only because being itself is already a gathering and holding together. What Parmenides and Heraclitus did with this original insight into being or this first conception of being is difficult for us to follow from the standpoint of a more articulated conception of being, but it must not be confused with the Wolffian idea of *ens in genere* understood as pure, abstract possibility. Our own first understanding of being is still one of concrete actuality, as it was at the origin of philosophy.

In a sense, this initial knowing of being can be seen as a kind of absolute knowing, even though it remains undifferentiated. It is absolutely certain and cannot be called into doubt. To doubt that we know being would be to claim that we know something else better and to know something else better would still be to know being in another form. Being presents itself in every act of intelligence, so that one cannot *intelligently* deny it altogether. One can only deny some particular form of it, but always in favor of some other form of being, whether it be materialist, idealist, realist, fluxist, or whatever else one might think. In the primordial act of knowing, where the identity of knowing and being is affirmed, no such differentiation is yet made.

Even without a differentiation, however, this initial absolute knowing is a knowing of something positive. It is not just a thinking of a pure indeterminate be, which is taken to be the same as pure nothing, as Hegel maintains at the beginning of his *Logic*. Being, as we understand it primordially, is not nothing, but everything or whatever is. In this immediacy it is neither indeterminate nor determinate. It is simply confused and calls for clarification through questioning. Even in his methodical doubt Descartes knew being already and was only looking for which ideas might correspond to it. Clarity and distinctness of ideas became for him the first criterion of certainty only because he lost sight of this first certainty from which we all begin in our quest for knowledge. Being is the first clearing from which we start. It is from this first certainty, or the principle of identity between knowing and being, that we proceed in our questioning of being, not as if it were clear and distinct from the beginning, nor as if it were pure or indeterminate, but as somehow everything, whether, as Plato put it in *The Sophist,* that be one, two, or many.

1.3.2   Different Ways of Knowing and the Idea of Metaphysics as First Way of Knowing

What we have, then, as a result of this first moment in our reflection on the primordial act of knowing as a knowing of being is the understanding of a certain polarity between knowing and being. In the second moment of our reflection let us now turn to the knowing side of this polarity and to the different ways of knowing we find on that side. Let us distinguish between two basic kinds of knowing to begin with: knowing *that* something is as a matter of fact *(to hoti)* and knowing *why* something is or what accounts for the fact *(to dioti)*. It is through some such distinction that we come to distinguish between what we call *scientific knowing* and the more immediate kind of knowing we think of as mere *observation*. Knowing something scientifically is knowing it through its causes as well as through observation, knowing why it is what it is. Over and above mere observation, science begins as an investigation into why things are what they are.

Here we take it for granted that there are already different kinds of science or different ways of accounting for facts, as Aristotle did at the beginning of his *Metaphysics*. Intelligence in experience gives rise to different ways of questioning about being as present in fact, whether it be in physics, biology, psychology, or economics, to name only a few examples. Each of these sciences delimits a realm of its own in being, its own subject matter, or *Sache,* distinct from that of other sciences, even though there is frequently a certain amount of overlapping within the initial fact that is being accounted for in these various disciplines.

It is important to keep in mind that, as forms of knowing, these are all sciences of being. In this sense they can be spoken of as *ontic.* They are particular sciences of being, each distinct and autonomous in its own right. They all relate to being as given in fact, such as the tree in my back yard, or to the same world as given in experience. But, as sciences of being, so related to the same facts and the same world, they do not remain unrelated to one another. The idea of some order among them arises necessarily, insofar as they all relate to being and, with this idea of some ordering among the particular sciences, we come to the idea of another kind of science in relation to being as a whole, a science that would be universal in its concern about being, and somehow first, or most radical, in its consideration of being beyond all particularization, a science of the ordering of the particular aspects of being in being as such.

We have already alluded to some of the particular sciences we can think of, each having to do with some particular aspect of being. Other particular sciences could be conjured up to deal with other aspects of being. But every one of them would still be operating on the same level with reference to being as given in concrete experience in accounting for different aspects of the initial known fact of being not accounted for in the other particular sciences. They would still be only particular sciences, like the first ones mentioned, relating to being as experienced in the same direct way. They would remain *ontic,* in that all have to do with being, but insofar as each remains separate from the other, it is only a particular science alongside other particular sciences or a science of some particular aspect of being. And if we were to come up with still other particular sciences deemed necessary to explore different aspects of being or of the world not yet explored, these would still be only particular sciences on the same *ontic* level of inquiry.

New empirical sciences could take us beyond our present knowledge of being, but not beyond the *ontic* level of questioning as a whole. We get beyond the *ontic* level of questioning about being only when we begin asking about the whole of being or about the ordering of the particular sciences on the *ontic* level. This is a level of questioning we could call *ontological,* because it is a second order of questioning, a level where being comes into questioning not just in a particular way as present directly in experience, but in a more universal way that encompasses the questioning of all the particular sciences as all relating to being. It does not matter whether we think of this level as higher or as deeper than the first. It still has to do only with being as given in experience, not with some object beyond all possible experience, as Kant had come to think after Suarez and Wolff. But it is important to understand it as having a certain priority over the first level of questioning in that it has to do with being in a way that none of the particular sciences do, in a way that encompasses all of the sciences and is reducible to none of them. In other words, it would be the ultimate and the first order of questioning, even though it comes only after the particular orders of questioning in experience.

Such a level of *ontological* questioning does not have to suppose that there is anything in particular beyond the world of experience still to be examined or accounted for, much as a new particular science on the *ontic* level has to do in defining its own particular subject. A new particular science expands our experience, so to speak, but it does not take us beyond experience as such. *Ontological* questioning does not expand our experience in the way that a particular science does. It simply takes experience and the particular sciences that relate directly to this experience as a whole and asks how it all comes together in being. It does not presuppose some other thing "in itself" hidden behind the things we know in experience. It does not try to indicate any particular thing "beyond all possible experience" still to be investigated and accounted for. It only asks about the whole of what is already experienced, but as a whole or as a presence of being.

Just what form this kind of questioning might take has yet to be determined. We shall do that when we come to reflect on the method we need to pursue this kind of questioning (see Chapter 2) and the meaning we attach to what we refer to as being (see Part Two). Here what is important is to understand how this kind of questioning is to be understood as first in relation to the questioning of the particular sciences.

As first, it could be thought of as an analytical philosophy of the particular sciences, whose subject might be the order between the sciences or between the particular accounts that they give of being in experience. It might also be thought of as a critique of the particular sciences. But in both of these cases the question would be to understand what its content is as distinct from the content of the particular sciences, since, without a content of its own it would be difficult to see how the first science or the first order of questioning could be distinguished from the other sciences as science or as knowing. An analytical philosophy of science might claim to be first philosophy for the natural and social sciences, but it could not distinguish itself from them as a first knowing if it only borrowed the whole of its content from them, as some analytical philosophers maintain. Such a pure analytical philosophy would not be a first science in any sense of the term. It could only be last. Lacking any content or subject of its own, it could only be absorbed in one or the other of the particular sciences, as in physicalism or economism.

Similarly, critical philosophy could also be thought of as first philosophy, as Kant claimed it should. But it too would have to have a content of its own. It is the absence of any content of its own other than the act of knowing itself that makes the *Critique of Pure Reason* so problematic in the end for both Kant and his successors. In positing a "thing in itself" Kant is admitting that there is a proper subject for a first philosophy that would be distinct from any of the particular sciences as well as from the critique of reason, but in saying that such a "thing" remains unknown and unknowable in itself, or "beyond all possible experience," he is saying that first philosophy cannot exist as a science for man. Along with merely analytical philosophy, a purely critical first philosophy lives only off a borrowed content, that of physics and mathematics, the only two properly constituted sciences for Kant. As a critical philosophy, it is left with this problem of an unknowable "thing in itself." How can it be truly critical if it is not itself the science of something other than just knowing?

The problem with a merely critical understanding of first philosophy may be that it is still too closely assimilated to the dogmatic metaphysics that it was trying to oppose or depose. The proverbial "thing in itself" is still viewed as a possible object of knowledge for which there is no proper intuition, Kant's prerequisite for any knowledge. If there is no intuition into the "thing in itself," it can only be taken as a possible. The conception of such a "thing" may give Kant some room for maneuvering with reference to the immortality of the soul and the existence of God in the realm of practical reason, but it does not take us out of the realm of pure possibility from the standpoint of theoretical reason. In our knowing we do not start from possible objects, but from being actually known in experience, and we ask why it is what it is.

The form of this initial question for first philosophy, or for metaphysics, must be understood very carefully. We must avoid thinking as if there were a gap between being and knowing, as Suarez did in starting from some "real essence" as the object of metaphysics. Such a gap would be unbridgeable, as Kant's *Critique* demonstrates. We have already seen that, where there is knowing, there is no such gap. The critical question arises only once we have begun to articulate what it is we know. When Aristotle raises the question of a first philosophy at the beginning of his *Metaphysics,* he phrases it in terms of seeking after the first and most universal principles and causes of things. The one who knows through such principles and causes is supposedly thought of as the wisest or the one who can best account for everything.

This is not to be taken as if we already knew at the beginning of this inquiry what these principles and causes are, or how they function as principles of being. It is to be taken in the sense that, of the two kinds of knowing, knowing *why* something is is better or higher than knowing just *that* it is, and in the sense that knowing the ultimate *why* of everything would be the best or the highest kind of knowing. One can think this without actually claiming to know any first principles or causes, or even that they are other than the being or beings we know more immediately in experience. All it presupposes is an idea of knowing as somehow principled, in the sense that it looks for principles and causes to account for what is given in fact.

The beginning of any science is in the knowing as well as in being. In the case of first science or first philosophy, the beginning is in the knowing that questioning ultimately leads us back to an inquiry into first principles and causes, whatever these might be. As first knowing or science it takes us through the *ontic* level of questioning to an *ontological* level that transcends any and all particular realms of questioning. It remains for us to understand what this *ontological* level of questioning means in a third moment of our reflection on the polarity of knowing and being. The question for us now is to see how the subject of consideration for this kind of questioning is to be formulated.

1.3.3 *Being as Being as the Subject of Consideration in the First Way of Knowing*

When Aristotle comes to determine the subject of what he calls first philosophy, he goes back to his initial definition of first philosophy as knowledge through first principles and causes and he asks: Of what are the first causes the cause? He illustrates the meaning of this question in terms of particular sciences such as that of health care or mathematics. "There is a cause of health and fitness; and there are principles, elements, and causes of mathematics; and in general every science that is intellectual or participates in intellect is about causes and principles considered either more exactly or more simply" (*Metaph* 1025b4–7).

The point of saying "either more exactly or more simply" at the end of the sentence, according to Aquinas in commenting on the passage, relates to a distinction between two ways of viewing the causes, either from our human standpoint *(quoad nos),* which calls for greater exactness, or from the standpoint of the cause itself *(quoad se),* which implies greater simplicity on the part of the cause. In either case, science is understood as knowing things through their principles and causes. The one who knows health scientifically knows the cause of health. The one who knows mathematics knows the principles of mathematics. The question that now arises for us is this: If first philosophy is an inquiry into the first and most universal principles and causes of things, of *what* are these principles and causes the cause?

We have already insisted that every science is of being. On the *ontic* level of questioning, every science distinguishes itself from every other science by determining a particular subject in being for its consideration and inquiring into the causes of this subject. Thus, we can say that physics is about being as quantifiable; biology about being as living; economics about being as produced by human labor. The causes that these sciences inquire into can only be particular, since they relate only to a particular aspect of being. If, then, there is a science that inquires into the first and most universal causes, it cannot be like any of these sciences on the *ontic* level or about any particular subject or aspect of being. Since, as a science, it is still about being, it can only be about *being,* not as any particular thing or under any particular aspect, but *simply as being.* As Aristotle puts it, "Inasmuch as we are seeking the principles and highest causes, it is manifest that they are necessarily as of a certain nature according to itself" (*Metaph* 1003a27–28).

The idea of "nature" here is used in a way related to the idea of the subject of a science. A science considers its subject as a kind of "nature according to itself." With the idea of a first philosophy inquiring into first causes, there has to be a corresponding "nature" as the subject from which the inquiry begins. Our claim is that this can only be being as being, and not about being according to any particular aspect.

It is important to note that we come to this understanding of the subject of metaphysics through a process of double negation. In the first negation we understand every particular science as having to do with only one part or one aspect of being. Each particular science is about this or that aspect of being, and *not* about any other aspect. It is from this reflection on what constitutes the subject of any particular science that we move on rationally to determine the subject of *ontological* questioning or first philosophy as something more positive through a negation of this first negation in particular science. First philosophy is about being simply as being in the most positive sense of the term.

To speak of being is the most positive way of stating the subject of any science. To speak of being as being expresses even more positively the subject of *ontological* questioning as transcending all particular subjects of inquiry. Without the mediation of some understanding of particular sciences as sciences of being on an *ontic* level, we cannot arrive at a proper understanding of metaphysics as transcending this level of questioning. The idea of "being as being," understood reflectively as we are coming to it here, is not simply a catch phrase that one can grasp immediately. It does not refer to anything beyond all possible experience, but only to being as given in experience considered as a whole. The phrase is the expression of a mediated understanding of what *ontological* questioning is about or of where it begins in experience.

Thus, the subject we are inquiring into in metaphysics cannot be directly indicated as anything in particular, as might be done for a science on the *ontic* level such as physics or biology, which can indicate their subject by pointing to one particular aspect or another of being as given in experience. To be sure, being is always immediately given or present, but not always as itself the subject of inquiry. Human inquiry immediately focuses on particular aspects of being as given before it comes to focus on being itself as being or as the subject of its inquiring. If one has not come into the idea of science intellectually, which for us first arises about a particular subject or a particular aspect of being as given in experience, one cannot have a proper idea of metaphysics as a science, or of its subject, being as being.

Though it is impossible for anyone with the use of intelligence to be without some knowledge or some conception of being, since knowing is always of being, it does not follow that everyone immediately raises the *ontological* question of being as we are raising it here. In fact, given the difficulty of any genuinely intellectual inquiry into being and the necessary mediation of inquiry on the *ontic* level for raising the *ontological* question of being, it may be that many will not raise it at all. Some may never even raise ques-

tions for scientific understanding on any *ontic* level. Others may become totally absorbed in the pursuit of questions about some particular aspect of being as given directly in experience. But those who pursue the enterprise of
questioning to its very end with regard to what might be the first and most
universal causes will inevitably come to understand that being itself simply
as being has to become the subject of some human inquiring.

    This is not to say that few people take any metaphysical stances with re-
gard to the ultimate meaning of being, for it is virtually impossible not to do
this in the use of one's reason. But it is to say that the adoption of such
stances will not be critically established through a reflective judgment on being as being. It will be an unwitting metaphysics, so to speak, without the
kind of critical reflection that validates it as a science. Those who undertake
to do metaphysics as a result of inquiry on the *ontological* level, however, do so
only through what Aristotle calls "intellectual science" or through thought
trying to encompass being as being.

    Metaphysics comes into its subject by denying the negation in any partic-
ular determination of being as the subject of a particular science. This is not
an empty negation. It has a very positive outcome as it refocuses on being,
but now simply as being, without any determination. It brings us to a consideration of being in its concrete wholeness. In stepping forth from the inquiry of particular sciences into the universal scope of being as such, it does
not cut itself loose from these sciences. Mediated by what is known of being
in these particular sciences, it does not ignore them as ways of knowing. Nor
does it deny them their own autonomy as sciences of being. But it does
affirm its own autonomy as a science on a higher or a more fundamental
level that we have characterized as *ontological*.

    It could be said that metaphysics has to do with the ground or the foun-
dation of what is thought about being in the other sciences. But this would
have to be understood very carefully. Strictly speaking, the proper understanding of being as being is not the ground or the cause for saying anything
in any of the particular sciences. Each science has its own ground for saying
what it has to say. The understanding we have at the beginning of metaphysics is simply a presence of being that gives rise to inquiry. If as a result of
the inquiry, it turns out that we have to affirm a cause of being as being other than any being simply present to us in experience, then we shall have to
examine precisely what that might mean with reference to being as studied
in the particular sciences. But being as being, as we understand it now, that
is, as only the subject of metaphysics or the beginning of our inquiry, does
not warrant such a leap. It only warrants a distinction of *ontological* priority

with respect to the being that all particular sciences study. If all particular sciences discuss being in one of its aspects or another, then at some point being itself should come under discussion simply as being. It is in this sense only that metaphysics arises as a science and assumes some priority over the other sciences, in that it tries to deal with what the other sciences presuppose as sciences of being, something that they usually do not even advert to in their particularity.

This priority of metaphysics with regard to the particular sciences does not mean that the ontological inquiry we are embarking upon should come before any inquiry of particular science, as Wolff supposed with his deductive mathematical model of science. Even if metaphysics does arrive at a first principle of being other than the beings we know in experience, there may still be no way of deducing anything *more geometrico* from such a principle as known in metaphysics. For us as we begin our inquiry, it remains to be seen whether there is such a principle to be distinguished from the being we know in experience, let alone whether anything can be deduced from it. Far from coming first in the order of human inquiring and learning, metaphysics should rather come last, or at least after some inquiring into the principles and causes of particular aspects of being, as the ancients thought, since, as we have seen, it presupposes a certain mediation from particular scientific endeavors and it is the most difficult for us to enter into in a truly critical or scientific fashion. Even if it does not depend directly on them for any of its conclusions, metaphysics has something to gain from the other sciences, since all of them have to do with one aspect of being or another.

Finally, when we speak of being *as being,* as the subject of metaphysics or of our ontological inquiry, we should note carefully that we are not speaking of a being in particular or of a plurality of beings. Strictly speaking, the subject of a science is never particular being, whether taken as singular or as a plurality. As Aristotle said, there is no science of the singular. What determines a particular science as particular is the particular aspect of being that it investigates. Such an aspect is understood as common to what may be thought of as a plurality of beings in our experience, but not as singular. Conclusions in a science are always universal, even when they are relevant only to singular beings. This is true of what we have spoken of as the particular sciences, which abstract different aspects of being for their consideration, but it is even more true of metaphysics, which does not abstract any particular aspect of being but considers being under what we might call the "aspect" being in the concrete, as long as "aspect" does not connote any kind of particularity. What we are speaking about in metaphysics is not being under any particular aspect, but as something common to whatever there is, what Aquinas spoke of as *ens commune* and what the Greeks spoke of as *to on xynon*.

As common to whatever there is, "being" transcends any particularity we might posit as being. As such, it does not exclude particularity. In fact, as we shall see when we come to consider the analogy of being, it can and has to include a wide diversity of being as well as a plurality of beings. When we speak of it in its commonality as the subject of metaphysics at the beginning of our ontological inquiry, however, we do not include any of those differences. Nor do we try to think of being as either singular or plural. We try to think of it simply as being, not in the abstract or as a possible, but in the concrete as a whole or as a concrete universal. This is not easy for us to do, since we are more inclined to think of being only under some particular aspect. But it is the condition for starting on the right foot in metaphysics. If we cannot do this, we are more likely to reduce metaphysics to just another particular science on the *ontic* level and to continue in a forgetfulness of the *ontological* question of being.

Having now asserted that the subject of metaphysics has to be being as being, we might ask ourselves whether that is enough, or whether we should not also add a further determination for the subject of our inquiry in terms of the be of being or the so-called ontological difference. As we know, Heidegger maintained that there had to be a second question of being, the question of be as be, over and above the question of being as being. The question for us, then, would be whether this would constitute a second inquiry into being, giving rise to a second science of being, one of be as be rather than of being as being, or whether it would be merely an extension of the question we are already raising. Heidegger himself insists that be cannot be understood except in relation to being in the ontological difference. The question after be as be, as he says at the beginning of *Sein und Zeit,* has to be asked of being as being. "Insofar as be [*das Sein*] makes up what is asked about [*das Gefragte*], and be means the be of being, it turns out that what the question of be is asked of [*das Erfragte*] is being itself [*das Seiende selbst*]" (*SZ* 9/26).

This suggests that the question of be as be for Heidegger would appear as part of the inquiry into being as being, after a proper deconstruction of metaphysics as the science of being as being. But it would be premature to try to make a case for that at this point, which is only the beginning of our inquiry. If we were to insist on the "difference" between be and being at this point, we would be skewing our question away from its universal intent on the commonality of being back into something particular or different from

being simply as being. To be sure, Heidegger insists that be is not to be understood as another sort of being than the different aspects of being on the
ontic level. "That which is asked about [*Das Gefragte*] in the question to be
worked out is be [*das Sein*], that which determines being as being [*das
Seiende als Seiende*], that whereunto [*woraufhin*] being, however it may be discussed, is already understood. The be of being 'is' not itself a being" (*SZ*
8/23–24). But to the extent that he wants to speak of be as "that which determines being as being," one has to think of it as some other essence than
the essence of particular aspects of being. Heidegger himself speaks of the
essence of be when he wants to focus on be as different from being.

Whether such a difference can be maintained in a science of being as being remains to be seen. It cannot be taken for granted from the beginning of
metaphysics. In the course of our inquiry, we shall eventually come to focus
on be, or the act of being, as something distinct in being, but not precisely as
distinct from being, unless being is reduced to essence. But we cannot do
this from the beginning, before having elaborated the logic of how we mean
being in the exercise of judgment. What we can come up with is not exactly what Heidegger had in mind when he spoke of ontological difference,
but we are not excluding any such consideration of difference in being. We
are only saying that in beginning of our inquiry we must first deconstruct
any such difference and start simply from being as being in its commonality.

CHAPTER 2

The Method of Metaphysics

~

I T IS NOT ENOUGH to determine the subject to begin a science properly. We must also determine a method for dealing with the subject. The
subject gives us only the content of what is at issue in the science of being as
being. We must now look into the proper form for this content as the subject for the science we are entering into. In other words, we must articulate
what our method will be in this science. This will determine the type of discourse that is possible with regard to being as being. What is there to be said
about the meaning of being precisely *as being?* Are there properties of being
precisely *as being?* Are there principles or causes that account for it *as being?*

It is important for metaphysics to understand its own method from the
very beginning. Particular sciences may be able to get underway without
properly reflecting on their own method. That may come only after the
method has been put in practice. But metaphysics cannot get underway
without a proper reflection on the method it is using even to get started. It
does not begin except in the secondary kind of reflection on the particular
sciences previously alluded to. Metaphysics has to grasp its own possibility
from the very beginning or else it cannot get underway. This means that the
philosophy of being as being has also to be a philosophy of this philosophy
of being at the same time. Without some understanding of a method mediated by an understanding of method in particular sciences we would not
have arrived at a proper understanding of being as being as the subject of
this science. As first science, philosophy of being as being must examine its
presuppositions. In this respect, Kant was right in wishing to do a critique of
knowing before proceeding in the elaboration of any metaphysics. He was
wrong only in ignoring that there is already some knowing of being in experience and in the particular sciences.

Thus, in its beginning, metaphysics starts from a certain circularity, going
from content to form and from form to content, or from subject to method

and from method to subject. Other sciences show the same kind of circularity in their beginning in that the subject determines the method while the method shapes the subject. But for metaphysics that circularity is critical. It makes an absolute beginning possible for metaphysics as first science or first philosophy of being as being. This is not to say that it has a fixed starting point, from which it can spring forth and which it can leave behind as it advances. But it is to say that, in the hermeneutic circle where it gets underway, it has a beginning that in no way depends on any other beginning. It is not an immediate beginning, as though the thought of being as being were immediately given. It is a mediated reflective beginning. But the mediation is that of its own act beginning by determining its own subject as distinct from the subject of any particular science.

If we think back on how we arrived at the subject of metaphysics, it becomes clear that we have already been doing metaphysics in determining its subject. If this were not so, this subject would not yet be established metaphysically as the subject of our consideration, and we would not yet have a science of metaphysics to speak about. Thus, as we now come to reflect on the method of metaphysics, we find that we have already been exercising that method in order to arrive at the subject. This should not be taken as a cause for embarrassment at this point of our beginning in this science. On the contrary, it constitutes a definite advantage as we come to reflect on the method we need and examine how to proceed in the investigation of the ultimate subject of all science, namely, being as being.

We do not have to go looking outside of the science for our method. We can only find it within the science itself, in the very act whereby we begin to consider being itself, or being as being, as our subject. If we had not exercised some metaphysical reflection in arriving at the subject of metaphysics, we would not have anything to reflect on at this point in our investigation. Having exercised some reflection on what is at issue in the knowing of being, however, we have something further to reflect on that we did not have before determining that being as being is our subject, something that cannot be separated from this subject as a form that cannot be separated from its content, but something that will nevertheless enable us to advance further into the investigation of being as being. If we cannot critically establish a method for doing metaphysics within metaphysics itself, then we shall have to conclude that metaphysics can only be a deconstruction of any particular science, without the possibility of a reconstruction in the order of being as being.

The importance of doing this as part of our beginning cannot be exag-

gerated from a critical standpoint. It is possible to raise the question of being, as Heidegger and others have done, without coming to a method for
dealing with it in its universality. Without a rational method for dealing with
this question, we can only come to a doctrine of metaphysical absurdity or
nihilism, as we find frequently in existentialism, or a doctrine of metaphysical agnosticism, as we find in a critical philosophy that stops short of some
unknowable "thing in itself" that it is nevertheless compelled to posit. Such
doctrines should not be accepted unless it proves absolutely impossible to
say anything meaningful about being precisely as such.

At the same time, however, we must look also for a method that is appropriate for the subject we have already enunciated in its universality. In this we
cannot adopt a method that is appropriate for only a particular science, since
that would be to reduce our subject to that of a particular science. What
counts for rational investigation in physics, biology, or economics is not
enough for rational investigation in metaphysics. Nor is the method of phenomenology, which the young Heidegger was enamored of, necessarily
sufficient for our task, since that too may be concerned only with a particular aspect of being, even if it be *Dasein* or the lifeworld. We must rather look
for a method for speaking about being in its complete and concrete universality.

What can we say about being as being, besides that it is? Being is what is.
What more is there to say? Apart from being as whole, there can only be
nothing, and, in saying "being," have we not said everything there is to say?
In a sense, yes. But do we know what we have said? Have we expressed
everything that we know in saying that being is whatever is? Is there more
to be learned about being as being that we do not yet know in our common
immediate knowledge of being as present, something that has to be mediated through rational discourse so that it becomes more intelligible to us?
Even though being is that which we know first and to which we refer
everything that we do know, is there not more to the intelligibility of being
than this first immediate knowing from which we begin?

What is in question here is an understanding of knowing that will open
the way for us to pursue the question of being as being systematically. We
shall begin with a reflection on how intelligence transcends mere experience even as it begins from it. Then we shall consider the twofold act of intelligence itself in order to come to the exercise of judgment as the activity
in which being presents itself for human knowing. This in turn will lead us
to distinguish between two kinds of judgment: a direct exercise and an indirect exercise. This will enable us to situate the exercise of judgment proper

to metaphysics in relation to being as it presents itself in experience. From this we shall then be able to demonstrate in what our method must consist in order to pursue our question of being as being.

2.1   Experience and the Twofold Act of Intelligence

The question before us concerns the relation between intelligence and experience in the process of learning. Learning is the way we come to know through a combination in which intelligence takes off from experience as experience accumulates. Though we insist on the necessity of starting from experience in any science, including metaphysics, we must not forget that science itself comes as an act of intelligence.

Experience entails a certain sense of being, a being attentive to being or a letting being present itself through intelligence. Intelligence is part of the presencing. This is already evident in the way we distinguish between different kinds of experience. Experience itself, as a whole, is massive and indeterminate. Through intelligence we bring discernment into it so that we may distinguish various aspects of it. Thus we come to acquire experience in one realm or another when we begin to recognize certain patterns or similarities in what happens under similar circumstances. We learn from experience, but it is the presence of intelligence in experience that makes us learn.

Moreover, intelligent learning entails more than just an accumulation of experiences. There are degrees of intelligence as well as degrees of experience. Sometimes we learn more from an experience than at other times. We also see that some seem to learn more from an experience than others do. The unintelligent individual does not seem to learn from experience as much as others do, even though his or her "experience" may be quite as long and quite as vast as that of others. To be old or well traveled is no guarantee of real learning. It is possible to remain confined to a very narrow scope even with an exposure to many realms of the world. Bias, whether individual or social, or the narrow focusing of intelligence in experience, can cut learning short prematurely or constrain it to only a part of what there is to be learned. It is partial to one thing or another as it ignores the more universal scope that intelligence can open up to. But it is also possible to learn a lot even from a relatively narrow scope of experience if intelligence intervenes by raising ample questions about what is given.

Intelligence, however, is not a simple act. In our consciousness of intelligence in experience, not as separate from experience, but as distinct from mere sense and as overcoming the sheer multiplicity and dispersion of sense knowing, we distinguish between two acts of intelligence within experience that can bring us more clearly to the point where metaphysics begins in the exercise of intelligence. In terms of learning, these two acts can be seen as answering two different kinds of questions, questions concerning *what* we can say about what we are experiencing and questions concerning *whether* what we say is true in reality or not.

These two acts or these two kinds of questioning are not independent of one another. They are in a relationship where the second kind of question arises only after the first kind has already found some answer or where we have begun to say something about *what* we are experiencing, as we turn to a more critical reflection on *what* we have conceived. It is important to understand this complexity of intelligence if we are to pass beyond the conception of human science as purely empirical and arrive at a proper understanding of where metaphysics begins as a science.

We can speak of these two acts of intelligence as *understanding,* in the first place, and as *critical reflection,* in the second. Both can be found in any science where there is learning from experience, whether it be what we commonly call "empirical science" or also what is called "phenomenology." In empirical science the first act takes the form of such questions as "What is it that presents itself in experience?"; "Why does it present iself as it does?"; "How regularly does it do so?"; and so on. The answers to such questions take the form of formulations or scientific hypotheses about what things are in their being.

What characterizes these questions as first acts of intelligence is that they derive directly from things given in experience as attempts to grasp or to apprehend and to express *what* they are. It is in this direct relation to experience that they find their meaning. So it is in the empirical or the physical sciences. So it is also in the social sciences. All of them are, in their first act of intelligence, attempts to understand or to grasp and express *what* things are as they present themselves through the senses.

Nevertheless, complex as this first act of intelligence might become in its attempts to grasp and express what things are, especially in the plurality of particular sciences, it is still only a first act and a relatively simple apprehension in comparison to the second act that is to follow, the act of *critical reflection* on what has been apprehended and formulated in the first act, since this second act consists in raising the further question of *whether* what has been formulated or understood is true or not. This is the more critical question, without which there is no *science* in the full sense of the term. It is the question of verification whether an interpretation of facts or data really corresponds to what is the case or to what we can simply refer to as being. It is an act of trying to compose what we have conceived with how being presents itself.

Empirical sciences have complicated ways of exercising this second act of intelligence or of answering their questions for critical reflection. All of them consist in a process of verification over and above a process of conceptualization. All of them issue into judgments that express either a yes, where a "composition" is found between the concept in question and being, or a no, where no composition is found but only "division," or a combination of yes and no, where the concept in question is thought to be partly true and partly false, or partly adequate and partly inadequate, to being. From this we have the understanding of this second act of intelligence as an act of composing or dividing, presupposing a prior act of conceptualization.

In phenomenology the same twofold act of intelligence comes to the fore, although in a different way than in the empirical sciences. There questions for understanding are raised less in terms of abstract aspects of being taken apart from other aspects, as physics considers the physical aspect of being apart from its living aspect, but more in terms of experience as a whole. Phenomenology is thought of as a return to the "things" themselves—*zu den Sachen selbst*—or to "matters" as they are lived precognitively. It has been described by Merleau-Ponty as more descriptive of the world than as constructive (Merleau-Ponty i–xvi). But ultimately it is still an attempt to form what we shall call a certain quiddity of things sensible or otherwise in our minds, or of what is given in experience as a whole such as it is (see Chapter 3.1). It is also spoken of as an eidetic reduction going from the fact of existence to the nature or the essences of things that are the business of human life—*Sachen.* Heidegger sees it as passing over from naive consciousness, which is not only absorbed in its unreflected immediacy, but also fails to differentiate between the accidental and the essential in experience, to a more analytical form of consciousness that distinguishes the more essential structures of everyday life from the arbitrary and accidental ones and, in so doing, brings them to light (*SZ* 23&49/38&61). Such is the analysis of the structures of *Dasein,* for example, in *Sein und Zeit,* prior to raising the question of being or of be properly.

All this, however, has to do only with what we call the first act of intelligence, understanding, or *Verstehen,* of what is given in lived experience. It is still only forming the quiddity of things in our own mind. It is only a first step in coming to know ourselves and the world. It does not close in upon itself, but rather calls for a second act of intelligence, that of critical reflection upon what is conceived, to see if it composes with being. Knowing critically cannot be satisfied with just bright ideas in forming its quiddity of things. It must check the truth of its ideas in relation to what is, or to being. The eidetic reduction is part of a resolve to make the world appear as it is prior to any reflection upon myself or any effort at conceptualization. Its ultimate aim is to make reflection equal to the unreflected life of consciousness. In this *lived* experience it looks for its criterion of truth and comes to its own judgment about being as given in the lifeworld. It too has its own act of composing and dividing in the relation between essence as conceived and essence as real. Only so can it be thought of as a critical science in its own right. Only so can we take it as properly an exercise of judgment with regard to what there is.

The question arises, then, as to whether either the empirical sciences or phenomenology can come to the question of being as being. As critical in their reflection they do refer to being in some way, but do they refer to it *as being*? If we understand them as particular sciences, as we understood such sciences in coming to our definition of metaphysics as the universal science of being as being, they do not refer to being in its fullness or in its commonality, but only to being in some aspect or some quiddity of what is given in experience. For them to refer to being *as being* they would have to cease being particular sciences and become sciences of the whole as whole, or become critical of our conception of being as being, which they cannot do without transcending their particular conception. In this sense, then, there cannot be a direct passage from any of these particular sciences, whether empirical or phenomenological, into metaphysics, even though all of them entail an exercise of the two acts of intelligence. But it is the exercise of these two acts of intelligence in any science that does open the way to a proper understanding of metaphysics, if we keep clearly in mind the twofold act of intelligence found in any exercise of judgment as part of experience.

2.2   The Exercise of Judgment and the Presence of Being

If we wish to focus on being as being as the subject of our inquiry, then, we must take the exercise of judgment as a whole as our opening. We may speak of being as being as a content of the first act of intelligence, but one that transcends the content of either empirical science, which inquires into the causes that determine various aspects of our experience, or phenomenology, which tries to make sense of our lived experience of the world. But we must also speak of being *as being* more positively as a content of the second act of intelligence, even as it distinguishes itself from the first act, a content that distinguishes itself as a kind of act or actuality over and above, but still in relation to, *what* has been formulated in the concept.

While science and phenomenology exercise judgment about different aspects of being as it presents itself in experience, they do not exercise judgment about this actuality of being. In raising the question of being as being, metaphysics tries to include this actuality of being to which reference is made in any exercise of judgment as part of what is to be understood in its subject. It does so by stretching the understanding so that it includes the actuality of being as well as *what* is conceived of it and by keeping reflection in constant relation to what has been understood or formulated in the first act of intelligence, as we do in any concrete exercise of judgment. If we can come to a proper way of conceiving being *as being* in our understanding, then we can come to a new kind of reflection in relation to actuality and a new way of exercising judgment about being *as being.*

Coming to the subject of metaphysics in this way brings out the special difficulty we have in conceiving its content. Starting from an experience of being, as every inquiry must, how are we to formulate the question about being as being without reducing it to another quiddity that would only parallel the first order of quiddities formed in premetaphysical inquiry and so miss what is distinctive of the question of being as being as a question for higher understanding and reflection? Is there another way of forming the quiddity of being as given in experience than the one already used in empirical science or in phenomenology? Can there be an understanding of being other than the one we already have in either one of these two forms of inquiry? If there is, we must come to it by stretching the understanding so that it includes actuality as part of its content without losing sight of the fact that this actuality presents itself only in the act of critical reflection. This is not a matter of intuition into something "beyond all possible experience," as Kant supposed, but a matter for discursive elaboration of the being we already know intellectually as well as sensibly in the exercise of judgment.

Kant had a very important point about human knowing, a point that Aristotle had made long before him. Every human inquiry has to begin from experience or "sense intuition" as a question for understanding. This has to hold true for metaphysical as well as for any other kind of inquiry. We somehow have to form a quiddity of being as being. We have to be able to say *what* we mean when we speak of being as such. Otherwise metaphysical discourse cannot get underway. And yet, if what we have said of the two acts of intelligence holds true and the question of being as being arises beyond all other understanding, this forming of the quiddity of being as being cannot take place on a merely prereflexive level of knowing. Nor can it remain fixed at the level of understanding as it relates directly to the level of experience. It must bring the level of understanding and the level of reflection on understanding together in a new way. It has to be an understanding that does not leave out the content of critical reflection, an intellectual content beyond mere experience and facticity, and a reflection that seeks understanding in its very transcendence of understanding.

How can this be done? Not by a reflection on mere intuition or directly on what is given in experience, which is required for human knowing. Nor just by analysis as it relates to intuition in a kind of hermeneutic circle. We must break out of the hermeneutic circle that binds understanding to experience and experience to understanding in empirical science or in phenomenology by insisting more on critical or judgmental reflection in its originality as a second act of intelligence, which, even when it is exercised in particular sciences or in phenomenology, includes a reference to being in its actuality. From this reference to the actuality of being we must go back to reflect on the exercise of judgment as a whole and bring out its structure, so that we may see how the concept of being itself is elaborated concretely for us in this exercise of judgment. It is through an understanding of this structure that we can come to a way of structuring our notion of being for the understanding.

2.3   The Structure of Judgment as Signifying Being

To get at this structure in the exercise of judgment we have only to go back to our analysis of experience and the twofold act of intelligence. In terms of this analysis, we can distinguish between three levels in the act of knowing or in the process of learning. First is the level of experience itself, which is the level of gathering things as data or as given, a level "open to understanding and formulation but by itself not understood and in itself ineffable" (Lonergan 273). This is the level of mere observation in empirical science or the level of mere facticity in the lived experience of phenomenology.

The second level is the level of understanding, which emerges through questions for understanding, whether by analysis or by eidetic reduction. This is the level of formulation or interpretation of what is taken as given in experience. It presupposes the level of experience, but it goes further into it by formulating *what* it is in its essence or how it comes to be what it is. This second level yields an understanding in the mind of the one exercising judgment. But the exercise of judgment does not end on this level, which is itself open to the further act of critical reflection by intelligence. This second level is a necessary mediation between the first level of experience and the third level of critical reflection. Without some act of understanding expressed in some formulation, where the one exercising judgment becomes conscious of his or her own conceptualization, there is no call for critical reflection.

The third level is the level of critical reflection as called for on the level of understanding. What is critical about it is that it brings in a formal reference to being as a criterion for the truth of what is in the understanding. Such a formal reference to being is found in any exercise of judgment, including that of the empirical sciences and phenomenology, though it is not formally adverted to in the exercise of these particular sciences. It is found in metaphysics as well, but there it has to be formally adverted to in order to bring out the proper subject of its consideration, namely, being as being.

It is not enough to distinguish these three levels of knowing, however; we must also understand the essential structure that binds them together as a single exercise of judgment whether in the empirical sciences or in phenomenology. For there is no proper understanding of hypotheses in empirical sciences without some need for verification and no proper understanding of eidetic reduction of lived experience without some reference to the existence placed in parentheses.

We can illustrate this structure in the exercise of judgment by reflecting on the judgment we have already come to exercise in metaphysics. De facto, we have already exercised a first judgment in this science in establishing its subject. If we think back on that first judgment we can both distinguish three levels of knowing in the way we arrived at the judgment and the structure in which it came together.

To begin with, we had no data of observation or no simple fact of lived experience to refer to directly as that about which the question of being as being turns. There was nothing in particular to point to or to indicate. Indeed, it would have been a mistake for us to point to anything in particular in our experience. We could only say "being as being" as an expression of a certain reflection on our part. But we did have the fact of certain utterances to work with in our first attempt to focus on a subject, ways of talking about being, whether as an infinitive or as a participle, and ways in which a number of metaphysicians had raised the question of being. We began our own questioning from these utterances as we found them in the tradition of metaphysics and sought to understand what was at issue in them, developing our own understanding of the question of being and examining *what* was implied in the different understandings that we encountered. Finally, after coming to some understanding of the question, we turned to reflect upon the different formulations of the question and to determine which seemed best suited to express the subject of metaphysics. We came to the judgment that metaphysics is best understood as the science of being as being, and not as the science of the possible as possible, nor of the "thing in itself" accessible only to some intellectual intuition, nor even of the be of being presenting itself through being.

This first judgment in metaphysics is final in one sense. We shall not have to go back on it as we proceed. But it is only a beginning for a whole new learning process upon which we are embarking and which we are now pursuing in seeking a method for the process. As we proceed, we shall shed new light on this first judgment, which remains obscure by itself, and we shall come to a further understanding of being as being, which will then call for further reflection, and so on, not indefinitely perhaps, but in a way that cannot be made definite at this point. Even with the question of method, we are already in the process of formulating an understanding for a new judgment about the way to proceed in metaphysics as a result of our first judgment about its subject that will lead to further questions about the meaning of being as being, its properties, its principles or causes, and so on. This second judgment will shed new light on the first and open the way to further judgments in the way of learning we have embarked upon in this science of being as being.

Another way of bringing out this same structure of judgment is to reflect on some particular judgment in which we affirm the truth of some particular understanding of something given in experience. Our point in this is not to examine the essence of truth. That is something we shall do later on, when we come to reflect on truth as a property of being. For the moment we are interested only in seeing how the structure of judgment relates to truth, or how the relation of truth appears in the structure of judgment.

In a question that is clearly formulated I already understand what is being talked about, the subject *(S),* and what is being said about it, the predicate *(P).* Is *S* truly or really *P?* Though I may understand both *P* and *S* clearly enough, as long as I do not know the answer to the question, there remains something for me to learn. In saying yes, however, *S* is *P,* or even no, *S* is not *P,* I am claiming to know something more than what I knew in merely understanding the question. Precisely what that "more" is, or what the truth is for any particular judgment, is not what concerns us here, but simply what there is in the act of affirming, or denying, that says more than just what is contained in the terms *(S* and *P)* of a judgment.

This is not to say that every particular judgment is true. There can be false judgments as well as true judgments. But it is to say that in the exercise of judgment something is being said about truth with some reference to being that is not being said in the terms of the judgment. It is being said in the *act* or the exercise itself, *in actu exercito,* and not in the terms, not *in actu signato.*

This is an important distinction to keep in mind. We shall have ample occasion to refer to it later on in our articulation of the meaning of being as well as of truth. But the distinction must not be understood as a separation between two acts. It is within one and the same act or exercise of judgment as a whole that the distinction is found between what is being said *in the act* and what is being said *in the terms* alone. There is no act of judgment without terms, nor are there terms for judgment without an act. The relation between the two is absolutely essential for the structure of any particular judgment. The act contains or expresses the assertion of truth, but the assertion is limited by the terms. I do not assert all truth in a judgment, but only the particular truth I claim to express through the terms of my judgment. The terms limit the act, no less than the act takes judgment beyond the content expressed in the terms alone.

Implicit in the act, though not in the terms, of a judgment is the claim that we already know, somehow, what truth is, and that what we are saying entails some truth or correspondence with being. The idea of truth here is not so much one of correspondence as one of relation or reference to being, which presents itself. Truth is that which we must correspond to in speaking. It is the presence of being that makes us critical of our understanding and initially causes us to reflect in the exercise of judgment. Indeed, it is this presence of being that gives us the very first principle of judgment, which is that we cannot both affirm and deny at the same time, and which, according to Aquinas, is founded on the notion of being and nonbeing—*fundatur supra rationem entis et non entis (ST* I–II, 94, 2, c).

In the exercise of the first act of intelligence, there is a certain apprehension of being. In fact, as Aquinas puts it in the passage just referred to, "that which first falls in the apprehension is being, the intelligence of which is included in all [things] whatever which one apprehends." This is why the notion of being and nonbeing is said to found the first, indemonstrable principle of judgment.

Apprehension here, however, must be understood very carefully, especially as it relates to being. It is not the apprehension of a genus or specific difference whereby we form the quiddity of things as given in experience, as one would expect if we were talking about the apprehension of some quiddity and not the apprehension of being. What we are talking about is a more fundamental apprehension that encompasses the quidditative apprehension of things in a broader perspective, that of being itself, which makes itself present in this apprehension. It is an apprehension that is more like a sense of presence within which everything is apprehended, ourselves as well as other selves or things. Being is what we apprehend first, in a sense that makes it prior to all categorizing, even though it is what we speak of last in the order of questioning and learning. It is apprehended at the juncture between the first and the second act of intelligence, which is why it not only gives rise to critical reflection but also grounds the first principle of judgment.

Another way Aquinas uses to express this same relation between being and quiddity is in terms of conceptions. "That which intelligence first conceives as what is known best [*quasi notissimum*], and in which it resolves all conceptions, is being" (*Ver* 1, 1, c). Whatever we conceive, we conceive somehow with reference to being, which is conceived first and is somehow known best. Knowledge is of being, as we have been saying from the very beginning. But what is conceived first and known best is not expressed in the terms of any judgment from the beginning. It is expressed more in the act or in the exercise of any particular judgment. It includes the terms of the particular judgment but goes beyond them. That is why the conception of being remains implicit in the exercise of everyday judgment and of scientific or phenomenological judgment. That is why also it has to be explicated in a special effort of conceptualization in metaphysics or, to put it more in terms of our present analysis, in an effort to bring it to terms, that is, express it in a better articulation of meaning.

Learning in metaphysics consists precisely in this sort of effort on our part, starting from what is said only in the act or the exercise of judgment and trying to express that in the terms of a different kind of judgment than the one we start from in common sense, in empirical science, or in phenomenology, a more indirect kind of judgment that explores the content of critical reflection or of the second act of intelligence in relation to the content of understanding or of the first act of intelligence expressed in the terms of judgment as part of one and the same structured act. We must now ponder how this more indirect kind of judgment of metaphysics differs from the more direct kind we find in common sense and in the particular sciences, and how this indirect kind of judgment relates to the direct kind of judgment we have been speaking about.

2.4   From the Direct to the Indirect Exercise of Judgment

In what sense is the judgment we exercise in metaphysics *indirect* as compared to the judgment exercised in the particular sciences or in phenomenology? This is an important question for us to consider at this point because it is as an indirect exercise of judgment that our systematic metaphysics will flow, as distinct from the more direct exercise of judgment that is characteristic of the particular sciences and phenomenology. As we have said, every type of science, every kind of human knowing, culminates in judgments in which something is affirmed about being, either under one aspect or another, as in particular sciences, or simply *as being*, as we have to do in metaphysics. What is affirmed or expressed in the terms of particular judgments such as those in particular sciences comes as an answer to questions for understanding that relate more or less directly to being as it presents itself in experience, depending on the relative complexity of the questions raised. What is affirmed in metaphysics relates to the same things present in experience, but only indirectly. They refer more directly to being as a whole or to being simply as being.

Of course, the judgments of these particular sciences do not explicitly refer to being in their terms. The judgments of physical science talk about quanta or energy and the judgments of biology talk about life and cells. But insofar as these judgments come as a result of critical reflection on what has been conceived in a first act of intelligence and express some claim to truth, as we have seen, they do include a reference to being, about which nothing is said in the terms or in the particular science as a whole. It is not part of their business, or their *Sache*, to attend to being as being, but only to being as it presents itself directly in experience and to seek verification for their hypothetical conceptions in this direct relationship. It is only in questions such as the one we are raising here, about knowing or the exercise of judgment, that this direct relation to being as it presents itself is set aside, for a moment at least, in order to ask what it is to know or to exercise judgment, and what it is that is known more universally when knowing takes place.

These are questions for understanding that relate directly to the act of knowing or to the exercise of judgment about being, and not to being as it presents itself directly in experience. They relate to being as it presents itself in experience only indirectly, since the act or the exercise of judgment to which they relate is one that begins from experience and somehow remains tied to this experience. In this way our questions can give rise to a science or to judgments that are only indirectly related to things as given in experience but that are more directly related to the act of knowing, as in logic, or even to being as being, as we have tried to show in establishing the proper subject of consideration for metaphysics.

Every exercise of judgment entails some critical reflection with its reference to being. In a science, every judgment one comes to is understood as an answer to a question for reflection upon some understanding. It is important to note, however, that our first judgments have to do directly with matters of experience, sensible things we see and feel and use and relate to, including other human beings. This is evident if we think back on our first experiences as children, when we were first learning to differentiate things, between red and green, hot and cold, living and nonliving, useful and not useful. The terms of judgment in this first experience were always sensible and always included a reference to a *this* or a *that*: "this is green" and "that is red"; "this is a dog" and "that is a doll"; "this is Mama, that is Papa." Yet even this most primitive kind of judgment entailed some reflection that made us ask questions and advance from this first knowing to a more penetrating and a more extensive knowing in a sort of spiral of reflection upon understanding giving rise to further questions for understanding, which then called for further critical reflection, a spiral that eventually gives rise to particular science and to more critical reflection. After we have differentiated and identified certain beings as human, for example, we go on to examine more closely what it means to be human, and so on of other beings that we differentiate or identify as part of what we experience.

The various sciences arise out of this speculative interest in understanding better what is given in experience as a *this* or a *that* and verifying one's understanding through critical reflection. Various aspects of being, various subjects of consideration, are defined for investigation and appropriate methods are devised for pursuing the investigation. Different disciplines emerge to explain or account for something at first just given in experience. As one advances in a science, the terms of judgment change; they become more specialized or technical. But even this technical terminology, which at times seems far removed from the initial terminology of "red" or "living" or "human," remains directly related to the things of experience. Scientific hypotheses have to be verified in terms reducible to some experience of a *this* or a *that*. Phenomenological reduction has to be brought back to the lived world. No matter how sophisticated the hypotheses or the reduction, the subject or subjects they deal with are always directly related to experience. They remain in what we refer to as the direct exercise of judgment, which has to do with being as it presents itself in experience.

In the indirect exercise of judgment, however, we step back from this immediate focus on being as given in experience to consider more how knowing takes place and what is known universally in such an act. Our first questions are about things given in experience, but once we have started asking questions about things and formulating answers to these questions, we become conscious of doing so and we begin to ask questions about this intellectual activity of ours. We go from a first order of questioning to a second order of questioning where the terms no longer refer directly to sensible things, as they did in the first order, but to the *acts* of our intelligence or to the exercise of judgment itself. We begin to ask how it is that we know or whether we even know at all. We begin to form the quiddity of what it is to know, which requires a new and broader perspective, one that remains related to experience, in that our intellectual activity begins and remains part of our experience, but only indirectly, in that the terms of our second order of questioning refer not directly to things as given, but to the activity of knowing these things. These second-order questions refer to our ways of categorizing things in exercising judgment, so that the terms of these questions are no longer directly sensible, but rather intelligible, in the sense that they refer to our intellectual activity directly and to sensible things only indirectly, namely, through the initial activity or the first order of questioning to which they refer.

To illustrate this second order of judgment we could refer to logic, which deals with second-order ideas, or ideas about ideas, such as "genus" and "specific difference," and not with ideas about things directly, such as "horse" and "man." But let us refer more concretely to some actual exercise of judgment.

A judgment could be defined as an act of intelligence in which I affirm or deny something *(P)* about something *(S)* with a consciousness of what truth is and a claim to having attained it in affirming or denying. In order to understand such a definition and to verify whether it is true, I have to have exercised some judgment of my own previously. If you have exercised some previous judgment of your own, you might want to qualify my rather simple definition somewhat, add to it or subtract from it. But in any event, in order for us to come to some agreement about a definition of judgment, or even to discuss a definition of judgment, we have to have exercised some prior judgment. Now that prior exercise of judgment, as part of human experience, had to do directly with sensible things. Its terms, *S* and *P,* were sensible. It had to be a judgment such as "snow is white" or, in the ultimate analysis, "this is snow." It is only after having exercised such judgment that we can then understand what it is to judge and put into the terms of a new judgment what was only in the act of the previous judgment. In this new judgment, however, the terms, "judgment" *(S)* and "act of saying something about something" *(P)*, are now intelligible and refer to some actual exercise of judgment as such, and not to what the first exercise of judgment was about originally, namely, snow, white, or this.

Note that the difference between the indirect and the direct exercise of judgment is basically a difference of terms, what is said *in actu signato,* or in the terms of judgment, and not of what is said *in actu exercito,* or in the exercise of judgment as such. The indirect exercise of judgment tries to express in its terms what is said only in the exercise of judgment, even though it is itself an exercise of judgment.

Note also that the exercise of judgment from which the terms for indirect judgment can arise can be indirect as well as direct. This could be seen as giving rise to an infinite regress in indirect judgment about indirect judgment about indirect judgment and so on. But that is not what happens in a proper reflection upon the exercise of judgment, whether the judgment be direct or indirect. What happens is rather a double sort of consciousness: first, a consciousness of an object as expressed in the *terms* of a judgment, S and P, especially in the direct exercise of judgment, where the focus is on things as given in experience; and second, a consciousness of the act itself in which the terms are expressed or a kind of self-consciousness that is not expressed in the terms S and P, but only in the act as distinct from its terms. In the indirect exercise of judgment we focus on the act itself as the "object" of our consciousness which we try to express in the terms of an indirect judgment, that is, one that focuses not on things as given directly in experience, but rather on the actual exercise of judgment itself and what it refers to as being.

In trying to bring this actual exercise of judgment to terms, however, in an indirect exercise of judgment, we find two things worthy of note. First, we find that we cannot adequately express in terms that are always determinate and finite the actual exercise of judgment itself, which in contrast to any determinate terms has something infinite about it. As I exercise judgment in whatever determinate terms I may have in mind, I find that my power to exercise judgment is not limited to any particular set of determinate terms but is always open, exercising itself in other determinate terms as well. In exercising judgment in terms of physics, for example, I know that I could also exercise judgment in other spheres of life or social existence. And in exercising judgment in any particular science, I know that I could also exercise judgment in a more universal science such as logic or, as we are about to say, in metaphysics.

Second, in the very same act of indirect judgment, we find also that we are still exercising judgment in an *act* that has not been reduced to terms and that is ultimately irreducible to terms, because every effort to bring this act to terms is always an act that is not and cannot be reduced to terms. If we try to bring this act to terms, we find that we are only repeating judgments that we have already made concerning the actual exercise of judgment so that there is no point in repeating such a judgment indefinitely. What gives rise to the appearance of an infinite regress is the disproportion between the actual exercise of judgment as such or as distinct from the terms of any particular judgment, which are always determinate in comparison to the actual exercise itself. But what gives the lie to this appearance is that the two, the actual exercise and the terms, are always part of one and the same exercise of judgment.

The direct exercise of judgment already contains the kind of reflection on the exercise of judgment that we try to bring out reflectively in an indirect exercise of judgment. The indirect exercise of judgment is still structured in the same way as the direct exercise in that the indirect entails an actual exercise of judgment along with terms, except that its terms refer to the actual exercise of judgment itself and what it refers to as "being" rather than to some being as given in experience. In reflecting on the actual exercise of judgment, I am not just reflecting in the present on some past judgment of mine, a present judgment that could then be reflected upon in some future judgment, and so on indefinitely. I am reflecting on this actual exercise in its composition with terms that express what I know in this judgment with the understanding that these terms do not exhaust or adequately express in their determinacy all that I know or refer to in the actual exercise of judgment. In other words, the actual exercise of any judgment is always in a sort of irreducible tension with its own terms, a tension that is already present in the direct exercise of judgment but that is now brought to the fore reflectively in the indirect exercise of judgment.

In this passage from the direct to the indirect exercise of judgment, one can readily understand the difference by the transposition from terms that still refer directly to sensible things to terms that are more strictly intelligible in that they refer more to acts of intelligence in which sensible things are known. One can easily overlook the actual exercise of intelligence that is common to both and that remains irreducible to terms in both the direct and the indirect exercise of judgment. In a reflection on the indirect exercise of judgment as well as on the direct exercise of judgment, however, we can no longer overlook this *act* that, as we have just tried to show, is irreducible to terms. In the actual consciousness I have of the judgment I exercise, through a definition such as the one given above, I am also conscious that the judgment I am actually exercising is not expressed in the terms of this judgment, since I still have to distinguish the act of this judgment from its terms, as I had to earlier. Nor will a further judgment bring that act to terms completely, since it too will be a composite of terms and act, still to be reduced to terms, and so on indefinitely. What I have to recognize is that the actual exercise of judgment contains an act that terms may be able to approximate but can never adequately represent. And this is seen immediately and reflexively only in the actual exercise of judgment even about the direct exercise of judgment.

This is not to say that the act and its content remain unknown to me. On the contrary, it is known in a way that cannot be reduced to terms or expressed in the terms of any determinate judgment. I know it and at the same time I know that I cannot adequately represent it through any concept I have, not even that of "the act of judgment." If we take intelligibility to refer primarily to the level of understanding in any exercise of judgment, then we would have to say that the act or the level of total reflection in the exercise of judgment is not *less* but *more* intelligible. It refers to a level of intelligibility we can strive for but can never completely attain in the terms of our judgment, a level that we can signify intelligently but cannot represent in the terms of our understanding. Such a level transcends experience and understanding, but it does so only in a dialectical relationship with them. We cannot signify the intelligibility of an act without representation, as our very effort to distinguish the act from the terms of judgment clearly shows. There is no actual exercise of judgment without some terms, representations, or concepts. We can get beyond them, into the meaning of the act as act, only by taking them seriously as mediating the intelligibility of the act.

To get into metaphysics as a science of being as being, however, and not just as a science of the actual exercise of judgment, in which being makes itself present, we must get beyond mere concepts or representations that can be expressed in the terms of judgment. We must come to some understanding of how act transcends any concept not just in the exercise of judgment, but also in the being we refer to as actual. At the same time we must be systematic in our use of concepts or in the terms of our approach because the act that transcends the conceptual remains in dialectical relation with the conceptual. We can get to the higher intelligibility of acts only if we proceed systematically through the intelligibility of concepts.

In other words, we must recognize that what we are trying to express in systematic concepts is not reducible to such concepts in its actuality. Just as the definition of judgment we arrive at through reflection on the actual exercise of judgment does not adequately express in its terms all that we know in the actual exercise of judgment, so also what we can say systematically in concepts about being as being may not be adequate to being in act over and above *what* a being is, which can be expressed in the terms of a judgment. Unlike Hegel, who tried to reduce everything to a system, or the Concept, we have to be systematically unsystematic, that is, not stop short of any system in self-defeating deconstruction, but rather transcend any system in the effort to understand being in act, something that cannot be adequately understood or conceptualized even as present in experience or as actual.

Hence the need and the difficulty of proceeding systematically in metaphysics. We must proceed according to a rational discourse. We must use concepts, which represent being for us, and order them properly, in order to signify clearly what we mean that cannot be represented through them. Without representations and concepts we cannot advance in metaphysics, but if we do not get beyond them we do not get to metaphysics properly, or we falsify it. We reduce being to our way of conceiving or representing it as possible instead of signifying it as actual, even though in the very act of doing so we know that the act in its own reality is irreducible to the concept or to the terms of any judgment.

Metaphysics is not the only science in the order of indirect or reflective judgment. Even if, unlike Hegel, we distinguish logic from metaphysics, we could think of logic as an indirect exercise of judgment, whether as the art of thinking or of exercising judgment or as the science of human knowing. In reflecting on our direct exercise of judgment we can consider only the activity of knowing according to its different forms. In this sense, logic involves the study of operations of intelligence such as forming the quiddity of things, affirming or denying, and reasoning. Such a consideration leads to the formulation of rules for proceeding in the exercise of judgment (logic as an art) or of laws governing purely formal systems (logic as a science). Such formulations have to do primarily with "second intentions," in that they do not refer to things as given in experience but rather to our way of thinking about things as given in experience.

These same formulations can also be used heuristically, as a means of opening up an access to things as given in experience. In this way, logic can give rise to *dialectic* as understood in the *Topics* of Aristotle, that is, as a way of considering things topically or according to what is probable, in the sense of what may or may not be provable about them. The formulation of hypotheses in empirical science could thus be viewed as a sort of dialectic in the direct exercise of judgment, just as Hegel's *Logic,* coming after the more experiential dialectic of the *Phenomenology,* can be viewed as an indirect dialectical exercise of judgment about how being is conceivable. In both cases we come up with notions or concepts that could be proved right or wrong in reference to being as actual.

Dialectical judgment, however, is not metaphysical judgment. As an orientation toward being, or at least toward what might be provable in reality, dialectical judgment takes us beyond mere logic, which considers only consistency in our way of thinking or, in its more mathematical form, sets that can be constructed from this way of thinking, independently of any reference to things. As dealing only with the provable, or with what remains to be proved, dialectic does not signify being in act. To signify the latter in its actuality we must proceed by way of a certain demonstration, which brings us into properly metaphysical discourse about being as being in act.

Metaphysics is thus in the realm of indirect discourse, but as a science of being it is not limited to a consideration of the exercise of judgment as such. It is not an epistemology or a study of human insight as such, although it does presuppose some epistemological reflection such as we are doing here in order to distinguish between the two acts of intelligence and the two kinds of exercise of judgment, direct and indirect. The structure of judgment that we have delineated does not give us immediate access to the structure of our subject here, namely, being as such, as dialectical thinkers like Hegel or Lonergan are wont to suggest. It does provide us with some means of approaching the question of being as being heuristically or dialectically. It could be, as Suarezians have long argued against Thomists, that the distinctions we have come up with are distinctions only in reason and not in reality. What metaphysics has to do further is to somehow bring to terms the actuality of being as it is expressed only in the actual exercise of judgment. It considers not the form of this actual exercise of knowledge, nor what could follow from that form, but what it refers to as being. As a scientific discourse, it tries to bring into *actum signatum* what is present only *in actu exercito* in direct judgment and to consider this content systematically as being in its actuality. In other words, it tries to make explicit what was known only implicitly in the direct exercise of judgment or to thematize what was unthe-matized there, and it tries to do this in scientific fashion, with its own kind of demonstration.

Human being can exercise judgment because, through intelligence, one stands at the horizon of being. Human being or, as Heidegger would say, *Dasein,* knows being. It represents or orders things in being. This it does, at first, in experience, through a direct exercise of judgment by differentiating between things and by ordering them as a world. But the knowledge of be-ing that comes into play in this first exercise of judgment is usually not brought to the forefront of consciousness for critical reflection or for exam-ination precisely as being. This first knowledge of being is only presupposed or taken for granted, not examined critically as it must be in metaphysics; it only serves to make us critical in other sciences. Metaphysics is the attempt to make this primordial knowledge of being critical precisely with reference to being in act through reflection upon the actual exercise of judgment in which we come to know being as being in act.

Since it is the direct exercise of judgment itself that concretely brings us to this critical questioning of being as being, it follows that we shall have to keep this direct exercise of judgment clearly in focus in our metaphysical re-flection. We have only one experience to start from in seeking an answer to the question of being. But it is not in any direct exercise of judgment that we can find an answer to this question we are asking. Metaphysics does not begin directly from experience, as do the particular sciences, although we can say that we do have some experience of reflection in the particular ex-perience of doing science or phenomenology. If we did not, we would not have what we need to begin metaphysics. Metaphysics begins directly, so to speak, only with reflection, which is found in experience or in the direct exercise of judgment, and which therefore presupposes experience, since it is always only a re-flection or a turning back on an already actualized exercise of judgment.

Because metaphysics is only an indirect exercise of judgment, however, with its own terms or discourse, derived from the actual exercise of judg-ment, and not from the terms of any direct exercise of judgment, its truth will not depend upon the correctness or the truth of any direct exercise of judgment itself. The truth of metaphysics does not depend upon the truth of any empirical science or phenomenology, but upon its own demonstration of what is at issue in the question of being as being—something it first has to formulate in its own original way as distinct from any formulation in the direct exercise of judgment.

We could speak of the method of metaphysics, therefore, as *transcendental,* but we must be careful to understand the term correctly. First, the method is transcendental in the sense that it transcends any method used in the direct exercise of judgment, such as that of empirical science or phenomenology, the transcendence that we have been at pains to bring out here. But it is not transcendental in the sense that it is concerned only with the form of knowledge, and not with a content of its own, as the transcendental method of critical philosophy or phenomenology seems to be. It is transcendental in this modern sense only in that, in order to bring out its peculiar content, it has to reflect upon the actual exercise of judgment that begins directly in experience.

This transcendentality of metaphysics is something we have become much more conscious of in modern philosophy, but it can already be found in the way the ancients and the medievals distinguished the question of being as being from any other question that could be raised in a particular science. Both Plato and Aristotle went to great efforts to formulate the question: *ti to on e on?,* as did Aquinas for the question: *quid est ens in quantum ens?,* and the effort had to do not only with transcending myths about the origin of being, but also with defining the question properly so that it could be dealt with methodically or scientifically no less than other questions, albeit in a different way.

At this point, then, we could give a definition of metaphysics in terms of the indirect exercise of judgment, but it would have to be one that remains purely formal and programmatic. We could say that metaphysics will consist of a series of indirect or reflective judgments about being as being that either follow immediately from an actual exercise of judgment, and therefore have only to be thematized, or that can be derived through rational discourse from this exercise, requiring in either case a special kind of demonstration that moves from experience or *a posteriori* to something ontologically prior. In keeping with the necessity of metaphysics to reflect upon or critically examine its own presuppositions, this is something we now have to demonstrate.

2.5 Demonstration of the Method

We have already arrived at a determination of the subject of metaphysics as the science of being as being. From this we have begun to move toward a method for developing this science by reflecting on the twofold act of intelligence as it relates to experience in the process of learning. What we have seen in this analysis can now serve as the terms for the judgment that we must now exercise with regard to the method of metaphysics. We have been forming the quiddity of human knowing in its complete scope for ourselves. We must now reflect on this quiddity as it relates to being as being in order to arrive at an appropriate method for a scientific elaboration of this subject.

Three points have to be made. First, we have to see how metaphysics as an indirect and therefore as an intellectual exercise of judgment follows from experience. Second, we must focus on where metaphysics as science of being as being properly begins in the act of intelligence proper to any exercise of judgment. Three, we must indicate how, from this beginning, a method can be devised to elaborate a discourse on being as being based on a reflective consciousness of the exercise of judgment itself.

2.5.1 How Metaphysics Follows from Experience

We say that metaphysics follows from experience. This can be viewed as a simple matter of fact. No one begins to do science, let alone metaphysics, without some prior experience and some learning through intelligence in that experience. Indeed, experience itself, as something that is acquired, can be viewed as a knowledge of particulars or of fact that is already rational in some sense, in that "the numerous memories of the same event end up producing the power of a single experience" (*Metaph* 981 a1–2). It entails a certain collation of particulars from which "science and art" take their beginning. "Art is generated when from many notions of experience a single universal assumption [*upolepsis*] is generated about similar [cases]" (981 a6–8). But experience itself is not yet "art" or science. It is only that from which "art" or science follows through rational assumption into the universal. As an indirect exercise of judgment, metaphysics is twice removed from experience, but it still follows from experience, if not directly, as do the first universal "assumptions" in particular sciences, at least indirectly.

To recognize the simple fact of the priority of experience for all human knowing, however, is not enough for a proper beginning of metaphysics. We must also recognize the necessity of this fact and its necessary consequence in the exercise of metaphysical judgment. Our point is not to account for this necessity, as one might do in a psychology of knowing or a phenomenology of perception, but to see how it enters into the very notion of being. If experience is necessary for the exercise of judgment, then the being we know through this exercise will entail an irreducible aspect of facticity or singularity, unlike the "pure be" at the beginning of Hegel's *Logic* or any innate idea given purely to intelligence, apart from all experience. The "being"

that is said to "fall" first in our apprehension or to be conceived first is a being given through experience, a *this* or a *that*.

In this respect Heidegger was quite right in beginning his approach to
the question of being with an analysis of *Dasein* as a fundamental ontology.
This was a way of making manifest not only the meaning of the be of being,
but also that from which such a meaning has to follow. Insofar as metaphysics follows from experience, it has to begin as a phenomenology, at least
in the sense that we have to begin by a reflection on how we experience the
lifeworld.

In this respect Hegel also was right in beginning his System with a Science of Experience, as the *Phenomenology of Spirit* was originally called. It
was a way of getting to what follows intellectually from experience. Once
he got to the intellectual or the spiritual, however, in absolute knowing or in
the absolute beginning for his Science of Logic, Hegel forgot how he got
there and tried to make everything follow from a "pure knowing of pure
be," apart from all experience. We recognize that metaphysical knowing has
to follow from experience, as Hegel did, but, unlike Hegel, we do not think
that this absolute knowing can cut itself off from its origin in experience in
a separate science or a pure knowing of pure be. Such a science would have
to do only with concepts, and not being in act, which, as we have seen, transcends the order of conceptual terms.

Insofar as metaphysics has to follow from experience for us, we cannot
simply leave experience behind in our elaboration of metaphysical concepts,
as if it were a ladder to be kicked away once we have climbed it through the
logic of the particular sciences or of phenomenology. Experience remains a
necessary component in what we know of being even at the highest reaches
of metaphysics. This is why we always think of divine being as a *this* or a *that,*
like any being given in experience, or as having a particular essence as well
as a *Dasein* or an existence, even when we deny that the ultimate divine being, or the first universal cause of all being, can be such a thing, as we shall
see when we come to the end of metaphysics. The necessity of following
from experience remains with metaphysics to its very end. Metaphysics as a
science always requires a stepping off from experience at every point of
demonstration in its articulation. As following from experience, then, it has
to proceed *a posteriori,* rather than in a way that is purely *a priori.* In this
sense it retains a certain phenomenological aspect in its method.

This necessity of following from experience can be demonstrated in several ways from the phenomenology of knowing we have formulated. First, it
can be seen from the standpoint of questioning, which gives rise to meta-

physics itself. It is clear that all questioning in the particular sciences or phenomenology starts from experience. Questions for understanding start from a level of presentation, while questions for reflection start from a level of understanding. Even if metaphysics does not start directly from an immediate level of presentation, since it begins in a reflection on the exercise of judgment, it still presupposes a level of presentation in a mediated way, since the exercise of judgment itself begins with "assumptions" in a direct relationship with experience. Questioning itself can be seen as an experience we have, but even with that we can still define experience as that from which questioning arises, for we can question even about questioning itself, as we do in logic or in epistemology or as we are doing here.

Another way of demonstrating the same necessity is through the structure of judgment, that is, the intellectual activity that entails a certain use of terms *(S* and *P)* and an assertion of truth *(S* is *P)*. Through this structure of judgment we can thematize the evidence that remains unthematized in the actual exercise of judgment. If anyone who has exercised judgment fails to recognize this evidence or denies that there is any such evidence, he can be brought back to it by retort or by asking what it is that he is talking about *(S)* and what it is that he is saying about it *(P)*. There is no escaping the necessity of this structure in any actual exercise of judgment.

To understand the terms of judgment, however, one must refer back to experience, either immediately or mediately, depending on the relative abstractness or universality of the terms. Physical theory, for example, can be many times removed from the reality of immediate experience, but unless one wants to postulate another world beside the one of immediate experience, the truth of the theory will depend not only on the correctness of its mathematical formulas, but also on how it relates to the real world of experience. Those who postulate another world are stuck with the problem of proving its reality, which will still come down to resolving it into some kind of experience.

Many judgments, such as "snow is white" in contrast to "this is snow," are universal. But such judgments do not claim to refer to reality directly; they presuppose particular judgments that mediate their reference to reality. When I say "snow in general is white," I do not mean that there is such a thing as "snow in general." I only mean that there is a *kind* of *this,* namely, snow, that is always white. When I say something about human being (universal *S*), I do not claim that human being as such exists, but rather that what I am saying applies to the individuals whom I know to be human beings. The truth of a proposition about human being as such does not presuppose the existence of human being *as such,* as one would in a Platonic world of separate ideas. It depends rather upon the experience that there are individual human beings to whom such truth is relevant. It is in this sense that we say that every exercise of judgment includes a reference to a *this* or a *that* known only in experience. This is a necessary part of the evidence for any judgment, an evidence that bears on the here-and-now and on the *this* and *that* of experience. To the extent that metaphysics follows from the same direct exercise of judgment as the other sciences, it will come under the same necessity, although in a way that is peculiar to itself as an indirect exercise of judgment.

Even the idea of an indirect exercise of judgment, properly understood, presupposes the same necessity of experience for the content of metaphysics. As indirect, it comes only after the direct exercise of judgment, as a universal judgment comes only after particular judgments. It is a special case of the relation between universal and particular judgment, though one of special importance for us.

We have already noted the fact that we begin to exercise judgment in logic or in metaphysics only after exercising judgment directly related to the experience of a *this* or a *that*. Without some direct exercise of judgment there is no occasion for any indirect judgment. One does not become concerned with the art of thinking unless one has exercised thought to a certain extent and feels the need to reflect upon the way of proceeding in thought. Similarly, one does not become concerned with the question of being as being until one has arrived at some understanding of things as given in experience formulated in view of judgment and begins to ask what it means for something to be simply in act, and not just some particular thing that can be accounted for in terms of other particular things. It is only upon reflection that we become aware of the further perspective of being as being in the exercise of judgment.

This fact of coming *after* contains or entails a certain necessity for metaphysics that it cannot get away from in its development. The reference to experience is essential to metaphysics even as it transcends experience. This reference to experience is not its ultimate point of intelligibility. Facticity, of itself, can be quite opaque. It is only that from which inquiry and enlightenment begins or follows. But it is a necessary condition for any reference to reality or being in act in our knowledge. In this respect Hume was quite right about knowing as a knowing of fact, and Kant was no less right in following him. Without some sort of "sense intuition" there can be no proper exercise of judgment, even though there is more in the *act* than sense grasps in a fact, as we shall try to bring out. Experience remains for us always a principle of knowing, even though in metaphysics, as an indirect exercise of judgment, it is neither the sole nor the direct principle from which it follows. For us at least there is no intellectual apprehension of being without some experience or some *sense* of being.

At the center of experience, of course, is the self, or *Dasein,* as Heidegger refers to it. It is one of the many sensible things of which I have to form the quiddity. I have an immediate experience of myself, but my understanding of myself is not so immediate. I begin with a simple presence to myself as well as with a simple presence of other things, especially other selves, to me. My sense of being is intimately tied to this simple presence. But to understand *what* I am or *what* another self is, more is required: a diligent and subtle inquiry, as Aquinas says, referring to the nature of the soul as distinct from its simple presence to itself or to another (*ST* I, 87, 1, c). Heidegger's phenomenology of *Dasein* represents precisely such an inquiry. But so too do other forms of inquiry into the self and its world. What makes Heidegger's analysis of *Dasein* especially interesting from the standpoint of metaphysics is that it brings out how human being is essentially one who raises the question of being.

We begin with an immediate experience, prior to all questioning. But that alone does not tell us all that we or other things are. Through inquiry and reflection upon experience we come to a better knowledge not only of *what* is, but also of some degree of being, the latter mediated by the former. Being itself is simply present in immediate experience, but through inquiry it appears anew in reflection as a diverse subject of inquiry in its own right. But its having appeared first as a simple presence here and now in *this* and *that* remains as a determination of the meaning of being for us.

We shall see how this affects our notion of being in speaking of the meaning of being. But before that we must examine more precisely where the metaphysical inquiry properly begins and how it develops, for we do not say that it begins in experience as such, but only that it follows from it. It begins in the reflection that occurs in any serious exercise of judgment, which can be viewed as a kind of experience, namely, an experience of reflection. But as reflection it contains more than simple presence; it contains an act as well as a fact.

2.5.2 *How Metaphysics Begins in Reflection*

As we have seen, a science begins with the determination of its subject, which consists in an intellectual act specifying something to be examined in being. Such a determination always presupposes a certain reflection on the knowledge of things as given. Biology, for example, determines its subject by focusing on things as living. Economics determines its subject by focusing on things as products of human labor for human consumption or use. These things are given in experience, but they become a subject of inquiry by a process of specification and abstraction from experience as a whole. Without this kind of specification for critical reflection upon experience, there is no science.

However, as we have seen, what distinguishes metaphysics from any of the particular sciences is that its subject does not have any particular specification. It is about being simply *as being*. The reflective moment of this *as* in the determination of the subject of metaphysics must be seen for all that it contains. Properly speaking, there is no experience of being *as* being, and there cannot be. It is only through the exercise of intelligence in experience that there can be reflection. Experience is always of a *this* or of a *that*. Even to specify a particular subject of inquiry for a particular science is already to go beyond the mere presencing of being in experience. It is to make a particular aspect of being present in a special way, but in a way that can still be related directly to experience. In biology, for example, we focus on the aspect of being we call "life" and we refer directly to some *this* or *that* that is living. To determine being only *as being* as the subject of inquiry for metaphysics, however, is to go beyond the mere presencing of being in experience even further, that is, in a way that can no longer be related directly to *this* or *that* in experience. In this sense, metaphysical inquiry appears much more universal than inquiry in any of the particular sciences. It begins as absolutely universal. Though being always includes for us some reference to a *this* or a *that,* being *as being* is not an aspect of any *this* or *that* that we can point to in abstraction from whatever else there might be. Being *as being* surpasses, as it encompasses, all particular aspects of being as well as all singular *this's* or *that's.* Metaphysics, for which being *as being* is the subject, thus seems twice removed from any *this* or *that* of experience.

In a more radical sense, however, metaphysics is much more concrete than any particular science, in that it reflectively encompasses not only the particular aspects of being studied in the particular sciences, but also the *this* and *that* of experience, for *this* and *that* too are real and are therefore included in being *as being*. Even as metaphysics passes beyond, or follows from, as we have just maintained, mere experience, it necessarily includes it, not only by referring to the world as a whole, but also by referring to *this* and *that*. It makes everything present in a new way, in the way of being simply *as being,* which transcends and assumes into a new kind of intelligible presence the presence of any particular aspect of being and of any *this* or *that* in experience.

If we characterize this new presence as the presence of an act, which is to be distinguished from mere fact, it is because it imposes itself only through the *actual* exercise of reflection in judgment. Facts impose themselves in a kind of brute way. Being imposes itself *as being* in a way that enlightens. As what falls first in the understanding, being is that in the light of which everything is understood. Through this first and most radical "impression" or presencing of being, we come to critical reflection on our understanding of anything, that is, we come to the necessity of measuring or verifying it with reference to the real or to being *as being*.

To be sure, this level of actuality in the exercise of judgment transcends the mere facticity of experience. But it is nevertheless something that appears in experience. Without reflection there is no exercise of judgment. But without the first impression or presence of being in experience there is no reflection. Thus, though we distinguish the level of reflection from both the level of understanding and the level of experience in the exercise of judgment, we can still speak of the exercise of judgment as something we experience, already containing some reflection in which the actuality of being is present and upon which we can reflect to begin metaphysical inquiry.

To illustrate this we have only to reflect on the judgment we are presently in the act of forming. We are in the process of forming a judgment about method in metaphysics. I am attending to the *actual* exercise of my judgment that is part of my experience, and you should be attending to the *actual* exercise of your judgment that is part of your experience. I cannot attend to your exercise of judgment for you nor can you attend to mine for me. Each one must and can only reflect on one's own *actual* exercise of judgment, though we are trying to come to a common judgment in a shared experience of judgment.

This actual exercise of judgment takes place here and now in an experience, starting from an understanding or an interpretation of the experience that is quite personal to each one of us. None of us has exactly the same experience as the other, and consequently none of us has exactly the same understanding as the other, although some aspects of understanding can be communicated and shared, as in a community of scientists. Thus our approaches to being through critical reflection can vary widely, but in all of them there is the search for evidence that will confirm our understanding in a composition or an affirmative judgment or undo it in a division or a negative judgment or, as is more often the case, that will lead us to revise the understanding in a combination of affirming one part and denying another part of it. The quiddity we form in our understanding is seldom adequate to the thing we are trying to comprehend. That is why knowing for us is an ongoing process of learning in which we try to discern what we know to be true from what we do not yet know to be true. The quest for evidence through critical reflection is the fact not of experience, but of intelligence, and its necessity derives from the reflective presence of being, over and above its merely experienced facticity, bidding us to make our understanding more adequate to it in its fullness. Hence the necessity of development and revolution in science. Our concern in the exercise of judgment, whether it be scientific or not, is not just to develop a clever understanding or a bright idea, although that is not to be overlooked, but rather to get to the truth of being in its actuality. Through critical reflection in judgment being compels me, so to speak, to speak the truth in my judgment or at least to seek it in serious questioning about what is given in experience. When I come to a strict necessity of affirming something in judgment, I have come not only to a necessary truth but also to being itself as present in this necessity.

This is not to say that every judgment is ipso facto true. It is entirely possible to be mistaken in one's judgment, as when I affirm that "this is a layer of snow on the ground" but eventually discover or learn that it is a layer of dust from a volcanic explosion. But even in such a false judgment, as an act of reflective intelligence, there is some sense that truth entails some adequacy of understanding in relation to what is actually the case in being, a sense that eventually allows me to recognize that my initial judgment was false and that my present judgment about this layer of stuff on the ground is more likely true, even though it may not be completely true and I may still have something to learn about what it really is even as a layer of dust rather than snow.

It is also possible to be mistaken in one's judgment in metaphysics, if one thinks one has come to an adequate grasp of being as being when one has not. But even in such mistaken or false judgment there is still some necessary truth expressed *in actu exercito* if not *in actu signato,* in the actual exercise of judgment if not in the terms of the judgment, to the effect that truth consists in some adequacy of thought to being in act and not just in some consistency of thought with itself. It is this necessary truth, initially expressed in the actual exercise of more particular judgments, that we are trying to thematize, or to bring to terms *in actu signato* here, in our metaphysical exercise of judgment.

In a question there is no assertion of truth. Neither is there one in a mere hypothesis. But in a judgment, whether it be affirmative or negative, categorical or hypothetical, there is an assertion of truth, with a reference to being that is either direct or oblique. If, for example, I say "the wall is not black," it is because I am thinking it is some other color in reality. Or again, to claim that "if the moon is square, it has angles" is to say that where there *are* squares in reality there are angles. Even the most abstruse judgment in terms of p's and q's contains, as an actual exercise of judgment, a reference to being and derives its necessity from that reference, at least in the sense that one cannot say both "p is q" and "p is not q" at one and the same time.

Sometimes we express judgments that are not our own, judgments to which we do not give assent. We are only reciting or quoting them as the opinion of another, or even as an opinion of our own, without any claim about their truthfulness. Such expressions posit a synthesis of S and P, formulated through the understanding, but no assertion of truth. This does not mean that we reject such opinions, or even that we withhold judgment on them, for that would already presuppose some judgment in the case at hand. It only means that we have not yet seen the necessity of saying yes or no, true or false, to what is said as it relates to being in act or as presenting some necessity. How the opinion relates to being is not yet taken as clear or evident. This remains to be seen in some critical reflection.

This distinction between affirmation or negation, on the one hand, and what is expressed in the terms of a judgment, on the other, brings out or demonstrates that in the exercise of judgment the act of reflection rises above the given of experience as understood or formulated in certain determinate terms and relates it to being as something prior and present only through critical or judgmental reflection, even though it is not present apart from experience and understanding. When we speak reflectively of being *as being* it is precisely this priority we refer to. Metaphysics, or the philosophy of being, is the attempt to formulate this reflective presence of being in an exercise of judgment that transcends the judgments of direct experience.

Here we could propose an argument by retort for anyone who would deny this fundamental beginning or principle of metaphysics. If one were to deny that there is any such reflective presence of being in the actual exercise of judgment, one would have to deny that there is any reflection in the exercise of judgment, which it is actually impossible to do in anything more than words. To deny the actual exercise of reflection in judgment, I would have to understand the structure of judgment and then deny that there is any distinction between the assertion of truth and what is expressed in the terms S and P. In other words, I would have to understand what I am talking about, that is, *S*, which in the case in point is the exercise of judgment, and what it is I am saying about it, that is, *P*, which is that it is an assertion of truth expressed in terms, and at the same time I would have to deny that it is such an assertion. In the act of doing so, however, I would be making an assertion that would have to be expressed in terms, that is, *S* and *P*, and which would presuppose some reflective grasp of being in act, namely, the being of my actual exercise of judgment. What I would be denying *in actu signato*, I would be affirming *in actu exercito*. Upon reflection on my actual exercise of judgment, I have to say that there is reflection in judgment and that this reflection entails some reference to being in act, unless I am willing to abandon all exercise of judgment or to say that all judgment is purely arbitrary or frivolous, as in the case of universal skepticism or pure deconstruction, a frivolity that, as Aristotle suggests, is beneath the judgment even of brute animals.

But even this is an impossible stance to maintain intellectually, for either it is a serious objection to my stance about judgment, or it is no objection at all. If it is an objection, it is an actual exercise of judgment that must be reflected upon and that will yield some assertion of truth expressed in some terms. There may be room for a revision of terms in our definition of judgment, but there is no denying that it entails an actual exercise of reflection. There is only the problem of formulating the structure of that act rightly. If, on the other hand, it is not really an objection, then there is no need to contend with it, but only to proceed along our own way as mandated by our reflection on the structure of judgment.

The absence of contention, however, may be a sign that there has not yet been a sufficient exercise of judgment to begin metaphysics. Metaphysics can proceed only through reflection on an actual exercise of judgment. Even skepticism or deconstruction can lead into metaphysics, on the condition that it takes itself seriously as an actual exercise of judgment. If it refuses to take itself seriously, then one must simply disregard it, as one would a plant that has nothing to say. Metaphysics can begin only with someone wanting to say something, not arbitrarily, but seriously and upon reflection with concern for the truth of what is being said with reference to being in act.

Our insistence on the act of reflection in the exercise of judgment could be construed as adding something that is missing in Kant's transcendental analysis of the human capacity to know or of the conditions for the possibility of the phenomenal object as such, something most crucial for the beginning of metaphysics. Besides the pure intuition of sense, Kant's transcendental analysis brings out the function of the *a priori* forms of sensibility, space and time, along with that of the categories of understanding and the regulative ideas of reason, as integral to the process of human knowing. In the end, however, this analysis is left with a gap between a problematic "thing in itself," defined in purely intellectual terms as noumenal, that is, apart from all sense intuition, and the intellect itself, a gap that would require an intellectual intuition to bridge. In the absence of any such intuition metaphysics is then declared to be impossible. The question remains, however, as to whether there is such a gap as is alleged between the "thing in itself" and the intellect. Did Kant uncover all the conditions for the possibility of the phenomenal object as such? Did he understand how the moment of critical reflection in reason itself enters into the constitution of any object in consciousness?

We have already seen that being is not to be thought of as some "thing in itself," some noumenal object hidden behind a phenomenal object. It is simply what is known when knowing takes place. Nor is there any need of a special intuition, other than that of experience, in order to know it. To start learning about it *as being* one has only to reflect on the actual exercise of judgment as it is already found in experience. In doing so one becomes aware of a presence of being that precedes every concept and intuition and in the light of which conceptualization and intuition take place. This is the radical *a priori* of human knowing that Aristotle characterized as a unity of the knower and the known and that Parmenides expressed in the simplest of terms, "is" or "is not." There is no gap to bridge between intelligence and being. There is simply knowing of being to begin with. Intelligence is already one with being from the very beginning of reflection and, as finite or limited in its understanding, it has only to make itself adequate to the being with which it is somehow one.

One could even think of this primordial unity of intelligence and being as the ultimate condition for the possibility of the phenomenal object as object, for without it the subject would be closed up within itself in a way that no sense intuition could open up or disclose. No matter how vivid, impression is still something only in the sentient subject. If we go from an impression to something "out there," it is because we are already out there intellectually with a sense of being as "object" or as present. It is with this intellectual presence of being that we begin, through critical reflection, to question our impressions and to rectify our understanding. Reflection can thus be understood as the beginning of metaphysics inasmuch as it is the ultimate condition for the possibility of the phenomenal object in the actual exercise of judgment.

2.5.3   How Metaphysics Proceeds by a Reflection of Its Own on the Structure of Judgment as Signifying Being

Finally, we come to the point of indicating how a discourse about being as being can be elaborated scientifically or systematically from this beginning in the reflective exercise of judgment. The beginning we have been trying to focus on seems very tenuous and difficult to lay hold of conceptually. How can it be thematized or brought to *terms*, without losing sight of its transcendent originality as *act?*

The difficulty arises from the fact that in the actual exercise of judgment there is always something that is absolutely irreducible to terms. The actual exercise of some judgment, as we saw earlier and as we can see from any reflection on an actual exercise of judgment, cannot be enclosed even in the terms in which I am speaking only of this or that judgment. The terms I use in speaking of this or that judgment never completely express the *actual exercise* of the judgment in which they are found, an exercise of which I am conscious as having an intelligibility of its own not reducible to terms or concepts. Nor do they express the actual exercise of judgment in which I am now speaking of that judgment. No matter what the actual exercise of judgment, direct or indirect, the terms of the judgment do not adequately express what I know or what I am conscious of in the actual exercise of judgment as actually exercised.

Now the grasp of being *as being* seems to be tied precisely to this irreducible aspect of act in the actual exercise of judgment. To express this actual grasp in terms proportionate to our understanding would therefore seem to be impossible, and yet what other way is there to express such a grasp so fundamental to our intelligence? How can we say *in actu signato* what can only be said *in actu exercito?*

The exercise of judgment is for us, as we have said earlier, knowing in its complete sense. It is absolute knowing in the sense that it reaches for being as the framework for all there is to be known. But it does this only as a movement of intelligence in its twofold act of understanding and reflection. Part of this movement can be represented through concepts, but part of it cannot. It can only be signified, albeit still through concepts. The intelligibility of *act* transcends concept, but it can be signified systematically only through concept. It can never be understood as a mere factual presence.

Our task in metaphysics, therefore, must be to espouse this movement of the exercise of judgment and to follow it in its structure as we try to elaborate the full meaning of being both conceptually and in act. We must not separate concept and act, but see them in their dialectical relationship. A mere dialectic of concepts would not be sufficient for the task, because it would leave out the highest intelligibility of being itself in its very act, and fix us on a level of mere opposition between representations. On the other hand, a dialectic of the act alone is impossible, since that would reduce it to a pure abstraction and make of it just another concept, the concept of pure be, admittedly the most abstract and the most empty. Ours must be a dialectic of act and concept where both are seen in their irreducible distinction and in their indissoluble unity. Being has to be conceived, but in a way that only signifies its act without representing it, while the act itself has to be signified in a way that transcends all representations, a process that requires the highest form of conceptualization. We cannot do without concepts. We must move through concepts to the act of being, taking our cue from the actual exercise of judgment as the act in which being presents itself most fully or actually.

What further complicates our task is that we cannot jump out of experience in order to do metaphysics, as we have already demonstrated in saying that metaphysics has to follow from experience. Not only do we have to think of being in concepts, but our concepts also have to entail a reference to *this* and *that* in the here-and-now. The actual exercise of judgment always takes place in and from experience. This is part of the historical rootedness for any metaphysics, even one viewed as absolute knowing. For us, at least, there is no perfect coincidence of pure act that rises above and escapes from historical experience. There is no annulling of time for metaphysics, as Hegel seems to suggest for absolute knowing at the end of the *Phenomenology of Spirit* (*PhG* 558/487). The concept cannot close in upon itself, without reference to a factual here-and-now. This is why some form of phenomenology or empirical science remains integral to metaphysics, though only in an indirect way.

How, then, does this affect the way we have to proceed in metaphysics? The beginning of metaphysics is in the exercise of judgment that takes place within experience but is not experience as such. It is in reflection upon understanding and experience. Hence it depends directly on reflection in the exercise of judgment, and not on experience or any particular interpretation of experience. But inasmuch as the exercise of judgment takes place for us only in experience, then the development of metaphysics will have to depend indirectly on experience, as its beginning inevitably does. The indirect exercise of judgment that is proper to metaphysics has an autonomy or an originality of its own, but one that relates still to the direct exercise of judgment.

This does not mean that the truth of metaphysical judgment will depend upon the truth of any particular judgment, whether it be in common sense, empirical science, or phenomenology. Metaphysics comes after some direct exercise of judgment, but it does not presuppose that this direct exercise of judgment has reached any final conclusion in its own order of questioning about anything given in experience. It only presupposes that one can enter into a different order of questioning, namely, one that encompasses being as being. One can still be quite provisional in most of one's judgments about things as given in experience or in the particular sciences and still raise metaphysical questions, as the history of metaphysical inquiry shows. What our claim about the beginning of metaphysics in reflection means is that some direct exercise of judgment in experience is required for metaphysics and that this direct judgment will have some influence on metaphysics, especially insofar as metaphysics has to proceed through some conceptual representation of what is given in experience.

This is why metaphysics has always appeared as a child of its time or of the particular interests of its author, even though it has always claimed to be a kind of absolute knowing rising above such particular claims. Both of these facts are in keeping with its nature as a human enterprise. We can only do metaphysics from where we stand in history, but we must do it as a critical exercise of judgment about being simply as being.

Ideally it might seem that metaphysics should begin only when we have arrived at a complete knowledge of the world as experienced, that is, once all the particular sciences have exhausted all there is to be understood directly in experience. But that has never been the case. In fact, it could never be the case. Development in direct experiential knowledge, it would seem, could go on indefinitely and always remain somehow provisional, as empirical science and phenomenology both show. At least, we cannot set any end to their expansion in the present or in any historical present. And yet beginning metaphysical inquiry does not depend on having reached the end in any development of experiential knowledge or in the direct exercise of judgment. It depends only on having exercised some judgment, which at first had to be directly related to experience. From such an actual exercise of judgment, which can be viewed in one sense as a part of experience, metaphysical inquiry can arise and pursue its own course of development without depending directly upon the developments of experiential knowledge, even though the latter might help indirectly in the formulation of appropriate concepts for metaphysics. The correctness of direct judgment is not a matter of indifference even for metaphysics, but it does not directly affect the exercise of judgment in metaphysics, which, while coming after, deals with something prior to what is expressed in direct judgment according to a method of its own.

Conversely, we should also note that, just as the development of metaphysical discourse does not depend directly on experiential knowledge, so also the development of experiential knowledge does not depend directly on the development of metaphysics. Physics and phenomenology can thrive as particular ways of knowing without metaphysics, even though they leave unanswered the question of being, which they presuppose. Metaphysics, by its very nature, is never in a position to replace any of the particular sciences. At best, it can only clarify the epistemological framework in which they operate. The most that one could say is that, just as a better understanding of the world of experience can be of some help in metaphysics, so also a better understanding of metaphysics can serve a certain heuristic function in the other sciences, including phenomenology, as they strive for a better grasp of their respective subjects, which is still some aspect of being, even though it is not fully being as being.

The general lines of our method can thus be understood as starting from the exercise of judgment and proceeding, first, to the formulation of our understanding of being as we first encounter it through intelligence in experience, in other words, as it first "falls" in our apprehension. Having done this and having discovered the analogy of being, we shall then inquire into what can be said of being in its analogy, how it is structured as it is given to us, and how it is communicated in its natural and historical diversity. From this we shall see how the question of a source or an origin for the whole of being can arise. But for now let us proceed to our first step, which is to disclose the fullness of actual being in its diversity and singularity as the subject of our consideration.

PART TWO

THE MEANING OF BEING

Introduction: Our Initial Concept of Being

≈

WE HAVE SEEN how our first understanding of being as expressed in the exercise of judgment entails a reference to being in act. So far we have reflected only on how we refer to being in act or as present, and not on how or what we mean by being in our first understanding of it. If we are to get to the fullness of the act of being in our understanding, however, we must reflect on our meaning in what we have spoken of as our first understanding or our first conception of being in the direct exercise of judgment, the conception into which all other conceptions are ultimately brought back or resolved.

Our understanding of being in the actual exercise of judgment includes a meaning as well as a reference to being in act. In reflecting upon our first conception of being, it is incumbent upon us to clarify this meaning as well as we can before proceeding to inquire into the properties and the principles of being as being.

We have argued that the subject of our investigation is best expressed in the participial form of the verb 'to be,' namely, as being, rather than in the infinitive form. The present participial form of a verb can stand for any particular or concrete form of the verb, including the infinitive, whereas the infinitive form is only general and abstract and in need of specification if it is to be used concretely, which means, of course, that it must cease to be infinitive. In the case of the verb 'to be,' the participial form expresses a concept of being that is both common to many forms, since it can stand for whatever *is*, and concrete, since it can stand for whatever mood in which being is expressed, indicative, subjunctive, optative, or even infinitive, and in whatever tense, present, past, or future. But what more precisely is the meaning of this *ens commune* or this *on xynon?* How is it meant or understood in the actual exercise of judgment, especially as it is first taken in the direct exercise of judgment with reference to things as given in experience?

In answering this question we must keep in mind that the concept of being is not like any other concept that can be expressed as a predicate in the direct exercise of judgment, not just because it is the first concept into which all other concepts are ultimately resolved, but also because, even as a concept, it does not represent any particular kind of being, as predicates like "animal" or "rational" do in the direct exercise of judgment. It rather signifies being in its presence through such representative predicates. Hence it cannot be reduced to a specific difference, which would divide a genus, or to a genus, which would still express some difference from other genera, or even to the highest genera, since such categorization always entails some exclusion as well as inclusion. As signifying being in its actual presence, the concept of being is more universal than all categories or kinds; it includes them all within its ambit insofar as they can be critically verified with reference to being.

This is so even with regard to the first and highest category of *ousia,* or substance, of which Aristotle said that it was to be the primary concern of the science of being as being. Even as the first or highest category, substance is still not as universal as being, which alone, as being, is the subject of metaphysics. The category of substance does not include the categories of quantity, quality, or temporality, for example, but rather, as a category, it distinguishes itself from these other categories, which can also be viewed as supreme genera along with substance. The concept of being is irreducible to any such supreme genera. It includes them all not as a higher genus, which would still make it only a category exclusive of other categories, but rather as encompassing their diversity in a higher unity, that of being simply as being. No category, not even the highest genus, is absolutely universal. Only the concept of being is absolutely universal in that it includes whatever *is* in what we shall call its transcendental order as distinct from the predicamental order of categories.

The concept of being differs from a categorical concept in yet another way. As a concrete universal, or as common to many, it is inclusive of the very differences in which it is diversified. Different categories express or represent some of these differences of or in being. In doing so, however, they not only set themselves off from other categories on the same level of abstraction, as substance sets itself off from quantity, or as quantity sets itself off from quality, and so on. They also abstract or set themselves off from the specific differences that divide each genus. Categories in the predicamental order of representation can be understood without including any of the differences, specific or individual, that might divide the genus or the species. The genus "animal," for example, can be understood without knowing whether the animal in question is rational or nonrational. Similarly, the species "human" can be understood without knowing whether the individual in question is Socrates or Plato. "Being," on the other hand, cannot be abstract in this way. Though it is common or most universal, it has to include all real differences, individual as well as specific and generic, because these differences too are part of what *is,* and hence come under the concept of being.

This is not to say that the science of being as being has to go into all of these differences in detail, which is the realm of particular sciences. It can focus primarily on what is substantial in being, as Aristotle suggests at the beginning of Book *Gamma* of the *Metaphysics.* But even in doing so it still encompasses the accidental in being as it relates to the substantial, as Aristotle shows by the example he gives of how substance is primary in relation not only to what is accidental but also to coming to be and ceasing to be. The concept of being thus has its own logic that has to be distinguished from the logic of ordinary concepts in the predicamental order of representation. Our first task, then, in exploring the meaning of our first conception of being has to be to bring out this peculiar logic, at least as it sets "being" off from the logic of other concepts. In doing this we shall come to a first understanding of what Heidegger calls "ontological difference." But we shall see also that this "difference" must be formulated in way that is slightly different from that of Heidegger.

After this clarification of the logic of being, we shall then proceed to a more positive consideration of how being includes its differences, that is, through analogy rather than through merely univocal predication. This will be a more dialectical consideration, as distinct from a merely logical or formal consideration, and it will lead us back to a better understanding of being in act as that in which differences are actualized or as that which is to be understood in composition with its differences, and not apart or in abstraction from them.

CHAPTER 3

The Logic of Being

INSOFAR AS METAPHYSICS follows from experience, the logic of our first conception of being must go back to the way we come to know being in experience. Insofar as it begins in the reflection that is found in any exercise of judgment, this logic must begin by a reflection on what we have referred to as the direct exercise of judgment. Though the logic we begin with in this way is itself an indirect exercise of judgment that turns or hinges on an actual exercise of judgment, the concept with which it begins is not a pure concept that has only itself as its content, as one might think in a Hegelian science of logic. It is a concept that is expressed in a direct exercise of judgment, which entails reference to things as given in experience as well as to concepts that represent these things in our understanding. How is being conceived in such an exercise of judgment? That is the question we must now answer in our reflection on the direct exercise of judgment. How is the concept of being expressed in such an exercise of judgment? Is there one key expression or are there diverse expressions for it that have to be brought back to one?

As expressed in the direct exercise of judgment, the concept of being does not represent things as other concepts do, or at least as they try to do in view of critical reflection. It signifies being in its actuality, as we saw in our reflection on the structure of judgment, not independently of representative concepts but through them. It is from this distinction between signification and representation in the exercise of judgment that we begin our logic of being. This will help us to understand how the concept of being can be both most universal and most concrete at the same time.

From that we shall see why the notion of being cannot be expressed in terms of genus and specific differences but rather as a structure in which essence, which can be represented through concepts, is distinguished from being as act. This will give us not only our first understanding of ontological difference, but also an understanding of how essence is to be taken as a mode of being rather than as a being. With this understanding of essence we shall then see why the concept of being does not yield either essentialism or existentialism, but rather a unity or a composition of essence and being in act in which essence limits the act. Thus we shall come to an understanding of differences as integral to the concept of being and conclude with the idea of the concept of being as transcendent.

3.1   The Mode of Signifying Being

Let us begin, then, by reflecting on the way we signify being in the actual exercise of judgment or the way the concept of being signifies when we use it as a substantive, as when we say something is a being. This way of signifying is the expression of our way of understanding our first conception of being. What do we think of as *being* when we say that something *is*? Aquinas writes that being signifies according to the mode of a certain concretion and composition. *Ens significat per modum cuiusdam concretionis et compositionis* (*Sent* I, 8, 1, 1, 3). Let us take this as the cue for articulating our first understanding of being.

First, we should recall that signifying is not the same as representing. We represent things through our concepts of *what* they are, but we do not speak of them *as being* through such representation. Being is what we refer to in the act of critical reflection on the representations in or of our understanding. We do not properly represent being *as being* through the understanding. We represent some particularity of being and through this representation signify being as we reflect on the representation in the exercise of judgment. In signifying we refer to being, which encompasses the representation, or *what* is represented, even as it transcends it in referring to actual being.

To say that being signifies according to a mode of concretion is to keep in mind that the exercise of judgment always starts from experience, which is for us the concrete. In experience we always refer to a *this* or a *that* here and now, in some place or other at some time or other. *This* or *that,* or what we shall refer to as "thisness" or "haecceity," will therefore be a necessary aspect of our understanding of being, since the direct exercise of judgment, from which we have to begin, always includes a reference to *this* or *that,* either immediately in particular judgments or mediately in universal judgments. For us being will always signify a *this* or a *that.*

But *this* or *that* is never understood as merely *this* or *that.* It is always understood as something to be interpreted, as having determinations to be understood. Being for us is not just a pure *this* or *that.* It is a determinate *this* or *that* or a thing with determinations. And it is to get at these determinations of being that we raise questions for understanding about *this* or *that* which presents itself. Answers to such questions are representations of the understanding which call for critical reflection.

Thus, in addition to *this* or *that,* our understanding of being also includes determinations, among which we may distinguish some that are only incidental to *this* or *that,* in the sense that they do not determine a being in what it is, and some that are more essential, in the sense that they do determine a being according to *what* it is. This distinction is not always easy to work out for any particular being, but our sense of being tells us that *what* a thing is is a necessary aspect of its being, perhaps even more than its haecceity, since *what* something is is always more significant than merely that it is a *this* or a *that,* prescinding from all determination. There is more to being this *human,* for example, than to being this *chair.* Concrete as *this* or *that* might sound, in itself it remains quite abstract apart from all determination. "This" can refer to the wall in front of me, to the chair I am sitting on, or to myself. "Now" can refer to 10:30 in the morning or to high noon as the day goes on. Concretion without interpretation is meaningless and therefore cannot, by itself, signify being.

Because interpretation answers to the question *what?,* we shall refer to this aspect of being as "whatness," or "quiddity." This does not necessarily include all the determinations of being, since quiddity refers only to certain determinations of a *this* we consider as pertaining to its very being in such a way that, without them, it could not be, or be *what* it is. Quiddity is so necessary to being as we understand it that we cannot think of being except as some thing or as some *what, aliquid.*

This does not exclude other, nonquidditative determinations from being thought of as being as well or from constituting a necessary aspect of being as we understand it. Accidental determinations as distinct from quidditative determinations of *this* or *that* are real, even necessary aspects of being as we know it in experience, and they have to be included in any complete articulation of the notion of being. But here we shall include them generally under the notion of quiddity in the same way that the questions why, or how, or how many times can be included under questions for understanding *what* something is. We shall deal with the complexity of these determinations of being later on. Here, in articulating our first understanding of being, it is enough to speak of it as entailing an order of quiddity or of determinations that constitutes another necessary aspect, along with thisness, of what we mean by being.

Besides these two aspects of being, however, that of haecceity and that of quiddity, there is yet an ulterior aspect that is expressed in the exercise of judgment by the very verb *is,* over and above what is expressed in the terms of judgment, as when we say that this *is* a human being or that *is* a chair or snow *is* white. This is a third aspect, so to speak, of what we signify in speaking of being and, though it is not expressed in the terms of any judgment, it is not to be overlooked in our logic of the concept of being. It is often spoken of as the order of existence over and above the order of determinations or quiddity. But the idea of existence tends to reify this third aspect of our understanding of being, as if it were a thing or another quiddity besides the quiddity already expressed in the second aspect. This is a danger we must guard against in speaking of ontological difference. What we signify in the verb 'is' must not be thought of as another quiddity than the first one we have already identified on the level of understanding, nor even as a difference from that difference, but rather as an *act,* the act of being, in composition with quiddity or difference.

To refer to this third aspect of our understanding of being in the direct exercise of judgment, it is better to use the infinitive, 'be,' as the ancients did and as Heidegger has done in the framework of modern ontology. If we prescind from haecceity and quiddity in the way we signify being, there appears to be something infinite about the act itself, whether of signifying or of being. If I leave out the subject *(S)* and the predicate *(P)* of any judgment in which I affirm something as being, I am left with only the infinitive *be,* which I do not say *is* as such, but which I always understand as limited or finitized by the terms of the judgment. I do not say "I be a human being" or "that be a chair." Whenever I signify something as being I always conjugate the verb in accordance with the terms of the judgment in which I express what I signify, which is to limit what I mean by *be* to what is expressed in these terms. But the *be* that is always conjugated with terms in this way is nevertheless something to be distinguished as the *be* of a *this* or a *that* and of this particular *kind* of determinate being or that particular *kind* of determinate being.

When we think of it this way, *be* may represent an ontological distinction, if not strictly a difference, which can be spoken of as the "be of being," as Heidegger was inclined to put it. But we should keep in mind that the difference or the distinction is not strictly between be and being. It is rather a distinction within the concept of being as a whole between *be* and the quidditative determinations of the *being* in question or the subject of these determinations taken as *this* or *that.* In other words, *be* is a third aspect of our concept of being with respect to the first two aspects of the same concept, not with respect to the concept as a whole, with reference to which it is understood as in composition with these first two aspects.

What is meant by *composition* here is the way in which thisness and whatness, as expressed in the terms of a judgment, limit *be* when it is conjugated with them in any particular judgment. Just as the exercise of judgment entails a composition of either affirmation or negation with terms, so also our concept of being entails a composition of what is referred to in affirmation or negation, *be* or *not be,* with a *this* or a *that* and its determinations. We come to some judgment about things only through asking questions about a *this* or a *that* given in experience, questions for understanding, which lead us to intelligible determinations of *this* or *that,* as well as questions for reflection. Questions for reflection, which refer to being in act, are mediated by the determinations we arrive at in our understanding so that what is understood as affirmed or denied in actuality is understood as limited by these determinations. We exercise critical judgment only insofar as we understand. Similarly, what we say *is* in answer to questions for reflection, whatever it be, is understood as being in composition with thisness and whatness.

There is no way of defining "being" according to genus and specific difference, since "being" as a concept includes whatever can be thought of as genera or differences in being, and is not itself included in any of them as concepts. But there is a way of expressing what we mean by the concept as that which is known or affirmed in the direct exercise of judgment. We speak of the exercise of judgment, rather than just a particular judgment, in order to bring out the performative *act* found in any particular judgment in composition with its terms, but not expressed by the terms. Such an act is common to many particular judgments insofar as they are part of an actual exercise of judgment, but in each particular judgment it is limited by the terms of the judgment.

So it is in the exercise of judgment. So it is also in the concept of the being that is affirmed in this exercise of intelligence. In it there is an act that is understood as entering into composition with thisness and quidditative determinations, which in turn are understood as limiting that act. Just as the actual exercise of judgment appears as infinite in comparison with any particular judgment, so also the *be* or the *actual* aspect of being appears as infinite in comparison with thisness and particular determinations of any sort. But in the concrete composition, whether of an actual judgment or an actual being, the act is always understood as limited and finite in accordance with the thisness and determinations of the being that is affirmed.

To sum up, then, we can say that our first concept of being, as it relates to what is given in experience, entails three aspects: an aspect of concrete this-ness; an aspect of determinations, which can be predicated of a *this* or a *that;* and an aspect of actuality, which enters into composition with determina-tions already in synthesis with a concrete *this* or *that.* These three aspects are not three of one and the same kind. In fact, we hesitate even to call them "aspects," since aspects are like determinations and could pertain to only one of the three ingredients of the notion of being we wish to distinguish. We hesitate to call them "ingredients" as well, things that go into something like one's favorite recipe, since that would give the impression that the three start off by being understood as independent of one another. This is not how our concept of being is first understood in the direct exercise of judgment. Each of the three aspects or ingredients we distinguish is to be understood in rela-tion to the others. There is no thisness without whatness and no whatness without thisness. Any *this* or *that* is always understood as having some deter-minations, which we try to express as predicates at least in some of the first judgments we come to, as when we say "this is green," "this is spherical," or "this is human." On the other hand, any determination is always understood as the determination of a *this* or a *that,* for it is not part of our judgment to say that there is greenness, or sphericality, or humanity apart from a *this* or a *that.* In fact the two together, thisness and whatness, or *this* with its particu-lar determinations, already constitute a certain synthesis in our understand-ing which is then related to actuality in the act of critical reflection, what we can call with Aquinas the synthesis of concretion.

The actuality, however, even as an aspect or an ingredient of our concept of being, is not like thisness or whatness. Nor is it like the synthesis of both. It is rather that with which the first or the concretizing synthesis of what-ness with thisness is understood to be in composition when we affirm some *this* with its determinations, as when we say, "this *is* a human being" or "that *is* a solar system." Actuality is a third within the concept of being, but not as a *this* or a *that,* nor as a quidditative determination of any kind. It is simply *be* as an *act,* something more positive than thisness or whatness in being, but yet found or disclosing itself only in whatness and thisness. Though we distin-guish actuality from thisness and whatness in our conception of being, it is not part of our direct exercise of judgment, in which our conception of be-ing is first expressed, to affirm that there is actuality apart from *this* or *that* which is given in experience with its determinations. Whether such an affir-mation could be part of our judgment in an indirect exercise of judgment remains to be seen. All that we can say here, with regard to the direct exercise of judgment, is that there is actuality only where there is thisness and whatness.

3.2   The Structure of Our Understanding of Being

Given this mode signifying being in the direct exercise of judgment, however, we have to think of our first conception of being not as a simple apprehension, but as a structured concept with a twofold synthesis, the concretizing synthesis of certain universal determinations with a *this* or a *that* and the composition of this synthesis with *be* or an *act* of being that has to be thought of as a higher synthesis than the first. To understand this entire structure properly we must begin from the higher synthesis as containing the lower synthesis.

Thus we begin our conception of being not with a pure concept of pure be, which is the same as pure nothing, as Hegel does in his *Science of Logic*. We begin rather with what he speaks of later on as determinate being, or *Dasein*. Pure be is not said to be in any positive sense by Hegel. It is only taken as a moment in a dialectic with pure nothing that immediately resolves itself into the totality of becoming, which is said to be their first and only truth, a totality that in turn subsides immediately into a stable unity "which is as being [*als seiend*] or has the form of a one-sided *immediate* unity of these moments [that is, the moments of 'pure be' and 'pure nothing'], is the be-there [*das Dasein*]" (*WL* I 93/106). What Hegel says about pure be makes some sense from the standpoint of becoming. If becoming is the first totality we can speak of in truth, as Hegel claims, then pure be can be understood as pure being in potency, but as such it is still without actuality or, as Hegel says, it is pure nothing. Becoming, however, is not the first conception into which all other conceptions are to be resolved, as we argued in establishing that being *as being* is the subject of our consideration. The first totality of which we speak in truth is being, not as being in potency, but as being in act in composition with determinations and thisness. We are not yet asking how such a totality has come to be, as we shall do later on in speaking of becoming. We are only asking how such a being is to be understood in its structure. What is truly at hand at the beginning of metaphysics is what Hegel calls *Dasein,* that which is there *(da)* as a *this* given in experience with determinations.

In speaking of the be of being as the subject of his consideration, Heidegger is much closer to the truth of this beginning for metaphysics. There is implied in his understanding of "ontological difference" some structure in this totality of be and being, even though at times Heidegger borrows

Hegel's language of pure be to speak of be in the ontological difference as the nothing of being. If we take *be* as something positive, rather than as nothing, in this totality we come to an understanding of being in act as something more positive than either thisness or whatness or both taken together in our first conception of being.

It is not clear whether Heidegger ever did this himself, because he always spoke of the ontological difference generally as a difference between be and being. What we are saying here is that the difference, or the distinction, is not precisely one between be and being. It is more one between be and the concretizing synthesis of thisness and whatness within the totality we name "being." In other words, the difference or the distinction we make is one between components of what we understand as being in its totality, and not between being and any one of its components. This is what enables us to speak of *be* as something positive in being, and never merely as nothing. It is also what enables us to think of *be* as more intelligible than the other components of our conception, and therefore as a subject for questioning beyond what we speak of as the determinations of being. But it does not enable us to raise the question of *be* as a second question of being independently of the determinations of being, as Heidegger appears to have tried to do. If we distinguish *be* from whatness and thisness within our conception of being, it is not to separate it from these determinations or to differentiate it from them as if it were another difference. It is only to understand it as in composition with these determinations. In what sense this distinction or composition is to be understood as real in being itself remains to be determined later on. For the moment we are only trying to understand it as part of our first conception of being as expressed in the direct exercise of judgment.

The actuality of being, which we can refer to as the be of being, has to be understood as an *act* that contains the intelligibility of the fact as understood or interpreted but in a higher order, the order of being itself, which is higher than the order of determinations, let alone the order of thisness and thatness, but this act is still conjoined for us to the first order of fact as found in experience. It is the act that can be understood as that which discloses things in their being for critical reflection and as the synthesis of syntheses in our concept of being.

It is well and good to call philosophy back, as Heidegger does, to the task of thinking the be of being at the end of metaphysics in technologized science. That is indeed the task of metaphysics as it continues or resumes *after* the modern metaphysics of Hegel called "Logic." But our conception of this task must not lose sight of the fact that be opens up for us only in composition with the determinations of a *this* or *that* that are understood as a part of being in technologized science. Whether and in what sense the be of being shows itself as the ground and how this ground shows itself as presence (*Ende* 62/374) is something that still has to be worked out metaphysically. But in the working out we must not try to think be, or *Sein,* as if it could be understood apart from its composition with determinations in the concrete. As pedestrian as this concept of being might seem, it is still the fundamental framework from which all intelligibility derives for us, including that of actual presencing. Even if the be of being is the ultimate opening for us of all that is, it is still known initially or originally as an aspect of the being we know concretely or as the *act* of this being that is at the same time a particular kind of being.

It is important to note that, if we think of pure be as pure act, this act has to be thought of as infinite, unlimited by any of the differences of whatness and thisness, not as something merely indeterminate, as Hegel did at the beginning of his Logic. It has to be thought of as something more positive and beyond all determinations. To be sure, the *act* of being does not present itself abstractly in this way in our first conception of being. As it first presents itself concretely in experience or in the direct exercise of judgment, it is the act of a *this,* which is not nothing by itself, but which is understood more positively with its determinations. These determinations, viewed abstractly, can also be understood as determinations in another *this* or *that,* like the color white can be a determination of that wall as well as this paper. As such they represent something more positive about a *this* or a *that* than just its thisness, especially when the determination represented is something essential to *this,* as when I say "this is a human being." The determination "human" is more positive than just *this* or *that,* for example, Socrates or Plato, as bare particulars not only in that it is found in both Socrates and Plato but also in that it entails more than just being a *this* or a *that,* which could be just a chair rather than a human.

Determinations can thus be understood as infinite, not absolutely, since determinations are still finite with respect to one another, in that one is not the other and is limited by the other even in one and the same *this,* but still as infinite with respect to just *this* or *that,* so that in its concretion or in its synthesis with *this* or *that* each determination is understood as limited by *this* or *that,* of which it is predicated. The white I affirm in being is not whiteness in general, nor the whiteness of many things, but the whiteness of only *this* or *that,* no matter how many thises or thats may actually be white. The human I affirm in being is not some separate form, nor the humanity of many individuals, but the humanity of this or that individual. Thisness is thus understood as restricting its determinations to only itself. Even if we accept the Platonic view of separate universal forms, these forms, or determinations, do not become the forms of things we know in experience except by restriction to some *this* or *that*. Aristotle rejected that view of separate forms or determinations of being precisely because it did not account for how determinations were found in the things of experience.

When we come to the third aspect of our concept of being, the be of being over and above its determinations, we have to think of something yet more positive than any determination, something that is infinite not only with respect to thisness but also with respect to the limitations that determinations represent for one another. We have to think of something positively and absolutely infinite, since there is nothing that can be thought of as limiting be from outside of itself, so to speak. Only something positive, like a *this* or a determination, can limit something else, like another *this* or another determination. Outside of be there is nothing positive. There is only or simply nothing, which in its purity as nothing is not a limit of anything, not even of being. One can only think of it as negating being and nothing more.

In this respect, our conception of the infinity of be or the act of being is different from our conception of the infinity of any particular determination of being. It is a conception of something absolutely and positively unlimited. But what is conceived in this way is not affirmed as being in this way. It is affirmed only as in composition with or as restricted by whatness and thisness. What is affirmed in the direct exercise of judgment is not some be, pure and simple, but the be of *this* with its determinations. It is a finite being, where the be is finitized, so to speak, by determinations and thisness. Just as haecceity restricts quiddity, so also quiddity, as the quiddity of a *this*, restricts the be of any being we know concretely.

To speak of an absolutely unlimited act of being could raise some interesting questions. It would be tempting to ask whether such an act can be by itself, without any restriction whatsoever. But that question would take us far beyond anything that pertains to the logic of our first conception of being into something that pertains only to the end of metaphysics, not its beginning. If there is such a pure act of being, it is certainly not like any being we know from experience. What we know from experience or in the direct exercise of judgment is an act of being or, more precisely, a being in act that is finite. What reflection on this direct exercise of judgment tells us is that this being is first conceived as structured, or with a distinction between be or the act of being and *something* that limits this *act* to its own finitude. How is this limitation within being as experienced to be understood? If be is to be taken as positively unlimited over and above thisness and its determinations, what is the principle of limitation in a finite being?

3.3   Essence as Mode of Actual Being

The first answer to this question of limitation is the one we have already given. The be of a finite being is restricted by its determinations and thisness or a synthesis of the two. But this answer seems to be too diffuse, if we are to speak more clearly of a principle of limitation in finite being. Can we speak more clearly of thisness and whatness as a single principle in contradistinction from the be of a finite being as coprinciple? How would we name such a principle especially as it relates to our conception of being as a whole, and how would it relate to being as a whole or to the be of being within being as a whole?

The name we would suggest for this principle distinct from the act of being in a finite being is that of *essence,* which has had a checkered history in metaphysical discourse but which has to be understood clearly as it relates to what we are speaking of as the act of being according to the logic we have been developing with regard to our first conception of being as expressed in the direct exercise of judgment.

The English word 'essence' is derived from the Latin *essentia,* which seems to have been derived from the verb 'to be' in its infinitive form, *esse,* much as the term *ousia* in Greek was derived from the verb *einai,* although *ousia* was derived from the participial form, and not from the infinitive. *Essentia,* however, was not used to translate *ousia* in all the senses in which it had been used in Greek, but in only one of the four meanings distinguished by Aristotle in book *Zeta* of the *Metaphysics* (1028b34), the one formulated in terms of the question *what?* According to this meaning, "essence" meant the what it was to be—*to ti en einai*—of something, which was rendered in Latin as *quod quid erat esse.* This is what has come to be rendered in English flatly as "essence." We shall see that the Greek term *ousia* was also translated as *substantia,* or substance, in another context, which is akin to the idea of essence, since what a thing is in its substance is also its essence. But on the whole the term essence has tended to be used mainly with reference to *what* a thing is according to its definition. Essence is what answers to the question: What was it for something to be? Or, if we simplify the expression of Aristotle, it is the answer to the question *what?* about something given in experience in the attempt to get a better understanding of its being.

Now, it will be remembered that the question *what?* pertains to the first act of intelligence and that the conception of being is somehow what comes first in this first act of intelligence as well as in the second. To answer the question *what?* about something is to give its definition through concepts, a resolution that cannot go back indefinitely into prior concepts but must come to some first concept. That from which the process of definition begins, as we have seen, is precisely the concept of being taken as that which identifies what is to be defined. Hence in thinking of *what* something is we think of it as its essence or as that which is most proper to it in *its* being. To be sure, when we define something in terms of genus and specific difference, we do not mention the idea of essence in the definition. As Aquinas writes, "it does not fall in the order of predicaments, except as principle" (*In Metaph* VII, 2, §1275). We only use the principle as a basis for definition. But as principle it is there in every definition and, in the exercise of judgment as a whole, it is expressed as entering into composition with and as restricting or defining what is said to be. Insofar as the definition of something expresses the mode of being of something, essence is then seen generally as the mode of being or, more precisely, as the mode of *be* within the structure of a finite being.

In this sense essence has to do with the determinations of being as given in experience. Insofar as all these determinations can be viewed as distinct from the act of being in a finite being, they can all be viewed as belonging in the order of essence in a broad sense with reference to the act from which they are distinguished. But we usually do not speak of the order of essence in this broad sense. We speak of it in a more restricted sense, as we shall do here, to include only certain determinations, those precisely that we consider essential to it according to *what* it is in its proper being, as when we say that what is essential to being human is being animal and being rational. "Animal" and "rational" are the determinations or the terms in which a human being is identified or defined as a kind of being different from other kinds of being. In other words, human being has its essence in these determinations as other kinds of being have their essence in other determinations. In every case of a finite being it is the essential determination or the set of essential determinations, or the *essence* simply, that limits its act of being. Taken in this stricter sense, essence can thus be understood as the radical principle of modification or limitation for the *act* of being at the core of any finite structured being.

3.4   Essence as Standing in Being or as Thing

To speak of essence only as the mode of being or as the principle of limitation for its act of being, however, is not enough. This already distinguishes it from the act of being, but only negatively. We must speak of it also more positively as a standing in being. To understand a being as finite is not just to understand it as a composite of determinations and an act of being. It is also to understand essence as a way of standing in being for a *this* with determinations. Though we do not include thisness when we define something according to its essential determinations in the abstract, we do think of these determinations as the determinations of a *this* that stands in being concretely in its own way. For us, in our first conception of being, an essence that *is* is always a *this* or a *that* determined in a certain way.

Initially, or as we first think of being in the direct exercise of judgment, we do not think of some abstract essence, an *ens in genere* that is only possible in that it could be or not be, as if *be* or actuality had to be added to it as an afterthought or as an "accident" *(kata sumbebekos)*. Essence by itself does not represent a being, so that *be* or actuality and *not be* or the lack of actuality are then thought of as modes of essence, as if essence were the "being" we think of first, as in Wolff's modern logic of "being in general" or of the possible as possible. For us essence represents the mode of being as a determination, or a set of determinations, of an actual being. In the direct exercise of judgment we think of an actual essence which we try to represent for ourselves through determinations. Essence is simply the mode that identifies a finite being for *what* it is. But as such a mode of being it is a standing in composition with its own act of being.

The name we have for this standing of essence in being is *thing,* which is not to be confused with the name *being* as we understand it in the direct exercise of judgment. Following Avicenna, Aquinas explains that the name "*being* [*ens*] is taken from the act of being [*actus essendi*], but the name of *thing* [*res*] expresses the quiddity or the essence of being" (*Ver* 1, 1, c). In the direct exercise of judgment what we say *is* is a *this* or a *that,* some thing, with determinations in actuality. When we focus on some determinations of this thing as given in experience to express what it is in its essence, we are thinking of it only as a thing that stands out on its own, so to speak, in being. The thing we are referring to is the same as the being in actuality, but in thinking of it as a thing we are thinking of it only as having its own determinations. A thing is a *this* with determinations, such as Socrates, the dog next door, or the tree in my backyard. When I name it or think of it as a being, I include the actuality of its being. When I name it only as a thing, I include only its essence or the order of determinations that constitute its essence. In trying to say *what* it is as a thing, I do not include the actuality of its being but only the determinations that make it what it is. Thinghood refers to *what* a being is in its modification, or to its essence. The danger or the mistake is to think that all there is to an actual being is its thinghood or its essence, which is also called its "reality" by Kant, without reference to its act of being.

We do, however, come to an order of essence, or of essences, within our first conception of being. If we think of many things as being, we think of them as each having or being an essence, for essence is thought of as something concrete initially, some *thing* given in experience. We speak of it first as something in being with a term that is derived from the verb 'to be,' before we speak of it as a quiddity, a term that is derived from the act of understanding, which raises the question *what? (quid est?)* in order to get at the essence of a being given in experience as a thing. To understand some thing ultimately is somehow to come to the standing of the thing in its essence. This is what we affirm in the exercise of judgment when we claim to have arrived at the truth about some thing, which is spoken of in Latin as *aliquid*, short for *aliud quid*, some *what* other than another.

To arrive at such truth about essence, or to come to an understanding of how things stand in being according to their essence, is not a simple matter of instantaneous recording, whether in visual image or word. It presupposes a vigorous use of intelligence as exemplified in the empirical sciences and in phenomenology, both of which strive to get at the quiddity or the essence of sensible things as given in experience. In this striving, determinations have to be sorted out in terms of which ones pertain to a thing according to what it is in its essence and which are to be predicated of the thing only incidentally or accidentally, that is, determinations that are real in a thing but that are not predicated of it *in eo quod quid est*. In this way we come to an understanding of an order of determinations even within one and the same thing in which some are understood as essential to the thing and some not, even though they may be necessitated by some other thing as well as by the essential determinations of the thing itself. Thus essential determinations can be seen as the ground for accidental determinations and the whole can be seen as an order of essence in contradistinction from the actuality of the being as a whole. Or, alternatively, the order of essence can be viewed more narrowly so that it includes only those determinations that are considered essential to a thing. In either case the standing that we discern in being as it discloses itself according to determinations is viewed as essential to things, whose fundamental standing is precisely their essence.

Essence in the narrower sense can be understood as ground for certain accidental determinations of a thing that do not pertain to its essence. But it cannot be understood as grounding its own actuality. *Be* or the act of being is not a determination or anything pertaining to the order of essence. Nor is it a mere accident to essence, as it was thought to be by Avicenna. It is simply the act of what is standing in its very standing. On the other hand, even as the act of what is standing in its essence, the act of being cannot be understood as the ground of essence or of thinghood, as one might infer from certain expressions of Heidegger in speaking of the ontological difference. The *be* of a thing does not make it be, as if this *be* were before or apart from the thing that is made to be. Neither *be* nor essence are apart from one another in our first conception of being. They are simply and immediately in composition with one another in being as it presents itself in experience, with essence understood as the mode of actuality, so that being is always understood as a thing or an essence standing in being. Essence, on the other hand, is simply being understood as *some* thing or other, which is then represented in our definition as belonging to some genus and species.

To get a better sense of this intimate composition of being and its modification as essence in things, let us reflect upon our own existence as thing in the world actualized through our own activity in the actual exercise of judgment or of personal decision. In one sense such activity is accidental to what I am as a thing in my essence, at least in the sense that I could be myself actually without being in the process of making this judgment or this decision or in the sense that I could be making other judgments or decisions than those I am actually making. Nevertheless, such activity is expressive of *what* I am in being, which is why I call myself a rational animal, and precisely as such an *expression* this activity is in composition with my act of being.

Think of this activity as both *real* and *mine.* It is determinately mine. In its actual exercise it could not be real unless it were mine and it could not be mine unless it were real. But the relation between *real* and *mine* in this activity is not one of merely mutual reciprocity. There is real exercise of judgment or decision, such as yours, that is not mine. This is not to say that there is real exercise of judgment or decision in general. There is real exercise of judgment or decision only in my activity or in yours or in someone else's. In other words, there is real exercise of judgment or decision only according to someone's personal mode. In my case, the activity is *real only on the condition that it is mine,* just as in your case it is *real only on the condition that it is yours.* In this we find the relation of modification that is necessary for something to be real in our experience. The actual exercise of judgment or decision cannot be real without being mine, or yours, or someone else's, always according to each one's standing in being.

At the same time, however, the activity I am reflecting on is not *mine* except *insofar as it is real.* Within the very spontaneity of my activity I experience a certain particularity within a more universal reality or a certain passivity with regard to being as a whole, which imposes itself, as it were, so that what I do I accept with a certain necessity as *really* mine. This is like saying that, while Socrates is actually sitting, it is necessary that he be sitting, even if he could get up at any moment. In my actual exercise of judgment or decision I still only find myself really exercising judgment or decision and I find that this activity is *mine only insofar as it is real.* This is how being discloses itself, with a certain necessity that I accept, at least to the extent that when I find myself acting in a certain way I have to say that it is part of my being or my part in being to be doing so at that moment. I understand my activity as part of what is real, as a participation in being which is at the same time a modification of being. The being that I experience immediately in my activity is a modified *be* or *act* of being from the very beginning.

Similarly, the being that I experience in myself as a whole, as a thing, as this human essence, or as subject, is a modified act of being. There *are* other human beings in my experience and other kinds of being or essences as well, each with its own act of being. There is no *be* in general. There is only the *be* that is I or the *be* that is you or the *be* of any other kind of being, with the understanding that *be* is always modified or diversified according to differing essences with their own standing in being. In other words, I experience being as diversified in different essences. In fact, I never experience being except as diversified and individualized, and it is the relation of this diversification and individualization in the order of essence to being or to the *be* of being that has to be interpreted metaphysically. *Esse est diversum in diversis* (*De Ente*, 6). How is this diversity to be understood in the logic of structured finite being?

3.5   From the Predicamental to the Transcendental Conception of Being and Its Differences

There can be no doubt that the notion of being is the most universal that we can have in mind. It can be said of everything that *is,* even of things that are not, for we do say that they *are* not. Even nothing comes under "being" in some sense, although not in the sense of any thing that is. Nothing is a limit for being. It "is" more as a limit for what we say *is,* for it is *not.* It is excluded from being, but what is excluded is nothing, which is another way of saying how *universal* "being" is: it excludes nothing, or it includes everything there is. If, then, there are differences in being, how does our initial understanding of being include these in its very universality or commonality?

Universality is associated with the predicate in the exercise of judgment. There are universal judgments in which the subject is universal, as when we say of human being that it is mortal or of snow that it is white. But such judgments usually come after judgments in which a *this* or a *that* has been identified as human or as snow. At least at the beginning, the exercise of direct judgment starts from individuals identified only as *this* or *that.* This is a human being. That is snow. But even in the most primitive judgment about *this* or *that,* the predicate *(P)* is always universal. There are no real judgments in which the predicate is simply *this* or *that.* Even when we try to make a predicate of *this* or *that,* we do not say, "this is this" or "that is that." We say "this is a this" or "that is a that." We turn "this" and "that" into universals, as we have been doing in speaking of thisness. The expression "that is that," as it is sometimes used to put an end to a discussion, is not a judgment. It does not predicate anything about "that." It simply stops at a singular *that,* without saying anything more about it.

Hence in the exercise of judgment a predicate term is always understood as universal, which means that it can be predicated of many and not just of one *this* or *that.* Even if a predicate, such as "mountain 29,002 feet high," is applied in fact only to one thing in the world, namely, to Mt. Everest, it is still thought of as applicable to other things. Once I have the idea of a mountain that high, regardless of how I get the measurement, I can ask whether it applies to more than one mountain. It is only after I have determined that there is no other mountain this high that I will speak of Everest as the highest mountain. In making this judgment I take a predicate, which is of itself universal, namely, "mountain 29,002 feet high," and say that it applies to only one mountain. I speak of Everest as the highest only because I know of no other mountain higher or the same height. As a universal, however, the predicate *(P)* does open up the question as to whether it is applicable to more than one thing. In its universality it is the medium through which questions for understanding arise about different things given in experience. That is part of its dynamic function in the exercise of judgment.

On the other hand, as we have just said, the subject *(S)* in the direct exercise of judgment is not understood initially as universal, but rather as a singular *this* or *that,* until we start speaking more theoretically about universal subjects. If we reflect on this singular function of *this* or *that* in the direct exercise of judgment, we find in it an ontological reference to something in itself, a thing in itself, as Kant put it, for which a predicate has yet to be formulated. Kant argues for the necessity of positing such a thing in itself in order to ground sense knowing of "phenomenal objects," or objects of experience. Though he posits the thing as noumenal, he finds nothing to say about it, noumenally, though there may be plenty to say about it phenomenally, that is, in predicates about a thing of experience.

The point about the ontological reference in *this* or *that* taken as singular, however, is that *this* or *that* as the subject *(S)* of a judgment stands directly for the thing as it is in itself prior to understanding. As such it cannot be predicated of anything else, but is thought of as a subject *(S),* or, as we are more apt to say in modern thought, an object about which different concepts could be predicated. It is what Aristotle calls "first substance," which he signifies simply as *tode ti,* "this something here," and which is to be distinguished from what he calls "second substance," or substance understood as a universal and therefore as predicable of more than one first substance, as I can predicate the second substance "human" of two "first substances" such as Socrates and Plato. Logically speaking, then, *this* or *that* is only an ontological point of reference for beginning to exercise judgment.

Eventually, as we do come to make universal judgments, in which we speak more theoretically of "second substance" rather than directly of "first substance," we do not think of the universal subjects of our judgments as *being* in their universality. We think of them only as universal concepts applicable, only presumably perhaps, to some *this* or *that* or to several of them. For example, in the judgment, "human being is humorous," the subject "human being" is predicable of many, such as Jane, Mary, and John. There have been those, like Plato and others, who, in order to uphold what moderns would call the "objective truth" of universal judgments, have claimed that universals as we conceive them do have a reality of their own in some separate sphere of being. But the truth claim of such universal judgments does not require such objectification or reification of universal concepts as such.

The proper exercise of judgment, in which truth is to be found, does not require a one-to-one correspondence between concepts or parts of concepts and reality or parts of reality. In the use of universal concepts as subjects in the exercise of judgment there continues to be an ontological reference as well as in the bare or preconceptual indication of *this* or *that,* but this ontological reference is not found in some direct correspondence between an abstract concept or determination and some separate sphere of being apart from experience. It is found only through the mediation of *this* or *that* in the ontological reference to being as given in experience. In other words, the ontological reference has to be concretized and it is concretized only in *this* or *that*. This does not take away from the truth of concepts in the exercise of judgment, but it does set concepts off as abstract, and therefore as cut off from being, so to speak, when the concretion of *this* or *that* is left out of consideration.

Abstraction, of course, is not of itself a source of error, unless we keep on trying to make a direct connection between abstract universals and a corresponding separate sphere of reality for our abstractions. Abstraction is an integral part of our inquiry into being as given in experience. Thanks to abstraction from *this* or *that,* concepts can exercise their dynamic function in the exercise of judgment. Without abstraction from *this* or *that* we would be without categories of understanding and hence without questions for understanding. In metaphysics we would be unable to speak of haecceity, or quiddity, or the be of being, all of which are abstractions in our indirect exercise of judgment, much as the categories of understanding and the different concepts of things are abstractions in the direct exercise of judgment, whether in empirical sciences or in phenomenology. Such abstraction opens the way for us into being itself, though always through reference to the concrete.

The use of abstraction, however, is not limited to the difference between a *this* and a *that*. There are also other differences from which we can abstract in focusing on one category of being rather than another. These are differences that can be expressed in concepts and that give rise to our understanding of different kinds of being, which we tend to classify according to categories that go from the more particular to the more universal, with the most universal understood as the highest or the supreme genera. As we rise from one degree of abstraction to another, we prescind from more and more differences and come to concepts that can be predicated of more and more beings in a way that is removed from concretion. We arrive at concepts like "body," for example, which can be predicated of all sorts of beings without reference to whether they are living or not, or like "substance," which can be predicated of something without reference even as to whether it is body or not. All this takes place within our universal conception of being that signifies according to a mode of concretion. It takes place according to differences that have to be understood as differences of being, but which nevertheless are conceived abstractly in our understanding.

The question for us, then, at this point of our logic is this: How do all these differences relate to being as we conceive it initially and how does the conception of being itself, in its concretion, differ from the conception of abstract categories that are expressed only as predicates in the exercise of judgment?

We do not merely classify things. We also conceive them in their different kinds. We see them as coming under categories according to genus and specific difference and according to different levels of genericity. The Porphyrean tree of categories is a good illustration of this. Suppose we define the human being as rational animal. "Animal" is then seen as proximate genus, with the specific difference of "rational" as opposed to "nonrational," another difference specified only negatively but referring to a wide diversity of animals thought of as merely sentient, which is what all animals are in common. "Animal" itself, however, can be seen at the same time as a difference in a "higher" genus called "living," where "animal" is now opposed to "nonsentient," another difference specified only negatively but now referring to a wide diversity of plants thought of as merely living. Similarly we can go on to think of "body" as a still "higher" genus, with "living" and "nonliving" as the differences, until we come finally to "substance" as the "highest" genus, with "material" and "nonmaterial" as the differences. This may not be the most searching way to formulate categories for understanding. Other ways of lining up categories and differences can be thought up, many of which might be more appropriate for certain purposes, scientific as well as practical. But this way can serve to illustrate the mode of categorical or predicamental thinking in any one of its forms, where abstraction is the rule.

Let us now come back to the definition of "human being" as "rational animal." What is the relation between the genus and the specific difference in this definition? Both of the notes in the definition are predicated of human being according to its essence or according to *what* it is—*in eo quod quid est*. In the concrete they must be understood together as pertaining to some *this* or *that*. In fact, the specific difference, "rational," cannot be understood apart from its genus, at least not in the way we understand "rational" initially, that is, as a specific characteristic of certain animals. But the genus, "animal," can be understood apart from the specific difference. In anthropology, for example, the remains of individuals dating from very early times can be identified as those of an animal without knowing whether that animal was rational or not. The genus, "animal," prescinds perfectly from the specific difference, "rational" or "nonrational." It is perfectly abstract, in the sense that I can understand something as "animal," that is, as sentient living thing, without yet understanding any specific difference.

This does not mean that there can be an animal without a specific difference, that is, that is not either rational or nonrational. But that is not due to the genus as such or in its abstraction. It is due to the fact that when I speak of a genus in the exercise of judgment I always understand that it has to be specified. The genus as such does not exist. What exists is a genus with a specific difference and, if I know the genus of a thing, I must further investigate to discover its specific difference, as happens in the study of fossils in anthropology, for example. I can understand the genus without understanding the specific difference. The genus contains its specific difference only potentially, so to speak, insofar as it abstracts from that difference. Conscious of a genus as abstract, however, I am led to inquire as to what its specific difference is in the concrete.

The same holds for every genus as we move up the Porphyrean tree. The genus "living" abstracts completely from its specific difference, "sentient" or "nonsentient," as does "body" from "living" or "nonliving" and "substance" from "material" or "nonmaterial." In fact, it holds not only in the category of substance, but also in any one of the other supreme categories, whether it be that of quality, quantity, relation, or any other supreme genus one might wish to distinguish. In the exercise of judgment we think of the modes of being as proportionate to the modes of our categoreal predication. But the modes of predicating are thought of as abstract, whereas the modes of being are not. Each genus delimits a certain aspect of being as distinct from other genera and applies only to that category of being, to the exclusion of other genera as well as specific differences.

The notion of being, however, while being more universal than any one of the supreme genera one might wish to distinguish, is not abstract in this way. As we saw, it signifies according to a mode of concretion and composition. We do not think being except as having modes. This is so true that we think of the most fundamental mode of a being as its essence. The categories we formulate are thought of as more or less adequate expressions of these modes of being. In our exercise of judgment we try to follow the mode of a determinate being as closely as possible, that is, we strive critically to arrive at an adequate conception of its mode of being in truth.

But our conception of being itself does not follow the mode of our expression in categoreal predication. Even as a universal, unlike any genus, "being" is not abstract. It has to include its differences, for these differences are understood as real and therefore as actually coming under the concept of being, unlike the differences of a genus which are understood as coming under it only potentially, that is, only insofar as the genus enters the actual exercise of judgment as a predicate. If the differences, whether generic, specific, or individual, did not come under "being," they would not be understood as being or real; they would be nothing, which alone is excluded from "being." Hence, as real, differences have to be included in the understanding of being, unlike specific differences, which do not have to be included in the understanding of their genus.

In contrast to this conception of being as the concrete universal, that is, as the universal that contains its differences, we might consider the notion of being as proposed by Suarez, who is at the origin of modern essentialism. For him the differences of being could not be understood in abstraction from being, much as a specific difference, such as "rational," cannot be understood in abstraction from its genus, namely, "animal." If individuality is a difference of being, it cannot be understood apart from being, much as rationality cannot be understood apart from animality. But for Suarez this did not hold if we reverse our consideration from the side of the particular to the side of the universal. Though the differences could not be understood apart from being, being could be understood apart from its differences.

For Suarez, the concept of being was not only one, but also most simple (*DM* II, 1 & 2), rather than structured or composed, as we have been arguing here. In this the concept was likened to a genus. In fact, Suarez argued that it had to be thought of as a sort of highest genus containing all differences, including not only those between substance and accidents, or the highest genera in the order of predication as understood by Aristotle, but also more importantly for an onto-theology those between created and uncreated being, since both the created and the uncreated had to be thought of as coming equally under the common concept of "being." As such, the concept of being was understood not only as most simple but also as completely abstract. It did not signify according to a mode of concretion and composition, as we have argued, but only according to the mode of an abstract name or genus.

For Suarez the "objective concept" of being as understood at the beginning or as defining the nature of metaphysics as a science was only a name (*nomen*) and not a participle (*DM* II, 4). As a name it signified only according to a mode of abstraction and simplification, as the name does when it is taken out of its place in the exercise of judgment. Whereas the participle includes some reference to time as well as to the concrete *this* or *that,* the abstract name in its simplicity does not. It prescinds perfectly from all differences, leaving us only with a concept of being as possible. Suarez speaks of this name as expressing "that which has real essence [*habens essentiam realem*]," which, he adds, means something not fictitious or chimerical. But what he means by "real essence" is one that is only apt to really exist *(apta ad realiter existendum),* not one that actually presents itself as being in experience. All that is required for such an essence to be "real," according to Suarez, besides its not being merely made up as a chimera by intelligence, is that it involve no repugnance in itself. This is how, in taking the place of the participle, the name "being" transforms the question of being into a question of the possible and opens the way to modern essentialism. It simply omits any reference to actuality, along with temporality and concrete thisness, as part of our initial conception of being. In other words, it prescinds completely from all differences and omits them from the universality of being, as if they were nothing.

Our claim is that the differences are included actually in the universal conception of being understood not only as a participle but also as a complex or structured concept. They are not included just potentially, as in the case of the differences for a genus, even though we may have yet to identify these differences clearly in a further inquiry followed by a further exercise of judgment. Our initial conception of being calls for clarification in terms of differences that are at first affirmed only confusedly.

When I know that something *is,* I include in what I mean by *is* all its real differences, even though I may not know all these differences clearly. In fact, I understand that in order to know this something as a being I shall have to discover its differences as it discloses itself to me, especially in its essential mode of being. When I see *X* approaching in the distance, I see it as something, a substance perhaps, then as a living body, then as a rational animal, and finally perhaps as my friend Socrates. The being that I first identified confusedly I eventually know fully and clearly in his differences. Similarly, when an astronomer discovers a new phenomenon in the heavens, or a new blip on an instrument, the astronomer has to go through a process of identification and clarification as to what it is, what kind of thing it is if it is more than a blip on an instrument, what size it is, and so on. Throughout the entire process of learning, the dynamic of our initial concept of being is at work even more radically than any particular concept within the science of astronomy. We have a sense of something real that at first is quite confused but that becomes clearer and clearer as we discover its being more precisely or as being discloses itself in its differences. Being, as it actually presents itself in experience, elicits the entire process of investigation and learning from start to finish. To know being more clearly, or to learn more about it, is to come to know it in its differences.

This tells us something about how being is understood in its commonality or as *ens commune* at the beginning of metaphysics. To know being only generally or *in communi* is not yet to know it fully. It is to know it only in a confused way, which calls for clarification through differences. To know being fully we must come to these differences, which are not added to "being" as a specific difference is added to an abstract genus, but are understood as already contained in "being," though not known clearly. It was with an unerring metaphysical sense that Descartes sought only clear and distinct ideas. He fell short, however, only in thinking that ideas could be clarified apart from, or prior to, any reference to our first conception of being in experience, which is never in doubt. It is from an understanding of differences as already contained in being that the process of investigation begins in any order of human inquiry. It is from this same understanding that we come to think of our categories as only abstract and as having to be specified and individualized through differences in the direct exercise of judgment. But the understanding itself is that being actually contains its differences and cannot be known fully apart from these differences.

Thus, before leading us into metaphysics, our initial conception of being as what is known *in communi* leads us into an investigation of the differences of being in particular sciences as well as in our more practical common sense. We learn about different kinds of being according to different categories of our understanding that come together in some order of generality and specification. This kind of learning about differences can go on indefinitely, since differences seem to be virtually infinite. At any given time our knowledge of being always seems only partial from the standpoint of being as a whole. To the extent that we do learn something from experience through questions for understanding and questions for reflection, however, we do come to know being as it discloses itself in its diverse ways.

This is not a futile exercise of judgment, nor is it to be forgotten as a preliminary for raising the question of being as a whole, where we do not turn away from the differences of being in perfect abstraction but rather try to think of these differences as they relate to being as we first conceive it *in communi*. To do this it is good to have understood some differences of being, but it is not necessary to have understood all these differences exhaustively. It is enough to understand the differences we do understand as differences of being and to see how in its relation to them the concept of being remains transcendental, at least in the sense of being irreducible to any one of them in particular and in the sense of including them in the universality of its own higher order of commonality. This transcendentality of the concept of being is an integral part of its concrete universality.

The term "transcendental" has been used in different ways by philosophers with reference to both knowing and being. But it is in connection with the differences of being that we introduce it here, especially as it denotes an order that surpasses what can be expressed as categoreal predication in the direct exercise of judgment. In comparing the concept of being to a category or a genus, we have been speaking of the relation between being and its differences, though not of any difference between created and uncreated, since we have no way of knowing yet whether or how that could be a difference of being as given in experience. In the course of this comparison between differences and the universality of being we have been led to recognize the being of the differences as the critical point. Differences cannot be excluded from the concept of being, taken not as a name but as a participle, because the differences *are*. There is no "being" as such or in the abstract that we can simply name as an abstract genus. There is only being in its differences, or the being of differences, whatever these differences may be, generic, specific, or individual, and it is in this being of differences or in being as differentiated that transcendentality first comes into our understanding as part of our initial conception of being.

It is interesting to note how Kant failed to grasp this transcendentality as it regards being. In the *Critique of Pure Reason* he refers to the transcendental philosophy of the ancients after drawing up his table of categories. In that philosophy, he writes, "there is yet another chapter containing pure concepts of the understanding which, though not enumerated among the categories, must, on their view, be ranked as *a priori* concepts of objects" (*KrV* B113). What Kant had in mind was the way Schoolmen spoke of being as one, true, and good: *quodlibet ens est unum, verum, bonum*. But in discussing these "pure concepts of the understanding," Kant focused only on one, true, and good in this proposition, without reflecting on the *ens,* or the conception of being, with which they were necessarily associated as properties, as we shall see in speaking of the properties of being. Moreover, having just finished a presentation of what he thought was a complete table of categories, he could only judge these "pure concepts of the understanding" or, as he also called them, these "*a priori* concepts of objects" in the light of his categories and not in the light of the transcendental concept of being in which they had been originally proposed. Hence he found them no less unthinkable than the concept of being itself. There was no place for them in his table of categories. To have accepted them would have amounted for him "to an increase in the number of categories, which cannot be."

In investigating the origin of "these supposedly transcendental predicates of *things,*" he was thus forced to reduce them to "nothing but logical requirements and criteria of all *knowledge* of things in general." He saw them only as prescribing "for such knowledge the categories of quantity, namely, *unity, plurality,* and *totality*" (*KrV* B114). The error of ancient transcendental philosophy would then have been, according to Kant, to take categories that, properly regarded, could only be taken as material, that is, as "belonging to the possibility of things themselves," and then to further apply them only in their formal meaning and "incautiously convert them from being criteria of thought to being properties of things themselves."

This, however, is not the way the ancients had come to think of the one, the true, and the good as transcendental properties of being, though it is in keeping with Kant's failure to think of being as transcendental. The precise way in which Kant accounts for the three properties of being mentioned as mere categories of quantity does not have to concern us here. Suffice it to say that, in trying to reduce them to a tale of category, he was ignoring their essentially transcendental character. As transcendental, they are not predicates of things or properties of things in themselves. They are properties of *being,* which cannot be understood merely as a particular *thing* or essence, but as a composite of a determinate essence, which also has its own determinate properties, and an *act* of being. The notion of being includes the notion of thing, but transcends it insofar as it includes an actuality as well that is distinct from the essence of a thing.

Being, understood as a participle, as we saw with Aquinas, is taken from the act of being, while the name *thing* is taken from the quiddity or the essence of a being. The German name *Ding* expresses what would have to be for Kant the supreme genus, much as the name *essentia realis* did for Suarez. In the Aristotelian logic of being the equivalent would have been *ousia,* or substance, not *on,* or being. In other words, the name "thing" relates only to categorical thinking and, for Kant, as well as for us, the categories of understanding are abstract. That is why they are said to be empty and to require a content from sense intuition in order to be applicable to objects. Intuition, we would say, provides them with the differences that they require as dynamic concepts for interpreting the real as given. "For," as Kant puts it, "we can understand nothing else than what brings with it in intuition something corresponding to our words" (*KrV* A277; B333). Kant's insistence on the necessary role of sense intuition in human knowing bears out the necessary aspect of concretion for a proper understanding of being. But it does not convey the equally necessary aspect of composition upon which transcendentality rests. Kant missed the transcendentality of the properties of being because he had already missed the transcendentality of being, which is neither a category nor a difference but encompasses them both in the totality of its *act*.

Kant, of course, had his own idea of transcendentality. He has a transcendental analytic and a transcendental dialectic. But this transcendentality applies only to the act of reflection, which has to do not "with objects themselves with a view to deriving concepts from them directly," as in the process of forming the quiddity of sensible things, "but is that state of mind in which we first set ourselves to discover the subjective conditions under which we are able to arrive at concepts" (*KrV* B316). All judgments require reflection, according to Kant, but this is "the act by which I confront the comparison of representations with the cognitive faculty to which it belongs, and by means of which I distinguish whether it is as belonging to the pure understanding or to sensible intuition that they are compared with each other, [and this] I call *transcendental reflection*" (*KrV* B317).

Reflection for Kant thus bears only on the subjective conditions of knowledge, and its transcendentality consists in the distinction and comparison of the different cognitive faculties to which concepts belong. Transcendental reflection is more than merely logical reflection, which is a mere act of comparison between concepts apart from any reference to faculties of knowledge. Transcendental reflection "bears on objects themselves [and hence] contains the ground of the possibility of the objective comparison of representations with each other" (*KrV* B319). But it considers objects only as objects of faculties, that is, of pure understanding or of sense intuition, and the relation between these in arriving at objective knowledge. Transcendental reflection for Kant has no bearing on being, which is simply left out of question. It is totally absorbed with the categories of understanding and the *a priori* forms of sense intuition, space and time, and how they combine with content as presented by intuition to give us knowledge of "reality" or of real essences.

Kant ultimately understands objects only as essences. Since we know these only as they appear through sense intuition, which provides a content for the otherwise empty concepts of pure understanding, they are known only as phenomenal objects. This is what raises the ever-recurring problem of the noumenal object or the "thing in itself "as having determinations of its own "behind" the appearances. Though this is a question of existence for him, Kant cannot think of it in terms of being, which for him is mere position of a subject apart from any predicate. With regard to objects, Kant never gets beyond the predicamental order of categories. He does speak of the noumenon as "transcendental object" (*KrV* A288; B344), that is, as something that the understanding thinks of as an object in itself, when he warns against sense intuition presuming to apply its intuition to things in themselves rather than just to appearances, but of this transcendental object there is no intuition on which some assignable positive meaning could be based. The only assignable positive meaning Kant can think of is one of the categories of understanding when they encounter a content through sense intuition. In his transcendental reflection on knowing, Kant remains locked in the relation between sense intuition and understanding. His is a critical reflection only on the act of knowing, not on the act of being, which, as present in reflection as the second act of intelligence, transcends both sense intuition and the concepts of pure understanding. It is only through critical reflection on being itself as present in act that we arrive at the proper transcendentality of being.

CHAPTER 4

The Analogy of Being

O UR REFLECTION into the meaning of being is an opening to what
we refer to as being. Though we have unpacked the notion of being
as a structured notion with three aspects, haecceity, quiddity, and be, or the
act of being, we have viewed it thus far only in relation to the predicamental
order of categorical thinking. Our reflection upon being in relation to this
order, however, has led us to recognize that what we refer to as being cannot
be properly contained within such an order of abstraction. The concept of
being is not properly a genus or a category even in the highest sense of the
term. Nor can it be a predicate that can be simply added on to other predicates in our characterization of something. In this sense Kant was right in
saying that "being" is not a real predicate. Even when we seem to use it as
predicate in so-called existential judgments, as when we say that something *is*
simply, without adding a predicate, it does not serve as a predicate like any
other predicate, because the *is* in the exercise of judgment refers to all the
differences of the something that can be expressed as predicates, even though
it may not express any of them clearly and distinctly. The affirmation of being expressed by *is* in the exercise of judgment is not added as a predicate. It
is added only as the complement to whatever is expressed in the predicate as
actuality complements the essential determinations of a thing. "Being" is
thus a transcendental notion in two senses, the first one, which was overlooked by Kant, as we have just seen, and the second one from which other
transcendental notions, such as one, true, and good, can follow, as we shall see
in speaking of the properties of being.

To be sure, there is no getting away from the predicamental order of categories in speaking about being. Suarez was right in saying that, as a name
taken by itself, "being" does not express any differences. But as a participle
containing its differences at least confusedly, it calls for some expression of
these differences according to the different modes of being given in experi-

ence. This is what we do when we speak of being according to our different modes of predicating. We experience being not only as *this* or *that,* but also according to different modes or degrees that we express as diverse categories or species of things. These categories do not strictly add anything to being, as though they were extrinsic to being, as a specific difference is extrinsic to a genus taken abstractly. But they do express a special mode of being that is not expressed by the name "being" alone. To the extent that the notion of being always entails some determinate quiddity and some haecceity for us, it will always have to be brought down to some order of predication in the exercise of judgment.

But that is not the only kind of order in which being calls for expression. There is also the transcendental order of being itself that we discovered at the end of our reflection on the predicamental order, the order that emerges when we try to think the being of differences as the differences of being. In this order "being" calls for a different kind of expression than the one according to abstract categories, which do not include the differences of what comes under them. It calls for an expression that will apply not to any special mode of being, such as that of substance or quality or quantity, or that of a special kind of substance, like a plant or an animal, but to every being commonly. It calls for some metaphysical expression according to its transcendental order, which raises an important question as to the unity of this further expression or of metaphysics itself as a science.

Other sciences define some determination of being as their subject matter and derive their unity from the unity of the subject matter so defined. Physics, for example, focuses on the physical object and has that, however it may be defined, as the unifying principle for all that it has to say. Similarly, biology focuses on life and has that as the unifying principle of all that it has to say. And so it is with all of the particular sciences. So also it must be according to our understanding of being as the subject of metaphysics, inasmuch as being, as we know it from the beginning, is determinate and can only be known determinately. What we have seen in our reflection on the notion of being and its structure shows us that there is a metaphysical exigency for the particular sciences as part of our knowledge of being. We can now understand this exigency. But can we understand the further exigency for the unity of metaphysics itself as the science of being as being?

In a way we have come back to our original question about being as being, only now it appears more clearly and with greater urgency. We have learned that being is discovered or discloses itself in its very differences or in its diversity. If this is so, what unity can there be to the notion of being as being, as distinct from being in any of its particular determinations, which will enable us to think of a unified science of being as being? We can understand now how there can be many sciences of being. But can we understand how there can be one science of being itself precisely as being?

Being is common to all the sciences. But it is for metaphysics to treat of it in its commonness. This commonness, as we have seen, cannot be understood in the abstract, as some sort of ground or background upon which or against which differences detach themselves. Differences are real only to the extent that they are part of being. If they were not part of being, they would be nothing, not even differences. Apart from being there are no differences. But if being can only be understood concretely, that is, with its differences, both specific and individual, how can it be understood as one without falling back into mere abstraction? What is the unity of being in the concrete?

It is at this point that analogy becomes crucial as integral to metaphysical discourse, for analogy expresses for us the precise kind of conceptual unity that we need for the science of being. There are many kinds of analogy. Empirical scientists reason through analogy when they develop models for understanding phenomena. Poets also use analogy in developing similes and metaphors that help us to represent reality better. Analogy is a way of comparing things and learning through comparison. A good analogy helps us to understand better, to see something new in what was only given previously, or even to discover something that was simply unknown to us before. In metaphysics, analogy is the way of access to being as being in the originality of its differences.

In fact, with being we have to do with the most basic form of analogy, or the ground of all analogy. It is difficult, if not impossible, to imagine a point of comparison for being as such. To what can being be compared? Things can be compared with one another. But apart from being there is nothing to compare being with. Comparison takes place only within being, and in this lies the reason of analogy. If things can be compared with one another in reality, it is because all of them appear in an order, the order of being, and this order is itself the basic analogy. The unity of being with its differences is a unity of order, and so our question is now to understand this order as the order of being. That is what the analogy of being consists in.

We have come to this question through reflection on the way we categorize being as we try to understand it in its determinations. But we have seen that what we refer to as "being" transcends all our categories. As such it implies an order of its own, a transcendental order as distinct from any predicamental order, and it is this order that we must now inquire into more positively. So far we have seen it only in the light of a predicamental order that is more proportionate to our understanding in the particular sciences or in the direct exercise of judgment. Other sciences, as particular, inquire into what things are as given in experience according to the different categories that they specify in the questions they raise about being. But, as such, none of them raises the question of the order of being as a whole or in its transcendentality. This is the question that is left for metaphysics and that is less proportionate to the categories of understanding. Metaphysics has to examine this transcendental order of being in its own light, which, though it transcends categorical understanding, still has to be brought to some systematic understanding, since it is the beginning of all understanding.

The first thing to note about this transcendental order of being is that, though we come to it only after discussing the predicamental order of our understanding, it is prior to this predicamental order even in understanding. It is part of our preunderstanding of being. Analogical thinking is frequently contrasted with categorical thinking and characterized as a lack of rigor and precision. Categorical thinking, we are told, is more logical and stringent, while analogical thinking is more vague and nebulous. This may be true for some kinds of analogical thinking, but not for all. In fact, analogical thinking about being has to be much more rigorous than just plain categorical thinking. This is why it is used in science as well as in poetry. The only reason why we think of categorical thinking as more logically compelling is that we feel more at home in it, as something of our own making. It is our instrument for coming to grips with what we think of as essential aspects of being.

But as such an instrument, categorical thinking is not adequate to all that there is to be grasped in being. We are biased in favor of categorical thinking from the standpoint of understanding, but if we can be critical of this bias it is because we already know, in some more rigorous fashion, that being transcends the categories of our understanding. To pursue the question of being as being, one must be more rigorous, not less, than in empirical science or phenomenology. We must enter into the analogy of being in its actuality, which requires careful thought in its most radical sense.

The categories we use in the direct exercise of judgment, especially those that can stand up to our most critical reflection with reference to being, detach themselves against a background of analogy that is at once more universal and more concrete. This is why categories are abstract not just with reference to individuals, but also with reference to the concrete whole. They give us only a piece of the whole. This is why also poetry can sometimes be much more incisive than science in its interpretation of reality. But most importantly for us, this is why metaphysics has to be the most rigorous science of all, because that is the only way of properly entering into the analogy of being. Even the categories themselves have to be understood in the light of analogy, as Aristotle intimates at the beginning of his work on the *Categories* through a reference to analogy in determining his subject.

If we come to the question of analogy through reflection on categories, it is not because categorizing is the first and most fundamental form of intelligence for us. It is because it is the easiest for us to talk about clearly. Categorizing is the act of intelligence that is most proportionate to our understanding and it is the aspect of intelligence that has been developed most extensively in our scientific culture. In one sense, therefore, it is better known to us than analogizing, and so we will begin there. But if we are to get anywhere in metaphysics we must get back to analogy as the form of thinking most appropriate for thinking being as being.

In his "Introduction" to *Sein und Zeit* Heidegger mentions this question of analogy in connection with the question of being. After quoting Aristotle to the effect that the universality of be is not that of a class or a genus, he writes: "The 'universality' of be *transcends* any universality of genus," alluding to the medieval notion of being as a *transcendens.* He goes on to say that "Aristotle himself knew the unity of this transcendental 'universal' as a *unity of analogy* in contrast to the multiplicity of the highest generic concepts applicable to things." "With this discovery," Heidegger adds, "in spite of his dependence on the way in which the ontological problem had been formulated by Plato, he put the problem of be on what was, in principle, a new basis" (*SZ* 4–5/22), a basis that did not consider being as some generic category in which all beings could equally fit but rather as an order of different beings unified conceptually by a reference to one—*pros hen.*

Heidegger, however, did not go on to explore this new basis for pursuing the question of being or the part of the metaphysical tradition that did explore it, though he surely knew of the controversy that took place about it with Duns Scotus, who denied the analogy of being, in opposition to Thomas Aquinas. Though he never denied the analogy of being explicitly, Heidegger chose rather to ignore it by insisting on what he refers to as the Platonic origin of the ontological problem and its culmination in modern technologized science—whence his concern for destroying the history of ontology. Whatever originality Heidegger might have seen in the Aristotelian notion of analogy for dealing with the question of being, it seems to get lost in this task of deconstruction, to the point that one interpreter of Heidegger can systematically argue, supposedly in line with the Heideggerian thrust, against any reference *pros hen,* the basis of analogy according to Aristotle, as just another source for metaphysics turning into technology (Schurmann 34, 39f., 75, 85, 87).

To be sure, the task of thinking being requires another kind of rationality than that found in technology. In fact, even analogy can be turned into just another form of technological rationality, as it does in the hands of Schurmann, as well as others before him like Cajetan in the metaphysical tradition. But that is not analogy as it can serve in the reconstruction of a metaphysics that is true to the question of being in its differences and in its diversity. We must learn to speak more properly of being as being with its differences, and in order to do so we must turn to the way in which the transcendental order of being is expressed through analogy.

4.1   The Logic of Analogy

Let us begin with a logic of terms. We can think of terms as either univocal or purely equivocal or possibly analogous. The question is to see how analogous terms relate to or compare with the other two kinds.

A *univocal term* is a universal predicated of many things according to precisely the same meaning. Such terms can express first and often undefinable notions, such as "white," which can be predicated of the paper I am writing on and of the ceiling above me. They can also be more elaborate notions, such as "human," whose definition includes a genus and a specific difference that can be predicated of Socrates, Plato, and Aristotle according to one and the same meaning. The categories we spoke of earlier, taken in the abstract, are expressed in univocal terms. It is only concretely in the actual exercise of judgment that we refer them to being or tie them into analogy.

A purely equivocal term is said of many things according to completely different meanings. Thus, both the left side of the Seine and the First National are called "bank" and both the outer surface of a tree and the sound of a dog are called "bark." In one case "bank" stands for "a rise that contains the flow of a river" and in the other it stands for "an institution specialized in the handling of money." In each case the term stands for a concept that is quite different from that in the other case. Similarly with the term "bark." These differences in the use of the same term may be accounted for by some etymological derivation. 'Bank' in the sense of "rise," for example, was derived from the Anglo-Norman, while 'bank' in the sense of "institution" was derived from the French. There may be some historical reason for the convergence of these two notions in the same term, for example, in the fact that a bank regulates cash flow. But in current usage the term "bank" actually expresses two quite different notions. Taken in the abstract, that is, apart from any context, the term is quite equivocal: it could equally express either one of the two notions, even though in a particular context it can become quite univocal. When I say "I am going to the bank to deposit my savings" no one should think that I am going to the rise containing the flow of a river, unless of course there is a bank on that bank. Again, from the standpoint of current usage, the convergence of these two quite different meanings in the same term can be viewed as purely coincidental or casual. The medieval logicians spoke of such a term as *aequivocum a casu,* equivocal by chance.

In such clear cases of equivocation as 'bank' or 'bark,' where the context can reduce the equivocation to a clear univocity, it is easy to see that it is not the notions, but the terms, that are equivocal. But in everyday language there can also be real equivocation of notions as well as terms. This can happen spontaneously before our ideas get clarified, or it can happen deliberately after ideas have been clarified up to a point, as when language is used not so much to make the truth appear, the whole truth and nothing but the truth, but rather to achieve some practical end, such as selling a product (through advertising) or achieving a political end (through propaganda).

When an advertiser tries to sell a product he often attempts to fuse, not to say confuse, the idea of the product with some other idea of something presumably attractive to the potential buyer. He does not just show a car, but he places a ravishing woman next to it or a dashing male in it driving along a steep mountain road. When a politician wants to sell himself to the nation he wraps himself up in its flag.

There is a kind of perversion of language in this kind of equivocation, especially when it tries to obscure concepts that have already been clarified. And there is perhaps more of it in our modern society than we like to think. It has even been raised to a level of science and expertise in some quarters, where politicians are marketed in the same way as products are marketed, that is, by the same experts, and where studied or designed equivocation plays on the still spontaneous equivocation of ordinary discourse, thus perpetuating the confusion of ideas and desires. But this kind of deliberate equivocation for practical ends presupposes a spontaneous equivocation, which it tries to maintain in its state of confusion. It is what medieval logicians called equivocation *a consilio,* equivocation by design, but only for practical ends, not for the purpose of getting to the truth.

There is, however, another kind of equivocation that does not arise only by chance or is not a perversion. It is *a consilio,* or by design, but for arriving at the truth, especially the truth of being. This is the equivocation we shall call *analogy*. It comes as an extension of the meaning of terms to get at aspects of reality that do not fit neatly into our clear and distinct univocal categories. The point of this equivocation by design is not to twist the meaning of terms with false or confusing associations, but to stretch meaning so that it will encompass more of the being we refer to in the exercise of judgment than a purely univocal use of terms will allow. This is not to obfuscate a clarity already achieved, but rather to strive for higher clarity about being itself as it presents itself in its differences.

One of the ideals of logical positivism or of analytical philosophy has been to reduce all language, whether scientific or ordinary, to some set of univocal terms, as if this were the only way in which meaning could be made clear. This seems very rational at first sight. But upon reflection it may not be as fully rational as it sounds, if rationality is understood as the effort to express being in the fullness of its diversity.

To be concerned exclusively with a purely univocal language may in fact be another perversion of language. We develop different kinds of language in order to express different aspects of what is. Poets do this. But so too do scientists, as is clear from the wide diversity of sciences dealing with the same global reality, or what we have referred to as the "ontic." "Science" itself is an analogous term, if we consider the diversity of discourses that it includes. We are always striving to stretch the meaning of our language beyond univocity. This is as it should be, since discourse entails a meaning that must encompass the richness of being. While it is incumbent upon particular sciences to try to define their subject matter as univocally as possible, inasmuch as they deal only with a particular aspect of being, it is incumbent upon metaphysics, or the science of being as being, to open up this univocity into the fullness of analogy, so that it will be more true to being in its differences. Without analogy, metaphysics as a science is impossible. But with it, we have the necessary complement of intelligibility for all the other sciences, which are abstract by reason of their particularity.

What we mean in the exercise of judgment is not restricted to what is expressed in terms that tend to be univocal. Meaning goes beyond what we say univocally to what we refer to as being. As long as we do not arbitrarily restrict meaning to that of one particular type of science or to what we have already said or clearly formulated, we are always seeking to grasp further dimensions of being, whether it be through new, less inadequate scientific theories or through poetic or symbolic representation. Metaphysics has to encompass this diversity of meaning as it reaches out to being as being. The kind of "equivocation" it must pursue through analogy is not the kind that stops short of univocity, which is still mere confusion in the face of being, but rather the kind that goes beyond univocity to a higher form of thought coming to expression in a new clarity about being as being in its differences.

In this context, then, an *analogous* term can be seen as one that is predicated of many according to a meaning that is *partially* the same and *partially* different. But such a definition hardly says what analogy really is or how it functions in language about being. It speaks only of a combination of univocity (partially the same) and equivocity (partially different) that remains extrinsic to the analogous term itself and seems to situate analogy somewhere between univocity and equivocity. Actually, a properly analogous term reaches out beyond univocity not on the side of equivocity, which is still only a state of confusion, but on the side of the truth of being itself. A truly analogous term is a universal term that can be predicated of many, not in the way of a univocal term, but in a way that includes differences, as "being" does. In other words, it expresses differences as they affect the very sameness expressed in the notion, so that its meaning becomes somehow *totally* different and yet remains *totally* the same.

To get beyond this purely paradoxical definition of analogy, let us look at one aspect of it that is not found in either univocal or equivocal terms: the aspect of relation suggested by the term itself or what Aristotle referred to as *pros hen,* the relation to one which gives us a focal meaning. It is from this relation that Aristotle himself proceeded in his discussion of analogy, not from univocity or equivocity.

What is the ground for predicating an analogous term of many? When I predicate a univocal term like "human" of many individuals like Socrates, Plato, and Aristotle, I do so on the grounds that there is something the same in these individuals. I do not claim that in reality they are absolutely the same. In fact, I view them as distinct individuals. But I prescind from the individual differences among them. I view them all as equally human. I also prescind from any order that might exist among them, whether it be as philosophers or as humans. I view each one absolutely in his humanity. In analogous predication, however, I do not prescind from either the differences among the individual subjects of predication or from the order that might exist among them. Not all the things that come under an analogous notion do so in the same way or absolutely. They do so according to a proportion or to degrees in some relation to other things that come under the same notion or, ultimately, to one thing that is at the center of the analogy and gives it its focal meaning. This one thing we refer to as the *analogand* or the *primary analogate.* It is the *one* to which reference is made in the relation *pros hen,* and it is with reference to this one that every other analogate has its meaning insofar as each is referred to it according to the way it is—*prout unumquodque secundum suam habitudinem ad illud unum refertur* (*In Metaph* IV, 1, §535).

We cannot properly think of analogy apart from an analogand or a primary analogate. It is from this analogand that the meaning of the analogous term begins to develop. Other things, or what we shall also call *secondary analogates,* come under the analogous term by extension of the original meaning according to some relation or order that is seen between the secondary analogates and the primary analogate.

Thus, the unity of an analogous term differs from the unity of a merely univocal term. In analogy there is a unity of meaning, but it is not abstract, as in univocal terms. It is a concrete unity of order. The univocal term says nothing of the order among the things that come under it. "Human" is as true of Plato as of Socrates, even though Socrates may be the father of Plato, his brother, or his son. An analogous term, however, always implies an order among the analogates, at least with reference to the primary analogate, and it cannot by understood apart from this order. As Aquinas puts it, it is understood *per prius et posterius:* "We must know that the one to which the diverse relations in analogates refers, is one in number [*numero*], and not just one in meaning [*ratione*], like the one which is designated by a univocal name. And that is why [Aristotle] says that being is said in many ways, not that it is said equivocally, but that it is said with regard to one [*per respectum ad unum*]; not, however, with regard to one that would be one only in meaning, but that is one as one certain nature. And this is clear in the examples given below" (Ibid.). Aquinas is referring to the example of "health" given by Aristotle to illustrate this "respect to one" in the use of an analogous notion.

To understand the analogy of being, therefore, we shall have to focus on one certain nature as our primary analogate, from which the meaning of being will have its beginning. But before we do that, we must ponder more carefully the key role of this primary analogate in establishing the first understanding of an analogous notion. This role is not exclusive, since secondary analogates also have a role in extending the meaning of the term. The first understanding of an analogous term is affected by the discovery of other things in their relation to the primary analogate. The primary analogate, nevertheless, remains the key for understanding the analogous term in that the primary analogate is the center from which the diverse relations fan out. Among these relations may be some, like similitude, which are univocal, but there are others that are not, like that of efficient cause, consequence, signification, participation, imitation, exemplary causation, final causation, and others.

To illustrate how these diverse relations can fan out from one primary analogate, let us turn to Aristotle's classical example of an analogous term, namely, "health." The meaning of the term is first seen as relevant to a living organism and is first understood as applying to this "certain nature" that is spoken of. The extended meaning of the term is then seen as centering on this first meaning of a healthy organism but as applying to other natures according to the diverse relations they may have to the healthy organism.

Initially, and most properly speaking, "health" means a proper disposition for the well-being of an organism, and in this sense, which is *unum ratione,* or one in meaning, it can be applied univocally to any number of organisms. But by analogy "healthy" is also understood as predicable of other things that are not organisms, such as medicine, diet, complexion, or urine, according to the diverse relations that they can have to health in an organism, whether it be as cause, condition, sign, or consequence. This extension of meaning by analogy is surely not arbitrary. It is grounded in an order of being, but the ground or the order cannot be reduced to univocity. It bespeaks an order and a rationality that transcends both mere equivocity and mere univocity and attains a higher kind of meaning, one of analogy itself.

When it is the analogy of being that we are thinking of, and not just the analogy of health, we touch upon the reason why human being is led inevitably not just to formulate myths in order to make sense of the universe in which he finds himself, but eventually also to seek causes and explanations in scientific fashion for what presents itself in experience. Such an inclination is due to the analogy of being as it makes itself present to and for reflection in intelligence as it leads us from effect to cause or from sign to signified.

4.2   The Dialectic of Analogy

The logic of analogy brings us to "being" as the most radical instance of all analogy. But of itself it does not bring us fully into this analogy of being, which has already begun to present itself in the way "being" contains its differences and in the way it signifies according to a mode of composition and concretion. All this is true only because being itself is analogous in making itself present. Let us try to enter more clearly into this radical analogy of being.

To do this let us follow a dialectic suggested by the young Aquinas in his *Commentary on the Sentences* of Peter Lombard where he speaks of a threefold division of analogy on the basis of the relationship between meaning and being or, as he puts it more exactly in Latin, between meaning *(intentio)* and be *(esse)* (*Sent* I, 19, 5, 2, ad 1). In the first case there is analogy according to meaning, but not according to be. In the second, there is analogy according to be, but not according to meaning. And in the third case, which is where the full analogy of being comes in, there is analogy according to both meaning and be. The dialectic, as Aquinas has it, leads progressively into the analogy of being itself.

4.2.1 Analogy According to Meaning but Not According to Be

First, there is the analogy according to meaning alone, and not according to be *(secundum intentionem tantum, et non secundum esse)*. In this case the analogous notion, which is one intention *(una intentio),* refers to many *per prius et posterius,* but it is understood as referring properly only to the primary analogate. This is the understanding of analogy we have seen already in the logic of analogy.

The way we predicate "healthy" of many different things besides living organisms is a good example of this analogy. The one idea of health is said of different things that relate to the health of an organism. But health in its primary meaning, which is univocal, is found properly, or has be *(habet esse),* only in the living organism. When we speak of health with reference to organisms, we are using the term not analogously but univocally. As predicated of living organisms, the idea or the intention of health has one and the same meaning. It is only when we speak of other things such as diet or complexion, which are not living organisms, as "healthy" that we use the term analogously.

This sort of analogy presupposes a certain interconnection among the secondary analogates and the primary analogate, as we saw, but what is predicated of the secondary analogates seems to remain extrinsic to them, unlike what is predicated of the primary analogate. Health, for example, is not predicated of its secondary analogates according to what they are in their essence as it is predicated of a living organism, the primary analogate.

4.2.2 Analogy According to Be but Not According to Meaning

Second, there is the analogy that appears as the reverse of this first one, that is, the analogy according to be and not according to meaning *(secundum esse, et non secundum intentionem).* This is the kind of analogy we do not think of immediately, but it enters into our thought at the moment of critical reflection in the exercise of judgment. In this case many things are thought of as coming under some notion, or into the meaning of something *common (in intentione alicuius communis),* but this common notion is not thought of as realized in the same way in the different analogates or, in other words, it does not have the be of one meaning in all the things of which it is predicated *(non habet esse unius rationis in omnibus).*

To illustrate this kind of analogy with the idea of health, we can say that the idea or the intention of health is understood as univocal or as having the same meaning when it is predicated of living organisms. Nevertheless, it is not understood as being the same in different kinds of living organisms such as a tree, a dog, or a human being, or in different organs such as the kidney, the liver, or the heart within one and the same organism. When we think of health critically as it is to be found in different organisms, we expect it to be different in different kinds of organism, though the intention or the meaning of the term is the same for all of them.

This second kind of analogy brings us closer to the analogy of being, but it is not yet fully the analogy of being. There is still something univocal about this analogy, even though the univocity is only according to meaning and not according to be. Analogy in this second sense implies a certain critical reversal of perspective that takes us from a merely logical consideration of concepts to a more ontological consideration of being. As such, it provides a crucial step for getting to the analogy of being itself. But the step is a tricky one, and has given rise to some misunderstanding in that it does require a reversal of the perspective we have followed until now in our discussion of the meaning of being.

We began by focusing on terms as either univocal or equivocal. This is the way we proceed in raising questions about being as given in experience. We formulate our questions according to categories and, in doing so in any particular science, we prescind from many aspects of being, or differences of being, in order to focus on one or another in some univocal sense. Thus, the natural scientist sets off one category of being as his subject of consideration, while the social scientist sets off another. From a logical standpoint, that is, from a standpoint according to meaning only, this gives rise to univocal terms that are articulated more or less systematically in the scientific discourse. The particular scientist, whether of natural or social relations, must know, however, that he is proceeding by abstraction and that, though his notions may be univocal by reason of this abstraction, he does not find them realized univocally in actuality. What he is talking about is actually analogous *secundum esse,* or according to be, even though he does not take this analogy into consideration in his univocal discourse.

Only the most naive form of reductionism, lacking all critical reflection with reference to being, denies this. Mass and energy, for example, can be dealt with univocally in physics, at least up to a point, but it seems gratuitous to affirm that mass and energy are found or realized univocally in such different material beings as atoms, rocks, trees, and animals. Insofar as mass and energy can be defined clearly and distinctly in physics, they are univocal according to meaning. But in reality they are not univocal insofar as the beings of which they are part include differences unaccounted for through mass and energy. The second kind of analogy we are referring to takes us out of the reductionism often associated with physicalism, without denying the validity of physics as an irreducible kind of knowing.

When we posit natural differences among beings we find in experience, such as those between living and nonliving bodies, or those between sentient and nonsentient living things, or those between rational and nonrational animals, we posit this second kind of analogy, which is according to be but not according to meaning. As natural, such differences tell us that "bodies," even if they can be understood in some univocal sense as physical entities, still have to be understood as analogous in the way they are realized in being according to these differences. Even physics itself, which operates with a univocal concept of physical entity, recognizes this kind of difference in that it distinguishes between plain physics and biophysics, so that the modern physicist recognizes differences in be that are not included in the univocal notion of physical entity. One could think, for example, of the difference between a visible physical object and a physical quantum in physics itself as an instance of this kind of analogy according to be but not according to meaning, since the term "physical" has the same meaning in both instances but is not understood as referring to the same kind of being in each case.

This second kind of analogizing is found in modern science no less than in ancient science, though examples of it are bound to be different. It comes with the realization that any particular science begins by a process of abstraction in its attempt to create a univocal discourse about a particular aspect of being. When it looks beyond this abstraction it recognizes that what it speaks of univocally is realized analogously in concrete actuality. Only reductionism fails to see this analogy, because it arbitrarily reduces what we refer to as being to what it can say about it univocally, disregarding the essential or natural diversity of what is given according to be.

The point Aquinas was making with this second analogy was tied not just to his physics but also to his metaphysical discourse. In fact, Aquinas speaks of the metaphysician *(metaphysicus)* as well as the natural scientist *(naturalis)* in connection with this analogy. He distinguishes both from the logician *(logicus)*, who, in inquiring only about meaning, without reference to being, remains in the univocal, in contrast to the natural scientist or the metaphysician, who both refer to the differences of being in their critical reflection beyond the univocal understanding of their concepts. With this reference to being, they are brought back to analogy, without, however, totally abandoning the univocity of their concepts taken in the abstract. The last step in coming to the analogy of being as being is taken only by the metaphysician.

4.2.3 Analogy According to Meaning and to Be

The third form of analogy supersedes the first two and brings us to the radical unity of both in being. It pulls the analogy that is only according to meaning and not according to be and the analogy that is according to be and not according to meaning together into one analogy according to both meaning and be at the same time *(secundum intentionem et secundum esse)*. In this analogy things that come under the analogous term are viewed as equal neither in the common notion nor in be *(neque parificantur in intentione communi, neque in esse)*, but as unequal or as belonging to different degrees of being. This is the analogy of being itself, which includes an order of differences according to meaning as well as according to be.

This is the most difficult analogy to understand because it transcends understanding, which clings to the simple clarity of univocity as much as possible. We come to this analogy only through reflection, by completing the reversal of perspective already begun at the second moment of analogy and recognizing the ulterior intelligibility of being in act as an intelligibility that is in composition with its diverse degrees of being and that can be understood only in this composition. The reversal is effected by bringing the first moment of analogy back into the second without making of it a simple return to the first. It is a passing beyond both moments into the analogy of being as being, which is the ground for all analogy. If there is any analogy of any kind, whether of the first or of the second moment, it is because being is already analogous from the very beginning according to both meaning and be at the same time.

This analogy of being itself can be expressed in terms of greater or lesser perfection *(secundum rationem maioris et minoris perfectionis)*, but this does not add anything to its intelligibility. It only specifies abstractly how we can speak of the order that analogy implies. Perfection, as we understand it here, is not extraneous to being. It is rather a way of referring to the differences of being as they relate to the one or the primary analogate from which they derive their meaning. Things can be thought of as more and less perfect, or as higher or lower, in the order of being. This is done with reference to one, the primary analogate of being. Whatever the primary analogate of being may be, other things will be seen in their difference as higher or lower, as more or less perfect in being, with the essence of a thing, or *what* it is, limiting its act of being or serving as a measure for it, so to speak, and with the act of being understood as the perfection that is so measured in a finite being relative to other finite beings.

This analogy of being, however, implies an order to be discerned in being with reference to one, *pros hen,* which will serve as the primary analogate. If we recognize differences of being or even different kinds of being in the direct exercise of judgment, the question then arises for us: Which will be the primary analogate in our pursuit of metaphysics beginning, as we do, from determinate being as present in experience? The question is important for us because, without a proper understanding of the primary analogate of being in experience, we run the risk of reducing the question of being to some lowest common denominator that would leave out the richness of the various degrees of being we find in experience.

4.3   Human Being as Primary Analogate of Being

To understand an analogous term, whether according to meaning or to be, we must attend first to a primary analogate as the one to which all the other analogates are somehow related. In the case of health, which is analogous according to meaning but not according to be, we attended first to the living organism as primary analogate before attending to the secondary analogates of which the term "health" could be predicated. Now, in the case of being, what are we to attend to as the primary analogate? Where does the idea of being begin for us? What do we say *is per prius,* so that whatever else we say *is per posterius* is understood as in some relation to it? What is this one being in our experience in which our understanding of being has its beginning according to both meaning and be? What is for us the one thing in relation to which all things will be understood as differing according to some degree of greater or lesser perfection in being?

If we follow Aristotle in answering this question, we would say first of all that substance is the primary analogate. For, after saying that being is thought of as diverse *(legetai pollachos)* and alluding to the analogy of health and medicine in Book *Gamma* of the *Metaphysics,* he goes on to show not only how the science of being as being must focus primarily on substance, but also how substance *(ousia)* serves as the primary analogate in the articulation of being in some of its diversity.

> Some things are spoken of as being because they are substances; others because they are modifications [*pathe*] of substance; others because they are a way to substance, or corruptions or privations or qualities or productive or generative of substance, or of things spoken of in relation to substance, or negations of the latter or of substance, whence we even say non-being is non-being. (1003 b5–10)

What we should note in this text is how all the diverse ways of thinking about being that can be distinguished from substance are understood as relating back to substance in one way or another. The text illustrates how an entire metaphysical system can be summed up in this kind of analogical thinking with reference to one thing *(pros hen)*.

In reflecting upon Aristotle's illustration, however, in the light of the dialectic of analogy we have just elaborated, we should note that the notion of substance itself is not analogous in the same way as being is analogous. Substance was for Aristotle a category, the first of the categories to which all the other nine categories were related as "accidental," or as going with *(sumbebekotos)*. Aristotle was using his scheme of the categories to illustrate the analogy of being as centering on some primary analogate. In doing so he was not thinking only as a logician, that is, as one concerned only with meaning, but more as a metaphysician, that is, as one concerned with the question of being. As a category, "substance" is not analogous. It is univocal according to meaning in the same way that "body" is univocal according to meaning. In this sense it belongs in the second kind of analogous terms we distinguished in the dialectic of analogy, not in the third, that of being as being. Substance can be defined univocally, for example, as "what has being in itself," as opposed to whatever has being in another in the case of "accidents" to substance. Substance is thought of as analogous only with reference to being in the consideration of the natural scientist or the metaphysician, where it is seen as analogous according to be, though not according to meaning.

Aristotle's use of the term "substance" in his illustration of the analogy of being has led to some confusion as to the kind of metaphysics he was aiming at, a science of being as being or only a science of substance. Some have argued that his was only a metaphysics of substance and not a metaphysics of being in the full analogous sense of the term (Gilson 43–47). Aristotle seems to lend himself to this interpretation later on in the *Metaphysics* when, in book *Zeta,* as he is about to enter into his investigation of actual being, he brings the question down once again to "being" in its primary sense, "clearly the what, which signifies the substance," while all other things spoken of as being are said to be "either quantities, or qualities, or modifications, or some other such thing" (*Metaph* 1028 a13–20). But this interpretation does not follow necessarily, if we keep in mind the three moments in the dialectic of analogy as laid out by Aquinas, especially the second.

With the understanding of "substance" as analogous according to be but not according to meaning, that is, as univocal in meaning, in the same way that "body" is analogous according to be but not according to meaning, we can see how one can speak of substance as the primary analogate of being without restricting the understanding of the subject in question, that is, of being as being, to the understanding of substance as a category. There is still room to make a distinction between the subject of metaphysics and the category of substance, even though Aristotle may not have been as clear about this as he might have been in focusing on substance as the primary analogate in his illustration of the analogy of being. When we bring in the third moment in the dialectic of analogy, that of analogy according to both meaning and be, which is most properly the analogy of being, we can see how the question of being remains open beyond any question of substance as understood in Aristotelian logic, not only with regard to "accidents" in relation to substance, but also with regard to an order of differences among substances in being or according to be.

This is the order that perhaps Aristotle did not sufficiently attend to in speaking of the analogy of being, but which we must now focus on to further clarify our conception of the analogy of being as being. The differences we must focus on in being are not only those between a substance and its accidents, which can be thought of as differences within one and the same being. More importantly for us, they are those that might set off one substance as different in being from another substance, or one type of substance as different from another type, as one might speak of a living thing as substantially different in being from a nonliving thing. If we think of the analogy of being as referring to different kinds of substantial being, over and above the differences within one and the same substantial being Aristotle alludes to in his illustration of the analogy of being, then we have to ask ourselves which one of the different kinds of substance we refer to in the direct exercise of judgment serves as our primary analogate and which ones have to be understood as being in analogy with this primary analogate?

This is a question we tend to answer spontaneously in the direct exercise of judgment according to the particular aspect of being we happen to be focusing on. The physicist, for example, tends to think of being primarily as something that corresponds to his representation of physical entity, while the biologist tends to think of it as something that corresponds to his representation of a living thing. But such judgments are not sufficiently critical in a metaphysical reflection and they tend to ignore or belittle what may be important differences or aspects of being that do not fit into the univocal categories of a particular representation. In other words, they tend to be reductionist rather than inclusive of all the differences there are in being. If we recognize that there are a diversity of substances in being, then our understanding of being as analogous forces us to raise the question of which one is to be taken as primary and how the others are to be understood as relating to it. The question must be faced clearly in an indirect exercise of judgment that is properly metaphysical with reference to being as being.

Metaphysical physicalism, which is not be confused with physics in the direct exercise of judgment, can be thought of as having faced this question and as having come to an answer that is not satisfactory. Without an explicit theory of analogy such as we have developed here, it takes the object of modern physics as what we would call its primary analogate of being. As one author puts it, "the rough idea is that only the basic entities and processes of mathematical physics exist, plus their complex combinations—often wholly novel—into stars, planets, life, consciousness, and more." Such a physicalism does not have to be reductive, according to the same author. It can allow for many "faces of existence." But it "claims to be a kind of unified theory or synthesis of all the diverse sciences, and indeed of all the domains of truth in or out of the sciences" (Post 159).

Clearly, this is no longer a question of physics. It is a metaphysical theory that implies a certain analogy of being and focuses on one kind of being as its primary analogate. It could even be understood as a science of being as being, inasmuch as it focuses on what exists and allows for an irreducible diversity in what are referred to as the "faces of existence." Like Aristotle, it focuses on some substance, or on *what* is *(ti esti)* or this something *(tode ti)* for its primary analogate, but this something or the *what* is taken as defined by modern physics in opposition to ancient physics. "Physicalism thus claims to provide the new, unified picture of existence that should replace the largely medieval one shattered piecemeal by successive discoveries in the sciences" (Post 160).

As a science of being, however, this physicalist metaphysics seems to subordinate itself to the particular science of physics, thus compromising its essential universal scope, much as Aristotle seemed to be doing in appearing to subordinate his metaphysics of being as being to a metaphysics of substance

or to his philosophy of nature, which also had its "basic entities and processes" as revealed not only in his work entitled *Physics,* but also in the whole of
his physical works, from the treatise *On the Heavens* to the treatise *On the
Soul.* It is not just set theory that seems too abstract and bloodless to identify the faces of existence even for a physicalist (Post 53), but also the categories of mathematical physics with reference to the full scope of differences
mentioned in the theory. If physicalism allows for higher forms of existence
or higher degrees of perfection in being than merely physical entities and
processes, it is not justified in trying to determine these higher forms or
higher degrees of being only with reference to what is thought of as the
lowest form or degree of being.

It is not that physicalism, or just plain physics, is entirely wrong in supposing some dependence of the higher forms of being on this lower form.
"Nothing at these higher levels can occur without some corresponding oc-
currence at the level of physics—not the flicker of an emotion, not a stir in
the womb. And the truths at the higher levels are in some sense determined
by or manifestations of truths at the level of physics" (Post 159). But this is
true only if there is something in the higher forms of existence that is not reducible to this lower form of being. Physical being in the concrete, that is,
"physical entities" as found in living and sentient things, entail ontological
differences that depend only on the higher form in which they are actualized.

In other words, these higher forms cannot be properly determined in
their differences as being in terms of physical entities. As higher forms, they
are more determining than determined. Even in its attempt to be nonreductive, physicalism has no way of expressing the higher degree of being found
in these higher forms because it is too conceptually constricted in its choice
of a primary analogate. As long as some differentiation is allowed between
higher and lower forms of being, it would seem better to start with a higher
form of being as the primary analogate in order to arrive at a more comprehensive science of being as a whole, for the higher forms encompass the
lower in a way that the lower cannot encompass the higher, just as the human form of being encompasses the lower forms, such as the sentient, the
living, and even the nonliving, in a way that the nonliving cannot encompass living or sentient forms, let alone rational forms.

It is difficult to think of a physicalism that can encompass the complete
analogy of being as given in experience and that is not in some sense still reductive as long as it understands determination as coming only from the
bottom up, and not from the top down as well. Even to recognize an emer-

gent being as higher than that from which it emerges is still to think of it only in terms of the lower. It is to constrain our conception of the perfection or the act of being in an unwarranted way, as if the lower essence were the first or the only measure of being. If there are higher kinds of being, there have to be higher essences that are less constraining on their act of being.

On the other hand, however, to start from a higher form of being as one's primary analogate of being is not to reach immediately for the highest form of being, if there be such a highest. A theologian, for example, might immediately think of God or the most perfect being as the primary analogate of being. But philosophically speaking, starting from an absolutely highest kind of being can be just as confusing as starting from the lowest, since we do not know at the beginning of our metaphysical investigation what such a being might be, nor even if there is such a being. Such an idea could only be an abstraction for us and could not be understood as referring to being as given in experience.

The appropriate place for us to begin is with a higher form of being or with the highest form of being as given in our experience that is still proportionate to our intelligence, namely, with human being, taken as the first or the primary being we know concretely in our first critical reflection. This is the determinate being we know most immediately in experience through confrontation with other human beings and in reflection into ourselves as self-conscious beings through this confrontation. Our first encounter with being in the fullest sense of the term is not with a physical entity as defined in mathematical physics but with another human being, in which we discover not just a "physical entity," but a whole being, another self, and our own self in the presence of this other self. It is in this radically reflective experience in the presence of another that we come to our first exercise of judgment and that we come to our first consciousness of being, namely, our own being as determinate in the presence of another determinate being, both human and each irreducibly distinct from the other in its actuality.

It would be difficult for us to reconstruct exactly how we first come to exercise judgment of our own in the passage from infancy to our own intelligent and self-conscious use of language. But it is clear that the passage takes place through a confrontation with an other in speech. Human infants who are deprived of this sort of human confrontation too early or too long never quite make it as human beings capable of exercising judgment of their own. It is in this confrontation that we discover what otherness is, or that there is otherness, the otherness of an other and of our own self in relation to that other. But this otherness is the otherness of two human selves, the otherness of one subject in relation to another subject. Each is a self-conscious subject in the presence of another self-conscious subject, so that the first other, the first object of consciousness, for each one is another subject.

When being first presents itself in the first exercise of judgment, therefore, it presents itself as a plurality through a sort of mutual recognition among selves conceived as determinate beings. At first what is understood is the difference between one self and another self. There are still many differences of being to be discovered and understood, both within ourselves and others identified as selves and among other beings we will eventually identify as objects or mere things, and not as human subjects. But our first inclination is to think of differences of being as differences between selves. This is why children have a tendency to treat pets, or dolls, or toys, or security blankets as if they were like the first subjects they differentiated themselves from in coming to self-consciousness. Learning what differences there are in being is in large part learning that not all others or objects are human selves, or sentient, or living, but that many things have their identity in something else than self-consciousness or life, sometimes even only in some abstract mathematical formulation of what we call a physical entity. When we come to such an abstract entity, however, we must not forget that this is not where our first conception of determinate being began. It began, or rather it still begins, in the confrontation through speech, including scientific and phenomenological discourse, among human beings as selves, with all the differences that a proper understanding of this world entails in its personal, living, and physical dimensions.

There is thus a definite advantage to beginning one's inquiry into the question of being with human being, as Heidegger suggests (SZ 9–20/ 26–35), not only because human being is the only one to raise the question of being, but also because it is the being that is best known to us in its immediacy. It is in the direct exercise of judgment, as we have seen, that being first discloses itself. This direct exercise of judgment can take many forms, as we have also seen, that of the particular sciences as well as that of phenomenology. But in its most concrete form it centers on a confrontation between human beings, myself and another self, a thou, where I first discover the importance of objectivity for my subjectivity in the "hardest science" of all, that of mutual recognition between two beings.

Thus, the first being we know or the being we know best is not just any substance, as Aristotle speaks of it in his initial discussion of the analogy of being. Nor is it any basic entity or process as determined in any particular science, whether it be mathematical physics or anthropology. Nor is it anything as obscure to us as some absolutely highest being. It is rather the human being known as a whole in its relation to another human being, myself in mutual recognition with another self. Aristotle would seem to agree with this when, at the beginning of his treatise on the soul, he characterizes knowledge of the soul not only as more honored or prized, but also as more exact or certain (*Soul* 402 a1–2). Perhaps the modern mathematical physicist would agree as well, if he keeps in mind the elaborate process of abstraction by which he arrives at positing what are for him basic entities. This does not render these entities any less real than he thinks they have to be to account for what is given in experience, but it does make them real only in a sense that is derived from the sense of being he started from in this process, namely, a sense associated more with human being than an object represented by some mathematical formula.

The way we name things or even categorize them initially is an indication of how we come to know them. We begin not with atomic or subatomic particles or quanta. Even in physics those are the last things to be named and they are known least determinately. We begin rather with the human being and we proceed from there to lower kinds of being by setting aside the more positive determinations of human being as self-conscious. At first we think of everything as human and the first individuals we identify as being are humans, others and ourselves. As we grow in discernment or judgment, we come to identify some beings as less than human, as nonrational, but still as sentient. From there we go on to identify further beings as nonsentient but still as living, until we finally come to nonliving beings. At each step along the way some particular science, such as psychology or biology or chemistry, can and does step in to define or specify more positively what is given at each level of negation or abstraction and to account for it, until we come to the most abstract level of physical science as such. But all along we are advancing within a more positive conception of being first set for us at the human level of existence.

The further we go from the human being, however, the more difficult it is to find any identity of being and the more indeterminate our concept of being seems to become. It is to the credit of mathematical physics that it has been able to lend greater determinacy to what appears at first as the most indeterminate. But this resourcefulness should not blind us to the fact that it rests ultimately on a principle of indeterminacy, which implies that it may not be dealing any longer with determinate being as we first understand it but with something less than being in a full, determinate sense. Where the line lies between determinate being and this something less than determinate being in the complicated reasoning process of mathematical physics, whether it be at the level of atoms or subatomic particles or further still, is very difficult to establish, if it can be established at all. But the difficulty itself is a sign that we are reaching the limits of identifiable being. This is not the point where being presents itself in its clearest form.

Mathematical physics, whether it be nuclear or astronomic, places us at the outer limits of what we experience as being. In the elaboration of our understanding of being, however, we do not begin at such an obscure limit. We begin rather at the center of our experience where being presents itself most clearly in the determinate form of human being. The particular science, or sciences, of this particular being can present no less difficulty than mathematical physics, as human psychology or the phenomenological analysis of a Heidegger can well attest. But it has its own clarity which mathematical physics cannot have. It is only by reason of its abstraction and oversimplification that the latter appears clearer to us than the human sciences or even literature and poetry. Nevertheless, it is with the clarity of human being that metaphysics must begin. Pascal, who was a mathematical genius in his own right, thought of man as the thinking reed somehow suspended between the infinitely small and the infinitely large, but he also thought of him as comprehending this twofold infinity. It is *from* the human being, as well as *by* the human being, that the order of being, which extends to other kinds of being, is to be comprehended.

The primary analogate of being is thus to be found in the human being, and not in any subatomic particle or galactic nebula. The whole order of being in nature or in the lifeworld is articulated with reference to human being at the center, not just in an evolutionary view of the world, but in the very direct manner in which we go about defining different levels of being in history and nature, some higher and some lower, by a process of negation starting from the rational animal who makes history by its own initiative. Physics is in no position to furnish metaphysics with the unifying entity it needs for its systematic elaboration, as physicalism claims (Post 211–13, 329). Physics operates only at the fringe of what we know as being and not at the center. It does not raise the question of being according to the full scope of its analogy, but rather seeks only to account for the order of being set up within its own abstract categories. Only in human being, understood as a determinate whole, can we find a "unifying entity" adequate to the analogy of being as it presents itself in experience without reduction and without monopolization, for the higher identity of the human being leaves ample room for the lesser identity of lower beings, thus allowing for the differences of being not only within one and the same being but also between different kinds of being. Only with a primary analogate properly located in the human being can we proceed to a metaphysical account of the differences of being as given in experience. For being can be understood in the full analogy of its differences only through reference to this one—*pros touto hen.*

4.4   Priority in the Order of Learning

To speak of analogy is to speak of an order of priority. We have just been speaking of the human being as having priority for us in the order of being. But it is important to understand in what sense this priority holds. When we inquire into the causes of something, we come to think of the causes as prior to their effect. That is the order of reality itself *(quoad se)* as we discover it. But it is not the order of discovery or of learning *(quoad nos).* In fact, these two orders are the reverse of one another and a proper understanding of the relation between them is crucial for a proper understanding of how analogy functions in the metaphysical thinking of being.

In any investigation we have to think of what we know first as the primary. When our investigation is into the causes of something, what we know first is the effect. It is what we name first as the subject of our inquiry. Thus, in the cause-effect relation, the effect is at first the primary analogate. It has to be as long as the cause is as yet unknown. Once the cause is known and thoroughly understood, it may then become the primary analogate, that is, that in the light of which we understand the effect, as when we come to see the secondary qualities of things in the light of their primary qualities, or what we call the properties of something in the light of its substance. Once we know the cause of something we first knew only as a fact, the order of priority in the analogy is reversed. But as long as the investigation is still underway or as long as the cause is not clearly understood, the effect remains the primary analogate. Indeed, if for any reason the cause cannot be clearly known by us, as is often the case in the particular sciences and as we shall see is the case absolutely with regard to the universal cause of all being, then the effect remains as the primary analogate and the cause is wondered at in the light of its analogy with the effect.

Thus, if in our search for the causes of what there is given in experience, whether it be in the particular sciences or in metaphysics, we are led to affirm causes that we cannot properly experience in their reality, whether it be subatomic particles, unconscious drives, or even a creator, we have to acknowledge that the being we start from, namely, the human being, remains our primary analogate. This is the situation in which we find ourselves as long as we are still learning or inquiring into what there is and what causes it to be so. We cannot avoid centering on the being we experience most concretely as the primary analogate.

The objection might be made that this gives rise to a reverse sort of reductionism to the one associated with physicalism, an exclusive sort of anthropomorphism or animism that does not take into account the differences of being other than the human or the living, whether higher or lower. In theology it would reduce God to human dimensions and in physics it would make of everything a living or even a rational thing. But this does not have to follow if the analogy of being is properly understood.

To be sure, there is a temptation in any systematic thought to reduce all things to some kind of unifying entity, whether it be physical or spiritual or a combination of both. Physicalism tries to do it in terms of the basic entities and processes of mathematical physics. Animism tries to do it in terms of life. Anthropomorphism tries to do it in terms of pure reason. But the point of the analogy of being is to say that none of these specific kinds of being can do justice to the differences and the diversity of being. None of the forms of being we know can monopolize being in all its differences, not even what we take to be our primary analogate. Even as we refer everything to one, it is to affirm the differences of being as well as the order between them, differences that we learn to discern through critical reflection with reference to being in common. We insist on a primary analogate of being only because that is where we begin in the process of discernment among differences of being in its commonality.

Strictly speaking, there is no unifying entity or set of entities that can determine the properties of all things (Post 211), whether it be the plenum of Parmenides, the formalism of Plato, the world spirit of Hegel, or the basic components of mathematical physics. There is plurality and diversity of beings, and being is what they all have or are in common. But being itself, or being as being, is not some abstract entity or some lowest common denominator that would be found in all this plurality and diversity of beings as a ground apart from the plurality and diversity. Plurality and diversity are themselves real. It is not even be that determines beings as being, as Heidegger would have it (SZ 8/25f). It is rather be that is diversified and thereby determined in its differences. Being as a whole includes its differences simply insofar as they are real and ordered.

Nor does there have to be any such determining entity or set of entities for there to be a metaphysics or a science of being as being. All there has to be is the unity of being itself, which is a unity of order in a plurality and an irreducible diversity of beings. The analogy of being is thus an invitation to learn more of this rich diversity of being in the universe, starting from the being we know first and proceeding to a better discernment of other kinds of being as well as a better understanding of the ontological constitution of each being. Even if it starts with subjectivity, so to speak, it is an invitation to the greatest objectivity possible and not just to an objectivity of quantifiable entities.

Even as first science, then, a metaphysics rooted in the analogy of being cannot replace or reduce all other sciences to itself. It allows not only for the analogy of being, but also for an analogy of science itself, where particular sciences can inquire into particular aspects or differences of being according to their own method and their own autonomy. Each of the particular sciences is different from the other particular sciences, in accordance with the subject it carves for itself out of the wholeness of being and with the method it uses to inquire into this subject. But each is also a science in that it is an inquiry into being according to some particular aspect.

The particular sciences are all part of an order of science, but none of them, as particular, is truly the primary analogate of science. Only the science of being as being, or metaphysics, can be this primary analogate as the overarching science. But it is overarching only in the sense that it raises the question that none of the particular sciences raises, the question of being as being. It is systematic not in the sense that it tries to impose an order that would determine everything, but in the sense that it tries to follow the order of being itself, starting from the being it knows first, namely, the human being or the self. For this reason, Heidegger's insistence on *Dasein* may represent a better beginning for metaphysical reflection than any of the sciences based on quantification, whether of the human subject or of objects, but only on the condition that it get beyond mere "being and time," which is still something particular.

4.5   The Truth of Analogy

Our approach to the analogy of being has been through the exercise of judgment or the concrete act of knowing. In the logic of being we saw how "being" signifies according to a mode of concretion and composition and that, as a structured notion, it contains the differences of whatever is said to be.

This is enough to take us beyond any notion of being as univocal. Univocal notions, by reason of their abstraction, do not signify according to a mode of concretion and composition, nor are they structured so as to include the differences of their inferiors. When they do include these differences as found in the concrete, it is by way of *be* or the *is* in the exercise of judgment. We can define "animal" univocally without reference to whether it is rational or nonrational, but when we affirm that *X is* an animal we also include concretely that it is either rational or nonrational, though we may not know determinately which one it is in a particular case. In anthropology, for example, we may know that the remains of *X* are the remains of what was an animal without knowing whether it was rational or not, but still knowing that, if it was *really* an animal, it had to be either one or the other, something to be settled only through further investigation in the differences of what is given.

At the same time, however, even if the notion of being contains the differences of its inferiors at least in some confused way, differences that are irreducible to one another because they are real, the notion is not purely equivocal. It has a unity of its own, which is a unity of order *per prius et posterius*. This is the insight of any metaphysical outlook that is not purely reductionistic and allows for *real* differences of being. Whatever may be thought of as the primary analogate of being or of the various orders of being to be distinguished, what we have to show or demonstrate at this point in the metaphysics of being is that we do, in fact, inevitably think of being with its differences in terms of some priority with reference to a primary analogate.

Even in the absence of any systematic objectification, we think of what is really given in experience as entailing differences. If, for example, we take the sense of touch or feeling as the most fundamental criterion of reality for us, we think of everything as "real" only in accordance with how it affects our sensibility or our feelings. We take what affects our sensibility or our feeling as our primary analogate for what is real, and, when we are forced to recognize differences in reality, we see them only as relating to what we *feel* is fundamentally or primarily real for us. Even if we do not abandon this subjective feeling as the locus for our primary analogate of reality, we come to see other things that do not affect our feelings directly as still related to feeling, or as real for us in this sense, in different ways or different degrees, according to an order of priority and posteriority where feeling still holds the first place. Some things are thought of as more real to us than others, while the ones that are thought of as most real are the ones that affect our sense of touch or our feeling most directly.

In fact, reductionism itself, whether it be objective or subjective, does not escape this analogous form of thought. It only tries to reduce the diversity or the differences of being, which it cannot ignore, to the univocity of its primary analogate. As a metaphysical system of being as being *in its differences,* it defeats its own purpose by arguing for the necessity of this reduction. It has already recognized the irreducible analogy of being in its differences or in the different "faces of existence." And it is these differences of being that have to be accounted for as well as the unity of all that we take to be real in its diversity which brings us to the point of acknowledging the truth of analogy according to both meaning and be.

The questions for us then are: How is this acknowledgment to be taken? How is it found in the concrete exercise of judgment? We began with a reflection not on our feeling, but on the critical act of knowing in the exercise of judgment in order to express what we mean by "being." We indicated what we mean by "being" operationally in terms of knowing. But in this reflection upon the act of knowing we have been led to recognize a certain necessity of differences in being, that is, a necessity of analogy, at least according to meaning at first, if not immediately according to be.

But whence is this necessity of differences in being for our understanding? Is it only from our way of thinking or is it from the necessity of being itself, that is, from the necessity of differences in being itself as we know it? The passage from the first moment to the second moment of analogy, from the analogy according to meaning but not according to be to the analogy according to be but not according to meaning, as we saw, entails a certain reversal of perspective. It is this reversal that we must bring to completion in order to bring out the truth of analogy, which has to be both subjective and objective, that is, according to both meaning and be at the same time.

We could, in idealist fashion, think of our own knowing as the primary analogate of being. But in the exercise of judgment we know that our knowing as such cannot be the measure of things. It has to be measured by things or what we *refer* to as being. Otherwise judgment would become purely arbitrary, lacking in what we call objectivity. When we make any claim to know truth, however, we are trying to reach beyond arbitrariness to some kind of objectivity. Our sense of truth is that knowing has to give way to being, or rather that it has already given way to the disclosure of being. We feel compelled by being, so to speak, when we make any claim to truth in judgment. We could think of the passage from analogy according to meaning to analogy according to be as a kind of argument *a posteriori,* from what is posterior, our knowing, to what is prior, being itself in its analogy.

But in the final analysis we have to recognize that it is not strictly an argument going from a known to an unknown. It is only an argument from something that we take to be known more clearly and distinctly to something that is already known more fundamentally, in order to bring the latter out more clearly and distinctly. It is a learning that goes from confusion to greater clarity in the disclosure of being itself. What we recognize in the end is that in making the distinction between the first two moments of analogy we were already within the hermeneutic circle of the third moment, which is not a closed circle, as a particular judgment might be, but an open arc as the exercise of judgment should be, that is, one open to the full diversity of being in its unity as an order of being or beings.

The dialectic of analogy serves to open up the heuristic structure of our questioning into being on the basis of an immediate evidence *a priori,* so to speak, found in the reversal of perspective going from knowing to the priority of being in knowing that opens the way to a realistic metaphysics as well as a possibility of many particular sciences dealing with different aspects of being. In one sense, knowing is a grasping of being, but more fundamentally it is letting being take hold in our knowing as it discloses itself so that we may become equal to it in its fullness.

As differences impose themselves in the analogy of being, the question arises for us now as to whether there is anything that can be said properly of being as being precisely in its analogy.

PART THREE

THE PROPERTIES OF BEING

Introduction: Transcendental Modes of Being

A SCIENCE MUST determine not only its subject, what it is about, but also the properties of this subject as it is understood in that science. Thus mathematical physics must determine its subject matter, what aspect of being it is about, and then say what the properties of this subject matter are, however these may be understood. So too biology, which is about life, must determine the properties of life. Similarly metaphysics, as a science or a systematic discourse, has to consider not only being as being, but also whatever pertains to being precisely as being, what we can refer to as the properties of being, though in a way analogous to being itself and not to any other kind of property. Having just arrived at the analogy of being we must not lose sight of this analogy in speaking of its properties.

In fact, given this analogy, we find ourselves in a perplexity with regard to any properties of being as being. If "being" signifies according to a mode of concretion and composition, can anything else be predicated of it apart from this mode of concretion and composition? If "being" actually contains the differences of whatever there is, since otherwise these differences would not be, is there anything that can be said of being as being apart from these differences, which, as differences of being, are not properties of being as being?

This perplexity must be understood clearly. The question of properties must not be confused with that of differences. To bring out the analogy of being we had to insist on the differences or the diversity of being. The question was to see how being could still be one in all its differences, whether essential or accidental. These differences, however, real as they are in their being, cannot be predicated of being precisely as being. What constitutes them as differences is what sets one kind of being off from another or one particular being from another being. What can be predicated of one as a property cannot be predicated of the other as a property because of this difference. This is true even of individual differences within one and the same kind of being. Properties, on the other hand, have to be predicated of their subject as such. They belong to their subject precisely as this subject has been determined in a science, as the properties of life belong to this kind of being, that is, the living, precisely as determined. Hence, since our subject has been determined to be being as being, the properties of being must be predicated of being precisely as being, and, since this subject has been determined to contain its differences, the properties must be said of the differences as well. The properties too must be analogous, for otherwise, if the properties were univocal, to predicate them of being would be to say that there is still something univocal about being. If being is analogous, so too must its properties be.

But how are such properties to be understood and what do they add to what we mean by "being"? To understand this question, let us reflect on how anything can be added to being. In one sense nothing can be added to being, inasmuch as being includes everything and excludes nothing. There is nothing that could be added to being that is not already included in it. But the thought or the concept of being does not immediately express all that being contains for us. As we saw, being signifies according to a mode of concretion and composition. It contains differences that the concept of being alone does not express. As a structured notion, it says not merely that something is, but also that as *something* and as *this* it has differences. In this it differs from a generic notion, which can abstract from its differences. But as a notion, being as being does not express the differences that it contains structurally. These must be added to it more expressly.

It is not as though these differences were added from outside being, so to speak. Even our first conception of being contains these differences. We do not conceive of anything in the direct exercise of judgment as being without differences. But as our first concept into which all our other concepts must be resolved, as into their first, it does not yet contain the differences expressed in these other concepts. As it presents itself, being is disclosed with its differences. But as we first conceive it, we leave out the differences to name only being as being. Having done so, we must then add the differences, or our conceptions of the differences, to our first concept, with which we begin. For, as we have said from the very beginning, knowing is of being. It is with being that we begin and being is itself the beginning of knowing. But it is only the beginning, to which other conceptions, or conceptions of differences, must be added. These further conceptions, as Aquinas puts it, express its *mode,* which is not expressed by the name of being itself (*Ver* I, I, c).

But this process of addition to our original concept of being takes place in two ways that must be clearly distinguished in order to get a proper understanding of properties of being. These properties are also added to being, but not in the way of differences. The first way of adding to our original concept of being is the way we have just seen in connection with the differences of being, where the mode expressed is a particular mode of being, such as living being or quantitative being. In this way we come to distinguish diverse categories of things on the basis of diverse modes of being that we recognize. This is the way that enables us to distinguish different ontic regions in what we referred to earlier as the "predicamental order."

In the second way, however, we transcend this predicamental order, which is still tied to the direct exercise of judgment and to the way we experience being immediately, and we enter more properly into the transcendental order of being itself. In this way what is said more expressly in adding to our first conception of being is not some special mode of being, such as could be expressed in a category, but a common mode that follows every being and therefore, like being itself, transcends all categories. Thus, if many different modes of being can be distinguished and all of them can be said to be, each in its way, so too whatever can be said more expressly of being in this common transcendental way will also be said of each mode of being, each in its own way. If, for example, unity can be said of being in this common way or as a common mode, then every being will also be said to be one in the same way or according to the same mode that it is. The more common mode does not express a difference of being, but follows the differences as being does. It is this more general mode of expression that gives rise to what we are calling the "properties of being," conceptions that can be predicated of being as being. We can refer to these conceptions as properly ontological, as distinct from ontic differences. But they have also been called *transcendental,* insofar as they follow the transcendentality of being.

Thing can be thought of as such an ontological conception distinct from the conception of being. Many are inclined to identify or to reduce the conception of being to the conception of thing. As we have seen, however, the two names or ideas are taken from different aspects in the structure of our conception of being. *Being* is taken from the act of being, which is the most comprehensive aspect of being as a whole, while *thing* is taken from the quiddity or the essence, which is the restrictive aspect of the finite being. The conception of being is thus ontological and transcendental in the broadest and most fundamental sense possible. But the conception of thing is nevertheless ontological and transcendental insofar as it signifies a being in its concrete essence.

In its own standing, or according to its essence, such a thing is not understood as transcendental. It has its own differences, specific and individual, that set it off from other kinds of being and other individuals of the same kind. But insofar as it has an essence or its own standing with its own differences, it is part of the transcendental order of being. Every finite being is understood as a composite of an act of being and an essence. What makes each specific and individual are its differences, not the composition. In defining a thing we include these differences, at least down to the specific differences, but not the idea of essence as such, which is the principle of definition and not one of the defining notes. The idea of essence is present in any definition of a determinate being but is not restricted to any particular definition. As taken from the essence as such, and not from any particular essence, the name "thing" is equally unrestricted. We speak of all sorts of beings and of many different individuals as things. In doing so we understand that they have their differences as things, but in speaking of them only as things we do not include any of these differences, just as in speaking of them only as being we do not include their differences.

In fact, in keeping with what we said about the primary analogate of being, what we first think of as a thing is a human being, which has its standing in being in the presence of another human being through mutual recognition. This is a thing with very specific as well as individual differences not expressed in the concept of thing but included in its standing or its essence. The human being is a thing that stands up to another human being in speech. It is also a sentient and living thing. In the direct exercise of judgment we also speak of other kinds of things that stand in being, but not as rational, though sentient and living, and others that are not sentient, though living, and of others still that are not living. Anything we think of as having a standing in being through its own essence we think of as a thing in some degree of being. Those things we think of as having their standing without the difference of rationality, or sensation, or life, we think of as mere things, but we do think of them as having a standing in being, albeit a very diminished one in comparison with that of a human being. On the other hand, we do not stop thinking of the human being as a thing with its own standing in being. We think of it as much more of a thing, or much more than a mere thing.

It can be argued, as we did for the primary analogate of being, that the diminished meaning of thinghood in a mere thing is not its first or original meaning. The first thing, literally, I come to discern as standing in being is a self, myself in the presence of another self or another self present to me. *This* and *that* originally refers to me and to you, the most primordial objects of human consciousness, so to speak. As we said earlier in speaking of the order of learning in the analogy of being, it is only from this first discernment of two different selves or things that we proceed to the discernment of further and lesser objects, extending our initial conception of thing as selfstanding to other kinds of things, sentient nonrational things, living nonsentient things, or nonliving things, all the way down to the entities or "things" of mathematical physics.

There, of course, the conception of thing is stripped of any personal difference it might have with reference to self, sensation, or life, but it still expresses a kind of standing in which basic entities and processes coalesce. The concept of thing, as has been pointed out even for mathematical physics, expresses a unity, identity, whole in data "grasped, not by considering data from any abstractive viewpoint, but by taking them in their concrete individuality and in the totality of their aspects" (Lonergan 246). This conception of thing, which derives from an initial conception centering on self, is necessary for the continuity of scientific thought and development and for keeping it related to the concrete order of being as a whole.

Thing thus has to be thought of as an ontological conception that follows being in its transcendental order. Whatever is thought of as being is thought of as thing, as standing in being with its differences. Inasmuch as it expresses only the quiddity of being or its essence, the conception of thing has to be distinguished from the conception of being. But inasmuch as it expresses only the quiddity or essence of a finite being in its proper standing as being, it cannot be distinguished as a property in the transcendental order of being. "Thing" refers to what a determinate being is in itself or in its essence. In fact, in the direct exercise of judgment, properties are thought of as properties of things, as whiteness is thought of as the property of the thing snow and as risibility, or the ability to laugh, came to be thought of as the property of the thing human being. These are properties only in one particular order of being. They are not properties in the transcendental order of being, that is, properties that can be predicated of being according to its transcendental conception, or as it includes its differences.

What we mean by the properties of being are those ontological conceptions that are not reducible to thinghood but that pertain to being as transcendentally ordered. These are the transcendental conceptions that were traditionally listed as the one, the true, and the good, to which we shall add the active in close association with the one. What these properties add more expressly to the thought of being remains to be seen as we come to examine how each one of them is derived from our first conception of being. But it is important to note at the outset that we do come to know them as derived from our first conception of being and that they do express more of the intelligibility of being than what we take to be our first conception of it in its structure as concrete and composite.

It is perhaps for having lost sight of these transcendentals, as we saw with regard to Kant in connection with the transcendentality of being, that modern metaphysics has found itself locked in essentialism, unable to reopen the question of the be of being. While it has moved from the pure conception of being to a conception of thing (res) or "reality," which expresses quiddity or essence, it has not moved on to the conception of the one, the true, and the good in relation to the order of being as a whole. Its forgetfulness of the question of being in the fullness of that term has been due, at least in part, to its forgetfulness of these transcendentals, which has left it unable to think through the question of being to any kind of completion. What we hope to show here is that, by reopening the question of the transcendental properties of being as being, we can open a new way into metaphysics or the philosophy of being that will allow for coming to some further exercise of judgment about being as being. If being calls for thinking, this thinking can proceed ontologically only through the thought of the transcendental properties of being. In this respect the transcendental properties of being as being are the key to our reconstruction of metaphysics.

Without these transcendental ideas, which are coextensive with the concept of being, it is difficult, if not impossible, to formulate any understanding of the transcendental order of being. We have seen how the idea of being contains the differences of its inferiors. But with only our first conception of being to work with, it is difficult to see how all these differences in their rich diversity compose with being. The diversity is something given to us in the very presencing of being. But how to conceive this diversity in composition with be or the act of being is the problem that metaphysics must solve. Can we say immediately that the diversity entails a multiplicity of beings or is it more a matter of diversity within one and the same being? And whether there is a multiplicity of beings or only one being, can there be diversity within a being as well as among beings? And if there is diversity of whatever kind in being, how is the relation between the different aspects of this diversity to be understood in being? These are questions that have been part of metaphysics ever since Parmenides.

They are questions we shall have to deal with in exploring the structure and the communication of being. But in order to do so rationally we must have the added intelligibility of the transcendental properties of being. These transcendental properties cannot add anything to being as though from outside of being. Nor can they add by way of special modes of being, as differences do. They can only mediate between our first conception of being and that of thing and of the differences of being.

As properties of being, they are not even distinct from that of which they are the property, as the properties of a specific thing might be. They are identical with being itself and yet enable us to articulate more of its intelligibility than we can without them. The distinction between them is not trivial or merely one of words. It is an opening of intelligibility into the transcendental order of being. Without the distinction of these properties, we would be reduced to speaking of being only as an abstraction or according to some of its differences in a particular order, as we do in the particular sciences. But with them we can plot a course or a discourse to include the whole of being in its be as well as in its essence or its many essences and differences. Though they add nothing to being as such, the transcendentals add considerably to our understanding of being, or to how we go about understanding being in its concretion and composition.

For them to do so, however, they must be derived purely from the thought of being as found in the direct exercise of judgment. The thought of the one, the active, the true, or the good are not precisely the thought of being. They add something to the thought of being. But what they add is itself derived from the thought of being, not through experience, which would only give us differences of being, but through reason alone or through thought as it expresses more completely how it understands being in its transcendental ordering.

Judgment about the properties of being, which has to be an indirect exercise of judgment, is thus *a priori* in two senses: it does not depend on experience in a way that would make it *a posteriori* and it proceeds from a prior conception, which is the original conception of being found in the direct exercise of judgment.

Though the properties of being come after our first conception of being, they follow from it necessarily. There is something that is immediately evident about them in the direct exercise of judgment, as we shall see, but some demonstration is necessary to show that they are indeed properties of being as being. Without a demonstration we might have some conception of these properties, since there is some immediate understanding of them in experience, but we would not understand them as the properties of being in its differences, which is what we must have if they are to serve in the elaboration of our metaphysical discourse.

Thus, like metaphysics itself, our conception of the transcendentals must follow from experience. It must rise *a posteriori* or *per posteriora* to what is prior conceptually not only with regard to being itself, as we have done in determining the subject of our inquiry, but also with regard to what we shall speak of as the one, the active, the true, the good, and whatever else may follow being as being. Some kind of phenomenological reduction is therefore required to bring thought back to what is evident *per se,* but it is in a transcendental critical reflection that the priority of this evidence is seen. Our demonstration will consist in opening up this evidence for thought. It will not be a demonstration *a priori* in the sense that we could give a strict definition of being and from that definition derive its properties. Such a definition of the transcendentals is impossible for us. Our demonstration will be *a priori* only in the sense that it leads us from or through what is *a posteriori,* from experience, to a prior evidence in thought itself. It will be a demonstration in that one has to be led to such an evidence from experience as we had to be led to the evidence that metaphysics is the science about being as being through critical reflection on the direct exercise of judgment in experience and in the more particular sciences.

This is what we have had to do already with regard to our first conception of being itself, which has had to be demonstrated in its primordial evidence. Now we must do the same with our conceptions of the one, the active, the true, and the good. Starting from experience, we must demonstrate how they too are part of that original evidence, that is, how they follow necessarily from the original conception of being itself. Our judgment with regard to these properties will be synthetic, inasmuch they add something conceptually to being. It will also be *a priori,* in that it will not depend directly on experience but on the thought itself in experience that proceeds thoughtfully, without the need of any further "intuition," from the conception of being in its transcendentality to the conception of the one, the active, the true, and the good. What it will depend on is the critical reflection found in any direct exercise of judgment that brings us back to the first evidence of being itself as it presents itself in actuality.

We shall proceed first with the conception of the one, which we most closely associate with the conception of being and of thing. Then, before proceeding with the conception of the true and the good, which require reference to a particular kind of being to be seen as properties of being, we shall focus on another property of being that was not usually mentioned among the transcendentals before modern philosophy, but which nevertheless is closely associated with our conception of being as one even as it opens the way for the inclusion of truth and goodness as properties of being, namely, the property of being as active.

We shall not include the conception of beauty, which is frequently mentioned as a transcendental, because in our view it is not coextensive with being precisely as being. It is coextensive with being only in a particular order, namely, that of being which is at once spiritual and material. To speak of beauty as a property of being, that is, as coextensive with the entire order of being and not just with this particular order, one would have to speak of it in terms of some combination of goodness and truth, leaving out any reference to the particular order of matter that is implied in the conception of beauty.

CHAPTER 5

Being as One

W E BEGIN WITH *one* as the first property of being because it appears
to be the one most intimately connected with being. This has been
clear from the beginning of metaphysics with Parmenides, who spoke of being as one and continuous (Frag 8, 1–6), and as undivided, since it is all the
same. He also spoke of it as even or uniform, inasmuch as being draws near
only to being (Frag 8, 22). Because his conception of being was still univocal, however, his conception of unity remained one of impenetrable density
that found expression only in the shape of perfect roundness and allowed for
neither movement nor multiplicity.

In his perplexity over being the Stranger in Plato's *Sophist* noted the same
connection between being and one and wondered why there are two
names, if being and one are the same (*Soph* 244b). This is the question we
must pursue here, but with the understanding that the notion of one does
not signify anything more in reality than what is already signified by the notion of being.

Even after speaking of the analogy of being, Aristotle still maintained this
parallel between being and one. He spoke of them as the same and as one
nature, or of the one *(to hen)* as nothing other than being *(to on),* showing
how both could be applied to a substance *(ousia)* such as human without
adding anything to what was already understood with the substance itself.
"As the substance of each thing is one not in any accidental sense, so also is
anything that is [*hoper on ti*], so that there are as many forms of being as there
are of the one" (*Metaph* 1003b 23–35). From this Aristotle concluded that
metaphysics had to be as much a discussion of the one as of being, although
he never gave priority to the one over being as Neoplatonism would later
on. By speaking of this connection between being and the one in the framework of analogy, however, he did establish the idea of a certain convertibility

between one and being that was to hold throughout most of the medieval period. *Ens et unum convertuntur.*

In the modern period the one who was to insist on the connection between being and one most emphatically was Spinoza with his conception of infinite substance as indivisible and unique (*Eth* XIIff). But this served only to exclude a plurality of substances in being and to reduce the analogy of being to that of one between substance and its modes. Kant, besides losing sight of the transcendentality of being, also did not admit the notion of infinite substance as having any gnoseological content. For him, the thought of unity was a pure concept of the understanding or a category under the heading of quantity, and so was bereft of any transcendentality (*KrV* B113f). Hegel, who sought to complement Spinoza's concept of infinite substance with that of subjectivity without falling into the empty transcendentalism of Kant, restored the concept of the one to the Logic of Being, but he did so only in connection with being-for-self, in a dialectical rebounding from determinate being's interplay of finite and infinite (*WL* I, sect. l, ch. 3). Coming before any discussion of quantity, Hegel's move allowed for a certain reopening of the transcendentality of the one, but the opening was closed with the conception of measure as the combination of quality and quantity that eventually collapses into the Logic of Essence.

After Hegel the ontological conception of unity seems to drop from sight altogether in metaphysics. It continues to be used in the elaboration of any metaphysical system, whether physicalist, personalist, or theistic, or to be abused in the deconstruction of any such system. But it is not itself the focus of any reflection as a conception that is coextensive with the conception of being. What we propose to do here, in our attempt at metaphysical reconstruction, is to refocus on this notion of the one as it is connected with the notion of being in order to see what intelligibility it can add to our first conception of being.

We have already had to use a certain conception of the one in elaborating the idea of analogy. An analogous notion, we said, is one, not so much by univocity or a unity of concept, as by a unity of reference to one—*pros hen.* This implies a twofold understanding of unity: that of a concept, in which differences are prescinded from, and that of an order, in which differences are taken into account. In the second sense, unity is seen in reference to different things that come under the analogous notion by reason of their relation to one thing, the primary analogate, as in the case of healthy, which is predicated first of an organism and then secondarily of various things that are signs or causes of health in the organism. As an analogous notion being thus refers first to a primary analogate, which we first think of as being, and then to secondary analogates, which we then think of as related to what we first think of as being whether as sign, cause, or simply as a coordinate in being with differences. Our recognition of differences of being leads us to the conception of being as analogous. The same recognition also leads us to bring these differences under some kind of unity, whether it be that of a single being with different aspects or modes, as Spinoza claimed, or that of many beings with their own differences in being ordered to one another, as we are more inclined to do in the direct exercise of judgment. It is to this unity that we must now turn to see how it follows from our very conception of being.

5.1   Undividedness and Identity

This conception of being, as it emerges from the direct exercise of judgment, is structured according to a mode of concretion and composition. It refers to things as we experience them, that is, not as a simple identity, but as a complexity of thisness or haecceity, whatness or quiddity, and be or act of being. Though the name being is taken from the act of being, we think of a being as a thing, which expresses its quiddity or essence. And it is this thing that we think of as one at the same time as we think of it as being. But we think of it as one only with relation to the differences of being and not simply to the thought of being as being. How does this come about in the direct exercise of judgment?

Just as being cannot be properly defined through genus and specific difference, since it is the principle of all definition, so also one, in its original and transcendental sense, cannot be properly defined. It can only be distinguished from being by introducing negation. To speak of being as one is to speak of it as *un*divided, as not divided, which presupposes some conception of division or of difference in being, a division or a difference that is then negated to arrive at the undividedness or the unity of being. This is the way Parmenides arrived at his conception of being as one. But this is also the way we arrive at the same conception through the exercise of judgment, with the difference that we start from experience and allow for real differences in being itself in accordance with the analogy of being.

In the direct exercise of judgment we posit many things as real or as being. We speak of nonliving things as well as living, nonsentient as well as sentient, nonrational as well as rational beings. Of each being or kind of being we also predicate different things as real. Of Socrates we say that he is human, white, sitting, and so on. Of human we say that it is rational, humorous, biped, and so on. In each case we assert a kind of identity, even though in each case it may not be a simple and direct identity. In fact, we seldom if ever assert a simple direct identity of anything with itself because we always suppose such an identity in any exercise of judgment. We think of a thing with its properties as one. Being not only presents itself in the act of reflection, but it presents itself as one with itself—*unum sibiipsi*. It is only through reflection on the exercise of judgment that we come to think of this primordial unity or identity of being with itself.

What this reflection shows is that judgment, in its direct exercise, is ultimately reducible to judgment about a *this* or a *that*. Universal judgments, such as "snow is white" or "human being is mortal," presuppose judgments about *this* or *that*, taken to be snow or human. In their application to being, such universal judgments have to be brought back to some *this* or *that*. Even verification in an abstract science like physics follows this structure of judgment by bringing its conceptions back to a verification that can be observed as *this* or *that* in experience.

This or *that* thus stands as some kind of ultimate subject of predication. When I say that human being is rational animal, I do not mean that human being as such exists, but only that, where there is such a thing as human being in a *this* or a *that*, it is rational. It is Socrates or any *this* or *that* like him who is rational, and not "human being" as such. The concept "human being" only expresses what *this* or *that* is when it is a Socrates or another being like him.

By itself, however, *this* or *that* expresses little about being. It only refers to the irreducible presence of a being in actuality. Without a predicate, which expresses what it is or how it is, it is barely or only negatively intelligible. If I tell you about *this* only that it is this, you still do not know whether the real thing I am talking about is the chair or Socrates. To know the reality of *this* is to know *what* it is as well as its thisness. What makes *this* one therefore is not just its thisness but also its whatness, which may be expressed, as when I speak of *this,* or of Socrates, as a human being. Or it may be left unexpressed, as when I ignore *what* this is as I refer to it simply as *this* rather than *that*. Even when I ignore *what* a particular is in its essence, I still must think of it as having or being an essence yet to be disclosed. This is why questions for understanding arise from the experience of *this* or *that*.

Such questioning, however, presupposes some unity or identity between *what* a thing is and its thisness which is found in what Aristotle referred to as the "substance" of a thing. In its first sense, as Aristotle understood it, substance refers to a *this* or a *that, tode ti,* this something here, whose quiddity is to be determined. In its second sense, substance refers only to the quiddity of this something. As such it is a universal, prescinding from its thisness or haecceity. In the concrete, however, both senses of substance have to be seen as one, which gives us our first conception of a thing as one. Every thing, whatever it is, is one through its substance.

In its first sense, as *this* or *that,* substance can never serve as a predicate. It cannot even be predicated of itself in any intelligible sense. To say, "this is this," adds nothing to our understanding of *this,* except to distinguish this here from that there and to insist on its identity as distinct from *that,* which is equally left without understanding. Pure *this* or pure *that* can only serve as subject of predication, awaiting, so to speak, the intelligibility that a predicate will bring to the purely posited identity. As such it stands for the thing as it is in reality, so to speak, while the predicate expresses how the thing is understood. In its second sense, substance stands for the thing only as we understand it, so that what is expressed in the definition of a thing can be predicated of *this* or *that,* or of substance in the first sense. The act of predication can thus be seen as an expression of unity in being grounded on the way in which being is present.

Needless to say, not all predication concerns only *what* a thing is in its substance, as when I say of Socrates that he is white, or learned, or sitting, or the owner of a field, as well as or besides just being human. This illustrates how complex the unity or the identity of a being can be, something that we shall have to take into account in our elaboration of the structure of being and the order or the communication among beings. But even this kind of oblique or indirect predication, which does not refer directly to the substance of a thing, is derivative from the predication that does refer directly to the substance of things. If we can understand that the unity or the order of being encompasses more than the simple identity of a substance, it is nevertheless from the idea of a substantial identity that our conception of one begins. Without such an idea we could not conceive of many beings or of an order among them.

To think of being as one, therefore, is not just to think of one thing or another, but to think of each thing as undivided in itself or as having a simple identity of its own. Though we may not know what the identity of each thing is, we do know immediately that each thing has an identity that sets it off from any other thing. This is so much a part of the immediate evidence of being in its presencing and standing that it cannot be questioned any more than the presencing of being itself can be questioned. *Non potest quaeri quasi ignoratum, sicut nec alia principia communia* (*In Metaph* VII, 17, §1654). It cannot be questioned as if it were not known any more than other common principles can. We know from the beginning that at least one thing can be predicated of any being, namely, itself, whatever that may be. It is undivided in itself or one with itself. To say this about a being is not yet to say much about *what* or how it is, but it is to affirm its unity and identity such as it is in itself, something that cannot be denied in any knowing of a being.

5.2   Multiplicity and Dividedness

In the direct exercise of judgment, however, we do not merely affirm each being as one in itself according to a principle of identity. We also speak of many beings. Just as the division in being associated with differences leads us to deny division in any being we affirm as a thing, that is, just as we speak of it as undivided in itself, so also this undividedness of each being in itself leads us to think of multiplicity and diversity in being wherever differences seem to enter into what each being is. From division and difference we go, by way of negation of this negation, to the idea of one; and from the idea of one we go to the idea of many, one thing and another each with specific and individual differences.

Difference thus appears as a kind of limit *(Grenze)* between one being or something *(etwas)* and another, as Hegel saw in his Logic of Dasein (*WL* I, 110–16/122–29). One thing is seen as ending at the limit where the other is seen as beginning, and vice versa, so that each thing is seen as limit for the other in being. Both are therefore seen as finite in relation to one another, with each having an identity of its own, and as caught up in an infinite order of being, which is not just another thing that would be opposed to the finite things as another finite but an order that allows for many finite things in being.

With this idea of many, however, another side of the idea of unity comes to the fore. The first side is the one we have just seen: undividedness in itself. The other side is dividedness from every other. Once we come to think of being as many things, we think of each thing or being not only as undivided in itself, but also as divided from every other, or, as Hegel would say, as for itself. Thus, if we say that the first thing to be distinguished from another is a self in the presence of another self, each self is immediately seen as undivided in itself and as divided from the other. Each is understood as standing in the presence of the other in its identity but as divided or separate from the other in some kind of confrontation.

In keeping with our understanding of the human self as the primary analogate of being, this is where our primordial conception of many beings or many ones originates, along with that of identity as undividedness in oneself and dividedness from every other, in a dialectic of recognition. In this recognition of one being and another, which is a first cognition of one-self and another or of another and oneself, a difference is made between equals. In other words, the equals are seen as many and each one is seen as reflected into itself from the other. Each is seen as standing in the face of the other.

Of course, this is not the only kind of standing that comes to be recog-nized in the direct exercise of judgment. We also come to distinguish differ-ent kinds of being that are nonrational, or nonsentient, or even nonliving, but that nevertheless have a standing of their own as things, as we saw in speaking of essence as a standing in being or as thing. In this we come to un-derstand that "many" includes not only many individuals of the same kind, as if our primary analogate of being were the only kind of being, but also many different kinds of being and many individuals of the many different kinds, each with its own degree of undividedness in itself and dividedness from every other as in the analogy of being. In other words, we come to under-stand the oneness that is coextensive with being as itself transcendental.

5.3   Transcendentality of the One

It should be noted that we are not thinking here of the one only as un-derstood in mathematics. The mathematical one is not the transcendental one as it derives from our first conception of being, but only the one as re-duced to the category of quantity. This is the one, as Kant understood it. In its truly transcendental sense, however, the one can also be found in other categories as well, besides quantity. It can be found in the category of sub-stance, as we have seen, where it means the identity of a thing in itself, its un-dividedness. It can also be found in the category of quality, where it means the similarity of a thing with itself, as Aristotle suggests (*Metaph* 1003b 37), or the being-for-self of something, as Hegel suggests (*WL* I, sect. 1, ch. 3). It is only within the category of quantity that the one is understood as the prin-ciple of discrete continuity or of number. Within that category, however, or within any category, the one is not simply convertible with being, since within each category the one specifies something according to that category, thus abstracting from other categories, and it adds a difference to our first conception of being, thus expressing it in only a special mode and not in the common mode characteristic of a transcendental property of being.

As a transcendental, the one follows more the transcendental conception of thing, adding only a negation of division to it. If we think of a thing as simple, then we think of that undividedness as simple as well. But if we think of a thing as complex or as composed of parts in any way, then we think of its undividedness as a whole, as we do, for example, of the self, our primary analogate of thing as well as of being. Wholeness is oneness as it is found in composite things. As the self is a whole in its identity, so also is any other self in an equal way. So too is any other lesser thing that can be identified; it is a whole, but in a lesser way. Whatever we can identify as a thing we identify as a whole before we can start breaking it down into parts. To be for it is to be constituted as a whole composed of parts. What is, at least as a thing, is not only one; it is the whole whose being must be viewed as whole before any of its parts. It can even be said that the be of any composite consists in its wholeness, just as the be of any being consists in its undividedness. *Esse cuiuslibet rei consistit in indivisione* (*ST* I, 11, 1, c).

Thus, as a transcendental, one is not opposed to wholeness, as it is to many or plurality. Nor is wholeness or totality "just plurality considered as unity," as Kant maintained (*KrV* B111). To be sure, wholeness can be understood as totality of things or their unity. This is part of their transcendental unity, insofar as they are not perfectly divided or isolated from one another, or insofar as together they constitute a world. But wholeness is also the wholeness of a thing or its oneness when the thing is composed of parts. A thing is not merely a simple mathematical unit. It is one as a whole with an identity of its own, undivided in itself. To think of more than one such whole, or of many, we have to think of each as a whole, as identical or undivided in itself and divided from every other. It is only after we have so distinguished between a plurality of things that we can think of wholeness as unity of a plurality. But then we are no longer thinking of wholeness as constitutive of a thing in its oneness but rather as constitutive of an order of many things somehow related to one another in a universe, a unity of many and diverse things.

At the same time, however, we also come to think of oneness or wholeness in such an order according to different degrees. At first we think of the oneness of the self as equal to itself and to that of any other self. But as we discern other things in reality that are not the equal of the self, but nevertheless things with an identity or an undividedness of their own, we think of them not only as lesser things, but also as less one, less undivided in themselves and less divided from every other. In fact, at the limit, where it is difficult for us to discern whether we still have to do with a thing as such, that is, a unity-identity-whole, say in the realm of the fundamental entities and processes of mathematical physics, it is also difficult to say whether we are dealing with something undivided in itself and divided from every other. This is the difficulty that physics itself runs into as it tries to determine what are the fundamental constituents of physical reality and finds itself torn between thinking of them as waves or as particles. In the order of being it is no longer clear whether we can still speak of things with a standing of their own or with an identity of any sort that can be numbered or measured.

This lowest degree, of course, is not where we first come to think of being in its oneness. This level of judgment is arrived at only by a process of abstraction from the more concrete sense of being we already have with the self and its oneness. But it illustrates how oneness adheres to being or, as Parmenides put it, how being draws near only to being, even where things can no longer be clearly discerned from one another as one self can be discerned from another. At the limit, oneness seems to resolve itself into a mere continuum without wholeness of any kind, whereas in the interval between the concrete sense of being as one self and an other and this abstraction of an indiscernible flow, many different kinds of wholeness are discerned in an analogy of oneness or wholeness as well as of being.

In this analogy we come to think of some things as more perfectly one than others, just as we speak of them as higher beings than others. The higher a being is, the more perfectly one or undivided it is in itself and the more perfectly divided or independent it is from every other. This is especially clear in our primary analogate of being, the self, which stands on its own better or more evidently than any other being of experience, even though it is not completely independent of every other. But it is clear also from every other kind of being that stands out in its essence as a thing, in proportion to its standing out. The better it stands out as a thing, the more undivided it is in itself and the more divided from every other. And the less it stands out, the less is it a thing undivided in itself and divided from every other, or the more divided it is in itself and the less divided it is from every other. Where we see a division among beings, we also see a unification among these same beings in a universe.

In thinking of the one as opposed to many, however, we must not think of it as simple rather than complex. The oneness of a being is not just a unit in some category or other. It is also a wholeness, which can be quite complex or made up of many units of different kinds. In the abstract, it might be tempting to think of something simple, like a basic entity in mathematical physics, as the primary instance of something one in being. But such an "entity" cannot be identified except in its relation to other entities. In its essence it is not really one in itself but part of a set. In the concrete, the set is more one than any one of its abstract entities. In fact, if we begin from our primary analogate of being in developing our conception of the one, we realize that the one can be quite complex in its wholeness. If every being is one, or undivided in itself and divided from every other, and if human being is our primary analogate of being, then it would appear that our first conception of oneness is associated with a high degree of complexity, so that less complex beings could be understood as less one and, at the limit again, the least complex or the most simple would be understood as the least one and as occupying the lowest level of being.

In between the most complex and the least complex beings we find others in experience with different degrees of complexity that constitute different degrees of identity and oneness for different kinds of being. And though it is difficult to make absolute comparisons in being, we could state as a general principle that the more complex a thing or a being is in its identity, the more one it is likely to be and conversely, that the more one it is, the more complex it is likely to be in its being. At least for being as it presents itself in experience, the degree of oneness in a being is in inverse proportion to the degree of its simplicity.

The things we know as more perfectly one are the more complex ones, like the self, and the things we know as less perfectly one are the more simple ones, or the ones made up of less differentiated parts. It is as though the greater unity of a thing required a greater diversity and complexity of parts. Rational beings are at once more one and more diverse in their complex makeup than nonrational beings. Their complexity may make them more fragile, physically speaking, but in it is disclosed a greater identity in the order of being. Being discloses itself to the rational being. But it also discloses itself more fully in the rational being itself than in any other being of experience that we judge to be less of a being. Similarly, living things are more complex than the nonliving, but they too stand out more clearly in being than the nonliving. And so it is as we go on down the line, until we reach the point where the parts of a thing are so much like one another that it can easily be divided into two things each of which retains the identity of the original thing, like the pieces from a block of granite or the buckets drawn from a body of water. In a higher living thing such a division is impossible, not only because of the greater diversity of parts that constitute the whole, so that one cannot function without the others, but also because of the higher identity of the thing. To sever it is to lose its identity altogether and to be left with parts that take on another identity as beings in themselves, as the whole disintegrates into a plurality of more simple beings.

Whether this proportionality between higher identity and higher diversity and complexity holds for the entire order of being or only for the order of being we experience in the direct exercise of judgment remains to be seen. It may be that this proportionality holds only for material beings, whose wholeness is constituted of parts. In any event, whether or not there are nonmaterial beings whose identity would be simple and not constituted of parts, this proportionality between higher complexity and higher identity serves to bring out further the transcendentality of the one taken as a property of being in the material order of things in comparison to the mathematical one, which, as the principle of number, cannot be taken as anything but simple. Before it is reduced to the category of quantity by the understanding, the transcendental conception of the one already expresses an identity of being, an undividedness of any being in itself proportionate to *what* it is and a similarly proportionate dividedness from every other.

Finally, in connection with this transcendentality of the one, we might note how the division of being is of two different kinds. First, there is the division according to species, such as that between living and nonliving beings or between rational and nonrational beings, which we characterize as higher and lower according to some order of perfection. Each species represents a certain degree of identity or wholeness in the order of being. But within each species, at least in the material order of being, there is also a further division of many individuals within the same degree of identity and wholeness. There are many individuals of one and the same species each of which is also identified as a being, undivided in itself and divided from every other. We can speak of the first kind of division as *formal division,* that is, as one yielding a *diversity* of forms, such as living and nonliving or rational and nonrational. We can speak of the second kind as *material division,* that is, as division yielding a *multiplicity* of individuals with the same specific form, such as Socrates, Plato, or Aristotle within the human species or the hundred and one Dalmatians within a species of dogs.

At the same time, however, this twofold division of being gives rise to the idea of a twofold order of being as well, a *formal order* of diverse species and a *material order* of individuals within diverse species. The two orders combine to constitute the material universe as a whole with a diversity of species of being and a plurality of individuals within the various species. How this order of the universe is constituted concretely in reality cannot be understood merely in terms of the transcendental one. It requires the conception of action and interaction as a kind of bond for this plurality of beings we call the universe. But the two sides of the transcendental one, undividedness in itself and dividedness from every other, open the way for the conception of such an active constitution of the universe as one in diversity and multiplicity.

5.4   The Judgment of Unity

It remains for us to see how this conception of being as one is indeed found in our direct exercise of judgment in the act where being first discloses itself. We have already alluded to judgment as the positing of an identity and to the act of predication as an expression of unity grounded on the way in which being presents itself in things. This is what opened the way for us into the thought that being is one. Our question now, which is a question for critical reflection, is to see whether this thought is truly the thought of being.

If we reflect on the exercise of judgment as affirming unity in being, we can think of the affirmation as having two sides: one, that every being is undivided in itself, and the other, that every being is divided from every other. In thinking through each side one after the other, we shall find that each side contains its counterpart as it refers to being itself.

On the side of undividedness or identity, we recognize that not all judgments posit the relatively simple identity of a thing and its quidditative determinations or even its properties, which are distinct from the quiddity of a thing but cannot be separated from it, nor it from them. We posit many sorts of identity or relations between things, such as that one thing belongs to something else, as the field belongs to Socrates, or is influenced by something else, as the field is warmed by the sun. But underlying all such positing there is a more fundamental positing of things themselves in some kind of identity. At the root of all judgment there is a principle of identity that says of every thing that it is one with itself or, conversely, that it cannot not be itself. The principle of identity is at the same time a principle of noncontradiction. If being is what discloses itself in judgment and if it properly discloses itself as an identity that has to be distinguished from other identities, then we have to say that every being, every such identity, is undivided in itself.

This is immediately evident in our first conception of being itself. Parmenides saw this, except that he did not distinguish between different identities in being. It is also immediately evident in any exercise of judgment where we distinguish different things as beings in experience and understand each thing as not the other. To bring out this evidence more positively, let us turn to our more immediate experience as human beings in confrontation with one another. In this experience, which is focused on our primary analogate of being, being discloses itself as determinate or as divided between two selves, you and me, for example, where I distinguish myself from you as undivided in myself just as you distinguish yourself from me as undivided in yourself and where we both come to the common understanding that each is an identity in itself.

This is an experience that is repeated many times with other persons and that is then extended to include other determinate beings that are not persons but that are also seen as undivided in themselves in being, albeit in less striking ways than as persons in themselves. Whatever we identify as a being we think of as undivided in itself. As we move further away from human being toward things characterized as nonrational and as nonliving, the principle of identification for each determinate being becomes more obscure, but we continue to identify things as undivided in themselves as long as some principle of identity can be found. At the limit, as we saw with regard to the fundamental entities and processes of mathematical physics, the light of any such principle all but disappears.

But this is not a loss of the immediate evidence that every being is undivided in itself. It is simply a failure to see how the principle of identity and noncontradiction applies in the case of such entities. Instead of a clear judgment about a determinate being, undivided in itself, we come rather to a suspension of judgment as to whether we are still dealing with a difference of one thing and another. This is not to say that judgments in physics have nothing to do with reality, but rather that they have to do with a reality of very diminished identity. It is not in such judgments that being discloses itself most clearly in its undividedness, but rather in judgments about one self and another confronting one another in mutual recognition.

This same immediate evidence that is available through reflection on the direct exercise of judgment can also be brought out through retort, if one tries to deny the truth of this evidence. If, for example, you try to think of being as not undivided in itself, you will have to think of it as divided. The thought of differences in being has already brought you there. But the thought of being as divided means a being and another being, or beings in the plural. Thus, in thinking of being as divided rather than undivided, you would no longer be thinking of a being in its identity, but of many beings, which brings us to the second side of the judgment of unity.

On this second side, which says that every being is divided from every other, we recognize that being discloses itself in a multiplicity and a diversity of beings. But with this recognition we also understand immediately that every being is divided from every other as the reverse side of its being undivided in itself. To think of many beings presupposes the thought of division in being, the thought of a being, and another, and so on. Such a thought implies a limitation or a negation in being. A being other than this being means precisely a being distinct from this one, divided from it, or simply not this one. A is other than or is not B, if B is not A. Thus, as we distinguish between beings in the exercise of judgment, we necessarily think of each one as divided from every other in the same way that it is undivided in itself.

Again this is most clearly evident in the dialectic of recognition between selves and less clear in the relations between the fundamental entities of mathematical physics. In confrontation with you, where our first conception of determinate being is most in evidence, I recognize myself not only as undivided in myself but also as divided from you just as you recognize yourself not only undivided in yourself but also as divided from me. The principle of identity in each determinate being is at the same time the principle of division from other determinate beings. This is especially clear in the case of division among persons. It is also clear in the case of division among different kinds of sentient and living things. But as we approach the limit of basic physical entities, once again we find the principle of division among beings more obscure and are forced to suspend judgment as to whether such entities are properly beings divided from every other.

Evidence for this principle that every being is divided from every other being can also be brought out by retort. If you try to think of every being as not divided from every other, you necessarily think of it as undivided from every other and therefore as identical with every other, which is to say that the other is not an other but rather that there is only one being, as Parmenides said. Such a thought is contrary to what is presupposed on this side of the judgment of unity, namely, that being discloses itself in some dividedness or as a multiplicity and a diversity of beings.

Thus any attempt to deny either side of the judgment of unity about things leads back into the other side and into a denial of being itself as known with its differences. It is impossible to think such an attempt through as a thought of being in its disclosing. It is, like any attempt to deny first principles of judgment, self-defeating as an act of intelligence. The only way to think the judgment of unity through as the thought of the being that discloses itself in truth is to think of every being as undivided in itself and divided from every other.

The two questions that remain with regard to the unity of being are that of the mode of its undividedness in itself, which can be complex as well as simple, and that of the mode of its dividedness, which entails a relative independence of things in a world of interdependence. We shall deal with each of these questions further as we come to speak of the structure of being and the communication of being, respectively. But before we can do that we must reflect on the other properties of being to bring out the bond that ties beings together in their very multiplicity and diversity.

CHAPTER 6

Being as Active

W̲E CONTINUE IN OUR ELABORATION of the properties of being with active as the second, before going on to the other two usually listed after the one, namely, the true and the good. When we think of a being as one, or as undivided in itself and divided from every other, we do not think of it as closed in on itself or as purely static. We think of it as active in its identity or in its very standing as a thing. In fact, as we shall see, we discover a being as a thing with its own essential standing only through its activity, so that a being is inconceivable as a thing without some proper activity.

In saying this, however, we must be careful to understand precisely how we come to think of "active" as a transcendental property of being. We speak of something as active with reference to action or to what it does as a thing. In the concrete this action, or what a thing does, is always particular: in a particular place, at a particular time, and of a particular kind. Not only is it the action of this or that being of a particular kind, which makes it an action of a particular kind, it is also particular even with reference to the being of which it is the action. For example, when I do something, such as some physical exercise or an exercise of judgment, I not only do it at a particular time in a particular place, or as a particularly human kind of action, I also do it as only one of the particular actions I could be performing. I could also be performing some other physical exercise or exercising decision making rather than some theoretical judgment. Even things that have less freedom or no freedom at all in their self-determination have a diversity of actions that we can observe, ranging from sensation and life functions to attraction and repulsion among inanimate things. Only the simplest of entities, like atomic particles, may have only one action proper to them, but even there, insofar as it can be located in space and time, it is still thought to be the particular action of a particular thing. All things have at least one action of their own and most, especially the more complex ones, like animals and humans, have many more.

Understood as particular in this way, the term "action" does not express a common mode of being. It is not convertible with being in its transcendental conception. It expresses only a special mode of being or a difference in being, not something that can be predicated universally of being as being. Even if we think of action as a general category containing all particular actions, it is still only a category, one of the ten supreme genera of being according to Aristotle (*Cat* chs. 4 and 9), which has to be distinguished from other categories of being such as quality, quantity, and substance, the primary category of being that expresses *what* a being is in its essence. In fact, if we think of the diversity of action in its particularities with reference to one and the same thing, we have to think of it as accidental to substance or as inhering in it or as flowing from it, rather than as part of the substance itself in its fundamental identity that persists as one at different times in different places and while exercising different activities.

How then is "active" to be thought of as a transcendental property of being if it entails a reference to something as particular as action? It can be done in the same way as we come to think metaphysically of being as common in a wide diversity of things, or as transcendental, in the exercise of judgment. In the direct exercise of judgment we refer to being as something particular, as a *this* or a *that* with some determination, as we do, for example, when we speak of this as a human being or that as a tree. In the indirect exercise of judgment we come to conceive "being" as a structured notion that entails the composition of an act with particular determinations in a singular *this* or *that,* or with what we can speak of as a concrete essence or a first substance, in the sense of Aristotle's *tode ti,* as we did earlier, for example, in our logic of being.

Action can also be conceived as a structured notion entailing a similar composition between an act and its specification, such as an act of judgment specified by its terms or an act of decision specified by the choice of a particular course over another. Even the acts of simple things such as purely physical entities are similarly specified according to the nature of the agent or the substance that produces them.

This similarity of composition in the concept, however, is not enough to satisfy the idea of complete transcendentality for action. Even as a structured notion, action remains one of the categories of being in contrast to passion and as such cannot be understood as including other categories, as the concept of being does, especially not that of substance, in relation to which action appears as something accidental. To think of "active" as something completely transcendental or as following the order of being in its transcendentality, we must think of action as following the diversity of determinate substances in being in its very relation to these substances, however "accidental" the action may be to the substance from which it flows. In other words, we must think of things themselves as acting, or as active, each according to its own way of being. Or, conversely, we must think of each way or mode of being not only as determined in an essence but *also* as giving rise to its own proportionate way of acting. We have to say "also" here with respect to action because an action is understood as flowing from a thing or an essence already constituted with its own act of being. The act of being does not flow from the essence that limits it in a finite being. It is simply in composition with this essence, as in the case of human being, where the concrete human essence limits its act of being. Action flows from this composite of an essence and its act of being.

With this understanding of the relation between a thing and the proportionate action that flows from it, no matter how particular the action of the thing, or between an action and the thing from which it flows, we can speak of being as active in a way that is completely transcendental in the same way that we speak of one and of being itself as transcendental. Unlike the case of being as one, however, where we are adding only a negation to our first conception of being, that is, a negation of division in what is undivided in itself, in the case of action we are adding something positive to this first conception of being as one or as a thing, namely, the idea of an inclination to act on its own, though not yet the idea of any particular or special mode of action. We are adding what can be called a "property" of being as being, because we are saying that every being, whatever it is, has such an inclination to act, or is active, in its own determinate way. We are saying that it is a property of being to be active.

It can be said that this insistence on activity as a property of being over and above the three usually mentioned, namely, unity, truth, and goodness, is due to an influence of modern philosophy and what has been called the "transcendental turn to subjectivity" in this philosophy, that is, the turn to the activity of the subject as a focus for philosophical reflection. This is a turn we have already taken here in this metaphysical discourse when we articulated what we mean by "being" or how we first conceive being by reflection on the structure of the judgment we exercise in experience. It is a turn we shall continue to take in arguing from the structure of our activity to a real structure or composition in the constitution of our finite being. It is in keeping with our insistence on human being as the primary analogate of being in this reconstruction of metaphysics, as well as with some of the more ancient adages about action or the inclination to act as following from being, like *agere sequitur esse* or *unumquodque agit in quantum est actu,* meaning that "to act follows from to be" or "each being acts inasmuch as it is in act," or again like *quamlilbet formam sequitur inclinatio,* meaning that from every form of being there follows an inclination to act. Such adages were spoken of transcendentally in the same way that we speak of transcendental properties of being here.

In affirming that every being is active, we are affirming what could be called a principle for all science, for it is through what a thing does that we come to know *what* it is in its essence. This is so for modern science as well as for ancient science. In speaking of being as active we are reaffirming an ancient principle for all science with regard to being in all its differences in a way that is congenial to modern critical philosophy's insistence on subjectivity, beginning with the proper activity of human being as our primary analogate. But we are doing so without departing from the ancient view by including, as part of the analogy of being and acting, the action of lesser beings as proper to these beings, including that of mere bodies or physical entities along with that of sentient and living things as well as that of rational beings.

In order to do this we shall begin by elaborating the concept of action as it comes to us from experience and how action relates to what we shall call the "underlying thing" or the thing as producing its action. Then we shall consider the two sides of action, the first as transient or as going out to other things and as affecting them, and the second as immanent or as remaining in the underlying thing that is acting and as perfecting it. From this consideration of action as two-sided we shall then go on to see how a being or a particular concrete essence comes to be thought of as a nature precisely insofar as it is the principle of its own action. Finally, before coming to the ontological understanding of action, we shall see how phenomenology views the entire life-world of the human subject as a world constituted by the action and interaction of a wide diversity of beings.

6.1   Action and the Underlying Thing

Let us begin by noting that action, like being and one, cannot be properly defined through genus and specific difference. If we take the term as a genus, "action" is among the supreme genera along with substance, quality, and quantity. It cannot be defined in terms of any higher genus. It can only be distinguished from other genera as sui generis. If we take the term as expressing a still broader notion than any genus, as we do here, it transcends any generic difference of being and follows being itself in its transcendentality.

In fact, what we know first about any being is its action. It is through its action that we come to know *what* a thing is. It is through different kinds of action that we come to identify different kinds of being. And it is through their action that we come to think of them as actual, or as being in act. Even the name we use to characterize the be of a being as distinct from its essence or mode of being betrays this relation to action. We call it the "act of being," implying that to be is always to be in action, just as to be human implies to be acting as a rational animal. This is not to say that the act of being, as understood in the structure of our conception of being, is just an action that flows from the essence of a finite being. On the contrary, the act of being has to be understood as constitutive of the very being from which action flows as an accident, so to speak, or as constitutive of what the being is in its essence or substance. It is only to say that a being discloses itself through action and is known only through its action. This is true not only of other beings we know in experience, but even of our own being, which we come to know only in and through our action or what we do precisely as rational beings. Reflection on what we are begins from our direct action. As Aquinas says, even our intelligence knows itself not through its essence, but through its act of intelligence (*ST* I, 8, 1, c).

To think of action in its primordial sense we must go back to experience itself. Experience is action. We experience ourselves through our action, including our spiritual action of thinking and willing as well as our physical action, and we experience other selves and other things through their action, which is not always spiritual and in the case of many things is only physical. When we say that we begin from experience in our knowledge of things, we mean that we begin from their action. The world of experience is a world of interaction among selves and things in which each comes to its own standing as what it is and takes its stand according to what it determines itself to be.

If all this conception of action seems somewhat anthropomorphic, it is only because experience itself is anthropomorphic. The common or analogous notion of action itself, which is understood as spiritual in human being, can be extended to include different sorts of action that are not anthropomorphic, that is, action that is nonrational, or nonsentient, or even nonliving. Although these are lesser kinds of action, they are nevertheless specifically different kinds of action through which different kinds of being disclose themselves or are identified in their being.

Like the other analogous notions, action is known first as it is found in the primary analogate of being, the human self. It is that of which we are first conscious in ourself or in other selves. Of course, concretely this includes all sorts of activities like feeling, seeing, hearing, imagining, judging, striving, desiring, and willing, all of which entail a certain immediacy in consciousness, a certain givenness in experience. But in keeping with our method here we should focus on the more reflective aspects of this activity, since it is in this aspect of our activity that we come to know not only *what* we are or how we stand in being, but also how being first discloses itself to us. It is in the activity of judging, as we have said from the beginning, that we come to know being as being in its presencing.

We could also add at this point that the same holds true for our activity of willing, since that too engages our self-consciousness at its highest level, in which we not only discover what we are but also determine ourselves to be what we are. It is in both activities of knowing and willing that the presencing of being has its first disclosure, both as my own being and as the being of others.

When I raise questions and seek answers, when I find answers and formulate them in concepts, when I organize these concepts in judgments, I am acting. When I entertain the possibility of different courses of action, when I deliberate about them, when I determine what I will to become, I am acting. Action begins further back in my being, so to speak, than in my intelligence and will, and it has ramifications not only in the obscure aspects of my being, but also in the world at large. But at the center of understanding and willing, action comes to a transparency in which the intelligent being knows itself as being and other beings equally as being, though not necessarily its equal in being. This is the reflective experience of being, so to speak, from which our first conception of being emerges. Without the experience or the action, the conception would not be possible, though being itself is what is first conceived.

But this kind of thoughtful action represents only a certain degree of action, and a relatively high one at that. Not all action is equally self-conscious or even conscious at all. We experience lesser kinds of action both in ourselves and in other beings. In fact, we experience action that is not conscious. Consciousness is not coterminous with action. There is action in myself that is not conscious and I do not have to suppose that every being is conscious, unless there is evidence to the contrary in its action. Conscious action is the form of action we know best and most immediately, but it is not the only form. There are lesser forms or degrees of action in what psychoanalysis speaks of as the subconscious and the unconscious or in the purely physical functions of the human body.

At the limit, there are forms of action that seem to have nothing to do whatsoever with consciousness, as in the case of nonliving things. However we may understand these forms of action, we do not have to understand them as conscious or self-conscious, though we do come to think of them in some analogy with conscious action, our primary analogate. It is not anthropomorphism to do so, for though we begin from a conception of action centered on human being, we extend it as disclosing different kinds of originality in being, including that of nonhuman being. We do this by differentiating other kinds of action objectively, so to speak, from our own and by insisting on the originality as something positive without being conscious. Different sciences can study these actions more positively in their specificity. But it is important for metaphysics to see them in their analogy with one another and with the primary analogate.

In the direct exercise of judgment we define or identify different kinds of being according to different kinds of action. We identify human being as rational animal or *homo sapiens,* indicating in this way what human being is by what human being does or by the action that seems proper to this being. We identify brute animals in the same way, but in contrast to human being we speak of them as sentient but nonrational. So too of nonsentient living things, and finally of nonliving things. At each step we recognize an absence of a certain degree of action, but we continue on down the line as long as we can identify a positive degree of action.

As we move further away from conscious activity, we find it more difficult to identify a positive content in action, obscure and minimal as it becomes, and so we find it more difficult to define the being or to give it a positive name. We think of force or of attraction and repulsion, but we do not think of these as identifying things as well as life and consciousness do. It is to the credit of modern science that it has devised better ways of speaking of this nonliving action or interaction without resorting to animism of any kind. Thanks to its highly sophisticated use of measurement and mathematics it has penetrated more deeply into the essence of nonliving being. Yet even this knowledge of modern mathematical science is still expressed in terms of what has to be called action or a functionalism that sets down laws of action and reaction between the different entities it distinguishes.

There is a problem, of course, in seeing precisely in what sense we can speak of functions expressed in mathematical formulas as referring to action in the concrete, but that is part of the problem of verification in natural science itself. It is not precisely our problem here in metaphysics. What we can say is that the difficulty of the problem lies in the very obscurity of the abstract formulations of science as they apply to reality. When we have only mathematical formulas to help us discern various elements of reality, it is because we are dealing with only a diminished kind of action, and hence with a diminished form of reality, and not with the full form we find in our primary analogate. In going from the one to the other we should keep clearly in mind what comes first both in the order of learning and in the degree of being

It is not the basic entities and processes of mathematical physics that come first in knowing, as physicalism claims, but human action and human being, as we have argued. There is a certain fallacy in trying to argue from what is more obscure to what is more clear in being, or from what is less known to what is more known. We could call it a fallacy of misplaced clarity as well as misplaced concretion. In our systematic articulation of being as we know it concretely, we must begin from what is better known to us in our own action, even if it cannot be reduced to exact measurement or mathematical formulation.

Along with the idea of action, however, we have also the idea of the agent or the *underlying thing* that is acting. To the extent that we think of a particular action as only accidental to a certain being or as flowing from it, we think of the thing as something posited under the action or of the action as belonging to this *suppositum*. In the words of the old adage, *actiones sunt suppositorum*: actions are actions of supposits. We shall speak of this *suppositum* as the underlying thing not to think of it as separate from its action, but rather to keep in mind that the thing is understood not by itself or apart from its action, but only as underlying its action.

To distinguish the underlying thing from its action in this way somewhat complicates the conception of action, but only by keeping the idea of thing, which follows the idea of being, present in it. Precisely how the underlying thing is to be distinguished from its action is something we shall have to work out. As in everything else for a metaphysics that takes human being as its primary analogate, this can be done more clearly through a reflection on human activity as it flows from and discloses the essence of its underlying thing, namely, human being or the concrete human essence of a Socrates.

In the diversity and the multiplicity of my actions, I come to think of myself as somehow distinct from them. Through them, through my judging and my willing, for example, I come to know *what* I am or the kind of thing I am. As the agent or the subject in all this activity, I discover or disclose my identity as a thing. I see myself as judging and as willing and in all of this it is I who judge and will. I am the thing that underlies all these actions and in all of them I am actualizing myself. I do not know myself apart from the actions, and yet in all of them it is only as one thing that I come to know myself as agent for all of them. I distinguish myself from all of them as an underlying thing because I see them as diverse and multiple and myself as one. I judge and I will. I also make many judgments and many decisions. And yet in all of these actions it is always I, this human being, who judges and wills.

This kind of distinguishing cannot be done as easily on the level of merely physical entities as it can be done on the level of the self or *Dasein*. But that is because of the greater obscurity of action at that lower level. Though we speak of basic entities for mathematical physics, it is much more difficult to identify them as things or to say what kind of thing they are, if in fact they are things in the proper sense of the term. If the action is difficult to define, the underlying thing is even more difficult to define, because it can only be defined through its action. At the limit, we may not know whether we are still talking about things at all or only about functions of things.

But this difficulty at the level of merely physical entities, which may or may not be actual things or bodies in the full sense of the term, serves to illustrate how closely tied our knowledge of things is to our knowledge of their action. We cannot identify things or say *what* they are apart from their action. But the converse of that is also true. We do come to identify things and say *what* they are through their action. Strictly speaking, there is no such thing as an unknown or an unknowable "thing in itself," as Kant was bent on supposing. Even if we do distinguish between the underlying thing and its action, we do not do so as if the underlying thing could remain hidden or undisclosed in itself. We distinguish the thing only because it discloses itself in its action. We affirm the thing as being only because it is known in action and we affirm it as known through its action.

This does not require any special intellectual intuition as of a "thing in itself," as Kant supposed for the possibility of metaphysics. All that it requires is a sense of the thing as it appears in experience through action and some reflection on the meaning we find in this disclosure. Through its action we know *what* a thing is, which is all there is to know about it, in itself as the *suppositum* of its action as well as in its relation to other things. To say that we know of a thing but that we do not know it in itself does not make sense. In saying what we know of it we are already saying that we know it in itself, even though we may not know precisely *what* it is in every respect. But we come to know what it is more precisely not by some pure intuition, but by further reflection upon its action or by closer examination of what it does. This holds true for our selves as reflective intelligent underlying things as well as for other things. And it holds true for metaphysical knowing as well as for the more "physical" knowing in the direct exercise of judgment.

In the indirect exercise of judgment that is proper to metaphysics there is no need for some sort of intellectual intuition into a thing in itself other than the intuition already found in the direct exercise of judgment. From the beginning we have seen that metaphysics follows from experience. It begins in the reflection found in any exercise of judgment, the critical reflection that is like a clearing in which being discloses itself. The question of being moves within the circle of this disclosing. When we distinguish between an action and its underlying thing, we are not distinguishing between two separate realms of being, one phenomenal and one noumenal, and declaring only one of them knowable, that is, the phenomenal. Nor are we positing some kind of noumenal object hidden behind the phenomenal. We are distinguishing an underlying thing only to say that it is what discloses itself in its proper action. That is what it is metaphysically as well as physically and that is all there is to it metaphysically speaking. The metaphysical knowledge of things or of human subjects does not double as another kind of physics or another kind of empirical psychology, with another kind of insight into things or into the subject than the one already operative in the direct exercise of judgment. Metaphysical knowledge is the knowledge of the thing already reflected upon, but as seen in the order of being as being in its transcendentality. It is a knowledge of being as including both sides of the distinction between action and the underlying thing.

6.2   Essence as Nature

In the thought of being as active we are led to the idea of nature and to the thought of being as nature. Let us reflect on how this happens starting from our first conception of being as it is signified in the direct exercise of judgment. In our initial reflection on the logic of this conception, we were led to distinguish a twofold structure in this conception, one, a synthesis of thisness and whatness, and the other, a synthesis of this concrete synthesis with be or the act of being. We spoke of essence in two ways, as referring to *what* a thing is in the abstract sense of a definition that does not include the thisness of a thing, or as referring to the combination of whatness and thisness of a thing in its concretion. We did all this without reference to the action of a thing, relying only on how we raise questions about *what* is given in experience, namely, questions for understanding and questions for critical reflection.

In speaking of the underlying thing with reference to action, we are once again referring to *what* a thing is or to its essence. But now we are speaking of it as it relates to the action that flows from it. In doing so we are introducing a new dimension into the order of essence, one that is usually ignored by static essentialism, but one that is strongly affirmed by existentialism. Essence, or *what* a thing is in the concrete, includes not only thisness, but also a natural inclination to act. Essence is not just a given in experience. It is something that makes itself be *what* it is. Essence is something to be achieved, something I have to make myself, for example. It is this act of achieving that is referred to as "existence." In affirming the priority of existence over essence, existentialism is affirming a certain priority of action over the merely given, at least in human being, if not in lower beings as well, but it is doing so within an order of essence as distinct from be or the act of being.

In other words, existentialism is affirming the order of essence in a new way, as something to be achieved, in opposition to a static essentialism that considers things only as given out of the past, whether by nature or by history in a human community. Existentialism is affirming essence as dynamic and, in doing so, it is, perhaps unwittingly, retrieving an ancient way of conceiving essence as nature. If it seems opposed to the priority of nature as well as of essence over existence or action, it is only because it continues to share the modern conception of nature as totally determined or as static in its givenness.

What was meant by "nature" among the ancients and what continues to be meant in the direct exercise of judgment is essence, or *what* a thing is, but viewed as a principle of action or as the principle of what we have to call its proper activity. This follows from the idea that every being is active according to its very nature. According to Aristotle, who was summing up the ancient view, "nature is the principle of a thing and the cause of moving and resting in that of which it is principle primarily according to itself and not according to some incidental factor" (*Phys*192b 21–23). In formulating this definition, Aristotle had only a particular set of things and their natural movements in mind, namely, the order of things that come to be by nature. This set of things was understood in contrast to things that come to be by art, which for Aristotle do not have a movement of their own as artifacts in the way that the things of nature do. Aristotle's definition, however, can be seen as applying to any thing having a movement of its own by nature, including the human being, even though it transcends its nature as merely given starting from this nature as the principle or the beginning of its own activity.

Insofar as every being is thought of as active, it is thought of not only as an essence, but also as a nature according to which it acts. When we ask: "what is the nature of something?" we are not asking for anything more than what is already intended by the simple question: "what is it?," referring to the essence of something. In saying, "what is the nature of?," we are only expressing how we expect to find the answer to the simple question: *"what?"* We are saying that we expect to find the answer through what appears to be its proper activity. *What* a thing is is known through what it does. The nature of a thing is thus only its essence viewed as the fundamental principle of its doing. As Aquinas put it in one of his first attempts to explain how we speak of essence, "the name *nature* taken in this sense [that is, as referring to essence or *what* something is] seems to signify the essence of a thing in accordance with its order or ordination to its proper operation, since no thing is without its proper operation" (*Ente* 1).

Needless to say, the metaphysical idea of nature will have to be understood analogously no less than the idea of action that it underlies as principle. To the extent that we speak of action as free and self-determining in the human being, for example, we shall speak of an open nature constituted concretely through the initiative of its own action. The human being does constitute itself in what it is historically through its own action. But this is also true, analogously, of other beings that do not exercise any historical initiative but are nevertheless active in their own natural way. All beings constitute themselves concretely in *what* they are through their action, whether that action be free and self-determining or not. Action is the ultimate determination of a being in the order of essence. It is that for which each thing exists, its ultimate perfection as an already existing thing.

To think of every being as active, therefore, is to think of it as having a nature of its own from which its proper activity flows. This nature is the essence of the being considered as the principle of its activity. To be such a principle, the essence or the nature must already be constituted in its fundamental or what we can call its *first perfection* as an essence or as a mode of being. It must already have a natural form as its first perfection in being, from which action will flow as its *second perfection*. We shall have more to say about this distinction between first perfection and second perfection in being when we come to speak of being as good. For the moment, however, it is important to ask why any being must seek or achieve its own perfection through action. The reason must be found in the way being is signified according to a mode of concretion and composition.

According to this way of conceiving determinate being, essence or the mode of being is understood as limiting *be* or the *act* of being. We have already made the point that what we refer to as the *act* of being is not to be confused with the action of a being. The action of a being flows from *what* it is according to its essence or from its nature. It may entail a certain openness or infinity of scope in relation to what is merely given in nature, but action, as we are thinking of it here, is not the *act* of being in composition with the essence or the natural form of the being already constituted in being. This *act* of being is understood as de facto limited by its essence in a concrete being, though as distinct from this composition with its essence it can be considered as somehow infinite in itself, or at least as entering into composition with a diversity and a plurality of other finite essences, so that its scope as an *act* is not limited to the essence of any determinate being but rather encompasses the order of all such finite beings. Through its *act* of being every finite being is in transcendental relation with other beings. However, it is in keeping with this transcendental relation that every finite being is active or has an inclination to act. Through its action it reaches out beyond its given finitude to other beings in order to find its own second perfection in communication with them. The *act* of being is like a call in every finite being to participate actively in the universe of beings through mutual interaction. To say that every being has its own activity is to say something that follows from its very ontological constitution. Action is that through which finite beings accomplish themselves according to their own nature and as a community of beings or as a universe.

At the same time, however, the action that flows from any determinate being does not cease to be the proper activity of this determinate being. As the second perfection of a finite being already constituted in its first perfection, it remains in keeping with this first perfection or with its natural form. A being acts according to *what* it is or its mode of being. What a thing does is not independent of *what* it is. This is why we can know *what* it is from what it does. Ontologically speaking, the second act is in some sense determined by the first act, even though it comes as its second perfection.

The inclination to act follows the form of the first act, whether that inclination be natural or intentional. In the case of an intentional inclination, the action follows upon an intentional form or one conceived through thought.

In the case of a natural inclination, it follows upon the natural form of the thing or the form of the thing existing independently of any thought of our own. This is how we come to know the nature of a thing through how it acts on its own, just as we come to know our intellectual nature through how we act on our own.

The lower we go in the scale of material beings, the more we think of form as absorbed in matter, the less form overcomes matter and the less it is a principle of action by itself, the more its action is only a reaction proceeding from an external form as well as from its inner form. Conversely, the higher we rise in the scale of material being or the more form overcomes the density of matter through knowing, for example, the less it is merely reaction and the more it is properly original action as we understand it in properly human activity. It is a certain regularity of action and reaction at different levels that leads us to think of the underlying things as having a certain determinacy in their nature that is open to perfection through action.

6.3   Phenomenology of Action

In our elaboration of the notion of action and its underlying thing and of being as nature thus far we have proceeded in a way that could be characterized as phenomenological. We have been saying what we mean by action and how that relates to being. The point we have been driving at, however, is the ontological turn in which action is seen not only as that in which being discloses itself, whether in ourselves or in other beings, but also as what follows from being itself in its disclosing. To make the point of this ontological turn more clear, let us review some of the significant aspects of action as we experience it and show phenomenologically how the ontological turn presents itself in this experience.

We begin from the fact of the universe as we experience it or from what has been called the *Lebenswelt*. This fact entails a certain polarity between consciousness and world or what we might refer to as an existential aspect and a cosmic aspect. Phenomenologically, we can begin from the existential center in a kind of fundamental ontology, as Heidegger calls it, where the action of *Dasein* is paramount. This action can be seen as only transitive or external to the self, as having to do only with things as given at hand in instrumental fashion, and as constituting only a world of instruments to be used in the pursuit of particular projects. Or action can be viewed as more immanent and internal to the self, as more thoughtful and willful, and as perfecting the self in its relation to the world. It is through this two-sided action, or experience as a whole, that being discloses itself to or in knowing.

Knowing, we say, is of being. But knowing begins as or in experience. Knowing is itself an action, but one that is intelligent. It is conscious not only of an object, but also of itself as real. It is self-consciousness as well as consciousness of an object. And it is through this reflection of self-consciousness that it becomes conscious not only of being, but also of being as being, at the same time as it thinks of being as something to be actualized. As an action, knowing is complemented by willing, both as the will to know and as the will to the fulfillment of being, which may coincide as one in the self-conscious being but which may also be kept apart in the transitivity of instrumental action.

All this about the existential center of experience is being said too quickly and would require much longer reflection to sort out. A proper existential analysis of *Dasein* would require much more thought than we can give it here. But that should not deter us from the task before us, which is to understand how this action relates to being as being.

As we have already said several times, we know the action first as real or as being. What is first for us in learning is action, whether it be our own or that of another, in the interaction, say, of mutual recognition between selves. But as we distinguish some underlying thing from action itself, whether it be our self or an other, we also come to understand that we know what that thing is through its action. We have no immediate intuition of what we or what other beings are. We have only a reflective understanding of being. We start from a second act, so to speak, and we are drawn into the first act of a thing, what we speak of as its natural form. Through our own action of understanding, we come to know, at the same time as we actualize it, the nature of understanding and hence the nature of our being as rational. Through our action of willing as well, we come to know, at the same time as we actualize it, the nature of willing and hence again the nature of our being as willful. Similarly, through the understanding and willing of others we come to know *what* they are as underlying things as well as what they make themselves to be.

Understanding and willing, however, are only the highest forms of activity we know directly in experience. They are not the only forms. There are also lesser forms, which we shall conceive in some analogy with understanding and willing, as the Greeks did, for example, in speaking of causality. The Greek term for cause, *aitia,* was originally taken from a legal context, where it meant a charge, an accusation, or an imputation. In that original context "cause" implied some kind of responsibility, which presupposes understanding and willing along with intelligence and deliberation. In lesser kinds of action where there was still some evidence of a thing initiating something of its own in being, which is the basis for imputing an action to a thing even when there is no evidence of understanding and willing on the part of the thing, the idea of causation was retained, though without any presupposition of intelligence and deliberation, as we continue to do in scientific discourse when we speak of a mere thing causing something to happen. In all of this we are extending our original idea of action wherever we can find enough initiative to warrant speaking of an underlying thing.

This extension, however, takes us into the more cosmic aspect of our experience as distinct from its existential aspect. The idea of being as active is relatively easy to conceive in relation to *Dasein* or the human self. I know myself only through my action and I know others only through their action. If I think of higher beings than the human being, I shall have to think of such beings as even more active in their intelligence and will. But what of the lesser beings of experience that seem to have little or no activity or initiative of their own? How are we to understand the proper activity of such things?

To answer this question is not precisely the task of metaphysics. It is more the task of the particular sciences in their specific concern with these lesser things or of the phenomenology of the life-world. But it is the task of metaphysics to show that, whatever there is at the limit, it is active. To say such a thing is to express a judgment that brings a set of terms together in some *a priori* fashion, for we come to know being as an underlying thing only through its action. But one way in which we come to this idea *a posteriori* or phenomenologically is through the observation of a certain regularity in action that enables us to identify different underlying things or natures on the basis of regular differences and to identify different relations of causation between different things through induction. This is how we come to the concept of an order of nature where there is action and interaction but no evidence of intelligence and will on the part of the underlying things. A phenomenology of science itself, as well as of the *Lebenswelt,* would bring this out by restoring the idea of nature in its pristine meaning, as referring to that order of things, which, according to Aristotle, happen always or most of the time—an order with exceptions, to be sure, but where things are still seen as acting according to their nature and identified as such by reason of their constancy or regularity in the moving diversity of the experienced world.

6.4   Ontology of Action

This brings us to the ontological turn in our reflection on action. How do we come to understand being in its most radical sense as active? Or how do we come to understand action as flowing necessarily from being in such a way that we have to say that every being is active?

To answer this question metaphysically we must reflect upon our most immanent activity, that of judging and willing, where we come to think not only of being as being, but also of being as active or as act that actualizes itself. How do we discover being or how does being disclose itself in its most radical sense in our exercise of judging and willing? We discover it in ourselves thanks to the act by which we coincide with ourselves. We discover ourselves as being in this activity and we discover being itself as this active identity in ourselves. We discover both at the same time, being and ourselves, in this activity that is most ours and yet that is a response to being as well as a disclosure of being.

Upon reflection I think of this activity as both mine and real. It is for me what is most real, and yet it is real only on the condition that it is mine. At the same time, however, I think of it as mine only insofar as it is real, or only insofar as it is. Though I make myself be in this immanent activity, I still find myself only participating in being. I discover this priority of being over me, so to speak, in the very act in which I discover the originality of my own being or in which what is can only be what makes itself be. Heidegger writes that *Dasein* "understands itself always out of its existence [*Existenz*]" (*SZ* 17/33), which he speaks of as "a possibility of itself to be itself or not to be itself," but which we can understand more concretely as action, or as *Handlung,* in which there is the possibility of making oneself one thing or another.

In other words, human being comes to know itself through its action. Because this action is free and self-determined, the essential determination of this being cannot be given as the *what* of a mere thing *(ein sachhaltiges Was).* "Its essence lies much more in that it has always to be its be as its own," which is why Heidegger says the name *Dasein* as pure expression of be *(Seinsausdruck)* has been chosen to designate this being (*SZ* 16–17/ 32–33). In this Heidegger is insisting on how being discloses itself in human being through human being's own action, which can only be as this being's own and which brings it to perfection according to *what* it is. But this cannot be understood only with reference to the be of this being.

Speaking of action, or of *Handlung,* Heidegger writes "bringing to perfection [*Vollbringen*] means to unfold something [*etwas*] into the fullness of its essence [*Wesen*], to lead it forth into this, *producere*. Therefore what already is is perfectible [*Vollbringbar*]" (Heidegger 1946, 313/193). So far, this is in keeping with what we have said of action as perfecting a being according to its essence. Unfortunately, however, Heidegger goes on immediately to confuse the issue by speaking of "is" in "what already is" as referring to be, or to the act of being, rather than to the essence to which he has already referred: "what 'is' above all is be [*das Sein*]" (*Hum* 313/193). This can only be construed as either reducing be to an essence in our conception of being or as treating be as if it were only an action in the order of essence, neither of which is acceptable in a proper conception of being as active.

In the composition of a determinate being, be, or the act of being, should be kept clearly distinct from its essence or what we are now referring to as the underlying thing. As such this act is not an action, but the actuality of the thing as given in experience. To be sure, this act can be conceived as a perfection of the essence it actualizes, which otherwise would have to be thought of only as possible. But action is not the perfection of an essence or of the underlying thing in the same sense as that. As the proper activity of an essence, action is a perfection only in the order of an essence as determinate. Action is an ultimate act for the finite being only in the order of the finite essence or of the underlying thing as proper to its nature. Be as the act of being is in composition with this entire order of essence as a whole, including action as its second or ultimate perfection. Even as distinct from its act of being, this order is quite dynamic, since every finite being is understood only as active and known only through its action. But action is only a part of this order as the proper activity of a determinate being, whereas be or the act of being has to be conceived as common and as distinct from the entire order of essence though ontologically in composition with it.

In terms of human being, this means that we can understand human action only as perfecting the human essence as the underlying thing. Without this concept of underlying thing, we cannot properly understand how action brings a being to its perfection. The act of being, on the other hand, or as distinct from its essence in the underlying thing, cannot be understood as the underlying thing, as Heidegger would seem to suggest. It is an act first appropriated by the underlying thing in its essence or its standing as a mode of being, and then further appropriated through the self-perfecting action of that same essence or *Dasein*. We cannot take *Dasein* as a pure expression of be, but rather as an expression of human being as a whole. *Dasein* has ontological meaning only in that it refers to human being as having its own immanent activity, which brings it to perfection in the order of its essence. Such a being still entails a composition between what is mine and what is real in what I am and what I still have to make myself be. I discover my being as being in this active identity.

I do not, of course, discover only my own being in this sort of self-perfecting activity. I also discover the being of others through their activity, which is immanent to them but external to me. Other selves discover their being in the same way as I do, through their immanent activity or as an active identity as well. But I cannot discover their being in the same way as I discover mine, through my own immanent activity. Nor can they discover my being in the same way as they discover theirs, through their own immanent activity. But in mutual recognition there is a certain communication in this immanent activity of selves. The ontological point to be made, however, is that each self is itself in a privileged position for the disclosure of being. It is, as we have said, the primary analogate of being. And it is that primarily as an active identity through the exercise of thought and will in relation to other active identities exercising thought and will.

When the actual exercise of this identity is suspended, thought and will disappear in us. They are no longer conscious in what we can call their "second act." But they remain in what we can call their "first act," that is, in the act that made their actual exercise possible in the first place. We speak of this as an act in the underlying thing, however, and not just as a possibility to be oneself or not to be oneself. If this first act of active identity were to disappear, it is our very being that would disappear. We would no longer be or would cease to be because we would be without any active identity. This is why being has to be thought of as fundamentally active, even where it appears to be inactive or passive.

This reflection into the first act of active identity brings out the identity of the self as underlying thing. I am directly conscious of myself as being only in the actual exercise of thought and will. But in the same exercise of active identity I am also indirectly conscious of being there *(Sein da)* as a *this* with a nature or a quiddity, or as a thing with an active identity. I do not know myself as a thing except as active identity and, to the extent that I am for myself the primary analogate of thinghood, I do not know of any other thing except as active identity. Whether that other thing can be conscious or not in its active identity, as I am, I can think of it as being only in an activity that discloses it to me. This is how being presences itself as a standing and how I come to know what different things are in their first act, namely, in their nature or essence, through the actual exercise of activity, my own as well as that of other things. No underlying thing, precisely as underlying thing, can be without its proper activity.

If this ontology of action is to include all things, the nonliving as well as the living, or the basic entities and processes of mathematical physics as well as the self, it must extend its understanding of active identity to include action without consciousness as well as with consciousness. It is easy enough to include living things in this extending, for life surely appears as an active identity. But how are nonliving things active and in what does their thing-hood consist?

This brings us back to the question of how far we can go in speaking of entities as active and therefore as identifiable things, a question that perhaps can never be completely settled but that could only be settled in an ontology of the particular sciences. The only thing we can say here in a more common ontology of action is that nonliving things, insofar as they are things, are active at least in the sense that they make themselves known to us. Kant saw this when he was forced to think of things in themselves as causing sense impression. We know them, or at least *of* them, because they act on the passivity of our senses. Without this supposition, Kant could not justify any objective knowledge, since without sense impression the categories of understanding remain empty with regard to ourselves as well as to other things. What Kant failed to see, however, is that there cannot be two things in experience, one phenomenal and one noumenal. There is only one underlying thing known for what it is in its first perfection through its proper activity. What he did see, nevertheless, was that every thing displays some activity in making itself known as well as in its interaction with other things in the world. In this he was quite right, for in the exercise of judgment, in our claims to be expressing the truth of being, we do not think of ourselves as acting arbitrarily, but as responding to being itself presencing itself as active and disclosing *what* it is through this activity. There is no way of thinking the being of anything except as active on us as well as in itself. If there is a gap to be bridged between knowing and being, as there seems to be when we begin to raise questions, we find the gap already bridged through action which discloses each thing according to *what* it is in its first act or its essence.

CHAPTER 7

Being as True

IT REMAINS FOR US to bring out the other two transcendental properties of being, the true and the good, in order to complete the thought of
being in its transcendentality. With the thought of being as one and as active
we already have a certain opening of being into multiplicity and diversity.
We have the thought of something and an other *(Etwas und ein Anderes)*, as
Hegel put it *(WL* 104/117), or simply of something *(aliquid)*, as Aquinas put
it, since some-thing refers to a thing that is other *(aliud quid; Ver* 1, 1, c). We
think of some thing always as a thing among others.

If a being is not perfectly simple in its identity, not perfectly undivided in
itself, it is also not perfectly divided from every other being; it is somehow
one with other beings. The idea of transcendental unity thus not only opens
the way to a certain multiplicity and diversity in being; it also implies a certain unification and interdependence in this multiplicity and diversity, a unification that takes place through action and interaction. We do not think of
beings as merely standing apart from one another in *what* they are. We also
think of them as coming together in a universe, as a unity of many and diverse beings. Being, thus, as multiple and diverse, takes the form of a world
of beings in which a center appears as bringing things together. It is in the
attempt to think through this concentration of being that the thought of
truth and the thought of goodness appear as properties of being, for it is
with reference to a thoughtful and a willful being that being itself is thought
of as true and good. But how is this thought of the transcendentality of being to be brought to completion through truth and goodness and with reference to what is thoughtful and willful being?

To think of truth and goodness as properties of being does present some
difficulty. Does not truth refer more to intelligence and good to appetite
than to being itself? A being, as that which is known, is thought of as in itself. As such, a being can immediately be thought of as one, undivided in it-

self and divided from every other, and as active or interactive with other beings. But can any being be thought of as true and good in the same way, that is, without reference to anything more than being itself? When we say that the thought of truth and the thought of goodness imply some reference to intelligence and appetite, are we not adding something that has to be construed as a difference of being rather than as a property of being? If so, can truth and goodness still be thought of as properties of being, as the ancients thought of them, or do they have to be relegated to some kind of being, thus allowing for some beings to be true and good and other beings to be false and evil?

This is a problem that ancient Pythagoreanism had struggled with. The solution it came up with was to split being into two orders, one good and one bad, and to posit a separate first principle for each order, one good and one bad, a solution that was later adopted and transposed into biblical terms by Manicheanism. But such a dualism of orders and of principles cannot be reconciled with the transcendental unity of being, which implies that there can only be one being or one order of being and that all being is ultimately reducible to one principle. Nor is it reconcilable with the idea that truth and goodness are properties of being, since it would imply an order of beings that are neither true nor good. If truth and goodness are to be understood as properties of being, then being itself or every being precisely as being must be understood as true and good.

But if truth and goodness can be understood only with reference to intelligence and appetite, how, then, can we understand them as properties of being itself? We can do so only by supposing that there is some being with intelligence and will that relates to all being or to which all being relates precisely as being. In an onto-theological framework it would seem that this can be done fairly easily through the notion of creation. Being is understood as created and creation is understood as flowing through intelligence and will. Thus every being is understood as related to the intelligence and will of the Creator. It is true insofar as it relates to the creative intelligence and good insofar as it relates to the creative will. Hegel thinks of creation in this way when he refers to the realm of Logic as "the truth as it is in and for itself without veil" and to its content as "the exposition of God as He is in his eternal essence before the creation of nature and a finite spirit" (*WL* I 31/50), as do other more traditional onto-theologians who are equally presumptuous in assuming for themselves God's viewpoint as the sole principle of being and as something given from the beginning in the thinking of being.

Whether God can be understood as sole principle of being, or even whether there is such a sole principle of being to be thought, remains to be seen. For the moment we can only say that being cannot be thought of metaphysically as flowing from any sort of creation here. In the beginning metaphysics can only take being as it presents itself and think it through to its properties as we first come to understand it. Before we can even approach the thought of creation through intelligence and will, as we shall find in raising the question of a summit of being, we must already have understood being in its truth and goodness. We are not in a position to adopt the view-point of a creator *ex nihilo sui et subjecti,* whatever that might be. We can only accept being in knowing, not create it. The only way we can come to a metaphysical understanding of being as true and as good is from the stand-point of our own intelligence and will. That is the pivot around which our initial thought of being takes place and it is pivot enough for coming to un-derstand being as true and good.

We have already seen how human being is for us the primary analogate of being. It is from human being and in relation to human being that we come to understand all of being. But this selfsame human being is not just a being closed in upon itself. It is a being open to all of being. Recapitulating what others had said before him, Aristotle wrote that the human soul is somehow everything that is, since to know something, whether sensibly or intelligibly, is somehow to be what is known, not in the sense that the known itself is in the knowing, but in the sense that its species is in the knowing, for it is not the stone itself that is in our knowing when we know the stone, but its species (*Soul* 431b18–30). Taking this thought of Aristotle and the ancients one step further, Aquinas finds in the human soul the ground for all being coming together and for thinking of being as true and good.

We have seen how he thought of the transcendentals as conceptions ex-pressing common modes of being that follow being as being in its transcen-dentality. One is such a conception. But one follows every being as it is in it-self. Are there not properties that follow every being in the order of one being to another? It is in such an order that we think of being as some thing, that is, as one thing other than another or as divided from others. But this order of one thing to another or of beings to one another can also be thought of more positively as a *coming together (convenientia)* of one being with another or of all beings with one another. Action and interaction can be understood as constituting such a coming together in a universe of being. But this coming together presupposes something whose nature it is to come together with every being—*aliquid quod natum sit convenire cum omni ente,* which, Aquinas says, is the human soul as understood by Aristotle, that is, the soul as somehow everything: *quodammodo omnia* (*Ver* 1, 1, c). According to Aquinas, then, it is through the human soul, which is at once sentient and intelligent, that we first come to think of all being as coming together; and it is through the same soul that we come to think of being as both true and good, since the human soul is open actively to being as both cognitive and appetitive. The conception of truth as a property of being thus expresses the *coming together* of being with intelligence or knowing, while the conception of good as a property of being expresses the *coming together* of being with appetite or willing.

This coming together of being with intelligence and will cannot, however, be thought of as purely incidental or external to being. It follows necessarily from our very conception of being as we try to express it more completely. Being is not something we think of as closed up within itself apart from all disclosure. On the contrary, we think of it only as disclosing itself in our knowing as that which is. When we think of being as true, it is of being itself that we think and not just of being as relating to our knowing. For without being there is no knowing. The truth of knowing has to be in being itself, since otherwise knowing would not be what it is, that is, knowing of being. Nor do we think of being only as disclosing and true, but also as appealing and good, that is, as an object of appetite, something to be striven for or acquiesced in. Being discloses itself as the most fundamental good, as that which is willed ultimately, whether in ourselves or in any other being.

Human being is thus the being that gathers all being together. It is the opening or the clearing in which being discloses itself as that which is willed ultimately, and it is by reason of our finding being in this opening that we necessarily come to conceive it as true and good. It is impossible to think of something as being without at the same time thinking of it as true or knowable, even if we do not actually know it. As knowable, however, it is also thought of as appetible, either precisely as something that satisfies the desire to know or as something that calls for a further response consequent on knowing. Being enters into this circle of intelligence and appetite precisely as being, so that the conception of true, which expresses a relation to intelligence, and the conception of good, which expresses a relation to appetite, both follow necessarily from our first conception of being in its transcendental analogy.

To say this, however, is not to think of being only in relation to human intelligence and appetite, which are finite or determinate in their mode of grasping. On the contrary, it is to think of being in its transcendental openness, even to the point of infinity, and it is to open human intelligence and appetite to this transcendental order, rather than to reduce being to only one of its determinate forms. Though being is thought of as gathered together through our intelligence and appetite, so that it has to be spoken of as true and good, it is not thought of as reducible to this particular gathering in the concrete exercise of our intelligence and will. Rather the gathering itself of being as true and good is thought of as a reaching out to being itself, which appears as that which stirs questioning of intelligence and appetite of will. It is being that gathers as it is being gathered by human being. This is why we speak of the true and the good as properties of being, and not just as objects of human faculties.

Though we think of true and good with reference to our intelligence and will, we do not think of them only with reference to what is given at hand in this intelligence and will. We think rather of intelligence as relating to the truth of being and of appetite as relating to the goodness of being. We experience intelligence as questioning only insofar as we experience being as transcending the understanding at hand and we experience will as desire only insofar as we experience being as transcending what we already hold and have to acquiesce in. In either case it is an infinitude of being that takes our intelligence and appetite beyond the finitude of what is at hand for them.

The thought of being as true and as good thus recenters metaphysics on the human being, as the thought of analogy did, only now it is to open up this being to the full scope of its intelligence and appetite, which is the scope of being itself in its fullness. The human being is the one who brings being as being into the open. It is the only being that can raise the question of being metaphysically. But it does so only in the pursuit of being and in the knowledge that being is the intelligible even before it is intelligized and the appetible even before it is desired. It is this foreknowledge of being as true and as good that we must now enter into, to see not only how it follows from experience, as metaphysics itself does, but also how it begins *a priori* in the reflection proper to the exercise of judgment and decision.

We begin with the understanding of being as true because the understanding of being as good presupposes the understanding of being as true, just as human willing or appetite presupposes human intelligence. In the end, however, we shall find that the good can also enjoy a certain priority over the true in their mutual inclusion of one another as properties of being. For even as true, being is a good that satisfies the desire to know, and as good, it comes under the requirement of truth.

7.1 The Essence of Truth

Just as being, one, and action cannot be properly defined in terms of genus and specific difference, since they are first notions through which other notions can be defined, so also truth cannot be properly defined in terms of genus and specific difference. It too is a first notion that we come to understand in our exercise of judgment and through reflection on this act. In fact, we have already encountered this notion of truth in our reflection on the structure of judgment, which always entails a truth claim, and we have been using it from the very beginning in recognizing that knowing is of being and that being is what is known. Already in this initial reflection on the hermeneutic circle of knowing and being in the exercise of judgment we were implying a conception of truth.

In his reflection on the original meaning of truth as expressed in the Greek term *aletheia,* Heidegger focuses on it as the disclosedness or unhiddenness of being. To say that a statement is true is to say that it discloses being in itself. It expresses or lets being be seen in its disclosedness. Phenomenologically speaking, this understanding of truth presupposes for Heidegger, as it did for Aristotle and Aquinas, a certain be-in-the-world *(In-der-Welt-sein)* on the part of *Dasein* or human being, which, in its care, relates to being in the world *(innerweltliches Seiende)* and through this openness attains the phenomenon of truth in its most original sense (*SZ* §44; 282–99/256–73).

The essence of truth understood in this way consists, then, not so much in some kind of agreement between a statement and the thing it is about, but rather in a kind of relating *(Verhalten)* that stands in the open and adheres to something open as something open. "What is thus opened up, and solely in this strong sense, was experienced early in Western thinking as 'what is present' [*'das Anwesende'*] and for a long time has been named 'being' [*'das Seiende'*]" (*WW* 184/124). What is present is what makes itself known and what makes itself known is being. In this relating, which is truth, being is understood as that which makes itself known.

But is it really being *(to on)* that the conception of truth expresses or is it rather the be of being *(to einai tou ontos),* as Heidegger would seem to prefer? "There is [*'es gibt'*] only be [*Sein*]," he writes, "—not being [*Seiende*]—insofar as truth is. And truth is only insofar and as long as *Dasein* is. Be and truth 'are' in an equally original sense" (*SZ* 304/272). But a question arises for Heidegger here, as it does for us: What does it mean to say that be "is" where be has to be distinguished from every being? The question can be raised concretely, Heidegger adds, "only if the meaning of be and the broad scope of the understanding of be in general has been clarified." This itself presupposes an understanding of be in its ontological difference from being, a difference that is not given in the question of being as we understand it here and the meaning of which we have yet to explore as something in being itself rather than just in our conception of being. How that ontological difference will affect our understanding of the truth of being remains to be seen in an exploration of the structure of being that the difference implies. For the moment it is enough to say, as has long been said, that the conception of truth does express being—not be—in a common way or as being in its relating to knowing, just as knowing in truth is of being.

This essential relating of truth has been conventionally described in terms of an agreement or a correspondence between understanding and reality or an adequation of intelligence and thing—*adaequatio intellectus et rei*. But we must not be misled by such a description. It is not a correspondence such as there might be between two things that are identical to one another, such as two coins or twins. It is a correspondence between an act of knowing and that which is known in that act. When I recognize a piece of earth for what it is, that is, knowingly and in truth, I do not become that piece of earth. I assert it in its reality according to what I know of it in the opening where I represent it conceptually. Nor do I assert it only in its representation, that is, as I conceive it or as it is in my mind, as I might if knowing consisted only in the first act of intelligence, which is to form a quiddity of things in one's mind. I also assert it in its reality, as I do in the second act of intelligence which comes only after the first act of intelligence or in conjunction with the quiddity formed in it, through critical reflection, as an act of "composing," when I say yes to what I have represented for myself in that quiddity, or of "dividing," when I have to say no to the representation.

Any conception of truth that fails to take into account this complex structure of judgment will inevitably miss the point of the conventional description of truth as correspondence or adequation. For when it is said that truth is found only in judgment, it is not meant that truth consists only in the bare yes or no of assertion or negation found in the second act of intelligence, but in a yes or no always determined by a representation in the first act of intelligence integral to the total act. Assertion or negation, the *is* or *is not* of judgment, rides on *what* is expressed in the terms S and P. Thus, in the metaphor of correspondence or adequation, truth remains an essential relating to being through the opening of understanding to being as present in critical or reflective intelligence.

7.2   The Truth of Essence

Relating, however, takes place in some kind of an opening between two terms. In truth this relating takes place between two sides, a subject and an object or an intelligence and a thing, whatever the thing may be. In our phenomenological approach to the conception of truth, we come at it from the side of the subject or intelligence. Truth, we say, expresses a relating in being to intelligence. The relating presupposes an intelligence that, in its care, actively relates to being or is somehow everything. When we speak of truth in its essence we speak of it only as a relating, without giving any priority to either side of the relating. The ancients referred to this as the *ratio veritatis,* the idea of truth in general as a coming together of two: intelligence and thing. But we can also speak of truth from the side of the object or the thing in the relating. Thus, if we speak of truth viewed from the side of the subject or intelligence as *logical or formal truth,* we can also speak of truth viewed from the side of the object or the thing as *ontological or material truth.*

These are all expressions that have been used to get at the various facets of truth in its essential relating. What sense are we to make of them? Are they all equally valid or valid in the same way? Can any one of them be understood independently of the relating or the *coming together* that is the essence of truth? What does it mean to distinguish ontological truth from logical truth, or material truth from formal truth? Can there be ontological truth without logical truth, or material truth without formal truth?

The idea of material truth, to begin with, should not be taken as referring to matter as such, as if truth could be found only in material things. In the context of Kantian critical thinking, "matter" refers more to the content of knowledge as distinct from its "form." Without content the categories of understanding are purely formal or empty and, since for Kant content comes only through sense intuition, there is no truth without some material component or sense manifold. On the other hand, since there is no knowing without the categories of understanding through which we represent things given in the manifold of sense intuition, there is also no truth without some formal act of understanding. Thus, in the Kantian perspective, the ideas of formal and material truth can only complement one another in a total act of knowing. Though the idea of content is not *per se* restricted to something material or sensible, since Kant allows for such a thing as an intellectual intuition that would have a purely intellectual content, it is in fact restricted to the material and sensible in human knowing, since Kant does not allow for any such intellectual intuition in human being, apart from sense intuition.

But the idea of material truth in the sense of a content of knowledge is not necessarily limited to that of a material thing in this way. Whether one wants to put it in terms of an intellectual intuition as such or not, one can still speak of a content of knowledge prior to sense intuition, as Hegel does in his *Logic*. In German such a content can still be referred to as *Sache,* a subject matter that does not have to be taken as a thing *(Ding)*. Even if it is understood as distinct from the form of the act in which it appears, however, this content is still not reducible to something material. This is why Hegel can claim to develop his Logic as an articulation of truth, that is, a knowledge with content, prior to any "creation" of nature or finite spirit, that is, independently of any reference to matter. In English we have some difficulty in following Hegel's move because we tend to think of *Sache* as subject matter or simply as the matter of a consideration. The use of the term "matter" in this way can be misleading, however, since the matter at issue is not strictly matter as such, but rather a subject of consideration, that is, of an act of intelligence able to consider an immaterial as well as a material subject. When we were speaking of being as the subject matter of metaphysics at the beginning, for example, we were not excluding matter from its content but neither were we restricting this content to material being as such. We were beginning to consider being simply as being, which includes a formal as well as a material content. In taking only be for his subject of consideration, Heidegger may have been simply falling back into the Hegelian move of trying to develop the concept of pure be without any reference to being present as present in experience or as grasped in the first act of intelligence.

Such a move results in an unwarranted restriction of the conception of being and truth to the given finitude of human understanding that is common among Heideggerians. But it could also be conceived as a move from the idea of material truth to a more common idea of ontological truth, although the move does present some difficulty for a proper conception of truth. Traditionally the idea of ontological truth had been opposed to the idea of merely logical truth. Kant understood this opposition as leaving the *Ding an sich* beyond the reach of human knowledge in the absence of any other intuition than sense intuition. In restoring a unity of form and content in pure knowing apart from sense intuition, however, Hegel seems to have only collapsed ontological truth into logical truth or, perhaps more exactly, to have expanded the idea of logical truth so that it includes or absorbs ontological truth.

What is to be made of this collapse or this expansion? Is it truly an expansion of logic into ontology, if the Logic begins only with pure be *(das reine Sein)*, which is then understood as pure nothing *(das reine Nichts)?* Or is it more a collapse of the two sides of an opening that should remain open? How is this relation between ontological and logical truth to be understood without collapsing the ontological into the logical?

The question brings us back to the idea of truth as a relating in an opening. What is doing the opening, so to speak, and what is being opened up? Human understanding can be seen as that which opens up and being can be seen as that which is opened. In accordance with this, logical truth can then be seen as truth on the side of human understanding, and ontological truth as truth on the side of being, as if the two sides of truth could be separated from one another. But truth is not a separating. It is a relating of two sides that cannot be understood in separation from one another. It expresses an identity between the knowing and the known. Hence logical truth and ontological truth cannot be understood as opposed to one another. They can only be understood as mutually including one another from either side of the opening in which truth appears, or rather in which being appears in truth, for it is being which makes itself known as truth. Logical truth makes sense only in relation to ontological truth and ontological truth makes sense only in relation to logical truth in this opening.

But does not this opening still imply some kind of opposition between the two sides of the opening? Would there be an opening without two sides that are somehow opposed to one another? Perhaps, but the opposition should not be thought of as one between ontological and logical truth. The idea of truth implies that the opposition has already been overcome in a relating. How else, then, can the opposition be thought? In modern philosophy it has come to be thought of in terms of an opposition between object and subject. Truth is spoken of as objectivity, and subjectivity or subjectivism is seen as a cause of untruth. The problem of truth is seen as one of overcoming one's subjectivity and entering into objectivity, as if truth itself were a thing that can be found only in objects.

This notion of objectivity in truth is, of course, very important for the essence of truth as relating. To speak of an opening is to speak of a distance between two sides. An object is that which stands over against *(Gegenstand)* a subject and the distance that separates them is that which has to be crossed by the subject desirous of knowing and thereby appropriating the object. In fact the object as conceived is what determines the form of consciousness in the subject, as Hegel shows when he distinguishes different forms of consciousness from one another in *The Phenomenology of Spirit*. This object, however, whether clearly conceived or not, exists only for a subject, which is a subject only as open to the object.

The term "subject" is not used here in the same way as we were using it earlier in speaking of a subject of consideration in a science. Here "subject" refers more to a thing, rather than to a way of considering things, albeit a thing with special characteristics. It is the thing that can be known immediately through the act of thinking, as Descartes thought, or the thing that still cannot be known *an sich* for lack of any intellectual intuition, as Kant thought. As such a thing, the subject can be thought of as an object, a *res cogitans,* and can become an object of investigation and appropriation. But it is not as such an object that it enters the opening of truth. The subject in the essential relating of truth is rather the opening itself as representing that which presents itself or takes its stand in being. As such, the subject is in quest of being as that which is to be attained, its objective, so to speak, and it recognizes being as that which is opened up in objects, including itself as an object or as a thing.

Thus, in the essential relating of truth, objects are not seen as closed in upon themselves, but as disclosing what is essential about being in the sense that "thing" expresses *what* a being is or its essence. The object appears as distant from the subject only insofar as this essence or standing in being has yet to disclose itself fully or to be fully appropriated. But this distance is overcome in the act of knowing where objectivity is attained, that is, where what presents itself is represented adequately. If human intelligence were not in quest, we would not have to think of truth as objective or having to be objective. We would think of it only as intellectual acquiescence in being itself as known in judgment.

There is perhaps some wisdom, then, in keeping the traditional description of truth as an adequation of intelligence to thing rather than as a static conformity between subject and object. Object suggests an opposition that cannot be overcome, a gap that cannot be bridged, which clearly is not the case where there is truth. Thing, which still can be opposed to intelligence, as that which takes its stand in being rather than just in intelligence, is not defined by this opposition. It is defined rather by what it is as it stands in being and as it presents itself to be represented, as that with which representation has to compose in the exercise of judgment.

It is perhaps because Heidegger thought of *das Seiende* or *das All des Seienden* as only an object at hand or a set of objects in the world, *innerweltliches Seiende,* from which *Sein* or be had to be distinguished in the ontological difference, that he could not accept being as being as the proper subject for the question of being. This is perhaps also why he thought of the entire tradition that accepted this definition of the subject of metaphysics as culminating only in technological science. But such a culmination does not follow from a proper understanding of being as being as the subject of metaphysics, nor from the understanding of thing as that to which intelligence relates in truth. It follows only from a conception of being or of thing as an object at hand to be handled or manipulated, which is only one particular mode of being and not being as including all its differences in its analogy. In his destruction of metaphysics, Heidegger appears to have had such a particular conception of being in mind and not the transcendentally open conception of being as being.

The conception of "thing," as we argued in the Introduction to Part Three, on the properties of being, follows the conception of being in its transcendentality, unlike object, which cannot include that against which it stands. "Thing" refers to *what* a being is or its essence and, as such, it can include any subject as well as any object. Kant could think of the human subject as a *Ding an sich* as much as of any other object. What a thing is in the concrete, or the conception of essence, can, of course, be understood as referring to many different ways of being, depending on the diversity and multiplicity of being itself as given in experience. The question of truth, then, as an adequation of intelligence to thing, becomes a question of discovering being in its differences, in what it is or how it is for this or that being, this or that kind of being, and so on. This is the passage from our first conception of being to what can be expressed as the special modes of being spoken of earlier. In this sense the quest for truth can be understood as that of the particular sciences. In the more transcendental quest that we are pursuing here, we try to express what being is simply as being and what its properties are simply as being.

In saying that being is true, we are saying not only that being as being is what truth aims at, but also that truth aims at every being in its essence or in the stand it takes in being, for being is found only in its differences, whatever they are. This is the aspect of essentialism that remains true not just for the particular sciences, but also for metaphysics, since knowing for us attains being only by representing for itself *what* presents itself or takes its stand in being as we experience it. The quest for truth is a quest for what things are in this standing and it does not attain the full scope of being beyond mere facticity except through such representation of what and how they are.

7.3   The Affirmation of Truth in Being

We have known that being is true from the beginning. In saying that knowing is of being, we were already expressing the relating that is the essence of truth. Knowing, as Aquinas puts it, is a certain effect of truth—*quidam veritatis effectus*. What the idea of true adds to that of being is a conformity between or an adequation of thing and intelligence, and knowing the thing follows from this conformity or adequation *(Ver* 1, 1, c). This, however, presupposes a priority of the conception of being over that of truth, since it is only with reference to being that the question of truth appears. If being were not for us the point of reference, so to speak, there would be no question of truth. We think we have the truth only when we think we have a conformity in our minds with what is and we seek such adequation when we think we do not have it.

We think of truth, therefore, with reference to being itself in its being opened up to intelligence, or as intelligible. To the extent that we know anything, it is being that we know, and, conversely, the being that we do know is surely intelligible. For how else can we know it if not by making it somehow intelligible to us? But are we to suppose that we know all being from the beginning? Can we not suppose that there is some being that we do not know? What of this being that is not yet intelligible to us? Is it intelligible in itself? If so, how do we know that it is intelligible in itself without having it as intelligible to us?

If we are going to say that truth is a property of being, we are going to have to say that being is intelligible in itself and not just to us. Indeed, we are going to have to say that our own sense of intelligence is modeled on being, and not the other way around. In truth it is being that has to have priority, and not just our understanding or what is in our mind, which can also be false or inadequate as well as true or adequate. But how can we know that being is true in itself otherwise than through our understanding what is in our mind?

This is the question we still have to answer if we are going to think of true as a property of being, whether we know all there is to know or not. We have approached the question of truth phenomenologically, or from its logical side. We have spoken of it from the side of intelligence, even though we have tried to think of it as an intelligence of being. Now we must try to think of it from the ontological side, or the side of being itself, to see if and how it is in being itself that truth is found. We must pass from our experience of truthfulness to the thought of truthfulness itself in being.

In doing so we have to go from what is *a posteriori,* or what is given in our understanding in the presencing of being, to what is *a priori* in being itself. Knowing is a certain effect of truth in us, as we have just seen. We must proceed from this effect to its cause, so to speak, that is, to being itself as truthful and as that which is the model for our idea of truth. Our aim, then, must be to reverse the perspective from which we begin in the experience of the essential relating which truth is and think it through to its other side, which is that of being itself.

This is a difficult task for us, since we are always left only with our own understanding to accomplish this task of reaching beyond any given understanding. But it is a task that is already begun for us in the exercise of judgment, which includes an act of critical reflection as well as an act of understanding. It is through this act of reflection that being presences itself and even imposes itself, so to speak, to make us critical of what we might be thinking only arbitrarily or uncritically. What we have to do, then, is see how reflection takes us beyond our understanding to being itself in its truth, or rather how reflection opens up understanding to let being present itself.

To understand is somehow to represent things for myself. When I begin to reflect upon my understanding in this representation, to see if it is true to reality, I begin to think back to what presents itself in what can be referred to as a process of verification. This process can take different forms in different kinds of judgment. But the reflection that is essential to any such process is an act in search of evidence or of how being shines forth in this or that representation.

The first evidence we have appealed to from the beginning of our inquiry is that knowing is of being. From this we can say immediately that the being we do know is intelligible in fact. But is the being we do know in fact all of being? Or is it only part of the being to which our intelligence is open as a whole? If it is only a part of being, if there is more of being than what we know, how do we know that this "more" is also intelligible? Can we think of this more as anything but intelligible, given the way being presents itself initially in our knowing? Is it possible to think of anything as being positively and as unintelligible at the same time? How can being ever present itself to intelligence itself except as intelligible? Is there any evidence for answering this question?

We should note that the question arises when we begin to introduce some differentiation in the initial evidence that knowing is of being. In this respect we are going beyond the original insight of Parmenides into being by recognizing some differentiation in our first conception of being. Being is thought of in many ways in the exercise of judgment. Affirmation, which is an affirmation of being, is expressed in many ways. It is always limited by the terms we use in a particular exercise of judgment.

At first affirmation tends to be purely positive. Our first representations, which are expressed in the terms of judgment, tend to be affirmed simply as true, that is, as expressive of a mode of being. But as we become aware of diversity in modes of being and of mistakes in identifying them through our representation, we begin to deny as well as to affirm and to differentiate between diverse modes of being. In this way we not only move from our first conception of being, which is still without any expression of particular modes of being, whether specific or generic. We also become aware that we do not know all of being or that our actual representation of being may not be equal to the whole of being itself. We do not lose our very first evidence that knowing is of being, but we begin to ask ourselves about being which we may not know about. And it is in this moment of questioning that the question we are now concerned with arises. Is the being that we do not know itself intelligible as well as the being we do know?

We cannot go back on our first evidence that knowing is of being, though we do question our way of representing being. We cannot knowingly deny our knowing of something, even when it is that we do not know anything. Nor can we deny that we know being when we do know something, though we may have some difficulty in relating that something to being as such. If we exercise judgment of any kind, directly or indirectly, we acknowledge this first evidence of being. But in doing so, we also acknowledge a certain convertibility between knowing and being. When we think of knowing in any strict sense, we think of it as a knowing of being, and when we think of being, we think of it as what is known when knowing takes place. Thus, when we try to think of some unknown being, we can only think of it as knowable in some fashion, as intelligible, or as true in itself, even though we do not presently know it for what it is.

Speaking subjectively, I can say that what is not known to me does not exist for me. But more objectively, I can also say generally that what is not knowable in any way whatsoever simply does not exist or is not. I cannot think of being except as intelligible. The only limit to intelligibility is nothing, which does not exist or is not, but which is still intelligible in some sense as negation, that is, as relative to affirmation or to what is.

Thus, the conception of truth or of the intelligibility of being necessarily follows our first conception of being, which is itself the very first intelligibility for us. Being is the proper object of intelligence, or what intelligence aims at, in the same way that color is the proper object of sight or sound is the proper object of hearing. Just as it is impossible to think of color as invisible, even though I cannot see it, or of sound as inaudible, even though I cannot hear it, so it is impossible to think of being as unintelligible, even though I do not presently understand it fully. This impossibility of thought is the sign of an immediate evidence in the way we know being or being makes itself known, even when being is not known fully or adequately.

In fact, the same evidence can be brought out in the sense we have that being itself is not known fully or adequately. This sense of inadequacy in knowing gives rise to wonder and to questioning. To wonder or to question is to recognize that we do not know all there is to be known. To begin to inquire, however, is to presuppose that there is some intelligibility to be understood, since otherwise we would not begin to inquire. Now some inquiries may terminate in the recognition of an absence of intelligibility or in the insight that there is nothing there to be understood. But even such inquiries are understood in relation to other inquiries giving more positive results in terms of intelligibility, an intelligibility that can only relate to being ultimately. It is being itself as that which is to be understood in its fullness that gives rise to our questioning, and not just some deconstructive agitation in an understanding that thinks of itself as inadequate.

This can be seen in a particular science such as biology, for example. When proteins were first discovered, a whole new line of inquiry was opened up to disclose what they were and what they did. The same can be said about the DNA molecule, the exploration of which is now the cutting edge of biological investigation. Even the discovery of any unique individual in the world will send us scurrying to see if there are others of the same kind in reality and to understand *what* that kind might be. Being, as that which is to be known, is what calls us to these inquiries. Though particular sciences may not think of it precisely as being, but only as some particular object of inquiry, insofar as they claim to be science or knowledge of reality, and not just an intellectual game, they presuppose the same convertibility of being and intelligibility as we are proposing here. Insofar as they exercise judgment properly, they affirm the same intelligibility of being as any other exercise of judgment does and they are aiming at that intelligibility through their own critical reflection or investigation.

Even the experience of inadequacy in knowing can be seen as pointing to this immediate evidence of being as true. When the human being faces what presents itself, it can not only represent it, but also misrepresent it. Falsehood can appear as well as truth through the understanding. In saying that every being is true, we are not saying that there can be no falsehood. What gives rise to truth in understanding can also give rise to falsehood. What is meant to disclose being can also foreclose on it or leave it undisclosed. But even to recognize this difference between truth and falsehood in knowing presupposes the thought that truth is rooted in being, and not just in our thought, and that only being can give rise to truth. Without the reference to being there could be no thought of truth in knowing, no critical reflection. There would be only an agility to represent or to fabricate without concern for what is, pure destruction or deconstruction without any regard for what is in its essence or structure.

Similarly, it can be seen that the recognition of error in the exercise of judgment presupposes the same evidence of truth in being itself. Our first representations of being are expressed positively in affirmative judgments. As long as we have not become fully critical in the exercise of judgment, we tend to take our representations as true at face value. With the rise of critical reflection in experience, however, we not only begin to doubt this face value of representations, but also begin to deny some of these representations, whether they are from ourselves or from others. We begin to make negative judgments as well as affirmative judgments, and many more that are partially negative and partially affirmative when we distinguish a part that is false and a part that is true in an initial hypothesis or supposition. These negative judgments, however, are based not on some representation of something else than being, which could only be nothing, as Parmenides understood from the beginning, but on some other positive representation that is seen as possibly truer to being. When I reject some representation as false, it is because I see some other representation as true or as calling for further investigation, always presupposing that it is in being itself that truth is to be found and doubt is to be resolved.

It may also be that, through a long effort of critical reflection and reconstruction of representations, we may arrive at some universal conception of being, such as that of Hegel, for example, which may still have to be deconstructed, but even such deconstruction, if it is to be taken seriously as a concern for truth, presupposes the conception of being as true in itself and as that which is to be attained ultimately.

7.4 The Impossibility of False Being

Given this understanding of being as true, is it then possible to think of being as false or even in any way doubtful? The question might appear facetious in some ways, but it can also help us to understand why Parmenides had to be so categorical in his separation of the two ways, the way of truth and the way of falsehood, and in his rejection of the second. If we take being as one of a kind or as univocal in the way that Parmenides did, then we have to say that being can only be true and cannot in any way be false. We have to oppose false to true in the same way as nonbeing is opposed to being. Falsehood is then something that can only apply to a way for human being, but a way that leads to nothing, not to being. It is a way not only of doubt, but also of total suspense in nothingness. The way of truth, on the other hand, which is the only way of certainty, is focused on the fullness of being.

When we allow for differentiation in being, however, or when we see this first conception of being as expressed in diverse modes of being, are we still held to this same kind of absolute opposition between false and true? Or is there some sense in which some beings might be spoken of as false, even though being in itself can only be understood as true?

In one way, even with the analogy of being, the opposition between truth and falsehood has to remain absolute, as stated by Parmenides. If being is true, then it is all that is intelligible, while unintelligible can only refer to nonbeing, so to speak. There is no limit to intelligibility other than being and no limit to being itself other than nonbeing, which, of course, is not an other in any way, since only a being can be an other. We cannot search for falsehood, as if it represented something, except as a possible hindrance to our search for truth, which does represent being. Falsehood can only be understood as a negation or as a privation of truth.

Yet, insofar as we think of truth as a property of being in its relating to intelligence and of being as differentiated, we can also begin to think of some representations of being as false in at least two senses. We are not stuck with only one representation of being, as Parmenides was. We have diverse representations of being, presumably of beings diverse in themselves. Thus we can represent one thing as something it is not, as when we speak of false gold. The thing we are speaking of is not nothing. It is something. But what it is is not what we represent it to be. When we discover that it is not gold, we may still have to discover what it really is in itself. But we already know that our first representation of what it is was false, that is, did not represent the thing itself but was rather a misrepresentation, and that the truth of being in this case is other than what we thought it was.

Representations can be thought of as false, however, not just in terms of what a thing is, but also in terms of expectations that follow from representations. Thus, when I represent someone to myself as a friend, I come to expect certain kinds of behavior from him in my regard. But when he does not meet these expectations, when he betrays me, for example, I start to represent him as a false friend or as no friend at all. This will not keep me from representing him still as a human being, but it will keep me from representing him as a friend.

Thus there is a sense in which I may speak of things as false, but I can think of them as false only in relation to the representation that gives rise to the relation of truth. It is not the thing itself that is false. It has its truth, which may or may not be known. It is rather the representation that is false, which then has to rectified or made true in the etymological sense of "verified." In any event the opposition between true and false remains no less absolute than the opposition between being and nonbeing. The question remains always one of disclosing being in its identity or in its diverse identities and interconnections or interaction.

CHAPTER 8

Being as Good

≈

W E HAVE ALREADY SPOKEN of the good as a property of being, in conjunction with truth. The conception of being as good arises in the same way as the conception of being as true, through the relating of being to human being, in which all being *comes together.* Just as truth expresses the *coming together* of being with the cognitive activity of human being, so also good expresses the *coming together* of being with the appetitive activity of human being.

As a property of being, however, the good still has to be conceived as distinct from the one, the active, and the true, because, in the being that is somehow everything or whose nature it is to come together with every being, the activity of appetite is distinct from the activity of cognition. Our conception of good has to follow our conception of being in the same way as our conception of truth follows that very first conception in its transcendental analogy.

Nor must we think that goodness is only relative to our appetite rather than in being itself. To be sure, the thought of goodness requires the thought of an appetite, since, as Aristotle says at the beginning of the *Nicomachean Ethics,* the good is that which all things aim at or go after. Phenomenologically speaking, therefore, we speak of the good in relation to our appetite. It is the appetible. But that does not make goodness itself something only relative to our appetite or something purely subjective, so to speak, as if being itself were not good or as if the good were not in being itself. It is being itself that has to be seen as good if we are to make any sense of appetite as distinct from just knowing, since appetite appears as a second movement toward the being that discloses itself in the clearing of truth.

Knowing is an activity that terminates in the mind or in an expression of the truth grasped through the exercise of judgment. But appetite is an activity that begins from knowing and terminates in being itself, which is why we inevitably think of being as appetible, something somehow good. Only through the conception of being can we come to a proper conception of the good as that to which appetite relates.

To arrive at this conception of being as good we must proceed as we did for the conception of being as true. We must think of being, or beings, not just as standing apart but as coming together in a universe, in a kind of concentration through human being. Being, as we have already said, is not thought of as closed up within itself, but as disclosing itself in our knowing. Knowing is thus a gathering of all being together, while human being is the opening or the clearing in which being opens itself. In this opening, however, there is not only a disclosing of being, but also an appealing from being that is not adverted to from the standpoint of knowing as such or in the modern concern for objectivity alone. But it is an appealing to which appetite responds. What we refer to as "appetite" is in response to this appealing. It appears as a second movement, after knowing, and it takes us beyond mere disclosure, which terminates in the knower as an expression of understanding, back to the thing itself in its goodness. *Verum est in mente, sed bonum est in re.*

This conception of being as good thus keeps open the circle of knowing and being we have spoken of in the exercise of judgment from the beginning in saying that knowing is of being, so that we not only acquiesce in the truth we come to know, but also remain in quest of it insofar as there is something more to be known and inquired into, for truth itself is something good for the intelligence. It is through the appeal of being that we come to its goodness, whether as satisfying our desire to know or any other desire. Just as the human being is the only one who brings being as being into the open in questioning, so also it is the only one that can embrace it or reject it in its appeal as good.

8.1 The Essence of Goodness

Good cannot be defined in terms of genus and specific difference any more than being, one, active, or true. Like the other transcendental ideas, it is a first notion through which other notions may be defined, but which is not itself properly definable. What it means is known only in the actual exercise of an activity we speak of as appetite as distinct from knowing in human being. The good, to repeat the classical formula Aristotle falls back on, which is not strictly a definition, is that which all aim at or go after. What is this aiming at or going after and how does it arise from our conception of being as good or from the appeal of being itself?

We have not dwelt upon this activity of human being which we refer to as appetite as we have upon the activity of knowing. To bring out the essence of goodness, however, we must do so, for it is only through this activity that this essence becomes manifest, just as it is only through the activity of knowing that the essence of truth becomes manifest.

Let us note first that, as we have already intimated, appetite is an activity that is distinct from that of knowing. We may think of it as coming before knowing, inasmuch as we can speak of a desire to know. In this sense we may even think of truth as good. Questioning is a questing after truth. Truth is something we desire. It is that in which we acquiesce in good judgment when we have found answers to our questions. In truth being is responding to our quest for knowing so that the relating of truth is already a relating of goodness in one sense.

But that is not yet the full relating of goodness, since appetite is also an activity that follows upon knowing. Appetite is itself a response to being perceived as good. It presupposes some form of consciousness and it starts from a perception of being as desirable or good. Knowing, as an activity, terminates in a word or an expression of what is perceived. As such it remains in the mind. But appetite goes out of the mind back to the thing itself. It is a response to the thing in its goodness.

How is this response to be understood? First of all it must be understood as following knowing. Without knowing or consciousness of some object, even if it be only a vague fantasy, we have no appetite. We begin to desire something or acquiesce in it only if we somehow fancy it as good. Even the desire to know presupposes some preconception of truth as good. We may think of appetite as a blind impulse at times, but it is not strictly blind. Appetite is a going after or an aiming at, beginning from a perception of something as good, even if the perception be false. It is even a sending of oneself after, as the middle form of the verb suggests in the classical expression for the good as that which all things aim at: *ephiesthai*. Appetite comes only after some form of integrated consciousness, whether sensible or rational.

But is it enough to say that appetite follows from knowing? Does it follow just casually, so that appetite may or may not come into play with regard to what we know? Or does it follow necessarily, so that willy nilly appetite does come into play with regard to everything we come to know? All human activity starts from caring or concern, including that of caring or concern for the truth. But this caring or concern does not stop with just learning. It is enhanced by learning, which only gives rise to a new dimension of caring and concern with regard to what is learned. Is there not some care about anything we do come to know? Is there not some necessary response to what comes to be known in any new awareness? The response may not be determined to go one way or the other. It may be one of acceptance or one of rejection or even one of indifference. It may be free. But even in freedom it is still necessary in the sense that some response is inescapably called for or some attitude is inevitably adopted with respect to what we are newly aware of.

Appetite is thus a responsibility that cannot be avoided. We become fully responsible only for what we do freely. We may choose some particular responsibilities over others. But we do not choose responsibility itself. We only find ourselves responsible in the response that follows any awareness of some good. It is in this sense that appetite is an impulse, though it is not blind. And it is from this necessary connection between appetite and knowing that we pass from the conception of being as true to the conception of being as good, for the necessary response we experience to any new knowledge of being is but a relating to being in the appeal of its goodness. The good is thus what we send ourselves after in the opening where we stand and where being is opened up, not only as present, but also as appealing in this relating. The essence of good is thus, like the essence of truth, a relating that, after standing in the open adhering to something open as something open, surges across the opening, so to speak, in response to the appeal of what is opened up in knowing.

We should note also that this relating to the good through appetite is not merely desire or a striving after something that is not yet possessed. To the extent that the opening in the relating implies a distance, appetite has the form of a desire or a striving after, as I crave food that I see but that I have not yet consumed or for a friend who is on my mind but absent. But it is the very same appetite that finds satisfaction in consuming the food or in enjoying the presence of the friend. Appetite does not cease with satisfaction or enjoyment. It simply finds fulfillment and acquiesces in the good. Without some sense of acquiescence, which somehow closes the distance in the opening where we stand in desire, there would not be any sense of desire, which implies some deprivation as well as distance. We have desire only if we can think of satisfaction, and the satisfaction is simply the passage of appetite from deprivation to fulfillment. Desire as appetite simply continues in its fulfillment through acquiescence. Satisfaction of one desire may give rise to other desires, but as the satisfaction of a desire it is the most perfect exercise of an appetite.

Appetite is thus an alternation of striving and acquiescing. It cannot be both at once. For when one is striving for something one cannot acquiesce in it and when one is acquiescing in some good one is no longer striving for it. But it is in the acquiescing that one best appreciates what the good really is. To know the good in this way is to know it better than we knew it when we were only desiring. To leave acquiescing out of appetite therefore is not only to cut appetite short but also to leave out what is most essential in the conception of the good. Even if we try to think of desire itself as the highest good, as we sometimes do when we think of the absence of desire as an absence of life and true existence, we are only thinking of desire as somehow fulfilling and as something to be acquiesced in. Desire itself is in this sense already a beginning of fulfillment and acquiescence.

If we think of appetite as a response in the opening where being discloses itself, we have to think of being itself as somehow appealing. Appetite, like knowing, emerges in the opening where being is disclosed. Truth is the disclosedness of being in this opening. It is a relating *(Verhalten)* that stands in the open and adheres to something open as something open, as we saw with Heidegger. But in this relating we find more than just disclosing. We find also a response to an attraction or an appealing of being that draws to itself or elicits care of some kind on the part of the knower. We not only care to know, we also care about what we come to know in response to its goodness.

Appetite can thus be seen as an effect of the good in human being, just as knowing can be seen as an effect of truth. If there were no good in being itself, there would be no appetite. If there were something that is not in any way good, there could be no appetite for it, no caring about it. But in speaking of being as good, we are saying that there is no being about which there is no caring. We are affirming what we have to refer to as an ontological goodness of every being insofar as it is. We do this not so much on the grounds that we happen to find some particular being desirable, whether that of another or our own, but more precisely on the grounds that we cannot think of any being except as appetible, as we shall argue in speaking of the acknowledgment of goodness in all actuality. To say that everything is good as being is not just to express a figment of our appetite, as Spinoza would have it in his Ethics of Absolute Substance (*Eth* Part I, Appendix). It is to recognize the necessity of goodness in being itself.

8.2   The Goodness of Essence

This is not to say much yet about the particular goodness of anything. But it is to affirm a certain goodness of essence in its very being and it is to open up a whole new perspective on being which the conception of truth alone does not give us, a perspective in which something can appear as good, bad, or indifferent in relation to some conception of goodness. This perspective remains to be articulated analogously, in keeping with the analogy of being itself, but in differentiating the good from the true as a property of being we are opening a new line of articulation in the analogy of being according to its difference, the line Platonism was more inclined to consider than Aristotelianism.

We are not saying that all beings are equally good or of equal value, for there remains a whole differentiation of goodness to be worked out, just as there is a differentiation of being on which to reflect. But we are saying that in every being, whatever it is, there is some ontological goodness. If we are repelled by one form of being, it is not because there is no good in that form but rather because we are more drawn by some other form. If we think of something as bad or evil, it is because we think of it as lacking a form or some good it should have. Our conception of the good appears phenomenologically through the twofold act of desiring and acquiescing, but it appears this way only because appetite itself is a response to the appeal of being as it discloses itself in truth. It is being that appeals in the disclosing and we come to think of being itself as good in our responding to the appeal.

8.3   Goodness and Perfection

It is not our task here to begin articulating the differentiation of ontological goodness as one might do in a discourse on ethics or a metaphysics of the different degrees of being or goodness. But it is our task to reflect upon one way in which the conception of the good differs from the conception of being, even while thinking of the good as convertible with being. Our conception of ontological goodness emerges through our responding to the appeal of being that we call appetite, as we have said. We might think of this response, which is rational as well as sensible, as most fundamentally an acquiescence in being itself as being. I acquiesce in being for what it is, which is not to constitute its goodness but to acknowledge it. But acquiescing in this way does not bring out an important difference in our conception of goodness that sets it off from our conception of just being as being or, better still, it does not bring out the dynamic aspect of our first conception of being as what relates to action.

This difference can be seen through the relation between the two sides or the two acts of appetite, which remains for us desire as much as acquiescence. If we think of appetite only as acquiescence, we are left with a conception of the good that is flat and undifferentiated. The good is whatever we acquiesce in. But is the good we acquiesce in all the good there is or is there some other good that we might also acquiesce in but that we can only desire at present? The thought of some higher good than that in which we presently acquiesce has to occur to us as long as we remain beings of desire as well as of acquiescence.

Thus, to think of the *good simply* we would have to think of a good that leaves nothing more to be desired, a good that would be totally satisfying and fulfilling. Anything short of that would not be good absolutely, or at least would not be *good simply,* but only good *secundum quid.* We could not think of any thing we do acquiesce in as simply bad, or not good in any way, since we do acquiesce in it. To acquiesce in anything is to enjoy it as good. But when there is still desire, along with the acquiescence, then we do not think of the present good, that in which are acquiescing, as *simply good,* but only as good in some respect, namely, in the respect in which we presently acquiesce in it.

Thus, the being that we know immediately can come to be thought of as good, insofar as it satisfies some appetite, but not as *good simply,* insofar as it does not satisfy all appetite. In other words, we can think of something as *being simply* without thinking of it as good simply. We can still say that every being is good ontologically, insofar as we can acquiesce in it, but we do not have to say that whatever is is good simply insofar as the being we acquiesce in leaves room for desire or striving. When we think of something as good simply or without qualification, we think of it as leaving nothing to be desired and as giving rise to full acquiescence without any further desire.

Whether we can ever experience such full acquiescence in any being or whether there is any being that can give rise to such full acquiescence remains to be seen. In any event, the conceptions of being and of the good remain essentially intertwined even in this difference between them. The being that we would think of as most fully satisfying would be the one that *is* most fully. On the other hand, even that which is not fully satisfying can still be thought of as *being simply,* though it is not *good simply* or fully satisfying. It is the conception of a good that is absolutely satisfying that is difficult for us to entertain. How can full acquiescence in such a good be understood as long as we remain beings of desire? It seems that every acquiescence only gives rise to renewed desire.

The idea of a full acquiescence and of an absolutely satisfying good can nevertheless be illustrated in some particular order of goodness where we can experience a fullness of acquiescence in some respect. Maturity and

health in a living organism, for example, can be thought of as such an acquiescence, and the good in such an acquiescence can be thought of as fully or
even most satisfying. Maturity and health are an absolute good, so to speak,
for the organism, though we still have to qualify this good in relation to other goods or to other orders of appetite and achievement. Nevertheless, with
reference to the organism, they are good simply and without qualification,
since no higher good can be thought of for that organism as such. Maturity
and health leave nothing to be desired in the nature of this organism. If they
could be maintained to perfection over time the organism would have
nothing to desire as organism. It could only acquiesce in its own goodness.

The same idea of fullness can be illustrated in other orders of appetite as
well. To get to the idea of a fullness without any limitation whatsoever, an
absolutely absolute goodness, so to speak, we have only to think of a good
that would satisfy all possible desire. This is the ultimate meaning of goodness in its transcendentality. On the one hand, it expands our conception of
being beyond what is merely disclosed in the opening where we stand as
open to what is open. But, on the other hand, it only enters into the expanded conception as that aspect of being in its appealing to which appetite
relates. Goodness itself, like being, has its differences which give rise to different appetites, rational as well as sensible, according to the different kinds
of consciousness from which appetite can begin, so that a total conception
of the good has to include an ordering of these appetites in their relation to
the good in all its differences.

Hence though we think of every being as ontologically good in its present appeal, we do not think of it as simply or absolutely good, but good only
in some respect as being. Good though it is in its being, it may still have
some good to achieve or be desirous of such good. It is in relation to these
two sides of goodness that the idea of *perfection* arises along with that of
goodness. In its relating to appetite, the good appears as that which fulfills or
makes it perfect. This is especially evident in human being, which is good in
its being according to its first perfection or natural form, but which also still
has to achieve its goodness or second perfection through its own activity.

In a being that has to achieve its ultimate goodness, *being simply* and *being
good simply* are not the same. The being may be already good insofar as it is
actually, but it is not yet good simply, insofar as it has yet to achieve its more
complete goodness, its own perfection or its goodness simply, through its
proper activity. The appeal of goodness in being calls for more than the fundamental or ontological acquiescence in being simply according to one's
first perfection. It calls for an achievement of goodness that is to come as

fulfillment of what already is simply, so that the idea of ontological perfection is integral to the idea of the good as we have it through appetite seen as both acquiescence and desire or striving. The same relation also allows for an idea of imperfection and defection in the beings for which the same twofold appetite of acquiescence and desire or striving holds. A being may be good or perfect insofar as it is actually, but still be imperfect or deficient with respect to the second perfection it should have or ought to achieve through its proper activity.

We are accustomed to think of perfection rather statically, much as Plato thought of the Good. In modern philosophy it is often thought of as pertaining only to God, whose idea is that of "Most Perfect." But this is not where or how the idea of perfection first occurs to us. It occurs first in our experience of appetite as both desire and acquiescence with reference to being in the concrete, and it is illustrated through particular instances of fulfillment such as the one we alluded to with reference to an organism.

Etymologically speaking, not to say ontologically speaking as well, the idea of *per-fection* presupposes a kind of dynamism, a coming to be, which may not be strictly applicable to God, who is thought of as immobile in his eternal being. What is *per-fect* in the strict etymological sense is something that has come to be and has reached a certain completion in its identity as a being, so that what has not come to be cannot properly be said to be perfect, or perfected. As Aquinas puts it, "*quod factum non est, nec perfectum posse dici videtur*" (SG I, 28, 268). What has not come into being or is not a *fact* as the result of a process, cannot be said to have come to the completion of its coming to be in what we have called its first perfection. We call this a "perfection" because we understand it as the good that was desired in the process and that is acquiesced in once the process has been completed. We call it only a "first perfection," the perfection of being simply, because we think that this being has yet to achieve its own further perfection through its proper activity. The idea of perfection, as it is first understood, thus implies that what is perfect has come to be such and that what it has become is not just a termination of the process but an end, its *telos*, desired and acquiesced in, in short, a good, even if it is only the good of being simply prior to any further achievement of goodness or perfection.

The idea of perfection is thus the same as the idea of goodness as goodness relates back to a process of coming to be that has come to some completion. That is the point of adding the preposition 'per' to the perfect participle of the verb 'fieri' or 'factum esse.' It expresses the idea that something has come *through* to the end of its coming to be and is a totality in identity, something *totaliter factum* (Blanchette 1992, 41–73). As such, a thing is understood as already good, even when it still has to achieve its own goodness through its proper activity.

8.4   The Acknowledgment of Goodness in Actuality

To argue for transcendental goodness as a property of being we cannot revert back to the exercise of judgment as we have done for transcendental unity and transcendental truth. We have to revert rather to the exercise of appetite that we experience directly as a consequence of judgment and which we had to refer to in formulating our conception of the good to begin with. It is because this exercise of appetite is distinct from that of judgment in the human self that we come to distinguish the good from the true in our conception of being. And it is because the exercise of appetite follows necessarily upon any exercise of judgment that we come to think of being as good, not because we want it to be so, but because we find it to be so as it appeals in the opening where it discloses itself. Just as knowing is an effect of being in its truth, so also appetite is an effect of being in its goodness.

What we have to show is that appetite is indeed a responding to the goodness of being itself as it appeals in the relating of goodness. How is this responding to be seen as related to the goodness of being itself and not just as a subjective disposition or a vain desire on our part or from our side of the opening? How is it a response to being itself, so that we have to think of being as good, or of the good as in being and not just as a figment of our mind? How is appetite a response to being itself? How is it an acknowledgment of goodness in the actuality of being?

We have seen how appetite is twofold. It is desire for the good not possessed and acquiescence in the good possessed. It is the relation between these two aspects of appetite that gives rise to the idea of goodness as perfection, that is, as that which brings a process to completion. For, as desire, appetite gives rise to the idea of something needed for satisfaction or fulfillment and, as acquiescence, it gives rise to the experience of satisfaction and fulfillment itself. Our experience of appetite combines these two in such a way that, without some acquiescence, we would have no proper conception of the good as perfecting and, without desire, which can recur even with acquiescence, we would have no proper conception of the good as a perfection to be achieved or aimed at. How does all this relate to the conception of being as good?

8.4.1   Goodness as Second Perfection

Let us think first of the *good simply,* or of the perfection that brings this good, that is, of second or final perfection, since only that which has its ultimate perfection is said to be *good simply.* This good is arrived at only through the activity of a being, so that, in relation to this good at least, appetite appears as a principle of activity, whether as striving or as acquiescing. In this sense the good or final perfection of a being is found in its final actualization through its own action. Short of this self-actualization a thing might be good in some sense, but not simply or without qualification.

To understand this we do not have to presuppose that any being ever achieves some kind of absolute perfection or goodness. We have only to understand the distinction between second and first perfection and understand second perfection as any kind of self-actualization that somehow completes the first perfection of a being. This can be illustrated in our own exercise of appetite. The good for us is not simply what we are given by nature. It is rather what we are to be through our own self-actualization. This is something we aim at or send ourselves after. Prescinding from what that good might or should consist in specifically as ethical perfection of human being, it is possible to see that it will be good in its very actuality, as something that is over and above what we are now, for, whatever that actuality may be, it will be that which we are already going or sending ourselves after and that in which we shall acquiesce as in the fulfillment of our appetite.

What we think of as the good to be achieved through action or as the good simply is thus the actuality we desire and in which we can acquiesce. This does not mean that any actuality is as good as any other. It is still possible to think of some actualities as evil, as we shall indicate, insofar as they do not conform to a true good. But even in the case of evil we still think of the actuality as good insofar as it is something positively achieved. Insofar as it is something it is still good, even though it is in contradiction with the true good.

How the good simply can be at odds with itself in this way depends on the fact that it issues from a free initiative, which can give rise to moral evil as well as goodness, or from a fallible power, which does not always achieve the good its natural development aims at. Frustration itself is a part of our experience of appetite, when the good we achieve is not something we can fully acquiesce in. But even in frustration as well as in evil, if we focus on the actuality achieved as something relating positively to appetite, we see it as good. It is in this relating to appetite that being appears as good. Any actual-

ity of a being relates to appetite in this way, even when it is not fully in accord with all that its appetite aspires to. What every being as active goes after
is its own good through self-actualization, which is the completion of its being or its second perfection. This is understood as good precisely as it relates
to appetite, the desire for some completion in being or the acquiescence in
such completion.

All this applies especially to human being, our primary analogate of being. If we go from this primary analogate to beings with an activity that is
less than rational but still conscious and sentient, the same relating of actuality to appetite can easily be seen to obtain. Other conscious beings too, as
we conceive them, find the good simply or their second perfection in the
exercise of their own proper activity and function.

With beings that lack consciousness of any kind we can no longer speak
of appetite properly, since appetite, as we understand it here, presupposes
some consciousness or awareness of something as good. However, inasmuch
as we can still speak of some proper activity on their part, we can still speak
of a good for them as what is achieved through this activity. We say this because such beings are still active as beings and because activity implies some
kind of inclination or appetite toward some good.

At the limit, only where there is no activity whatsoever, and hence no
fullness of being, will we say that there is no good to be achieved through
self-actualization, just as we said that anything lacking any activity of its own
could not be thought of as being with an identity of its own. Conversely,
nevertheless, to the extent that we shall be able to speak of matter not as being in act, but as being only in potency, we shall think of this being in potency as an inclination, if not as an appetite properly, toward some act as to
its good or its perfection or its actualization, for the act of a potency is all
these things at once, as we shall see more clearly later on.

8.4.2 Goodness as First or Ontological Perfection

Every being that achieves some actuality of its own is thus good, since
such an actuality is the ultimate object of appetite. Appetite, however, presupposes a being already in existence with some degree of completion and
identity that has its own appetite as well as its own consciousness. Is this being in its first identity, prior to any actualization through activity of its own,
also good or is the idea of the good restricted to that of an achieved self-
actualization or second perfection? Can we speak of any being in its very
first identity as a being as already good in some sense, if not in the complete
sense of something that is *good simply* in its full actualization? In other words,

can we say there is an ontological goodness in any being precisely as being prior to any exercise of initiative on its part? If so, then we shall have to say that every being precisely as actual is good in some sense, even though it is not good simply according to the fullness of its self-actualization.

How can we show that this follows from our first understanding of being as it relates to appetite? To answer this question we must reflect on being in its given actuality, for being is given or at hand only in some actuality. Even if this actuality is thought of as in no way achieved by the being itself that is at hand, it is still an actuality, and as such it is a good, something to be desired or to be acquiesced in, at least by the being itself, in the way that a living thing clings to life. It is actuality as such that relates to appetite and that is therefore good, even when it is taken as merely given.

When we speak of being as being as the subject of metaphysics, we speak of it not as possible, but as an actuality that is already something to be thought of as a good or as the first perfection of a potency that yields a being that is somehow complete with an identity of its own, that is, an active identity. To think of being only as possible, as Wolff does, or as pure be supposedly equal to pure nothing, as Hegel does, is not yet to think of it as good any more than it is to think of it as true being. But to think of it as in act, or as actualized in any way, whether as merely given or as perfected through its own activity, is to think of it at the same time as good. *Be,* or the act of being, is thus what everything desires or acquiesces in from the beginning, regardless of how it further actualizes itself in its second perfection or its final goodness. Even in its truthfulness, being is already a good, for the exercise of judgment entails a certain acquiescence in the actual truth of being.

To put this in the reflective terms of a human being, this idea of being as good is clear to me as I reflect on my own being as given to me as it must be clear to you as you reflect on your own being as given to you. Now if I think of you as another being like myself and you think of me as another being like yourself, then we must also each think of the other as also good in its actuality. In other words, neither one of us, in our own given identity, is the only good. There are many such goods relating as otherness in actuality, not only to their own individual appetite, but also to my own or to any rational appetite, which responds to this otherness of the good. For to recognize another as being other in actuality is to recognize it as a good in itself, even though I may not want it as the good for me individually.

This is especially clear when the other appears as another self like myself in the primordial experience of being through mutual recognition. In this we have the very first acknowledgment on an intellectual level of otherness in being or of being in otherness, where each one and the other is known as one and as active. In such recognition, the other is a good equal to my own good in its actuality.

But the same thing is also clear with regard to the recognition of lesser beings, which are also seen as good to the degree of their actuality. I cannot rationally desire or acquiesce in them as I would in a being of equal dignity, since they are not an equal good in actuality, yet I can desire and acquiesce in them in various ways, recognizing their true otherness and identity in actual being. I may want to know them better, so that I may use them better both for their own good as well as for my good or the human good. Once again, it is only at the limit of actuality itself that I stop thinking of anything as good, just as I stop thinking of it as one, active, true, or simply as a being. Otherwise, whatever is said to be in any proper sense of the term has to be thought of as good in its actuality.

To speak of this ontological goodness of any being in its first perfection or actuality is not to say much about the degree of goodness of anything in particular. Nor is it to absolutize the goodness of any particular thing, including that of human being, our primary analogate of being. It is only to recognize different degrees of goodness in a diversity of actuality such as is given to us. The ontological goodness we recognize in the actuality of any being is only relative. It is relative to its own final goodness, to be achieved through its own action, and to the goodness of other beings in their actuality and in their own striving for their final goodness. In fact, as we view a multiplicity and a diversity of beings striving each for their final goodness, we have to say that the goodness of each, given or achieved, is relative to the goodness or the perfection of all taken together as the universe in its actuality. Indeed, it is in this striving that the many and diverse beings come together as a universe.

We have spoken of ontological goodness as first perfection in contradistinction from the second perfection or final goodness achieved through a being's own initiative. To speak of this goodness as a perfection, however, is to suggest another way in which the actuality of a being can be acknowledged as good even as merely given. The idea of *per-fection* in its original sense, as already suggested, implies the idea of a process coming to some completion. What is perfect is what has been perfected through some process. Thus to speak of actuality as a perfection is to say that, even as given, actuality has come to be, and that what is given at the end of the process is a good arrived at that was somehow desired from the beginning, so that it can be acquiesced in as the end that fulfills. Acquiescence is itself a recognition of perfection. Thus, as a thing stands out in being or in its actuality, it stands out as something that was desired in some way and that can now be acquiesced in, even if it still has to achieve its own second perfection. The good, as we understand it, or as perfection, is tied to our conception of change and time, but, taken in its fullness or its ontological proportions, it transcends this particular mode of being and applies to any being as being in any actuality, whether higher or lower than our primary analogate.

8.5   The Possibility of Evil

It remains for us to reflect on how evil is to be conceived in the light of this ontological goodness we affirm of every being. We have already alluded to the possibility of evil in speaking of achieving goodness through self-actualization. How is this possibility to be conceived, if whatever is achieved or actualized positively is somehow good? Is there such a thing as evil and, if there is, in what does it consist? Can it be thought of as a thing of any kind?

The possibility of evil appears in the relation between what we have spoken of as the first and the second perfection of a being. It is only the second perfection of a being that allows us to speak of it as good simply, for a being only in its first perfection as a being is good only *secundum quid,* that is, in respect to its being actual, but it is not good simply, that is, in respect to its complete self-actualization. Evil is the opposite of good, but it is the opposite of the good simply, not of the good *secundum quid,* or of the ontological good as such. The possibility of evil appears first in the transition from first to second perfection when a being is free to choose the form of its own final actualization or when it can be frustrated in the achievement of this actuality. It is in this self-actualization that a certain contradiction can occur between the form a being actually takes and the form required for the good simply of the being.

The being that is simply and is already good *secundum quid* comes to be in a certain way or *secundum quid,* which may or may not be in conformity with what is good for it simply. When it is not in conformity with that good simply, we think of it as having become evil. In its most general sense, evil is this lack of conformity between what a thing becomes, or has become, and what it ought to be for its good. If we can speak of an absolute good simply for any being, we can also speak of an absolute evil for it as the opposite of that good. Such an evil, however, is still only a lack of that good which, in fact, may take many forms, each of which is positive in itself even as it falls short of the good for that being. If there is no absolute good simply for any being, but only relative good, evil is still only a lack of that good and the opposition between good and evil remains somehow absolute as an absence or a privation of the proper good.

Thus, evil is very real. It is even something positive in being, in that what is thought of as evil has a certain form. But as evil it is not a thing other than this positive form that is good in itself. Evil is experienced as frustration or as guilt. It is assessed on the basis of some good that is desired or to be acquiesced in, but it is judged to be only a lack of that good, which may be the good of an individual alone, the good of an order of beings, or the good of all beings in common.

As a lack or a privation, however, evil is not a thing or a being of any kind. In itself, so to speak, it is nothing or, better still, it is a privation of some good and therefore of being of some kind. Moral evil is a privation of moral good due in or to persons. Physical evil is a privation of any form a being should have or be able to acquiesce in according to its nature. In either case, real as the evil may be, it is still only a privation and not a being as such. It is actual only in the sense that the appetite in which it is experienced is actual. It is not experienced as a thing, but as a lack or a privation of goodness in a thing.

While it is possible to speak of physical and moral evil, as we have just done, is it possible to speak as well of an ontological evil as such in a way that parallels ontological goodness, as some authors sometimes try to suggest? If we take being to be good as being, as we are maintaining here, the only way this could be done would be by taking finitude or the limitation of determinate being as evil in some ontological sense, as these same authors attempt to do. But what ontological sense could this make? If evil as such is the privation of good, ontological evil would have to be the privation of being itself, or nothing at all, since actual being as such is at least good *secundum quid*. Nothing as such, however, is neither evil nor good nor being of any sort. The differentiation between good and evil in things presupposes that something is, which, as we have argued, is already a good, though not necessarily good simply or as it should be.

Moreover, finitude or limitation in being, however it is to be understood, is not a negation or a privation of being as such. It is a positive stand in being which is also good, no matter how finite or limited. If we associate negation with finitude or limitation, it is not with reference to being as such, since any finite or limited being is still thought of as being in its finite or limited way. Negation in this instance is with reference to other beings, which a determinate being is not. *This* being is not *that* being. This kind of being is not that kind of being. In either case there is being on either side of the *not* or the limit. Both are beings in a positive way and hence are at least ontologically good. In fact, the kind of negation implied in finitude as such entails no privation on the part of the being that is affirmed positively. Finitude as such speaks not of an absence or a lack, but of a presence that not only is, but is good in its presencing, that is, insofar as it is.

Thus, while moral and physical evil are quite possible and real as part of our experience of being, there can be no such thing as ontological evil, in the same way as there can be no such thing as nothing. To say that some thing is evil will always imply that it is good at least in the sense that it is actually, but that it is not all the good that it should be simply. Even the being who is damned is good ontologically in its first perfection or actuality as a being, though it is not good as it should be in its second perfection. Its damnation consists precisely in the recognition of this privation of a good it should have in keeping with its active identity.

CHAPTER 9

Being as Universe

WE HAVE SPOKEN of four properties of being: one, active, true, and good. Whether there are other properties of being that could be conceived as we have come to conceive these is debatable, depending on whether anyone can think of any more such properties of being precisely as being in its transcendental sense, which includes actual differences of being. With the four properties we do have, however, our first conception of being has developed considerably and can now be expressed in terms of a universe of being. Just as each property is a common mode of expressing being in its transcendentality, so also the idea of the universe is a common mode of expressing being as a whole, that is, as a unity in its diversity. To see this we have only to keep the four properties of being clearly in mind.

In developing our first conception of being through the properties of being we have not sought to express being according to any of its differences or any of its special modes. We have not gone from our primary analogate of being, for example, to other kinds of being. We have focused only on the primary analogate, that is, on human being, while encompassing other beings in their analogy with this one. Given the differences of being as we acknowledge them in the analogy of being, the question arises as to how these differences relate to being in the light of the properties of being. Parmenides, who did not include any differences in his conception of being, still thought of it as some kind of whole that was round and without parts or motion of any kind. While including differences within our first conception of being, we do not abandon this idea of wholeness in being. In fact, our inclusion of differences enables us to speak of parts and motions in being and their coming together as universe through the different properties of being. How does this come about conceptually?

9.1 The Conception of the Universe through Unity in Difference

As we include differences in our first conception of being, we are led to a certain conception of nonidentity or dividedness in being. We then begin with unity as the first property of being, which is taken as a certain undividedness in being or a negation of dividedness. We say: Every being is undivided in itself and divided from every other. From this comes the conception of many beings divided from one another. If we admit a plurality of beings, we can still think of being as one, but in a way that is much more complex and differentiated than Parmenides did. We can think of it as a universe of many and diverse things in some relation of unification. We can also think of each single thing as a whole with a differentiation of parts, as we have already suggested in speaking of being as one even when it is a complex whole.

To speak properly of the universe as a whole made up of many beings, however, we should keep a twofold understanding of division clearly in mind. First there is the understanding of division or nonidentity among a plurality and a diversity of beings, which entails some separation of one being from another. Then there is the understanding of division or nonidentity as it is found in a difference of parts within one and the same being as a complex whole. In general, "division" or nonidentity can mean either one of these two ways of differentiating, but more specifically it should be taken as the first way of differentiating, that is, as a matter of some separation of one being from another, as distinct from the second way, that is, as a distinguishing of constituent parts within a single whole being. As a specific term, "division" refers to the division of one being from another or the division between beings in the plural, each with an identity or a unity of its own. This is the way we shall use the term "division" in this discourse on being as universe. To keep the second understanding of division or nonidentity as applying within one and the same being clearly in mind, however, we shall speak of it only as "distinction" between different parts or constituent principles of one and the same being, not as one whole being divided from another whole being, but as constituent parts of one and the same being that are nevertheless distinct from one another in the sense that one "part" is not the other "part" while the two constitute one single being in its identity. This will be something especially important to keep in mind later on when we come to speak of the intrinsic structure of beings prior to speaking of the communication among them. The idea of distinction, as we shall use it, will not entail any idea of division in the specific sense mentioned here as between one being and another being, even when we come to speak of a *real distinction* between intrinsic principles within beings as we know them in experience or in the direct exercise of judgment.

In admitting division in being, that is, a plurality of beings, we do not abandon the idea of being as one. We only come to think of each being, if there are many beings, as undivided in itself and divided from every other, and of different kinds of being as differently undivided in themselves and divided from others. All this is still to speak very generally of being in its oneness, but it does show how we come to think of oneness in being as a wholeness that is two-sided. On the one hand, we think of any being or each being as a composite of parts in its unity, so that oneness is not thought of as mere simplicity, which entails an absence of parts. In this sense being is not thought of as perfectly one in every case, but as a whole composed of parts. This allows for different degrees of identity or undividedness in different kinds of being.

On the other hand, the idea of these different degrees of identity or independence in different kinds of being gives rise at the same time to the idea of different degrees of interdependence among the different beings, which in turn gives rise to the idea of another kind of wholeness, a wholeness of many and different interdependent beings. Different degrees of independence among beings imply different degrees of dependence on one another, so that all, though many and diverse, are still thought of as one, that is, as a universe of beings rather than as one simple being.

Thus, through the idea of being as one in its differences, we are led to the idea of being as a universe or an allness of being. In positing a plurality or a diversity of beings, we do not stop at positing any one of them in some sort of independent isolation. We go on to see them all as relatively independent and as relatively or proportionately dependent on one another. If a being, as a composite of parts, is only relatively undivided in itself, it is also only relatively divided from every other. As only relatively independent, it is also relatively dependent. For each degree of being, the two, undividedness and dividedness, are proportional to one another as they are to the degree of being.

The lower we go among the secondary analogates of being, the less we find of independence in being and the more we find of dependence on other beings. Similarly, the higher we go, the more we find of independence in being and the less we find of dependence on other beings. In either direction, however, we find a universe of beings in their interdependence. A unity of composition in the structure of limited being implies a correlative unity with other beings.

9.2   Action as Bond of the Universe

This dividedness and undividedness of beings, however, is not just a static juxtaposition of different beings in the universe. To speak of the universe only as an interdependence of beings or as a unity of differences in being is still too abstract. Seen in their plurality and diversity alone, beings are separate from one another. To understand them as universe we must also see them as coming together concretely through action and interaction. Without action and interaction, beings would only stand next to one another, so to speak, in a plurality and diversity, each with its own standing or identity in being according to what it is, but each left apart from every other in its own standing and identity. The unity of beings, or their order, would be purely abstract and quite incomplete as universe. To understand this order of beings in its concrete completion we must understand each being as active at the same time as undivided in itself, for it is through action that a being *comes together* with other beings.

If, as Aquinas argues, "we take away the actions of things, we take away the order of things to one another: for there is no gathering of things that are of diverse natures together into a unity of order except through the fact that some act and some are passive" (SG III, 69, 2447). To deny, therefore, that every being has its own proper action is not only to deny our proper understanding of being as active; it is also to deny that the universe can *come together (convenire)* as a unity of diverse beings. As Aquinas concludes, it is *inconveniens,* that is, contrary to their *coming together,* not only in the loose sense that it is not fitting, but also in the more strict sense that the order of things in their diversity cannot be seen as truly one, that is, as a universe.

Being as universe is thus a coming together *(convenientia)* through action and interaction as well as an interdependence of many and diverse beings. Through its action every being is seeking its own completion as a being or what we have referred to as its second perfection. In a plurality and diversity of beings, however, beings seek this completion in interaction with other beings also seeking their own completion. Together they thus constitute a universe of beings that has its completion in the completion of all the particular beings.

To understand this idea of the universe in its *concrete* order, therefore, that is, in an order that has come or *grown together (con-creta)* out of a diversity of beings, we must not only think of every being as active. We must also think of the action of every being as flowing from its being according to its first perfection in a way that is distinct from this first perfection or from what it is as a kind of being. In being active or passive a being is open to other beings and so can take them in, as it is taken in by them, each without losing its identity as a being. In this way each being, in seeking its own perfection, is at the same time, by reason of the order of the universe, as Aquinas also maintains, seeking the perfection of the universe, which is common to all and the highest perfection of all things given in experience. By distinguishing the action of a being from what it is in its first perfection as a being, we are able to see how each being is maintained in its own identity and goodness even as a part of the common good of the universe.

We are thus led to distinguish two levels of goodness with regard to the universe as such, as we did for diverse beings as such. First, there is the level of first perfection or goodness, which is constituted by the totality of diverse beings conceived simply as being in actuality. This totality is already a perfection in the sense that it is the complete set of all that is, the *universitas rerum*. It lacks nothing of what is, like being as such, or, to put it more positively, it includes all that is and it is already good and perfected *secundum quid* in respect to its being all that there is in actuality.

Over and above this first perfection, however, there is also a second perfection to be achieved through the self-actualization of the constituent parts. What this final good should consist in concretely will depend on the nature of the beings that constitute the universe and on how well they achieve the good they desire. But it is clear that it will be a common good, that is, a good common to all beings in their plurality and diversity, in the same way that being itself is common to all these beings in their different identities.

9.3   Human Being as Center of the Universe

In speaking of the analogy of degrees, or of diverse modes, in our first conception of being in its transcendental universality, we were led to focus on human being as our primary analogate. In order to arrive at the last two properties of being we distinguished, namely, truth and goodness, we had to focus once again on this same human being as that in which all things come together or as that which is open to all things as coming together in it. Truth and goodness are properties of being precisely in this relating of all being or beings to human being as both intelligence and appetite.

This does not mean in any way that truth and goodness, or being in its truth and goodness, are created by human being. The truth that is in human knowing is an effect of being, not a cause, while appetite itself in human being is an effect of being as good. Nor does it mean that human being is necessarily at the summit of being, or the norm of all truth and goodness. Human being remains a mode of being among other modes, higher than some in the transcendental order of being, but also possibly lower than others in that same transcendental order.

However its place in such an order may be assessed ultimately, human being is the being around which our conception of being as given in experience is ordered. Human being, as far as we actually know, is the being in which being discloses itself as truth and to which it appeals as good. Being, or rather beings, come together as universe around this being. It is in relation to this being, our being, that we come to think of all diversely ordered being as a universe of truth and goodness.

Even if we come to think of higher beings than human beings, for whatever reason, we continue to think of human being not only as our primary analogate, but also as our center of being, because it is from this being that we reach out toward all being and around which we gather all being. This is the being that is somehow everything, as Aristotle said (*Soul* 431b19–20), in its being intelligent and sentient, relating thus to all intelligible and sensible being, and it is the being whose reaching out is of itself unlimited or infinite, whether below or above itself. In this reaching out, human being may be responding to an infinite being, which would then have to be a true summit of being other than human being or any other finite being, as we shall see when we come to raise the question of a summit of being. But even in this responding to a possibly infinite being, human being remains the center of the universe in our science of metaphysics as the being in which and to which the different degrees of being disclose themselves.

We think of ourselves as less limited in being than other beings, which we think of therefore as lower beings. And if we think of yet other beings as less limited than we are, we think of those as having a higher degree of being and therefore as more perfect in their actuality than we are in our human actuality. Such higher beings can still be thought of as finite, though they are relatively infinite in comparison to ourselves and other finite beings we know experientially, just as we are relatively infinite in comparison to lower and hence more finite beings than we humans are. In other words, such higher finite beings than ourselves would still be only parts of the same universe as we are along with lower material beings, and they would still only represent different degrees of being in relation to a universe that we would then have to think of as greater than the one we now have to think of in relation to experience, and ultimately as possibly relating to a highest or an absolutely infinite degree of being not known in experience.

In thinking all this, human being is itself somehow infinite or open to such higher infinity, so that it can still be the being around which the universe is ordered as known by us. It is the being that still understands itself as finite, nevertheless, in that it is not all being, so that it is limited by other beings to which it relates as lower or higher than itself, if not as equal to itself. It thinks of itself as part of a universe of being with a diversity and a plurality of beings and it thinks of this universe, such as it may be in all its fullness of diversity and plurality, as relating to itself. It belongs to the universe in its finitude, but the universe with its different degrees of perfection in being enters into it as in a being that is infinitely open to being.

9.4   Analogy and Homology in the Properties of Being

Just as the properties of being enable us to conceive being as universe, so also the idea of the universe enables us to understand what used to be referred to as the "convertibility of the properties of being with being itself." Such convertibility is not merely an interchangeability between being, on the one hand, and the one, the active, the true, or the good, on the other, because that would imply that one, active, true, and good are only synonyms of being. As we have seen, these are not synonyms of being. Nor is the distinction between them and being trivial or nugatory. They are different ideas that express our first conception of being according to its more common modes, as we saw with Aquinas at the beginning of our reflection on these properties of being. To say that a being is one, active, true, or good is not the same as to say that it is a being. These properties express something about being distinct from being as such, even though what they express is not outside of or really distinct from being itself. They are not merely interchangeable with being, therefore, but convertible with it in that whatever is said to *be* in some sense also has to be said to be *one, active, true,* and *good* in a corresponding sense. And conversely, as the idea of convertibility implies, whatever is thought of as one, active, true, or good also has to be thought of as being in a corresponding way. Every mode of being is illustrated in its own proper mode of unity, activity, truth, and goodness, while every mode of unity, activity, truth, and goodness illustrates a mode of being precisely as being.

To speak of being and its properties is thus a form of synthetic *a priori* judgment that opens the way to a metaphysical discourse about being as being, on the condition that we do not reduce any one of the properties to any category of being, as Kant did when he thought of unity as coming under the category of quantity. As a transcendental concept, unity is not reducible to the one that is the principle of numbering. Beyond mere plurality, there is also diversity in which unity is also diversified according to different degrees of identity, such as the difference of active identity between the unity of a human being, that of a dog, that of a tree, or that of a stone. Similarly, activity is not reducible to that of a single kind of being but is diversified according to different degrees of being. Nor is truth reducible to that of one particular science, like that of physical science or mathematics, but it is diversified according to the entire range of being that is to be understood, including being itself in its transcendental analogy, an analogy that goodness itself follows according to the different degrees of perfection in being. This is the idea of the transcendentals that is lacking in Kant as well as in the modern philosophy that he was criticizing and which opens the way to a properly metaphysical discourse about being as being in its transcendentality.

To get this idea in all its fullness, however, we must keep in mind two lines of thought that have been converging in our reflection on these properties. First, we must understand the properties of being as analogous in the same way as being itself is *analogous,* in keeping with its differences. The same transcendentality holds for the properties as it does for the notion of being. If it did not, if any of the properties were univocal in any sense, as Kant's concept of unity is, then something could be predicated of being univocally and being would no longer be thought of as analogous in the strict sense we have tried to signify. Like the concept of being itself, the concept of each property of being has to include the differences of unity, activity, truth, or goodness that are convertible with the differences of being according to the plurality and the diversity of beings in the universe.

At the same time, however, as we think of these differences in the properties of being, we must also think of the properties as proportionate to one another and to being for each degree of being, whether it be the degree of unity, activity, truth, or goodness. This is the second line of thought about properties that comes together with the thought of the analogy of differences in being. If we think of the differences as different levels of being, we must also think of each level as having the same level of unity, activity, truth, and goodness. If analogy represents a kind of vertical line in the transcendental order of differences in being, then horizontally, for each level of being, we must have a kind of *homology* among the properties and being itself. For each degree of being, we must say that there is a corresponding degree of unity, activity, truth, and goodness and, similarly, for each degree of any one of the properties, there is a corresponding degree of being and of the other properties. Without this homology there would no convertibility of the properties with being itself.

We have thus a principle of homology that goes with our principle of the analogy for each degree of being according to its differences. This principle will enable us to argue from the structure of a property such as the activity of a being to the ontological structure of the being itself. This principle will also enable us to think of being as good in different degrees, so that we think of different degrees of being as entailing different degrees of perfection. The universe is the totality of these different degrees of being and perfection that entails its own perfection as a totality or as an order of many and diverse beings.

9.5   The Perfection of the Universe

We have not begun to speak of being in any of its differences. We have been speaking only of the common and transcendental properties of being in its analogy. These properties, as we have said, express our first conception of being in a common way that is in keeping with *ens commune,* the subject of our consideration in metaphysics. To arrive at the concept of the universe, however, as distinct from our first conception of being, we have allowed for these differences of being and have thought of the totality of being as an order of beings in some kind of plurality and diversity.

In thinking of each being in its ontological constitution, we think of it not only as one, but also as active and hence as seeking its own final perfection through its own action. Inasmuch as we think of this final perfection as a second perfection achieved through a being's own self-actualization, we think of the being itself in its original ontological constitution as having a first perfection in its very identity as a being that has yet to achieve its second perfection. How does this translate into the thought of the universe as an order of many and diverse beings?

The universe first appears in experience as an interaction of many and diverse beings, that is, as an interaction of many and diverse beings seeking their own second perfection. As such a totality, the universe is understood as on the way to its second perfection through the action of its constituent parts. We cannot say that the universe, taken abstractly as a set of beings, is seeking its own second perfection, since it is not a being but an order or an ordering of beings. But if the second perfection or the good simply of some of its constituent parts, like the human being, can be identified with the good of the universe as such, or if the good of the universe can be identified with the good of such constituent parts, then the perfection of the universe can also be thought of as having to be achieved through this process of self-actualization of its essential constituent parts.

In thinking of this final perfection of the universe through the self-actualizing interaction of the many and diverse beings as also a second perfection, we are then led to the thought of the universe as having its first perfection in its own ontological constitution or, more exactly, in the ontological constitution of its constituent parts. If we omit the thought of the passage from first to second perfection along with the thought of a plurality and diversity of constituent parts, we are left with Parmenides' thought of being as a totality that is unchanging and purely one. But if we include these two thoughts with our concept of being, as we have been trying to do, we come to the idea of a first perfection of the universe as the totality of all the beings that *are* in their plurality and diversity, the *universitas rerum* that is complete or perfect in that it includes all that is given in actuality, even though its second perfection is still to be achieved through the self-actualization of its parts.

Though it can be said, with Aristotle, that First Philosophy or the philosophy of being as being has to focus first on *ousia* or substance in its ontological constitution, this should not be interpreted as excluding the universe of substances in its totality. If we allow for the differences in the analogy of being, and even for a plurality and a diversity of beings in transition from first to second perfection, our question still concerns the whole of being, as it did with Parmenides. If, as we come to focus on differences as integral to our conception of being, we arrive at establishing a true plurality and diversity of being, as we shall try to do in examining the *structure* of being in Part Four, we shall then have to examine how they remain or become one as being, or how they *come together* as a universe of being, as we shall try to do in examining the communication of being in Part Five. It is the idea of being as universe, mediated by the properties of being, that opens the way to these next two parts of our metaphysical inquiry and ties them together as a reflection on being as being.

PART FOUR

THE STRUCTURE OF BEING

Introduction: Facing the Differences of Being

❧

W E TURN NOW from a consideration of being in its transcendental commonality to a consideration of being in its differences. We have alluded to these differences in connection with the logic and the analogy of being, but we have not yet attended to them directly as adding something to our first conception of being. We have already seen how the transcendental properties of being add to this first conception, but only as common modes that follow being in its transcendental commonality. Now we have to see how differences add special modes to this first conception of being and what further questions arise for metaphysics from this addition.

Differences of being cannot, of course, be separated from being. If we considered them as separate from being, we would have to consider them as nothing. But they can be separated from one another in being, or at least distinguished from one another, for otherwise it would make no sense to speak of real differences in being. *Difference* means that one thing is not another thing or one aspect of a thing is not the same as another aspect of one and the same thing. However we may think of difference in being, we have to think of some kind of otherness *within* being—not of otherness than being, which is nothing, as Parmenides saw quite clearly. Otherness within being, however, introduces the question of a relation between the different "others" in being and how these different "others" relate to one another. Does one have priority over the other? Is one the cause of the other? And so on.

It is in this way that science as an investigation into causes arises, not just for the particular sciences, but also for the universal science of metaphysics. We began with our concern for determining the subject of our science and the method for dealing with this subject. We then went on to elaborate our understanding of this subject on the basis of a transcendental reflection on the exercise of judgment, which led us to the analogy of being. This conception of being as analogous enabled us to inquire into the transcendental properties of being. As we saw from the beginning, however, it is the task of a science to inquire not just into the properties of its subject, but also into its causes, for only through causes or principles do we come to a complete understanding of a subject. This is the part of our task that we are now beginning to address in turning to the differences of being.

We are not asking about the cause of being as a whole. Such a question may come up later, in connection with the summit of being, but we are not yet ready to deal with such a question. The question of causes first arises metaphysically in connection with the differences of being as given in experience and the relation between them. The idea of cause and effect presupposes some kind of otherness in being, where one thing is understood as influencing another, or at least one principle is understood as relating to another within one and the same being. The effect is understood as being, but as being other than the cause, and the cause is understood as cause precisely because it is not the effect. Without this idea of otherness in being there would be no idea of cause and effect in being. In speaking of the differences of being, we are speaking not only about how one thing differs from another or how one principle is distinct from another within one and the same being, but also how they relate to one another or depend on one another.

Causality implies some kind of priority of the cause over an other that is its effect. But this priority must not be understood too narrowly, as it usually is in a particular science. Causality itself is an analogous notion and must be understood in accordance with the various kinds of otherness found in being. There are different kinds of cause, as we shall see, each with its own kind of priority over its effect, a priority that is ontological as well as historical, temporal, physical, or whatever else it might be. It is our task to explore these different modes of causality as we turn to the differences of being, for it is through causes or principles that we account for differences either among beings or within one and the same being. Only through some accounting for the differences within being as we know it in the direct exercise of judgment do we come to the question of whether there is any accounting for being simply as being in its transcendental commonality or in its actuality as being.

In turning to the differences of being we are thus beginning an inquiry into the causes of being. But where should such an inquiry begin? What difference should it focus on first? What determinate being should it attend to first? Given what we have said in connection with the analogy of being, the answer that comes spontaneously to mind is that of our primary analogate of being: the human being. Having focused on human being as our primary analogate, should we not focus on it as the first difference in being to be considered? We have already done this in part in the very fact of focusing on human being as our primary analogate of being or, more exactly, as only our primary analogate, leaving room within our conception of being for other kinds of being in analogy with this one.

But just as we had to warn against anthropomorphism in doing so, so also here we must warn against the danger of reducing metaphysics to anthropology or to a phenomenology of the life-world. In a way human being will be at the center of our consideration as we turn to the differences of being, just as it was at the center of our consideration for the analogy of being. But it is not precisely as human or as the center of the life-world that it becomes the center of our consideration in metaphysics. It becomes the center of our consideration rather as the being that we know best or as the being in which being discloses itself most intimately. In considering the differences of being, it makes sense to begin from this being, not as a specific kind of being, but as a being that exhibits differences paradigmatic for the differences of other beings present in experience.

Speaking more critically, we could say that what we turn to now is the being that we know in the direct exercise of judgment, for it is with reference to this direct exercise of judgment that we first elaborated the structure of our notion of being. After insisting only on being in its commonality even as it is known in this direct exercise of judgment, we are now turning to the difference that is disclosed in the selfsame exercise of judgment. What I say is, is a *this* and a *something* or other. The *this* may be myself or Socrates, both of whose *something* is to be human. But it may also be my dog, whose *something* is not rational, or my pet rock, whose *something* is not even living. These are differences that I recognize in the direct exercise of judgment and that can be spoken of generally as differences of being even though human being remains our primary analogate of being. In fact, they are differences that are defined in relation to human being when we speak of these different beings as either nonrational, or nonsentient, or nonliving, respectively. But as differences of being they can be spoken of commonly as applying to the beings or the different kinds of being that are disclosed in the direct exercise of judgment or experience.

Human being, however, happens to be the most prominent kind of being for us in this realm of disclosure, for, though human being transcends the merely sensibly given in its self-consciousness, it is still disclosed as being in an activity that is sensible as well as intellectual or voluntary. Human being is not only geared for and open to the quiddity of sensible things in the direct exercise of judgment; it is itself a sensible thing that exercises such judgment and which is known in this exercise of its proper activity. It is also a sensible thing with feelings that exercises deliberation and choice, another side of its proper activity that also discloses its being as something more than an inanimate thing or a purely sentient animal.

Thus, even if we say that the being known in the direct exercise of judgment, namely, the sensible thing in its quiddity, is the one we know best and is best suited for our understanding of being in its differences, we can still focus on human being as our primary analogate, since human being itself is such a sensible thing. In fact, it is the sensible thing that gives us the best access to differences of being as such because it is the being we know most intimately through an activity that is our very own at the same time as it is that of a being, our being. It is in human being that being first discloses itself not only as being, but also in its very differences, as our reflection will bear out.

What differences, then, must we attend to as the differences of being? In a sense, all real differences are differences of being, those that are accidental to a being as well as those that are substantial. But it is not for any science to go into all the differences that might affect its subject in particular, as it is not the task of anthropology to examine what difference race or profession makes in relation to one another or to being human. These may be important differences for an individual human being for all sorts of practical reasons in certain societies, but they do not pertain to what it is to be human, which is the primary concern of anthropology. So too with metaphysics, even if its subject somehow includes all real differences, it does not have to go into all the particulars of these differences or account for all these details in particular. It has to do only with differences as differences of being, that is, with differences that are essential to being as such in its disclosure, and it has to account for such differences in terms of being itself, that is, in accordance with what we shall call "principles of being."

There may be many differences of being as such, but here we shall begin with those that are common to being as we know it in the direct exercise of judgment or in experience. This includes, first of all, *becoming,* which is the most fundamental kind of difference and which seems to affect beings as we know them most commonly. All beings that we do know are becoming in one way or another or are part of a real becoming. How does this becoming relate to their being? Or how is their being to be understood in the context of this becoming? Can we account for this becoming through being or must being itself be accounted for by becoming?

Along with becoming there is also the difference of *multiplicity* in being.

In the direct exercise of judgment, we do not speak of only one being, as Parmenides did, but of many beings. How is such multiplicity to be accounted for metaphysically or in terms of principles of being? Can it be understood independently of becoming or is it intimately tied with becoming as such? Is the principle of multiplicity the same as the principle of becoming or is it some other principle of being? If it is the same, how does it account for both multiplicity and becoming at the same time?

Beyond mere multiplicity there is also the difference of *diversity* in things. In the direct exercise of judgment we speak of different kinds of being, some living and some nonliving, some sentient and some nonsentient, some rational and some nonrational. There can be many individuals of the same kind. But there are also diverse kinds of being, some more perfect or more accomplished and some less perfect or less accomplished, or capable only of lesser activities. How is this to be understood in terms of being? What is the principle of this diversity and how does it allow for these different degrees of accomplishment in being? How does it affect our very conception of being according to different degrees of perfection?

Finally, there is *finitude* itself as the ultimate difference of being. Our first conception of being, as being, does not express any sort of finitude. It is neither definite nor indefinite. It expresses no special mode and, as such, it is simply infinite in its universal transcendentality. But this is not being as we know it. The being we affirm in the direct exercise of judgment is always a *this* or a *that* and of this kind or that kind. This here ends at that there, or is rendered finite by that, while one kind of being has its limit in another kind of being, of which it is not the same kind. A dog is not the same as a tree, nor is a tree the same as a carbon molecule. This is true even of the highest kind of being that we know directly, the human being, which has its limitation in lesser kinds of being as well as in its own thisness. Each kind, however, is thought of as being in some degree or as having its own stance in being. How is this to be understood? How is the seeming infinity of being as being to be reconciled with the finitude of being as we know it? How does finite being take its stand in being, so that we can truly speak of many and diverse things in a universe of being?

These are the questions we must contend with in our consideration of the differences of being and how they are to be accounted for in terms of principles of being. After considering becoming as such in being, we shall consider two different kinds of becoming, one we shall call "accidental" and one we shall call "substantial." This will bring out why metaphysics must focus primarily on substance in being, as Aristotle claimed, and on the principles of substance in being. Having elaborated on these principles of sub-stance as we know it in the being of direct experience, with reference to which we first come to judgment, we shall then turn to the final and most difficult question for this part of our inquiry: How is be or the act of being to be understood as really distinct from the finite essence of which it is the act without being separate or separable from it? How is this act to be differ-entiated from the pure potency of mere matter and how is an essence, which is already understood as the actuation of a potency in matter by a form, to be understood as still in potency to this act of being?

Before we can come to this ulterior question, however, we must begin with a more direct consideration of becoming, which, as we shall see, is itself an actuation of potency in matter by a form.

CHAPTER 10

The Principles of Becoming in Being

D IFFERENCE IN BEING can be understood in diverse ways, as when we speak of diverse kinds of things like human beings, dogs, trees, and rocks, or as when we speak of different individuals of the same kind, like John, Jane, and James, each a human being in its own standing. These are differences that refer to beings divided from one another, each with an identity of its own. But there are also differences that can be understood as pertaining to one and the same being in its identity even as divided from every other and undivided in itself. This implies that such an identity is not absolutely simple, but rather has within itself some kind of otherness or complexity. Something in it is other than something else in the very same being.

This otherness within one and the same being can also be understood in diverse ways. Synchronically, it can refer to different sides or aspects of one and the same being, as when I distinguish between my intelligence and my will, or between my mind and my body, all of which are part of my being even in differing from one another. Diachronically, however, otherness can also refer to a difference within one and the same being or even within one and the same aspect of that being, as when I become physically sick, which I was not before, or learned, which I also was not before. Being sick, or having become sick, and being learned, or having become learned, are something other than what I was before in my standing as a human being. To the extent, then, that becoming occurs within one and the same being, it can be thought of as the most fundamental kind of difference in being and as that kind of difference that must be accounted for first.

It is possible to distinguish between different kinds of becoming, as we shall do between accidental change and substantial change, once we have established a distinction between accident and substance within a being. But it is not necessary to do that yet. Nor is it advisable at this point. It is better to deal simply with the question of becoming as a whole or as a change in being, because that is where the entire question of difference in being has its beginning. The first question for us, as it was for Parmenides, is: How can there be change in being and how can it be accounted for in terms of being itself? If it cannot be accounted for in terms of being, then it will have to be set apart from being, as some sort of untruth or false being, as it was for Parmenides. Only if we can account for this most fundamental differentiation in being can we go on to speak of the other differences of being that we have alluded to.

The question of becoming can thus become the most radical question of metaphysics, as it does in Whiteheadian philosophy, even to the point of displacing the question of being as the proper subject of metaphysics. If there is becoming and if becoming is seen as a trait of all things we know, then is it not becoming that is most common in reality rather than being? The suggestion is intriguing because it entails recasting the entire subject of metaphysics so that it will no longer be *ens commune,* as we have maintained from the beginning, but some sort of *fieri commune,* or what Whitehead refers to as "process in reality" (Whitehead 1929). But can the subject of metaphysics be recast in this way and what would be the consequences of such a recasting for the science itself as a whole?

The attempt to do so goes all the way back to Heraclitus, who can be seen as opposing Parmenides in his original casting of the question by insisting on flux rather than being. Everything is in flux, he is alleged to have said, meaning that all things give way—*panta chorei (Crat* 402a). This gives the appearance of setting the idea of being aside as that which intelligence first conceives and as that to which every conception is ultimately resolvable as to the first, a point we made in establishing the subject of metaphysics in terms of being as being. But such is not the case, even if we agree with Heraclitus that all things give way or with Whitehead that reality as we know it is fundamentally process. To be sure, what is being set aside is a certain fixed concept of being, which seems to have been what Parmenides had in mind in opposing being to becoming. But strictly speaking, being is not opposed to anything. The only thing that can be opposed to being is nothing, which, of course, is neither a thing nor an opposite of any thing. Opposition can only be thought of as something in the realm of difference within being. Instead of the fixed Parmenidean idea of being, we have insisted not on becoming or flux as such, but on the analogy of being itself according to both meaning and be, which allows for, or rather begins from, differentiation within the very concept of being.

Being is what we first conceive in the direct exercise of judgment not as fixed or as set apart from difference, but as differentiated in its very analogy. Even with this differentiation, being remains both a common concept and our first concept to which all differences, including becoming, are reduced in the sense of being brought back. As a difference of being, or even as the most fundamental real difference in being, becoming cannot replace being as the proper subject of metaphysical reflection. It can only be conceived as a difference in being and hence as what might be only a particularization of being to which other particularizations might be opposed, such as that of fixity or even that of substance as opposed to pure process. To be sure, becoming is a kind of differentiation that a metaphysics of being has to contend with, as we shall try to do in what follows, but it can be conceived only as coming under the conception of being precisely as being, which is the only proper subject for a metaphysics of being. It is being that encompasses difference and becoming, and not difference or becoming that encompasses being. It is not being that has to be accounted for in terms of becoming, but becoming that has to be accounted for in terms of being. How is such an account to be found? That is the question that Parmenides could not answer, but that Aristotle did answer in a way that has remained unsurpassed since he first raised the question in the first book of the *Physics*.

10.1   The Idea of Coming to Be and Ceasing to Be

Let us begin with the very idea of becoming, which is often not only distinguished from being, but also opposed to it. Heidegger, for example, speaks of "this distinction and opposition [*Entgegensetzung*]" between being and becoming as "standing at the beginning of the inquiry into be" and as being "still today the most current limitation of be by something other; for it comes immediately to mind from a representation of be that has hardened into the self-understood" (*Einf* 103/81). This is said in terms of Heidegger's own understanding of the question of being as the question of be. But we must ask: What is this representation of "be" that has hardened into the self-understood? Is it the conception of being in the concrete that we say is the first in our intelligence and from which our own inquiry has begun? Or is it an abstraction from that first conception fixed in some kind of opposition to any other-than-being, no less fixed in its opposition to being, even as becoming?

Our first conception of being cannot be hardened into a representation that is self-understood apart from becoming or any other difference of being. We first signify being according to a mode of concretion, as a *this* or a *that,* and of composition between be and an essence, not purely as be. What we refer to is a being with differences that include becoming, if that is how being presents itself in experience. These differences, including becoming, are not understood as opposed to being, but as contained in it.

To speak of becoming as the opposite of being is to speak of it as nothing. This is what Parmenides did when he reduced all opposition to that between "is" and "is not." Caught in this opposition, he was bound to deny all reality to change or, more exactly, to see it as not pertaining to being in any way. Heraclitus is often thought of as having taken a stance that was the exact opposite of this. For him everything was in flux or in becoming, presumably as if flux were opposed to being or as if being had to be thought of as inflexible or as unchanging and unchangeable. But was this really the thought of Heraclitus, or was Heraclitus speaking simply of becoming as something fundamental to being as we know it in experience? If being in its concept is common *(xunon)*, as Fragment 2 of Heraclitus suggests, can it not accommodate strife and opposition at the heart of everything? Could we not say that Heraclitus was beginning to introduce analogy into our first conception of being as fixed by Parmenides?

To be sure, we cannot think of becoming without some kind of opposition or otherness. But this is not opposition to or otherness than being. It is opposition or otherness within being, which is itself common in the very otherness of becoming, whether the latter is conceived as opposition and strife or not. Becoming entails a difference of standings in being. What comes to be is not what used to be. But this is a difference of being or an otherness in being, not in opposition to being.

What, then, is this otherness that becoming represents in being? To conceive becoming properly, we must think of a standing in being that has come to be. Such a standing has to be thought of as something positive and as different from or other than what was before. In other words, the concept of becoming hinges on a standing in being understood as new and as the end of a process or a movement. This new end of a process is referred to as the *terminus ad quem* of the becoming. Without a proper focus on the *terminus ad quem* of a process, we cannot properly conceive becoming of any sort. Coming to be cannot be understood except as coming to be something *determinate.* Even if this something determinate is not an absolute end of becoming, so that becoming can continue after it, the becoming that we try to understand can be understood only in terms of something that has come to be at some point and that represents a standing that differs from what was before. We understand water as having become hot only by understanding it as having reached a certain degree of temperature that is higher than what it was before. We understand a tree as having come to be only by understanding it as having grown where it was not before from something it was not before. Without a clear conception of the heat or the tree as the term of some coming to be, we have no understanding of their coming to be.

We understand becoming thus from the standpoint of some term. We begin from an end in which we can look back on some process. But we understand this term or this end as having come to be only as opposed or contrary to an other earlier state of affairs. Becoming entails a negation of what is or was, in favor of something other or, perhaps more exactly, the recognition of a prior state of affairs as having been negated. We do not understand the term of a becoming without reference to some prior standing in being that was other than what has come to be. In the absence of any reference to some other prior state, we are left only with a fixed representation of a being that leaves out its having come to be. In other words, as Heidegger says, the term of a becoming is hardened into a self-understood standing that is opposed to a no less hardened self-understood standing in being.

To understand becoming is thus to understand flexibility and negativity in being. It is to understand something as new in being, as other than what used to be, and as having come to be such through a process. This idea of process perhaps best expresses in English what the Greeks meant when they spoke of becoming as *genesthai* or *genesis,* from which we have our terms "generation" as well as "genesis." We associate the process with coming, as in coming to be or *be-coming,* but the Greeks thought more of the passing itself from one standing to another as a *pro-ceeding,* a going forth from one thing to another. This was to think of becoming in a very positive way, as we have been doing, but without ceasing to look back on what was negated. It was from this positive view of becoming that the question of accounting for it began to arise among the early natural philosophers.

On the reverse side of this positive view of becoming, however, there is also the negative view of ceasing to be. To understand ceasing to be in its relation to becoming we must think of change as either coming to be or ceasing to be or both simultaneously. Change can be thought of as going or giving way in either direction. Ceasing to be is the reverse of coming to be. If we think of becoming as a *pro-cessing* toward some standing, we should think of ceasing to be as a *re-cessing* from some standing. Proceeding is a giving way to something positive. Receding is a giving way from the standpoint of what was before. Though 'proceed" and 'recede' are spelt differently in English, both stem from the same Latin verb, *cedere,* which can be thought of as either eventuating in some positive result or as a passing away from. Like *ire,* "to go," which expresses a going to that is at once a going from, *cedere* expresses a giving way to something from something. The prefixes *pro-* and *re-,* in Latin as well as in English, each restrict the two-way idea of *ceding* to one of its directions, whether toward something in the case of *pro-* or away from something in the case of *re-*. Thus change is understood as a kind of ceding either way or a *con-ceding* that may be viewed positively in terms of what comes to be or negatively in terms of what ceases to be. In this sense every coming to be of something is at the same time a ceasing to be of something else.

In order to understand becoming as something positive we had to focus on its *terminus ad quem*. In order to understand ceasing to be we must focus on the *terminus a quo* of a change. Once again this term-from-which has to be thought of as some positive standing in being, whether it has come to be or not. But contrary to what we think of as coming to be, we think of ceasing to be with reference to what was and is no longer, that is, when there has been a *re-cessing* from the positive term we began with. Water has cooled off or the tree has died and rotted away. This may be in exchange for something else that has come to be, but from the standpoint of the term we start from it is cessation in being. In every change there is a kind of exchange of terms, so to speak, which we shall have to look into and account for. But for the idea of ceasing to be, it is enough to see how it begins from a *terminus a quo* understood as having ceased to be, for, like coming to be, ceasing to be is understood from its end state seen as an absence of some standing that was once present. Without this reference to some standing once present, an absence is not understood as a having ceased to be.

In sum, then, we must say that to understand coming to be or ceasing to be, we have to have clearly in mind a certain term in relation to which we think of either a process toward some positive standing, in the case of coming to be, or a recess from some positive standing, in the case of ceasing to be. Such a term is a positive presence in being to which an absence of that term is opposed, either before the presence, in the case of coming to be, or after the presence, in the case of ceasing to be.

This is to speak very generally about coming to be and ceasing to be, but it should be understood that such change does not take place or is not understood as taking place except with reference to very particular terms in the concrete, such as this water becoming this hot or this tree growing in my backyard. This is why, in trying to conceive becoming as real or within the concept of being, we must pay particular attention to particular terms in the concrete. To understand becoming in being clearly, it is not enough to think vaguely of flow, as is often done in process philosophy, without refer-

13

ence to a *terminus ad quem,* which has come to be, or to a *terminus a quo,* which has ceased to be. It is in such terms that the differences of being appear as differences of becoming.

10.2   Accounting for Becoming through Principles

As we have just seen, becoming is a change toward some positive standing, whether it be heat, a tree, or a new idea when we change our mind. With this idea of something positive and new coming into being comes also the idea of accounting for it in terms of its beginning, its origin, or its principle. We might say that this is where scientific investigation begins in the concrete, that is, with becoming. This is how it began with the early Ionians. This is the way it still begins in the modern sciences. Recognizing that something new has come into being, we ask whence it is, in order to account for it in its actual being.

Because becoming entails some kind of differentiation or otherness in being, however, the question soon becomes whether the beginning or the origin entails only one principle or several principles. To speak of a principle is to speak of a beginning, just as *principium* in Latin means beginning as well as principle, while the same word, *arche,* in Greek means both beginning and principle. But the beginning from which something comes to be is not necessarily simple. It can be quite complex, just as that which comes to be is also complex. In this way, we may have to distinguish between different principles in the beginning of what comes to be in order to account for the differences that come to be. This is the question we must now examine, for, if becoming entails some kind of opposition between what comes to be and what used to be, can it be accounted for without some contrariety in the principles of becoming?

Among the very first philosophers of nature there were some, like Thales and Diogenes, who tried to insist on only one principle for all things in nature, whether it was water, air, or vapor. But this alone could not account for the diversity of things that come into being. In order to account for diversity, they had to introduce some kind of distinction within this one principle or a distinction of principles such as condensation and rarefaction. Different things came to be by different degrees of condensation in the fundamental principle. Others, like Anaximander, spoke of diversity and contraries as being drawn out of the one fundamental principle, where they were all mixed together and confused. But eventually, after insisting more on the diversity of nature or of things that come to be, most naturalists were led to posit a plurality of first principles that became more clearly differentiated as the cosmos took shape for them. Some posited only two, fire and water, others three, fire, air, and water, until Empedocles came up with four, fire, air, water, and earth, which became the generally accepted number after Aristotle gave a systematic account of the four with their various motions of up or down and their various qualities of hot or cold and dry or wet.

All this, of course, was still a very primitive way of accounting for what comes to be in the universe. But it does illustrate the way of accounting for what comes to be in its diversity. In modern science we have far more sophisticated ways of accounting for what comes to be which go far beyond the reduction to only four elements and some basic qualities attributed to them. Nevertheless, even in this modern science, we find a way of appealing to principles that are contrary to one another in accounting for the diversity of what comes to be in nature. We have, for example, the opposition between positive and negative charges as the fundamental forces of nature and the apparently irreducible difference between mass and energy illustrated in the difference between classical physics and quantum mechanics.

Without claiming that there is any simple correspondence between our modern science and ancient science, we can still see that the question of accounting for what comes to be remains somehow the same and that the way of doing so remains the same in many fundamental respects. Reference is made to a diversity of things in their identity followed by a reduction to principles that have to remain diverse in their unity in order to account for the diversity of what comes to be. It is a general understanding of such principles of becoming that we are seeking here in order to account for this most fundamental difference of being.

It seems, then, as Aristotle concludes from his review of physical theory as he knew it, that everyone arrived at positing some contrariety in principles. Even Parmenides, who said that being is one according to reason, admitted diversity according to the senses and in this diversity posited hot and cold as contrary principles, the first of which he associated with fire, and the second with earth. For the naturalists who posited only one principle in nature, there was still the difference between rare and dense to account for diversity, while for Democritus, the atomist, contrariety appeared in the form of the void and the full as well as in position, figure, and order (*Phys* 188b 19–27). If we include modern physics as arriving at a similar recognition of contrary principles at the origin of coming to be, we can agree with Aristotle that this is indeed well said or *eulogos,* at least as far as it goes.

The question arises, however, as to how precisely such principles are to be understood as principles of becoming. Let us follow Aristotle in his analysis of this idea of contrary principles. To begin with, as *principles,* the contraries must be first: they are not from others, whereas others are from them. There may be all sorts of contraries or differences, some of which may be principles for others, but when we refer to the first contrary principles we mean the first contraries from which all others come to be.

Second, as *contraries,* these principles are not from one another. Hot, for example, is not from cold or dry is not from wet. This implies at least a duality of first principles in becoming.

Third, to have a duality as principles is to have everything else as coming from them. But this must be understood in accordance with the idea of coming to be and ceasing to be with reference to a *terminus ad quem* and a *terminus a quo.* Not anything comes from anything. If I become learned, for example, it is not from being white. My being white is only incidental to my becoming learned. *Per se* I become learned from being unlearned. Similarly, if I were to cease being white, *per se* I would become not something like learned or unlearned, but black or some other color in between white and black. To come to be or to cease to be always includes *per se* the other of what is said to come to be or cease to be in a specific way. It does not include anything else that is only incidental to this *per se* relation or to the particular term of becoming we are referring to.

The same is true of complex things like houses that can also be thought of as coming to be. What a house is is a certain harmony of materials that comes to be *per se* from a disharmony of those materials or some other harmony of the same materials, for example, the way they were stacked in various warehouses. In short, everything that comes to be or ceases to be comes to be *per se* from its contrary and ceases to be *per se* in its contrary.

This is the idea of contrary first principles that had been used by many before Aristotle in trying to account for becoming, though in different ways, depending on whether they proceeded from sense observation or reason in setting up their first contraries. Even in the differences, however, there remained a certain convergence in that all fell back on the same kind of relation or proportion, not to say analogy. All started from some coordination of contraries. All also saw one of the contraries as positive and the other as negative. And, no matter what they posited as the principles, all saw them as accounting for what follows from them in some way.

Following Aristotle still, the question then arises as to whether there are two, three, or more such principles of change or becoming (*Phys, Alpha,* ch. 6). There cannot be just one, since the principles are contrary to one another. Nor can there be an infinite number of them, as Anaxagoras had maintained, since that would be contrary to what they are as principles, that is, as accounting for what comes to be. As infinite, they would be unknowable and none of them could be understood as first in any way or as a point of reference for any kind of *per se* order in coming to be and ceasing to be. In fact, if the order of coming to be and ceasing to be can be accounted for with a finite number of principles, as will be borne out, there is no need to posit an infinite number.

We begin, then, with a need for a minimum of two principles in accounting for coming to be and ceasing to be, no mater how such principles might be understood for the time being. Are two enough? If we view them as contraries, as we have been doing, they cannot be enough, for, as contraries, how can they account for everything else coming from them? We cannot say that one of the contraries will derive everything from the other, for nothing makes anything out of its contrary. It is not in the nature of density to convert "rarity" itself into anything, or conversely. Concord does not move discord or make something out of it, nor conversely. Heat does not heat cold as such, but some other principle that is subject to cold and then becomes subject to heat. In order to understand how two contraries can be principles of becoming, we must come to a *third principle* that is not like the first two mentioned but that underlies or is subject to *(hupokeimenon)* both of them and through which there can be an interchange between them. Without this third principle there can be no accounting for change. This is the principle we shall refer to as the *material principle* distinct from any form seen as coming to be or ceasing to be.

Finally, the question arises as to whether three principles will be enough to account for any coming to be and ceasing to be. If so, then no more than three should be posited. In fact, given the way we have come to these three principles, it would be difficult to suppose that there could be more than three, two formal and one material. We have posited the material principle only in relation to a set of contraries presumed to be first. To posit another material principle other than this first one would require another set of contraries, which would cast into doubt our initial supposition of only one set of first contraries to account for all coming to be and ceasing to be. It is not in the nature of the material principle we have arrived at to be multiplied in this way. We must stop at only one such material principle, along with a pair of contrary first principles, to account for any change. We shall see that, in conjunction with the diversity of determinate forms in nature, this is enough to account for any change.

In his commentary on Aristotle's *Physics,* Aquinas points out that all this is said only dialectically *(disputative)* in relation to what others have thought in accounting for change and through an induction based on different kinds of change in the world *(In Phys* I, 11). It starts from an idea of contrary principles that many, if not all, have taken for granted and it explores the various difficulties connected with such an idea as accounting for becoming only to arrive in the end at the need for positing a third, a material principle, if we are going to stay with the initial idea of contrary first principles. Whether all this is true as a way of accounting for change, and in what sense it is true, remains to be seen or demonstrated in a reflection focusing more properly on coming to be itself as a way of being.

10.3   The Three Principles of Becoming

To understand becoming, as we have said, we must focus on something as the point of arrival for a process, a *terminus ad quem* at which the process is thought of as terminated, at least provisionally. Water has reached a certain degree of temperature. The tree has grown to a certain degree of maturity. As a point of arrival, however, this is seen in contrast to a point of departure, a *terminus a quo* from which the process began. At some point the water was cold, from which it became hot, or the tree in my backyard was not there or was only a seedling. The water is understood as having become hot by going from cold to hot. The tree is understood as having become this tree by going from a seed to what it is now.

But what precisely is understood as having come to be? Is it just heat *as such* or treeness *as such* or is it a composite of these with something else? Let us reflect on the example of someone like myself becoming learned. I understand this as a becoming only once I have become learned in some respect, say, in the history of philosophy. Until then I cannot refer to a real becoming in this respect. But once I have become learned in the history of philosophy and I begin to think about this term of becoming, I do not think only of the being learned in the abstract, but of myself as being learned or as being perfected in learning. I include myself in the term of becoming as well as the new form of learning. What has become is a composite of learning and myself. Similarly, when water has reached a certain degree of heat, what has come to be is a composite of heat and water. In the case of the tree that has grown in my backyard, the kind of composition in the *terminus ad quem* is more difficult to express, but it is analogous to that between my learning and myself and between heat and the heated water. We shall say more about this kind of becoming later on. For the moment let us just say that it is a composition of a tree, or the form of a tree, that is new with a material principle as its subject.

Here let us concentrate more on this idea of a *subject* in becoming as illustrated in myself becoming learned or water becoming hot. Such a *subject* is crucial for understanding becoming or change. Without a *subject* or some underlying principle found in both the *terminus ad quem* and the *terminus a quo,* there can be no change. There can only be substitution of one thing for another, not properly a becoming. When I become learned in some respect, it is I who become learned. There is not just learning that takes place, but learning in me or you, in a subject that is, who from being unlearned becomes learned. Similarly, there is not just heating, but the heating of something like water or some other subject that, from being cold, becomes heated. This subject is part of the composite, not just in the *terminus ad quem,* but also in the *terminus a quo.* Unlearned *I* become learned *I.* Cold water becomes hot water. If there were no subject of learning, there could be no call for examining individual learners, since learning would then be thought of as detached from any learning subject, nor would there be any learning in reality, since there is no learning without a subject who learns. If there were no subject of heating such as water, there would be no preserving of heat even for a moment.

The presence of such a subject in becoming is made clear in the very way we differentiate between "coming to be from" and "becoming." The two expressions are not completely interchangeable when we speak of becoming or coming to be, as Aristotle points out (*Phys, Alpha,* ch 7). We speak of coming to be *from* only with regard to the opposite from which the becoming is understood to have begun *per se,* not with regard to the subject. Thus I speak of coming to be learned *from* being unlearned, not from being a man or a learner. With regard to myself as a learner, I speak only of becoming learned. I become learned, but I do not come to be learned from myself. I come to be learned *per se* from being unlearned. Similarly, when water becomes heated, it does not come to be such from being water, but from being cold. It is the presence of a subject or an underlying principle in becoming that forces us, so to speak, into this kind of discernment between coming to be from and becoming.

Moreover, this same presence of a subject indicates a certain permanence in change, while the opposites express what is not permanent. When I become learned, I cease to be unlearned, but I do remain myself. Similarly, when water becomes hot, it ceases to be cold, but it does remain water. It is this permanence of a subject that makes the difference between change and mere substitution of one thing for the other.

This does not mean that permanence is unchanging. Permanence is not the opposite of change. *Per-manent* means that the subject of change *remains through* change. Only in change is there permanence of this kind. It is characteristic of the subject or the underlying principle of change to remain *(per-manere)* as it changes. In other words, remaining is a characteristic of what changes and is itself in the change. I remain myself when I become learned, but I do not remain unchanged. I keep my identity as a self, a self who is improved by learning. Similarly, when water becomes hot, it keeps its identity as this water, but it is changed in its very permanence. Permanence in the subject of change indicates a certain readiness for change, a certain dynamism that is open to new forms and even desirous of them. We shall see more about this in due time.

All this, then, adds up to three principles to account for any becoming. One is the subject of change we have just been talking about. It underlies both the term of arrival and the term of departure as that which remains through the change. This subject is what becomes or comes into being in one way or another. As *subject* it is one, but as a principle of becoming it has to be understood as twofold, itself as the subject that remains and as the opposite or the privation of what is to become. I am myself and I am *un*learned until I become learned. What becomes learned is not just myself, but myself unlearned. Similarly, what becomes hot is not just water, but water that was not hot.

Being unlearned, or the privation of learning, is thus a principle, along with the subject that remains, of becoming learned, at least in the sense that privation comes before learning. Being cold, or the privation of heat, is also a principle, along with the subject, of becoming hot. And these two, the subject and the privation, are principles only in relation to the third, or the term of arrival, from which reflection on becoming begins. This is the learning that is finally attained or the degree of heat that is reached. After the becoming, the subject is now in composition with this new form or it is now twofold in this new way. I am now learned after having been unlearned. The water is now hot after having been cold. In either case, it is one subject that remains through the change while a new form comes forth from its opposite, which does not remain. It is with regard to this opposite that we speak of *coming to be from,* while we speak of the subject as that which *comes to be* with a new form.

These three, however, are not all principles of becoming in the same way.

To be sure, all three have to be understood in any coming to be, but they have to be understood differently in relation to what comes to be. Only two are constitutive of what comes to be, the subject and the term of arrival or the new form of what has come to be.

This becomes clear if we try to define or say what has come to be. We cannot mention just the subject alone, since that would leave out the very term of becoming. Nor can we mention only the new form alone, which is the term of becoming, since that would leave out what becomes or has become. In saying that I have become learned, I cannot speak only of myself without including the learning. Nor can I speak of the learning without including myself as the one who becomes learned. Similarly, in saying that water has become hot, I cannot speak only of the water without including heat, nor of heat without including the water. What comes into being is thus a composite of two such principles that account for its final way of being.

Moreover, these are not only principles of its becoming. They are also principles of its being, since we are speaking of a being that has come to be. In things that come to be, being is not something apart from becoming. It is what *comes to be*. This is why we can speak of these two principles as ontologically constitutive of what comes to be in the same way as Aristotle speaks of them as *per se* principles of what has come to be (*Phys, Alpha,* ch. 8).

What, then, of the other principle that we have distinguished in our accounting for change: the opposite of the form that has come to be, or its privation? In what sense is this a principle of what has come to be, if it is a principle at all? It is not constitutive of what has come to be, as the two *per se* principles we have just distinguished are. And yet it is essential in accounting for change and for understanding coming to be as *coming to be from.* Of itself this other principle is negative, but as accounting for a determinate change it is a determinate negation. With reference to learning it is *not-learned,* which has no name, and with reference to heating it is *not-hot,* which has the name cold. How is such negativity essential in accounting for change?

We should note that form and *subject,* the two *per se* constitutive principles of what has come to be, are not enough by themselves to account for change as *coming to be.* It is entirely possible to think of a composite of form and matter without thinking of it as coming to be or ceasing to be, as Aristotle did, for example, with regard to the heavenly bodies. For him, the matter of these bodies was not affected by any privation, like the matter of bodies we have an immediate experience of that do come to be and cease to be.

Of course, he was wrong in thinking that the heavenly bodies did not come to be or cease to be or in setting them apart from the bodies "here below," as we know now. But the example of the heavenly bodies as he thought of them shows that his hylomorphism, his theory of form of matter, as it is frequently presented, does not account for change or coming to be if we leave out privation from the account. What comes to be comes to be only *from* its not being. Without reference to this not-being of what comes to be, or its privation, there is no understanding of coming to be.

No doubt, Aristotle was led to this insistence on privation as a principle of becoming by the idea of contrary principles that he found in his predecessors as well as by the contrariety or the otherness he found in any change. But he did not leave this idea hanging loosely above change, so to speak. He saw it in change itself, first, by distinguishing a third principle besides the two contraries through which they could interchange, and then by focusing on this third principle as the subject of change, as that which comes to be something from not-being that something. It is through this *subject* of change, the *hupokeimenon,* that privation remains as a principle of coming to be, for, in its duality as subject of change, it is subject not only to the form of what has come to be, but also to the privation of that form.

Privation is not a *per se* principle of what comes to be, as the subject itself is along with its new form, but it is a principle *per accidens,* insofar as the subject, in its permanence, remains subject to privation while being subject to its new form. What comes to be learned was at one time deprived of this learning. What comes to be hot was at one time deprived of this heat. It was subject to privation and, as such, it was open or in potency to the new form. It was not mere privation apart from any subject, since that is nothing. It was privation in a subject or in something positive with a dynamic aptitude to a new form, that is, subject to the privation of that form that it has or gets when it has come to be. It is because the subject, as subject of change, was still *only* a dynamic aptitude to the form it acquires in coming to be that we can speak of privation as a principle of becoming, albeit only *per accidens,* that is, as affecting the subject of change, one of the two *per se* principles of what has come to be.

We might add that as long as the subject of what has come to be remains subject to privation, or in potency to other forms, what has come to be can also cease to be or give way to other forms, of which the subject is now deprived. But that would be to begin considering some other coming to be than the one we have been considering. There are further distinctions to be made within coming to be, but before we go into those let us sum up how far we have come in our accounting for becoming.

We have seen that just setting up a dialectic of contrary principles is not enough to account for change. We must come to a *subject* of change in what comes to be that enters into composition with the new form of what comes to be. These two, the subject and the form, are the *per se* constitutive principles of what comes to be, while privation remains a third principle of sorts, *per accidens,* insofar as it affects the subject of change. Contraries remain as part of accounting for change, but the contrariety should be kept where it belongs. It is not between the form and its subject, as is often supposed in modern accounts of hylomorphism. The form and its subject are now one being. Properly speaking, the contrariety is between the form and its privation. The contrariety is in the subject, since it is subject to both form and privation, but the subject itself, as distinct from both form and privation, is something positive. It is not a mere negation of form, nor is it a mere privation or mere nothing. It is potential being, which, as we shall see more clearly, enables us to account for change as *coming to be* and not just as a negation of being.

Finally, we should keep in mind that all this has been said from a reflection that focuses on the form of what has come to be understood as having come to be. As we said earlier, becoming is understood from the standpoint of a *terminus ad quem*. The subject of change that we have distinguished from the form of that terminal standing is understood only in relation to this form or through its proportion to this form. This will be especially evident when we come to speak of the subject of change as pure potency or as lacking any form whatsoever.

As for privation, it has to be spoken of only in relation to the form that has come to be as well, since we have been speaking of determinate negation only, the privation of this form that has come to be, and not of negation in general or mere nothingness. *Coming to be* is not from nothing absolutely. From nothing in this sense nothing comes, as Parmenides saw and as Aristotle and Aquinas both concurred (*Phys* 191a 33ff and *In Phys* I, 14, §5). *Coming to be* is from a determinate nothing or nonbeing, the nonbeing or the nothing of what comes to be in a subject that was something other before becoming what it becomes, whether that be learned, hot, or the tree in my backyard.

Nor is *coming to be* from being as such, as Parmenides also saw and as Aristotle and Aquinas also both concurred (*Phys* 191b 17ff and *In Phys* I, 14, §6).

Coming to be is from some otherness in being or a privation in a subject of change that has to be thought of ultimately as a pure potency, which is neither total privation, or nothing, nor an actual being, but still is something positive in the way that *becoming* is. It is with this idea of *being in potency,* which Parmenides did not have and which we have arrived at with Aristotle, that we can ultimately account for becoming. We must now reflect on how it is realized in different kinds of becoming.

CHAPTER II

Substance as Being-in-Itself in Becoming

Iᴛ ɪs ɪɴ ᴛʜᴇ ᴄᴏɴᴛᴇxᴛ of becoming that the question of substance arises in metaphysics as integral to the question of being. Even if we do not think of becoming as the opposite of being, that is, as nothing or as nonbeing, but rather as part of being, the idea of being itself seems to suggest something more permanent than what only comes and goes, something that underlies change as such. To think of being in this way is to think of being as substance, as distinct from accident, and of the question of being as having to be refocused somewhat in keeping with the new wrinkle that has entered into our concept of being.

We have just seen how becoming can be accounted for in terms of being, that is, in terms of three principles, two that are *per se* constitutive of the being that comes to be, one that is *per accidens,* inasmuch as that which has come to be was not what it has come to be. The key to this threefold understanding of principle in becoming is in the idea of the *subject,* or of being in potency, which is not nothing or pure privation, but something positive oriented to different forms that can actualize it, each of which entails a negation or privation of other forms when it is the actualizing form. Being in potency is thus one as subject of change but many in its dynamic orientation to different forms.

To explore this newly disclosed being in potency, however, we must reflect more carefully on what it is that comes to be and in precisely what sense it comes to be. For we can speak of coming to be in two ways. We can speak of one and the same being as changing in a way that does not take away from its identity, as when we say that Socrates has become learned. Or we can speak of the being itself in its very identity as coming to be or ceasing to be, as when we say that Socrates himself has come to be or ceased to be, not in any particular respect such as coming to be or ceasing to be learned, but simply as Socrates, who was not and now is or who was once and now is no longer.

To focus on Socrates or any other such being in this way is to focus on being in a new way. It is to focus on being as a subject of change that may not change in its identity as to who or what it is, or else may change even as a subject in its very identity, in which case we would have to cease speaking of Socrates or of the being as being itself in its identity before or after the change. To understand this difference in coming to be, which is referred to as a difference between accidental and substantial change, we must interpose some idea of being as substance, or what the Greeks referred to as *ousia,* which is no longer the idea of being in the fullness of its transcendental scope, but being in a more restricted predicamental order as distinct from accidents, being which may or may not come and go.

It is with reference to change that the Greeks seem to have come to their idea of *ousia,* or substance, as distinct from *on,* or being. Substance was understood as referring to the being *in itself,* as distinct from what only affects or modifies such a being. What only affects or modifies being in itself, on the other hand, was thought of not as nothing or nonbeing, which is the opposite of being simply, but rather as being *in another,* as in the case of learning *in* Socrates. In this case Socrates is the being understood as in itself or as substance and the learning is understood as being in another or as accident, in the sense that it accedes to Socrates, no matter how necessary or how good this might be for Socrates. Learning is thus a part of the being of Socrates, since it is his learning, but it is not what Socrates is in himself as a substance.

The idea of substance thus refers to *what* something is *in itself.* This question can be asked of anything that is, as Socrates does when he asks Euthyphro what holiness is in one of the earliest uses we find of this idea of *ousia.* In his answer Euthyphro speaks of holiness only as something that is loved by the gods. "When you were asked what holiness is," Socrates tells Euthyphro, "you were unwilling to make plain its substance [*ousian*], but you mention some accident [*pathos*] about it, namely, that it is loved by the gods. But what the being is [*ho ti de on*] you did not say" (*Euth* 11a 8–10). The question *what?* thus seems to go after something *in itself* in being, and not after what may be just happening to it. It can be asked of something like holiness or learning, which seem to be only in another. In this case one might end up saying that holiness and learning are something in themselves and not just in another in any way, which is true insofar as they are real. But most fundamentally the question is asked of what is thought of as being in itself absolutely and not in another. Holiness or some accidental goodness may be such things in some separate realm of being, as Plato claimed, but not as found in our experience. In our experience, they appear more like accidents, like learning in Socrates, that is, as being *in another,* while substance is that other than accident which is *in itself* and not in another, like Socrates in himself, whatever else he may come to be. Substance is what stands by virtue of itself or in accord with itself *(kath' auto).*

11.1   The Logic of Substance

The idea of substance as it comes up here is closely related to the idea of subject in the direct exercise of judgment in the same way that the concept of being is related to its structure. This is clear from the way Aristotle developed the concept of substance as the first of ten categories by going back to the way of predicating in the direct exercise of judgment.

Aristotle begins by distinguishing between being *predicated of* a subject and being *in* a subject, so that the idea of substance could not be reduced simply to that of a subject of predication in the exercise of judgment. He speaks (1) of things that could be predicated of a subject but were not in a subject, such as man, which can be predicated of a certain man but is not in a subject; (2) of things that are in a subject but are not predicated of any subject, such as the science of grammar, which is in a subject such as the soul but is not predicated of a subject; (3) of things that both are predicated of a subject and are in a subject, such as science, which is both in a soul and is predicated of grammar as its subject; and (4) things that neither are in a subject nor are predicated of any subject, such as this man or this horse, neither of which is in a subject nor is predicated of any subject (*Cat* 1a 20–1b 6).

The difference between (4) and (1) in this enumeration is very important for understanding the idea of substance properly. In (1) there is reference to something that could already be understood as something substantial, namely, the form or the species of an individual, because it pertains to the identity or to *what* a certain thing is of which it is predicated. But it is not substance in the primary sense of the term. Only (4) refers to substance in that primary sense, which is *ousia,* or being-in-itself. Numbers (2) and (3) refer only to being in the order of accidents or being-in-another and need not detain us here, except to note that in all four cases Aristotle is referring to categories of being, or *ta ton onton.* It is only in a *this* or a *that,* which neither is in a subject nor is predicated of any subject, that we find the category of substance in its fullest sense.

Now *this* or *that* is always some kind of a being, such as a human being or a horse, to repeat the examples of Aristotle. But it is not simply as "human" or as "horse" that it is thought of as substance in the first or the highest *(malista)* sense of the term *(Cat* 2a 11–12). Such predicates or what is referred to by such predicates pertain to substance only as giving a *this* or a *that* its substantial identity. Only a *this* or a *that* is the ultimate subject of predication that cannot be predicated of anything else and cannot be in anything else as in a subject. The subject we speak of as substance is not just the subject of a predication, but a being-in-itself that, as Aristotle goes on to point out, underlies all other things, while the latter in turn will be either predicates of this substance or be present in it as in its subject *(Cat* 2b 15–18).

In deference to Plato's idea of the forms, perhaps, Aristotle allows for a second sense of substance, or secondary substances, namely, the species within which the substances spoken of as first are contained and the genera of the species of these substances. For instance, this man or this woman is contained in the species "human" and the species is contained in its turn in the genus called "animal" *(Cat* 2a 13–18). These are the predicates that can be said of a substance inasmuch as they express what it is in itself. The idea of containment used here by Aristotle is similar to that of participation in Plato, but it does not imply any separate being of the secondary substance, the species or the genus, apart from the primary substances, which are clearly material as well as individual. This idea of secondary substance as containing individuals will have some bearing on Aristotle's understanding of the perpetuity of species in being and the cause of this perpetuity, but the perpetuity itself of the species will not presuppose a substance apart from the succession of individuals embodying the diverse species in nature.

Thus, according to our direct exercise of judgment, it is only with reference to a *this* or a *that* that we think of something as a substance, so that we include *this* or *that* as part of our idea of substance just as we included it as part of our concept of being. As merely *this* or *that,* it is inexpressible in any concept, except in the most vague and abstract concept of thisness and thatness, which expresses nothing of *what* the substance is in itself. But substance is not simply as *this* or *that,* without any identity. It is always as something about which we have to ask the question *what?* To ask *what?* of any *this* or *that* is to begin to focus on it in its substance as this can be expressed conceptually and to enter into a disclosure of being in *this* or *that* as to *what* it is. We spoke earlier of action and the underlying thing, which is supposed in any action as the action of a thing. Here we must come to understand this thing as substance or as being-in-itself.

What we refer to as *this* or *that,* which appears only as a subject of predication and can never be predicated of anything else, has in itself *what* it is to be something. It is substance or being in the first and most fundamental sense. But as *this* or *that* it is not a single being, nor is it always of the same kind. To speak of a multiplicity in being is to speak of many substances, which are in themselves. To speak of a diversity in being is to speak of a diversity of substances or of different degrees of being, each with its own mode of being. Each individual substance has an identity of its own, both as *this* and as *what* it is, and so it is one and undivided in itself. But as only *this* or *that,* or as only one kind of being, it is imperfectly one, and so imperfectly divided from every other, so that the many and diverse substances constitute a world of diverse species each perpetuated in a multiplicity of individuals all in interaction with one another. There is not only one substance or only one kind of substance referred to in the direct exercise of judgment, so that the univocal logic of substance must yield to an analogy of *being-in-itself* with human substance as primary analogate.

11.2   The Analogy of Substance

As a category in the predicamental order, substance has to be understood as univocal. It is one of many categories, each with its own demarcation from other categories. As actualized in being, however, substance is not univocal, if we recognize that there is a diversity of substances as well as a plurality of substances in being.

In our dialectic of analogy we spoke of three kinds of analogous terms: one, like health, which is analogous according to meaning but not according to be; another, like body, which is analogous according to be but not according to meaning; and finally the third, namely, being itself, which is analogous according to both meaning and be, inasmuch as being includes all the differences of being even though these are not known distinctly in our first conception of being. If we ask to which of these three kinds of analogous terms substance belongs, we have to say that it belongs to the second and not to the third, which is the analogy of being itself and its properties as being.

Substance is not analogous in the same way that being is because, according to its meaning, substance is not as inclusive as being. As a concept, "being" includes all differences, those of all categories as well as those of substance. As a concept, "substance" does not include categories in the order of accidents. It refers only to being-in-itself, for example, and not to being in another. It refers to only one category of being, albeit the most fundamental, and not to others. In this sense it has to be thought of as univocal and determinate, not as analogous.

It can, however, be thought of as analogous, if we think of substance according to be and not just according to meaning, that is, according to how it is found in reality and not just according to how we conceive it. In other words, though we can give a univocal definition of substance, such as that it is being-in-itself and not in another, when we think of substance in being we do not have to think of it as being of only one kind. If we did, we would end up having to think of all being as only one substance, as Spinoza did, without any thought of the analogy of being or a diversity of substances. It is the thought of the analogy of being in its diversity that leads us to think of substance itself as containing differences in being. In other words, we come to think of substances as differing in being, so that there can be different kinds of substance, which are to be discovered in their differences, as it is for us to discover the differences of being. In this way we come to think of different kinds of substance or of being-in-itself as different modes or different degrees of being. Without this idea of real diversity within the category of substance based on the analogy of being, we would have either to reject the very category of substance with reference to being or to stay with Spinoza's rather flat view of being which follows from a rather univocal conception of substance.

It follows from this that substance expresses being in a way that is quite different from the way one, active, true, and good do. These four notions, which we spoke of as transcendental, along with being, are said to follow being according to its modes. They are common ways of expressing being in its common aspects. Hence they are said to be convertible with being. Every being is thought of as one, active, true, and good in proportion to its being. But this does not entitle us to speak of the order of being or beings as if it or they were one substance. Substance is not convertible with being, since being includes all modes of being, accidents as well as substance. Nor does substance express being in the common way of being itself. Substance expresses being only in specific ways or, more exactly, according to the diverse ways of being which we can refer to as substantial in the very diversity of their being.

Moreover, the concept of substance is not opposed to the concept of coming to be and ceasing to be, but rather includes it as part of its analogous meaning. We see this in the way Aristotle first spoke of substance as the primary analogate of being: "some things are spoken of as being because they are substances [*ousiai*]; others because they are accidents [*pathe*] of substance; others because they are a way to substance, or destructions or privations or qualities or productive or generative of substance, or of terms relating to substance, or negations of one of these terms or of substance" (*Metaph* 1003b 6–10).

The text illustrates not only how the analogy of being is to be understood with reference to substance and accidents, but also how substance takes priority in this analogy. It shows not only how accidents relate to substance, but also how coming to be and ceasing to be are equally thought of in relation to substance. Substance does not preclude becoming any more than it precludes accidents. In fact, it seems that the idea of substance was originally thought of as much in conjunction with change as it was with accident. It does not imply a negation of change in favor of stasis. It only affirms a unity of being or an identity in what a thing is in itself as it changes or comes to be one thing or another while it ceases to be something else.

This is clear in Aristotle, but it is also clear in Plato, from whom Aristotle adopted the idea of substance. In the *Sophist,* when the concept of *ousia* is first introduced, it is closely associated with that of *genesis* (*Soph* 245D). It comes up after the discussion of not-being and being has been going on for some time. Plato recognizes the disagreements about *ousia,* as to whether it consists of matter or only of ideas, but he uses the concept to get himself out of the impasse in which Parmenides' pure idea of being leaves him. Being is eventually considered a third in relation to motion and rest, while these two are taken or seen as belonging to the community of substance *(pros ten tes ousias koinonian),* so that both can be said to be *(einai)* (*Soph* 250B). *Ousia,* as that which is shared or participated in, is then seen as that which allows a certain commingling of certain things with certain other things in some kind of harmony, like the letters in a language or the sounds in music, the sorting of which commingling in being is the art of dialectic or the task of the philosopher (*Soph* 251D–254B). The idea of being thus remains as a brilliant light that is difficult to see in itself, but it is mediated by the idea of substance that is participated in diversely by diverse things in motion and at rest.

Plato and Aristotle can thus be seen as concurring in their view of substance as something to be distinguished from being simply as being and as associated with coming to be and ceasing to be. In this view, substance was not understood in opposition to change or process, as it frequently is in modern philosophy, but rather as presupposing it. Substance was rather understood as that in which coming to be results or that from which ceasing to be begins. It was also understood as giving rise to the gigantic battle as to whether substance was completely material or whether there were not also immaterial substances to account for what we see happening among the material substances.

11.3   The Question of Substance as Primary
in the Question of Being

It is interesting to note that the Greek word for 'substance,' *ousia,* is a nominalized form of the verb 'to be,' just as the Greek word for 'being,' *to on,* is a nominalized form of the verb 'to be.' This suggests a much more concrete reference to actuality in using the term *ousia* than is often supposed in the modern use of the term "substance," as has been shown in recent studies on the verb 'be' in ancient Greek (Kahn 453–62). Like *to on, ousia* also, by reason of its participial form, which can stand for any finite form of the verb, was used concretely to refer to beings or to *what is.* What was meant by *ousia* was not just some abstract essence that might be or not be, but something in actuality about which the question *what?* could be raised. As a nominalized form of the verb, it could be understood abstractly as representing only the *what* or the essence of a being, but it was also understood as referring concretely to a *this* or a *that* so characterized.

To be sure, there could be some disagreement as to *what* precisely *this* or *that* might consist in, especially as to whether it was material or immaterial, which was the point of the battle over *ousia* referred to in the *Sophist* (246A). But no matter how one came down on that question, whether true *ousia* was something in matter or something apart from matter, it was seen as having to do with being in the concrete. Aristotle disagreed with Plato as to where this primary sort of being or substance was to be found, but both agreed in thinking of *ousia* in this concrete fashion as being in itself or according to itself *(kath' auto),* as distinct from any other being that might accrue to it accidentally, or *kata sumbebekos.* And it was this conception of *ousia* that led them both into the fuller question of being as being.

In this regard Gilson was quite right in saying that Aristotle was thinking of substance in the same way as Plato had done before him, that is, as something that existed concretely in itself. But he was wrong in saying that for Aristotle *ousia* remained unknowable in itself (Gilson 47–48). This is to read back into the Greek understanding of substance something characteristic only of modern philosophy, whether substance be taken as abstract essence, separate from its accidents, or as an unchanging "thing-in-itself" hidden behind appearances. For Aristotle substance was not primarily a "thing-in-itself," whether separate from matter or hidden behind appearances. The thing, or the *pragma,* was the whole being in its state of becoming, including accidents as well as substance. Substance, or *ousia,* was this being-in-itself, that is, as distinct from whatever could be thought of as only in it or only happening to it. As such, substance was knowable through any determination as to *what* a thing is. To define a thing in a science was to say what it is in its substance. In this view substance became the special concern of metaphysics in that, as the being-in-itself of any being, it is what is to be known or disclosed first, if there is to be any science of being as being. All other kinds or categories of being, including coming to be and ceasing to be, as well as accidents that also come to be and cease to be, are to be understood as being in relation to this being-in-itself. The question for Aristotle was to understand how this being-in-itself is to be distinguished from being-in-another, or *kata sumbebekos,* even when it is not posited as separate from matter or as apart from coming to be and ceasing to be, as Plato was more inclined to think of it.

In speaking of *ousia,* a nominalized form of the verb 'to be,' the Greeks emphasized the idea of *being* enclosed within the idea of being-in-itself as distinct from being-in-another. In speaking of substance we have lost this terminological emphasis on being, but we have gained something else in our understanding of being that was originally associated with the idea of being but that was not expressed in the verb 'to be' as such. This was the idea of standing that comes out when we contrast being with becoming, or *ousia* with *genesis.* In his account of "the unity of *eimi* [I am] as a linguistic system," Kahn brings out the stative-durative value of the verb 'to be' in contrast to the mutative value associated with verbs of becoming (Kahn 388–89), a stative value that at times may be expressed by the verb *histamai,* "I stand," a verb that functions like the verb 'to be' at times (Kahn 219). Thus "standing" can be understood as a part of being just as "I stand" can be seen as contained in "I am." In translating *ousia* as "substance," we emphasize more this stative value of being and, with the Greeks, think of it still as the aspect of being that "stands under" *(sub stat)* every other aspect of being in our categoreal scheme.

Substance is the category of being in relation to which all the other categories of being make sense by analogy *pros hen.* It refers to that which stands under all the accidents inhering in it as in another than themselves. To be sure, in categorizing being this way, we run the risk of conceiving it as purely static in opposition to accidents, which supposedly change. But that is a misconception of the stative value of being. In calling the first and central category of being "substance," we are rather representing being as something in which a stand is taken. Substance is still only a representation of being in our exercise of judgment as a whole, but it is a representation of being-in-itself as taking its own stand in being, as being *what* it is, whether human or dog, that is, as human being taking its own stand or as dog taking its own stand, or tree, or any other being that can rightly be thought of as a substance, that is, as each one being in its own way. For without such taking of a stand there is no substance, no disclosure of being-in-itself, and consequently no disclosure or knowledge of being in any sense. The understanding of being as being begins with what stands under in itself.

We spoke earlier of action and the underlying thing, which is supposed in any action as the action of a thing. Here we must come to understand this underlying thing as substance, or as being-in-itself. What we have been speaking of here as the subject, either of predication or of inherence, is spoken of in Greek as the "underlying," *to hupokeimenon*. It is the subject as that which is thrown under, *sub-jectum*. Whatever this thrownness may be, *this* or *that,* which appears only as a subject of predication and can never be predicated of anything else, has in itself *what* it is to be. It is substance or being in the first and most fundamental sense. But as *this* or *that* it is not a single being, nor is it always of the same kind. To speak of a multiplicity in being is to speak of many substances, which are in themselves. To speak of a diversity in being is to speak of a diversity of substances, each with its own mode of being. We enter into metaphysics when we begin to consider these many and diverse things in their transcendental unity as substances.

This is the way Aristotle first approached metaphysics as *ta meta ta phusika,* namely, as after *ta phusika,* or after the treatment of the physical, when, in the first book of the *Metaphysics,* he examined how his philosophical predecessors had come to focus on *ousia,* or failed to do so properly, in connection with coming to be and ceasing to be. This is the way he pursued his own investigation in book *Zeta* of the *Metaphysics,* when he argues from the priority of substance that to ask *what* is being is to ask *what* is substance. "And so for us too the highest and the first and the only concern, so to speak, is to investigate what is with regard to being in this way [*peri tou houtos ontos*]" (*Metaph* 1028b 2–8). This was to distinguish substantial being from accidental being as the special concern of metaphysics. But it was also to focus metaphysics on physical reality to begin with, for he goes on to add immediately: "substance appears most manifestly to be present in bodies," the list of which includes animals, plants, the four elements, and the heavens. It is from this that the further questions would arise: "whether these are the only substances, whether there are others as well, or some of these, or some of these and some others, or none of these but certain others" (*Metaph* 1028b 10–16).

Thus the idea of substance which figures so prominently at the begin-

ning of metaphysics, though connected with that of body, is neither reducible to body, which is only one kind of substance, if it is one and if there
are other kinds of substances, namely, immaterial substances. The question as
to whether there are immaterial substances arises from the consideration of
material substance. Plato's idea of substance is still very much in the picture
or in the purview of the question, but it is no longer the starting point in its
immateriality. Of the four senses in which the term *substance* is used, namely,
the essence, the universal, the genus, or the subject, the last "is the one of
which the rest are predicated, while it is not itself predicated of anything
else, so that we must first examine this subject, since the first subject appears
to be substance in the strongest sense" (*Metaph* 1028b 33–1029a 3). It is this
first subject that we ultimately can indicate only concretely as *this* or *that* in
the direct exercise of judgment, but which is understood as having determinations that can be expressed in univocal universal terms and predicated of
the subject in accordance with *what* it is.

This is the idea of substance as something given in experience according
to a wide diversity of natures. It is not reducible to something produced or
given at hand for production, as Heidegger suggests when he argues that the
whole idea of *ousia* and its attendant concepts of species, form, essence,
genus, definition, and nature were modeled on a basic comportment of *Dasein,* namely, one of producing or placing-here *(Herstellen),* which means at
the same time "to bring into narrower or wider circuit of the accessible,
here, to this place, to the *Da,* so that the produced being stands for itself on
its own account and remains able to be found there and to lie-before there
[*vorliegen*] as something established stably for itself" (*GPP* 152/108). According to Heidegger, the Greek term *ousia* simply sums this up as that which is.
"What is thus tangibly present for dealing with [*vorhanden*] is reckoned by
everyday experience as that which is, as a being, in the primary sense"
(Ibid.). But that is not all that substance meant for the Greeks. Far from being just something at hand for manipulation, it was more something to
wonder at in nature for them as it is for us still in an age where technology
has come to replace not only science as inquiry into the nature of things but
also nature itself, as Heidegger himself shows by reducing the idea of substance to that of an artifact.

It is interesting to note that Heidegger attributes this reduced conception
of substance not only to the Greeks but also to Kant, from whom he takes
his departure in raising the question of being. He quotes Kant as saying that
"finite substances cannot of themselves know other things, because they are
not their creator" and that "no being except the creator alone can cognitive-

ly grasp the substance of another thing" (*GPP* 213/150). This explains Kant's agnosticism with regard to substance as something given in nature. It is not that substances are unknowable in themselves, but rather that they are un-knowable to our finite understanding. They are knowable only to the one who produces them. This means that, though we may be able to understand the "substance" of a bridge or a house produced by us, we cannot under-stand the substance of anything given by nature or supposedly produced by a higher being.

If, however, we liken Heidegger's conception of the be of being to the Greek idea of *ousia,* as Heidegger appears to do frequently, we see how he comes to think that it is his own conception of the be of being that has been reduced or ignored in Kant, for he writes: "Be of a being must be under-stood here as being-produced, if indeed the producer, the originator, alone is supposed to be able to apprehend the substance, that which constitutes the be of the being [*das Sein des Seienden*]" (ibid.). In raising the question of the be of being, of course, Heidegger is not prepared to settle for the agnosti-cism of Kant with regard to the be of being. Nevertheless, it is not clear how Heidegger proposes to distance himself from Kant when he writes that "be of a being means nothing but producedness [*Hergestelltheit*]" (ibid.). If this reflects his own view of what is meant by the "ontological difference," it is difficult to see how he can escape from the reduced conception of knowable substance he attributes to Kant. There are other places where Heidegger seems to associate his concept of *Sein* with Aristotle's concept of *ousia* (*GBM* 50), but he never adverts to the broader framework in experience where the concept of substance opens up to the analogy of being. For him the treat-ment of substance reamins within the realm of artificial producedness, and as such it does not do justice to the understanding of substance as it is affirmed in the direct exercise of judgment with reference to a wide diversity of things given in the concrete, natural as well as artificial.

This is not what Plato and Aristotle had in mind when they spoke of things as *ousiai*. They may have thought of them as simply extant or as *vorhanden* in some sense, whether they had come to be what they were or not, but in speaking of them as *ousiai,* whatever they were, material or im-material, they thought of them as being simply according to what they were, with Aristotle insisting on pinning this down to a *this* or a *that, tode ti* or simply *tode.*

Heidegger makes too much of the fact that this same term, *ousia,* was synonymous with property, possessions, means, and wealth, and that this meaning carried through to the end of Plato's and Aristotle's time (*GPP*

153/108). What Heidegger says of *ousia* could be said equally of "being" or "beings," *to on* or *ta onta*, for the same period. If *ousia* had meant only property or possession for Plato and Aristotle, there surely would never have been any *gigantomachia* over it, nor could anyone have advanced the thought, as Plato did, that true *ousiai* might be immaterial, which would make them anything but present at hand for use around the house. More careful studies of the Greek have shown that there is no direct connection between these possessive uses of the participial form of the verb 'to be' and the more metaphysical uses we find in Plato and Aristotle (Kahn 453–62). The battle over substance cannot be put to rest as easily as Heidegger would have it, nor can it be absorbed into the question of the be of being, least of all if be is taken as producedness.

In fact, Heidegger only fuels the battle further by limiting the concept of substance to producedness or to what is at hand for use or when he speaks of it as only extant at-hand and says that *ousia* does not belong to the ontological constitution of *Dasein* or human being, as he claims at one point (*GPP* 169/119–20), but only to the ontological constitution of lesser things, if indeed they can be thought of as having an "ontological constitution" at all. Hence the need for him to go beyond this "*average concept of be* in the sense of *being-produced*" (*GPP* 219/154). Heidegger, however, claims "that this interpretation of being was developed *with a view toward the extant, toward the being that the Dasein is not.* Consequently [for him] the question becomes more urgent: How must we determine the be of being that we ourselves are and mark it off from all the be of being not of the type of *Dasein*, but yet understand it by way of the unity of an original concept of be" (Ibid.)?

It is out of this question that the theme not of analogy, but of temporality arises as "the ontological condition of the possibility of the understanding of be [*Seinsverständnis*]. Temporality takes over the enabling of the understanding of be and thereby the enabling of the thematic interpretation of be and of its articulation and of its manifold ways, that is, the enabling of ontology" (*GPP* 323/228). This is to bring the question of ontology back to the question of *Dasein* or of human being, not to the question of the analogy of being. It enables us to see why Heidegger had to oppose temporality to "substance" in the access to any understanding of be. But the opposition arises only because he has so restricted the understanding of substance to what is extant at-hand, which he refers to as the "average concept of be." Such a conception of substance allows no room in it for subjectivity, as Hegel would have it, or for *Dasein*, who is also extant at-hand and appears as substance even as human being, though more as producer than as merely produced. It also restricts the concept of substance to only one kind of substance, not to the full range of substances in the order of being given to us in experience.

This was not the original understanding of *ousia* in Plato and Aristotle. In his attempt to settle the battle over *ousia,* Plato referred to the soul and to certain virtues in order to break out of a purely material conception of substance. In his discussion of the *Categories* Aristotle uses *anthropos* as his most prominent instance of substance, while in *Metaphysics Gamma* he uses human being once again to illustrate how "being" and "one" refer to the same thing (*Metaph* 1003b 25–37). The point to be made here is that Heidegger's approach through *Dasein* and temporality is not in opposition to a proper conception of substance, but rather that *Dasein,* or self-conscious human being, is itself a substance extant at-hand in its self-consciousness, but only one kind of substance. Even if we focus on it as our primary analogate of substance in its temporality, it is not to lose sight of other kinds of substance but rather to bring out their differences in the order of being.

11.4   The Real Distinction of Substance from Accident

We wish to speak of substance here as the thing that presents itself in experience or in the direct exercise of judgment, the thing understood as the ultimate subject of predication that cannot be predicated of anything else, whether this be you or I or any other thing that presents itself in understanding.

As such this thing has to be thought of as being somehow absolute in itself in contradistinction from whatever else may be in it as in another. What is only in another, as color or size is in a substance or as learning is in Socrates, is not absolute. It is only as relative to that in which it is. But substance, as distinct from that which is in it as quality or quantity or some other accident, is not in another. It is only itself, or in itself, in its own identity. In this sense it is absolute, at least in comparison to what is in it or to that whose identity is only to be in another, even though it may not be absolute as by itself in relation to other substances.

The thing as a whole, then, or as a being, includes more than substance. It includes what we can refer to as accidents, whose being is to be in another or in a substance. When we speak of substance itself, however, we refer to the thing only as being-in-itself, without reference to whatever else may be in it as accident. The idea of substance thus expresses something absolute about any thing thought of as substantial, to which everything else in the thing is relative as an accident or a mode. Such an idea does not have to be understood as referring to only one substance. It can also be understood as referring to a plurality and even a diversity of substances such as we find in experience.

The question for us, then, is whether there are any such substances given to us in experience and how they are to be understood as distinct from whatever accidents may be included in their being. For, if there are accidents really distinct from their substance within one and the same being, this does not mean that the accidents are beings unto themselves or in themselves. That would make them substances stuck onto other substances, and not accidents inhering in a substance. As accidents their only being is a *being-in* their substance. Even as distinct from accidents the being of a substance includes the being of accidents or is the being upon which the being of accidents depends in their very distinction from the substance in which they inhere.

In making a distinction between a substance and its accidents, we are not setting up a separation of different entities from their substance, each complete in itself or an entity unto itself. If we are speaking of only one substance, we are speaking of only one entity, no matter how many accidents or modes we may distinguish from that substance. That is what Plato and Aristotle referred to as *ousia* in being. Even though we may ask *what* an accident is—for example, what is learning? or what is being white?—we do not think of such whatness as an entity in itself. We think of it only as *being-in* whatever entity is learned or white. And that which it is *in* is what we think of as substance.

This is true even of the faculties or powers of a human being when they are distinguished from their substance. The power to think or the power to see is not an entity that thinks or sees by itself. Each of these two distinct powers is in a subject or in a substance that thinks or sees through it. The powers are distinct from the substance as well as from one another, for otherwise they could not be distinct from one another while being powers of one and the same being. We distinguish the powers because we distinguish thinking and seeing as two distinct types of activity in the being that both thinks and sees. Yet in that same being we distinguish only one substance as the underlying thing that thinks and sees and has the powers of thinking and seeing. This thing or substance both thinks and sees for itself through these powers inhering in it.

In order to understand this distinction between substance and accidents more properly and critically, let us turn not just to what is referred to as *this* or *that* rather generally and abstractly in the direct exercise of judgment, but to the actual exercise of judgment itself as the *act* of one who comes to judgment in a process of learning. This is in accordance with our understanding of every being as active, beginning with our primary analogate. The exercise of judgment is the proper activity of a being that is referred to in its substance as a rational animal. The point is not to see how it comes to be called rational animal, but rather how in its actual exercise of judgment it is distinct from that operation in its own substance. In this case the *this* or the *that* is the *I* or the *you* exercising judgment in our confrontation as learners and teachers.

If we reflect on exercising judgment as a kind of learning, we can say that it begins in wonder or in raising questions. When I arrive at an answer to my question, I express it in a judgment, which is now for me an action of mine. As an answer to a question I had, it is really new, in that I did not have the answer or it was not "in" me when I was still only asking the question. This newness of the answer is immediately evident to me. It presents itself as being and as being new. If answers to questions were not new, there would be no concern for learning and no worrying about examinations, for example. To learn or to pass an exam one always begins with questions. These are given, so to speak, or they are raised. Though they presuppose some intellectual activity and some conception of being, as we saw from the beginning of questioning being itself, as questions, they do not contain the answer. If they did, not only would examinations present no problem for students, but also there would be no need for scientific investigation of any sort. Everything would be given in the formulation of a question or in the initial concept of being, which, as we saw in saying that every being is true, is the source of all questioning. The initial concept of being would contain explicitly from the start every answer to every question. The answer, therefore, is something new in being for the being coming to this answer, even if it is not entirely true about the being that was in question.

This claim about the real newness of answers to questions is a judgment of mine, something I have learned. It comes as an answer to a question about the exercise of judgment as a kind of learning. If you wanted to object to this claim, you would have to concede my claim in the very act of objecting to it. By raising your objection you would be raising a new question for me, and by expecting me to answer the question in your way, you would be expecting something new from me, which is all I claim about any answer to a question, whether the answer is right or wrong.

On the other hand, however, in this transition from question to answer, it is always the same I who is going from the one to the other. It was *I who was asking* the question in my eagerness to learn and it is *I who have learned* or remembered the answer. In this sense the *I* is *not new* like the answer to its question is new. This too is immediately evident to the learner, since if one were not interested in finding answers, one would show no concern for questioning and one would have no problem with exams, inasmuch as the answers to questions already exist, presumably in the mind of an examiner. The point about exams is to verify whether a particular individual has learned or at least remembers certain answers to questions, the self-same individual who did not know them before or at least was thought of as not knowing them. Exams do not necessarily prove that one has learned, only that one knows something in the end, which would be new to that individual if one had to learn it.

Again this claim about the *I* not being new in going from question to answer is another judgment of mine, something else I have learned. It comes as an answer to the question as to the identity of the learner in learning. If you wanted to object to this claim, you would again have to concede it in the very act of objecting to it. You would want me not only to reopen my question, but also to find another answer for it so that I could be in agreement with you. You would want the same *I* who is not in agreement with *you* to agree with *you,* which is all I claim about any *I* answering questions, whether in agreement with *you* or not.

Now the *I* who is the same in the transition from question to answer is what we refer to as the substance here in this instance of learning. This substance, we say, is really distinct from the answer or the particular operation of judgment that is new in the learning process. This substance is the subject of this change not just in the sense that it is the underlying thing of the operation, but also in the sense that it is the initiator of this change. It is a human subject with its own temporality and concern for learning. And it is as such that it is substance, with its own identity through time and change. It is the self-same *I* who raises questions in its being open to the truth or to the disclosure of being and who finds answers to its questions.

In speaking of self-sameness here we should note the *ambivalence* of sameness in change. We speak of the same *I* before and after learning and we distinguish this *I* as substance from what has been learned. Hence we say it is the same *I* before and after. But in what sense is it the same? Is it that the *I* has not changed in learning or is it that the *I* has changed but not substantially, that is, not in its identity as this *I?* It seems that we have to say two things at the same time, both that the *I* has changed and that it has not changed, in order to think of the *I* as learning or having learned. To leave either one out is to lose sight of something happening to or in the subject of a change.

This ambivalence is characteristic of any subject of change or becoming, as we saw in speaking of the three principles of change. Before acquiring the new form it was subject to privation: it was *not yet* what it was to become. Before becoming learned in some respect I was still unlearned in that respect. This being subject to privation as well as form is what we refer to as the *potential nature* of the subject: while it is subject to one form it remains in potency to other forms. But in the case of *me* or *you* learning or becoming learned we are not talking about a pure potency. The unlearned *I* is already subject to some form, that of being this *I* or this rational animal, while remaining in potency to learning. It is as such a subject that it is a substance still in potency to learning and that it remains the same substance in having actualized some learning. But the learning does not come to it as a layer of change spread out over an unchanging substance, as if it were covering it and hiding it from view. Even if learning is only an accidental change, as it may be spoken of in relation to the identity of the substance that remains before and after the change, it is still a change *in* the substance. That is in the nature of an accident, to *be in*. The only sameness of the *I* between its being learned in some respect and its having been unlearned in that respect is a sameness of identity as this rational animal. The *I* who has become learned is identically the *I* who was not learned. Without this identity there is no learning of anything new. While there has been a change *in* the substance, there has been no change *of* substance. If there had been, there would have been not learning as such, but a substitution of one learned *I* for another *I*, one who was unlearned and would remain unlearned. In learning, the self-same unlearned *I* at some time becomes learned *I*.

This understanding of accident as being-in explains how we come to know substance as being-in-itself even as we distinguish it from any accidental being accruing to it. The being-in-itself is not understood as static or unchanging, but as potential, even as initiating its own change through an active potency of its own. The unlearned *I* comes to learning through its own intellectual initiative, although it can be helped in this initiative by another *I*, a teacher.

At the same time it is fair to say that the substance is not some unknown or unknowable thing in itself which remains hidden behind the appearances of its activity. It is precisely the being-in-itself that discloses itself through these activities, especially when they are understood as proper to it, as in the case of reasoning for the rational animal. We do not distinguish substance from accidents in order to keep it hidden behind appearances, so to speak, but rather in order to bring it out in the open as being-in-itself through these appearances, especially those that are the proper activity of this being-in-itself. We come to think of an *I* or a human being as rational in its substance through this activity of learning viewed as proper to it and as disclosing what it is in itself.

In speaking of every being as active, we speak of action as giving us an ontological access, so to speak, to the being-in-itself of substance inasmuch as we affirm that there is no being without its proper activity. Even as distinct from its proper activity, substance is known through this activity, for it is not distinguished as in-itself except through it. Substance is not affirmed as being-in-itself in any other way than through its proper activity, so that it cannot be unknowable even to human understanding. To speak of it as distinct is to speak of it as already known.

All this has been said with reference to a human being learning, our primary analogate of being. It shows a distinction between substantial being and accidental being and brings the focus of the question of being to substance as the primary instance of being to be considered even in our primary analogate. Human being in its substantial identity as *I* or as *Dasein* is what we first conceive as substance in the very exercise of its proper activity. Such a substance is by no means static, nor is it unchanging in its substantiality. It is known in this substantiality only as exercising its own activity. Nor is its substantiality opposed to its subjectivity. It is precisely as active or as a subject in act that it is a substance.

When we think of substance in this way, as distinct from accidents inhering in it one way or another, we can speak of it as a univocal concept meaning what is in-itself as distinct from what is in-another. Such a concept, however, is not thought of as realized only in the human mode of being. To the extent that we recognize other modes of being, such as nonrational beings, nonsentient beings, and even nonliving beings, we have to recognize also different modes of substantiality in being. These are not different modes of one and the same substance, as Spinoza would have it. These are different kinds of substance and even different individual substances, each with an identity of its own. Aristotle speaks of horse, as well as of man, to illustrate his idea of *ousia*. We cannot speak of this horse as learning in the same way that I do as a human being. It is not a rational animal. But it is nevertheless an animal and as such it is a substance with a proper activity of its own through which we identify it as this horse. We can also speak of a tree as a living substance with a proper activity of its own, and even of some nonliving things as substances, also with a proper activity of their own, albeit in a very diminished sense, but an activity that nevertheless enables us to identify them as this kind of substance rather than another kind and even as this individual rather than that one.

In this we are thinking of substance as somehow absolute or in and through itself, but not as infinite, as Spinoza would have it. Spinoza was absolutizing his conception of substance as conceived abstractly and univocally. This is why he had to think of substance as unique as well as infinite, and of everything else as a mode of the one substance. In the direct exercise of judgment, however, this is not how we come to think of substance. We think of many and diverse things as substances, each with an identity of its own in itself. Though the concept of substance is univocal according to meaning, in that it is specified as being-in-itself as distinct from being-in-another, it is not univocal according to be or according to what is referred to in being. Even if the human subject is the first kind of substance we come to identify, it is not the only kind there is. We also speak of lesser substances in referring to nonrational, nonsentient, and even nonliving beings. And we may even speak of higher substances with reference to higher intellectual beings than human beings, as Platonism was inclined to do.

We see, then, how the concept of substance, like the concept of body, is analogous not according to meaning, but according to be, in accordance with the second moment in the dialectic of analogy. This allows us to think of many and diverse substances, each somehow absolute in-itself and yet finite or limited by other substances in the total order of being. Our initial concept of substance, univocal as it may be in meaning, is analogous in being. We think of substance as realized in different ways in being. Though being-in-itself always entails an identity such as that of the human being, there are different kinds of identity, each of which is thought of as substance insofar as it is distinguished from its activity and each of which is identified through its proper activity, diminished as this may be in extreme instances of nonliving things which can still be thought of as beings-in-themselves.

We do not have to say here where the limit might lie for speaking of a being-in-itself, whether at the level of molecules, atoms, or subatomic particles. It is not immediately clear that any of these can properly be called beings-in-themselves in a way that is still analogous to human being, our primary analogate of being-in-itself. But it is clear that they are not the first or the only instances of being-in-itself, as physicalism tends to suppose, if in fact they are substances at all. Apart from human beings, animals and other living things are much more clearly instances of substantial being, as are also many compounds whose properties can be readily identified. The critical point of evaluation is in the identity of a thing according to what it is in-itself, which is much more clear from the top down, that is, starting from the human being, than from the bottom up, that is, starting from atoms or subatomic particles, which are impossible to identify except as quanta in abstract mathematical formulas.

What all this implies is that the category of substance is not to be thought of as realized primarily according to what modern physical science refers to as elements, atoms, or subatomic particles. It is not excluded that these might be thought of as substances, if proper criteria for identifying them as such can be agreed upon. But other things are much more clearly identifiable as substances, even if subatomic particles cannot be so identified, namely, living things, sentient things, and most of all, human beings, in relation to whom our understanding of substance first emerges. Substance refers to each thing identified as substance as it is in itself or in its identity as it appears in its proper activity. It is as such that we focus on it as what is primary in the question of being and what is capable of being elucidated even if we have not yet elucidated what might be the elements or the particles into which physical substances might be broken down if and when they cease to be what they are as a certain kind of being, as when a human being turns into a corpse and starts to decompose.

As a science of being in the concrete, metaphysics inquires not into a naive or unexamined concept of substance associated with some particular science such as physics, chemistry, or biology, but into a more critical concept of substance as being-in-itself first seen as distinguished from its accidents or being-in-another in the temporal identity of an *I* or a human being, and then seen by analogy in lesser beings, or what can also be referred to as lesser substances, even though each has its own identity as a kind of being and as an individual, like the human being in this respect even though it is a different kind as well as a different individual in being. It is to the investigation of how such being-in-itself is constituted that we now turn.

CHAPTER 12

Matter as Indeterminate Being in Potency

IT MAY SEEM THAT, while being-in-itself allows for change, just as I can sit and stand or learn and forget, it does not change in itself. We have spoken about it as an identity, that which remains itself even as it changes. Substance is spoken of as permanent in being: it remains through change. This may not mean that it is unchanging, as we said, since it is the substance that changes even in accidental change. But it does mean that things change in it while it retains its identity. From the standpoint of its identity, substance has to be thought of as remaining the same, whether it is the solidity of a rock, the stiffness of a tree, the adaptability of an animal, or the temporality of a human being. In all these changes *what* the thing is remains what it is in itself, no matter how it changes, at least for as long as it remains in itself. But there is also death or the destruction of a thing in its identity to be considered, which appears to be the ceasing to be of a substance or of *what* a thing is in itself, and conversely there is the coming to be of substance, as when animals and plants are generated.

We are accustomed to think of this ceasing to be and coming to be of substances as such in terms of decomposition into or composition from more simple elements. Thus, we think of death as the decomposition of a body or of conception as a combination of sperm and ovum. We have come to understand a great deal about the mechanics, so to speak, of these processes. But we may be forgetting a greater perplexity about what is happening on the level of substance or of being-in-itself. Do we realize what we mean when we speak of a substance as a being-in-itself and of this same substance as coming to be in its new and original identity or ceasing to be in that identity? This is something Spinoza could not allow for in his abstract conception of Substance as Absolute and Infinite.

To speak of this coming to be or ceasing to be of a substance in our experience merely in terms of a mechanical composition or decomposition,

however, is to leave out of consideration precisely what is essential for a substance, namely, its identity as being-in-itself. I am not just a set of molecules
held together by a certain force. In my substance, or in what I am, I am myself as a self, this human being, and I know myself in this identity. I also
know you as another substance like myself and other substances as well,
many of which are less than human. It does not matter right now just how I
know this. What matters is that, if we think of anything as a being-in-itself,
no matter how complex in its composition, how can we think of it as coming to be simply as a substance or ceasing to be? Do we not have to think of
a substance simply as being, at least for as long as it is what it is in itself?

This is the question that arose at the origin of metaphysics and that the
philosophers of nature, like Thales and Empedocles, touched on as well as
the philosophers of being, like Parmenides and Heraclitus. It is a question
that remains for us, because, just as in ancient times physiologists and
philosophers of nature failed to posit *ousia* or substance as a cause of being, as
Aristotle pointed out (*Metaph* 988b 28–29), so also in our time scientists or
philosophers of science fail to consider the being of anything in its identity,
that is, as this or that substance. Thus, far from being perplexed about how
being-in-itself can come to be or cease to be, they are perplexed only by the
question itself as to how it arises.

For these scientists or philosophers of science change is conceived only as
a rearrangement of particles, not to say a rearrangement of symbols, and the
closest thing to a substance they can think of would seem to be one or several of these particles referred to as basic physical entities. Whether or not
such "entities" are truly substances, a *this* or a *that* with an identity of its
own, remains itself a matter of perplexity, as we have seen. But if we conceive all change only as a rearrangement of particles, then we are forced into
saying that there is only one kind of substance, namely, that of particles, and
that all change is accidental, that is, a matter of rearrangement, while the
"substances" or particles remain always the same in their identity. In that case
there is no such thing as a self or a human being, a horse, or a tree in itself.
There are only unchanging particles of some kind and varying arrangements
of such particles. There can be no question of coming to be or ceasing to be
of substances. Whatever else may change, "substances" or the "basic physical
entities" do not come to be or cease to be, for if they did, it would appear
that the supposed laws of physics would be groundless. It is only with the
principle of indeterminacy in physics that the perplexity about coming to
be and ceasing to be returns with regard to physical being-in-itself. The

question, then, from a metaphysical standpoint, is to focus the perplexity more properly on the coming to be or the ceasing to be of a substance.

If we take the idea of substance more concretely, however, that is, as referring to a *this* or *that* which is a human being or to any other being with an identity that is analogous to that of a human being, the perplexity appears more immediately in death and in generation, which appear to be a ceasing to be and a coming to be of some *this* or *that* in its identity as a living thing.

We have already begun to reflect on coming to be and ceasing to be in order to arrive at the three principles of becoming. In doing so, however, we were reflecting only on a kind of change that has to be thought of as accidental, as in the case of learning, which is only accidental in relation to what I am and remain in myself. I come to be learned or cease to be learned in forgetting. Such coming to be or ceasing to be is accidental to myself as a substance. It is a coming to be or a ceasing to be *secundum quid,* that is, according to some aspect of my being, in this case, learning. With the concept of substance as being-in-itself clearly in mind, however, we can raise the question of becoming in a much more radical sense, one that somehow touches on the question of being simply, since substance refers to being in its most radical sense. If substance refers to what a thing is in itself, how can we think of it as coming to be *simply,* as if from nothing, or ceasing to be *simply,* as if into nothing, rather than only *secundum quid,* as in the case of a merely accidental change like learning. If we take a living thing such as a human being to be a substance with an identity of its own, then surely the genesis or the death of such a being is an instance of such coming to be simply or ceasing to be simply. How is such a radical change in being to be conceived and accounted for?

12.1   Matter as Principle of Being

It will be noted that with this question we are back with the perplexity that is at the origin of metaphysics. Parmenides, who had not yet distinguished *ousia* as a category of being from the concept of being, or *to on,* found himself incapable of allowing for change or multiplicity in being. For him coming to be simply could mean only either one of two things. It could mean coming to be either from being or from nonbeing, neither of which makes any sense in terms of being simply. Being, as being, does not come to be. It simply is. Nor does being come to be from nonbeing, since from nonbeing nothing comes to be. Nonbeing is simply the opposite of being and, just as hot does not come from its opposite, cold, so also being does not come from its opposite, nonbeing. From nothing nothing comes.

This is why for Parmenides there could be no change in being. His univocal conception of being did not allow for any escape from the horns of this dilemma. This is why also for him being could only be one, and not many, since multiplicity would also require some opposition in being, one being as *not* another, while the only opposite of being is nonbeing. Thus becoming and multiplicity had to be a predicament for Parmenides from which he could not escape except by retreating into his pure concept of being, without difference and change.

As we have seen, however, the introduction of a category of substance along with the analogy of being opens a way out of this predicament, so that we can allow for some change in being on the level of what happens to a being if not on the level of *what* that being is in itself. But the question for us now is: Does this allow for what we are now speaking of as substantial change, as we seem to find it in experience with the coming to be simply or the ceasing to be simply of a human being or any living thing? Or does the Parmenidean predicament remain on the level of substance, if not on the level of accident? Should not substance itself, or being-in-itself, be conceived as unchanging and unique in its absoluteness, as it was by Spinoza, or as an absolute multiplicity of unchanging physical entities, as it is by physicalists? Are we not still in a predicament about what coming to be or ceasing to be simply on the level of substance might mean, regardless of what we might think of as substance? And does not this predicament remain a perplexity for anyone wishing to speak about coming to be simply, as Aristotle did perhaps for the first time and as many have done after him? We have already seen how Aristotle began to find his way out of this predicament in speaking about three principles of change in general, but now we must examine what manner of being must be disclosed to account for this coming to be simply.

It is interesting and important to note that Aristotle, even with the idea of a category of substance within the analogy of being, did not directly challenge either one of the two horns of the Parmenidean dilemma. For Aristotle as well as for Parmenides, as we noted earlier in section 10.3, being cannot come to be either from being or from nonbeing. In fact, even a theologian like Aquinas does not challenge this assumption of the Greeks when he speaks of *creatio ex nihilo,* since creation is not a coming to be like the coming to be of individuals we experience in the world, as we shall see when we come to discuss the summit of being as "cause" of being. What

Aristotle did was to find a way around the dilemma without denying either one of the two horns, a way that Aquinas wholeheartedly accepted without giving up anything of his idea of "creation from nothing," a way that focused only on *coming-to-be-from* and nothing else. What is this way?

It was not a way of creation from nothing, for it is not clear whether Aristotle ever had such an idea associated with his idea of the Unmoved Mover. Nor was he in a position to bring up such an idea at the point of the inquiry into being where we now find ourselves. The question of "creation from nothing" properly arises only with the question of the summit of being, a question that we are still far from having reached in this investigation. Whatever may be meant by "creation from nothing," here we are considering only what is meant by coming-to-be-*from*, and it is through this preposition *from* tied to *coming to be* that Aristotle finds his way. Let us follow this way as he presents it in his first approach to the question of coming to be simply at the beginning of the *Physics* (*Alpha,* ch. 8).

We cannot think of coming to be except as coming to be from, as is clear even from Parmenides. He dismissed all thought of coming to be because he thought it had to be *from* either being or nonbeing, neither of which makes sense. Hegel tried to do otherwise at the beginning of his *Science of Logic.* Hegel appears to begin with pure be *(Sein)* as what is present *(vorhanden)* in the determination of pure knowing *(Wissen)* (Blanchette 1981). This pure be, however, in its indeterminacy, turns out to be the same as pure nothing, which is also an absence of all determination and content. The two are thought of as distinct and yet as having passed over into one another to give rise to becoming *(Werden),* the first whole for Hegel in which truth is to be found (*WL* I, 67/82–83). In this hasty passage from a distinction between pure be and pure nothing, where becoming is seen as the whole to appear in truth, Hegel was leaving the distinction between being and nonbeing in utter confusion, where being and nonbeing are spoken of as the same and yet as not the same, because both are utterly indeterminate. In this dialectic some determination is being presupposed, if only to say that one side is *not* the other, at the same time as all determination is being denied on either side or both sides, since pure be and pure nothing is said to be the same indeterminacy.

What Hegel was speaking of is not the coming to be of anything in particular. It was becoming pure and simple, *Werden,* made up of an interplay between pure be and pure nothing, both or each of which is pure indeterminacy. This shows that for Hegel the thought of becoming needs to be accounted for through some interplay of being and nonbeing, but it does not get Hegel to anything determinate in being or becoming. The only way Hegel can do this is by supposing that this teeming of being and nonbeing somehow quiets down in a vanishing of becoming that collapses into a quiet result on the side of be. This quiet result Hegel calls *Dasein* (*WL* I, 93/106), what is *da* as a determinate being.

Thus, for Hegel, though there was talk of becoming before any talk about determinate being, there was no talk of coming to be *from*. Determinate being simply appears *there* out of a supercession *(Aufhebung)* of becoming and no more thought is given to that *from* which it might come, as in Aristotle. The idea of a real principle of becoming as distinct from a mere dialectic of pure indeterminate concepts is simply overlooked.

In taking issue with Parmenides and with all those who saw all change as only accidental to some unchanging substance, Aristotle focuses not on being as such, but on a particular being and the coming to be of something quite determinate, in accordance with the analysis of change we have already seen. Coming to be is understood not only in relation to some *terminus ad quem,* but also as having started from some *terminus a quo.* This relation of *being-from,* however, can be taken in two ways, which Aristotle illustrates with the example of a doctor doing different things, like building a house and healing a patient, or becoming different things, like an architect or just ceasing to be a doctor.

It is one and the same individual who both builds and heals, the one we are referring to as the doctor. In both cases the building and the healing come from the doctor, but not in the same way in relation to this individual being a doctor. In one way, in the case of his building, the relation of coming *from* is only incidental to his being a doctor. The building is *from* the doctor, not as doctor, but as builder. It is only healing that is *from* him *per se* as doctor. It is only because the doctor happens *(per accidens)* to be a builder as well that the building comes *from* the doctor. Only the healing comes *from* the doctor as doctor.

Similarly, if the same individual becomes something else, say a tennis player, it is also incidental that this is *from* being a builder or a doctor. In fact the same individual could become a tennis player even while remaining a builder and a doctor. But if the individual ceases to be a builder or a doctor, this is *from* having been a builder or a doctor as such. Aristotle speaks of the doctor becoming pale. This is not *per se from* being a doctor, but *from* being of ruddy complexion, whereas ceasing to be a doctor would be *per se from* being a doctor.

Now, what does this have to do with coming to be or ceasing to be simply? It illustrates how we can think of coming to be from being and from nonbeing not *per se,* but *per accidens* or *kata sumbebekos.* We cannot say that something comes to be *from* nonbeing simply, as Parmenides saw, but we can say that it comes to be *from* nonbeing *per accidens,* understanding being now as a *this* that is new and that was *not* in being before. That from which this new being comes to be *per se* is not nothing, but something in being which, *per accidens* to what it was, was *not* this new being. We cannot say that this same new being comes to be from being simply, as Parmenides also saw, but we can say that it comes to be from some being *per accidens,* understanding that earlier being as some other being in itself.

To illustrate this second side of coming-to-be-*from per accidens,* that is, not just of coming to be *from* an opposite, as in the case of an accidental change, but of being coming to be *from* being, Aristotle makes up an example that seems strange at first sight but that focuses on the point at issue here very well, which is that of a substance simply coming to be. Suppose, he says, a dog comes to be *from* a horse, not in the sense that a horse produces a dog, but in the sense that a dog comes to be from what was once a horse. Whether this could happen or how it could happen is beside the point. The point is in the coming-to-be-*from.* What comes to be simply and properly is the dog, which is an animal. But what about being animal as animal? Does that come to be as well? In one sense, yes, since the dog is an animal and being animal comes to be coincidentally with the dog coming to be. But being animal comes to be only *per accidens,* that is, insofar as the dog, which properly comes to be simply, "happens" to be animal. Being an animal as such does not properly come to be simply because the horse was itself animal. Thus being an animal ceases to be *per accidens* insofar as horse ceases to be and comes to be *per accidens* insofar as dog comes to be, but it is present before as well as after the horse has become the dog. It does not come to be *per se.*

This is the point that has to be understood about being coming to be *from* being. What comes to be properly is a being that was not before, namely, this substance as being-in-itself. It cannot come to be *from* nothing *per se,* since nothing comes from nothing. Nor can it come from another being *per se,* since that being, as being, simply is, although it may cease to be. Nor can it come from being as such, since that would exclude being from what comes to be and thus negate the very coming to be of the new being. Being thus does not come to be *per se,* but it does come to be *per accidens,* that is, in the coming to be of any particular being. In coming to be, a particular thing becomes a being.

In this sense we can speak of a new being, a substance that has come to

be simply. But this does not mean that all being is new. There was being before this one came to be in other beings and there remain other beings beside this new one. In the coming to be of a substance we can say that there is
really new being that has come to be, but this new being does not come to
be precisely as being but only concomitantly with this particular thing that
properly comes to be. In other words, being comes to be only *per accidens*,
because being, as we have seen from the beginning, cannot be understood
abstractly, apart from what comes to be, but only concretely as this something that comes to be, as we see now. Just as when this animal, say a dog,
comes to be from that animal, say a horse, or this body comes to be from
that body, not all body or all nonbody and not all animal or all nonanimal is
taken away from that *from* which a new being comes to be, so also not all
being or all nonbeing is taken away from that *from* which this being comes
to be, because that from which this substance comes to be has some being,
in that it is or was itself a substance or part of a substance, and some nonbeing, in that it is or was not the new substance.

All this enables us to get around the Parmenidean predicament and to
understand how coming to be can be from being or nonbeing, not *per se*,
but *per accidens*. This concrete individual being comes to be not from nonbeing as such, but from the nonbeing of itself, which was not nothing before
but something else or some other concrete individual which, *per accidens*,
was not the new being to be. There was being prior to this new being's
coming to be, so that it is not being as such that properly comes to be from
being, but rather this concrete individual substance, so that there is truly a
coming into being on the occasion, so to speak, of this individual coming
into being simply.

This does not make being only an accident of the substance that comes
to be. On the contrary, being is integral to a substance insofar as it *really*
comes to be and is, for, as we have seen from the beginning, being is signified according to a mode of concretion. It is by reason of this concretion of
being as such that we can understand how a being comes to be *per accidens*
both from the nonbeing of itself and the being of something else.

Having said this, however, there remains a very important question to be
asked about coming-to-be-*from*. If what comes to be simply as a substance
comes to be *from* nonbeing or *from* being only *per accidens*, *from* what does it
come to be *per se*, for, as Aquinas says in commenting on the text we are par-
aphrasing, what is *per accidens* has to be brought back to what is *per se* (*In
Phys* I, 14, §126[7])? This is the question that leads us to the disclosure of a
principle of being and becoming that Parmenides and others had not seen

before Aristotle and which Hegel failed to bring out in his initial dialectic of being and nonbeing leading up to becoming, the principle that has to be thought of as the subject of change, according to the analysis of becoming we saw earlier in this chapter, a principle we now have to call *matter*. Aristotle does not develop the idea of this principle at the beginning of the *Physics*. He merely mentions that it has to do with the distinction between being in potency and being in act and that the idea of it is developed more clearly elsewhere, that is, in the *Metaphysics,* book *Eta,* chapter 1.

12.2   Matter as Being in Potency

How is this radical principle of becoming and being to be understood? We speak of it as matter but in what sense is it matter in things that come to be and cease to be? Is it the things themselves or is it an originating principle *from* which they come to be? To answer this question we must go back to our earlier analysis of change in terms of three principles, two *per se* and constitutive of what comes to be and one only *per accidens,* in that it pertains to the subject of change prior to the change. It is as a *subject* of change that we must think of the principle we are now looking for. As this *subject* it enters into what comes to be as one of its two constitutive principles along with its new form, the other constitutive principle of what comes to be. But inasmuch as we are now speaking of coming to be simply, and not merely of coming to be *secundum quid,* we must understand this *subject* as something that differs radically from anything we have seen up to now.

In the case of an accidental change, as in learning, which we spoke of earlier, the subject of change is actually a substance, as I am and remain myself in learning. In coming to be simply, however, as we are now conceiving it, the *subject* of change can no longer be a substance, since it is of a substance as such that we are speaking as coming to be. One substance cannot be the *subject* of change for the coming to be of another substance, nor can it be the constitutive principle of a new substance. When a substance gives way to another substance that comes to be, it simply ceases to be as a substance, as a horse would cease to be in becoming a dog. In order to conceive the coming to be of a substance properly, we must conceive of a *subject* of change that is not a substance but that is constitutive of a new substance along with its new form.

Thus, while substance is a substrate for accidental change, there is a radically different kind of substrate in the coming to be of a substance. This substrate is not a *this* or a *that* like a substance, nor does it have any of the characteristics we commonly associate with substance, such as quantity or quality. It is purely substrate of coming to be, nothing more, without any actuality by itself. It can be thought of as a process, but only as one terminating in an actuality, like the form of a new substance that has come to be. It is what Aristotle speaks of as *being in potency,* which is to be distinguished from *being in act.*

What comes to be simply is a being in act. It comes to be *per accidens from* its not being in act and *from* the being in act of another being. But what it comes-to-be-from *per se* is its own being in potency. This potency, as the substrate of coming to be simply, say of a substance such as myself or a dog, is constitutive of what comes to be as a *per se* principle, according to the understanding of the principles of becoming we arrived at earlier. As a substrate, before the coming to be, it was subject to another form than that of the substance that has come to be. But even as subject of that other form, it was in potency to another form, that is, the form that now actualizes it as this particular being that has come to be. For this reason we can say that this form has been educed from the potency of its substrate, or from the potency of its matter, in which it was contained as in a process or a matrix.

Thus we come to understand matter as a radical principle both of becoming and being in things that come to be. As such we can speak of it as *prime matter,* not as though it were a particular material thing, but rather as a principle of particular material things. As first or as prime, it is not a thing like the things we speak of in the direct exercise of judgment, but it is a principle of such things in their being and coming to be. Insofar as it is distinct from the other *per se* or constitutive principle of what comes to be, namely, the form, it is indeterminate and imperfect or in need of perfecting. Form, the other constitutive principle of what comes to be, is the principle of its determination and perfection, as we shall see when we come to speak of form as distinct from matter in the composite substance that comes to be.

But even as indeterminate, matter is not nothing. Nor is it reducible to nothing, like Hegel's concept of pure indeterminate be. *Prime matter,* as we have just come to understand it, is not to be thought of as something actual by itself, but it is something potential or, better said still, it is something *potentially,* since as potential it is close or in relation to becoming actual. As Aquinas puts it, it is close to being a thing, *prope rem*; it *is* in some sense, *aliqualiter,* because it is in potency to the thing; and it is even the substance of the thing in some sense, again *aliqualiter,* because it enters into the constitution of the thing (*In Phys* I, 15, §132 [4]). As a principle of being, matter is something positive, something dynamic, even if it be only an orientation to being in act, a potency or a *dunamis* to form and actuality. It is understood distinctly as that *from* which something comes or, rather, as that *from* which something has-come-to-be properly and *per se,* since it is only upon reflection on what has come to be that we come to know *prime matter* as a principle. Hegel saw this when he spoke of truth as neither be nor nothing, but as the passing over or, rather, the having passed over of each into the other (*WL* I, 67/82–83.). What he failed to see was that our understanding of becoming itself requires not just a concept of pure be and pure nothing, but a positive principle of *being in potency* which we call matter.

12.3   Matter as Distinct from Privation

As we distinguish matter understood as being in potency from its form or actuality in being, we must not confuse it with nothing, for if we do, we lose sight of Aristotle's disclosure of matter as a positive principle of being. What we say *is* simply or without qualification is being in act. Matter as distinct from form is only being in potency. As such it is not in act and it cannot be said to be simply, since that is true only of being in act. With the idea of being in potency, however, we are not left with a simple opposition between being and nonbeing. Something of that opposition remains, in that privation is opposed to form, but it is mediated by a kind of being that is neither being in act nor nonbeing, but something in between, so to speak, as *being in potency.* In other words, matter, even as only indeterminate *being in potency,* is more on the side of being than of nothing, since it is something potential and not pure privation.

In terms of our earlier reflection on change in Chapter 10, the opposition between being and nonbeing comes down to an opposition between form and privation. In order to understand any kind of change in being, we saw that it is necessary to keep privation in mind as a principle *per accidens,* inasmuch as the new form has appeared from its *not* being. I understand myself as having become learned only from having been *un*learned. Socrates really comes into being as a substance only from the *not* being of Socrates. Now the *substrate* from which I come to be learned or Socrates comes to be simply is not the privation either of learning on my part or of being simply on the part of Socrates. The substrate, which is already in potency before coming to be in act, is subject to those privations before becoming either learned, in the case of myself, or a new substance, in the case of Socrates coming to be. Hence there is some opposition in coming to be and ceasing to be, but it is not an opposition between form and matter or between act and potency. It is an opposition only between a form or an act and the privation or negation of that form or act. Taken with reference to a determi-

nate change, privation or negation is determinate: it is the privation or negation of the determinate form that has come to be. It is with reference to the
statue that I think of the block of marble from which it was shaped as lacking the shape of the statue. Prescinding from the determinacy of any change,
however, privation or negation can be thought of simply as nonbeing, or as
the nonbeing of whatever comes to be.

In thinking of privation, however, rather than just nonbeing in opposition
to being, as Parmenides did, we are not only getting around his predicament.
We are also keeping our attention clearly focused on matter as dynamic or as
being in potency. At the same time we are avoiding the confusion in which
Hegel leaves us with his opposition between pure be and pure nothing. To
be sure, there is a passing over in becoming. But it is not a passing over of being into nothing or of nothing into being. It is a passing over into some determinate being from the nonbeing of that determinate being, a passing over
that, as being in potency, is itself constitutive principle of what comes to be.
If there is a dialectic in coming to be and ceasing to be, it is not between
pure be and pure nothing as both still indeterminate, nor between form and
matter, nor between act and potency. Nor is it precisely between one form
of being and another form of being in the coming to be of a substance. It is
rather between a form and the negation of that form or its privation. But
such a dialectic presupposes a substrate that is being in potency, as we see in
reflecting on matter as being in potency or as a principle of becoming.

As the subject of change, or as matter, this substrate is one numerically,
but it is one only potentially. That is, prior to the change it is subject to privation as well as subject to some form. In this sense it can be thought of as
nonbeing *per accidens,* in relation to the form that is yet to be educed from its
potency, but not *per se,* since it is not privation as such. As something positive, matter or being in potency, while still subject to privation, is close to
being a thing in act, as the marble of the statue is close to being a statue,
while its shapelessness in relation to the statue is not. *Prime matter,* while not
being a thing we can point to in act, still *is* somehow by being in potency to
some thing and by entering into the substance of the thing as a constitutive
principle, which cannot be said of privation or nonbeing in any way.

This idea of matter as being in potency and as positive principle of things
that come to be can be seen as quite original with Aristotle, especially in its
distinction from privation or nonbeing. It could be said that Plato had arrived at a certain conception of matter, if not of prime matter as such, at
least in the sense of some kind of nature or principle underlying all natural
forms, as Aristotle acknowledges near the end of his discussion of matter in

the opening book of the *Physics*. But Plato did not clearly distinguish matter from privation, as Aristotle also points out in this same discussion. In fact, according to Aristotle, Plato did not mention privation and ended up confusing matter with privation or negation of form. As a result of this confusion, which is not unlike that with which Hegel would later begin his Logic, Plato lacked the idea of matter as being in potency and as a positive principle of being as well as becoming.

Understood properly as a positive principle of being, along with form, matter is a cause of things that come to be according to nature. It is a receptive cause, in the manner of a mother or a matrix, as Plato pointed out. But if we distinguish it clearly from privation, which Plato failed to do, we see why privation is not a constitutive principle of things that come to be, since it is only the opposite of what comes to be. Privation is the nonbeing of what comes to be. We think of it as a principle of what comes to be only *per accidens,* or dialectically, inasmuch as it is in the subject of change as being in potency prior to the actualization of a new form. Strictly speaking, privation is *per se* a negation of being, what Parmenides referred to as nonbeing in general and what we now refer to as determinate nonbeing. While we associate privations with matter as being in potency, matter itself is not privation, nor is it the pure nothing that Hegel opposed to pure be, but something positive constitutive of things that come to be in a new form.

Matter is thus a certain desire for form, which is not only educed from its potency but also comes as a fulfillment or a perfection of this desire or potency. In this sense form can be thought of as a good for matter, whereas privation has to be thought of as an evil. Form too is something positive, even more so than matter. It is an act or a participation in act, since everything is in act insofar as it has form. As such, form is a good, even an *optimum,* for what comes to be, since it comes as the perfection of its potency. It is therefore an object of appetite in coming to be, where everything seeks its own perfection. In contrast to this, however, privation is no more than an absence or a removal of form, a *remotio formae,* and hence an evil in the sense that it expresses a lack of perfection or of goodness. Matter, on the other hand, even as recipient of form, is neither evil nor negation of form, but it is a positive desire, a dynamism or a potency for form and, as such, is already good insofar as it already is potentially a principle of being.

12.4   The Order of Matter

Matter, as we are now representing it to ourselves, can be understood only in its relation to form or, as Aristotle puts it, by its analogy to form, from which it is distinguished as a principle of being in what comes to be. Whatever comes to be has to be understood as a composite of a form and a substrate. Matter is the substrate for the new form in whatever comes to be as a substance. Thus, to complete our understanding of matter as a principle of being, we must turn to the form with which it enters into composition as a principle.

Before we do that, however, let us dwell more on this principle of matter as it now presents itself in our reflection on coming to be simply or as constitutive of material substances. The term "matter," as we use it commonly, is ambiguous. This is so not only because material being is the least intelligible, but also because our mode of knowing is through abstraction from matter. Our concept of matter is derived from our experience of material things, but the concept itself is not material.

We speak of matter in many ways. We say "matter is heavy," but we do not mean that matter as such is heavy. We mean rather that material things are heavy and that weight is a property of these things inasmuch as they are material. Similarly we say "matter is colored," but we mean that material things are colored and that color is a property of these things inasmuch as they are material. Even colorless gases are spoken of as material in this way. We also use the term "matter" as a whole when we mean the totality of material beings or of all the beings that have materiality in common, regardless of the diversity of these beings.

It is, however, with reference to this diversity of material beings that the question of order in matter arises, first with regard to matter itself as dynamic or as being in potency to form, and second with regard to the diversity of forms among material beings. The very idea of being in potency, as we have seen, entails an idea of order or an inclination to form. If there is a diversity of forms among material things, as we find in the direct exercise of judgment, the same idea will entail a diversity in the potency of matter and an order in this potency to the diversity of forms. Even if we speak of prime matter as a radical principle of being for any substance that comes to be, this does not mean that it is a sort of flat potency to any form whatsoever, a sort of lowest common denominator for all bodies that we might refer to as "bodiness." It means rather that this principle must be understood according to its analogy to the diversity of forms as they appear in matter, since it is only in its analogy to form that matter is understood. How is this to be understood in terms of what we refer to as the natural process of generation as a whole?

Let us go back to our initial reflection on any process of coming to be. To understand such a process we must have a concrete *terminus ad quem* clearly in mind and we must understand this term as coming *per se* from the opposite or the privation of itself, and not just from anything indiscriminately. Healing or getting better for a patient, for example, comes from being sick, and not from being white or tall or anything else not relevant to healing. When we relate this to being in potency, it means that potency must be understood always in relation to some specific act. Thus, for example, it is not anything that can become healthy, but only a living organism that is already actualized as such but that is not healthy. The potency to health resides in the nature of a living organism, and it can be actualized either by that nature itself, by the art of medicine, or by both at the same time. But in order for health to be actualized, the organism must be properly disposed or in a sort of immediate potency to health. Without a well-articulated organism there is no disposition or potency for health. Similarly, without an intelligence there is no disposition or potency for learning.

This much can be said with regard to any form that comes to be, whether accidental or substantial. It is educed from an immediate potency for it. But in the case of a substance coming into being, as in the case of Socrates coming to be, we are talking about educing a substantial form from the potency of matter as such. How is this to be understood as coming from the potency of matter? Does Socrates come to be immediately from the pure potency of what we have spoken of as prime matter? Or does he come from a more immediate potency of a matter disposed more immediately for a human form?

Keep in mind that in speaking of a human being, our primary analogate of being, as coming to be, we are speaking of a rather complex material being. Such a being does not come to be immediately from the pure potency of prime matter as such. It comes to be from a matter that has been already predisposed for such a form. We could think of the human egg and sperm as such a matter, or even of the early stages of formation of the individual being. In any event we have to think of a matter that is not only apt for the form that is educed from it but also quite removed from whatever we might think of as the simplest kind of material substance. In fact, we have to think of the potency of matter as having been built up, so to speak, so that it could come to be an immediate potency for the human form or soul.

This is entirely in keeping with the idea of matter as being in potency. For if we begin with material beings in their simplest form, whether these be the four elements of the ancients or what are referred to as the basic physical entities in modern science, we have to think of the matter of these beings as in potency, not only to their actual forms, but also to other forms that we would characterize as higher, and ultimately as in potency to the human form as the highest in nature, with many other forms mediating between the lowest and the highest. In this way we come to an order of potency in the natural order of being going from the lowest to the highest which has been outlined as follows by Aquinas: "Prime matter is in potency first to the form of an element. Existing under the form of an element it is in potency to the form of a compound, and for this reason elements are the matter of the compound. Considered under the form of a compound it is in potency to a vegetative soul, for soul is the act of such a body. Similarly vegetative soul is potency to sensitive soul, while sensitive soul is potency to intellective soul" (*SG* III, 22, §2030). Aquinas goes on to illustrate this in terms of the process of generation of a human being, as he understood it. First, he says, there is the fetus living the life of a plant, after that the life of an animal, and finally the life of a human being.

It is interesting to note that Aquinas said all this without presupposing any evolution of species in nature, as we now understand it. For him the ontogenesis was not a repetition of a phylogenesis. But it was an illustration of the dynamic order of potency in matter, an ascending order of potency in nature according to different degrees of being, all the way up to human being, after which "there is not found in things that come to be and cease to be a later form or a higher one" (Ibid.). If we now include an evolution of the species as part of this ascending order of matter, we come to an even greater affirmation of this potential order rising from the lowest to the highest through a multitude of intermediate forms. The idea of matter, taken as being in potency and as principle of being for things that come to be, is the ground for any theory of evolution offered in nature.

It is not for us to go into the complex mechanism through which this process of evolution is supposed to have come about. Suffice it to say that it has been aptly characterized as a process of complexification (Teilhard 1959), going from the most simple to the most complex corporeal substances. But we must also add that it has also been a process of progressive integration. Each new stage in the evolution is a new kind of integration into a higher unity, so that at the summit human soul appears as the most integrative form, which is not to be confused with the material simplicity of an elementary body. In the human substance all the parts are integrated as one body formed or informed by an intellective soul. Form can then be seen as somehow overcoming the dispersion of matter as found in simpler bodies and making it more one in a diversity of beings, so that at the summit, through the intellective soul, it becomes more one than in any other material being. "The more form overcomes matter, the more what results from it and matter is one" (*SG* II, 68, §1453).

With this idea of evolution in the ascending potency of matter, however, we must be careful not to confuse prime matter, the common principle of material being, as we have come to think of it here, with any kind of primordial matter that is presupposed as having existed at the beginning of the evolutionary process. Such a primordial matter, whatever form it might have taken or however we might conceive it, would not *be prime matter* as common principle of material being as we have spoken of it. *Prime matter* as such, that is, as a radical principle of being constitutive of material things, does not exist as such independently of a form. Nor did it ever so exist in the past, nor can it ever so exist in the future. It can exist, if this term is allowed with regard to it, only as a constitutive coprinciple, along with form, of material things, which do exist, in the more proper sense of the term. Whatever primordial matter may have existed at the beginning of evolution, it was already a material being, so to speak, that is, a composite of prime matter and some form no matter how imperfectly integrative. It is spoken of as formless or as chaotic only in contrast to or as the privation of the more integrative forms that eventually developed from or in it. As such a composite being, the primordial matter was already a formed prime matter that was subject at the same time to a privation of the forms that were yet to be, or in the sense that it was only in potency to them.

Besides, prime matter is not merely something of the past. It is a constitutive principle of material things in the present as well as in the past. In fact, it is precisely as such that we know it best, since we know it by its analogy to form in actual composite beings. It is only by reflection on actual beings as having come to be that we understand matter as being in potency. This being in potency of matter is not some property added on to its essence, but rather, as Aquinas puts it, matter itself "according to its substance is potency to being substantial [*potentia ad esse substantiale*]" (*In Phys* I, 15, §131 [3]). Prime matter is not a complete substance by itself. It is substantial only in the sense that it is constitutive of a substance, along with form, as we have seen. But it is constitutive precisely as being in potency, subject to privation as well as form.

It is as subject to privation that we think of matter as imperfect apart from form and of coming to be as a process of *per-fection* or as a way of completion, which is the opposite of what was previously incomplete. The terms of this coming to be simply are privation and form. According to the way it exists under privation, matter has the idea of something imperfect, whereas according to the way it exists under a form it has the idea of something perfected, so that coming to be simply is seen as a passage from something imperfect to its opposite, which is perfect or perfected in the sense of having reached a positive *terminus ad quem*.

Clearly, this entails an order of succession and time, for the passage from the imperfect to the perfect in nature is always gradual. It takes place little by little, *paulatim,* which is also according to the nature of matter as being in potency. This can be illustrated in the coming to be of a single complex substance such as a human being, where the perfection of the substantial form comes only at the end of the process, but it can also be seen in the process of evolution as a whole, where the higher forms come only after the lower or less perfect forms. Regardless of what we may think about how this process is effected by causes external to the substances that come to be, the process has to be viewed as natural because it is quite in keeping with the dynamism of matter as being in potency and as constitutive of substances that come to be.

In the end, however, understood as the substance actualized in being, matter remains as that which is actualized. It may still be subject to a privation of other forms, which keeps it always subject to change, but as actualized by a form it remains a *per se* constitutive principle of the actual substance that has come to be, and it is as such that we must now view it as the principle of individuation and multiplicity in material substances.

12.5   Matter as Principle of Individuation and Multiplicity

The question of individuation is a sticky one in metaphysics. The principle of individuation was a matter of intensive debate for a long time in the history of metaphysics (Gracia 1994). If, however, we consider that there is no science of the individual, as Aristotle claimed, we might wonder if metaphysics as a science can have anything to do with the individual as such? And if it is the science of being as being, we can wonder how it can include the individual as such in its consideration? Is not the individual somehow the direct opposite of being in its commonality?

On the other hand, however, do we not have to say that the individual is a part of being even as an individual? Do we not consider individuality as essential to our primary analogate of being? We speak of any human being as an individual. In fact, do we not think of the person as the Individual par excellence, almost as if that were a proper name common to all persons? And do we not distinguish other kinds of individuals from these human individuals, whom we refer to as ends in themselves and never just as means, according to Kant's third formulation of the categorical imperative?

All this bespeaks a very high consideration of individuality as essential to being as we know it not just among human beings, but also among lesser beings. It is still something to be accounted for in metaphysics. But in accounting for it we must be very careful to understand precisely how the question arises and what is at issue. In our reflection on the conception of being we saw that it is a structured notion integrating three levels, thisness or haecceity, whatness or quiddity, and the *be* of a thing, and two distinct syntheses, that between whatness and thisness and that between these two taken as one, or as the essence of the thing, and *be* or the *act* of being (see above, section 3.2). When we speak of individuality or the individual, we focus on the thisness of being as distinct from the whatness and the be, although we do not separate it from the structure of the notion in which it is embedded. And from the standpoint of experience it is important that we do so, for being always appears to us as some *this* or *that* in the direct exercise of judgment. What I think of as being first and foremost is myself as an individual, or another self as another individual, or of both at the same time as individuals facing one another.

To raise the question of individuation, however, is not to ask about what these individuals are in their essence, as we seem to presuppose when we speak of the *Individual* as though that were the name for a certain kind of being with a certain dignity, namely, the human person. *Individual* in that sense seems to refer more to the nature in which these individuals share as human beings than to their individuality as such. Of course, in the concrete this nature cannot be separated from the thisness of each individual, but in raising the question of individuation we are not focusing on that nature as such. That pertains more to the question of the determination of being or its whatness, as we shall see. In raising the question of individuation we are focusing only on what constitutes a being in its individuality or thisness, which can refer to "this tree" or "this dog" as well as "this human being."

As such, this question pertains not just to human individuals, but to any being that can be identified as a *this* or a *that* in being, or what we can now refer to as a *substance* in the primary and concrete sense of the term. To the extent that there are individuals other than human beings, lesser beings, so to speak, which are nevertheless individual substances, we have to speak of the principle of individuation in a more common and ontological sense so that it will account not only for human individuals, but also for any individual substance of whatever kind in nature. In this sense the principle of individuation will be the same for all individual beings, whether human or not, and the human being will be seen as accounted for as an individual in the same way as any other individual substance in nature.

How, then, is this principle of individuation to be understood? We can think of many things that individuate beings from one another. Among them are the actions of each individual that are proper to each and that set each one off from any other. We could also include any number of qualities by which individuals, even of the same species, are distinguished from one another. The place that an individual occupies in space or the time in which it appears also distinguishes each one from others. But Swartz speaks of theories that focus on these accidental factors as individuating principles as "negative" because they invoke "*nothing more* than a thing's properties" as distinct from its "substance" (Swartz 279). While insisting on substance, however, he thinks of it only in the Lockean sense, that is, as some property-less substratum unknown and unknowable in itself or as some kind of "ontological glue" for sets of properties we associate with or in individual things (282–83). Swartz rejects most of the negative theories he reviews, but he argues for a more radical theory that focuses on the concept of "physical object" as "more primitive than that of *space*" or any other such relation that presupposes numerical difference (308). In this he is returning to the more primordial concept of substance or to the idea of primary substance as found in Aristotle. But he does not raise the further question that we are raising here, namely, the question of a principle of individuation for any such "physical object" on the level of substance as such when there are many individual substances of the same kind to be accounted for.

On this level of substance as such, one could appeal to causes external to an individual substance as individuating that substance, as when we speak of someone as the daughter or the son of so-and-so. But none of these individuating factors goes to the substance itself in its individuality, which has to be the ground for all of them as pertaining to this individual. If the substance itself is not an individual, none of these other principles of individuation can come into play. What is the principle of individuation of the substance itself in its individuality?

To answer this question we must look to the constitutive principles of an individual substance, namely, matter and form. We cannot look to the form, as some try to do, because, as we shall see more clearly, form is the principle of determination, in which many individuals of the same species can be seen as the same, that is, as not distinguished in kind. A human form is what makes Socrates and Plato both the same kind of being, namely, human. What makes them distinct from one another radically or substantially as individuals of the same species has to be their matter or, more precisely, the individual matter that is constitutive of each one in his individuality. How is this to be understood, since matter as a radical principle of being is only being in potency?

We must keep in mind what it is precisely that comes to be. We alluded earlier to an example of Aristotle where dog comes to be from horse. This served to illustrate the difference between coming to be *per se* and coming to be *per accidens*. Dog, which happens to be animal, comes to be *per se,* but not animal, since there was already animal in horse. Animal comes to be only *per accidens,* insofar as what comes to be *per se* happens to be animal. The same point was made with regard to being and notbeing with regard to coming to be simply. Now, however, we must bring the point to bear more on the individual as such of any species, for that is what comes to be *per se* or most properly. Whatever comes to be as a substance is always an individual and it comes to be precisely as an individual, as this substance and not any other even of the same kind. It is thus the principle of becoming that itself is the principle of individuation, and this can only be matter as the subject of change. It is matter that makes this individual be this individual and not another even of the same kind.

Having said this, however, we must now ask in what sense matter is the principle of individuation. Is it as prime matter as such or as matter *in communi,* which, as we have seen, does not exist as such, or is it as matter that is already actualized by some form, which nevertheless remains in potency to other forms? In speaking of matter as the principle of individuation, we are referring to matter as being in potency that has entered into composition with a form in the constitution of an individual substance. As such it is actualized by the form, but in being actualized it also constricts the form, so to speak, to being the form of this individual and not of another. While Plato and Socrates share in the same substantial form, one is not the other thanks to the matter of each that is actualized as human in each instance.

In being actualized the potency of matter becomes individualized. Matter becomes designated, or *signata,* as the Scholastics used to say, something we can point to as *this* or *that*. But it does not become designated as *this* or *that* by reason of the form, which is principle of specification, and not of individuation, but by reason of itself as being in potency. Just as being in potency is the very nature of matter, so also it is of the nature of this potency to be individualized when it is actualized. Hence, matter is not individualized unless it is actualized, but it is in the nature of matter to be individualized when it is actualized. Just as we do not understand matter except as being in potency to form, so also we do not understand it except as individualizing the substance in which it is actualized.

In saying that matter is the principle of individuation we do not mean that it is principle of personality in human being, since personality cannot be reduced to mere individuality, something that can be said of things that are not persons as well as of persons. Granted, every person in our experience is an individual. But not every individual is a person, unless we want to make the case that only persons are individuals. But that would seem to go against our experience in the direct exercise of judgment, where we do seem to recognize other individual substances besides persons not only on the level of other kinds of living things in the animal and plant kingdoms, but also on the level of inanimate objects. They too have matter as the principle of their individuation, like persons, while persons have a higher principle of determination in their form, which is their rational soul. It is the soul that makes the person *what* or *who* it is, not its matter. Matter only makes it this individual, which is significant, but not fully determinative of what it is to be a person.

Concretely, through the direct exercise of judgment, we come to this question of individuation in metaphysics from the standpoint of persons, our primary analogate of being even as substance. It is interesting to note, however, that Strawson, in his more descriptive account of how we identify particulars, focuses first on what he calls "material bodies" as the basic particulars long before he gets to the question of persons, which for him present a special problem with regard to the ascription of states of consciousness to the same thing as that to which we ascribe corporeal characteristics (Strawson 1959). This difficulty in dealing with persons as individuals comes from considering only "material bodies" as primary analogates of substance and not persons, who are also "material bodies" among other bodies along with having different states of consciousness. The question of individuation on the level of substance is the same for all beings that are thought of as bodies or material substances. It must not be confused with the question of what determines different individuals according to different kinds or species, like persons or other kinds of living things, or even nonliving things. Every substance we know in experience not only has a form of its own, but also *signate matter* as its principle of individuation that sets it off from other individuals with the same form as well as from other individuals with different forms, whether conscious or not.

Thus, even if we grant that there is no science of the individual as such, this does not mean that the individual as such is not real or not intelligible. Individuality is not nothing. Nor is it a privation. It is something positive in reality. It is often what we focus on first and foremost in being, especially in the case of a human being, which we refer to as the Individual. In fact, we sometimes focus on individuality to the exclusion of *what* a thing is, forgetting that what a thing is, or its specific form, is also part of its identity along with its individuality. Not all individuals are of the same kind and the difference of kind affects individuality as such, while individuality alone does not express any of these important differences. It expresses only the difference between this one and that one as individual substance that is, nevertheless, real and accounted for by matter as a radical principle of being.

In expressing this, however, individuality also expresses how matter is principle of multiplicity in being, a multiplicity that can be seen in the plurality of individuals of one and the same species in nature or in the sheer plurality of the wide host of individuals taken indiscriminately from the diversity of species. This multiplicity pertains to the differences of being we have spoken of earlier. But it is not the only kind of difference we have to account for in the order of substances. There are also the differences that come from the diversity of forms, which we have yet to speak of and with which this difference of multiplicity has to be correlated.

12.6 The Reality of Matter as Distinct Principle of Being

We have come to an understanding of matter as a first principle of things that come to be simply or on the level of substance. This is the principle that the pre-Socratics sought, but could not find, so that they were forced to think of every change as only accidental and never as substantial. This is the principle that Plato did find, but did not adequately distinguish from privation. It is the principle that many today still have not found, either because they still view all change as only accidental or as a mere rearrangement of unchanging particles, or because they still do not adequately distinguish being in potency from nothing. It is the principle whose reality must now be affirmed as constitutive of material beings as such.

We do not claim that prime matter is itself a material thing. It is not, nor can it be. It does not exist except as actualized by a form in a substance. Of itself, it is only being in potency. But we do claim that it is real as a constitutive principle of any material substance and that it is distinct from its form in such a substance. We have tried to explain or understand how it is so. We must now come to a critical judgment of our own as to whether it is really so, that is, a principle really distinct from its substantial form, restricting this form to this individual, and constituting with that form the individual substance that comes to be and *is* in the primary sense of the term, while remaining itself in potency to other forms, so that what has come to be can also cease to be.

This is the question of the real distinction of principles of being that used to be debated in the Schools. To speak of the distinction as "real" does not mean that each principle, in this case matter and form, is a thing unto itself or a substance. The matter and form of a substance are not distinct from one another as one thing is distinct from another. We would refer to this kind of distinction as a division or a separation of one being from another in accordance with the understanding of transcendental unity we proposed earlier in Chapter 5. This kind of division or separation presupposes a plurality of things so divided or separated. In speaking of a real distinction of principles within an individual substance, however, we are not presupposing such a plurality. We are assuming a substance as only one thing and, within this one thing, we are maintaining a distinction of principles that are understood only in relation to one another as constitutive of this one thing. They cannot be separated from one another as such principles of one thing. But they have to be thought of as really distinct because the only way of accounting for material substances as coming to be and ceasing to be precisely as substances is by affirming this duality of principles as real.

We are inquiring into the very idea of substance in being and how substance comes to be. Let us recall where we are starting from: not the obscure region of material being of so-called basic physical entities as defined in mathematical physics, but the human being, which is the first to be identified in our experience as a substance, or as a plurality of substances. We are proceeding not from the bottom of the order of material beings, where bodies appear to be more simple as well as more obscure, but from the top of the order, where bodies are more complex but also more clearly identified as beings in themselves, starting from the rational animal in all its complexity as a unity-identity-whole and going on to the nonrational sentient animal, then to nonsentient living substance, and on to whatever can be identified or interpreted as substance in the realm of the nonliving. For, even if we start from the living in our understanding of substance, we do not exclude any body with an identity of its own, even if it is not living, from this category, and we view it as any body, that is, as constituted from matter or being in potency. Thus, though our argument appears clearest from the standpoint of a living substance, given its more obvious unity-identity-wholeness, nonetheless it has to be true of inanimate substances, which also come to be and cease to be in their own way.

Let us consider three arguments for maintaining a real distinction between matter and form in things that come to be simply, one based on the very conception of such things, one based on the way we conceive such things as concrete, and one based on a consideration of the proper activity of such things.

12.6.1 The Argument from the Understanding of Coming to Be Simply

This argument starts from the interpretation of some changes in material being as substantial, that is, as the coming to be simply or the ceasing to be of a substance, as experienced in the genesis or the death of an individual like Socrates. Such a change is not to be confused with a merely accidental change, as in the case where Socrates becomes learned or forgets what he has learned, where the substance of Socrates is the subject of change and remains the same identity throughout. But it has to be understood as another kind of change with another kind of subject, which can no longer be thought of as a substance with its own unity-identity-wholeness, since it can be only as constitutive of a substance. Thus, the argument proceeds by analogy with accidental change, but we arrive at a totally different kind of subject of change, namely, prime matter as constitutive principle of being distinct from form.

We must keep in mind that even substantial change is not a mere substitution of one thing for another, or the annihilation of one thing and the creation of another. As a change, it is a transmutation of one thing into another, where there is something permanent that was before and that remains after, a subject of the change, as well as a new form in which the change terminates. In other words, there is a subject of the new form in what comes to be that is really distinct from that form and that is continuous with what preceded this coming to be, a being in potency that calls for a new form as the old one disappears. *Corruptio unius est generatio alterius.*

Inasmuch as the change in question is substantial, we have to speak of the new form as the substantial form of the new being that has come to be. This is the principle of its quiddity or of *what* it is as such an individual, while the subject of this form in the new composite is its matter, which is undetermined in itself, except as being in potency to its form, even as it restricts this form to being only the form of this individual.

This is essentially the argument in the book *Zeta* of the *Metaphysics,* chapter 7, where Aristotle is arguing that the forms found in material things are generated not from separate forms or forms existing apart from matter, as they would be for Plato, but rather from forms existing in matter, whether these be in nature itself, in the case of natural generation, or in the thought of an artificer, in the case of generation by art. The argument includes bringing in form as part of the process of generation, whether it be the form of the natural agent of generation, which generates something similar to itself, as when a human being generates another human being or a plant generates another plant of the same species, or the form in the thought of an artist, as when a sculptor produces a statue from bronze. In both cases, however, whether natural or artificial, the process of generation presupposes matter. "All things which are generated naturally or artificially have matter; for it is possible [*dunaton*] for each one of them both to be and not to be, and this is the matter in each individual" (*Metaph* 1032a 20–23). In other words, what has come to be is in potency both to being and to not-being by reason of the matter *from* which it is constituted.

It is important to note that possibility or potency *(dunamis)* is spoken of here only as being in individual things, and not as anything in itself. As matter it is that which remains as the subject of the form in what comes to be. It is that which *could* be this thing before it came to be and it is that which could still be something else after it has come to be this thing. The potency of matter is found only in individual things and it is that which makes each thing changeable, even to the point of ceasing to be. While it is really distinct from the form of which it is the matter, it is not itself a thing and cannot strictly be spoken of as coming to be or ceasing to be. Only individuals come to be and cease to be *per se,* and not matter as such. Only material things, and not matter as a constitutive principle, can come to be or cease to be. Prime matter is only the potency of a material being to be or not to be, but as such it is a constitutive principle of its being.

12.6.2   The Argument from the Individuality of Concreta

Another argument for this real distinction of matter from form can be formulated in terms of the structure of the notion of being articulated earlier, in section 3.1, or in terms of the way we signify being in the concrete. In this conception we saw a twofold synthesis, one between the *be* of a thing and its essence, which we called a *composition,* and another within the essence itself between *what* a thing is or its quiddity and its being a *this* or a *that,* its haecceity, which we called a *concretion.* In referring to a plurality of beings such as yourself and myself, or Socrates, Plato, and Aristotle, which are all of the same kind, we refer not only to their being in *act,* but also to the quiddity of each in its own self as something human and to their respective individualities or haecceity. It is this latter synthesis between quiddity and haecceity that is relevant here for coming to the distinction of matter, which, as we have seen, is understood as principle of individuation.

If we consider that there are many individuals of one and the same species, like yourself and myself and any other individual recognized as human, which come to be, and that all these individuals really are human in themselves, then we can ask: On what basis are they separate individuals from one another, even while being of the same kind? They are the same, that is, human in their being, by reason of the form that is common to all of them. What makes them separate from one another as individual beings cannot be their form, since it is common to all of them and therefore is the same for all. It has to be a distinct principle that is proper to each individual and individuates this form in this individual from that form in that individual. This principle we call *matter* as distinct from *form* in the individual that comes to be.

Now, it could be said that matter too is common to all material beings. But this would be matter taken only in abstraction. In the concrete, or as signate, matter is always individuated. We can also speak of thisness or haecceity in abstraction, but this does not amount to any concrete this or that common to many. The point in distinguishing between *this* and *that* individual is to express that each is a separate being from the other. As an individual being it has to have within itself the principle of its own individuation distinct from its principle of specification. When there are many beings of the same kind, that which specifies them as a certain kind of being cannot be that which distinguishes them from one another as individuals of the same kind, because this principle makes them all the same in kind. Without a distinct principle of individuation for each, these individuals would all be collapsed into one and the same being, of the sort that was represented in Plato' s separate forms. Only matter as a principle of being distinct from form can establish them as separate individual beings, which is the reverse side of its being the principle of transmutation and multiplicity within one and the same form of being.

The question arises here as to whether this argument establishes a real distinction in things themselves, or one that follows only from our way of thinking about a plurality of substances of one and the same kind. To be sure, the distinction is necessary from the standpoint of our thinking. It follows from our understanding of the notion of being in its structure as a *this*

and a *what*. But this is only the understanding of a notion or a way of referring to being in itself. Is the distinction in being itself or is it only in our way
of signifying?

It would seem that in raising this question we wish to separate being
from knowing once again, as if it were not being that is known when knowing takes place. To do this would be to open a gap between being in itself
and knowing that can never be bridged by any sort of intuition, whether
sensible or intellectual. We have seen from the beginning that there is no
such gap to be bridged whenever there is knowing. Knowing is always of
being. Nevertheless, even admitting this, it does not follow that every notion
of ours or every structure in our notion necessarily corresponds to being in
itself even if it is necessary for us. With Kant, we must recognize the limits of
our understanding and ask whether our notions are true or express what is
the case with being itself.

This argument from the expressed individuality of *concreta,* then, does not
do this. It is valid, but only up to a point. It is what Aristotle or Aquinas
would have referred to as only a dialectical or a logical argument. It does not
go far enough to be strictly demonstrative. It is true as far as it goes, but it
does not bring us to a scientific conclusion. It brings us only to something
probable not as something that may or may not be true, but as something
that remains to be proved or is provable. Is there a more demonstrative argument for the sort of real distinction we are trying to affirm?

12.6.3   The Argument from the Structure of Proper Activity

Let us consider the proper activity of the beings we say come to be simply and cease to be. If we find a structure or a composition such as the one
we are affirming in the proper activity of these beings, we can argue to a
similar structure or composition in the substance of the being on the basis of
the principle we established with regard to being as active in Chapter 6. As
we saw in reflecting on activity as a transcendental property of being, not
only is every being active, so that action necessarily follows upon being, but
also the proper activity of each being is proportionate to its being. In this instance we shall focus on the activities of judging and deciding, seen as proper to human being, our primary analogate of being, and argue from the
structure of these activities to a proportionate structure in the substance of
our being.

Let us first recognize that the exercise of judgment is a genuine proper
activity of the self in which we form definitions and formulate hypotheses
to be reflected upon for verification. For our purposes here we do not need

to go into the second act of intelligence involved in this exercise of judgment, namely, that wherein we reflect upon some understanding in order to come to some agreement or disagreement with it or to say "yes" or "no" to it. We need only focus on the first act of intelligence, in which we come to some understanding or formulation concerning something given in experience. In this act there is, as we said before, a concretizing synthesis in which some understanding, as expressed in some formulation, is united with a *this* or a *that* in the concretizing synthesis of direct judgment.

The exercise of judgment begins around a *this* or a *that* given in experience and expressed in the subject *(S)* of the judgment. "This is a human being." "That is an elephant." "This is Socrates." "That is Plato." We do go on to make universal judgments, in which *S* is a universal. "The human being is mortal." "The elephant is big by nature." These universal judgments claim to express something about reality. But they do not claim that the universal, the human being as such or the elephant as such, exists as such. They only claim that what can be said of the universal *S* can be said of all the individuals that come under *S*. There is no reality except that of individuals and whatever is claimed about universals is claimed about individuals defined or determined as coming under these universals. It is not human being as such that is mortal, since human being could be thought of as going on immortally in the succession of individuals that are human. It is the individual human being that is mortal. Similarly, elephant as such is not big, but only individual elephants, or at least they are expected to grow big according to their nature. This relation of the universal to the individual is sometimes expressed in a syllogism: "All men are mortal; Socrates is a man; therefore Socrates is mortal." But the syllogism does not demonstrate anything. It only expresses a subsumption of an individual, which is presupposed in the direct exercise of judgment, under a universal.

The same relation holds not only of universal concepts, but also of hypotheses or theories formulated with universal concepts. In empirical science we do not think of any hypothesis as true unless it has been verified in this or that experiment with this or that state of affairs. We do not say that what is expressed in the theory exists as such, that is, as it appears in the theory, but only as it explains this or that fact in a state of affairs. This is why the philosophy of logical atomism as proposed by Bertrand Russell cannot ultimately make sense. It confuses logical entities, which are only parts of a universal theory, with existing individuals. Even when a theory postulates the existence of certain entities to account for the existence of individual states of affairs, not to say substances, it does not posit them as a *this* or a *that* that can be signified concretely but rather as a postulate that is still on the abstract level of theory. Only if we conjure up some experiment that will make this entity appear as a *this* or a *that,* independently of all theory and interpretation, can we speak of such entities as individuals in the concrete sense of the term. Always, the truth of an empirical theory in the direct exercise of judgment depends on how it relates to some *this* or *that* in experience.

The point here is not to argue about the ontological status of any entity mentioned in a scientific theory, but rather to reflect on the structure of the activity in which we think of such theories or formulate the quiddity of any sensible thing. Although the old criterion of meaningfulness proposed by logical positivism, namely, that according to which the meaning of a proposition is reducible to some sense content according to the so-called principle of verification (Ayer 5ff), has proven altogether too simplistic and untenable, it was right in pointing out that meaning and truth for us always entails some reference to a *this* or a *that* in experience. This is especially evident in the direct exercise of judgment, whether in common sense, in empirical science, or even in phenomenology. Regardless of how universal the predicate may be, this exercise of judgment always implies some reference to a *this* or *that,* when it does not explicitly contain such a reference as its subject. In its structure it always entails a concretizing synthesis of something on the level of universal quiddity with some *this* or *that.* This is a necessary structure of the activity.

From the necessity of this structure in the activity we argue to a similar structure in the substance of the being that produces the activity, because this activity, the direct exercise of judgment, is seen as a proper activity of this substance, namely, the self. Just as in my activity of judgment there is a determination expressed in the predicate that needs haecceity for any reference to being in truth, so also in my substance there is a form that needs another principle to concretize it as *this,* namely, *matter.* And just as haecceity limits the validity of any universal determination in the direct exercise of judgment to some *this* or *that,* so also this other principle limits the form of *what* I am to this individual that I am. When I speak of whiteness as real, I do not mean that it exists as such, but that this white thing is really white, so that *this* limits what I refer to as white. So also in my substance, humanity does not exist as such, but only as this individual self, and so on of every other individual self recognized as similarly exercising judgment. And just as every singular judgment, by reason of its haecceity, is distinct from any other singular judgment, so that one may be true while the other may be false, so also I am really separate from you and you from me, even though we both share the same human form, by reason of a principle that is really distinct from our form and that individualizes this form as real in each one of us.

In this argument we start from a real exercise of judgment that we experience phenomenologically and we bring out a structure in it, or a distinction of principles, one restricting the other, which, of itself, is more positive than the first. "White," for example, or "human," expresses something more positive than just "this" or "Individual," even though "white" or "human" does not exist except as *this* or *that*. They are more positive at least in the sense that they are found in more than one individual. They are found in this way by "entering" into composition with a principle distinct from them that individualizes them, a material substance in the case of white, which belongs in an accidental category, and a designated matter in the case of human, which refers to a substantial form.

It should be noted that what we propose is an isomorphism not between knowing and the *known*, as Lonergan does in establishing what he refers to as the "elements of metaphysics" (Lonergan 483–87), but between knowing as the proper activity of human being and the same human being as *knower*. Our argument is transcendental in that it starts from a reflection on our activity of knowing, but not in the sense that it goes from a structure in the knowing to a structure in the known. Even if we grant that knowing is of being, as we do from the beginning, it does not follow that the heuristic structure of our knowing is of itself grounds for affirming a parallel structure in the reality known or in what Lonergan refers to as "proportionate being," the being we have been speaking of as coming to be and ceasing to be, or the being known in the direct exercise of judgment.

It is true that it is by a reflection on the heuristic structure of knowing that we arrived at our understanding of being as a structured notion earlier in the logic of being. But this was only a transcendental reflection in the Kantian sense, as is any reflection on insight. While it does give us an understanding of what it is to experience, understand, and judge, and of the notions contained in this experiencing, understanding, and judging, such as the structured notion of being, it does not necessarily give us an understanding of being itself, unless we make some kind of dogmatic rationalist leap from the structure of knowing to the structure of the known. Taken in this sense, the so-called transcendental method does not yield a knowledge of the structure of being itself, but only of knowing, as Kant understood very well. Even after having established the necessary structure of our notion of being, we still have to demonstrate a structure in being itself, especially with regard to substance.

Now the fact that we have demonstrated a structure in our notion of being does open the way for this further demonstration with regard to being itself. In this way Lonergan is quite right in proposing an isomorphism between knowing and *known*. But this is only a dialectical argument at best for a real distinction of principles of being. It yields only a probable result, like our argument from the individuality of *concreta*, that is, one that still has to be proven or demonstrated of being in itself or in its substance. In this sense the transcendental method based only on knowing as such and its structure does not go far enough in reaching for the known. What is needed is another kind of transcendental method based more on knowing as the activity of a subject and as disclosing the structure of that subject in its substance. This second kind of transcendental method has its roots not so much in Kant, but much more in the ancient understanding of every being as active, and it rests not just on the activity of knowing, but on any proper activity of human being, deciding as well as judging.

In fact, an argument for the real distinction of matter from form in the human substance that would parallel the one we have just seen from our activity of knowing could be constructed from our activity of willing. Such an argument would focus on the concretizing synthesis found in any exercise of choice for us, where there is always a *this* or a *that* to be chosen or, more exactly, where we are ultimately reduced to choosing between this or that, each of which is tied to a distinct individual motion or potency within our being (Blondel 1984, 109–44). From the distinction between these individual motions and our universal power of deciding in our voluntary action we can argue to a parallel distinction between the material principle of movement and individuation in our substance and its substantial form.

The argument in both instances, whether from knowing or willing, is phenomenological in that it starts from an activity immediately experienced. In each activity it brings out a real distinction of two factors irreducible to one another and constitutive of the particular phenomenon as a whole. From this the argument proceeds to a similar distinction of constitutive principles in the substance of which the phenomenon is a proper activity. The demonstration is *a posteriori*, that is, based on experience, and not a dogmatic or rational leap from knowing to *known*, in that it begins from what is immediately evident to us but then understood as derivative from something ontologically prior to it, namely, the substance. It is demonstrative in that it gives us knowledge of the substance or of the being in itself which produces this activity as constituted of two really distinct constitutive principles, matter and form, neither of which is anything independently of the other. The substance appears as the sort of thing it is in this distinction, a composite of matter and form.

In arguing only from knowing or willing, however, we have shown only that human substance is a composite of matter and form. What of other substances? Are there other kinds of substances and, if so, are they also composites of matter and form? While a transcendental reflection on our own proper activity might give us knowledge of a distinction of principles within our own substance, there is no possibility of such a reflection on the proper activity of other substances. If there are other kinds of substance, as we say there are in the direct exercise of judgment, they too have to be understood as having their own proper activity. And though we cannot reflect transcendentally on their proper activity, we can reflect on it as it appears to us in direct experience, as we do in empirical science or phenomenology.

In all that we can clearly affirm as a material thing, we find an activity that is similar to ours in that it synthesizes a particular kind with a *this,* as this plant photosynthesizes carbohydrates from this water and this carbon dioxide, or as these two parts of hydrogen combine with this part of oxygen to form this water. In fact, it is through such activities, viewed as proper to each kind of thing, that we come to identify them as material substances. One individual thing acts in this way on other things, while another acts in a different way. In all this sort of activity there is always a synthesis, which is a form, with a *this* in some manifold, a synthesis, which discloses a radical composition in the substance of material things between a principle of determination and a principle of becoming and individuation.

The question could arise at this point as to whether there are only material substances to be considered in metaphysics. Our insistence until now has been on human being as a substance that is at once intelligent and material. But is that as far as the analogy of substance could go? Could we not think of substances that would be intelligent and not material or dependent on any composition with matter, in other words, pure intelligences as substances. If there are such substances, then they too would have to be thought of as having a proper activity of intelligence of their own, which would also have to be immaterial, that is, not dependent on any sense experience. It would be difficult to understand how such substances could appear in our experience, since their proper activity would be quite immaterial. But if we had access to the activity of such beings through our own intelligence by way of abstraction from our dependence on experience, we would have to think of it as a pure activity without composition with thisness or thatness, and from that we would have to infer a purity or a simplicity of form in a substance that would not be a composite of matter and form. If they were such pure forms, without matter, could they still be thought of as coming and ceasing to be or even as individuals, since matter is the principle of coming and ceasing to be and of individuation in being?

These are all questions that would follow upon our affirmation of matter as a principle of being in beings known in the direct exercise of judgment, once we start thinking of immaterial substances. Before we can answer any of them in any way, we must reflect more attentively on the nature of matter's coprinciple of being in material substances, the substantial form, which we have referred to frequently in matter's relation to it but which we have not yet considered in its own right as a distinct principle of being.

CHAPTER 13

Substantial Form as Principle of Determination of Being in Potency

~

H AVING CONSIDERED THE NATURE of matter at some length, we now turn to consider the nature of form, its coprinciple in the constitution of a material substance, keeping in mind that what comes to be properly is neither matter as such, nor form as such, but the composite of matter and form. In our reflection on coming to be simply we did speak of the form as new in contradistinction from the permanence of the material principle or the subject of change. In a transmutation an old form disappears, that is, the form of the being that ceases to be, and a new form appears, that is, the form of the being that comes to be. But this new form comes into being only by being educed from the potency of matter, that is, as the form of this new composite that has come to be. Only the composite comes to be in the proper sense of the term.

We have said that matter, as a principle of being, can be understood only in its analogy to form. It *is* only as in potency to an act. As subject to privation it is thought of as imperfect in relation to its act, albeit not as nothing, while the act or the form is thought of as its perfection at the end of the change, at least with respect to what has come to be. The form comes as a certain completion for the change; it is the *terminus ad quem* toward which the potency of matter was ordered and which remains in the composite as a constitutive principle. All of this speaks of matter as real but always as ordered to form. If this is so, why did we not consider form first in bringing out the intelligibility of matter? Would not that have made matter more intelligible to us, given its natural analogy to form?

In one respect, the point is well taken. We have in fact found ourselves forced to refer constantly to form in elaborating our understanding of matter. In other words, we have been operating with a preunderstanding of form that we needed in order to bring out our understanding of matter. This preunderstanding, however, was immersed in the movement of matter, so to speak, which we had to establish first as a principle of being for the beings we come to know first in the direct exercise of judgment. Form was seen only as the *terminus ad quem* of a transmutation and not according to its own nature as a principle of being distinct from matter.

This is, of course, how we first come to know and understand form in the direct exercise of judgment, that is, as involved in change and as expressing a *de-termination* of change, that which enables us to determine a change as having taken place. In the case of coming to be simply or of a substantial change, form is that which determines what has come to be according to *what* it is. It is what we have already begun to speak of as the substantial form, coprinciple of being with its designated matter. It is preunderstood in our understanding of change, which is where all of our understanding of being begins in the direct exercise of judgment, since the being we know first is one that comes to be and ceases to be according to our experience even of our own being. But this preunderstanding must now be developed or articulated more fully insofar as form has also disclosed itself as a principle of being in what comes to be.

It has been suggested that form is the perfection of a potency in matter. How is it such a perfection? Can it be such without matter? Can there be forms that are not perfections of matter but that are really "perfections" in themselves, separate from matter, as Plato thought, or are such "forms" merely abstractions from matter, that is, unreal, as we understand being in the direct exercise of judgment? Can a form be a being or a substance unto itself, without matter? If so, how would the existence of such a form be known to us? How can such an existence be understood, when it leaves out what is now for us a necessary component in our conception of being, that is, thisness, as well as a necessary principle of being, that is, matter?

These are questions that remain for us with regard to our preunderstanding of form as the term of coming to be and as a principle of being for a substance that comes to be. Through a discussion of them we can come to a better understanding of form as a principle of substance or being in itself.

13.1   Form as Principle of Determination

In articulating the structure of our notion of being earlier, in section 3.2, we spoke of determination as anything more positive in a being than mere haecceity in the order of essence. In this order we distinguished between two different kinds of determination, those that appear secondary and accidental and those that are more quidditative in that they pertain to *what* a thing is in itself.

This is a distinction that often gets lost in contemporary discussions of individuation. Starting from the Lockean conception of substance, determinations are usually understood only as properties and qualities, without any reference to a substance, which presumably remains unknown and bereft of properties in itself. All predicates are understood only as expressing properties or qualities pertaining to a subject or a *this,* which supposedly has no determinations of its own as a thing in itself. The idea of determinations that pertain to *what* a thing is in itself, as distinct from those that are only qualities, relations, or even properties of the thing, is simply ignored, even though such an idea is necessary for understanding the question of individuation in its most crucial form, namely, in the case of many individuals of the same kind. How can we speak of many individuals of the same kind unless we understand at least some determinations as pertaining to these individuals according to *what* they are? Moreover, how can we speak of such determinations as unknown or unknowable, if in fact we recognize a diversity in things such as that between the living and the nonliving or between the rational and the nonrational as well as a multiplicity of individuals in the different kinds or species of being? Such determinations are predicated of beings according to *what* they are or according to their standing in being, and not just as properties or qualities distinct from substance. This is what we do, for example, when we say of Socrates that he is rational animal.

We must not confuse the properties of a thing with what is predicated of it according to *what* it is in its substance. Even those who ignore the substance of things still speak of their properties. In the strict sense of the term, a property is predicated necessarily of its substance, but it is not predicated properly of the thing according to *what* it is. The property of a thing does not enter its definition. It only follows from that definition, as Aristotle shows in the *Posterior Analytics.* A property is only an accident that differs from other accidents in that it is predicated necessarily of its substance, while other accidents are not predicated necessarily. It is a property of being human to be able to laugh, for example, but not to be white or colored in some other way.

We speak of "quidditative determinations," but we must not understand them in a purely static fashion, as the modern understanding of substance seems to suppose. If we keep in mind that we are speaking of substances that come to be, we understand the determination of *what* a thing is as the termination of the process whereby it comes to be simply. We refer to the "substantial form" as this determination that constitutes the thing that has come to be along with its matter. Aristotle spoke of this form as the *entelecheia* of a thing, which we translate as its actuality, but which etymologically expresses the fact that the thing has attained an end *(telos)* in itself or has been actualized from its potency to some degree of completion, even though it may still have a further completion to actualize through its own action. The substantial form is the *finis generationis,* the end of the process of coming to be simply, which is not to be confused with the *finis rei generatae,* the end that the thing generated still has to achieve through its own proper activity.

It is this idea of substantial form as the end of a process of generation that enables us to speak of it as a certain kind of perfection. In connection with the understanding of being as good discussed earlier in Chapter 7, we spoke of a distinction between the first and the second perfection of a thing. In the complete or final sense of the term, the perfection of a thing is achieved only through its own proper activity. A thing is said to be good simply only when it has attained its appropriate end. This is what we have called its second perfection. But in coming to be simply, as a substance, from the potency of its matter, a thing can also be said to attain a certain perfection, which we have called its first perfection. This is in keeping with our understanding of matter as being in potency or as a certain desire for form, which not only actualizes it but also brings its coming to be to a certain substantial completion, a certain standing in being according to *what* it is as a being. Substantial form is thus understood as the first perfection of a being that has come to be, from which it launches itself toward its second perfection.

The idea of *de-termination* also implies a certain delimitation in being. What is determined as only a plant is not an animal. Even the rational animal is not any animal but only a certain kind of animal. We have spoken earlier of differences of being in connection with becoming in general. Now we are speaking of differences in the order of substances that set one kind of substance off from other kinds of substances. Each substance of whatever kind has a certain completion in itself. Yet it belongs to only one kind of substance and it is only one individual of that kind. What individualizes it is its matter, but what determines it to be of a certain kind is its form.

We alluded to these differences of substantial form earlier, in section 12.4, in speaking of the order in matter. Matter as such is being in potency to form and, when it is actualized through certain lower forms such as those of nonliving substances, it remains in potency to higher forms such as those of living substances. The different determinations of substances at various levels enable us to speak of different degrees of being among the diversity of material beings that we experience and claim to know in the direct exercise of judgment.

We can speak of these different degrees of being according to an ascending order, as we did in connection with the material principle of being and becoming. But in connection with the formal principle we can also speak of them according to a descending order, starting from the highest material being we know, human being, our primary analogate of being, and going to the lowest that we can identify as a substance. In either order there is delimitation of one level of being from other levels as well as a diversification of being, but the richness of the diversity appears much more clearly from the top down than from the bottom up. It is in the form of the human substance that being is disclosed most amply to us. This form, like any substantial form, is the principle of being for the composite human being. It is the principle of its subjectivity and its activity, just as the form of a plant is the principle of its life. It determines the indeterminate being in potency of matter to be *what* I am, not any kind of individual, but a human individual. Lesser beings are thought of as lesser because they do not disclose the same amplitude as the human being. But to the extent that they too are substances according to their own degree, they too have forms that are the principle of being for *what* they are as our form is the principle of being for *what* we are.

13.2   The Idea of Pure Form as Separate Substance

We have spoken of matter as something positive, that is, not as nothing or privation but as being in potency. We have spoken of form as something even more positive, as that which actualizes the potency of matter to be this or that kind of being. In our understanding of the composite substance we can speak of the pure potency of matter insofar as we distinguish it from the form that actualizes it. We have to think of it as real insofar as we think of it as something positive, especially if we think of it as a principle of being really distinct from its form. But is that enough to make us think of it as something actually existing?

It all depends on what we mean by "something actually existing." Here we have been taking it to mean that which is affirmed to be in some complete sense in the direct exercise of judgment as a *this* that is one kind of thing or another. What actually exists is a substance understood as being in itself. In existential philosophy, existence usually connotes more than this bare subsistence of substance, especially with regard to human being. There, to exist authentically means more to constitute oneself in one's own final identity through one's own activity. "Existence" in that sense has more to do with one's second perfection than with one's first or essential perfection. Here we are taking "existence" in a more restricted sense, that is, as applying to whatever is in itself as a substance, prescinding from its activity and how it constitutes itself in its ultimate perfection. But we do take it as something actual, and not just as potential. Hence, matter, understood as only being in potency, cannot be thought of as actually existing. What actually exists is an actualized potency of matter with form as the actualizing principle. Matter cannot properly exist without form.

But what about form as distinct from matter? Can it exist without matter? If we take "form" strictly as we have understood it up to now, that is, as the coprinciple, with matter, of a composite substance that has come to be, we have to say no. What exists properly is what has come to be properly, the composite, and not just the form alone. From this we shall argue for a certain necessity of matter on the part of form, at least in the case of essentially composite substances. But could we not also think of another kind of form as actually existing alone, a pure form totally separate from matter?

Let us reflect on what is involved in such an idea of a pure form separate from matter. First, we should note that the purity we are speaking of can apply only to form and not to matter. When we refer to the potency of matter as pure, we do not refer to anything intrinsic in matter as such. We refer only to what it is as distinct from form. In itself, precisely as being in potency, matter is totally related to the actuality of form. As such, it is quite "impure," in that it is a desire for form. A pure form, on the other hand, would not be such a desire. As pure act it would be complete unto itself, without matter and quite separate from matter in its ontological makeup. Even if that is not the kind of substance we experience in the direct exercise of judgment, there would be no contradiction in thinking of a pure form as a substance, as there would be in trying to think of a "pure" potency as a substance, that is, as a complete being in itself, since being in potency only is understood as essentially incomplete, whereas being in act can be understood as complete in itself without potency.

Such a pure form would be like the infamous "thing in itself" of Kant or the "noumenal object." It would be something beyond our experience, unknown and unknowable to us according to *what* it is in itself. Unlike Kant's "thing in itself," however, which was still posited in relation to sense intuition, it would have to be posited as completely independent of anything having to do with sense experience. It would not be the form of anything we know in experience. And if it were to be posited as existing, we still could not know it according to *what* it is, as we know the things we directly experience.

Hence we could not say anything positive about such forms, except that they would be more positive or would represent higher degrees of being than the forms we do know in experience, including the human form. If we thought of a plurality of such forms, we would have to think of each as a principle of determination unto itself, setting itself off from other forms as of a different kind and not just as an individual of the same kind, since there would be no matter as principle of individuation in any one of them. We would have to think of them as intellectual substances, since intellectual activity is the kind of activity in human being that seems to transcend the conditions of matter more than any other. But even that would fall short of *what* they are in their higher form of intelligence. Most of what we could say about them would be by way of negation with reference to our limited form of intelligence, which is tied to matter as principle of individuation and limitation.

We could say that pure forms or purely intellectual substances are simple, but that would only mean for us that they are not composites of form and matter. This would not tell us *what* they are in their simplicity. We could also say that they are immaterial, in the sense that they are not tied to any matter in their ontological constitution or according to *what* they are in themselves. A number of conclusions would follow from that, since matter is the principle of becoming and of individuation in the things that come to be.

First, we would have to say that such purely intellectual substances do not and cannot come to be or cease to be, since they are not composites or in composition with a principle of becoming for their being. They simply have to be in themselves, without coming to be or ceasing to be. This would hold true even if they were created, since to be created, strictly speaking, is not a coming to be from a subject, but from the nothingness of a subject *(ex nihilo subjecti),* as we shall see in the relation of the things we know from experience to the summit of being (section 19.2). There could be pure forms that are not only higher than the human form but that also have a subsistence of their own that does not depend in any way on the potency of matter for their being. They would be immaterial substances, even though they would not be at the very summit of being.

Second, we would have to say that such pure forms are not individuated in the way of material substances. In the absence of any matter as principle of individuation, each one would constitute a species or a degree of being unto itself. We could think of such forms as many, as some philosophers have done, beginning with Plato, but only as many different kinds of being, as we think of the different species among the material substances, rather than as individuals of one and the same species. In their case there would be no problem with the preservation of the species, since each form would neither come to be nor cease to be, but simply be of itself, without requiring a succession of individuals to preserve the species. Only at the material level of substances is a succession of individuals necessary for the permanence of some specific form. But for each different pure form we would have to think of a different degree of being that neither comes to be nor ceases to be, but *is* simply.

Of course, whether there are such pure forms remains an open question for us here. They certainly do not enter into our direct experience of being. They represent something that is strictly beyond experience. In this sense they do not enter into what we begin from in our metaphysical inquiry, namely, being as known in the direct exercise of judgment. Plato posited the existence of such separate ideas in order to account for the different kinds of form found in the realm of coming to be and ceasing to be. It is important to understand that he took these ideas to be more real as substances than the things we experience in the realm of appearances, which were thought of as participating in those forms. But Aristotle, who understood the things we do experience as true substances in their own right, argued against Plato's position of separate ideas as unnecessary and inadequate to account for what is to be accounted for. Aristotle himself argued for the existence of separate substances on other grounds, as did the Neoplatonists, and as did Aquinas, who did not accept the grounds of any of his Greek predecessors (*SpirCreat* 5; Blanchette 1992, 275–78). But this is not the place to go into any of these arguments about separate substances.

We bring up the idea of such substances here only to clarify something about our understanding of form as a principle of being even in material substances. Form could be a substance by itself, although matter could not be, but such form would not be of the kind we can say we find in our direct experience of being. While it would be determinate in some sense, it would not be a determination that appears as the completion of a process. While it would represent a certain degree of positive perfection in being, it would not be one that has come to be. In this sense it would be perfect in itself, but it would not have come to its perfection as the substances that come to be do. But in its unmoved and immovable perfection, such a form focuses our attention on the positive nature of any substantial form as a principle of being, even in things that come to be and cease to be. In this respect we are indebted to Plato for this very positive conception of form as a principle of being.

13.3   The Necessity of Matter for Form
in Composite Substances

Let us return our attention to these things that do come to be and cease to be in experience, from which our reflection into the principles of being begins. Theirs is not the case of a pure form, even for human being, but the case of a form in matter or, more precisely, the form of a material substance. We have seen that matter needs form in order to be actualized as a substance. Now we must see how the substantial form of beings we know in experience is one that essentially requires some matter.

This is not just something that follows analytically from the idea of form as the form of a composite. If the form is to be the form of a composite, it needs something else than itself to enter into composition with. This idea of form needing matter does not follow from the idea of form as such. We have just seen that there could be forms existing as substances that do not need matter, pure or immaterial forms that would be separate substances unto themselves. But these are not the kinds of form we are speaking of in our reflection on substances that come to be and cease to be. Rather we are speaking of the forms of substances that do come to be and cease to be. As such, these forms have to be understood as needing matter for their own self-actualization.

There is a paradox in recognizing such a necessity on the part of form. We have seen that form is what actualizes matter. As such it is principle of determination and it is in a real sense the perfection of its matter. But in saying that it needs matter, are we not saying also that it is imperfect in itself? A pure form can be thought of as imperfect in that it may be only a determinate form limited by other determinate forms or, as we shall see, it may still be in potency to a further act, namely, the act of being. But a pure form still has to be thought of as perfect or complete in itself in that it does not need matter. On the other hand, the form of a composite substance cannot be thought of as perfect in that way. It can be perfect only as the form of some matter, wherein it is individualized, so that it does not exhaust the totality of its species. What is thought of as perfect in this case is the composite or the concrete substance, for example, this human being.

Let us examine how this perception of form as still imperfect by itself is reflected in our manner of speaking. When we speak of any form by itself we usually speak in the abstract. Thus we speak of the human form as "humanity." This name, "humanity," is only our abstraction from what is given in the concrete. It is an abstraction from matter. It is only a part of what we take to be a whole. We do not take the part to be perfect or to exist as such, but only the whole, which is the form with its individuating matter. This whole, which we take to be more perfect or complete in itself than the abstraction, we speak of with more concrete names, such as "human being," referring to what it is in itself. In its abstraction from matter, form is seen as imperfect because it is not seen as subsisting by itself but only as the form of a composite.

This is not to say that, as imperfect by itself, the form of a composite has then to be seen as in potency to its matter. This would make no sense whatsoever. Matter, as we have seen, is being in potency to form. That is its nature, such as it is. Form can be understood only as an act for this potency, its actualization and perfection. The relation between two such principles cannot be reversed. If there is some potency in the form, it has to be in relation to something else than matter, either to the whole composite as more perfect than the form in abstraction from its matter or perhaps to a further act of being of the whole composite. We shall examine this question more closely in speaking of be as the act of determinate being in the next chapter. What is of concern now is how form depends on matter even though it is its principle of perfection. How can we demonstrate this dependence and what are we to make of it?

The demonstration is pretty much the same as the one we saw in distinguishing matter as a principle of being from its substantial form. What makes it necessary for us to make this distinction is also what makes the dependence of form on matter necessary. The form we are speaking of is not any kind of a form, especially not a separate form. It is the form of a composite, which comes to be and ceases to be. Thus, it is not a form that is thought of as existing apart from matter before being zapped into matter. It is only the form of a composite that has come to be, its principle of determination that is an actualization of the potency of its matter. No matter what its degree of perfection, this is all that we know of it and this is all that we say it is as a principle of being.

We have argued for the distinction of matter from form mainly and primarily from the standpoint of human being, namely, through our experience of our own body as this thing that I have come to be, and from the structure of our proper activity on the level of sensibility. Now, if there can be any doubt as to the ontological dependence of the substantial form of a composite on its matter, it is more likely to occur on the level of the human

form than on any other level of experience, since that form is the one that
seems to transcend or overcome matter more than any other material form,
so much so that many, like Descartes, are inclined to say that it is completely
separate from matter. But this is contrary to the way we experience ourselves as embodied souls. By drawing our argument for the distinction of
matter from form primarily from the human composite, we have forestalled
this Cartesian doubt about the human soul as the form of its body. Because
matter as a principle of being is really distinct from form even in the human
substance, we have to say that the human soul, which is the form of this
composite, is ontologically dependent on its matter or on the matter that individuates it, just as its own act of sense consciousness depends on a sense
organ. Without this dependence of form on matter, there is no understanding of Socrates as this human being.

13.4   The Transcendental Meaning of Form and Matter in the Diversity of Composite Substances

We live among a wide diversity and a great multiplicity of material beings and we are ourselves individuals of a specific kind among these material beings. We have been reflecting mainly upon the ontological constitution
of individuals that come to be and cease to be in this world in which we live
and have our own being. In this reflection we have been brought to distinguish between a substance and its accidents in the beings we know from experience and, within the substance, between matter and substantial form as
coprinciples of being in itself. In this way we have been able to account not
only for a diversity of action and interaction in the world, but also for a diversity and a multiplicity of beings according to different degrees of being in
this material world. How, then, is this world to be understood metaphysically in terms of the properties of being that we have distinguished?

Beginning from the distinction between substance and its accidents,
among which activity is the chief one to be considered, since every being is
active, we note how the substance of a thing does not remain unknown to
us, but is known through its proper activity. As an accident, action has no being apart from the substance in which it inheres or from which it flows. Its
entire being is to *be-in,* which, of course, means to be in a substance. As
such, action is that through which a substance discloses itself and in which it
is disclosed. It is through reflection upon its action that we come to know
what a thing is in its substance. So it is in empirical science, which does try
to say what things are in themselves. So it is also in phenomenology, which
tries to get back to essences. And so it has been for us in our effort to distin-

guish between the two constitutive principles of material or composite substances. It is by a reflection on the real composition of our activity as it appears in experience that we have established a real composition of principles
in our substance.

With this composition, however, we are able to understand the constitution of any and all material beings, including human being, along with their
diversity and multiplicity in being. Taking matter as indeterminate being in
potency, which means that it is not only capable of determination but is also
desirous of it, we understand the substantial form of a material being as the
principle of its determination which is at the same time a perfection of its
being in potency. But taking determinations as something that can be common to more than one individual and the same for several of them, we also
understand matter itself as the principle of individuation for the material
substance, so that substantial form is not something that can be found as a
universal anywhere, but rather is always individualized in its union with its
matter. In other words, the substantial form of any being we know in experience is always the form of an individual composite. Its commonality to
many individuals does not require that we posit any universal forms existing
as such apart from matter, since, as we shall see in speaking of the communication of being, this commonality can be accounted for through the influence or the action of one being on another. What is important with regard
to matter and form of material beings is that we understand them first in
their internal relation to one another within the individual being. Form determines the matter to be that of a certain kind, while matter individualizes
the form to be that of this individual.

In this relation, we understand how form determines matter according to
different degrees of perfection that are at the same time degrees of being,
with some higher than others and with human being as highest of those we
know directly in experience. Even though each individual counts only as an
individual by reason of its matter, some individuals count more than others
by reason of their form. Different substantial determinations represent real
or ontological differences among substantial forms, each with corresponding
degrees of identity or unity, activity, truthfulness, and goodness.

With regard to identity or the undividedness of a being in itself, form is
the principle of internal unity in any substance, while matter is a principle of
dispersion and multiplicity. Though form overcomes the dispersal of matter
in its unification, it is still not perfectly one as a pure or separate form would
be, since it still needs matter in order to be simply. It is only the form of a
composite. The same kind of form, however, can be multiplied in many indi-

viduals, since by entering into composition with matter, it is always individualized.

With regard to the dividedness of every being from any other, the degree
of perfection is contingent upon matter as being in potency and as principle
of individuation. On the one hand, matter is the principle of multiplicity
and, on the other hand, it is the principle of dependence. Material beings
can never be totally independent of one another. Matter depends on form
for its actualization and the educing of a form from matter for a composite
depends upon another being with the same form already actualized in it, as
we shall see in speaking of the communication of being. The dependence of
form on matter implicates it in this dividedness even as it diversifies matter
according to different degrees. The dividedness and interdependence among
essentially social human beings is not the same as that between stones in a
pile, trees in a forest, or even bees in a hive.

The same dividedness also entails a greater complexification in the human being than in any other material being. The higher a form, the more it
emerges from mere materiality, the more complex is its matter, as we see in
the progression from nonliving things to living things, from the merely living to the sentient, and from the merely sentient to the rational animal.
Complexity of substance is proportionate to the degree of form, which is
the principle of unification in being, but it is contingent on the potency of
matter. Even the lowest of pure forms would not require such complexification, as it would not require matter.

With regard to activity, we find the same complementarity of form and
matter according to different degrees. Form, as we have said, is a principle of
activity. Matter is a principle of passivity. It "receives" form even as it individualizes it. Thus, in those beings where the form overcomes the dispersal
of matter more, there is a higher degree of activity and identity, while in
those where it is more immersed in matter, or more material, so to speak, or
merely material, as in nonliving substances, there is a lower degree of activity and hence a lower degree of identity.

Even at this lower degree, however, activity remains the bond unifying
whatever dividedness of being we find. Through their activity the different
and many beings *come together* as one universe of being. Among those where
the form is more immersed in matter, the activity is hardly distinguishable
from passivity; it is more an interaction or a reaction than a proper activity
of a particular being. Among those where the form emerges more from
matter, as in living things, we have a more distinguishable activity than that
of merely material beings, and in the human being we have the most distin-

guishable activity of intelligence and will. It is in the latter that we find the highest unification of beings in the world, for it is in human consciousness that the wide diversity and multiplicity of individualized beings is gathered together as one universe.

With regard to truthfulness or intelligibility, we should note that matter, as indeterminate being in potency, is least intelligible. As a really distinct constitutive principle of a substance, matter is something positive, as we emphasized in opposition to Plato and Hegel, something distinct from mere privation or nothing, and therefore something intelligible. It is intelligible, however, only in its relation to form. If there is no science of the individual, as Aristotle claimed, it is because matter is principle of individuation and matter is least intelligible by itself. On the other hand, since matter is intelligible through its relation to form, there has to be some science of the individual by reason of the form that actualizes it. This form is more intelligible in itself, but not without its essential relation to individualizing matter. In this sense we have to say that all science is of individuals, at least in the direct exercise of judgment, inasmuch as science is of being and matter is a constitutive principle of being in the being we know directly. In saying that there is no science of the individual, Aristotle was thinking only of the way we demonstrate the properties of a thing from its definition, as he explains this in the *Posterior Analytics*. This does not require the inclusion of an individual that can be defined, as when we say that a sense of humor is a property of being human because it follows from the definition of being human. But the definition does not apply to a pure form that would be universal in itself. It applies only to individuals of the kind specified by the definition.

Finally, with regard to goodness, we can see how form, as the *de-termination* and the *per-fection* of a process, its *terminus ad quem,* is the good "sought" in that process. Form is thus a good, an object of appetite, something desired when it is not had and acquiesced in when it is had, and as the principle of actualization in being for a potency, it is what grounds our thinking of any actual being as good or as a fulfillment of appetite. This is not to say that matter is evil. Good does not enter into composition with evil any more than form enters into composition with privation or heat enters into composition with cold. Form enters into composition with matter, which is to be distinguished from privation as well as from form and which is therefore good at least in the sense that a positive desire for the good is itself also good. In fact, we could say that matter is good even in a stronger sense, in that it is required for the form. Though it would make no sense to speak of the form as being in potency to matter and therefore as "desiring" it in the same way as matter itself is desire for form, still insofar as a substantial form needs matter we could say that matter is a positive good for that form, or better yet, for the composite which is said to have come to be simply. Matter is good not as a thing in itself, since it is not such a thing, but as ordered to the thing of which it is a constitutive principle. In this sense the body is for the good of the soul and matter as a whole is for the good of the universe, while the soul is the form of the body, and the order of the universe, which includes a wide diversity as well as a great multiplicity of beings, is the form of its very complexified matter.

CHAPTER 14

Be as the Act of Determinate Being

O UR INVESTIGATION into the principles of becoming on the level of both accidental and substantial change has led us to a distinction of two principles, matter and substantial form, as constitutive of things that come to be and cease to be in their essence. These two principles can be understood as truly ontological and the distinction between them as truly an ontological difference, a difference that can account for there being different kinds or different degrees of being in nature as well as different individuals of the diverse kinds of being in the universe. They do not, however, account for the fullness of being in its actuality. They account for becoming as a difference of being in essence, but not for being as encompassing in its *act* the order becoming.

If we go back to the distinction we made earlier in the logic of our first conception of being between the order of essence and the order of existence, we have to say that matter and substantial form, as ontological principles, pertain only to the order of essence, and not to the order of existence. They account for things that come to be and cease to be in their substance, and not in their *be* or in the *act* of their being. This *act* of their being or this order of existence is something we still have to inquire into. Is it really distinct from the substance of things or the order of essence or is it reducible simply to substance and the order of essence, as we have understood it up to now?

The question arises from the very structure of our conception of being as given in experience. If *be* is irreducible to quiddity and haecceity, or to the synthesis of the two, in our conception of determinate being, can we say that it is equally irreducible to the form of whatever we say is according to the direct exercise of judgment? Is the act of being really distinct from its essence or substance in the finite being we know?

This is the question that we can say was forgotten in modern philosophy, after Suarez reduced the question of being to the question of essence. It is the question Heidegger rightly tried to return to or to recover with his insistence on the ontological difference between be and being. We only touched upon this question at the beginning of our inquiry in maintaining, against Heidegger, that be as be cannot properly be the subject of metaphysics, saying that the question of be as be could only be a part of the broader question of being as being. Having clarified our conception of essence or substance as part of the question of being, we must now recover the other part of the question having to do with the be of being. In speaking of the ontological difference, Heidegger was still inclined to think of be as an another kind of essence than *what* a thing is in its essence, as if one could ask what is the essence of be as different from being. But here we must avoid even this last remnant of essentialism. We must not look for *be* as something other than being. We must look for it as constitutive of being precisely as being. We must focus on *be* as the *act* of any being in the concrete, but as something positive irreducible to any sort of essence, which only expresses *what* a being is. We must deconstruct Heidegger's understanding of the "ontological difference," which allows for turning the question of be into a question of essence, in order to come to a new understanding of what we shall call the "ontological structure" of any determinate being as a composition of essence and its irreducible *act* of being.

According to the logic of our first conception, "being" encompasses both substance, or the order of essence, and be. Being is a composite of both essence and be. In this sense, be is not distinguished precisely from being, but rather from essence, within being as a whole. Nor can it be a composite in itself, as Heidegger initially suggested in relating his conception of the ontological difference to the Scholastic debates about the distinction between essence and existence (*GPP* 15, 21/11/16). It can only be understood as an act in composition with some essence, and not as an essence with a composition of its own. As such it can only be a part of being as a whole which is not distinct from the being as such but rather from the essence as its coprinciple of the being as a whole. The question for us here is to recover this understanding of *be* as an *act* with reference to being as given in experience.

14.1   The Passage from a Metaphysics of Substance to a Metaphysics of the *Act* of Being

Our investigation into being according to its differences has given us an understanding of substances in the concrete as things that come to be and cease to be, including matter and substantial form as constitutive principles

of such substances. This understanding of composition in material substances, however, is restricted to what we spoke of earlier as the order of
essence. It does not yet refer to what we have spoken of as *be* or the *act* of
being, which is itself understood as composing with essence or substance as
a whole. But the principles of determinate substances do not give us an understanding of the composition in being precisely as being. The composition
of matter and substantial form gives us an understanding of composition in
being only as becoming or as being in itself. If there is a distinction between
what we have spoken of as *be* or the *act* of being in our first conception of
being as it is given in experience, we must pursue the metaphysics of the
structure of being one step further. We cannot stop merely at substance or
becoming in general. We must inquire further into this distinction of the *act*
of being from its determination as essence. Over and above a metaphysics of
becoming or substance, we must articulate a metaphysics of being as *act*.

Let us consider first how we come to such a metaphysics. In keeping
with the logic of being we developed earlier, we can think of being as divided in two different ways. One way is to think of it as divided in accordance
with our categories or the diverse genera in the diverse ways of predicating
we use in the direct exercise of judgment which follow the diverse ways of
being we encounter in experience. Being is spoken of in many ways and
these categories or "predicaments" limit or contract being to diverse ways of
being, so that being is understood according to the diverse ways of predicating, which presumably follow the diverse ways of being. If we take Aristotle's
list of the highest categories, we then have certain predicates that signify the
substance of a being, certain that signify its quantity, certain that signify its
quality, and so one. Thus, for example, to say that a human being is animal is
to refer to the being of its substance, to say that it is tall is to refer to the being of its quantity, to say that it is white is to refer to the being of its quality,
and so on.

Being is thus divided according to what we referred to earlier in section
3.6 as the predicamental order, with substance as the center or the primary
analogate of this order. In our consideration of the structure of being up to
now, we have been operating largely within this order, for substance has
been understood not only as being in itself but also as coming to be and
ceasing to be. The predicamental order of being can thus be understood as
referring to the order of material being or of the being in motion we have
been considering up to now.

But there is also another way of dividing being that has emerged in our
reflection on being in becoming, the division according to potency and act,

which is first discovered in connection with things that come to be and cease to be, but is not necessarily confined to such material being. For, as Aristotle suggests at the beginning of Book *Theta* of the *Metaphysics,* "potency [*dunamis*] and act [*energeia*] extend to more [*epi pleon*] than what is spoken of only according to motion" (*Metaph* 1046a 3–4). To be sure, we first learn of this division with reference to being in motion, where we come to our first conception of matter as being potency, for it is from a reflection on being in motion that we first come to these notions of potency and act. Nevertheless, the notions are not necessarily confined to the particular order of becoming, which is only a particular order of being. They can also be used to explore the further composition we find in our first conception of being between the act of being and its determinate essence, which can then be understood as somehow in potency to this act in the broadest sense of being as *ens commune,* according to the expression of Aquinas (*In Metaph* IX, 1, §1770).

Let us follow how this has been done by Aquinas, for example. Taking his cue from Aristotle, Aquinas speaks of a composition between substance and *esse* as something of an other order *(non eiusdem rationis)* than the composition between matter and form, even though both orders entail compositions of potency and act (*SG* II, 54). Presupposing the understanding of matter and form as constitutive principles of substance, he proceeds by saying, first, that matter is not the substance itself of a thing, because from that it would follow that all forms are accidental, as the ancient philosophers of nature opined and, we might add, as many modern scientists and physicalists still do. Matter is only a constitutive principle of substance as something that comes to be or ceases to be. As being in potency, matter requires its own proper act, which is its substantial form or the form of the composite. Second, and more importantly, Aquinas adds that *esse* itself is the proper act not of matter, which is only one of the two principles constitutive of a composite substance; it is rather the proper act of the whole or the composite substance, so that the composite substance itself has to be understood as somehow in potency to this act of being. For, as Aquinas argues, "be is the act of that about which we can say that it is. Be is not said of matter, but of the whole. So that matter cannot be said to be that which is, but substance itself is that which is" (Ibid. §1289).

What then of the substantial form? Does it thereby cease to be understood as the principle that actualizes the potency of matter? Is it to be taken simply as the be or the *esse* which is supposedly distinct from the essence? Aquinas says no to this as well. "Form is not the be itself, but the two are related according to an order: for form is compared to being [*esse*] as light [*lux*] is to shining [*lucere*], or as whiteness [*albedo*] is to being white [*album esse*]" (Ibid. §1290). The question for us then is: What is this order of form to the *act* of being and how is it to be conceived? The example suggests something of an act *(lucere)*. Aquinas goes on to say that the form itself *(lux)* is related to being itself *(ipsum esse)* as to its act. But of what precisely is be the act? Have we not said that the form is the principle of actualization for the composite? How is this *act* still related to be as to a distinct *act of being?* "In composites of matter and form, the form is said to be the principle of being [*principium essendi*] in that it is the completion of substance, of which [namely, the substance] be itself is the act" (Ibid. §1291). It is as a constitutive principle of a composite substance that form is an act. At the same time, however, this substantial form is in potency to the *act of being* only insofar as the composite itself is in potency to that act.

Hence, Aquinas concludes, "in substances composed of matter and form there is a twofold composition of act and potency: the first is that of the substance itself, which is composed of matter and form; the second is composed of the substance itself and be" (Ibid. §1295). This second composition is the one we are more interested in exploring now. Our first understanding of such composition begins with the material or composite substances, but, as Aquinas further concludes, implicitly referring back to Aristotle, "the composition of act and potency is in more [*in plus*] than the composition of form and matter. Hence matter and form divide natural substance, whereas potency and act divide being in common [*ens commune*]" (Ibid. §1296).

We have already spoken of the transcendental meaning of matter and form with regard to the order of substances that come to be and cease to be. But now we are coming to a broader transcendental meaning, which can no longer be spoken of merely in terms of matter and form, confined as these are to the order of "natural substance." We now have to speak in terms of potency and act in relation to the order of being as being in a broader sense, rather than just as material or natural being. In speaking of the broader meaning of the composition between act and potency in relation to being in common, Aristotle and Aquinas both had in mind the idea of immaterial substances which they would want to include under being in common, along with material substances. To do so they had to move to a different understanding of potency than the one we first have in connection with material being or being in motion, an understanding that is no longer tied to coming to be and ceasing to be.

"Whatever is proper to matter and form as such, such as to *be generated* and to *be corrupted* and other [things] of that sort, is proper to material substances, and is in no way appropriate to created immaterial substances" (Ibid.). Without going into this question of created immaterial substances at this point of our investigation, what more could we say of a relation between potency and act that would not include generation and corruption? What could we say of this composition, or what follows from it, which could be common to any mode of determinate being, whether material or immaterial, that does not still have to do with process and motion? To begin to answer this question is to come to some understanding of *be* as the *act* of being even for the composite substance of matter and form.

14.2   The Disclosure of Essence as Potency with Reference to Being in *Act*

We should note, to begin with, that our first understanding of the distinction between potency and act does not have to do with *be* as the *act* of being. Far from it. Our first understanding of this distinction begins with the experience of motion and the power to move or be moved.

The power to move something else is understood as an active potency, while the power to be moved by something else is understood as a passive potency. In fact, as Aristotle points out, the first thing we think of as being potent is a thing capable of affecting another in some way. "Potency [*dunamis*] means the principle of motion or change which is in another or in itself as other, as the art of building is a potency not in what is built, while the art of medicine is a potency which may be in the one medicated, but not as medicated. Hence in general the principle of change or motion is called potency in another or in itself as an other, or by an other or by itself as an other" (*Metaph* 1019a 15–21, 1046a 4–30). In the case of the building, what this means is clear: the potency to build is in the builder, who is clearly another than what is being built. In the case of "one being medicated," or a patient, it may not be as clear, because the one being medicated may also be the one doing the medicating. But even when it is one and the same person on both sides of the equation, there is still a distinction to be made between what is being medicated and the potency to medicate or the art of medicine. Even when the doctor is his own patient, it is not as patient that he medicates himself but as doctor or as having the potency to medicate, which is not the same as the potency to be medicated.

Though the power to move in this way is an active potency, it is spoken of as only a potency in order to refer to it as something that a mover *has,* whether one is actually exercising the potency or not. Thus the actual mov-

ing of another is the act of this potency, but the potency is the power that
the mover has, whether it is actually moving another or not. Corresponding
to this power to move is of course the power to be moved in the thing
moved. This is called a potency, because the thing moved has the power to be
moved, just as the thing moving has the power or the potency to move. In
the second case, however, the potency is called passive because it is moved
only by this other than itself. The entire meaning of the idea of potency derives from this first understanding of an active potency as other than what is
moved.

Though Aristotle illustrates this idea of potency with an example taken
from building, the understanding of it does not refer to the building as such,
but rather to the *art* of building as the potency to build, or to the art of medicine, or to any art or science. The possession of a science or an art, or even
of a virtue, should be thought of as active potency, for each one of these
habits, or things had, is a power to act on others or on oneself as on an other. Though they are perfections of a subject, and in this sense they are actual-
izations of this subject, they are still thought of as only potencies in relation
to their proper act, which is the exercise of their power on another.

Such, then, is our first understanding of potency as a power to move another. How do we go then from this first understanding to that which we
have already seen with regard to matter as being in potency?

First, let us note how we distinguish potency from act even with regard
to active potency. The Megaric school tried to maintain that a thing is in
potency only when it is in act and that it is not in potency when it is not in
act. This, Aristotle argued, could not make sense. It would be like saying that
a man who is not actually building cannot build, so that only the man who
is building would have the potency to build, and only at the moment he is
building. It is easy to see the absurd consequences of this claim. For, as Aristotle points out, building is an art that is acquired by practice or by acting in
a building way, and in acquiring this art one becomes a builder, that is, one
enters into the possession or the habit of this art. The same can be said of
any other art that the rational human being can acquire, all of which must
be viewed as active potencies. Now, if it is impossible to possess these arts
without acquiring them at some time, and then also impossible not to possess them without having lost them at some time (for example, by forgetting), whenever the artist stops in the actual exercise of his art, he will no
longer possess the art, and if he has to start up again immediately, how can
he ever acquire it (*Metaph* 1046b 29–1047a 10)?

The same argument can be made with regard to the qualities of things by which they affect our senses, which qualities are also active potencies in things. Neither hot nor cold nor sweet nor bitter nor anything sensible in general will be such unless it is being sensed. According to the Megaric school, there is no power of sensation unless it is being exercised in act. This would be like going blind or deaf each time we close our eyes or stop listening. It would be impossible to begin actually seeing or hearing. More generally, the possible itself would have to be thought of as impossible. For if something is deprived of its potency to act when it is not in act, it cannot act; or, as Aristotle puts it, it will be impossible for anything that is not happening to happen, since that is precisely what "impossible" is supposed to mean.

In short, as Aristotle concludes, anyone who denies the distinction between potency and act ends up having to deny both motion and generation. That which is standing, for example, will always be standing and that which is sitting will always be sitting, because if it is sitting it will not get up, since it is impossible that anything that is incapable or does not have the potency of getting up will get up. This is no small thing to deny in experience. If, on the other hand, we wish to maintain that it is possible for something to be and yet not be and possible for it not to be and yet be or, for example, if we wish to maintain that it is possible for something to walk and yet not be walking or possible for it not to be walking and yet to be walking, then we have to maintain a distinction between potency and act (Ibid. 1047a 11–29).

This is the argument of Aristotle for maintaining a distinction of potency from act in general. What we saw earlier with regard to the composition of substances that come to be and cease to be is a special case of this argument, which tries to account for both motion and generation. In bringing out the real potency in things, however, we must not forget that this potency has to be understood in relation to its proper act, whether it be the act of standing or walking, the act of seeing, the act of thinking, or, with reference to what we are now trying to understand, the act of being. We have just seen how Aristotle speaks of this act of being, corresponding to the potency of being or not being, in the conclusion to his argument against those who would identify potency with act. How do we come by such an idea of act? Do we start with it as a pure abstraction, or do we come to it through our understanding of motion, much as we have just done with the idea of potency? Do we understand it first in isolation from potency, or do we understand it in its relation to potency?

There is a sense in which act must be understood first, since a potency can be understood only in its relation to an act, just as a motion can be understood only in relation to its *terminus ad quem*. But this idea of act as distinct from potency in turn is itself something to be understood prior to potency. It is something first known in our experience of motion, which, as Aristotle points out (Ibid. 1047a 32–33), is the first act we come to know. The idea then is extended to other things, such as the form or the entelechy of a substance that has come to be, as we saw earlier. While we can think of nonexisting things as conceivable and even as desirable, we cannot think of them as moving or moved, "for of non-existing things [*ton me onton*] some are in potency, yet they are not, because they are not according to completion [*entelecheia*]" (Ibid. 1048a 1–2). To be in motion is to be in act, whereas to be only in potency is not yet to be in act. To speak of anything as being in act is to speak of it as having a certain completion, which presupposes that we have already begun to think of motion as an act or as a process of coming to completion. Thus being itself, or rather be, in our way of thinking, is associated with motion as act. Only that which is actually is thought of as in motion and as motion itself, or coming to be generally, is thought of as terminating in be as a completion of the process. *Fieri terminatur ad esse*. Coming to be is precisely what it says: coming *to* be, *ad esse*.

How is this *be,* then, the completion of a process or the *act* in which the process terminates? How is it still an act if it terminates a process? We have seen that substantial form is the act in which the coming to be of a substance terminates. It is what Aristotle calls the "entelechy of the substance," its having in itself its completion or perfection. In this sense we speak of it as the principle of the substance's being *in act* rather than just in the potency of its matter. Is *be,* then, simply the same as the form of the substance or is it another act, a further act, an act of this act or a perfection of this perfection, to which the form or, more exactly, the composite of form and matter would still be in a relation of potency to act? The latter is the idea we have seen Aquinas draw out of Aristotle, but how can it be justified?

Aristotle defines motion as the act of something existing in potency insofar as it is in potency (*Phys* 201a 9–10). This definition presupposes a distinction between potency and act and focuses on motion precisely as act, that is, as no longer mere potency, but as act still in potency, that is, as still not having reached its term, in which the particular motion will be completed or perfected. This definition could apply to any kind of motion or change, whether accidental or substantial. In speaking of a substance as having come to be simply, we spoke of the same distinction between potency and act, but then it was with reference to what could be understood as the term of a process now understood as a composite of matter and form, two constitutive principles, one of which is being in potency to an act and the other is the actualization of this potency. What *is* simply or what has come to *be in act* is neither just the matter nor just the form, but the composite substance. But such a composite, in its very completion as a substance, is not all there is *in act*. The composite is only a particular kind of being among other beings and it still has to perfect itself in being through its own activity. It is still in potency to many acts and, most fundamentally, it is in potency to the act of being by which we say that it *is* even as it has *be-come*.

14.3   The Transcendental Meaning of *Be* as *Act*

With this understanding of be as an act, we have come to what might be the purest idea of an act, one without any determinations whatsoever. The form, as the act of a composite substance, is a principle of determination that differentiates this substance from that substance. Be, however, as an act distinct from any potency, entails no such determination. It is the act for which determinations are the potency. Potency is understood only as relative to act, but in and of itself act is not understood as relative to anything else than itself. Other than itself there is or can be only nothing. Act is limited only by the determination of which it is the act, as the substantial form of a composite is limited to this or that individual by its designated matter.

At this point we might still be tempted to ask for a definition of *act* to show what this act of being is. But such a definition cannot be given, since, as Aquinas remarks, act is one of those first simple concepts that cannot be defined, because we cannot go on indefinitely in definitions (*In Metaph* IX, 5, §1826). We must start with some *first* ideas, like that of being or one or true or good, and *act* is one of them. The idea itself is discovered by a sort of induction *(epagoge),* where what we mean is made clear in each particular case by an analogy that goes from one case to another, as when we speak of building in act in comparison to the potency to build, or of being awake or conscious as distinct from being asleep or only in potency to being conscious, or of actually seeing as distinct from having our eyes shut but still with the potency to see, or that which has been differentiated from matter as distinct from matter itself, or that which has been shaped as distinct from the unshaped. In all of these examples cited by Aristotle, and in others as well, "act refers to one side of this distinction while potency refers to the other. Not all, however, are spoken of in the same way, but rather according to an analogy, so that this is in this or related to this as that is in that or related to that, for some are as motion to potency and others are as substance to matter" (*Metaph* 1048a 35–b 9).

This analogy of act and potency thus follows the analogy of being itself. In the end it leads to the most fundamental way in which this distinction is to be understood: that between *be* as the *act* of being and what a thing is in its substance or essence. If we take this way to transcend even the order of coming to be and ceasing to be or of becoming in general, what is there in the distinction between act and potency that remains to be understood? What is there to the distinction that remains if we prescind from motion as such, so that we could speak of a distinction between potency and act even where there is no motion in the strict sense of the term and no coming to be or ceasing to be?

In a text we have already quoted at some length in the passage from a metaphysics of substance to a metaphysics of the act of being, Aquinas suggests two verbs to express what remains of the distinction between potency and act when we prescind from motion or becoming and think only in terms common to being as such or to any kind of substance, whether material or immaterial, as in the case of a pure form that would be a separate substance apart from matter and motion. If the distinction between potency and act is found in more than the distinction between matter and substantial form in natural substances that come to be and cease to be, we have to speak of it in terms that prescind from coming to be and ceasing to be or, as Aquinas puts it, from *being generated* and *being corrupted,* which pertain to material substances but not to immaterial substances as such. The language he proposes is that of *receiving* and *perfecting.* To maintain the distinction between potency and act in its most common sense, even where there is no question of motion, we can speak of potency as that which *receives* and of act as that which is *received* and, conversely, of act as that which *perfects* and potency as that which is *perfected* (SG II, 54, §1296).

This means that we have to prescind from the notion of motion or coming to be implied even in the notion of *perfecting,* since we still come to our first understanding of this notion through our experience of motion. Aquinas does this by speaking of an immaterial created substance as still in potency to its act of being. In speaking this way, which is that of a theologian, he appears to be starting from the notions of creation and immaterial created substance, as well he might in a *Summa* that is essentially theological. But that is not the way he is proceeding philosophically. It is not the notion of creation or the notion of immaterial created substance that determines his understanding of the broader distinction between potency and act, as Thomists often sugest, but rather this broader understanding of the distinction between potency and act in terms common to any being, whether in motion or not, that determines his understanding of an immaterial created substance and of creation itself.

If we follow Aquinas's argument carefully, we find that he is proceeding by analogy from the distinction between potency and act as we first understand it with reference to being in motion to the broader distinction in terms of receiving and perfecting that prescinds from motion, even though it is still applicable to material substances as composites as well as to any other finite or determinate substance there might be. For him to speak of an immaterial created substance is just another way of speaking of what we have spoken of as a pure form, separate from matter and yet determinate in itself. What we must do here is follow this philosophical analogy from composition in the order of becoming to composition in the order of being simply as being that is expressed in terms of *receiving* and *perfecting*.

To begin with, the idea of *receiving* here does not presuppose a giver or any relation to a giver from outside the composite. It only expresses a relation of the potency in the composite to its act, which is received in the potency, as a substantial form is received in the potency of its matter, except that, in the order of being simply as being, the act is understood as received without reference to any motion or becoming in the substance that receives it as the potency of this act. Hence in this more common and inclusive distinction of potency from act, we are speaking of substance itself as a passive potency, one that only receives its act and does not in any way produce it, as an active potency does. The potency receives the act as the subject of this act in a way that is analogous to the way matter receives the form in a composite substance. It is not some kind of an objective potency, which might be thought of as something on its own, like some abstract possibility, prior to receiving its act. It is strictly a subjective potency that exists concretely in being actualized or in receiving its act. We speak of this as a *reception* only because we distinguish the potency from the act in the composite of a determinate essence and its act of being.

With regard to the idea of *perfecting,* the analogy with the composition in the order of becoming or of material substance requires even more careful unraveling. Strictly speaking and according to its original meaning, as we have just noted, *perfecting* or *perfection* presupposes a process of becoming, "for it seems that what has not come to be [*quod factum non est*] cannot be said to be perfected [*perfectum*]" (*SG* I, 28, §268). In Latin becoming is spoken of as a *fieri,* which is the passive form of the verb *facere*. In its active form *facere* means to make, but in the passive form, *fieri,* it means to be made or to become, and in the past tense it means to have been made or to have become *(factum esse)*. Thus, the idea of *perfectum* means that something has reached the end of some becoming. The prefix *per* simply intensifies this idea of some process having reached its end.

Interestingly enough for us here, Aquinas explains all this in terms of act and potency. "Because everything that comes to be [*omne quod fit*] is reduced from potency to act and from not-be to be [*de non esse in esse*] when it has come to be [*quando factum est*], it is then rightly said to be perfected [*perfectum*], as though it had become totally [*totaliter factum*], when potency has been totally reduced to act, so that it retains nothing of not-be but has a complete be [*esse completum*]" (Ibid.). This would be unequivocally true of any substance that comes to be, as it attains the perfection of its form. The form is itself this perfection relative to the imperfection of its matter. It determines what something is when it has reached the fullness of its being or, as Aquinas puts it, retains nothing of its not-be or the not-be of itself.

How, then, can we go on to speak of a composition between potency and act that prescinds from becoming as still a relation of perfecting, if coming to be does not come into consideration? This is where analogy comes into play. But in what does the analogy consist? It consists in thinking of the *act* as something positive that somehow completes a potency, regardless of whether the substance now in question has come to be or not. "Because in things that come to be, something is then said to be perfected [*perfectum*] when it is educed from potency to act, this name perfected [*perfectum*] is transposed to signify every being to which be in act [*esse in actu*] is not lacking, whether it has this by way of becoming [*factionis*] or not" (*ST* I, 4, 1, ad 1). In saying all this Aquinas is thinking of the way we come to think of God as absolutely perfect, even though God does not come to be or cease to be. But in order to do so Aquinas has to think of be itself as an act that is as a *perfection* for whatever *is* according to its own determination. As such, *be* is the act of a substance that has its act of being as its proper perfection.

This is how *be* or the *act* of being can be thought of as *perfecting* a substance that already has a certain perfection of its own in its substantial form. But how precisely is substance perfected as being? This is where the idea of potency comes in with regard to substance as it relates to its act of being. If we distinguish a determinate substance from its act of being, we have to think of it as a potency in this composition with its act. As distinct from the act in this composite, the substance as potency is that which is *perfected,* as it *receives* this act. As a subjective passive potency, it is the subject of this perfection, just as the matter of a composite substance is the subject of its substantial form.

The question then arises: In what does this potency consist? Is it merely the potency of prime matter once again? Or is it another kind of potency? As we have seen, potency is understood always in relation to some act proper to it. As we have also seen, the potency of matter is understood in relation to a substantial form as its proper act with which it enters into composition as a whole substance that comes to be. In other words, the material substance is already a composite of potency and act. It is this composite, which already includes its own determinate act, which in turn relates to be as a potency to its proper act of being. *Be* is the *act* of something that is already in act in some determinate sense, the perfection of a perfection, while the substance, which is already viewed as having come to be, is also viewed as in potency to its act of being. Any determinate substance, even one that would be an immaterial form, that is, one that does not enter into composition with matter and hence does not come to be or cease to be, would still be viewed as in potency to its act of being in a proper understanding of the distinction between potency and act where the act is taken purely as *act* of being.

To understand this relation of substance to the act of being more clearly, let us come back to the idea of being as determinate. Every substance is a determination of being. As distinct from its own act of being it is a potency to that act; it is positively ordered to that act in its own standing; it *is* its own potency or capacity to be, so to speak. As determinate, however, it limits this act as it *receives* it, so that the act is its proper act of being, and not that of any other. Only thus can this act be its *perfection*.

Moreover, substance is a limitation only in relation to the *act* of being. When we first think of determination, we think of it with reference to motion or coming to be. *Determination* is the termination of a movement. To the extent that the substantial form is the essential determination of a substance, it is not a limitation of matter, but a specification of matter according to some determinate actuality. Taken in abstraction from any determination, the potency of matter entails a certain infinity. This infinity of the potency of matter, however, is only a *privative* infinity. Without a determination it is unfinished. As mere potency, matter lacks a finitude or a determination that it is in its nature to have. As matter is actually found in being or as having come to be, the determination comes as its completion or perfection. Though the determination of something that has come to be delimits it in relation to *what* it could have become, in the sense that it only this kind of being and not another kind of being, and in relation to *what* beings are in actuality, it is not strictly a limitation in relation to the privation in matter as indeterminate or as mere potency. It is a determinate negation of that privation and, in the resulting composition of potency and act, designated matter limits the form, so that it is the form only of this individual, and not of other individuals of the same kind.

It is by analogy with this limitation of form by matter that we come to the understanding of the limitation of the *act* of being by a determinate substance. As the potency in the composite of substance and *be,* substance is the principle of limitation for an *act* that otherwise would be not merely indeterminate, as in the case of matter as being merely in potency, but positively unlimited, as form itself is positively unlimited in comparison to any one of its individuations in matter.

Thus, through a proper understanding of determination in being we come to our appreciation of the difference between *be* as the *act* of being and prime matter as indeterminate being in potency, which have often been confused in the history of metaphysics. We can speak of both *matter* and *be* as principles of being, as we have done, but in quite different senses.

Matter is a radical principle of being in material substances. Without matter as indeterminate being in potency, we could not account for beings that come to be and cease to be. It has to be understood as a real principle of being in whatever comes to be and ceases to be. And yet it is a principle only in composition with its substantial form, which is its determination or its proper act. When we raise the question of an act of being distinct from substance as a whole, we are not going back to this radical principle of being of material substances. We are raising a question of being *in act* and we are raising the question precisely in relation to the composite of matter and form as a whole, which we take for granted as given in experience. We are moving to a higher intelligibility of being, not to the lower one of matter as indeterminate being in potency, and we are moving toward this higher intelligibility precisely in its being *actual*.

For us, then, be is an act that constitutes its own composition with a substance as its potency, a potency that itself may consist of a further composition between matter and form, as in the case of material substances, or that may consist of no such composition in itself, as a pure form without matter. We could illustrate this idea of a twofold composition in one and the same being through the exercise of judgment or of decision making, which entails the same kind of twofold composition, and we shall do so when we come to argue that there is a real distinction between a composite or determinate substance and its *act* of being. But before we do that let us sum up what is entailed in the idea of a composition of act and potency without any reference to being in motion or to generation and corruption.

14.4   The Composition of Potency and *Act* in Determinate Being as Such

We have spoken of potency as receiving its act and thereby limiting it in a composite. Apart from any composition with a potency, therefore, an act by itself would have to be thought of as unreceived and therefore as unlimited, at least in the sense that it is not limited by any potency receiving it. We can see this already in the composition of matter and form. Matter receives the form and thereby limits it to being the form of this individual, whereas, apart from the composite, the form is thought of as unlimited with reference to its individualization. This is not to say that form thought of in this way is absolutely unlimited, since the form is still only of a particular kind of being, say, of a human being, or a dog, or an oak. It is determinate and, as such, it is limited by other forms of determinate being. This would be true of any form of determinate being, even those that would not be in composition with any matter. The form of any determinate being would be unlimited only in its particular order.

Moreover, this same form of determinate being, whether it be the act of a composite substance, as in the things we know through experience, or a substance unto itself, apart from any matter receiving it, can also be thought of as in potency to a further act, since it still entails some limitation in itself. When we transpose the understanding of the composition of potency and act, initially arrived at through determinate being in becoming, to this further kind of composition between potency and act as that between substance and the *act* of being, we come to the understanding of an act that, apart from the composition, has to be thought of as positively and absolutely unlimited in itself.

This is not to say that such an absolutely unlimited act exists in itself apart from any consideration of ours, whatever such an existence would mean. The only act that we can speak of as being so far is an act that is in composition with a determinate substance or essence, hence an act that is received and hence limited by its passive potency or the determination of which it is the act. But the idea of such a determinate act, or of such limited acts, does open the way for understanding how there can be a diversity of determinate beings as well as a plurality of individuals of one and the same determinate kind, just as the idea of being in potency opened the way for understanding how there can be change and becoming in being. It also opens the way for the idea of an act that could be thought of as absolutely infinite in itself, if we consider it apart from any composition with a potency. Such an act would be limited in a composite by the potency that receives it, namely, by the determination of *what* a being is, and it would be diversified according to the different quidditative determinations in being that limit not only one another but also the respective acts of being which they each receive. The act of being is what all beings have in common, each in its own way. It includes all perfection of being and is itself the perfection of all perfections standing in being.

Even if we do not suppose the existence of an infinite act, however, the idea helps us to understand how finite being as such is constituted ontologically in terms of potency and act. To think of this act as infinite in itself, all we have to do is think of it as *unreceived,* which implies that it is *neither limited nor multiplied,* since the receiving potency is principle of limitation and of multiplication. What follows from this in terms of composition between act and potency can be understood in two complimentary propositions.

14.4.1   An Act Is Not Limited Except by a Subjective Potency That Receives It

Only if it is received in such a potency is it limited. This can be shown in two ways, one through the very notion of *act* and the other through the notion of transcendental unity.

14.4.1.1   *Act Understood as Unlimited Perfection.* From the notion of act we can argue as follows. Act is understood as the perfection of a potency. But as distinct from any potency it is understood purely as perfection. Hence, by reason of this understanding, act means only perfection. The understanding, however, says *what* something *is.* Hence act, by reason of *what* it is understood to be, has only perfection, or unlimited perfection.

On the other hand, a limitation is a lessening of perfection. As such it is not a perfection. Therefore, act does not have any limitation of itself. The internal reality whence limitation comes to an act in something limited is not the act itself. Therefore, that internal reality whence the limitation comes is a subject of the act that is really distinct from the act, much as prime matter is really distinct from form in the order of becoming, except that now we are talking about a composition in the order of being as such, where be is the act and the subjective potency is substance or some determination of being.

14.4.1.2   *Potency Understood as Limiting in a Composite.* From the notion of transcendental unity, we can argue as follows. Every being is one, but it is one to the degree of its perfection in being. Hence a being that is not infinitely perfect in some respect is not perfectly one under the same aspect.

Therefore, under that aspect, it has a unity only of composition—that is, it presents itself as having a distinction. Such a distinction cannot be one between two separate things, since we are talking about only one being as one in its composition. We are talking about a distinction of principles in one and the same thing.

What, then, are these distinct principles within the one being? They are not opposites, since opposites repel one another and do not constitute one being. As distinct they must be correlated under the aspect of the perfection in which they are not perfectly one. Hence one of them must bring something of that perfection that the other does not. Therefore, one must be the principle of that perfection, while the other must be the principle of limitation of that perfection. In the case where being itself is the perfection, one must be the *act* of being and the other must be the potency of this act.

14.4.2   An Unreceived Act Is Neither Limited Nor Diversified Nor Multiplied

Conversely, this means that an act, such as the act of being, which is diversified in species or multiplied in individuals, is limited. In other words, if an act is found to be common to many things, and thus diversified or multiplied, it has to be limited in each derivative case, if not in the first. This too can be shown in two ways, one through the idea of diversity and again through the notion of transcendental unity.

14.4.2.1   *Diversity and Multiplicity as Departure from Unlimited Pure Act.* From diversity we can argue as follows. If many beings have the same perfection but in different degrees, then, even if the first of these beings were to have that perfection in an infinite degree, all the other beings would have to have that same perfection in some finite degree, and if they were diverse even in this finite degree, they would have to have that perfection according to diverse finite degrees, as, for example, plants, animals, and humans have the perfection of life in diverse degrees.

Moreover, if we think only of multiplication without diversity, in other words, if we suppose that all the beings with a certain perfection have that perfection in the same degree, as all humans have the essential perfection of human life in the same degree, we still have to say that each one of these beings is distinct from the other and that each has something proper to itself that the others do not have. This "something proper" cannot be that which brings the perfection in each being, for example, human life in the case of many individual human beings, for what is proper to one cannot be proper to the other. The something proper has to be something distinct from the perfection in question in each individual that multiplies this perfection by limiting it in each individual case.

In other words, where there are many beings with the same degree of one and the same perfection, each one limits that perfection to its own individuality, for none of them exhausts the whole of that degree of perfection. This is the side of the question we saw in connection with matter as the principle of individuation. When there are diverse degrees of the same perfection, such as diverse degrees of life or diverse degrees of substantial form as such, which represent diverse degrees of being, we have to say that the subject or the receptive potency that diversifies the perfection in each case is also a principle of its limitation.

14.4.2.2   Diversity and Multiplicity as Limiting Composition with an Act. From transcendental unity we can argue as follows. Again, even if we suppose that the first of the beings with a certain perfection is unlimited, the others with the same perfection can have it only as limited. That is the condition of their being other than the first with respect to that perfection. If they are multiplied according to some perfection, each one is limited according to that same perfection. And if they are multiplied according to different degrees of that perfection, they are also limited according to different degrees.

Note that it is not inconceivable that the first of many beings having a certain perfection is unlimited in its possession of that perfection. Its very unlimited possession of the perfection will distinguish it from all the others, while the others will be distinguished from the first and from one another according to the varying limited degrees in which they possess the perfection. The question is how to conceive of an unlimited possession that leaves room for a limited possession by others and how others in their limited possession can be other than this first in its unlimited possession. To conceive such a thing we may have to posit a radical ontological distinction in the way a perfection is possessed between the unlimited and the limited as well as a radical ontological dependence of the limited on the unlimited.

It should be understood that at this point in our investigation we are speaking only hypothetically of a perfection possessed by a positively unlimited act, since we are talking about the idea of an infinite act only to clarify the idea of a composition between act and potency in the broadest common terms. It is in relation to such an infinite act that we come to think of the beings we know as finite, as composites in their multiplication and diversification, and therefore as imperfectly one or imperfectly undivided in themselves. Corresponding to this degree of imperfect undividedness of finite beings there is also a degree of imperfect dividedness from every other that will lead us to the question of an interdependence among finite beings and an ultimate dependence of all finite being on the perfectly one infinite being, in which there would be no composition of any kind, and therefore no passive potency whatsoever distinct from what would then be an absolutely pure infinite act.

With regard to the finite determinate being from which we begin in our investigation into being as being, this understanding of *be* as an *act* of being in composition with substance itself as its subjective potency gives us access to an ontological distinction in its most radical sense, the distinction that accounts for finite being in its very finitude. Every being is itself in its own standing as a substance. It has its own identity, its own first perfection, which it must further actualize in a second perfection through its activity. But this reality or this essence *is* what it is only *by an act,* which in itself or in its commonality might be infinite or does not of itself entail any limitation, an act that is finite or limited by being received in the potency of different essences.

Essence, as we have seen, refers to a thing according to *what* it is. It is what Kant thought of as the reality of a thing or what Suarez thought of as being, understanding being only as the name for a "real essence." According to our logic of being in section 3.4, however, essence expresses the whole of *what* a thing is in its own standing in being. This includes the actuality of a thing insofar as it has come to be and attained the perfection of its substantial form, which is the principle of its being as having become. What we refer to as "essence" does not include the actuality of the thing insofar as it *is* simply or insofar as the standing it takes is still only a standing in or a participation in being. This actuality of the thing must be distinguished from the essence of a thing as a whole as an act is distinguished from its subjective potency. It is the act by which the thing as a whole *is* and to which the thing as a whole or the essence stands as a potency to its *act.*

Clearly such an act cannot be understood as a thing in itself, nor as another essence. It is not different from its essence, as another essence might be, nor can it be thought of as ontologically different. It is constitutive of a thing as a whole in its very being. But can it be understood as *really* distinct from the thing as a whole, or from its reality or its essence? This is the question that has been debated among Thomists and their Suarezian adversaries and that we must now examine in order to understand how we can say yes to it and what it means to say yes, without positing *be* as ontologically different, or as another essence of some kind.

14.5   The Argument for a Real Distinction between a Determinate Essence and Its Act of Being

In arguing for a real distinction between essence and existence, Thomists frequently start from an idea of creation and from the idea of God as pure uncreated act in which there is no composition whatsoever. It is supposed that only created beings have a composition, in the way we saw Aquinas speak of "created immaterial substances" as pure forms in potency to their act of being. What this proves, however, is not a real distinction between essence and existence, but only what Suarez would call a "distinction of reason," that is, a distinction based only on ideas, somewhat like the distinction we arrived at earlier in arguing from the idea of transcendental unity to show that any act that is multiplied is limited, if not in the first instance, at least in all the others. In fact, in supposing that created beings have composition, the argument is presupposing what has to be proved, namely, that there is a real composition of essence and existence in any finite or determinate being.

If there is to be any demonstration of a real distinction between the substance of a thing and its act of being, it must be made independently of any idea of creation or of an uncreated act as pure act. Not only is the idea of creation or of an uncreated act too much for us even to understand, so that we could hardly demonstrate anything from such an understanding, but also the idea itself is impossible to arrive at philosophically without some prior understanding of the real distinction between the essence of a thing and its act of being. If there is any connection between the idea of a real distinction between essence and existence and the idea of creation, it can be arrived at philosophically only through the idea of the distinction itself, and not through the idea of creation, for the philosophical idea of creation can only be derived from the idea of this distinction, and not the other way around. In other words, we cannot arrive at any idea of creation in being except through some idea of a composition in the determinate being we begin from in our reflection. Thus to argue from some idea of creation, presumably given in faith, as Suarez did against any real composition in finite being or as Thomists also do in favor of a real composition of essence and existence in finite being as such, is at best to take what can only come as a conclusion as the principle for an argument and at worst to confuse the intelligibility of being itself with some still very tenuous ideas about being in *act*.

To argue for a real distinction of *be* as the *act* of being from its limiting substance, therefore, we cannot proceed onto-theologically. We must proceed from the determinate being we know immediately in experience. Here again, as before with regard to the distinction between form and matter, we must proceed phenomenologically or *a posteriori*. We already have elaborated the notions of act and potency in their mutual implication as relevant to this question. While this elaboration of the idea by itself is not enough to prove a real distinction between a finite substance and its act of being, it does indicate dialectically what is at issue in this question of a real distinction. It points us in the direction of something probable or something to be proved. To prove that the distinction is real, we must now join the dialectic we have elaborated with our experience of being in its presencing and show how the affirmation of a real distinction follows from a proper reflection on determinate being as finite being.

We have already argued from transcendental unity for a certain composition in finite being. To the extent that a finite being is not absolutely perfect in being, as a positively infinite act unreceived in any potency would be, it is not perfectly one. Its unity can only be one of composition. Moreover, to the extent that beings are diversified and multiplied, they have to be finite. Even if the first being is infinite, the others can only be finite in order to be distinct from one another as well as from the first, while the first is singled out from all the others in being infinite. Thus we come to the conclusion that finitude in being and composition go together. But this does not tell us precisely in what the composition of finite being consists. It brings us to the idea of a composition in being, but it leaves the idea of a real composition open or in need of demonstration. In this sense even the argument from transcendental unity is only dialectical or logical. It needs to be complemented by an argument from experience or *a posteriori,* just as our understanding of transcendental unity itself follows from a reflection on the being present in our experience.

Where, then, in our experience do we find the kind of transcendent act that we suppose the *act* of being to be as distinct from its limiting finite essence or substance? The question must be understood with great care and precision, for we are not asking about any kind of an act. We already have the understanding that substance itself, in the order of becoming, is a composite and already has an act of its own, the substantial form, perfecting its matter. What we are asking about now is a perfection of this perfection, a perfection in the order of being over and above a perfection in the order of becoming and substance.

The *act* of being that we are now inquiring about is not the constitutive principle of a composite substance, like the form in such a substance, though it has some analogy to such a form in that it is the act of a potency. Much less is it like matter, the other constitutive principle of the composite substance, which, as distinct from its form, is only being in potency. We are inquiring about an *act* that does not entail any potency whatsoever unless it is *received* in one. We can think of it only as a simple presencing of the finite being as a substance.

Any finite substance, whether composite or simple, has a certain completion in itself. As a presencing in being, the *act* of being is a completion of this completion, the perfection of this perfection, the ultimate principle of the substantial being as something that simply *is*. If we speak of the substance as that which is *(quod est),* then we have to speak of the *act* of being as the principle by which that which is *is*. If it were another substance or another essence, another *quod* or another *quid,* it would not be the principle of the substance we speak of first as being. It is not a *pricipium quod,* but a *principium quo id quod est est*. It is the principle *by which* something *(aliquid) is*. The act of a finite being is not another thing than *what* is in itself, but it is distinct from it as the act *by* which it is, so that the substance relates to its own actuality as that to which it is still in potency.

In experience we have an instance of this kind of twofold composition in the exercise of judgment, as we have shown in section 2.4. We have, to begin with, the composition of a predicate *(P)* with a subject *(S),* which ultimately is reducible to saying something *(P)* about *this* or *that (S)*. But this composition of *P* and *S* does not constitute an exercise of judgment by itself. It only expresses *what* is to be affirmed or denied about some *this* or *that*. It is not itself the affirmation or the denial, which is a further act following upon critical reflection.

What is expressed in the terms of a judgment, *S* and *P,* follows from questions for understanding. Once a formulation has been elaborated for understanding, which is concretized in a *this,* a further question arises before there can be any proper exercise of judgment, the question for reflection that leads to agreeing or disagreeing, saying yes or no, to *what* has been formulated. Without this further question, and some answer to it, there is no proper exercise of judgment, which consists in the affirmation of some truth. With the affirmation or negation, however, we come to a second composition between that which is expressed in the terms of a judgment, that is, the first composition, and the *act* of judging or the exercise of judgment itself which is in composition with the first composition as a whole.

Now it is clear that in the concrete there is no exercise of judgment without the first composition, expressed in the terms of a judgment. There is no judgment unless one is saying something about one thing or another. On the other hand, the exercise of judgment itself, or the *act* of judging as such, is not restricted to any particular judgment. Having affirmed something about one thing, it is still possible to affirm something else about another thing or even about the same thing. The latter would be another judgment than the first, but it would be no less an exercise of judgment, another *act* of judging in composition with another composition or set of terms, *S* and *P.*

If we prescind from the first composition as a synthesis of terms, we have to think of the exercise of judgment or the *act* of judging as somehow un-limited in and of itself. It can enter into composition with any set of terms, whether in a direct or an indirect exercise of judgment. At the same time, however, it cannot be or exist without being in some composition with terms or a composition of *P* and *S.* It has to enter into some composition with terms or, rather, it is truly as an exercise of judgment only in such a composition. To judge without saying something precise about something is not to judge at all, but only to toss words about or rehearse opinions vaguely.

In the concrete exercise of judgment we thus have a composition in which something finite, the composition of terms, is understood as partici-pating in something infinite in itself, or at least not limited to the finite terms that restrict it concretely. The exercise of judgment or the *act* of judg-ing as such is irreducible to the terms of any determinate judgment and, in that sense, it is of itself unlimited in itself. In reality, however, that is, in the concrete exercise of this act, it is *received* in certain terms and limited by them, so that when I am saying something about one thing, or denying it, that *something* which I am saying restricts the bearing of my affirmation or denial. Thus the exercise of judgment for me concretely is not some infinite act affirming truth in general but a series of determinate acts in which dif-ferent truths are affirmed. Each act of judgment has its own limited claim to truth, with which one may agree or disagree without calling into question any other limited claim to truth or the more general claim that some truth has been attained. We can disagree about particular judgments in one realm or another without disagreeing about all particular judgments in all particu-lar realms or without denying all capacity to judge in one another. At the same time, however, in each particular judgment, the act of judging comes as the perfection of what is expressed in the terms of the judgment from the standpoint precisely of judging. Questions for understanding are ordered to questions for critical reflection. Answers to questions for critical reflection, that is, particular judgments as formulated, come as the perfection of answers to questions for understanding, that is, as the perfection of our formulations in complete acts of knowing.

Thus, we have in the exercise of judgment a composition of precisely the kind that we claim is the case with *be* as an *act* of being distinct from its finite essence. It entails a second composition that includes a first composition as one of its members along with a proportionately limited act. The composition expressed in the terms of a judgment remains in potency, so to speak, to the proper act of judging, while the same composition limits this act in *receiving* it according to the second composition or that of the judgment as a whole.

This, we can now say, at least illustrates the kind of composition we have in mind in speaking of a real distinction between essence, or *what* a thing is, and its *act* of being. But does it prove that such a distinction is real for a determinate being? Not directly, but indirectly it does, if we go back to our ontological principle as enunciated in sections 6.3–5, according to which the proper activity of a thing is proportionate to its being.

To exercise judgment is a proper activity of human being. The second composition we have just brought out in the exercise of judgment is an essential structure of that activity. From this essential structure of a proper activity, we can argue to a similar structure in the being as a whole, or at least in the case of the human being for whom judging is a proper activity. Just as in the exercise of judgment there is a real distinction between the content of the judgment as expressed in the terms and its proper *act* of judging, so also in the presencing of human being there is a real distinction between *what* it is as this determinate being and its act of being. Just as the terms of a judgment limit its act, so also *what* a human being is, or its substance, limits its *act* of being. And just as the *act* of judging perfects the thought formulated in the terms of the judgment, so also the *act* of being perfects the substance of human being as being, not by adding anything quidditative or accidental to its being human, but by making it present or actual as being, to which presencing or actualizing the substance of human being is still only in potency. Thus, we can conclude, at least for the human being, that there is a real distinction between essence, or *what* it is, and *be* as its *act* of being.

A similar argument for the real distinction of essence and be as the act of being could be worked out from human being's other proper activity, the exercise of willing. In this activity also there is a twofold composition, one between a particular motive for action and the act of willing as such, and the other, within the particular motive, between an individual impulse and the corresponding conception of a good desired. I do not exercise my will without reference to a plurality of motives for action among which I have to choose. For me, to will is to choose between this course of action or that. Each course of action is itself a composition of an impulse within me and some good that I envision for myself. But as long as I have not chosen it, as long as I am still deliberating over which course to take, each course is still only a possible action. Only one of them can become actual or real, even if I do not know yet which one, and it becomes real only once I choose it, once I will it. In other words, a possible course of action becomes actual only in composition with the act of willing.

At the same time, however, the particular course of action that I choose upon deliberation receives this act of willing and so limits it. I do not will simply to will in some infinite way. In willing, I always will this or that course of action, and, through this choosing of particular courses of action, I exercise my willing in a series of actions, each of which is in composition with my willing as it restricts it to this or that particular course. In willing I am choosing only this particular course of action at this time, with the possibility of choosing another course at another time. From this composition in the concrete exercise of willing we can conclude also to a similar composition in the ontological constitution of the being for whom this is a proper activity.

Just as in the exercise of willing there is a real distinction between the particular course of action chosen and its proper act of willing, so also in the actualizing of human being there is a real distinction between *what* it is as this determinate being and its *act* of being. Just as the chosen course of action limits its act, so also *what* a human being is, or its substance, limits its *act* of being. And just as the act of willing perfects what, prior to the choice, was only a possible course of action by making it actual, so also the act of being perfects the substance of human being as being not by adding anything quidditative or accidental to its being human, but by making it actual as being, to which actualizing the substance of human being is still only in potency. Thus, on the basis of this phenomenological reflection on the exercise of willing, we can conclude once again that, at least for the human being, there is a real distinction between essence, or *what* it is in its substance, and *be* as its act of being.

To forestall any recurrence of the Suarezian objection, we should note that in this argument from the structure of a proper activity to the ontological constitution of a finite being, while insisting on a real distinction, we are not talking about a division between one thing and another, *sicut res ad rem,*

as some Thomists were maintaining in the time of Suarez. We are not arguing from two different judgments or from two different choices, even
though both the exercise of judgment and the exercise of willing each
involve a series of different acts. We are arguing from the structure of any
particular or determinate judgment or choice and bringing out a real distinction in that particular act as a whole, a distinction of what we call constitutive principles of one particular act, not of different acts. The distinction
is real only to the extent that we have to distinguish a principle of limitation
from the actual exercise of the act in each one of these particular acts. Similarly, with regard to being, we conclude to a distinction not of beings, but
of constitutive principles of being for the determinate being for whom
these are proper activities, namely, a distinction between its essence, which
expresses *what* the being is, and its proper act of being, on which its presence or actuality as being depends.

Suarez speaks at one point of an "actual exercise of being or existing"
(*DM,* 4, §3) in connection with "being" understood as a participle cosigni-
fying time. Can we accept this as a way of talking about the *act* of being? Is
be an *act* that we can actually exercise, as we exercise judgment or willing?
We have just been reflecting upon the actual exercise of our judgment and
willing in order to arrive at the kind of distinction we are trying to establish
between essence and the *act* of being. If the act of being is the kind of act we
can actually exercise in the same way as we exercise judgment and willing,
can it still be the proper *act* of what we are in our essence or substance?

To be sure, as proper activities of human being, judging and willing are
proper acts of this kind of being. But they are proper acts that flow from active potencies of this determinate being. Though reflection upon their
structure gets us back to the ontological structure of human being itself, the
act of being that we distinguish from the essence or the substance in this ontological structure cannot flow from this essence as from an active potency
or as an action flows from its substance. If this is how Suarez thought of the
act of being, that is, as an actual exercise of some activity flowing from the
active potency of a real essence, then he was quite right in rejecting the idea
of an act of being as really distinct from essence. For what was at issue in the
controversy was not the distinction of some activity from its substance, but
the distinction of an *act* from its substance as having its stance in being.

In speaking of an actual exercise of being or of existing, Suarez sounds
somewhat like a modern existentialist, who focuses only on the exercise of
some activity as the defining feature of a human being. In this the existentialist is missing the point of distinguishing an *act* of being from the essence

of a determinate being, an act constitutive of the being precisely as being. Nor does it clarify the issue to insist on the *act* of being as some kind of existentialism, as is sometimes done (Sweeney 1964). We must rather see this *act* as prior to what we can speak of as the existentialism of self-actualization through one's proper activity.

The act of being is not something appended to *what* a being is in its essence or exercised as an activity once the being is constituted in its substance. It is constitutive of the very being in its essence or substance prior to any exercise of activity or in the very exercise of any activity. A being can exercise its proper activity, as we do in judging and willing, only insofar as it already *is in act*. The act of being cannot be properly exercised as an activity, but it is out of its enduring abundance as perfecting a limiting determinate substance that the proper activity of any determinate being flows. In this sense *be* is an actualizing of a determinate being. As actuality, without reference to any determinate being, this act would be unlimited. But there is no actualizing of actuality. There is actualizing only of determinate being, which *receives* the *act* of being and limits it to the standing of this determinate being. What there is actual in being is only a determinate essence relating to other determinate essences each in composition with its *act* of being.

What is actual concretely in experience is *this* or *that* determinate being, including a wide diversity of determinate beings, for each of which actuality is as a *perfection* of its very standing according to *what* it is in its essence. The standing of a determinate being in its own essence is actuated by *be* as its *act* of being amid other determinate beings each with its own act of being. A being is established in *be* or is understood as complemented by *be* according to its own essence in the concrete as it takes its stand or comes to a stand in being through a process of becoming only because, in its standing as an active essence, it is still a potency to this *act* of being.

In one sense, this is to understand the act of being as "added" on to a finite essence taken as only potential being or as a possible. But this is not reverting back to Wolff's idea of *ens in genere* understood only as possible. In affirming a real distinction between essence and the act of being, we are not starting from some abstract essence that would be merely possible, which then leaves us with the problem of making it actual. We are starting from an actual essence that is concretely a *this* or a *that* and we are distinguishing this essence from its act of being in the *actual present*. We are abstracting the essence, or even subtracting it, so to speak, from its *act* in the whole of a being, not as a mere possible or as a nothing by itself, but as something positive in the concrete that is still in a relation of potency to its act of being. We are only backing into the idea of finite essence as a subjective potency through reflection on the actual, not starting from it as merely possible. The essence or the substance we are speaking of is the one that presents itself in experience or is presented, made present or actual, through its own *act* of being.

To be sure, once we affirm a real distinction between essence and its act of being in a finite being, we can then speak of the essence as only possible insofar as it can be distinguished from its act of being as a potency to that act. *Ab esse ad posse valet illatio.* This does not warrant our speaking of that essence as real, however, apart from its *act* of being, as Suarez did in speaking of *essentia realis* without admitting any consideration of the *act* of being as part of the subject of metaphysics. The subject of metaphysics for us includes the *act* of being of any finite being in the concrete, not just its essence or its possibility. Nor does it include that *act* only as an afterthought, as it did for Wolff who spoke of "being" first and foremost as a possible and then found himself having to explain how he could go from the possible to the actual. In a metaphysics of being in the concrete, as it presents itself in experience, we begin from a being that includes its *act* of being as well as its essence, even though we come to understand how this act is to be distinguished from its essence in a finite being only later on, after we have understood how potency and act can be distinguished in any transcendental order of finite beings, with potency understood as principle of limiting receptivity, and act understood as principle of perfection, including the perfection of being positively.

Moreover, in affirming this distinction or this composition in any finite being, we are not just affirming what Heidegger calls the ontological difference between be and being. "Being" for us is not just an essence from which *be* or the *act* of being is to be differentiated. Being, as it is given or present in experience, includes both essence, or *what* a thing is, and its act of being. In fact, if we distinguished between essence and its *act* of being with reference to a finite being, it is not on a basis of difference. Difference has more to do with how we distinguish one finite being from another, one essence from another essence. The *act* of being is not something different from its essence in a finite being. That would make the act another essence than the essence of which it is the act. Far from being a matter of difference, the act of being as distinct from any finite essence differing from any other finite essence is something common to all of them, an *esse commune* that is limited differently in a plurality and a diversity of finite beings. What we affirm, then, is not an ontological difference between being and be, or between essence and existence, but rather a real distinction between any finite essence and its act of being, presupposing the difference of a plurality and diversity of beings as given in experience and justifying these differences as real in a transcendental order of being or *esse commune*.

The argument for this real distinction between essence and the *act* of being, as it has been presented thus far, however, applies only for the human being. In fact, insofar as it flows from a reflection on my own proper activity, it proves a real distinction only in my being. What of other human beings? Insofar as they exhibit the same kind of proper activity as mine, they too can be demonstrated to have the same kind of ontological constitution as mine. In fact, it is by reason of their being constituted in their own essence as determinate beings that they can exercise their own judgment and willing and so be seen as really other beings than this being that I am. What characterizes all of us as human beings is not only that we can exercise judgment and willing as our proper activity, but also that through this activity we have access each to our own ontological constitution. It is through this activity that we are the clearing in which being discloses itself in its real composition as finite.

What, then, of other beings, lesser beings, such as nonrational animals, plants, and nonliving things? Is there a real composition also of essence and an *act* of being in them, even if they do not exercise any activity of total reflection such as we do? To be sure, lacking this kind of total reflection that has led us to the twofold structure of our activity and, through that, to the twofold structure of our being, they do not have the same kind of reflective access to their ontological constitution as we do to our own. But this does not mean that they are not similarly composites of an essence and an *act* of being proportionate to their essence or that we cannot know whether they are so constituted as finite beings or not.

We do know them and we know them as being through their activity. In fact, we know *what* they are in their essence through their proper activity as we know what we are in our essence through our proper activity. What we know in their proper activity is not a greater act than that of the human being, but a lesser act, one that is constrained by its principle of limitation even more than our own act of being is constrained, whether that act be one of mere sensation, mere life, or of bare inanimate thinghood. This indicates not a lack of composition, but an even greater degree of limitation and therefore of composition in their essence than in the human being, since their standing in being is not equal to that of human being. In fact, it is the thought of this real composition in them that justifies our speaking of them as determinate beings in themselves, albeit as lesser beings than we are.

On the other hand, however, to the extent that these lesser beings are still presenced in their own standing as substances, they are determinate beings in a way that is analogous to human being. They too come to their own standing in being according to their own essence as they are established in be and complemented by *be* as their *act* of being, an act that is even more limited in being received in this lesser standing. As a being, each one of these lesser beings is one. But as a lesser being it has less of an identity, and therefore is less perfectly one as an essence with its own *act* of being. If it is not an essence with a standing of its own limiting an act of being, however, it is not a being.

Conversely, it follows from this that, to the extent that a lesser is a composite or not perfectly undivided in itself, this lesser being is also not perfectly divided from every other. Even as a being in itself, it is dependent on other beings and subject to their influence more than other beings that are more perfectly undivided in themselves and therefore more perfectly divided from every other, that is, less dependent on others in their own standing in being. The understanding of the real composition in finite beings thus not only justifies our speaking of many and diverse beings, but also opens up the question of the interdependence and the interaction among them in the order of being as a whole that comprises these many and diverse beings. To this question we must now turn, not only regarding lesser beings, but also regarding all finite beings in the order of being as a whole, that is, in the universe.

PART FIVE

THE COMMUNICATION
OF BEING

Introduction: Intercommunication among Beings

⤬

WITH THE UNDERSTANDING of the twofold real composition in the constitution of finite beings in becoming, that of form with matter in the substance and that of the act of being with substance itself as a whole, our inquiry into the causes of being shifts into a different mode than the one we have followed up to now. Our reflection has brought us to a recognition of what we have called "constitutive principles of being," which can be understood as causes of being. But the causes we have come to distinguish are only those that are intrinsic to the beings that they constitute. They cannot be understood as separate beings in themselves, but only as distinct principles of the composite beings they constitute.

Through these causes we come to a certain originality, not to say a certain absoluteness, of determinate beings according to *what* they are in themselves as constituted by their form and matter, in the case of composite substances, and how they are constituted in their essence in composition with their *act* of being. The latter composition allows us to include even simple substances, such as pure forms that would not come to be even as determinate beings, as well as composite substances that do come to be and cease to be, since it would not be excluded that these simple substances would also be finite or determinate in their own way. In affirming this diversity and this plurality of beings, however, we are brought not only to recognize particular beings in their own ontological constitution, but also to raise the further question of how these beings interact with one another or how one is the cause or the effect of an other. How is the communication among a diversity and plurality of beings to be understood?

Are the constitutive principles of determinate beings the only causes to be considered, so that with these principles we have arrived at the complete intelligibility of being? Or are there causes extrinsic to the various determinate beings we know in experience that also influence their being, so that we have to look beyond the intrinsic causes of determinate beings in order to arrive at the full intelligibility of their being? Can the coming to be of determinate beings be accounted for adequately only in terms of their intrinsic principles? Or do we have to look further in the way beings communicate in the order of the universe as a whole?

We began our investigation by dwelling at some length on how the subject of this inquiry is to be determined in terms of being as being. We also dwelt on the logic of this subject in its transcendental and analogical dimensions in order to bring out how differences are included in this subject in its very commonality. Moreover, it has been understood from the beginning that a science not only has to determine the proper subject of its consideration, but also has to inquire into the properties of its subject and into its causes in order to arrive at the fullness of truth in what is to be known of being.

Thus, after our elaboration of the analogy of being, we turned to a consideration of its properties as one, active, true, and good—properties that do not express any specific differences of being but only general modes that follow being in its very transcendental commonality. While this entailed some consideration of the differences of being, in order to bring out the transcendental character of these properties, as we had done for our first conception of being, it did not yet focus on any differences as such or as differences of being.

This we began to do only as we approached the question of the structure of being in its differences. In moving toward this question we were not only passing from a consideration of being in its commonality to a consideration of being in its more specific differences, we were beginning as well a consideration of the causes of being. For, as we saw in the Introduction to the preceding part of our investigation, the question of causes with regard to being arises first in connection with the differences of being, before it arises with regard to being or beings as a whole in becoming.

This is especially true in the direct exercise of judgment and in the way particular sciences, such as physics, biology, or economics, arise by focusing on a determinate subject of consideration in being as known in this direct exercise of judgment and by inquiring more critically into the properties and causes of what is given in experience in accordance with their determinate subject. In physics, for example, attention is given to being as measurable in certain ways and to the properties and causes of such being. In biology, it is given to being as living; and in economics, it is given to being as product. In each particular science a particular subject is determined and inquiry is made into its properties and causes.

But the same should also be made clear in the more indirect kind of judgment that we are exercising in metaphysics, where the subject has been determined as what is most common in being, namely, being itself as being, in comparison to any particular determination of being, and where we have already inquired into the properties of this common subject before beginning our inquiry into its causes in connection with the differences we necessarily express as part of the being we know in experience.

The idea of cause and effect, as we have already remarked in the Introduction to Part Four, presupposes some kind of otherness between the two, cause and effect. One thinks of an effect as real only as other than the cause, and therefore of cause as really causing only if the effect is other than the cause. If this were not so, there would be no problem with causality, as there was, for example, with Hume, since there would be only an identity of effect with cause. It is the otherness of the effect in relation to the cause that makes for a problem with regard to any principle of causality, especially specified as efficient causality.

Hence, to inquire into the causes of being, whether in particular or in common, is to presuppose some otherness in being, just as the idea of accounting for anything in being arises from a recognition of difference in being, the most common form of which is becoming. It is when we see something as coming to be from something else that we begin to inquire as to whether that something else might not be the cause of this something that has come to be.

Otherness is a matter of difference in being, whether it be the difference of one being from another or the difference of one aspect of a being from another aspect of the same being. Thus, as we turn to consider differences as differences of being as being, and acknowledge the reality of these differences through distinct ontological principles in determinate beings, we are led to ask whether some differences take precedence over other differences or whether some determinate beings take precedence over other determinate beings in the accounting for what is or comes to be and, if so, which differences and in what sense do they take precedence. Understanding a cause as taking precedence over its effect in some way is to raise the question of causality, the answer to which accounts for the way the diversity and plurality of beings are given concretely in their respective differences.

In our reflection on the structure of finite being as we know it in the direct exercise of judgment, we have already rendered one account of being in its differences. Starting from becoming as the most common mode of difference in being, we have arrived at a distinction of three principles, two of which are *per se* constitutive of the being that comes to be and one of which

is only *per accidens,* in that it is not constitutive of the being but is only dialectically connected with its form through the permanent subject of the
change that remains in potency to different forms even as it is actualized by
one specific form. Of these three principles, two can be thought of properly
as causes of being in that both are in a positive sense constitutive of the term
or of the being that has come to be. The third is not a cause properly speaking, because as distinct from the other two principles it is not anything positive, but only privation or nonbeing, even though it is dialectically necessary
to account for the coming to be of anything.

In this sense, the idea of cause is more restrictive than the idea of principle, which can apply to anything that comes first *(arche)* or before something
else, as the privation of learning, or being unlearned, comes before learning.
This privation is a principle of my learning in that I have to become
learned, but it is not constitutive of my being learned, which includes only
myself as subject and learning as a new form in this subject. Nor is it a cause
of learning, as is the act of my own intelligence, by which I learn for myself,
or the influence of a teacher in this act of learning who is thereby an extrinsic cause of my learning.

Here a question could arise as to whether the intrinsically constitutive
principles of being we have distinguished are truly causes. Where in them is
the otherness implied in the idea of cause and effect? Are they not constitutive of one and the same being, namely, the one that has come to be? In
what does the otherness of their causality consist? What distinguishes them
from privation, as we have just seen, is that both are positive constituents of
the being that has come to be. But is that enough to warrant speaking of
them as causes, if they are still intrinsic to the determinate being of which
they are the principles?

If we think of causes only as extrinsic to their effect, as we tend to do in
modern thought, then these intrinsic principles of being are not causes. Under this supposition the cause of a being has to be another being than the
effect, as one being is other than the other. But is this the only way of thinking the otherness of causality in being? Is there not also the otherness of
principles in relation to one another, which we claim are really distinct,
within determinate beings, which beings, for their part, are really divided
from one another as beings by reason of their being constituted by their respective principles?

Each determinate being is a substance unto itself with its own act of being. As really distinct from one another, the constitutive principles of composite beings are not in simple identity with one another, nor is the com-

posite that they constitute in simple identity with either one of them. It is not as if each of the distinct principles were first a thing in itself and the composite would then be a result of their coming together, as in the case of a new chemical compound, where the elements can be thought of as substances each in its own right before they combine to make another substance. Each of the principles we distinguish is real only as constitutive of a determinate being. It is not a substance by itself, nor did it exist as such before the composite. Each principle is only a principle intrinsic to a substance that is distinct from its coprinciple in the same substance. Yet, even within this identity of substance, there is still enough real otherness to be accounted for not only between the two principles, but also between the whole and its constitutive principles, to warrant speaking of true causality intrinsic to the one being.

In this sense we can speak of a substance as the cause of its proper activity and of a signate matter and a determinate form as the material cause and the formal cause of a particular substance. To do this is not only warranted by the understanding of composite substances; it will also give us a better way of raising the question of a more extrinsic kind of causality among beings, namely, final and efficient causality.

Modern discussions of causality tend to focus only on this extrinsic kind of causality between two complete beings in themselves, or what we can now think of as composites. They take the otherness of determinate beings, in the plural, as a given and do not try to account for it in any way. They simply dismiss the thought of really distinct intrinsic constitutive principles of finite being and so leave the plurality and diversity of such beings unaccounted for. They raise the question of causality only at a point once removed from the intrinsic constitution of beings in their plurality and diversity.

In doing so they tend to consign the question of causality to one of merely external mechanics, as Descartes did even before Bacon, while overlooking some important aspects of determinate being as we know it in its coming to be. In distinguishing constitutive principles of individual determinate beings, we are taking a more fundamental view of causality, one more characteristic of the ancients in their understanding of the question of being, which includes the otherness of principles of being in relation to one another and to the whole of which they are principles. In doing so we can account for the plurality of beings as well as their interaction and at the same time come to a better understanding of extrinsic causality among the many and diverse beings.

Instead of taking the otherness or the plurality of beings for granted, we can account for it by distinguishing matter, or the subject of change, as the principle of individuation in this plurality of beings, and substantial form as the principle of determination and diversity among the different kinds of being. In doing this we have begun to answer the question about the causes of being. Moreover, even as they account for the plurality and diversity of beings, these intrinsic principles lead to the further question of extrinsic causes that we must now face.

If there is truly a plurality and a diversity of beings, how are they still one in being? How do they relate to one another in this otherness? How is there communication among beings? Besides being composite substances, or even as simple substances, each of these determinate beings has its own act of being, so that it is radically other in its own being, at least to the extent of having its own standing or its own determinate essence in being. What communication is there among beings in this radical otherness of many and diverse beings? How do they influence one another or how is one influenced by another in its very being? Can one come into being without the influence of another?

This is the question we must now face in our exploration into being as being. It is the question of causality in the broader sense, where one being is thought of as influencing another in its being by causing it to become or by changing it in some way. We speak of communication here because we start from the plurality and diversity of beings as accounted for by the ontological structure of each. We are no longer thinking of being in its purely transcendental commonality, but of beings in some kind of community of interaction and interdependence in their being.

This can only be taken as a communication, because it presupposes the plurality of beings as established. But it is a communication *of being* in that we find many similarities as well as dissimilarities among these many beings and in that these similarities and dissimilarities seem to have some connection with one another even as they appear in one being and in another. So far we have spoken of coming to be in relation to one determinate being at a time. But communication is something that happens among many beings at the same time and often with many similarities going from one being to another.

We have spoken of a new form being educed from the potency of its matter in the coming to be of something. But we have not asked how this happens or by what agency. Is it by an agency of matter as such, which, in addition to being a passive potency, would also have an active potency to produce its form? Is it by the agency of the form that would educe itself from the matter as if by its own initiative, in the same way that it initiates the activity of the composite once the latter is constituted? Or is it by the agency of another being altogether, which produces by actively inducing a form into the matter from which it is educed? If there is such an external agency in the active constitution of a being, in what does it consist? How is it a communication of being from one to another?

We should note that in this, as in the reflection on the structure of being, we begin from being in becoming or, better still, beings that are understood as having come to be. If there is any communication from one being to another, it is through movement, in the sense that one thing is moved by another, which is therefore the moving cause. What the moving cause communicates to the moved being or to its effect may be only some local motion, as in the case of one ball striking another. But even that is a communication in being in that the motion in the second ball is something real that has come from the first. It is communication at least on the accidental level of being, even though the second ball is not changed substantially by this new motion in it that has come from the first.

In the case of a more substantial change, as in the procreation of a new living being, there is a communication of being on a more substantial level in that the procreated shares in the same substantial form as the procreator, or at least so it seems from the specific similarity of the second understood as coming from the first. If we have a clear understanding of matter and form as constitutive principles of what comes to be, whether substantially or only accidentally, it is much easier to understand how this passage of something from one being to another through movement is at the same time a communication of being, for coming to be is then understood as a passing from potency to act or as the eduction of a form from the potency of matter where neither the form nor the matter by themselves can account for this passing.

The form of what comes to be is nothing actual apart from the composite that comes to be. Nor is it actually contained in matter before the composite comes to be. It is "there," so to speak, only in potency and needs to be reduced to act by something else already in act. This is the way Aristotle speaks of the principle of efficient causality in its most radical sense (*Metaph* 1049b 3–1051a 4). The new being, as we shall see, comes to be in act through the agency of its procreator, which is already in act and which, at least in some cases, as we shall also see, appears to be acting in view of an end. The coming to be of the second composite being is thus at the same time a communication of being from the first.

Thus it is from a prior understanding of the material and the formal cause of determinate being that we pass to an understanding of efficient and final causality in the universe. It is with these efficient and final causes that we must now concern ourselves in this investigation into being as being.

These are thought of as the extrinsic causes in contrast to matter and form, which are thought of as intrinsic or as constitutive of determinate beings. They are not, however, extrinsic to being as such or to beings as a whole. The are said to be extrinsic only with reference to some determinate being of which they are the cause. Unlike the distinct constitutive principles of determinate beings that are not separate beings, they are themselves determinate beings other than or extrinsic to the determinate beings of which they are cause. Whether there is a cause extrinsic to the totality of determinate beings, and in what sense such a cause might be extrinsic, remains to be seen after we have explored this more immediate communication among determinate beings.

In this part of our investigation we are concerned with the extrinsic causes of being only in the sense that one determinate being is seen as extrinsic to another determinate being and yet as communicating being in some way to another determinate being either as moving cause or as what is intended by the moving cause, namely, its final cause.

We begin here, as always, from being as it is known in the direct exercise of judgment. But we take this being now as a plurality and diversity of beings that have come to be in some kind of interdependence with one another. We take this interdependence to be somehow related to the coming to be of composites of matter and form. Being only imperfectly undivided in themselves, as composites, they are only imperfectly divided from one another. The being of one somehow influences the being of the other. Not only is each determinate being finite and limited within itself, but it is finite and limited with reference to other determinate beings. How does this interdependence work, so to speak? How is it a dependence among beings, to begin with, and how does it account for the community of determinate beings, as we know it concretely in the universe?

Since we have to do first with beings that are composites in their substance, we take our cue from their constitutive principles, form and matter, which we have already identified as causes of being.

First, from the formal cause we shall pass on to the final cause as part of what accounts for certain determinate beings. In this we try to bring out an aspect of causality that has been rejected or at best ignored in modern science and philosophy due to a metaphysical confusion between how coming to be is to be understood and a mechanistic frame of mind that allows only for quantifiable impulses as accounting for what happens in reality. We try to present a more intentional view of causality not only in spirit but also in nature itself.

Second, from the material cause we shall pass on to the moving or efficient cause, which is what modern science thinks of first when there is any mention of causality but which is not always understood clearly in more general metaphysical terms as relating to being over and above the determinate or specific form of a quantifiable impulse.

Having distinguished final and efficient causality in the communication among beings, we shall then go on to bring out their mutual implication in the constitution of a twofold order among beings, one of nature and the other of history, as integral to the universe understood as the concrete order of determinate beings in their diversity and multiplicity.

CHAPTER 15

From the Formal to the Final Cause

IN THE QUESTION of the communication among beings we presuppose a plurality and a diversity of beings as something established and accounted for by our understanding of the ontological structure of determinate being. Our question now, given this plurality and diversity, is: How is the communication among them to be understood? How does this communicating enter in as a part of our accounting for being? In what does the communicating consist?

The way we understand this question depends a great deal on what we take to be our primary analogate of being. If we take the basic entities of physical science as our primary analogate, as physicalism does, perhaps without giving sufficient thought to the analogy of being, the tendency will be to understand the communication among beings mainly, if not exclusively, in mechanical terms, that is, in terms of quantifiable impulses that go from one entity to another but remain extrinsic to the entities in question. In this view, the world is bound to appear as little more than a complicated pulsating clockwork, expanding and contracting according to forces that do not penetrate the intrinsic being of the entities that make up the mechanism.

If, on the other hand, we take human being as our primary analogate, as we have done, then the question of communication among beings takes on a much broader scope, one that includes intentional interaction among conscious beings as well as the more external interaction of a mechanical contact often conceived without any trace of intentionality. In this view, the world appears more as a region inhabited by conscious as well as unconscious beings whose action and interaction is not merely mechanical, as between mutually impenetrable entities, but rather more vital and penetrating into the very being of the other.

These two contrasting views of communication among beings are not necessarily exclusive of one another. There is something to be said for the physicalist or the mechanistic view, which we shall have to consider when we come to the question of the efficient cause. But before we can come to that we must open up the question of the final cause, which is also an extrinsic cause, but one best understood from the standpoint of human being, our primary analogate.

This question has been largely dismissed in modern science with regard to nature, to the point that it is often rejected even with regard to human action, where it is most paramount in the question of motivation for action. It has also been largely ignored in modern philosophy, after Descartes and Spinoza set it on its more mechanistic course *more geometrico,* except for Hegel and Whitehead, who could not ignore it by reason of their insistence on becoming and process as fundamental to being.

We begin with final causality because that is the mode of extrinsic causality that appears most prominently on the level of human activity, our primary analogate of being. In what does this causality consist?

15.1   The Idea of Final Causality among Determinate Beings

The idea of cause and effect implies not only a certain otherness between the two, but also a certain priority of the cause over the effect. The cause somehow has to come before the effect. But there are several ways of understanding this "coming before." In the case of a composite of form and matter, for example, we can speak of a certain priority of the constitutive principles or causes over the composite, but not in the sense that they exist separately prior to the constitution of the composite. They have priority only in an ontological sense in that they are really distinct from one another even as they come together to constitute the composite. What comes to be strictly speaking is the composite and not either matter or form as distinct from one another. In other words, what there is before a composite comes into being is not some matter totally deprived of form or a form separate from matter, but some other composite, which ceases to be in the generation of the new composite. In this sense we can speak of the coming to be of one being as a transmutation from another being.

In what we take to be a communication among beings, or from one being to another, however, the cause of an effect is taken as coming before the effect in some sense, either as efficient or final cause. It is in this sense that we speak of these causes as extrinsic in contrast to the formal and the material cause, which are understood as intrinsic to what is produced. It is clear that the efficient cause, which produces its effect, comes before its effect.

Whatever produces something else than itself comes before what it produces. But how can we say that the final cause comes before its effect and in what sense can we say that it causes its effect, if it does not actually exist before the effect is produced?

To answer this question we must focus clearly on what we mean by *intentionality*, or the intention to produce an effect. Does that not also come before the effect and is it not part of the causation in the very production of the effect? If we are to understand final causality as distinct from efficient causality in the communication among beings we must focus upon this intention as distinct from execution. It is precisely as an intention that the final cause comes before the effect or the execution. For even if it is difficult to discern any kind of intentionality in inanimate beings, it is clear that there is such intentionality among rational agents, if not in other living and sentient beings as well, who *affect* one another as well as other kinds of beings. For a metaphysics that takes human being as its primary analogate of being, such intentionality in one being is not to be overlooked as something that influences the being of another.

But we must first ask: How is the intention of an agent a cause? The easiest way of answering this question is to look at how human beings come to produce things. Let us take the example of producing a house or an airplane. This does not happen just out of a spontaneous arrangement on the part of materials or a spontaneous exertion of force on the part of human beings. A house, for example, comes into being ultimately because we are aiming at some purpose in building it, whether it is to dwell in it, to work in it, or whatever else it might be being built for. Similarly, the airplane comes into being for the purpose of flying. If we did not intend such ends, neither the house nor the airplane would come into being, so that the end is truly a cause of such things coming to be. In fact, we should even say that the intention or the final cause is the cause of the other causes that effect such things as houses and planes, for if there were no intention, the agent would not act, nor would matter be transformed so as to constitute a house or a plane.

This is not to say that the final cause is a sufficient cause by itself. It has its influence in being only through the agent or the efficient cause. But it does have its influence, which is not to be confused with the exertion of the efficient cause. This influence can be understood not only in that it causes something to be simply, which would not be without the intention, but also in that it causes it to be the kind of thing it is or *designs* it in a certain way. The way a house is designed, for example, really depends on the use we intend to make of it, the way we intend to live in it, or the kind of work we intend to do in it. Similarly, the way an airplane is designed depends on the use we intend for it, whether it be to carry passengers, freight, or guns and bombs. Design *affects* the form of what is produced, but the design itself is affected by the intention or the idea of the intended use. Thus both the coming to be of the product and its form are affected by the intention or the end the producer has in mind in producing some determinate object such as a house, an airplane, or any other artifact of human ingenuity.

Clearly, the intended use does not exist before the product as such comes into being, as does the producer and the material with which one is work-ing. The thing cannot be used until after it has come into being. Yet in saying that this coming into being and the design of what comes into being is affected by the intended use, we are speaking of this intention as a cause both of the coming to be of the thing and of its form. Marx saw this quite clearly when he spoke of "labor in a form that stamps it as exclusively hu-man. A spider conducts operations that resemble those of a weaver, and a bee puts to shame many an architect in the construction of her cells. But what distinguishes the worst architect from the best of bees is this, that the archi-tect raises his structure in imagination before he erects it in reality. At the end of every labor-process, we get a result that already existed in the imagi-nation of the laborer at its commencement. He not only effects a change of form in the material on which he works, but he also realizes a purpose of his own that gives the law to his *modus operandi,* and to which he must subordi-nate his will. And this subordination is no mere momentary act. Besides the exertion of the bodily organs, the process demands that, during the whole operation, the workman's will be steadily in consonance with his purpose" (Marx 1906, 198).

In writing this, Marx does not abandon his insistence on the material conditions of human production. He sees man as opposing "himself to Na-ture as one of her own forces, setting in motion arms and legs, head and hands, the natural forces of his body, in order to appropriate Nature's pro-ductions in a form adapted to his own wants. By thus acting on the external world and changing it, he at the same time changes his own nature" (Ibid.). We could say that in changing himself he is also aiming at his own perfec-tion as well as some new perfection in external reality. But what Marx brings out more clearly for us, even as materialist, is the causality of human purposefulness in the appropriation of "Nature's productions." What hu-mans produce through their own intervention in the forces of nature has to be counted as real and as original, that is, as something that would not be except by the willed initiative of a human being. Yet what makes that be cannot be attributed merely to the "motion of arms and legs, head and hands," those peculiarly human forces of nature, but also to the purpose that is imagined by the human agent, what we are referring to as the intended end, which not only sets one in motion but also guides the whole operation in consonance with the purpose. In characterizing human production in this way Marx was describing it as something that transcends merely natural forces and introducing a more historical dimension of reality into nature itself, something we shall characterize as spiritual, though Marx was quite reluctant to do that in opposition to Hegel. It is in the sociocultural realm of history as distinct from mere nature that we can see much more clearly how intentionality influences being, for there it is the basis not only of an original production in nature, but also of communication among beings in mutual recognition.

Before we look more carefully into that, however, let us reflect more closely on how intention influences the being even of physical objects like buildings and airplanes. Intention can be said to be really a cause of what comes to be, at least as a result of human production. But how precisely is it really a cause? In what sense does it account for what comes to be in a way that nothing else can? We cannot say that it exerts power in the same way that the producer exerts power. To say that would be to say that the end has to be actualized before what is produced in the same way as the producer is actualized. What is intended, however, or the intended use of what is to be produced, as we have just seen, can be understood as actualized only after the product has come into being. It cannot exert any power as the producer does or as matter does in the production of what it presupposes for its own actualization. Nevertheless, as an intention in the producer it does influence being by determining that something new come to be which would not come to be without its influence.

Moreover, intention does not influence only the coming to be simply of artifacts like houses and airplanes. It also influences the way they are formed as determinate objects. The form of what we produce as well as its being is influenced by the use we intend to make of it. Precisely what they are is a result of our intentional intervention in the forces of nature where the outcome is determined by our intention. If it is the efficient cause that exerts the power for an artifact's coming to be, it is the final cause that orients the exertion of that power toward a new form that is determinate. Even without exerting any power of its own, the final cause can still be said to be the most fundamental of causes insofar as it sets the efficient cause in motion both absolutely with respect to its causing something new in being and relatively with respect to the form of what comes to be.

The existence of artifacts like houses and airplanes, however, is part of the broader sociocultural realm of history as distinct from or as transcending nature. They are products of the human spirit that is in pursuit of its own ends as spirit. If we focus more directly on the spiritual aspect of spirit's historical activity, we see in it not only an initiative that transcends nature but also an initiative that is driven and guided by intentions, many of them explicit in certain initiatives and many others still only implicit in them.

The evidence for this intentional orientation is in the satisfaction we experience in such typically human achievements as learning, the formation of communities, or aesthetic enjoyment of both nature and works of art. The satisfaction comes as a fulfillment of what was originally only an intention. It is an actualization where the intended use coincides almost perfectly with the productive act itself as self-actualization. Such spiritual self-actualization among human beings should not be considered any less real than physically productive activity, nor should the crucial influence of intentions in the constitution of this reality be overlooked, even when the intended use can no longer be separated from what is produced, as in the case of artifacts like houses and airplanes.

If we wish to distinguish the causality of the end from that of the efficient cause more clearly, we could think of it as an *affecting* rather than as an *effecting*. What is produced by human activity or what is actualized in a historical initiative is not strictly an effect of the intention involved in production or the initiative. The effect as effected is what comes to be. *Factum est.* It is effected by forces that produce it, including some human resolve or the workman's will, as Marx put it. These effective causes precede it in being, whereas what is intended does not. What is intended, the use of a product or the completion of an initiative, can only come after the product or the initiative has been actualized or effected. The final cause of the production or of the initiative precedes the effect only as intended. As a cause it is first in intention but comes to be last in execution. Though my intention of dwelling or working in it precedes any effort to build a house, and in this way sets the entire process in motion, the realization of that intention comes only after the product has come to be. And though human being intends some fulfillment first before taking any historical initiative, this end is actualized only as an achievement.

In other words, there is a real influence of being from the intended end, but it is not an *effecting*. It is rather an *affecting*, as we have said from the beginning, not only setting the effective cause, namely, the producer or the historical initiator, in motion, but also determining the design of what is produced or achieved. The kind of use I have in mind or the kind of communion I intend with others *determines,* that is, sets the limits for, the kind of house I build or the kind of association I form.

This brings us to a further observation to be made about the final cause or the causation of an intended end. While it does determine our *designing* in production, it does not necessarily determine the *outcome* of production. If there were no intention of some use for a product, there would be no designing and no production. If there were no production, there would be no product, nothing effected. If there were no historical initiative, there would be no achievement. But what comes from the production or the achievement does not always meet the requirements of the intended end. In other words, the product is not always successful for the intended use or what is effectively achieved does not always satisfy the intended end. What was intended was some perfection in the effect or in the historical subject, but the result does not always have that perfection because of some *defect* in the material cause or the efficient cause.

This opens up a certain distance between the intention in a process of production or in an historical initiative and the actual effect of the process or the initiative. What is intended is a certain effect, but the resulting effect may not be what was intended. Whatever the reasons may be for this failure, which leads us to look into the material and efficient causes as well as the final cause, it is important to note that it is *judged* to be a failure *in the light* of the intended end. Thus, while this end does not necessarily determine the outcome of the process, it does determine our judgment as to whether the effect is perfect or defective. This too is a sign of how real final causality is.

There is thus an important distinction to be made in our understanding of an effect as the result of a process of production. As an actual result it may or may not correspond to the end intended. This makes for a certain ambiguity in speaking of the *end* of a process. When we think of a process as stopped, we speak of its end-result, what has actually been effected. This is what most people have in mind when speaking of the "end" of a process, whatever its final result may be. But this is not what we mean when we speak of the final cause or the intention that orients a determinate process. Here we speak of the end as intended, an end-intended and not just an end-result. The end-intended is the cause of the entire process. The end-result is only its effect.

Insofar as intention aims at some realization, we can speak of an effect as intended, but that is only when the actual effect corresponds to the end as intended. In that case we think of our action as having achieved its purpose and of the effect as satisfying our intention. If a process or an intervention has other effects besides those intended, as often happens, we speak of those as "side effects," that is, as aside from what was directly intended. In cases where we achieve our purpose or the intended effect, our action may also have side effects that must come into consideration, and in some cases we may not achieve our intended effect and still have many side effects, or effects not directly intended, which must still be taken into consideration. These side effects too may be judged as good or bad, perfective or defective, in the light of the actually intended end or of some other good we might also be intending. But in any case the end-intended as final cause is not reducible to the end-result of a process. The end-result is always judged in the light of an end-intended. The end-result may be good or bad, but the end-intended is always understood as some good in the light of which we judge a result good or bad.

15.2   Finality in Nature

Most people would agree with this assessment of the final cause as influencing being in the realm of human action, both in the production of artifacts and in the immanent action of communal self-betterment, where there is clear evidence of conscious intentionality. The question arises, however, as to whether there is any such influencing of being by an end in the realm of nature, where there is no rational consciousness and hence no explicit intentionality prior to what happens or what is produced, as there is in historical initiative.

This is a difficult question to understand properly, for it is often supposed that in raising the question we are presupposing there has to be some conscious intentionality hidden in nature. This is the way empirical scientists usually understand the question when they say that there is no finality in nature because there is no consciousness in it as there is in human activity. But the point is not to know whether there is any kind of consciousness in nature, but rather whether there is still some finality in what happens and comes to be in natural processes, even where there is no consciousness. There is no question here of introducing some kind of conscious intentionality into beings that have none. That would be to deny the very question we are trying to raise. The question that arises for us here in metaphysics is whether there is finality influencing beings that appear to have no conscious intentionality of their own.

Up to now we have spoken of the final cause only in terms of conscious intentionality, as we know it in human action. If there is any question of final causes in nature where there is no evidence of conscious intentionality, it must be understood in a sense that does not include this sort of intentionality and yet that does include some kind of orientation toward an end. This is why we now speak of "finality" in a more common or analogous sense, and not just of conscious intentionality, which is a specific kind of finality proper to our primary analogate of being and finality in action. Now we are asking whether there is finality in a broader yet real sense even where there is no conscious intentionality.

The question is like the one we had to raise with regard to action in saying that every being is active. Our first notion of action, or the locus of our primary analogate for action, was tied to human action, which includes the exercise of judgment and deliberation. The question that arose then was whether beings that do not appear to exercise judgment and deliberation really are active, as human beings are active, without having the same degree of activity. The answer that we arrived at was that they are active, since it is only through their proper activity that we come to identify them as beings, but that the degree of their activity was far more obscure and difficult to discern than the degree of human activity. With regard to finality, we have seen what it consists in more fully on the level of human activity in elaborating the very notion of final cause. The question now is to see what it consists in on lower levels of activity, where there appears to be no consciousness.

We could argue to some degree of finality on these lower levels of activity through analogy, as we did for action and the other transcendental properties of being, starting from the proposition that every agent acts in view of an end, as Aquinas does (SG III, 3). We would take this proposition as true on the basis of our understanding of human action, which, as human and deliberate, is always in view of an end. From this we would have the understanding that every action entails finality or orientation toward an end. Thus in recognizing lesser degrees of action, where there appears no conscious intentionality, we would have to admit some degree of finality as well, proportionate to the degree of activity.

Needless to say, this degree of finality would be obscure and difficult to discern, but that would be in keeping with the degree of activity in question. To discern it, however, would not presuppose that we have to introduce some kind of conscious intentionality into beings that appear to have none any more than we have to introduce some kind of judgment and deliberation in order to recognize some kind of action in beings that are not conscious. It would only require a willingness to look for final causes in the processes of nature, as we are willing to look for final causes in human action and initiative.

This is something that modern sciences of nature have been reluctant to do. In fact, they have insisted mainly on the material and the efficient cause, often to the exclusion of the final cause. In this they have been justified up to a point, in that insistence on the final cause in Aristotelian science at the time of Galileo had led to a neglect of consideration for the other causes in nature, especially the material and the efficient. The idea of what nature was supposed to do, based on an observation of nature that was still naive and superficial, was keeping the defenders of ancient science from actually looking at what was actually happening in nature. Galileo did well to make them look into his telescope and Bacon was quite right in insisting on the need for experimentation to get at the secret forces of nature. Unfortunately, this opposition to the exclusive consideration of the final cause led to a complete break not only from what had been only a superficial view of teleology in nature, but also from all understanding of teleology, giving way to what has come to be an exclusive consideration of the material and efficient causes.

In an effort to restore a proper consideration of final causality in nature, without excluding consideration of material and efficient causality, let us say that an end is aimed at in nature in the sense that it is what enables us to distinguish one process from another. It is one process that produces an oak and another that produces a human being, and if we can distinguish one from the other, it is because we see one as aiming at one form and the other as aiming at another. In this sense we could say, as Aristotle did, that the end of certain processes in nature is the perpetuation of certain species of being in a succession of individuals. To be sure, we do not see or have any vivid impression of this aiming any more than we see any relation of cause and effect in nature, as Hume pointed out. What we see is a result, the oak or the human being, but insofar as it is seen as a result of a particular process distinct from any other process, it is seen as the *intended* effect of that process.

The same could be said about nature as a whole or about the cosmos as a set of determinations in motion. Insofar as the entire set of determinations in motion tends to result in a certain unification or a *coming together* of all things, we could say that nature intends the formation of a universe. This end does not have to be understood as fixed in advance of its coming to be, especially if its orientation can be changed by the original intervention of human labor, which has its own end over and above that of mere nature. It could be understood as an open design that would allow for different possibilities, depending on the originality of new natures that might appear in time and on the free initiative of historical individuals like human beings. But it would be understood as an end in the sense that it is something aimed at or *intended* in the very process as a whole.

We do not have to ask who does the intending in order to understand an effect as *intended*. We only have to understand it as determinate, that is, as tending toward a determinate end, as in the coming to be of any substance composed of matter and form, even if the end is determinate only as an order distinct from chaos. There are some processes in nature that we do not yet understand. We do not know toward what end they are tending. We begin to understand a process only when we begin to conceive of an end for it, as we saw with regard to any movement and its *terminus ad quem*. Then we proceed to investigate into the mechanism of the process. In this sense, teleology is not excluded from scientific investigation. It is presupposed by it in the very understanding of any determinate process.

If we did not presuppose some kind of *telos* in the processes of nature, we would have to think of every process as purely random and even as without anything we could properly call a result or an effect. Anything could come from anything, and there could be no science of nature, where we expect at least some valid predictions in the sense that from certain processes certain results follow, as conclusions follow from a demonstration. We expect certain determinate results from nature because we have discerned certain tendencies in it, tendencies that are precisely what we have to think of as finalities in nature, in that the tendencies aim at what has to be understood ultimately as some value or as its form, viewed as a certain *convenience* in being.

This does not presuppose an absolute or unfailing determinism in nature, as we have already suggested. Quite the contrary, it can be understood as a kind of indeterminism such as we presuppose in human action, when we do not think of it as always successful in its intent. Discernible natural processes aiming at some *convenience* in being do not necessarily always produce the same result. To discern tendencies in nature, as Aristotle shows (*Phys, Beta,* 8), it is enough to discern a regularity in what happens always or most of the time as a result of a certain process. From this regularity we infer a certain kind of finality in nature, that is, a certain orientation toward an end, as a part of the rationality of nature and, from there, we proceed to inquire into the material and efficient causes as part of the same rationality or as a sort of means to the end intended.

Now we may be wrong or naive in inferring certain finalities in nature, due to an insufficient observation of natural processes, which may send us completely off track in the search for material and efficient causes or keep us from seeing the true material and efficient causes of an effect in nature. But the inquiry itself into these latter causes starts from the discernment of a tendency toward a determinate end, that is, of a finality, which has to be explored, and perhaps eventually to be exploited for some other finality of human being or possibly even of nature itself, as in the case of health care, which is human caring about natural processes and which exemplifies a remarkable coalescence between human finality and natural finality, since the tendency of both is toward one and the same end, namely, health.

A particular human nature is not always successful in its tendency toward health. Nor is the complement that the art of medicine adds to this tendency. In fact, nature may even be thought of as ruthless in its resistance to human ministration, when the natural mechanisms necessary for health simply are not present. But successful or not, the tendency is there, in nature as well as in human caring, as determined by the end–intended, not the end–result, which often is contrary to the end–intended, as in sickness and death.

The difficulty for us lies more in understanding the tendency that is proper to nature as such, not just as it is found in particular individuals but in nature as a whole. To illustrate the difficulty, let us take an example that Aristotle discusses in his argument for recognizing finality in nature (Ibid.).

Rain is an important factor in the growth of grain. The growth of grain can therefore be seen as an effect of rain. But is it only an end–result of rain, not to mention other factors in the growth of grain, or is it also an end–intended? Does it rain so that grain will grow or does it rain simply as a necessary result of certain atmospheric conditions? Clearly rain cannot consciously intend anything. But can the growth of grain still be thought of as somehow intended by rain and would this be an instance of what is meant by finality in nature?

The objection was made that rain could be adequately explained in terms of atmospheric conditions without reference to the growth of grain and that it could even ruin crops as well as increase them. Rain was itself simply the result of certain atmospheric conditions, just as the growth or the ruination of crops was a result of too much, too little, or just the right amount of rain. In answer to the objection, Aristotle did not try to argue that *this* rain was for the benefit of *this* grain in purely mechanistic fashion. In fact, he readily admitted that it did rain out of necessity when certain material conditions were realized. But he still recognized a general tendency of rain to be for the benefit of crops, even though it did happen that it also ruined crops at times.

More precisely, what he recognized was a general tendency, according to his model of the natural cosmos, to perpetuate a diversity of species in being through a cycle of generation and corruption of perishable individuals, a cycle of which rain was a part. Seeing this preservation of species as an end or a *convenience* in being worth aiming at, not unlike modern-day environmentalists, enabled him to recognize a certain finality in nature as well as the material causes that did bring it about. Without the thought of some *convenience* or benefit in being, some positive value or end intended, there can be no thought of finality.

Interestingly enough, as we have already remarked in passing, Aristotle thought of the perpetuation of species as an end intended *in* nature, if not *by* nature. This is an end that environmentalists also intend in their support of nature against the abuse of technological development, which has its own ends that are not those of nature. But the perpetuation of species is not the only end one can think of in nature.

In the context of a theory of evolution of species in nature, we can think of the appearance of new species also as an end intended in nature. Aristotle had no idea of such an evolution from his observation of nature. His method of scientific investigation was still too limited to particular places and particular times still relatively close to the Greeks. Had he discovered the evidence for such an evolution in the broader cosmos, however, he would have had no trouble integrating it into his idea of finality in nature, especially if we think of the later species to appear as higher than those from which they evolved, for such later species would represent a higher value or *convenience* in being than their predecessors.

The fact that they come last, or later, does not present any difficulty for understanding them as intended ends. In fact, it reinforces the idea. For, as we see in the development of a complex organism such as an animal, that which is intended from the beginning, the mature form of the individual, comes last in the process. In his understanding of the development of anything, Aristotle usually took that which came last as the indication of what was intended from the beginning. I say "usually," because what comes last is not always in keeping with the end-intended. It can be a failure or a monster. What is intended in nature is some positive *convenience* in being that happens always or most of the time and it is what appears later in any natural process of generation and growth rather that at first, as in the case of maturity for an animal.

A new and higher species in being, such as human being or animal being or living being relative to nonliving being, is certainly a more positive *convenience* in being than lifeless being. But how can it be said to be that which happens always or most of the time when it appears for the first time? Aristotle's understanding of finality in nature seems to work well for established species. But does it work as well for understanding the arrival of new species? Modern science usually thinks of the appearance of a new species as purely random, without finality. It supposedly accounts for higher species not as a matter of *development,* for that would entail some kind of finality, as in the development of an animal to its mature form, but as a mere matter of survival of the fittest. Among the new beginnings of being, which have to be thought of as somehow infinite or chaotic from the standpoint of the established order, inasmuch as they are totally random, only those survive that win in the struggle for existence. They are dubbed fit, or fittest, only because they survive, and not because they represent a new *convenience* in being. Because this idea of *convenience* or of the good of being is left out of consideration, the higher species are seen only as an end-result in the process of evolution, even as a failure from the standpoint of the established order, and not as an end-intended.

There is much to be said for this modern understanding of evolution. It brings out both the material conditions and the moving causes of the evolution of new species in a way that was not understood before. But it does not account for any kind of *development* in this evolution or the appearance of *higher* species in time. It is a theory of evolution without development and without discernment of progress toward an end, as if one could understand the evolution of an organism without understanding the mature form of that organism, which is the end-intended of the development. The ultimate rationality of any development lies in the end-intended of that development. Without an understanding of that intended end, there is no understanding of development and no understanding of failure or success in development, let alone of a form or a *convenience* in being.

Hence any understanding of an evolution of the species must begin from the end, which is, of course, where the theory of evolution begins anyway as a theory. We have come to understand that there has been evolution only because we stand at the end, and not at the beginning. This is how we understand any movement, starting from the *terminus ad quem*. Standing at the end, however, once we get the intimation of an evolution of species, we begin to see ourselves also as standing better, or *higher,* in being, not only than other species of being contemporaneous with ourselves, but also other species that preceded us. Without standing at the end we could not have such a discernment and without the discernment of some finality in the process we could not think of the movement as a *development* or an evolution.

Even the thought of "the survival of the fittest" presupposes some discernment of finality, for survival is taken as the end-intended, something better than annihilation. The problem with the thought of mere survival is that it thinks of fitness, or what we have called *convenience* in being, only in terms of some lowest measurable common denominator, namely, survival, which can be attributed to a mere stone as well as to a complex or highly evolved organism. There is more to standing in being for an organism or a human being than mere survival. And this more, this greater *convenience* in being, such as life, sensation, and intelligence, this higher identity according to *what* a being is, this *higher* form of being, even when it is much more precarious than a stone from the standpoint of mere survival, must be taken into account in any understanding of evolution. This is why a theory of evolution without some understanding of finality in nature remains ultimately irrational or fails to account for what comes to be, by one-sidedly insisting only on the mechanisms or the material conditions of evolution. Such a theory is in contradiction with itself because it denies what it has to presuppose in order to speak of *development* or *evolution* toward *higher,* more *convenient* forms of being.

This kind of exclusive insistence on the material and efficient causes was not totally unknown to Aristotle. Some of it could be found in Empedocles with his theory of the four elements as that out of which everything else evolved. According to this theory, things could be understood adequately as coming from their material conditions, as rain could be understood as coming from certain atmospheric conditions. There was no need to posit any finality in nature.

In countering this position Aristotle insisted more on the pattern of development within organisms, especially that of higher, more complex animals, where he saw a *convenience* of being always ordered to a greater *convenience,* which is ultimately the *convenience* of the whole in the dignity of its being according to its essence or species. In such patterns, where what came last also appeared as the most *convenient,* Aristotle discerned an orientation to an end-intended as well as the effect of previously existing causes. He was disposed to see this by his metaphysical understanding of change as a passage

from potency to act and of matter as being in potency to form according to
an order, namely, the order of matter we spoke of earlier in section 12.4. But
in positing finality in nature he was not one-sidedly denying the order of
the material and the efficient cause. Rather he was affirming it, but only
within the order of the final cause.

Failure to understand finality in nature is closely connected with the failure to understand the coming to be of a substance or even to understand
substance as such, all of which presents a real difficulty for the modern sciences of nature, as we have seen at every turn. If, however, we reflect on the
coming to be of a substance, we can see most clearly how deeply finality influences or *affects* natural processes. What comes to be simply, as we have
seen, is a composite of matter and form and it is understood as a composite
precisely as having come to be through a process. At the origin of that
process there is matter, which is in potency to the form of what comes to
be. As still only in potency to that form, it does not yet have that form, but it
entails a certain orientation to that form as its end, of which it is still deprived and which it somehow desires, although not consciously. This is why
we came to speak of the substantial form as a perfection of its matter according to *what* it is as a substance. In this understanding of form as perfection we have an understanding of it as the end of the process of generation
for this substance, that toward which it was tending from its beginning and
in which it terminates as a determinate being. In the case of a living being,
we think of this perfection of form as having been reached in the mature
healthy individual. To be sure, this substance is a result of the process, but it is
a composite or a substantial whole precisely because of a tendency of this
matter to find its perfection in this form. The coming to be of a substance,
whether living or nonliving, is *affected* by a finality from its very inception,
and the end of that process is its form. This is what we speak of as its "dynamism," which is taken from the Greek word for potency, *dunamis.*

The substantial form of anything in nature can thus be seen as the first
and the most fundamental kind of end or final cause in nature. It comes as a
result at the end of its process of coming to be, but *affects* that process from
its beginning, thus making the result at least possible. It may also fail to *affect*
the process sufficiently, by reason of some deficiency or defect in the material or the efficient cause, so that the actual result may not be in accordance
with the end-intended in the natural process according to what the substance is or is supposed to be. In that case we may speak of the resulting
substance as deficient in some way or even as a monster, not as something

that terrifies us, but as something that declines from or falls short of the end intended in nature in the process of coming to be simply.

What we have in the case of such a deficiency is a substance, but one that is not perfect according to the potentiality of its nature, even though it may be perfect in many other respects. But even in such cases, the result is judged to be not perfect or imperfect in the light of the end that is thought to be intended in nature. If there were no tendency toward certain kinds of perfection in substances, no matter of how many differing degrees, there would be no grounds for speaking of anything like deficiency or imperfection, just as there would be no grounds for distinguishing between health, which is an end or a *convenience* for living things in nature, and illness, which falls short of that end.

This finality in the process of generation as such, however, is only the first instance of it in nature. There is also another finality, which is that of the thing generated *(finis rei generatae),* and not just that of the process of generation *(finis generationis).* Not only is there a finality in coming to be. There is also a finality of what has come to be. This finality presupposes a plurality of beings and affects the relation between them, and not just the process of coming to be one substance or another. It is a finality that *affects* being precisely as finite.

15.3   Finality in Finite Being as Such

We have seen that every finite being is a composite of essence or substance and be or an act of being. This is a composition of potency and act that is different from that of a substance that comes to be, in that it does not necessarily imply a coming to be or ceasing to be, but that is still analogous to it, in that it still implies a relation of receiving on the side of the substance and of perfecting on the side of the act of being. The act of being is received in the substance and it perfects the substance as being. Substance as such already entails an act, which is its form, but the act of being is the act of this act, or the perfection of being in the concrete of this perfection. Just as matter receives its form, and so limits it as the form of this or that individual, so also substance receives its act of being and so limits it as the act of this being and not another. Thus the act of being is multiplied and diversified in being received in diverse and multiple substances, while, as an act distinct from any one of these substances, it entails a certain kind of unlimitedness or positive infinity that goes beyond any finite substance, just as the form of a material or an individual substance entails a kind of unlimitedness or a positive infinity that goes beyond the individual as such, since it is received in other individuals as well, as the human form is received in Socrates, Plato, and other individuals of the same species.

All this has been said in accordance with an understanding of the ontological structure of the beings that we know in the direct exercise of judgment centered on a common understanding of the distinction between or the composition of potency and act in being. This twofold distinction, that between matter and form and that between a substance and its act of being, accounts for the multiplicity and the diversity of beings as we know them in experience or as given where being is disclosed. But is that all it accounts for? Does it not account as well for the fact that every being is active and for some further finality in substantially constituted beings over and above the finality that has affected their coming to be, namely, the finality of action and interaction among finite beings?

In our initial understanding of the distinction between potency and act, in connection with the principles of becoming, we distinguished between not just two but three principles. Two were understood as constitutive of the thing that comes to be, namely, the new form of what comes to be and its subject or matter. The third was understood as a privation to which the matter was subject before the coming to be, namely, the privation of the form yet to come. This privation, clearly, is not constitutive of what comes to be, since it disappears, so to speak, in the appearing of the new form, but it is a principle insofar as it affects the subject or the matter, which is constitutive of what comes to be. In fact, even while it is under one form, matter remains under privation of one kind or another in that it remains in potency to other forms. This is what makes for the mutability of material things, and even for their eventual corruption, for if and when this potentiality of their matter to other substantial forms is actuated it entails the corruption of the thing in its present form. The generation of one thing always entails the corruption of another.

Privation, even if it is not a positive, *per se* constitutive principle of becoming and of beings, is thus integral to any understanding of potency and act as principles of becoming and being. Without privation there is no proper understanding of the dynamic relation between these two positive principles, for we must maintain a distinction between being in potency as something positive in the constitution of a being and privation, which in itself is merely negative or nothing. Privation is a determinate negation only in relation to the form of which it is the privation, as cold is a privation of heat or being unlearned is a privation of learning. In the case of Socrates' learning, the privation of learning is part of the dynamic relation between his becoming learned and his being or having been learned only in potency. In the case of his coming to be simply as a substance, the privation of the human form was part of the dynamic relation between his becoming a human substance and his being or having been such only in potency in the seed and the egg from which he came.

As we extend our understanding of this relation between potency and act to the composition between a substance and its act of being, however, is there still any place for privation as integral to what has to be understood? We might be inclined to say no, since, as we saw, this instance of the composition does not necessarily entail a strict coming to be or ceasing to be. It is a composition that obtains between any finite substance and its act of being, whether it comes to be and ceases to be or not. In other words, if there were a pure finite form, which would be a substance unto itself and would not be constitutive of a composite material substance, it would neither come to be nor cease to be, but as finite it would still be in a relation of potency to its act of being. If there is no coming to be or ceasing to be for such a substance, is there still any privation in the relation between itself as potency and as act of being, or is the relation purely static, or again, as some might say, is the relation purely formal?

Similarly, when we speak of this composition between substance and act of being for a substance that does come to be, as in the case of Socrates or the tree in my back yard, we mean a composition that transcends that between matter and form, in which we find privation as part of the dynamic relation between the two in becoming. Insofar as this composition between a substance and its act of being transcends this first composition, does it still entail any privation or is it also purely static and formal? If it does entail some kind of privation, how is the dynamism of the relation that follows from that to be understood? Will it be just one of becoming, as in coming to be strictly and ceasing to be? Or will it be one of action and communication with other finite beings?

15.4 Action and Communication as Transcendence of Ontological Limitation

As distinct from the act of being, substance is principle of limitation of that act. If this act were not received in different substances, as each limits it to its own standing, it would not be diversified and multiplied. On the other hand, in being diversified and multiplied it is limited to each substance of which it is the act of being. What there is, then, is a diversity and a plurality of beings each sharing in an act that is somehow common to all of them. Each finds something of this act in itself and in others. In its commonality to the diversity and plurality of beings, the act of being is not limited to any one of them. It is somehow infinite. In its composition with the diverse substances, it is a finite act of each finite substance, but as common and infinite, it overflows this finitude in a dynamic relation to other beings sharing in the same act. In limiting the act of being to its own standing, an individual substance does not isolate itself. It finds itself in communication with other substances within the infinity of their common act of being.

There is thus in every individual substance not only potency to the act of being, but also a certain privation in relation to the being of other substances. Not only does each limit its own act of being, but each also limits the other in its being. It deprives the other of being all of being, so to speak. Thus, among the finite beings of our experience, there is a mutual deprivation of being, so to speak, which does not leave them isolated from one another in a static coexistence but draws them together in a dynamic relation, not just of coming to be, as in the dynamic of matter and form, but of action and communication. This privation of a substance in relation to the act of being regards not just its own act, but also the act of other beings. It takes the form of a desire for the other as other, which it cannot become without ceasing to be itself, but which it somehow desires as the perfection of its own limited being in the only way that this is possible, that is, as an end to be attained through action in some kind of communication.

Every being clings to its own being. A material substance, which is constituted of a matter that remains in potency to forms other than the one it now has, has to struggle against these different potencies in itself to survive in being. But it cannot rid itself of this potency to not-be or to nonbeing. In desiring an other as its end, however, it is not actuating this potency not to be, so to speak. It is still clinging to its own being as a substance. It is maintaining its standing in being and from this stand, which is its first perfection, it is proceeding to act in its own way, which is its second perfection. The privation we are speaking of with regard to the other is one that gives rise to action among substances that have some endurance in being and not just to a process of generation and corruption. It presupposes the separate actuality of substances and sets them in action in relation to one another. It entails a finality of communication among beings extrinsic to one another that does not take away their first perfection as substances but rather enhances this perfection into a higher form or *convenience* in communication with others.

We speak of action here in connection with this finality of extrinsic relation among beings, and not just of a process or a coming to be and ceasing to be intrinsic to a substance, because action is an ultimate act of substances that is not necessarily tied to any process of coming to be or ceasing to be. In one sense, be or the act of being is the ultimate act of a finite substance, insofar as the substance is something *actually* or has its standing in being. However, insofar as substance limits this act of being, that is, as a potency to such an act, it is also in potency to the being of other things, not as desiring to be other than itself, but rather as relating to them, as other, as part of its own final perfection. In this way a substance aspires to transcend itself in its initial ontological constitution not by ceasing to be itself, but by acting in its own way and according to its own form in relation to other substances. For this reason, to be for a finite being is never just a static standing. It is always an inclination to act, to overcome its initial ontological finitude, and to seek its ultimate perfection in some conjunction with all of being.

15.5   The Ontological Inclination to Act

We have been speaking of finite being in its propensity to act in a way that is common to finite beings as such. But there is a diversity of finite beings as well as a multiplicity. Not all are the same, even as finite, and not all are inclined in the same way to act or inclined to act in the same way. There is a diversity in finitude and this diversity affects the inclination to act in different beings. How is this diversity to be understood?

Let us recall that the principle of diversity among determinate beings as well as the principle of perfection in any determinate being is the form. The substantial form of a being is what specifies it to be the kind of being it is. It is from this form that the inclination to act follows. As the ancient adage used to say, some inclination follows from any form. *Quamlibet formam sequitur aliqua inclinatio.* If the form is intentional in the mind of an artist or a craftsman, the corresponding inclination is to produce or to reproduce it in some matter. If the form is that of a thing in nature, the corresponding inclination is to reproduce itself in another thing or to seek another thing of its own kind.

The inclination to act follows from form in a twofold sense. First, it follows in the sense that we have been arguing for, in that the finite being, precisely as finite, is inclined to transcend its own ontological limitation through action and communication with other finite beings. A being is finite by reason of its form, whether it is the form of a composite or a simple immaterial form. As the potency in its composition with its act of being, form limits this act as it receives it. The inclination to act follows from this very limiting of the act of being. As form, albeit still in potency to the act of being, it is not purely passive potency, as matter is in relation to form. It has some kind of active potency through which it is inclined to act in order to equal in some way the infinity of being as common to many beings. The tendency of a finite being as such to transcend the limitation of its ontological constitution follows from its form as in potency to the act of being. In this sense, the inclination to act follows necessarily from any finite form actuated by an act of being shared with other finite beings.

The second sense in which the inclination to act follows from form is closely related to this first sense, but it adds an important specification. The inclination follows from the form, which is specific to each being, and not from the act of being, which is common to all beings even though it is that which is most intimate to each being as being. Thus the inclination to act is in accordance with the form, and not with the act of being. Through its action, a being transcends the limitation of its ontological constitution, but it does so only in the measure of its form. If a form is totally immersed in matter, so too is its action, while its transcendence, even though it goes out to other beings, is restricted to material conditions. If a form emerges from its material conditions, as in the case of a conscious being, so too does its action, which comes to include the forms of other beings as well as its own intentionally, although not physically. The form that entails consciousness, especially as found in productive human labor, opens up the scope of transcendence through action far beyond the physical limitation of any individual, as Marx did not hesitate to point out, and, we should add, the form that entails self-consciousness, opens it up infinitely through the spiritual inclinations of intelligence and will.

The inclination to act thus means different things for different beings. It is best known to us and first known in our own proper activity. There it has the form of an appetite, which is an inclination to act that follows upon the consciousness of an object to be desired or acquiesced in. We spoke earlier, in Chapter 8, of the will as an appetite or an inclination to act in this sense, in developing the idea of the ontological good. We could also speak of the intelligence as a similar appetite or inclination to act, in that it desires truth as its object, which is the truth of being, and in that it acquiesces in it in the affirmation of judgment. Truth, which is a disclosure of being, is the good for intelligence that inclines it to seek and wonder, as being itself is the good for the will once it is known. This is known in a kind of self-consciousness that takes in or wonders about the whole world along with itself, for self-consciousness gives a universal scope to the human inclination to act as well as the possibility of acting in many different ways in determining itself. It is by reflection upon these two inclinations to act in our human being that we arrive at the notions of truth and goodness as properties of being.

But we do not suppose that all beings have such a universal and self-conscious inclination to act. There are others that have some consciousness, but do not appear to have intelligence and will. Theirs is only a sense consciousness, with an appetite consequently that is only sensual. Their inclination to act can still be called an appetite because it follows from some consciousness of objects as desirable and as satisfying. But this appetite does not have the same universal scope as the human appetite, which is intellectual as well as sensual, nor does it appear to have the same level of reflection into self. It is more caught up in its material conditions in that it depends intrinsically on sense organs and on merely physical affection, and its scope is far from being as universal.

Moreover, while merely animal consciousness does entail a certain transcendence over its immediate physical being, the wonder and satisfaction of animals is still confined to very particular worlds of their own. Each animal has a world of its own, in which it lives and breathes and dwells. Each has its own inclinations to act in this world of its own. But neither this world nor these inclinations have the full scope of being that opens up in human inclination through intelligence and will.

On the level of plant life, we may no longer be justified in speaking of appetite, if we restrict the idea of appetite to an inclination that follows from some kind of consciousness, even though there does appear to be some kind of sensitivity to environmental conditions in some plants. Our differentiation of animal life from plant life seems to rest on a distinction between, on the one hand, sensation, which definitely entails a form of consciousness, although not self-consciousness, as in the case of humans, and on the other hand, whatever is proper to plants in their interaction with inanimate elements. In this interaction, however, there is certainly an inclination to act on the part of the plant, even if it be only to absorb and to discharge as it holds its own in being through its vital functions.

The place among beings where the internal inclination to act is least distinct and most difficult to discern is in nonliving things. This is in keeping with the lower degree of their identity or of their standing in being and the greater immersion of their form in their matter as mere things. In them the form barely overcomes the potency of matter, so that the inclination to act is barely more than a reaction, a force caught up in an interplay of forces. Even at this level of being, however, and to the extent that we are still talking about a plurality of beings, we have to think of an inclination to act in each being relating it to other beings as to ends, for the other is that toward which the being is inclined to act. In fact, this inclination may not be strictly to act, as in the case of the living. At the most basic level of physical activity, the inclination may be more to a place, according to the scientific model of Aristotle, who thought of the four elements that he distinguished at the base of physical reality as inclined to opposing places, with earth inclined toward the center of the cosmos and fire inclined away from this center toward its periphery, while water and air were intermediary, one on the side of earth and the other on the side of fire. Or the inclination may be nothing more than a relation to an opposing force, as in the case of negative and positive charges at the atomic level as defined by modern physics. In any case, it is to some inclination that we are brought back as most fundamental to any being and as consequent upon its form.

Modern physics has gone much further than ancient science in distinguishing elements and basic entities, but it still distinguishes these elements and these entities on the basis of what we should call different inclinations it finds within them relating to other elements and basic entities, even though these inclinations are expressed mainly as mathematical equations. Even at this level of minimal inclination, there is still an order of finality among the different things distinguished always in relation to one another as distinct from one another, an order that is analogous to that among self-consciousnesses in mutual recognition.

15.6   The Necessity of Finality among Finite Beings

To speak of the end as an extrinsic cause is to speak of a being that is other than the being for which it is the end. We have spoken of a certain finality in the process of coming to be, where the form of what comes to be is the end-intended of the process. This is the process of generation as the process of growth and development of a being. But this is a finality that is still only intrinsic to the being that is coming to be. It is not finality in the fullest sense of the term, that is, in the sense that one being is somehow the end for another being as an object of desire or acquiescence. We have spoken of a certain desire for form in matter as being in potency in Chapter 12. But this was not the desire of one being for another, or for an object other than the subject. It was the desire of a subjective principle for its coprinciple in the constitution of a composite being, a desire found only in matter in its relation to form as the fulfillment of its potency. It was not the desire of one thing already constituted in its being for another thing also constituted in its being. Only the latter is the sign of a finality among finite beings over and above the finality intrinsic to each in its coming to be, the sign of a need among finite beings for one another.

How does this need relate to the inclination to act that follows upon the form of any being? On the one hand, the inclination to act is a positive orientation to all of being on the part of form, including the being of others. But, on the other hand, it is also an appetite for the other in its being and goodness. This appetite can be understood as either desire for the good, when it is not possessed, or acquiescence in the good, when it is possessed. But in either case it has to be understood as a kind of need for the other on the part of the finite being as such, a need that manifests itself in the passing of the finite being from its first or ontological perfection to its second perfection (Chapter 7), for it is in this passage from first to second perfection that each finite being encounters other finite beings also passing from their first to their second perfection as part of the universe in which they all find themselves.

In order to show that every being is good, we argued from our experience of appetite, which is an effect of goodness in us. The goodness we were speaking of is that of being which is divided among finite beings in varying degrees and according to different needs. For the finite being, who has to achieve its second perfection through its proper activity, the experience of desire, even for a being constituted in its first perfection, is an experience of some otherness in being, of some object that stands opposite the desiring subject, which it does not have, and which it desires.

We can think of this as the experience of animals, to speak only of beings that show a certain degree of consciousness and hence of appetite in the proper sense of the term. Animals desire things outside themselves, which they seek out in their roaming, to satisfy their own needs and so maintain themselves in their second perfection as animals. But the place to think about it most properly is in the experience of human beings, who desire not only mere things but also other human beings for the satisfaction of their needs and the maintenance of their second perfection as human. In this experience, which is our own proper activity, we can reflect directly on the need of a finite being to transcend its own ontological limitation in the encounter with another finite being like itself. From this reflection on human being in its second perfection we can then extend our understanding of this need by analogy to other kinds of finite being, especially lesser kinds.

In what does the second perfection of human being consist? Most properly, it consists in self-conscious activity. But how is this activity constituted

in its self-consciousness? From what need, from what desire, does it follow?
We are well aware of our needs and desires on the animal level of being,
even though we may not understand all of them as fully as we might. These
are the needs and desires that can be satisfied through things outside ourselves, but in the satisfaction those things are often consumed and cease to
be, which gives rise to a constant recurrence of needs and desires for more
things outside ourselves. It also gives rise to our desire for accumulating such
things in anticipation of future needs.

But these are not the needs and desires that give rise to self-consciousness
as such, as Hegel has shown in his phenomenological passage from mere
consciousness of objects that stand over against *(Gegenstände)* consciousness
to genuine self-consciousness, where the other is now another self-consciousness *(PhG* 124–43/98–113). This self-consciousness has to be associated
with another kind of need or desire, which is for another kind of good,
namely, a spiritual good, and which Hegel calls recognition *(Anerkennung)*.

In the satisfaction of this need and desire, the object or the other is not
consumed and does not cease to be, but rather is affirmed in its very being
and in its own self-consciousness as other than the first to which reference is
made. In the mutual recognition of self-consciousnesses among finite beings, the goodness of each being is preserved and maintained for the other,
since this is the condition for its coming to be and its continuing to be such
as it is. It is as other than itself that a self-consciousness needs another self-
consciousness in its desire for recognition. Only so can it come to self-consciousness in the presence of another self-consciousness.

How does this mutual recognition spell itself out as the satisfaction of a
need for an other in the finite being? To distinguish oneself from an other in
one's own self-consciousness is to distinguish oneself as finite, as not the other. To distinguish the other as distinct from oneself in being is equally to distinguish it as finite, as not oneself. All this is implied in mutual recognition,
but it is implied concretely in such a way that the distinguishing of one self
from another takes place in a mutual presence of the one to the other. Each
discovers itself as being in its self-consciousness and as finite in the presence
of an other who is also discovering itself as being in its self-consciousness and
as finite in the presence of the other self. In fact, each needs the other in order to discover itself in its own self-consciousness and has to affirm the other
as other in order to get the recognition that it needs, for without the other in
self-consciousness there could not be the satisfaction of recognition.

In the need or the desire for mutual recognition between selves we thus
have one finite being drawn to another as to its end in the very act of

achieving its own second perfection as self-consciousness. In fact, we have that only among several self-consciousnesses each seeking its own perfection through the other as a good for itself. In the achievement of mutual recognition we have a certain acquiescence in this goodness of the other for oneself as well as in one's own goodness as self-conscious. As mutual between two selves or among several selves the relation is reciprocal. It constitutes a community of finite beings where the good of each is at the same time the good of the other, a common good that begins as mutual recognition but that can open up into friendship, a further acquiescence in the goodness of the other.

All this illustrates how one finite being is an end for another finite being at least on one level of being, that of human being. Insofar as mutual recognition is a necessary condition for self-consciousness, it illustrates a need or a desire for the other as part of the end-intended in intending one's own perfection. For the achievement of its own perfection even as self-conscious, the human being has to go through or will the perfection of another human being in its self-consciousness. But is all this true of other finite beings or is it true only of human being? Can it be extended by analogy to other realms of finite being, where there appears to be no self-consciousness?

We began our reflection on the need for an other in finite being with self-conscious human being not only because that remains for us the primary analogate of being, but also because that is where the need for an other or the orientation to an other might seem least apparent. Self-consciousness entails a kind of self-centeredness or absolute self-standing that has seemed to preclude any necessary relation to an other for modern thought beginning with Descartes and Hobbes. In the need or the desire of self-consciousness for recognition, however, we have found that such is not the case. We have found that self-consciousness is itself a limited being, both by reason of *what* it is in itself and by the presence in being of other self-consciousnesses. We have found also that self-consciousness transcends this limitation through recognition of and from the other.

In fact, we might argue that we first become conscious of an object as other than ourselves in being, and consequently of ourselves as a being distinct from that one, in the confrontation with another self. The first object we come to know objectively is another self in relation to whom we come to know ourselves as a self or as a subject affected by another self. Lesser objects, that is, merely sentient beings, merely living beings, or even nonliving beings, appear to us as objects only subsequently, so that the objectivity of mere thinghood depends on the objectivity in intersubjectivity, that is, a relation of mutual recognition among selves. It is in this relation among selves that we come to our first conception of being in its finitude and in its plurality at the same time as in its tendency to overcome its finitude through communication and interaction with other finite beings.

The fact that this takes place only on a level of self-consciousness sets self-conscious being off as the highest form in which this communication and interaction takes place among the beings we know in the direct exercise of judgment. For the lower forms of being and their need for an other, we have only to proceed according to our understanding of lesser forms of consciousness and lesser forms of desire to the point where there appears no conscious desire and no life but only an inclination to some other which is barely an other on the level of basic physical entities, as in the case of mere negative charges in relation to mere positive charges.

To speak of a conscious being without self-consciousness, such as what is called a brute animal, is to speak of being with a lesser self-standing, and therefore of one that is more finite and more in need of an other, even though this is no longer a need or a desire for recognition. The form of this lesser being does not give rise to this higher inclination or appetite for recognition any more than it gives rise to the capacity for mutual recognition and self-consciousness in the full sense of the term through symbiosis.

To speak of living but not conscious beings, such as plants, is to speak of even more finite beings and beings more in need of an other in order not just to arrive at their own self-standing or essential identity, but also to actualize themselves in their second perfection.

Finally, to speak of nonliving beings, where the level of self-standing seems to be most diminished, is to speak of the most finite kind of being and the kind most in need of an other for whatever self-standing can be achieved. This is the level of being that physics studies, in abstraction from all higher levels of finite being. But it is a level in which there is still some inclination as to an other from which all motion, conscious and living as well as physical, begins, to the extent that there is still a discernible distinction between entities in their mutual relations. At the limit there is only a pure passing over without distinction of terms and therefore without order and without finality, a pure force or a pure bang that may not be the inclination of anything.

In speaking of the *higher* activity of human being and of its inclination to act, however, we should keep in mind that these are not detached from the lower forms of activity and inclination in nature. The human being is not a pure self-consciousness. It is also an animal, a living thing, and a physical entity with its own physical organs, including arms and legs along with head and hands. In its self-consciousness it integrates these lower forms of activity and inclination into a higher unity, that of a self-conscious being and that of a community of such self-conscious beings. Conversely, however, the lower forms of being not only exhibit proper activities, but also in these activities manifest inclinations to some things rather that others and in this way form specific parts of an order that can be thought of as a kind of community of beings, the community of natures as a whole that is tending or intended in many different ways at many different levels toward the historical community of human beings at its summit.

CHAPTER 16

From the Material to the Efficient Cause

To SPEAK OF THE ORDER OF FINALITY among determinate beings is
not enough. Finality accounts for why finite beings tend to transcend
their initial ontological limitation through action and how they need other
beings in doing so. It accounts for why separate beings tend toward one another in their very separation, but it does not account for how they come
together effectively in the communication of being from one to the other.

In the discussion of finality in nature, we saw how a one-sided consideration of the final cause in reality can come to displace and even to replace all
consideration of the material and the efficient cause. We argued against the
one-sided reaction to this tendency which tends to look only to material
and efficient causes in accounting for things, to the exclusion of any consideration of finality, but we did not deny the necessity of considering the material and the efficient cause along with the final cause. On the contrary, we
affirmed the necessity to do so, since the end does not *affect* what comes to
be as an effect, whether by art or by nature, except by the *effective* power of
an agent. We have already given a good deal of thought to the material cause
of being in composite substances, and it is from this side of the composite
substance that we shall proceed to our consideration of the efficient cause,
just as it is from the side of the form that we proceeded to our consideration
of the final cause.

We should keep in mind, however, that the composite substance we are
focusing on is not just a mere physical entity, but a living, sentient, rational
thing, the human being, our primary analogate of being. In doing so, we are
avoiding the kind of separation between the order of efficiency and the order of finality, or between the order of nature and the order of freedom,
Kant was left with in his critical philosophy. We are keeping these two orders
together as part of a single universal order of beings in relation to one another. In *The Critique of Pure Reason* Kant was left with the problem of a

"thing in itself" that had to be affirmed but that could not be known as such. In this way the question of "metaphysical knowledge," as conceived by Kant, remained quite problematic, but not the question of "physical knowledge." Through the *Critique,* Kant claimed to have resolved the question of experiential knowledge through a combination, so to speak, of the categories of the understanding with a content from sense intuition. This synthesis of sense and understanding gave us a knowledge not just of things outside ourselves, but also of ourselves as things of experience, that is, as things that are subject to the same necessity as all other things in nature. While it did not allow for a more total reflection upon the activity of thought itself as the appearance of the self in its substance, it did allow for knowledge of human being both as knowing and as caught up in the determinism of nature in its being.

It was only in abstraction from this realm of determinism that Kant allowed for the freedom of the human subject in the realm of Pure Practical Reason. He allowed for it speculatively as part of what was hidden in the unknowable "thing in itself." He did not claim to know this as such, since there was no intuition connected with Pure Practical Reason as there was for Theoretical Reason. But he claimed it as a postulate of Pure Practical Reason, for without this postulated freedom there could be no thought of a moral order as distinct from the natural order and as governed by pure practical reason.

In this dualism of Pure Reason Kant managed to preserve both the order of efficiency and the order of finality. One he saw as the order of nature and the other as the order of morality, where at least the human being was seen as an end in itself in a kingdom of ends. But he preserved them only as juxtaposed to one another or as superimposed upon each other, depending upon whether we come at them through theoretical reason, where the order of necessity is thought of as holding sway, or through practical reason, where the order of freedom asserts itself. He did not bring them together as one order, as German Idealism tried to do after him or as we shall try to do here in our understanding of the universe.

It is through our focus on the composite substance of human being as our primary analogate of being that we keep these two orders of finality and of efficiency from diverging into two separate realms. In the composite substance we already have an understanding of two principles of being, matter and form. In the relation between the two we already have an understanding of some finality in this relation, inasmuch as matter somehow desires form and form is the intended end in the process of generation. From the form there also follows the inclination to act in the finite being that reaches out to some other being as to an end. It is from the side of matter that we discover as well some influencing of being from an other or some dependence in being from an other in the finite being. This is the order of efficient causality in the relation between finite beings, which now comes into question for us. In what does it consist? How is it a pouring out of being, or an *influencing,* from one being to another? How is it a dependence of one upon another even though each is somehow self-standing?

16.1   The Idea of Efficient Cause

In elucidating our idea of the final cause we started from the way human beings come to produce things such as houses and airplanes. Let us begin with the same kind of activity to elucidate the idea of efficient cause, which is presumably better understood in modern science and philosophy but which is still not always understood as clearly as it might be. In what does efficiency consist as distinct from finality? How is the efficient cause to be distinguished from mere matter as a cause of what comes to be?

In the production of things like houses and airplanes the end, or the final cause, of the production is the intended use of the product. We build houses in order to live or work in them. We build airplanes in order to fly in them. In speaking of the efficient cause, however, it is of the actual building of such things that we are speaking, the producing of them into being. In what does this consist? How is the product an effect of the producer? How is one thing *effected* by another?

In raising the question of efficient causality among finite beings we are raising the question of causality in a way that is irreducible to any of the other causes we can distinguish in being. As we noted from the very beginning of our reflection on the communication of being, the idea of cause and effect presupposes some kind of otherness between the effect and the cause. The effect is real as effect only as other than the cause. It is from this otherness of the effect that the question of efficient causality as external arises. How does this or that, which is thought of as an effect, relate to its efficient cause?

Part of the answer to this question relates to the end for which the effect is produced. Part of it also relates to the form and matter of the product which, as distinct principles of a composite, are other not only than one another but also than the whole that they compose, and hence can be thought of as causes of the composite. But in its most radical sense the answer to the question still relates to how one being depends on or is caused by another being once a plurality of beings or the otherness of the effect is recognized.

All questions about the final, the formal, or the material cause at some point converge upon this question of the efficient cause, which has to do with one being *effecting* an other or one being understood as *effected* by an other, not to be confused with the *affecting* and the being *affected* of final causation. The final cause, or the end-intended, does not exert its influence in being except through the efficient cause, nor do form and matter come together as an actual composite except under the influence of some other composite that is already actual, as we are about to show. The question of accounting for being that first arises with coming to be, as we saw at the beginning of our reflection on becoming, culminates in this one about the efficient cause, beyond that of the material and the formal cause. How does the actuality of one being account for the actuality of another?

In answering this question we must begin from the thing *effected* and see it as a thing, just as in answering the question about any motion in being we had to begin from the *terminus ad quem* of the motion. It is in the product that we understand a production, just as it is in its term that we understand a change. Now in the case of a house or an airplane, the product is clearly a composite of matter and form that is a thing other than the producer. As such a thing it has a form of its own actualized in its matter, which are the materials out of which it was formed.

To understand a thing as a product of human activity, however, we must understand the form as having first been thought by a human being. The form of the house or the airplane that comes to be was first conceived by a human being before it could be actualized in its matter. As merely conceived, the form is not yet the form of the thing produced or to be produced. Before it becomes that, some actual disposing and shaping of materials will have to take place, which begins after the initial thought of the form has reached a certain completion. But the *conception* itself, as distinct from the end-intended we spoke about earlier, must be seen as part of the efficient causality for the house, or the airplane, or any other human artifact, including a work of art. The conception is the invention of what is to be produced and we certainly think of the inventor as the efficient cause of what he invents, even when he does not give a hand to the actual production of his invention. The same is true of the artist or the designer, who may not always be an inventor but who operates out of a certain habit or an art that is still basically a conception.

To be sure, the conception alone does not make the thing produced. Not all bright ideas come to fruition in external reality. Measures must be taken to bring certain materials into shape according to the conceived form. But even these measures follow from the conception, which is truly that whence the entire process begins. In the actual production of an artifact or of a work of art, the conception is the beginning of the efficiency, which must be distinguished from both the final cause and the material cause of the product. In this sense, it is *conception* that is the true origin of the work of art rather than just be or *Sein* in the abstract, as Heidegger claims. What is produced in being is something someone had to think of first. Without the thought at the origin, the thing would not have come into being, the thought, not just of a certain use or a certain purpose for which the thing could be used, but of the thing itself or the work of art according to its own form, that which had to be produced in being, and the thought from which a conclusion had to be drawn as to where to begin in the actual disposition of matter for the production of the thing or the work of art.

In fact, the thing, as artifact or as an effect of art, which is more than just a force of nature, has to be understood more as a product of thought than as a product of mere nature because the principles of motion in nature alone could not account for its coming to be. Even though the materials did have a certain potency to the form of the product or the artifact, there was nothing in nature to educe this form from this potency at this time. The thought had to intervene, so to speak, as a new beginning, as an origin of something new in being. This is an aspect of labor or human production Marx did not sufficiently attend to in his analysis of the forces of production.

This idea of human efficiency presupposes that we understand the product as a thing distinct from its producer. The house and the airplane are original artifacts of human being that clearly stand outside the producer, even though they are in some sense expressions of our originality. We could also think of a certain kind of human efficiency that stays within the human being through which one shapes oneself rather than something else. There is always something of this even in the shaping of things outside ourselves. In producing things we are also cultivating ourselves. As Marx puts it, "By thus acting on the external world and changing it, [human being] at the same time changes its own nature" (Marx 1906, 198).

But even in this kind of internal or immanent efficiency, we would have to maintain a distinction between what is produced and what produces, or what is caused and what causes, a distinction that is seen much more clearly when the product is something separate from the producer or the effected is separate from the cause, as the house and the airplane stand in being in their own way apart from any human being. When we see them as things in themselves, so to speak, even though they are not things of nature, that is, when we see them as artifacts or as products of human art, we see much more clearly how the efficient cause is something else than the effect, even as the origin of the effect, in a way that is not true of the material cause, which is a constitutive principle of the effect as a composite.

We spoke earlier of matter as that out of whose potency forms are educed, whether it be by nature or by human initiative. In speaking of this relation of material causality we spoke of coming to be *from*. Matter is that *from* which something comes to be. As a principle of being, however, it is only a subject of change. It is constitutive of what comes to be along with the form educed from it. To express the relating of efficient causality we must speak of origin in a different way than we do for the material cause. That which comes to be does not originate from its efficient cause in the same way as it comes to be *from* matter. The house or the airplane comes to be from the materials out of which it is produced. Its form is educed from this matter. But the efficient cause of the house or the airplane is not the matter that constitutes it or *from* which it comes to be.

Nor is the efficient cause the form that is actually educed from its matter, the form that is constitutive of the being produced. It is another being that has produced it in being as the form of this matter, starting from a conception of the form. The efficient or the moving cause is the source of the motion through which an effect comes to be, for we are speaking of production still for things that come to be. As such the efficient cause is something that stands apart from and is prior to what comes to be and yet causes it to come into being.

Aristotle speaks of the efficient cause as that *whence (hothen)* the first beginning of change or rest comes. He gives as his first example of such a cause the one who has conceived a plan *(ho bouleusas)*, before mentioning the father of the child or, more generally, the producer of a product or that which changes that which is changed (*Metaph* 1013a 30–34). In the order of coming to be, the efficient cause is the moving cause of that which is moved or comes to be through change.

16.2   Teaching as Efficient Causality in the Historical Order

Discussions of efficient causality in modern philosophy usually focus only on physical or mechanical interactions among things. This is the way causality was still viewed by Hegel, who tended to minimize it as something immersed in the mechanical forces of nature. So far we have illustrated the idea of efficient causality only in terms of human production having to do largely with external objects at hand, though we have insisted on the conception of ideas, or on art, as an essential aspect of this causality. Nevertheless, physical interaction is not the only kind of efficient communication among the beings we know in experience. There are other kinds of communication, especially among human beings, that can be viewed as instances of efficient causality on the level of spirit as well as nature.

In keeping with our understanding of human being as the primary analogate of being, we should insist on human interaction even on the level of thought as a kind of efficient causality, prior to asking about efficient causality in mere nature or among merely physical objects, for it is in this human kind of interaction that we can understand how one being *effectively* influences another better than in merely physical interaction. Human beings themselves, even in their self-consciousness, begin historically in an interaction or a confrontation of individuals that issues in mutual recognition among them. Human being as we understand it in history presupposes a plurality of individuals. It emerges in a communication among them that is intentional as well as physical. This interaction is no less worthy of metaphysical consideration than merely physical interaction, since as intentional it represents a higher degree of being than the merely physical.

There are, of course, many ways efficient causation takes place in human interaction. Mutual recognition is already such a way. Another way is the kind of influencing that takes place through counseling even in the exercise of free will. But it is perhaps in the activity of one human being teaching another that we find the clearest example of an efficient cause in the intentional order of human action, for there we have not only a distinction between two individuals but also the understanding of one depending on another for something that comes to be in the understanding, namely, learning in one individual as separate from the other.

To speak of teaching is to speak of a communication between two separate individuals. We sometimes speak of teaching oneself something, but this is not strictly teaching. It is learning by oneself through own's own intelligence from experience and possibly from beings other than oneself in experience. This learning, however, is the activity of the one who learns and it comes to one as a second perfection of one's being through the act of one's own intelligence. In this sense the individual human being is the cause of its own learning and, if it were the only individual involved in that process, it would be the sole cause of that learning, without the intervention of an external teacher. When another individual human being intervenes in this process, however, and strengthens it or enhances it, as in the case of teaching, then this other individual has to be seen as an additional cause of the learning, an efficient cause external to the first individual becoming or being learned.

How is this intervention by another in the process of one's own learning to be understood? Let us look first to the learning process itself. In its most basic form it consists in a certain kind of syllogizing, a certain kind of rational collecting from experience. We learn from experience and we have experience in something when we have come to recognize and to connect certain similarities in it. We learn more about the thing when we can account for it through an understanding of its causes, which include matter and form as well as its end and its efficient cause. We can think of all this learning as taking place within one and the same individual, who is going from potency to act in learning.

In one sense this individual is reducing itself from potency to act through its own discourse. But even in this sense we have to distinguish an active principle of intelligence from a passive principle, for nothing is brought from potency to act except through something already in act, as we shall come to understand more clearly with this principle of the efficient cause. This is why Aristotle distinguished between an active intellect and a passive intellect in human being, because in learning by oneself one is both actively integrating being as given in experience and receiving it in one's intelligence before expressing it in concepts and in acts of composition and division or judgments.

In the context of mutual recognition among humans, however, this learning does not take place in one individual without the presence of other individuals who may also be learning, and who have also or are actually learned. We could argue that learning of this kind, which entails self-consciousness as well as consciousness of objects, does not take place without the active presence of others in the relation of mutual recognition, due to the finitude of each individual human being, who needs the other for its own self-perfection. But whether this represents an essential need or not on the part of human beings as such, in the case of a situation where one is more learned in act than an other in some learning process as a whole, we can have a situation in which one becomes a teacher for the other, that is, someone who can somehow *effect* learning in the other. This is true, for example, in the case of Anne Sullivan teaching language to Helen Keller as well as of an advanced physicist teaching the discourse of his science to a beginner in that science, not to mention the metaphysician teaching the discourse of his own science, as we are doing here.

Now it should be noted that this teaching does not take place automatically in any interplay between individuals. It requires a certain resourcefulness and initiative on the part of the teacher as well as a desire or a potency to learn on the part of the one who is to learn. To be sure, there is no learning without a positive act of intelligence on the part of the learner. But this act is not just an act of remembering something already known, as Plato suggests in the *Meno,* nor just of remembering what the teacher has said. It is a movement or a passage in which something that was not known comes to be known as a conclusion to some reasoning process. It is a passage from potency to act, as Aristotle brings out in the *Posterior Analytics,* and in this passage another, the teacher, can intervene to suggest a middle term or a form for the student's own syllogizing that will hasten the passage, make it more *effective,* or even make it happen where it otherwise might not happen at all.

We see this very clearly in the case of Helen Keller's first coming to language as portrayed in *The Miracle Worker* (Gibson). We know that Helen had the potential to learn because she did learn. This is something the family did not know before Anne took over, since they were thinking of committing her to an institution, and which Anne herself did not know for sure, although she did see signs of intelligence in her charge. We also know that Helen did not learn until the language came from her own intelligence, internally, and not just from merely external signing and discipline merely remembered mechanically, so to speak. No matter how much Anne forced language on Helen, Helen did not understand it until she understood it for herself or until she put a concept and a thing together in her own mind. This first concept/thing could have been anything, but for Helen it was water, and through that first word of hers a disclosing was opened up which could then quickly encompass the entire world of being. We see this in the way she rushes about asking the names for things, beginning with persons, like mother, father, and, soon after, teacher. Once the syllogizing of intelligence has been set in motion, it tends to rush about in a quest or a questioning for understanding more and more, especially in one like Helen who has a lot of catching up to do.

But this new thing in the intelligence of Helen was not just the work of her own intelligence. It was also the work of Anne who provided forms for Helen to work with and who recognized her intelligence in its budding, a recognition that was very essential for Helen in this first venture of her own understanding. Those forms and that recognition from Anne were a cause of Helen's coming to understanding in the same way as the forms conceived by an architect are the cause of the building that gets constructed through the efforts of many others. And they were a cause as coming from another being, who is then recognized as the teacher, Helen's teacher, in an act of mutual recognition between two persons. This was clearly a first for Helen. But it was also a first for Anne as well, who saw herself in a new light, as a teacher, as one who had effected learning in another, even as she saw the learning come forth in and from the other. For this, Anne too needed the recognition of Helen, and for the turn that her life took as a result of this miraculous encounter for herself as well as for Helen.

All this may be thought of as a miracle in the life of two human beings, where the two come to a new understanding of themselves and of one another. But it must not be understood as having been caused by a special divine intervention, as miracles are usually understood. Anne, not God, was the "miracle worker," as the teacher or the particular efficient cause in this case. What Anne did was "miraculous" in the sense that it was extraordinary in overcoming a handicap and in helping Helen bridge a gap in her syllogizing, something no one else had been able to do up to then. This was a handicap for everyone else as well as for Helen, inasmuch as everyone wanted Helen to come to understand but no one knew how to help her do it. Anne did and designed ways for helping her do what she could not do by herself. In this she became the efficient cause of learning in Helen, even though Helen still had to learn for herself. We know this because Anne was successful in teaching where no one else had been before.

But what she accomplished was "miraculous" in another sense as well, which is more fundamental in the sense of its being *mirabile,* or admirable, and which may not be so extraordinary. Anne brought someone else to a new kind of consciousness and a new self-consciousness. What was extraordinary in doing so with Helen were the steps she had to take because of Helen's sense limitations, not rational limitations, which had kept her from learning as children with all their senses usually learn. But just coming to one's first understanding and to self-consciousness is itself something to be wondered at and admired in any child. We look for that first word from a child and we cheer it when we think we have heard it. The wonder, however, is quite ordinary, and it is taught by others in all sorts of subtle ways that we hardly ever advert to, especially when they are mediated by all the senses, especially those of seeing and hearing.

Humans come to full consciousness and self-consciousness as human beings not just in a physical contact with other beings. Humans come to full consciousness and self-consciousness only in communication with other humans, who use language as well as make physical contact. This is why humans who lose contact with other humans, especially in the early stages of their development, never seem to come to a fullness of human consciousness and self-consciousness. They are handicapped not by sense limitations, as in the case of Helen, who did not lose physical contact with other humans, but by the absence of other humans. They are lost as human in a world of silence. They remain in the dark of nature.

In all these ways of using language with infants, *infantes,* which means those who are yet speechless, there is an *effecting* of speech that enables them to go from potency to act in a speech of their own. In this sense learning speech even for oneself is caused by others who use speech in their contact with the speechless. The extraordinary case of Anne Sullivan with Helen Keller only highlights an intersubjective relation that comes into play for any awakening to human consciousness and self-consciousness, a wondrous learning experience for a human being in which another human being always has an effect.

In the teaching of science at a more advanced level the same kind of intersubjective and causal relationships can be seen to obtain. If we begin from the understanding that learning is an act of the learner and that learning is itself a perfection of the one who has learned or is learned in some science, then we have to say that learning is primarily the effect of the learner's own act of syllogizing or gathering. One does not arrive at scientific conclusions by just remembering what has been said by others, although that is not excluded from the process of gathering that precedes concluding on one's own. Remembering is an important part of learning, but not just of words spoken or written by another. A properly scientific conclusion has to be one's own, even when it is a repetition of someone else's, that is, one's own appropriation of a previously established conclusion. One can only see and follow a demonstration for oneself.

Nevertheless, even in this process of coming to one's own conclusions, there is the intervention of an other who can also be thought of as a cause of the learning in the learner's mind. This is clear in the elementary teaching of a particular science like physics, biology, or economics. The good teacher, who looks for more than just memory of the textbook from the student, is the one who knows how to elicit questioning on the part of students and who can furnish appropriate middle terms for their rational gathering or syllogizing from experience and experimentation. This is something that the student might not do by himself, or might not do so expeditiously, without the help of someone more advanced in that science. In other words, the teacher has to *demonstrate* for the student, which, as Aristotle understood in

the *Posterior Analytics,* means furnishing an appropriate middle term for syllogizing and gathering an answer to a question about a subject, an answer
that is *apodictic,* literally, one that makes the other know *(alium faciens scire),* so
that the other comes to his or her own conclusion (*PA* 71b 17–19). Through
such *demonstration,* then, if the student responds to it or takes up the middle
term in his or her own syllogizing, the teacher can also be called a cause of
the student's own conclusion.

The same kind of intersubjective and causal relations can also be found in
more advanced forms of scientific discourse, where questions still remain to
be answered and where conclusions may be advanced before a scientific
community in the form of hypotheses to be verified. Whenever anyone arrives at a new theory, as Einstein did with relativity in physics, one that better accounts for what is taken to be given in fact, his first task is to explain
what he means by his hypothesis, how it arises from questions that remain
for a particular scientific community, and how it answers these questions. In
this case, through his publication of "results," he is presenting himself as a
teacher for this community, explaining the question to be raised and offer-
ing his demonstration for his conclusion to be tested or critically evaluated
by the other members of the community, who then have to come to their
own conclusion, whether it be one of agreement or disagreement or a mixture of both leading to a revision of theory. All this happens in a process
where the new theory functions as a complex middle term for discussion
and syllogizing and, insofar as the new theory is the basis for discussion, the
one who initially proposed it is thought of as the teacher or as the cause of
the new learning in the community of scientists. This is why Einstein was
thought of as an original genius in his field, an original thinker who was
able to teach others his conclusions.

All this is not usually thought of as a case of efficient causality, but if we
take learning to be something real and really new in the being of learners,
and if we accept that learning takes place from teaching as well as from one's
own act of intelligence, then we have to understand it as caused by another.
In fact, it is a case in which we see efficient causality most directly at work,
for we know that our own act of intelligence is the cause of our learning
and we have experienced the presence or the actual influence of others in
this very act of learning. That is how Helen Keller experienced Anne Sullivan as teacher in her own act of learning language, through which she came
to self-consciousness as human being. That is how we experienced our own
teachers, who, as we say, had an influence in our own intellectual self-conscious development. They were the ones who turned us on, as we also say,

and led us along a way that became as much ours as it was theirs. In this they were efficient causes of our learning, which has to be thought of as both a result or an effect as well as an act, the perfection of a self by another as well as one's own self-perfecting.

16.3   Efficient Causality in Nature

The question of efficient causality, however, does not end at the spiritual level of intersubjective communication. It can be illustrated in terms of human or artistic production, as in the case of a house and an airplane. It can also be illuminated in terms of a human being teaching another in so much as learning is something real in oneself caused by another as well as by oneself. But both of these types of efficient causality presuppose a cause that is intelligent and can conceive antecedently the effect to be actualized, whether in production or in teaching. It is the concept that is at the origin of the efficient causality. What of those beings in which there is no such conception or no concept as such? What of those beings that act without a concept of their own but only out of their nature? Can they too be thought of as efficient causes of other beings? If so, in what sense are they efficient causes? In what way do they *influence* being in other beings?

In beginning to answer this question we must keep in mind the kind of being we are speaking about as the effect. It is a being that comes to be, a *factum* or, better still, an *effectum,* an effected, which has been brought to some perfection or determination in being under the influence of another. For us the question of the efficient cause arises in the same way as the question of the material cause, which is in need of determination. The question of the efficient cause starts from motion and has to be thought of as the question of a moving cause other than the thing in motion. We can think of the thing in motion as moving, but to think of it as an effect or as effected we must think of it as *moved* or as *perfected* in some way and of the efficient cause as the *mover* or as the moving cause of what comes to be, as the designer is the cause of the airplane or as the teacher is the cause of learning in another. The communication of being from cause to effect is a communication from one being that is mover to another that is moved. How is this communication to be understood?

From the side of the cause it has to be understood as an action influencing another. Presupposing a distinction between one being and another as understood through the ontological structure of individual beings, with designated matter understood as principle of individuation, we think of the efficient cause as acting on another and causing it to be something in *act* that it would not be without the influence of this cause. This is a kind of *making* *(facere)* something else be something in act, the understanding of which cannot be simple. We have to understand the something that comes to be in act from the side of what we take to be the effect or the effected, where we must consider the different ways of coming to be.

As we saw in Chapter 10 in our reflection on becoming and coming to be, a thing can be thought of as changing or coming to be in two ways, either accidentally, that is, as coming to be according to one aspect or another of its being which is only accidental to its substantial identity, or substantially, that is, as coming to be simply, as this or that substance, from its not being. In both of these ways of changing or coming to be, a thing can be thought of as *moved* and therefore as dependent on a cause other than itself for its movement, and in each case the cause must be understood in relation to the movement that is effected or perfected, that is, brought to some sort of a term, for, again as we saw in our reflection on becoming, a movement or a change can be understood only in relation to its *terminus ad quem*. To understand an efficient cause, we must understand the effect of which it is the cause as having been brought to its perfection under the *influence* of this cause.

Thus in our reflection on the question of the efficient cause we are brought back to our reflection on the material cause in coming to be. But the distinction between the two causes must be kept clearly in mind, even though we cannot clearly understand either one without the other. We have seen how matter is a constitutive principle of what comes be. It is only in this sense that we speak of it as a cause, insofar as it is distinct from its form, with which it constitutes a composite whole. The form too, as the other constitutive principle of that whole, can also be called a cause, but still not in the sense of an efficient cause. As constitutive principles of what comes to be, form and matter can only be intrinsic causes of a being. Here we are inquiring into the extrinsic causes of what comes to be and, more specifically, into the efficient cause. We are trying to see how another being, a properly efficient or moving cause extrinsic to what comes to be, comes into play or *influences* the being of what comes to be.

The main objection to speaking of efficient causality in nature came from Hume in modern philosophy. He thought of it as a matter of constant conjunction between two facts, each perceived separately through a vivid impression. Supposing that one fact, the effect, is distinct from another, the cause, the idea of efficient causation arises only when we see a certain "effect" always following from a certain "cause." For example, supposing that the fact of heat in the water placed on the hot element of a stove is other than the fact of heat in the element itself, we get the idea that the hot element causes the water to become hot because the water always gets hot when we place it on the hot element.

For Hume, this connection of two facts was only an idea, not a matter of vivid impression. As an idea, it was at best a vague impression due to an association or a constant conjunction between two determinate facts. For him, it was based only on an association of past occurrences or past impressions, from which there was no guarantee that the same conjunction would always occur in the future. While we could have a vivid impression of a conjunction in the past, we could have no such impression of anything that has yet to happen. Hence, since for Hume knowledge of fact could only be a matter of vivid impression, and since the idea of cause and effect could only be one of a necessary conjunction of an effect with a cause, one that would hold in the future as well as in the past, then there could be no knowledge of cause and effect, just as there could be no knowledge of what a thing is in its substance. There could only be bundles of impressions associated together as one "thing" or another and there could only be bundles of associations between one "thing" and another, which we thought of as effect and cause only by reason of the constant conjunction between two separate occurrences associated with two separate "things." For practical purposes, to be sure, we had to do as if there were really substances that we had to use in order to sustain ourselves, as substances, and we had to do as if certain things did cause certain effects in other things in order to live in the way that we chose to. But we had no way of *knowing* any of this for certain, at least not as a matter of vivid impressions, which was for Hume the only way of knowing matters of fact or of truth about being. Hence the matter of cause and effect in nature could never be anything more than a vague idea for him, arrived at by some association of vivid impressions.

This is what is generally understood as the empiricist critique of causality. Bunge has shown, however, that it does not correspond to what is properly understood by causality in modern science any more than in ancient science. He has shown, for example, that the understanding of causality does not necessarily involve the kind of contiguity that is presupposed in the Humean critique (Bunge 58–62). Nor does it necessarily involve the kind of temporal antecedence of the cause that is also presupposed by Hume (Bunge 62–68). The understanding of causality is compatible with action at a distance, as in the case of an architect causing a certain building to be built through his design without laying a hand on it or of the sun heating the earth without coming close to it. It is also compatible with instantaneous links, as in the case where building depends on actual laboring or where the warming of the earth depends on the actual shining of the sun. If the work of the builders stops, actual building comes to a halt, and if the sun is clouded over, the surface of the earth begins to cool down.

These examples appear simple and gross in comparison to the complexity and the intricacy of physical reality posited in modern physical science, but they illustrate the essential point about efficient causation. Bunge makes the same point in a much more complicated way in terms of modern physics and relativity. He distinguishes between states of physical objects and causal efficacy. States of physical objects as such are not properly causal. "Initial states cannot therefore be causes but may be produced by previously acting causes" (Bunge 87). It is the various physical objects that are causes of various effects in a given state or in a succession of states. The upshot of this distinction is to show that "predictability by means of laws of succession is a criterion not of causal connection but of the validity of nomological hypotheses about time sequences" (Ibid.). In other words, we can still understand a certain causal connection between certain physical objects without supposing an absolutely necessary conjunction for the future. Nomological hypotheses about time sequences are not necessarily causal statements.

Hence, whatever may be said of Hume's idea of necessary predictability as a criterion for any true knowledge of nature in its successive states, it does not properly apply to our discernment of efficient causality from one thing to another in nature. There can be causality even where there is no necessary predictability. Aristotle, who surely thought we could discern some efficient causation in nature, spoke of what happens by nature as "that which happens always or most of the time" (Phys 196b 10–24). Thus, while some predictability could be expected on the basis of efficient causation among things in nature, it did not entail an absolute necessity for the future. Things could fail to achieve their expected result, either by reason of a deficiency in the matter on which they were working or by reason of a weakness in their own power to act.

Aristotle spoke of efficient causation in nature as it relates to final causality. Things of nature were thought of as aiming at a certain determination not only in their coming to be, but also in their action upon other things. This natural end or determination could be discerned in experience through a pattern of how things happened always or most of the time. It did not, however, involve any absolute guarantee of what would happen in the future. Even with a certain natural determinism in the orientation of the forces of nature, things could still fail to achieve their natural end. After all, nature could still produce monsters or results that could be deemed defective, judged to be such precisely in terms of the proper determination conceived for a particular nature. Even if we do not go all the way with Aristotle in his understanding of final causality in nature, it is still possible to understand a certain teleological determination in nature, as Bunge also suggests (Bunge 19), which in turn redounds to our understanding of efficient causation, for these different kinds of causation cannot be understood as functioning independently of one another.

What is crucial for the discernment of efficient causality in nature, then, is not so much guaranteed predictability, but rather a certain regularity in similarity between the effect and its cause. To understand this we must go back to our understanding of every being as active. In speaking of activity as a transcendental property of being, we distinguished between an action and its underlying thing. This was to speak of the action of a thing as distinct from its substance or its essence, in other words, from *what* it is in its nature, nature being the essence of the thing understood as the principle of its proper activity. It is through this proper activity of a thing that we come to know its nature, what it is in its essence, and to understand its substance. All this is said on the basis of some similarity between *what* a thing is in its essence and its action. Phenomenologically speaking, we come to know what a thing is through what it does. But conversely, or ontologically speaking, a thing acts as it does by reason of what it is. *Omne agens agit sibi simile.* Every agent acts in a way similar to itself.

Now, insofar as action is not merely expressive of *what* a thing is in its essence but also communicative with other things, the understanding of this principle of similarity between *what* a thing is and its action must be extended to include how communication with other things takes place. In one sense, the principle that every agent acts in a way similar to itself applies to its own action as expressive of itself. I come to know *what* Socrates is in his essence as I observe his acting rationally. I also know him to be virtuous, which is something more than what he is by nature, by observing how or what he chooses as a rational being.

But I also observe that Socrates has a certain influence on other human beings, even if it be only by talking with them and not actually teaching them something. I recognize this as an effect caused by Socrates in these other human beings through a certain similarity in what they do in response to what Socrates is doing, that is, by talking back to him. Even if they only talk back, without learning anything from him or with him, there is a certain similarity in what they are doing to what he is doing, and inasmuch as they are talking back in response to his talking, that similarity in them is understood as depending on him to begin with. They become the talking beings they are as a result of his talking to them.

If Socrates actually manages to teach these others something through this talk, then we have an even greater similarity between them and Socrates, which is a learning on their part in response to Socrates. To be sure this learning on the part of others is an act of their own, which therefore expresses what they are in their essence and as learners, but insofar as it depends on Socrates' initiative as actually teaching them, or at least getting them to reflect, it is also an effect of Socrates in them. The communication from one being to another is seen in the similarity between them and the causation is seen in the dependence of the similarity in determination in the effect upon the corresponding determination in the cause.

This is not to say that every similarity of determination between two beings is a matter of efficient causation from one to the other. Two things can be quite similar in nature without being causally connected, just as two people could learn exactly the same thing independently of one another. We speak of causality only where we discern dependence in similarity between one thing and another. Nor do we speak of causality when the similarity in one merely comes after the similarity in the other. When there is merely a succession in similarities, we cannot conclude *post hoc ergo propter hoc*. We must discern an actual dependence of the similarity in the second on that in the first to speak of a relation of effect to cause, which may or may not entail a temporal succession.

To speak of the efficient cause as the cause *whence* something else comes is not to presuppose a temporal priority of the cause over the effect, but only an ontological priority, that is, a real dependence of determination *in the effect* on a similar determination in the cause. Such dependence can be instantaneous or simultaneous as well as chronologically successive. The reason why we speak of the efficient cause as the cause *whence* is that our first understanding of efficient causality is always associated with the process of coming to be, which entails a temporal succession. But this does not restrict the ontological priority of the cause to a temporal priority. It is entirely possible to have a thing that is ontologically dependent on another that is not temporally prior to it, even though temporal priority may be an indication of ontological dependence in certain circumstances, as seems to be implied in the method of verification in experimental science.

The crucial factor in understanding efficient causation from one thing to another is the discernment of the dependence of some determination in one thing upon a similar determination in another in accordance with our understanding of the ontological principle that every agent or cause acts in a way that is similar to itself.

Such a discernment, to be sure, is not a matter of vivid impression alone. In limiting what he calls knowledge of fact to vivid impression, without understanding and reflection, Hume was quite right in denying any certain "knowledge" of cause and effect, especially when the link from the cause to the effect was understood as requiring a necessary conjunction. Understanding the relation between two things, or even between two vivid impressions, is not a matter of mere impression. It is a matter of interpretation in what may start off as only an impression but calls for understanding, which is also part of our knowing of being in the facts.

The exercise of judgment, in which being presents itself and in which we express our knowledge of being, involves much more than mere impression. It includes understanding, through which we come to grasp *what* things are and what relations obtain between them, one of which is that of effect to cause. It also includes reflection, through which we relate the expression of our understanding to being as it presents itself. Hume's failure to see any certain knowledge of cause and effect was part of the general failure in his theory of knowledge. Just as atomizing knowledge into vivid impressions kept him from understanding substance as anything more than a bundle of impressions stuck together by some vague process of association, so also it kept him from understanding cause and effect as anything more than a constant conjunction between two sets of impressions also brought together by a process of association.

Given his narrow conception of knowledge, therefore, Hume was quite consistent in denying any certain knowledge of cause and effect as well as of substance. However, inasmuch as this theory left out any consideration of similarity in determination between impressions, which is also part of what we know in experience and which gives rise to our understanding of substantial identity in things, along with any consideration of dependence in similarity from one thing to another, which gives rise to our understanding of cause and effect between things, he was foreclosing not only on the ontological understanding of cause and effect as well as of substance, but also on the direct exercise of judgment as it relates to experience in any of the particular sciences. For in their ontic concerns with any particular kind of being, these sciences include an ontological reference to being which they do not explicitly reflect on but take for granted in the proper exercise of their particular judgment. What we are doing here in metaphysics or in the universal science of being as being is expressing in more ontological terms of cause and effect what particular sciences express in particularly ontic terms.

16.4   Efficient Causality in Coming to Be Simply

So far, in our exploration of efficient causation, we have spoken mainly of accidental change. The determinations we have spoken of, such as warming or learning, have to be thought of as accidental determinations of the beings in which they are found. At the same time, however, the idea of cause and effect has been closely associated with the idea of coming to be. Even if we allow for a certain amount of self-determination in things that come to be, especially in human beings and other living things, there is still some determination that takes place from one thing to another so that we can speak of some determination in one thing as depending on the *influence* of another thing. If we admit a plurality of things already in existence and a certain communication among them, all this can be readily understood as a matter of efficient causation from one thing to another or as a matter of some dependence of one thing on another.

But what if we begin to think of things coming to be simply, rather than as already in existence? If we focus on substantial change, rather than just accidental change, how is determination to be understood as going from one thing to another when the other is coming into being simply, prior to its having any determination of its own as a substance? How is this thing that is only coming to be determined by another prior to its having any determination of its own? This is the question of efficient causation in its more radical sense, where one being is to be understood as producing another in its substance, just as coming to be simply as a determinate being is coming to be in its radical sense.

To understand this question properly we must go back to our understanding of how things come to be simply as composites of substantial form and matter. We saw earlier how things come to be *from* matter, understood as being in potency, not to be confused with privation or nothing. Now we have to see *whence* they come to be as determinate beings in their substance, for matter as such, or as only indeterminate being in potency, does not account for the new determination that is educed from it. If we focus more on the form, which is the principle of determination in the composite that comes to be, we have to ask *whence* is this new substantial determination, if it is not from matter as such. This is what distinguishes the question of the efficient cause from the question of the material cause in what comes to be simply. How does the new determination depend on some other being extrinsic to the being that comes to be?

We have spoken of the form of a composite as educed from its matter. This is an expression of how matter and form have to be understood as essentially related to one another in the constitution of a composite substance. We do not think of matter as something that can be separated from form, but only as being in potency to form. Nor do we think of the form as existing separate from matter prior to entering the composite, but only as actualizing some potency of matter in its determinate way. In distinguishing these two constitutive principles of a thing, we do not start from a separation, but from an actual composition of the two. Nevertheless, in saying that the form is educed from the potency of matter, we have not said how this is done through the agency of another than the composite that comes to be.

Given the idea of the form as educed from the potency of its matter, however, we might think that the form is actually hidden in the potency of matter. This would then lead to the thought that the agency of the external cause consists only in disclosing what was already there as an actual form, like remembering discloses an actual thought that was previously hidden. But apart from the fact that the idea of something *actually* hidden in a potency seems at odds with the very idea of being in *potency,* which does not include anything actual, the idea of the external cause only disclosing an actuality that is already there seems to take away from what one expects of an efficient cause. If the form is actually there in the matter, though hidden, it is not an effect of the agent, nor is its being in composition with matter. We could compare this to helping someone to remember certain ideas without any sort of effective teaching toward learning some new conclusion. It would be like reminding matter of a form it already has without causing anything new.

We could also think of efficient causation as disposing matter so that it can receive a new form that is not actually in it. This is a more positive conception of efficient causation than that of mere disclosing in that it entails a certain ordering of the potency of matter toward certain forms not yet in any composition with matter, especially more complex ones. But it still does not express the idea of efficient causation fully enough. To express this idea more fully we have to speak of a communication of form from one thing to another, as the production of a work of art is the communication of a form to some material object or as teaching is the communication of a demonstration toward a conclusion to a student. In the understanding of an efficient cause and its effect we see not only a similarity of form between two things, but also a certain dependence of the form in the effect as communicated from the cause.

This can be illustrated best in the procreation of human beings, where we understand several beings as self-standing with some as having produced others of their own kind, that is, with a similar substantial form, through a natural process. While the intrinsic constitutive principles of matter and form of these several beings account for their being individuals of the same kind, they do not account for the actual coming to be of any one of them. In order to account for this actual coming to be for some of them at least, we turn to their parents as having set the process in motion and as giving this process its human determination, so that their human form is communicated to their offspring. This is a natural process in which an actual form is communicated from one generation to another.

The precise physical and biological details in which this process takes place need not detain us here. Those are the domain of more particular sciences, where all sorts of further distinctions can be made between cause and effect among the elements of the process. The only thing we would say in this regard is that the process of human procreation should not be reduced to what happens in the isolation of the physical womb. If the upright stance and speech are part of what characterizes human being according to its nature, as zoologists are more willing to say, then human procreation must be understood as continuing beyond the physical womb in what has been called the "social womb" (Portmann 1990a, 1990b), where we learn to walk and talk as human animals. Parenting has a social and cultural dimension as well as a physical one. It extends even beyond the social womb of the family. But in any event, it is the active communication of a truly human form to new individuals who might not otherwise attain it.

In recognizing our parents, we are acknowledging the efficient causes of our being and our dependence on them in our original coming to be, which is very important for understanding who or *what* we are in our identity. For the dependence is not merely biological, as for all animals, but also rational, in that even our coming to self-consciousness as human beings depends upon a dialectic of mutual recognition with an other, the dialectic in which we first come to understand the difference between one being and an other, namely, myself and this other or these others, each a self-standing thing in the face of the other, the dialectic also in which we recognize our dependence on these others as being *what* we are, intelligent as well as cunning animals, and as having learned to walk and talk from them. Thus, even if we admit the most extensive self-movement in our subjectivity, we still find some real dependence on other human beings in this coming to be simply *what* we are in our substance, and in this we acknowledge some dependence on these others as on efficient causes in our coming to be and hence in our being even though we think also of our coming to be as a self-actualization.

Given a certain constancy or regularity in this process of coming to be, in that human beings come to be only from other human beings and what usually comes to be from a human being is another human being, we are also led to understand this original dependence on others as the result of a certain causal efficiency in the nature of things themselves. This does not warrant any absolute certainty that every being in nature will always produce another like itself or that every individual produced by another will always be the equal of its producer. As noted earlier, there remains the possibility of certain deficiencies either in the matter of what comes to be or in the power of the efficient cause that we have to acknowledge in the presence of what we see as monsters or aberrations. But it does warrant a certain kind of anticipation of what we should expect from nature with regard to what comes to be, the anticipation that enables us precisely to see what is an aberration or a deviation, and what is not. In the case of human beings at least, given the complexity of the matter from which they come to be and the immense power that is required to effect such a being, it should come as no surprise that there be aberrations or deviations at times. But this does not take away from our understanding that one being or several beings are the cause of another in its coming to be simply.

In fact, the anticipation that we should expect something from nature gives rise to a further understanding of how an effect depends on its cause in its very movement. According to the adage we have already seen, every agent acts in a way similar to itself. *Omne agens agit sibi simile.* From the standpoint of efficient causality, this means that the effect will be like its cause, and it is on the basis of this similarity in dependence that we will assign a relation of cause to effect.

But if we insist on the otherness of the effect from the cause, as we should in speaking of efficient causality, how does this similarity appear from the side of the effect? Is the effect immediately like its cause or does it still have to become like its cause? When we recognize self-movement in the coming to be of an effect, is this purely haphazard or is it oriented toward a certain completion of the effect where it will be more like its cause? Would we recognize it as self-movement if it were not oriented to some kind of completion and would this be the completion of an effect if it were not somehow like its cause? Would Socrates be completely human if he were not somehow like his parents, at least as far as being human is concerned?

What we find from the side of the effect is a certain tendency to become like or to be assimilated to its cause or origin. *Omne effectum intendit assimilari suae causae.* This is why knowing one's origin is always important for oneself in one's very identity. The similitude that is communicated by an efficient cause becomes, in the effect, a tendency to be assimilated to the cause, even to the point of reproducing another offspring like itself in the same way as the offspring itself was produced. The dynamism of nature is not purely haphazard. It is more a dynamism of assimilation in the effect toward the cause that flows from the *influence* of the cause on the effect. In this sense we can see how teleology *affects* the very process of coming to be simply, through matter, back to the efficient or the moving cause.

We have illustrated the process of efficient causation in coming to be simply in terms of a human being, our primary analogate of substance in being. Such a substance in its coming to be has to be understood not only as constituted by two distinct principles of matter and form, but also as effected by another substance of the same kind that actively educes the form of the new substance from the potency of its matter. This is to be understood, however, not just of the human substance, but of any substance that is understood as coming to be simply. It is easy to see how this understanding applies by analogy to other living things such as animals and plants in their coming to be, since they too disclose a kind of substantial identity like that of the human being as well as a dependence on other substances of the same kind, their "parents," in their coming to be. But can we extend the analogy to nonliving things? Can we still speak there of one thing effecting another in the same way as we speak of one living thing producing another?

This is the question we have encountered before in focusing first on human being as our primary analogate and then extending our concepts from what is proper to human being to lesser beings by way of negation. At the limit we always come to a point where it is difficult to identify anything as a thing or as a substance with a proper activity of its own, as we can more easily with the human being and its proper activity. At that point it also becomes more difficult to discern what there is that is coming to be simply, whether it is even a thing or a substance at all. This is a problem Aristotle did not have in his physics because his analysis stopped at "elements" that could be identified as "substances" such as earth, water, air, and fire.

To the extent that we can still speak of something with a substantial identity of its own and as coming to be simply, we can also speak of it as depending on another being as on an efficient cause in its coming to be. This only supposes that we can clearly distinguish between two beings, one thing and an other, and see one as depending on the other in its coming to be by reason of a dependence in similarity. Where no such distinction can be made in the way being presents itself, we cannot properly speak of a relation of dependence on an extrinsic cause, which is presupposed in the idea of efficient causation, though we may still be able to speak of some determination common not to a plurality of beings, but to a sequence of aspects in some matter as a whole.

16.5   The Absolute Priority of Act over Potency in Coming to Be

What remains to be demonstrated is the necessity of positing an extrinsic efficient or moving cause, in addition to the intrinsic material cause, for a thing's coming to be. This is a task for metaphysics, whereas it is the task of particular sciences to investigate the particular efficient or moving causes, in addition to the material cause, of the different things that come to be. It is a task that is similar to the task of demonstrating the necessity of distinguishing the substance of a thing from its accidents and it follows upon that task, inasmuch as the question of extrinsic efficient causes presupposes that we understand how a plurality of substances is posited in being. Having shown how a plurality of things is constituted metaphysically, we must now show how the coming to be of one thing has to depend metaphysically on the *influence* or the motion of another thing.

We can do this starting from how a human being comes to self-consciousness only in the presence of another self-consciousness, as Hegel argues in the *Phenomenology of Spirit*. If we take coming to self-consciousness as coming to be simply for a human being, presupposing all the material conditions this already requires in the natural process of birth and growth, we can say that a human being comes to be simply as a self-conscious being through a process of recognition from another, who normally is already self-conscious in act. In other words, the necessity of recognition from another self-consciousness for one being's coming to self-consciousness demonstrates the necessity of *influence* or motion from another in this coming to be simply self-conscious. Without this influence from another there would be no coming to self-consciousness for an individual.

We can see some of this necessity in the necessity of a teacher for a student's learning. Even if one can learn by oneself, one still needs a teacher who has already come to certain conclusions in answers to questions raised in order to learn one's own conclusions more efficiently. But learning at this level presupposes self-consciousness in the student as well as in the teacher. It can be considered as only an accidental change or coming to be. The necessity of a teacher there is relative only to what is learned. On the more substantial level of coming to self-consciousness as such, there is a more radical need of *influence* from another in coming to one's own self-consciousness, as we see, for example, in the quite abnormal case of Helen Keller's coming to self-consciousness. Without the *influence* of Anne Sullivan finally getting through to her, she would never have come to her own self-consciousness.

Even if we take an absolutely primordial case of two individual human natures both coming to their own self-consciousness for the first time through mutual recognition, we can still see the necessity of influence from another for this coming to be simply. In such a case, neither individual is actually self-conscious at the beginning, so that neither one actually has anything to teach the other, as Anne did for Helen. Both have yet to learn even what it is to be self-conscious. But insofar as they can only come to self-consciousness through confrontation and mutual recognition, they do so only through reciprocal influence and motion from one another. Without this reciprocal influence or recognition, there would be no coming to self-consciousness simply. Each one becomes actually self-conscious as it is actually influenced by the other and as it actually influences the other, who in turn is simultaneously becoming actually self-conscious as it is influenced by the first and as it actually influences the first. Even if there is perfect equality of actual self-consciousness between the two, the necessity of mutual recognition between two individuals for their coming to self-consciousness simply and respectively still shows a necessity of influence or motion from another on the side of either individual for coming to be self-conscious.

Even when there is no question of coming to consciousness or self-consciousness, we can still speak of the same kind of necessity for *influence* from an extrinsic efficient cause wherever we can speak of something determinate coming to be, either accidentally, as in the case of water heated by the hot element of a stove, or substantially, as in the case of an animal generated by its parents. The key thing is to understand that the form of a thing cannot educe itself from the potency of its matter. Though we can speak of the form as educed from the potency of matter, we cannot speak of any determinate form as necessarily educed from matter because matter as matter always remains in potency to many forms. What determines the form educed from matter for any individual is the same or a similar form already actual in another individual. This form in the prior individual is communicated to another individual by educing it from the potency of some other matter. Before a determinate form can be educed from the potency of its matter, there has to be another form of the same determination already actualized in some other matter and this other form has to exert its *influence* on some other matter than its own to educe another form or produce another being like itself. From this follows the necessity of positing an extrinsic efficient or moving cause for a thing's coming to be, in addition to its intrinsic formal and material causes.

What this necessity means is that there is an absolute priority of act over potency in being, though there is a priority of potency over act in time. If we consider a thing as having come to be, we think of it as having been in potency before being in act. Being in potency is being in matter, but not yet actualized. In order for something to be actualized as some determinate being, however, something more is required than just being in potency, which is not nothing but which nevertheless is not being simply or being in act. This "something more" is the *influence* of another being already in act that will transform what was merely in potency into an actual determinate being. The reason why we have to posit the necessity of an extrinsic moving cause for anything that comes to be is that nothing that is only in potency to some act contains that act. The act has to be communicated, through the *influence* of some other being already in act, to what is only in potency for it.

What this means also is that nothing is moved unless it is moved by another. *Quidquid movetur ab alio movetur.* Whatever is moved is moved by another. Expressed in the passive in this way, the adage sounds like a tautology. To say that something is moved is to say that it is moved by another. But to speak of another is to introduce a duality in the adage. One could speak of being moved by oneself. What the adage wants to say is that wherever we speak of being *moved* we have to speak of being moved *by another.* There is no motion, no passage from potency to act, in something except under the motion of something else already in act. Even when we speak of something as moved by itself, we have to understand that some part of it is moved by some other part of it, as my body is moved by my mind. When we speak of a thing being moved as a whole, we have to understand that it is moved by some other thing as a whole. In this case we are positing the necessity of an extrinsic moving or efficient cause for whatever is moved or in motion, that is, going from potency to act.

To demonstrate this, let us begin with what we have spoken of as accidental change, as with the heating of something like water or learning by a human being. In the case of learning by a human being, we recognize an active principle on the part of the learner, for without this active principle of intelligence in the learner there would be no learning. In some cases it would seem that the learner does learn all by himself, as when someone comes to a new insight or discovers something new about being without the help of a teacher. In such cases at least it would seem that learning is by oneself and not by another. But are there such cases of learning purely by oneself without the help of another and, even if there are, do they come about without any help whatsoever from a teacher? Does not the very process of learning itself begin under the *influence* of a teacher who is already learned in some sense?

We do not have to think of some advanced learning here, as in the case of nuclear physics or capitalist economics, although such learning usually does not come without a good deal of teaching by others to orient and hasten the learning process. We can think of just the beginning of learning or the first use of one's intelligence, which does not seem to take place except under the influence of another, who has already understood and learned something in act.

We see this dramatically illustrated in the case of Helen Keller finally coming to learn for the first time through her first use of language only under the influence of Anne Sullivan and in the immediate recognition by Helen of Anne as her teacher. We find the same kind of recognition among scholars for their teachers and we should find the same recognition in all of us at least for those who first taught us to think for ourselves and even to just begin to use language intelligently, for without them we would not have begun to learn.

What this implies is a certain efficient causality by another in someone's own process of learning. This does not preclude the fact that learning is always original with and for the learner, nor that learning through the teaching of another does take place in many different ways. But it does point to a certain dependence on another in learning such that the learning that does take place would not take place without the influence of that other, who is already in act what the learner, or the one who has yet to learn, is still only in potency.

If we recognize this kind of dependence of learners on teachers as necessary in the very learning process for human beings, we come to see a certain necessity for some efficient causality at least in the process of human learning. This necessity can be expressed as a certain priority of being in act, that is, as being already learned on the part of the teacher, over being in potency, that is, as having yet to learn on the part of the one who is still unlearned.

But it should be understood that this is a necessity of dependence on an efficient cause in its effect, and not the necessity of the effect flowing from the efficient cause, as Hume conceived it. Here, as we did earlier in speaking of the constitutive principles of a thing in becoming, we are arguing from the term of a becoming, from the *terminus ad quem,* or from the effect to an extrinsic efficient cause, and not from the cause to an effect. What has the power of acting on another does not always exercise that power effectively. One who has the power to teach does not always find students who are receptive or willing to learn. It is only when we know that there has been learning under the influence of a teacher that we can say some efficient causation has come into play. And when we also know that this learning would not have taken place *as it did* without the *influence* of the teacher, we understand the necessity of another, an extrinsic moving cause, to bring one who was only potentially a learner to the act of learning. Such an extrinsic cause had already to be learned *in act* in order to bring the learner to the same learning *in act* as that of the teacher. It is through this sameness in actual learning between the learner and the teacher that the dependence on an extrinsic moving cause is recognized even in the very act of learning. Anyone who actually learns from another is usually quite grateful to the teacher for the learning, and quite rightly so, since the learning is not purely from oneself.

The same point of dependence upon an extrinsic moving cause can perhaps be seen more clearly in the case of one thing becoming heated by another, as in the case of water placed on the heating element of a stove. If it is not always clear that learning takes place only under the influence of another who is already learned in act, it would seem to be more clear that something does not become hot except under the influence of something that is already hot in act. This is what we suppose when we place the water on the heating element. We know that the water *can* be heated or is potentially hot, but not actually so. From past experience we also know that placing it on the heated element will cause it to be heated. Thus, from the standpoint of the water itself, there is a certain temporal priority of being in potency over being in act: the water is at first only potentially hot and then becomes actually hot, if the heating element exercises its proper effect on the water.

From the standpoint of the heating, however, as a proper effect, there is a more ontological priority of being in act over being in potency: if the water is brought from being hot only in potency to being hot actually, it is only because there was already something else already hot in act to make it so. To understand this, we do not have to presuppose, as the ancients did, that fire is an element that is hot in and of itself and so is the cause of everything else being hot directly or indirectly, as though it were the first cause of all heating as such. What we have to understand is that something becomes hot actually after having been hot only in potency, only under the influence of something else already hot in act. Water cannot reduce itself from being hot only in potency to being hot in act by itself. It can become hot only by another, which is already hot in act by whatever cause it may be so.

This is what was meant by the old adage: *Quidquid movetur ab alio movetur.* Whatever is moved is moved by another. This is true not only of one thing being bumped by another, like one ball being hit by another on a billiard table, but also of other accidental changes in certain substances like heating or becoming agitated. It is also true of learning, at least where we recognize that learning takes place only under the influence of a teacher, who is other than the learner. In all these cases we find this ontological priority of being in act over being in potency that requires that we posit a moving cause outside the thing in movement in order to account more fully for its coming to be in the way that we see it come to be.

This does not mean that we can know a cause before knowing its effect. We come to know the cause only through its effect. Much less does it mean that we can know a cause by itself and deduce it from it all its effects. Even after we have discovered one thing as the cause of something else, we cannot be certain that this effect will always follow from that cause. In this Hume was right about the relation of cause to effect. But the proper understanding of an effect depending on an extrinsic moving cause does not depend upon any such certainty about the future, even though scientists do use predictability as a criterion for the truth of their hypotheses about causes in nature and in history. All that knowing a cause requires is some similarity in dependence on the part of the effect with that cause, in accordance with another adage we have seen: *Omne agens agit sibi simile.* Every agent acts like unto itself.

If we go from merely accidental change to more substantial change, or coming to be simply, we find the same kind of ontological priority of being in act over being in potency even more emphatically. In the case of coming to be simply we are speaking of the coming to be actual of a substance as *this* or *that* thing after its not being simply or after its being only in potency. Here again we have a certain temporal priority of being in potency over being in act from the standpoint of what comes to be. After having been only in potency, it comes to be simply *in act*. But this coming to be *in act* cannot be accounted for sufficiently by the being in potency alone of what comes to be. A thing cannot produce itself into being by itself from its being merely in potency.

To be sure, as we saw earlier in speaking of prime matter, being in potency is not nothing. As distinct from mere privation, it is something positive. It even implies a certain desire for form as its perfection. But it cannot give itself or acquire this form for itself by itself. Being in potency by itself cannot actualize itself in being without the influence of another being that is already actual in being. In other words, to return to our primary analogate, Socrates cannot become the actual human being that he is without the influence of his parents who are already actual human beings.

The process by which Socrates comes to be is not a simple one. It is as complex as his actual being is. But it is a movement from being in potency to being this individual human in act. As so moved, regardless of the complexity of the movement, Socrates is moved by an other, or others, the like of whom he actually becomes. With all its understanding of the complex mechanisms whereby this comes to be, modern science cannot change the understanding of the fact that Socrates is still the son of his parents as one substance depending on other substances for his coming to be. It is not that his parents have to know all of the biological mechanisms by which he is conceived and develops into a human being like themselves. Nor do they have to consciously or conscientiously preside over every aspect of the movement by which he comes to be, as an artist presides over the coming to be of his work of art. It is enough that they set the entire process in motion and and that they be there as speaking rational animals for the moment of self-recognition, so that Socrates becomes a speaking rational being actually other than themselves. It is once again in the likeness of the effect to the cause that we recognize the son or the daughter as the procreation or the product of the parents, but a likeness that is as complex as the coming to be and the beings in question.

In short, insofar as Socrates comes to be through a movement, he is moved by an other as by an extrinsic moving cause. The ontological priority of being in act over being in potency remains no less true in the case of coming to be simply as it does in the case of coming to be *secundum quid*. Regardless of how natural a movement may be to a thing in its growth and development, it is still true that it does not move from being in potency to being in act only by itself. It is set in motion, at least in its very beginning, only by an other that is already in act. Such is the understanding of the necessity for an extrinsic efficient cause for any coming to be, a causation that is recognized in the dependence of likeness in the effect on the cause.

The argument here begins, as always, with the human being, our primary analogate, and its coming to be simply. We take this to be a matter of fact, not just in the sense that a human being is given, but also in the sense that as a given it is a *factum,* something that has been made or has come to be in its very substance. That in which being actualizes itself most intimately to us is at the same time a being that has come to be, that is, as having gone from being only in potency to being simply in act. This *factum,* precisely as *factum,* cannot have come to be only by itself, but must have come to be by an other, or by others, namely, those we think of as parents or as causes of this individual who has come to be simply.

We think of this kind of causation not just as production, as in the case of anything we produce by art, but as *re-production,* for what comes to be is of the same kind as that which produces it, a reproduction of the same nature, another substance of the same kind as those who produced it. We use this term, *reproduction,* not just for the coming to be of human individuals, but also for the coming to be of other animals and of other living things, whether sentient or not, where we still see clearly that what is produced is of the same kind as that which produces it. If we do not use it for the coming to be of other, nonliving substances, it is perhaps because we see less clearly, especially in the context of modern physics, that what is produced is in fact a substance, a thing in itself with its own identity, let alone that what comes to be is in substance like that *whence* it comes to be. In other words, the question of substance is less clear for nonliving things than it is for living things, and so we hesitate to speak of reproduction in the case of nonliving things as we do for living things.

The question of *reproduction* is one of recognizing a similarity of identity in substance between two individuals, one of which comes to be simply by the other. We recognize this kind of similarity in dependence more readily in complex beings like the human being and among other living things that have their own self-standing and living identity. But wherever we do find a coming to be simply of something with its own identity as a substance, we can extend our understanding of reproduction to include any coming to be of a substance in nature by another substance. This is not to say that every coming to be in nature is a reproduction of one being by another being of the same kind, for not every coming to be in nature is a coming to be simply or the coming to be of a new substance with an identity of its own. But it is to say that, wherever there is a coming to be simply, or the coming to be of a substance with an identity of its own, there is a kind of reproduction taking place similar to that among human beings and other living things.

Wherever such reproduction takes place, there is one being coming to be by another.

This is what our argument demonstrates, not only for human being, but for any being that comes to be simply, that is, that passes from being only in potency to being simply in act. Such a being cannot come to be except by another being already in act that communicates the form of its actuality to the new being by educing this form from the potency of the matter that is constitutive of the new being. This is recognized in the similarity of dependence of the new being upon the prior being already in act communicating its actuality to another which, without this communication, would not become a being of the same kind or the determinate being that it is.

We can think of this kind of communication along the line of a teaching/learning relation, where one individual, who is learned only in potency, comes to be learned in act under the influence of an other or by this other who is the teacher in a particular case of learning. Unlike the case of learning, however, where the learner can actually learn by himself as well as by another, since the learner, who is already a substance in act, has an active potency to learn, in the case of coming to be simply, there is no such active potency to being or coming to be simply. There is only a passive potency to become something determinate, a pure potency, so to speak, which is not nothing, as we argued in sections 12.1–2, which is even a positive orientation to some perfection or form, as we also argued in section 12.3, but which cannot be actually oriented to any determinate form except by some other determinate being with some form already in act. Thus while matter is truly a principle of being in whatever comes to be, along with the form with which it constitutes a composite, it is not sufficient by itself. It requires the active intervention of an efficient cause, another already in act with which it comes to communicate in form.

CHAPTER 17

The Universe as Order of Nature and History

❧

IN GOING FROM THE FORMAL to the final cause and from the material to the efficient cause we come to a fuller understanding of how being is to be accounted for in its diverse determinations. One determinate being needs another determinate being as part of its total good and so finds itself as part of a universe along with other determinate beings. The same determinate being finds itself also depending on another determinate being in its coming to be or in its determinacy even as it influences other determinate beings through its own effectivity. Being discloses itself as communicated and as communicating among determinate beings, and so it discloses itself not as a single being, but as a universe of determinate beings interacting with one another. Being is one not as a single substance, but as a plurality and a diversity of substances acting and interacting with one another; and it comes together as one in an order of both final and effective causality.

Earlier, in reflecting on the transcendental properties of being, we came to our first understanding of being as universe in terms of a certain proportion between the two sides of transcendental unity, namely, the undividedness of every being in itself and its dividedness from every other. To the extent that a being is imperfectly undivided in itself, it is also imperfectly divided from every other. Only an absolutely simple being would be perfectly divided from any other, whereas any composite being entails not only some distinction of principles within its own identity, but also some relation of dependence on some other being. We come to this understanding of composition in a being not only as we reflect on its coming to be, but also as it presents itself in its difference from any other being. Thus we come to understand one being and an other, each undivided in itself and divided from the other, but also each relating to the other in some kind of unity or interdependence among them.

This interdependence can already be understood in that each being has something in common with other beings, whether it be a determinate form or just being in common, as well as something that differentiates it from the other, whether it be as an individual or as a kind of being specifically different from other kinds of being. Individuals can share in the same form of being or in different forms of being. But the full understanding of the interdependence implied in the concept of transcendental unity among beings comes only with the kind of communication we have arrived at among determinate beings with the understanding of final and efficient causation.

This interdependence, however, is not to be understood in purely static terms. It is not just a juxtaposition of things in space-time. To be sure, we have to understand individual things as separate from one another in space and time. We also have to understand them as sorted out into different species of being. But they do not constitute a universe together simply by standing next to one another or coming after one another. Sheer plurality and diversity do not a universe make, as the term *uni-verse* indicates. What constitutes the universe concretely is action and interaction among the many and diverse beings. To speak of "the universe" is to speak of a certain coming together, a *convenientia,* of beings through action, which is the bond of the universe in its ultimate form, as we indicated earlier in section 9.2. This is what now has to be thought through concretely with the understanding of final and efficient causality as an ordering of beings in their plurality and diversity.

It could be argued that we first come to know being in precisely this kind of ordering between at least two beings. What discloses itself as being is never something purely common and abstracted from its differences, but something analogous that always entails some difference of one thing from another. We could say that being first discloses itself in reflective self-consciousness, where the act is at once the disclosure of a determinate being, myself. To the extent, however, that this act of self-consciousness does not take place initially except in the presence of another self-consciousness, our first conception of being is never one of a single being in isolation, but always one of one being and another. I distinguish my self from your self in being as you distinguish your self from my self in being, and so we both understand being as divided in this confrontation from the beginning. Being discloses itself in this difference between you and me and in the many differences that go into the makeup of the universe, which is to be understood as a kind of horizon for a plurality and diversity of beings.

We sometimes think of the universe as if it were a thing, one of a kind, a universe among many "possible universes." But this is not what is truly meant by "*the* universe." As a name, like any other name, "universe" means a certain kind of thing, of which many can be thought of as possible. We can speak not only of this world in which we find ourselves, but also of other possible worlds in which one thing or another, like an elephant, now present would be absent, or at least different from what it is, or a world in which you or I would be absent, or in which we would not be doing metaphysics now. But this meaning of "universe" is only an abstraction that prescinds from what we refer to when we speak of "*the* universe" more concretely, for the idea of the universe can only refer to one "thing," the totality of what there is. Regardless of what the parts of this totality are in actuality, or regardless of whether we know or understand all of them, when we speak of "*the* universe" we refer to something in actuality that can only be one concretely, namely, as this totality of what there is. Even when we distinguish between what we know of the universe and what there might be of it that we still do not know, we still think of it as this one "thing" or this totality of things that we know only in part and have yet to know fully.

In this respect the concept of *the* universe is somewhat like the concept of being. As a concept, "being" is the most universal concept. But as we have argued from the beginning, it refers concretely to something in actuality and it gives rise to questioning about *what* there is that we are referring to. So too with the concept of the universe as horizon. It is quite universal. It refers to, or encompasses in its scope, all that there is and that can be known in the direct exercise of judgment. To the extent that we think of the universe as this all-encompassing horizon, we have to think of it as only one. For, if we try to say that there is some other "universe" or some other part of being not included in what we initially conceive as the universe, we are only expanding the horizon in which we are already exercising judgment. We are not exchanging it for another. What we previously thought of as the whole we now think of as only a part of the greater whole that now comes into view. When my horizon expands to encompass your horizon and that of many others as well, it is always the same horizon in which more is encompassed. What the concept of the universe does express that our first concept of being does not, however, as we tried to show in speaking of being as universe in Chapter 9, is a greater recognition of differences in being, a greater diversity than was initially thought of in our first conception of being, but one that is still gathered in some unity that has to be thought of concretely.

Perhaps it is the idea of *concretion* that is most crucial for understanding the idea of the universe properly. Other ideas may be understood abstractly, which means that they can be concretized in different ways or at least in different instances. For example, when I have the idea of a human being, I can think of it as concretized in Socrates or Plato. Not so, however, with the idea of *the* universe. I cannot strictly think of it as *a* universe in the abstract, for in doing so I am no longer thinking of what I was originally thinking of as *the* universe. I can only think of *the* universe concretely, or as *this* universe, even though I may be able to entertain the thought of another universe in abstraction from *this* actual universe, just as I am able to entertain the thought of possible being in abstraction, starting from actual being that discloses itself. Like the concept of being, the concept of *the* universe has to be a concrete universal.

In fact, we might even say that we come to this concept of the universe through an understanding of concretion in its etymological sense of *growing together* or of having grown together: *con-cretum*. There are different ways of thinking about this in terms of the different causes we have distinguished. One is the order of matter, which we spoke of in section 12.3. This is an order of being in potency to different forms, where matter is understood as being in potency to a wide diversity of forms, from the lowest to the highest, from the most elemental to the most complex in the human being. Taken as a whole, the order of material beings is seen as growing together in a diversification and a complexification of forms, not by the elimination of elemental forms, but by a development of new forms from the potency of matter, the result of this development being the *con-creta,* those things that have *grown together* from the potency of matter.

Implied in this understanding of the *concrescence* of the universe is, of course, the order of formal causes, which gives rise to diversification in the universe. This is the order that we discern in the different degrees of identity and being and the different kinds of substances that come to take a stand in being, or in what has been referred to as "the different faces of existence" (Post 51–53). It can be viewed as an ascending or as a descending order, depending on where we take our stand in understanding it.

If we take our stand at a lower form of being, as in physicalism, which focuses first on physical being or being in its most elemental form as measurable and quantifiable, then the other forms of being appear as higher and perhaps as less "substantial" than the lower, if we let the lower form in its dubious identity totally determine what we understand by substantial being. In the ascending order, or from the bottom up, the substantiality of higher forms of being is more difficult to discern because the order that they represent cannot be properly defined within the order of the lower form. Each new form that appears in an ascending order of being transcends any lower form and has to be defined in its own original terms. Hence, the order of forms or of different degrees of substantial being is more difficult to discern in the ascending order, or from the bottom up, because each new form represents a higher and more certain kind of identity not found in the lower form.

If, however, we take our initial stand in a higher form of being or in the human being, as we have done here, and proceed in a descending order, or from the top down, so to speak, the order of forms is more easily discernible because then we begin from an understanding that not only transcends but also includes lower orders, such as the merely sentient animal, the merely living plant, or the merely physical inanimate object. In taking our initial stand with human being to understand a substantial being in its identity, we encompass lower forms of being that can still be taken as substantial, even though they do not have the fullness of form and identity that human beings show forth. This was part of the reason for focusing on human being from the beginning of our consideration as the primary analogate of being as being. It is easier to discern the different forms and orders of being in a descending order insofar as the lower forms are contained in the higher forms, whereas the higher forms are not contained in the lower ones. This does not, however, dispense us from having to understand lower forms of being as also having a substantial identity of their own.

Metaphysically speaking, it is important to maintain this distinction between different kinds of substantial being as part of our understanding of the universe, lest we fall into anthropomorphism, which is no less reductionist with regard to the transcendental order of being than physicalism. Without an understanding of the diversity of forms or of faces of existence, there can be no proper understanding of the universe in its *concrescent* unity.

Beyond this order of material and formal causes, however, there is also the order of the final and the efficient causation. In our understanding of this order, we presuppose the plurality and the diversity of beings constituted in their own identity and think of them as *coming together* through action and interaction. More than an order of *concrescence,* this is also an order of communication among beings. Most immediately, this order appears on the level of human action, where mutual recognition among individuals gives rise not only to a sense of otherness in being, but also to a desire for this other as good and as a complement to one's own goodness. Through mutual recognition, being is disclosed as a horizon of beings in which one *influences* the other and is *influenced* by the other.

For the child, this horizon is still very limited, to only a few individuals, all of them human at first, but in this first recognition of otherness in being there is already a first understanding of a universe, or rather of the universe, an understanding that will develop and expand as being is disclosed more fully in all its diversity. Not only do more individual human beings come to be recognized in different contexts and in different types of social configuration, but also other kinds of being are recognized more objectively as different parts of this universe of persons, each with its own proper activity and its own standing in the order of the universe, all influencing one another in diverse ways in some order of communication.

Given the way being discloses itself initially in the direct exercise of judgment, however, there is no way of understanding it for us except as individual and determinate and as something to be accounted for in its coming to be through principles such as matter, which accounts for its coming to be as this individual, and form, which accounts for its determination as this kind of being.

Accounting means getting to more of the truth of determinate being in its principles and causes, as we do when we come to understand matter and form as constitutive principles of composite substances. It means gathering in what is given in experience according to its substantial constitution. It also means gathering the plurality and the diversity of beings according to the extrinsic relations of *appeal* and *dependence* they have with regard to one another, for, as we have argued, a determinate being, as finite, needs another determinate being for the perfection of its own being and depends on another determinate being in act for its own coming to be in a transition from potency to act. The quest for truth concerning determinate beings thus leads us beyond any determinate being in our accounting, to an order or to a diversity of orders, among determinate beings within the horizon of being we call *the* universe.

In determining the subject of our questioning at the outset of this inquiry we spoke of being as being, or being as common to many different kinds of things, without focusing on being as any particular thing or on any particular determination of being. In reflecting on being as common to many things in the concrete, in accordance with the structure of the direct exercise of judgment, however, we were brought to understand this commonality of being not as a genus, which totally abstracts from the differences of its species, but as an analogy that contains differences even when they are not expressed. We illustrated this analogy in terms of human being, which we took as our primary analogate, and other kinds of being given in experience or in the realm of the direct exercise of judgment. We spoke of an or-

Causes

der in our understanding of being as analogous. But we did not pursue the question of this order in its ontological bearing, as we can do now, with the understanding of extrinsic causation as an order of *mutual appeal* and *mutual dependence* among a plurality and a diversity of beings. How can we do this now without turning aside from our initial project of accounting for being precisely as being?

It is not our task to go into any particular account for any particular determination of being. That is the task of the particular sciences, from which we have distinguished the more common science of metaphysics. Metaphysics is not in any position to replace or displace any of these particular sciences in their inquiry into the particular causes of particular beings, as we have recognized from the beginning. But it is in a position to uncover the more common principles or causes of being, such as matter as a principle of becoming and form as its coprinciple in determining *what* comes to be. These are in a way first principles of being as it is given in experience or in the direct exercise of judgment. Metaphysics is also in a position to uncover some necessity for extrinsic causation among determinate beings as finite and as having to go from potency to act, without going into any particular modality of such causation, which is still the realm of particular sciences. It may even be in a position ultimately to raise the question of an absolutely first universal cause of all being common to all determinate beings.

But we have not yet come to any such position in this investigation into the causes of being as being. The constitutive principles we have arrived at are still only the principles of finite essences and the final and efficient causes we have spoken of are still only in the realm of determinate beings of which they are causes. As such they cannot be taken as strictly universal or common to all being as such, even though some may be more universal than others in the scope of their appeal as good or their power as effective. The appeal of a human being in its goodness, to speak once again of our primary analogate of being thus far, or of the power of this being to produce or to reproduce, may be more universal than any lesser being in nature whose form is totally immersed in matter. But the appeal and the power of human being are still only *relatively* universal. They are still only part of the universe and must be considered as part of this order.

What remains for us to do here, then, with regard to the universe, is to consider the order of final and efficient causes as a whole within the horizon of being as we experience it or as it presents itself in the direct exercise of judgment. It is in this sense that we will come to speak of the totality of beings truly as *uni-verse,* or as one in its diversity. How is this to be understood as an essential part of the truth of being to be accounted for? How is the universe constituted truly as a universe when there appears to be such a plurality and such a wide diversity of beings?

17.1   The Transcendent Constitution of the Universe as the Concrete Order of Being

We have spoken of composite substances as constituted by two distinct principles, that is, matter and form. Through these principles we account for what we think of as basic differences in being, those we associate with the diverse kinds of individuals and those of individuals as such. Matter is the principle of individuation, while form is the principle of determination. But through these principles we also account for a true plurality of beings, each with its own standing in being or its own substantial identity, and a true diversity of kinds among these many beings. The composite being we know in the direct exercise of judgment is a whole whose parts are not beings in themselves, but principles that constitute one being as a whole. When we speak of the universe we mean a very different kind of whole. As a whole it is constituted of parts. But its parts are not principles of one being, but rather they are the many and diverse beings constituted of such principles. As a whole the universe is constituted of parts each with its own standing and substantial determination in being, even where there is plurality of individuals to perpetuate the diverse species in time as parts of the universe.

We can speak of this whole as if it were only a sum of its parts, the sum of all beings, or, as physicalism is more inclined to say, the sum of all physical entities in space and time (Post 125–28). As such, the conception of the universe refers to a concrete whole, namely, the whole of what there is, but it is not yet a concrete conception of this whole. It is like our very first conception of being, before the transcendental properties or any of the special modes of being are expressed in it. In order to conceive of the universe more concretely we must conceive of it according to the different degrees of being it contains and according to the order in which they *come together* as one universe. This order is like the form of the universe as a single whole composed of its many diverse parts.

In a complex individual such as a human being the substantial form represents a certain kind of wholeness in relation to the different parts that make up the whole being. The wholeness of the universe can be thought of as a kind of form, through which we come to think of it as a single universe. This wholeness, however, cannot be that of a substantial form, since the universe is not a single substance, but rather a plurality of diverse substances, and since it does not come to be as a single substance, but rather as a diversity of specific substances, each actualized in a plurality and a succession of individuals and each inclined to act according to its own nature or essence. The wholeness of the universe is a wholeness of order among the many diverse substances we come to know in experience. We may not know everything there is in this order, but when we speak of the universe concretely, or as the totality of what there is in experience, we include the differences we do know in being and we even refer, in some confused way, to whatever other differences there may be in the universe, differences to be explored not only in metaphysics but also in the particular sciences.

The conception of the universe at the end of our consideration of final and efficient causation brings us back to our first conception of being with its differences. The idea of the universe is closely tied to our understanding of being in its analogy. In the universe we distinguish different degrees of being, different kinds of substances, but not as isolated from one another. Within the different degrees of being, such as the particular species we come to identify as parts of the universe, we distinguish different individuals of the same kind or species and we see them as belonging to the same order of determination, some coming to be *by* others and developing into the same kind of being. Among the different kinds of being we find not only differences but also interconnections and interaction that coalesce into a wholeness we call the universe.

This we do in the direct exercise of judgment in diverse ways and according to different particular sciences. Different particular sciences can give rise to different conceptions of the universe as a whole, such as the physicalist conception based on the physical sciences, or the anthropomorphic conception based on the human sciences. But the truly metaphysical conception of the universe arises only in the indirect exercise of judgment through reflection on how being discloses itself as a whole in its very differences, not as an abstract sum, but as a concrete order of many and diverse beings, where the diversity itself is most essential to the order. The universe is made up not just of many things of the same kind, as if all things had the same form of being, but more properly of the different kinds of beings, with different forms of being giving rise to different kinds of action and interaction among the different kinds of being.

If we insist on the different kinds of the beings in the universe, it is to bring out the transcendental aspect of its order. Far from being confined to only one order of being, the universe, metaphysically conceived, entails a transcendental order of different kinds. It is like a house made up of different materials, each with its own determination adding to the order of the house as a whole. Without the different materials the house could not be what it is. So also the different species of being make up the universe and in this diversity of species the universe finds its consistency, even with the coming to be and ceasing to be of individuals within the diverse species. Individuals themselves participate in this concrete order through their participation, for a time, in the species of their being.

But to think of the universe properly, it is not enough to insist on the different kinds of being. We must insist even more on their *coming together* as a universe through their action and interaction, which is made possible by the very differences we begin by insisting on, for it is by reason of these differences that some beings are active and some are passive in relation to one another. Without true diversity among beings there would no way of understanding how one being can influence another or how one being can be influenced by another or how they all constitute one universe together (Blanchette 1992, 118–40).

This action and interaction of diverse beings is most essential to the universe in the concrete, for the order we are speaking of is not just one of location or static juxtaposition of many and diverse beings existing absolutely in isolation from one another, but a dynamic ordering of the many and diverse beings to one another through the proper activity of each and every kind of being. This is how we know the universe most concretely, through the activity of its components, for what we know first of any being is not what it is in its substance without action, but rather what it is in this identity through its proper activity, wherein it is in communication with other beings in the universe. Every being is active. Through its proper activity we come to know what it is in its substance. We discern one thing from another within this order of action and interaction that constitutes the universe, where being discloses itself through the initiative of different beings in relation to other beings. What we refer to as "the universe" is what we encompass as the whole of this action and interaction.

We can speak truly of the universe in this way without having grasped all there is about it either as a whole or in its diverse parts. Our initial conception of being as universe arises spontaneously in the direct exercise of judgment the moment we begin to discern different ways of acting and, consequently, different kinds of being. As we saw earlier in section 9.1, this conception follows from our very understanding of being as one and as active, once we have begun to distinguish one kind of being from another through their different kinds of proper activity. We do not do this always in the precise formal terms we are using here, but we do it as a way of thinking of being as a whole even after we have begun to think of it as many and diverse.

The conception of the universe occurs at the limit of any particular conception of things. It is the conception of something that cannot be reduced to any particular order of intelligibility. Because of this, some authors are inclined to speak of the universe as a mystery (Post 128–31; Munitz 6), or as something that remains undisclosed in any rational investigation into the intelligibility of what there is. But this is not strictly true for a metaphysics that purports to inquire into the fullness of being as being. It is true only for a metaphysics that restricts its fundamental conception of being to a particular order such as that of physical entities and processes. The broader or more common conception of being we have spoken of as analogous should not be thought of as mysterious or unknowable, even though it cannot be reduced to any particular understanding of a particular order of being. The idea of rational inquiry into being should not be reduced to any particular science, as we tried to demonstrate from the beginning of this inquiry in arguing for a rational necessity to raise the question of being as being over and above any particular science, which cannot but leave the question open. To be sure, from the standpoint of a particular science, the question of being as being remains unintelligible and therefore, in that sense, mysterious. But in pursuing the question of being as we have done here, that is, as a matter of rational discourse, we have been saying that being as being still comes under a broader conception of reason, so that what discloses itself in this investigation is not strictly a mystery but rather a higher form of intelligibility for us, which includes that of the universe, the encompassing form of intelligibility. Knowing, as we said from the very beginning, is of being. Being is what discloses itself in knowing. Now when being discloses itself as many and diverse, it discloses itself as universe, which is being understood as a total frame of reference for intelligence.

In distinguishing the *act* of being from its essence in any finite being earlier in sections 3.2 and 14.1, we saw in this act the ultimate point of intelligibility in the beings that present themselves in experience. In also distinguishing one being from another, or one kind of being from another kind, we see that the *act* of being is not only multiplied but also diversified according to the different essences or modes of being in which it is received. In each case the act of being is truly limited to the thing of which it is the act. It is the ground for understanding different beings as truly separate or divided from one another as beings.

At the same time, however, insofar as the *act* of being is also the act in which all share in common as beings, it is also the ground for thinking of them still as one or as undivided, that is, as ordered to one another in the universe. Given the distinction of the *act* of being from its essence in finite being, and given the plurality and diversity of finite essences in experience, the *act* of being has to be understood as one that presents itself only in an order, namely, the concrete order of the universe. The be that discloses itself in experience or in the direct exercise of judgment is be with order: *esse cum ordine.*

Let us explore the dimensions of this transcendent order that we speak of as nature, on the one hand, and history, on the other.

17.2   The Universal Order of Nature

Within the order of the universe as a whole, there are two aspects that deserve special consideration in metaphysics because each pertains to the order of the universe as a whole and each relates to the other as part of the transcendental order we have just spoken of. These are the order of nature and the order of history. The one comes from things as given in nature and the other comes from human being's initiative amid things, including human beings, as given by nature.

We have seen that human being holds a special place within the order of the universe. This is so, however, not only because it holds a special place as given in the order of nature, but also because through intelligence and will it gives rise to a new kind of order over and above the order of nature. This is an order of reason we refer to as historical, which is irreducible to the order of nature and in fact raises the order of the universe to a higher level of being than it would achieve by nature alone.

We shall reflect further on the basis for this distinction between history and nature in human action when we come to consider the order of history more fully in itself. But before we come to that let us consider the order of nature as somehow prior to the order of history and as that out of which the order of history emerges.

17.2.1   Order

The order of nature is the order of becoming as a whole. Insofar as matter is the principle of becoming, we can think of it as a kind of matrix out of which all the different kinds of being come to be, not indiscriminately, as we saw in section 12.3, but according to an order of potency, where matter is at first in potency to the simplest material things or to fundamental elements, in which it is first actualized. While it is so actualized, however, as we also saw earlier in connection with the order of matter, it remains in potency to more complex kinds of things, compounds that come to be from the matter of elements. From the matter of such compounds come to be living things, which not only represent a new kind of identity and actuality in being but also are oriented to a new kind of activity, a new kind of *convenience,* life itself, for it is by a diversity of acts that life defines itself. From the matter of living things such as plants come to be sentient beings, a yet higher order of life, and from the matter of sentient beings come to be rational beings, the highest kind of being we know in the direct exercise of judgment to which matter is ultimately in potency in the order of becoming. With human being we come to the highest form to which we know the potency of matter is actualized.

This understanding of the order of matter is not necessarily a representation of what we have come to think of as the evolution of the species in the universe. In fact, it was first formulated prior to any such theory of evolution, and prior to the discovery of evidence in nature for positing such an evolution. It was even formulated when the different species of being in nature were still thought to be perpetual in the order of the universe, perpetuated by the supposedly perpetual motion of incorruptible heavenly bodies as well as by the succession of individuals in the different species. But it was formulated on the basis of another kind of evidence in nature, the evidence of different degrees of being and life and a certain gradualness in passing from one degree of perfection in being to a higher degree which could be accounted for in terms of matter as being in potency always to a higher form until it reaches the form of human being (*HA* 588a 18–b 3; *Caus* 31, §445).

This evidence of different degrees is much clearer when we come to think of higher substances such as human beings, animals, or living things in general. It was available for interpretation even in the less sophisticated sciences of antiquity, which relied more on observation of nature than on experimentation and mathematical calculation. But even as modern science develops and reaches further into the recesses of nature, past and present, the same evidence remains before us to be interpreted and accounted for, not just in particular, but also as part of the order of the universe.

We no longer think of the heavenly bodies as incorruptible or of their motion as perpetual or merely circular. Nor do we think of all the species that make up the transcendental order of nature as perpetual or as present from beginning to end. We know that some species of being that once were have disappeared from the order of the universe. We know also that the motion of heavenly bodies is not essentially different from the motions of bodies closer to our own. We even have good reason to think that many of the species of being we now take for granted as part of the order of nature appeared only relatively late in the cosmogenesis, after many other species were already present or disappearing. But we still have to think of these different degrees or species of being and understand the order among them as an order of potency in matter taken as a whole going from a lower form to a higher form of being, not just in one individual that comes to be and develops to maturity, but also among the species themselves, with a certain continuity and gradualness in the passage from the lower to the higher. Without this understanding of matter as being in potency there is no understanding of being as it presents itself through becoming as a whole.

Along with this order of matter in nature we must also consider the order of form, for matter, as being only in potency, is not actualized except through form. This implies that there is a certain order to form in matter in the very constitution of any composite substance in nature. What comes to be according to nature is not just anything, but some determinate thing or another. We think of this determinate thing as having come to be as a substance when we think of it as having reached a certain completion in its process of coming to be. What has come to be is now this determinate being, which was not before, and it is thought of as a substance insofar as it has reached a certain identity in itself. Without this identity as the term of the process we would not be thinking of anything determinate as having come to be. In this identity there is not just an individual but also a certain determination of that individual according to its specific form. What comes to be is never just an individual as such, but always an individual of a certain kind. While matter is principle of individuation, as we have seen, form is principle of determination.

From the understanding of form as ontological principle of determination we can see how process is oriented in coming to be. As determination, a substantial form marks the end of a process in two senses. It marks a certain point at which the process of coming to be is somehow terminated. But it marks this point not just as a cessation of motion in coming to be simply, but also as a certain completion or perfection in what has come to be. The determination of a thing at the end of its coming to be is something positive for the thing that has come to be, over and above its mere individuality or its mere having come to be as an individual. In this sense the substantial form can be understood as final cause in the process of coming to be and so, in hindsight at least, as having affected or determined the process as a whole leading up to this form of the thing.

In observing a process for the first time, we usually cannot predict its final determination. But once that final determination has appeared, we understand it not just as a result, but also as that to which the process was leading. This understanding is further confirmed when we observe a regularity of the same result or the same form appearing at the end of the same process. Nature does not necessarily guarantee certain determinate results, but the things of nature do tend to reproduce themselves according to determinate forms with some consistency. It is in the light of this regularity that we judge what is according to nature and what is not. We think of something as falling short of its nature when it does not attain its proper completion in its final determination, either because its coming to be is cut short by a cause outside the process or by a deficiency in the matter of the thing, or we think of it as abnormal or monstrous when its final determination deviates from the expected or natural end in its process of coming to be.

17.2.2 *Law*

It is not that we find any conscious intentionality in judging what comes to be by nature. It is just that nature discloses itself according to certain patterns in various processes of coming to be and we take the final form in which a process of coming to be terminates, or is determined, as the norm for the process as a whole. From this comes our idea of *law* in nature. Lawfulness is not opposed to finality in nature, but is rather an expression of nature as it relates to a final substantial form that appears with a certain regularity in results. Lawfulness in a process is an orientation to certain determinate results that we take to be the completion or the perfection of the process, its final end. This is clear from the way we exercise judgment in any experimental science. We come to identify certain things according to *what* they are, or according to their nature, through what they do or through their proper activity. But insofar as we identify them as resulting from a natural process, we think of them as the final determination of a process, the law of which was to arrive at this final determination.

At the limit, this idea of law in nature takes the form of a complete determination, or what is also called absolute determinism. This means that what we initially take to be a certain regularity of outcome or results in various processes of coming to be, allowing for some deviation, or in what happens always or most of the time, as Aristotle puts it in speaking of what happens by nature, comes eventually to be taken as an absolute necessity that does not allow for any deviation whatsoever. This is the more modern conception of law in nature that comes with the more mathematical analysis of processes, especially in physics.

The ideal of such an analysis is to arrive at a formulation of the most basic and universal laws that supposedly govern any process of coming to be according to the quantifiable conditions of space and time, without regard to the final determination of any process or to the variety of such final determinations as found in the higher forms of life, sensation, and rationality. In this respect, it abstracts from all evidence of concrete finality in nature. It focuses only on what can be expressed in mechanistic terms such as force, mass, and energy, and it tries to account for everything that comes to be only in such terms, ignoring other kinds of causality in nature such as life itself, which is oriented to different qualities of being and higher types of activity that are as much part of what appears in observation as bare space-time coordinates.

If mathematical physics were able to succeed in its ambition, it would not only abstract from the concrete determinations of the beings we start from in experience, but also from the very conception of one thing and another. It would end up with a pure lawfulness expressed in mathematical formulae, through which everything would be seen as absolutely determined, so that from any given point at any given time one could calculate the relative position of anything at any other time, past or future. Such was the ideal formulated by Laplace in the nineteenth century, for example. In its dogmatic form this ideal is not only deterministic, but also antifinalistic, that is, opposed to any view that might allow for any really new form emerging in nature from the potency of matter, that is, one that is not already written into the determinism of nature. At the limit it aims at a conception of the universe that resembles Spinoza's conception of substance from which differences of modality flow with absolute necessity.

17.2.3 Indeterminism

We must recognize that the science driven by such a mathematical ideal has arrived at remarkable results in accounting for coming to be in nature. Even when we insist on the original identity of higher beings that are not reducible to space-time coordinates, such as living things or rational human beings, we must admit, with physicalism, that change on these higher levels of being does not go without some change at the level of basic physical entities and processes. There is "no difference without a physical difference"

(Post 174–80). But we must recognize also that this science leaves us with a blank space-time at the heart of its conception, which it can express only as a principle of indeterminism, according to the self-imposed limitation of its categories, but which also opens the way for a more positive conception of final determination in coming to be allowing for life, sensation, and rationality as more positive forms of being, differences that cannot be expressed in purely quantitative terms.

This is not to say that, from the principle of indeterminism in physics, one can simply reason to these higher determinations of being, as perhaps Descartes would have liked to do in his mathematical reconstruction of the cosmos, where the whole was conceived in univocally mechanical fashion, leaving the soul, or the *res cogitans,* totally separate from the *res extensa*. These higher determinations of being, including those of life, sensation, and rationality, are taken concretely as part of the way in which being discloses itself in its analogy, with human being as the primary analogate. They do not have to be deduced. They are part of our initial understanding of being in its differences or of what there is in its diverse determinations, along with whatever is taken to be basic in mathematical physics. In its inability to get beyond indeterminism, however, physics may be at a point where some consideration of finality and potency to higher forms in matter would have to be reintroduced as part of our accounting for what comes to be through nature.

The principle of indeterminacy is associated with the idea of basic entities or particles that cannot be properly known in themselves, so to speak, to the extent that "knowing" in this case means "measuring." To measure them is to disturb these basic entities, so that we cannot know them without changing their position or their mass or adding to their energy. If they have a nature of their own, it escapes us because their proper activity is so faint that it offers no resistance to the slightest pressure required for measuring anything. To physical science they are undetermined because they cannot be measured. But in themselves, if they are things distinct from other things, however this distinction may be conceived in physics, they do have an identity and a nature from which some activity flows insofar they are determinate in any way. Mathematical physics tends to think of these basic entities as unchanging elements, of which everything else is made up, as if change were proper only to more complex entities and as if it were only one of rearrangement of such unchanging entities, a view found in ancient atomism as well as in modern physics.

But that is not the only way of viewing these entities. If we transcend the purely mathematical outlook that has led us to identify these basic entities as something determinate, we can also think of them as subject to change and transmutation. As such they could be understood as composites of matter and form of the simplest kind, and hence as having come to be and ceasing to be. As distinct from their form, their matter would be in potency to other determinate forms to which it could be actuated by the interaction among basic entities themselves or by higher forms already existing in nature. In this way process would be understood not only as a rearrangement due to another form than that of the physical basic entities as such, but rather as originating in the basic entities themselves through the matter with which their forms are in composition.

The important thing would be not to confuse this matter, which is being only in potency, with the basic entity, which, as something determinate, has a form and is a composite of potency and actuality. As an actual entity the basic element is something original in nature. But as a composite of matter and form, its matter remains in potency to other forms than the form it has at any instant. In other words, it remains in potency to becoming some other actual entity that would be no less original in nature and of a higher order, whether as an inanimate compound, a living thing, all the way up to the rational animal. When this potency to a higher form is actualized the lower being or entity ceases to be and gives way to the higher being or entity that comes to be. From the standpoint of measure as understood in purely physical science, the higher being is seen as measureless or as undetermined. But from the standpoint of the higher being in question, we have another kind of "measure" or determination that can be the subject of consideration for other kinds of science such as biology or psychology, whose "measuring" is of a different order than that of purely physical science and irreducible to it.

To be sure, we cannot know the full extent of the potency of matter as a principle of being from a mere inspection of just the basic entities posited by mathematical physics. Nor can we know it from an inspection of other nonliving things or even of lower living things. We know it only when we include the rational human being as a part of what is to be considered in our understanding of nature as a whole. But this is not something we discover only at the end of a process. Even if human being did appear in fact only at the end of a long natural process of evolution, our understanding of the process begins with the presence in nature of what is given in that end. Concretely, it begins with ourselves as actual entities at the center of the picture, and surely with an identity that is quite original in nature, a determination that is not be overlooked in the consideration of nature as a whole.

17.2.4   The Anthropic Center

As we move away from this center of our experience into the more re-
mote areas of biology and physical science, we cannot forget this actual entity, namely, human being, as part of what is given in the direct exercise of
judgment and as part of the order to which we refer in our consideration of
nature. Being does not just disclose itself to human beings. It is also human
being itself that discloses itself in its originality and as the central part of nature as a whole. In doing biology or physical science, we can prescind from
certain aspects of this actuality at the center of the natural order while focusing only on life in general or on nonliving physical being in general. In
doing so we can come to a better understanding of different actual entities
in nature such as basic forms of life or basic physical entities. But these cannot be fully understood in abstraction from other actual entities and from
the order of nature as a whole.

The deeper we penetrate into the recesses of nature, the more we have to
understand how each part, even the most basic, relates to the whole, which
is not just an abstraction as it relates to the highest actuality in it. In prescinding from being in its human form, and even from being in its living
form, physical science brings us to a consideration of material being in its
most basic form. In this prescinding, however, which seems like a precision
but which is in fact an abstraction, it cannot consider higher forms of being,
which are, nevertheless, actual entities in nature to which we eventually have
to refer what is discovered in physical science. To understand things better,
we isolate them from the rest for a time of consideration. But when we discover them as coming to be, and therefore as composites of matter and
form, we have to see the potency in them not just to the form which they
are already have actually, but also to other forms, including higher forms as
we look back on them, so to speak, from our own higher vantage point. Going deeper into the things of nature means discovering not only their determinate actuality, but also their potency in an order of forms that brings them
back to the highest form of concrete actuality. Only in this way can we say
that the particular physical and biological sciences contribute to our understanding of nature as a whole.

To understand this order of nature as it is given in actuality, therefore, we
must distinguish the different degrees of being from the highest to the lowest and give each its due as a standing in being or as a mode of being. Metaphysically speaking, it is especially important not to reduce one mode to another, whether it be a higher to a lower or a lower to a higher. Each must be

given the full force of its identity. For the differences are essential to the transcendental order of the universe. It is equally important, however, to understand these differences as a matter of degrees in being, some higher and some lower, with perhaps one as the highest and another as the lowest, and with all the others in between according to their different degrees of being.

17.2.5 Evolution

We may also want to understand these different degrees of being as having appeared successively in time from the lower to the higher, according to a theory of the evolution of species or of the different degrees of being. This would be more in keeping with our understanding of the order of matter as being in potency to different forms and as passing from one form to the next gradually or by degrees. But to understand the order of evolution of species as modes of being, we could not view it merely from the standpoint of what is presumed to have come first in the evolution, namely, the lower forms, as is usually done in the Darwinian conception of evolution among the species in nature. Each form determines not only a certain mode of being, but also an order of many beings, or individuals, belonging to that mode or species of being. The form of a cat determines not only what it is in itself, but also how it will reproduce as a cat and how it was itself produced by other cats.

This is an order of individuals within the same species or the same mode of being. According to this order, cats reproduce in time only as cats. If the offspring of a cat turns out to be deficient as a cat, it is still possible to understand this deficiency in terms of the order we call cat, namely, as a privation in the order of what a cat ought to be according to its nature. But if the offspring turns out to be more than a cat, rather than just a deficient or even a complete cat, this can no longer be understood merely in terms of the order of cat as such. From the standpoint of this order, the mutation is random. It cannot be accounted for by anything that has come previously in the order of cat. It can be accounted for only in terms of a new form that is original and transcends the order of cat. In terms of the order pertaining to this new form, however, it is not random, but quite determinate, and it gives rise to an order of beings, which may or may not survive, but has a standing of its own in the being of nature.

In a truly evolutionary perspective, the randomness that results in a new or a higher form of being in nature from a lower form is not the same as the random deficiency that occurs in the normal or the natural order of reproduction within a particular species. It is randomness that has to be understood in terms of a higher order of being that has appeared with the new form as something more positive and transcending the lower order but not as merely random. In other words, when a new and original form of being appears in nature, it is the entire order of nature that is transformed into something higher.

This is illustrated in the way a human being is understood as coming to be biologically. What it is at first is a single cell that immediately divides or reproduces itself as a second cell of the same kind, both of which then go on to divide and reproduce, and so on, until there are enough cells for diversification of functions. With this diversification there comes the diversification of organs and the gradual development of a complex organism that eventually makes up a complete human being. If we consider the human being at any single stage of this development, which entails an order of being that can be considered from its own standpoint, and only from the standpoint of that particular stage, we find nothing to account for the next stage in the development of the whole. The next stage in any development always appears as random from the standpoint of the previous stage, however minute the difference may be between the new stage and the previous one. However, as a stage in the development of a single human being as a whole, it is understood as leading up to the next stage or as creating the conditions for its appearing in being. In other words, it is understood only as a part of a higher order, which, even if it appears last in the order of time, accounts for what it is in its own order.

The original cell from which a human being will develop, and which is not yet ordered as the developed human being will be, is already a human being, not just because it already has its own individual genetic code, but also because in the actuality of its composition it has the potency to develop into the full-grown human individual. To think of the original cell without this positive orientation to an end and a fullness of being is not to understand it for what it is in its very makeup. To understand it in the light of that fullness of being that we call human, however, is to understand this original cell in the light of a higher order that transcends what it is in its initial stage of development. The final order to appear in the process of becoming is the one that determines the entire process and all the particular orders that appear between the beginning and the end.

This is what we have to think as we observe the process in which a human being comes to be in its own subsistence. We cannot understand the process without some understanding of the finality or the determination that pulls it together only in the end. This is also how we have to understand the evolution of species in nature as a whole, whether it is understood diachronically or synchronically. Mere randomness does not account for going from a lower form to a higher form of being. Nor does the idea of selectivity through a struggle for survival yielding only the fittest. Such a struggle accounts for nothing in the differentiation of species as higher degrees of being. It only presupposes this differentiation. Worse still, at the limit, it denies differentiation of higher species and gives way to complete entropy in nature, where the final state is understood as a return to some original amorphous state without any accounting for anything new that has *actually* taken place between the beginning and the end, which is, of course, the actuality that has to be accounted for in our experience. In the absence of any understanding of finality in nature, the Darwinian view of evolution stops short of understanding the true order of nature, which appears only in the end, or in the highest order of material being, namely, human being.

The Darwinian hypothesis falls short of what there is in nature because it tries to read everything in nature from the bottom up in purely mechanistic terms, which, for all their mathematical exactness, remain quite obscure in relation to the different modes of being we have to account for in experience, whereas the entire order of nature can only be read from the top down, as we have argued in connection with the analogy of being. In other words, the order of nature has to be read from what appears last in the order of evolution. As in the case of the coming to be of a human being, it is the highest and the final form of material being, human being itself, that determines the entire order of nature and all of the particular orders that make it up in space-time, not by reducing all to its own specificity, but by recognizing all in their diversity and necessity as conditions for the order of the whole understood as the phenomenon of man (Teilhard 1959).

It is possible to understand nature as a whole from a purely physical standpoint. But this comes to only a partial and abstract understanding of the order of nature. While it gives us an understanding of how things relate to one another mechanically in space-time, so to speak, it does not encompass the higher order of life as part of nature, much less that of sensation and of reason. In the vast expanse of what we now take to be the physical universe, this order of life may first appear only as a microscopic cell, the likes of which may not be replicated anywhere else or at any other time in this universe. But the originality of this new order of life in the universe is not to be denied on the basis of an understanding of being that is only abstract and univocal, without any capacity for understanding *higher* orders of being. The presence of life in the universe elevates the order of nature to a new degree of being that includes the merely physical order as it transcends it. Minute as it may seem from the standpoint of the totality of mass and energy, it entails an infinity with respect to the finite understanding of merely physical being. This is why we have to understand it as a new and higher form of being, with its own determinations that can vary as no purely physical determinations can, as if these new forms of being were less deeply immersed in their matter and were, in a way, more free to act on their own.

In nature understood only in physical terms, things are related according to mathematical space-time. In nature understood in biological terms, the very same things, or at least those physical things that share in life, are related in a wide diversity of ways that can no longer be understood in mere terms of mathematical space-time but that nevertheless have to be understood according to determinations proper to life, where there is much more diversity and a higher kind of order that cannot be reduced to the purely physical terms of space-time coordinates. Part of this higher order entails some finality not just in the coming to be of living things, but even in the relation between the order of life and the physical order in space-time.

From the standpoint of abstract physical science, this finality is indiscernible. This is why, in the life sciences, those who model their understanding on the so-called hard science of physics tend to deny finality even in life as distinct from a purely physical arrangement in space-time as they look only for space-time relations among elementary particles in microbiology. While this may yield good results in our understanding of living things according to their abstract physical determinations, it does not include any understanding of life in itself as transcending these merely physical parameters. In terms of space-time alone, there may not be any discernible finality in nature. But once life is introduced into nature, or, more exactly, into our understanding of nature, as it is concretely in the direct exercise of judgment, finality appears not only in the process of life itself, but even in the way the purely physical comes to relate to life, since what were previously understood as only physical relations in space-time are now understood as necessary conditions for the new order of life.

From the standpoint of this new order, it is possible to understand this finality of the purely physical order as a necessary condition for life, not as something to be read in its actuality as spatiotemporal, but as something contained in it as a potency, for matter is understood as being in potency to form and, even while actualized by a lower form, as being still in potency to a higher form. While there may be some finality in the various orders of nature, living and nonliving, so that what comes to be is always some determinate thing and such a determinate thing always tends to reproduce itself as part of a species of being, the most fundamental finality is the transcendental finality among the diverse species themselves in nature as a whole, the finality that discloses itself better and better with each new order of living things until we come to human being, from whose vantage point we can view the order of nature as a whole best. As the name itself suggests, it is only in the end *(finis)* that finality makes itself known fully. And it makes itself known only in what is yet a higher order of being and finality than mere life, namely, that of a rational consciousness, which is not just an epiphenomenon on the surface of space-time coordinates or of merely vital functions, but a culmination in the order of nature itself. Human being is what determines the order of nature as a whole as it includes all the lower orders of space-time, the living, and the sentient. Even physics seems to be coming to recognize this with its consideration of what is referred to as the "anthropic principle" (Barrow 1986).

With the rational species of being at the summit or at the end of the development of nature as a whole, however, we come not only to the highest kind of self-determination in the order of nature, but also to a whole new dimension in the transcendental order of the universe which we must now consider as integral to the universe, for the universe is more than just an order of nature. It is also an order of history, which does not leave the order of nature behind but integrates it into the higher order that human being creates through its own initiative, an order of human providence or an order of spirit in matter.

17.3   The Universal Order of History

It might seem that we have already been speaking of history in speaking of evolution in nature. In a sense, we have, insofar as history means a succession of events following one another and insofar as evolution appears to lead up to the human species of being. In this sense nature has a history of its own, which includes a certain kind of self-determination in passing from one level of determination to the next. But this is not the order of history in the full sense of the word. It is only a prehistory leading up to history in the proper sense, which begins with human initiative and self-determination in being. What we mean by "history" here, as the part of the order of the universe that distinguishes itself from what is merely given in the order of nature, is the order of being, or beings, that is constituted by human initiative through intelligence and will, which is free and hence original, over and above the order given by nature.

History thus represents an order in which being discloses itself no less than in the order of nature in a way that is still integral to the order of the universe or to the order of being as a whole. In fact, it is the order in which being discloses itself to the one capable of questioning after the truth of being as well as initiating its own determination of being in a way that transcends nature as given. For human being is not only the maker of history but also the one in whom being discloses itself historically as well as naturally. If we keep in mind that human being remains our primary analogate of being at the center of the universe, so to speak, and understand history as the order properly initiated by human being in the order of finite being, then we have to say that history is the order in which being discloses itself most immediately even as it is initiated by human being. It is the order that metaphysics can least afford to overlook because it is the order in which being is opened up in the fullness of its transcendental scope beyond mere nature as well as within it, since human being remains a part of nature even as it transcends it.

17.3.1   Historical Transcendence

But how is this order to be understood as transcending nature? How do we come to it in its disclosing? Clearly, we come to it through the initiative of human being, which is more than just a thing of nature and has to be characterized as spirit. Spirit oversteps nature as something that entails a composition of form with matter. In our consideration of human being as the culmination of self-determination in the order of nature, we were regarding it as a composite of form and matter and as a thing of nature, albeit as the highest form of being in matter. Now, as we turn to human being in its own originality as historical self-determination, we find that there is more to it, and to being, than can be accounted for strictly in terms of nature or of a composite of matter and form, as any reflection on the proper activity of knowing and willing will show in contrast to the activity of sensation and emotion in the human soul, which is still only on a more natural level. What we mean by the spiritual dimension of being is what discloses itself through these activities of intelligence and will in human being, and what we understand as the historical order as distinct from the natural order in being is what is constituted through such activity.

If we reflect upon our activity of sensation and emotion, we find that these are somehow tied to what we can still call physical organs such as eyes or feelings, even though such organs entail a much higher kind of determination than what can be expressed purely in terms of space-time coordinates. In other words, a proper understanding of such organs already entails more than what can be accounted for in merely physicalist terms. Nevertheless, insofar as they remain physical organs, they are made up of basic physical entities in a specifically determinate arrangement which may or may not be discernible in physics or chemistry alone, as when we recognize a loss of function due to an injury to the necessary arrangement of basic entities for a determinate species. Thus, as high as the acts of sensation and emotion, both of which entail some consciousness, might be in the order of determinations of being, they are still tied directly to something physical. They are still acts of the composite thing of nature even in human being, and not yet spiritual or historical as is the act of reflection itself we are now exercising upon such activities.

If, on the other hand, we reflect on the activities of intelligence and will, we find that they are no longer tied directly to anything physical, although there remains some dependence on the physical, inasmuch as we cannot exercise reflection under certain physical conditions and inasmuch as in our exercise of reflection there is always some physical activity that is presupposed. In reflecting self-consciously we rise above the merely physical and natural and function in a way that is autonomous with regard to nature. Raising questions for understanding in experience, for example, or formulating hypotheses to account for what is given in fact, does not depend directly on any particular organ of sensation, but rather on an exercise of thought. Inhibiting the flow of our emotions, at least momentarily, in view of deliberation prior to choosing a particular course of action does not depend on any particular emotion within oneself, but rather on a more universal power of will that transcends all particular emotions and places itself in one of them rather than in another by choice.

I say "does not depend directly" in both cases because clearly in my exercise of intelligence and will there remains some dependence on physical conditions. There is no intelligence for me without some physical experience. And there is no will for me except through deliberation over what emotions present for me as motives for action and through the choice of one of these, all of which also entails all sorts of physical conditions. But these conditions, as necessary as they may be for intelligence and will on my part, are not sufficient conditions for the proper exercise of intelligence and will. The sufficient condition for the proper exercise of intelligence and will is in the power of intelligence and the power of willing itself, neither of which is tied to a physical organ, as the powers of sensing and emotion are. Hence, though we can speak of a necessary dependence on physical conditions for the proper exercise of intelligence and willing, we cannot speak of this dependence as direct, as in the case of sensation and emotion, but only as indirect for an activity that is in itself spiritual even in its relation to the physical. In the order of history based on human initiative we have an activity that flows from a power that transcends any physical power, even those of sensation or emotion, and that can be properly called spiritual, which constitutes an order of being higher than anything nature alone can produce.

Needless to say, this higher order of being in the universe discloses itself only in the proper activity of human intelligence and will, which always entails some reflection and self-consciousness. But consciousness of this order is part of our experience of being, just as the reflection or the indirect exercise of judgment from which the knowledge of being as being itself flows is a part of our first experience or the direct exercise of judgment. This is why we say only that there is no direct dependence on any physical organ, just as we say there is no direct dependence of metaphysics on physics or any other particular science. For there is some dependence of intelligence and will on sense faculties and emotions, since there is no intelligence for us without sense experience, and no will without some deliberation and choice, which always entails a diversity of particular emotions. But, real as it is, this is only an indirect dependence for an activity that flows directly from a power of reflection and self-consciousness that is self-determining and cannot appear on any level of mere sensation and emotion. In their own self-determination, intelligence and will are independent of any physical organ. This is what determines them as spiritual rather than just natural.

This is how the spiritual order of being discloses itself in relation to our own personal experience and in relation to the natural order in which this experience takes place. This is how also, in the advent of human being with intelligence and will, the order of nature is taken up into a new and higher order, which we call the order of history, for nature is not just the ladder of ascent for human being that is then left behind, but rather the instrument that human being needs and takes with itself in its own self-actualization. The question that arises now is how to understand this spiritual order as constituting a new order for the universe as a whole in relation to the order of nature? How is it an order of being even as it transcends the natural order through human self-conscious initiative?

To answer this question we must go back to our original and originating experience of self-consciousness through mutual recognition. Coming to self-consciousness does not take place in isolation for any individual human being. It takes place only in a relation of mutual recognition between individual consciousnesses, who come to self-consciousness through this confrontation. I become conscious of myself in my understanding and willing only in the presence of another who is also becoming conscious of himself or herself in his or her understanding and willing in the presence of myself. This, we can say, is the first act of history in which we begin to transcend our merely natural being. It takes place through language as a new kind of communication in which one being recognizes its distinction from the other as it recognizes the other as distinct from itself, or rather where two or more individuals recognize one another as distinct from one another in their very communication.

17.3.2   The Beginning of History

This has to be understood as a new and radical departure in the context of natural evolution and growth. It is like coming to the age of reason for an individual or for a community. It is difficult to pinpoint any particular time at which this takes place in the normal development of any individual, but we watch for it in the first genuinely human smile of recognition of an infant and in the first word that a child utters meaningfully. Different children come to this differently, but they all come to it through a language they pick up from those around them and begin to use to make themselves present for others and for themselves. They may not speak of themselves at first. In fact, they speak more often of the other, mama or papa or whoever is first to become significantly other for the child and in whom the child discovers itself as significant. But whatever the word or the name, even if it be that of a thing like water, it expresses a new act of understanding with a new self-consciousness through which the child enters into the spiritual world of communication with other selves. If such moments are more difficult to pinpoint in the normal development of a child, they are more easily discerned in the positive development of a handicapped person such as Helen Keller, where breaking out into the world of spirit through language takes place much more dramatically, as it is admirably represented in *The Miracle Worker* (Gibson 1963), or negatively in the lack of sufficient development for those whom we think of as retarded.

Language is crucial for this passage from the order of mere nature to the order of history. We see this most clearly in any individual's coming to the age of reason or to the age of adulthood. Living in a society that defines itself by its language, the individual comes to self-conscious understanding and willing in a language that is already established historically. In the context of an evolution of the species, one has to wonder how such a passage took place when there was no previously established language and no earlier spiritual generation of individuals. What must the first word have been? How did it first come about between the two individuals who first uttered it in mutual recognition? We can represent this original development as having been very gradual and incremental, as in the case of the normal development of a child. But we must not lose sight of its originality, as the first moment of historical consciousness for an individual or a community, with reference to which what comes before in nature is prehistory. To distinguish it more clearly from all previous evolution in nature, we might think of it as a revolutionary moment, in which all that was given or previously established is set aside or integrated into a new kind of determination.

Marx spoke at times of actual history in bourgeois society as only prehistory in relation to true history, which was to begin after the communist revolution (Marx 1859), as if the actual state of society in which he was living were only a natural state to be overcome. He also spoke of the universal proletariat revolution as the time when "the shedding of all natural limitations will be accomplished" (Marx 1967, 468; Blanchette 1983, 117). But in this he was betraying his original insight into the meaning of history as distinct from nature, or of human labor as distinct from the activity of spiders and bees. History is something in the present and it began with the first word uttered between two individuals long before our time. If it were not so, if language had not opened the way for us, we would not be here to reflect upon it, in communication with one another. Whatever the future may hold for us in this communication, we cannot deny this actuality of real presencing in the present through language. For, without language and a self-conscious understanding of language, there is no understanding even of labor as a primordial historical activity (Blanchette 1974, 325–82).

Marx was right in wanting to keep historical actuality one with nature through labor. But he was wrong in maintaining a priority of labor over language in the constitution of history. As we try to represent for ourselves what must have been the first word or how it first came about between two individuals in the context of evolution, we must ask ourselves as well: What were these individuals doing at the time as things of nature? Were they just continuing to "labor" as things of nature, as ants and bees do? Or were they beginning to act in a new way as human beings in self-consciousness? How did they begin to *labor* as human beings, that is, as conceiving an end to be actualized prior to getting to work on nature, if not through language and a confrontation in language rather than through merely a struggle for domination? There have been different ways of representing what must have been this original state of nature or this transition from mere nature to properly historical being for human being. It has been represented as a state of war by Hobbes or as a state of peaceful labor by Locke. But in neither of these representations do we get to the essential confrontation of mutual recognition in which history begins as history not just in the distant past, but in its present actuality as well, the confrontation through language prior to the confrontation through labor as production of commodities for human living.

In fact, labor itself, as properly human and as a properly historical act, presupposes language at its origin. Even Marx describes labor not as anything that any other animal can perform. It is peculiar to human beings and it depends on an ability to envision an end to be achieved and some means to achieve it. It presupposes a language of some kind and some of what goes with this kind of consciousness, some understanding and some resolve or willing, without which it is not human and not properly historical. It presupposes some kind of mutual recognition through language such as we find exemplified in *The Miracle Worker,* where we see Helen passing from a state of pure nature, so to speak, to a historical state in her own self-consciousness.

In trying to represent what must have been the first word between individuals just coming out of a pure state of nature or how this leap came about, we could very well represent it as taking place with regard to a task that they began to envision together and for which the first word was uttered not as a command, but as the expression of an idea shared by both. The division of labor and the domination of one over the other, as Marx points out, come only later, as do competition and struggle for exclusionary possession. The first struggle of labor is with nature itself and it begins as a cooperative understanding between two individuals expressed in a language that, although closely tied to a task to be performed in nature, is a first opening into the world of spirit. It is unfortunate that Marx saw this opening only in its relation to nature, as an understanding and a domination to be advanced technically for the liberation of all human beings and the end of all class struggle, and not also in its own originality as already a new and higher order of communion in being. Hence his materialism, even with his keen sense of the spirit, for in his struggle against idealism he could not escape the reductive identification of human being with only matter or nature. Though he was for a humanism that could not be reduced to a pure naturalism, he could not think of this humanism except as another kind of naturalism. This is why he kept playing back and forth with the idea of history and prehistory. He could not see the complete spiritual originality of history as an order of being in present actuality.

17.3.3   Historical Consistence as Community

In what, then, does this originality consist? In its most fundamental sense, it consists in a new level of self-consciousness in which being discloses itself as a world of spirit. This self-consciousness is not the consciousness of an individual isolated from every other individual consciousness, as it has been represented in the modern conception of human being. Nor is it a self-consciousness that arises only out of an initial conflict unto death that gives way to a relation of master and slave, as it has been represented in Hegel's *Phenomenology of Spirit*. It is more a self-consciousness that arises in a loving and cooperative confrontation between two or more individuals in their struggle with nature. This self-consciousness in mutual recognition first expresses itself in a language they share from its very inception. It is a world of spirit in which there are always two or more self-consciousnesses present to one another and communicating in this mutual confrontation.

It is not a world that stands over the world of nature, but rather a world that integrates the order of nature into a new order of culture. It is not a world in which one individual simply stands over against or in competition with another individual like a bare thing of nature. Rather, it is world where one individual is truly distinguished from the other as a self-consciousness in a recognition that sets each one free in its own standing as they communicate in setting one another free and in transforming the world of nature given to them.

Most importantly, this is the world in which two beings are distinguished from one another in their mutual presencing to one another. It is the world in which we begin to exercise judgment and in which being discloses itself as one being in the presence of another being who is at the same time in the presence of the first. In terms of metaphysics as an indirect exercise of judgment, it is the world in which we first distinguish between one thing and another in the most radical ontological sense, where one thing is a self-conscious subject in the presence of another thing, who is another self-conscious subject.

The first thing we come to know as an object other than ourselves, as we have said before, is another subject, who also knows the other self as an object other than itself, prior to any other kind of object that is differentiated from self-conscious subjects altogether, such as merely sentient beings, or merely living beings, or even nonliving beings. For in the direct exercise of judgment, the world is constituted in our consciousness not from the bottom up, but from the top down, as we saw with regard to the analogy of being. In the indirect judgment that we are now exercising metaphysically, we come to recognize the primacy of mutual recognition even for reflection upon being as being. We do not come to know phenomenal objects first, independently of any reflection on the subject, and then go on to reflect on the subject in its self-constitution as free and ethical. On the contrary, subjects are the first phenomenal objects to be distinguished in this radical experience of being as mutual recognition, which only spiritual beings come to; and they are seen, or recognized, immediately as interdependent in a world that is objectively ethical, a world that integrates the order of mere nature into its own order.

In speaking of transcendental unity in Chapter 5, we were brought to speak of the one as undivided in itself and divided from every other. Every being is one in the sense that it is undivided in itself and divided from every other. Where we see this most clearly is in mutual recognition between two self-conscious subjects, or between you and me in this confrontation through language. I am myself a being, undivided in myself, as distinct from you in this confrontation, as you are another being undivided in yourself. I come to think of myself as one, as having my own identity, as undivided in myself only in the presence of another, from whom I distinguish myself. This adds nothing to who I am, except the negation of not being the other, but it is a recognizing of who I am in the presence of the other.

The other, of course, or *you* in this historical confrontation through language, are also coming to think of yourself as undivided in yourself and as recognizing who you are in the presence of this other as well. I am a part of your world in my identity and you are a part of my world in your identity and together, in this confrontation, we constitute a world of beings, each undivided in itself and divided from every other, but not isolated from one another. In this world, other beings are recognized as well, not only those who are equally subjects confronting us through language, but also those who confront us as only sentient and not rational, or as only living and not sentient, and even as nonliving. If each or any one of these could be thought of as perfectly undivided in itself, or as perfectly simple, it could also be thought of as perfectly divided from every other or as totally independent of any other. But this is never how we experience being in the direct exercise of judgment. We experience beings only in relation with one another as we experience ourselves only in relation to one another within a horizon that we think of as the world of beings, which is a world of self-conscious subjects as well as a world of things, an order of history as well as an order of nature.

This historical world is not just a flat horizon or a kind of abstract background of space-time against which things or events take place, because every being that we distinguish is not only one in itself but also active. Here again, with transcendental activity as spoken of in Chapter 6, as in the case of transcendental unity, we understand the historical order most clearly in the mutual recognition among self-conscious subjects. The identity that discloses itself in this recognition is not just something static or passive. It is something quite active that discloses itself in its very activity. I do not first discover the identity of my being, which I then proceed to exercise according to its proper activity. But rather, I discover my identity as a being in the very exercise of my activity as one recognizing and being recognized by another; and I discover the identity of the other in the other's very exercise of recognizing and being recognized.

To be sure, this is a spiritual activity of intelligence and will as well as one of sensation and emotion, and it constitutes a world of spirit as well as a world of nature. But in either case the world that is constituted is a world of interaction among the beings that are distinguished from one another as beings. This world is not just an afterthought that comes after the beings have been constituted. It is part of the thought of being itself as it discloses itself, since being, or every being, discloses itself only in its activity and, insofar as we distinguish more than one being, as we do from the very beginning in mutual recognition, we can only understand them as parts of a world in which they confront one another actively.

Moreover, insofar as this confrontation is mutual between two or more beings, we can understand immediately how this activity entails what we have referred to as extrinsic causation. It is an interaction among several beings in which one needs the other even for its own good as self-consciousness and in which one influences the other for that same good in the other. I need the other, since it is only in the presence of an other, whom I need precisely as other than myself, that I come to my own self-consciousness. In this sense the other is final cause for me, an object of love or appetite, or at least an object of regard and respect. And the other needs me in the same way, and so must also respect me objectively, that is, as a self-conscious subject. I also need others in order to learn about other things. And I need the things themselves, to satisfy not just my natural needs, but also my need to know and even to respect them for *what* they are. In this sense, all things are objects of desire for the human community along with other human beings in mutual recognition. This kind of extrinsic final causality is most evident in the world of spirit, but it is also present in the order of nature wherever we understand one thing as satisfying the need of another.

With regard to efficient causality, it is similarly in mutual recognition that the extrinsic causation is most in evidence. This is not just a physical confrontation, although there is always something physical in any confrontation between one individual and another. It is more fundamentally a spiritual confrontation expressed through language, in which one being affects or *influences* the other in a way that produces or reproduces it as a self, so to speak, or as one who speaks for oneself.

We spoke earlier of reproduction in the order of nature in section 16.4. In mutual recognition between two self-conscious subjects, we have another kind of reproduction, one that is more spiritual and one that may be more radical than anything in the order of nature alone. In the normal course of events reproduction among human beings begins in the order of nature but it continues in an order of culture. Normally, parents not only beget children but also begin to educate or to form them as human beings, that is, as social beings in communion with others. If parents are not there for that, or if the family is not functioning properly in this basic education of children, someone else has to intervene for the formation of a fully developed human being, that is, one who is able to participate in human activity rationally. In emphasizing teaching as a kind of efficient causation in actuality in section 16.2, we were not just alluding to some esoteric example of such activity. We were focusing on a central activity in the order of history as part of the order of the universe, an activity that begins in the family or some other form of intimate intersubjectivity but that eventually brings in many others at different levels of association, an activity that can be the object of its own scientific investigation as much as the activity of nature, the activity that constitutes human communities in history.

17.3.4   Social Science as Science of Historical Being

This is not the place to go into any long description of what we now refer to as the order of history as distinct from the order of nature. That would entail bringing in too many of the particular social sciences which we can now distinguish from the particular physical or natural sciences. But we should note that these particular social sciences, such as economics and political science, are no less sciences of being than are the physical or natural sciences. We are inclined to think of physics as the only hard science, or as the prototype of such science, while the others are considered science only insofar as they approximate the mathematical hardness of physics. But that is only another form of reductionism, this time in the very conception of science. The social sciences deal with beings no less than the physical sciences and, while these beings are less predetermined in their activity than are the beings of physics or biology, they do entail real determinations that require a science no less rigorous and hard than physics. The key thing in this scientific rigor is not so much rigor *more geometrico,* which is not appropriate for every subject of inquiry, but rather, as Aristotle pointed out at the beginning of the *Nicomachean Ethics* (1094b 1328), a method suited to the subject as defined in the particular science, which in the social sciences tends to be much more complex than in the natural sciences and also much more free in its own self-articulation.

Suffice it to say that this order is properly a social order constituted by the initiative of individuals in communion with one another. Insofar as this order entails an appropriation of nature for human purposes, we think of it as economic. History, as Marx has pointed out, is to be accounted for, at least in part, in terms of production and industry, that is, as human labor contending with nature. It is an order of civilizations, some of which have come and gone and some of which continue to develop in their diverse ways. But insofar as it is properly human and spiritual, it is more than just an economic order. It is a whole that constitutes itself as a human community or, perhaps more specifically, as a number of communities, each of which is an ethical whole with its own specific determination that transcends all purely natural determinations.

Hegel spoke of history in linear fashion as a sequence of such ethical wholes leading up to the modern state, with freedom or liberation for all as the ideal determination for the order of history as a whole (*PH* 20–23). But in doing so he spoke too exclusively or, as he would have said, too one-sidedly of one kind of human community, the one that found its fulfillment in the modern European state, the origins of which he found in the language and the constitution of earlier states, especially the Chinese and the Greek. In this he found a way of unifying history as a whole under his ideal determination of liberation. But he did so at the expense of many human communities that he did not recognize as ethical wholes or as integral parts of history. Though he spoke of a World Spirit working out its purpose in a succession of particular spirits through time, this World Spirit ended up always as a particular spirit that was supposed to be the absolute spirit at that particular time with the right to dominate all other spirits or communities or to destroy them, as it saw fit.

So it was at any given time in the past, according to Hegel, and so it remained for him in his own actuality, with a certain contempt for any community lying outside the geographical concentration in which the World

Spirit was supposedly centered or lacking in any language or constitution as conceived for the modern state. Hegel's idea of spirit was not completely locked into this particular conception of the modern European state, for he did envision the possibility of the World Spirit moving on to different determinations in the future and to different geographical locations, but this more universal idea of spirit never lessened his insistence on a particular state as the only absolute spirit in history. He remained resolutely opposed to any idea of a cosmopolitan spirit, which Kant had already begun to advance.

What Hegel did understand quite rightly, however, was the idea of a human community as an ethical whole constituted through mutual recognition among human beings. Such an idea could be understood as existing only for spiritual beings who are able to interact socially through intelligence and will as well as in labor, and it had to be understood as transcending any given natural order, including human individuals as merely given by nature or by the past, since the whole was constituted only by the interaction among several human beings or the recognition that constituted them in their self-consciousness as well as in their interrelation. Such a whole had to be conceived as somehow absolute in relation to anything given by nature and as a new kind of whole in the light of which truly ethical judgment was to be exercised. Truly ethical judgment, as Hegel showed in his early writings, is never purely individual or purely formal (NR 59–92). It is exercised always in the light of a people or a community or in the spirit that draws individuals into a community, namely, the actual recognition that they show one another.

In this whole, which is an order among several individuals, there is no opposition between the whole and any one of its parts, since it is only in the whole of mutual recognition that any one of its parts finds its actualization even as self-conscious and free. If there is opposition, it is only between one part and another, where one part may sometimes claim to speak in the name of the whole in totalitarian fashion. In fact, there is a certain identification between the good of the whole and the good of any one of the parts, so that in finding oneself as a spiritual individual in a community one is also finding the good of the whole.

But this good of the whole should not be understood merely as the good of only a particular community at any given time. This is still to limit it to something particular, even though it is not limited to a single individual generated by nature. It has to be understood as something absolutely universal, wherein the good of all particular communities as well as of individuals is to be found. If the good of any particular community is absolute for the individuals that make up the community, it is still only relatively absolute as a particular spiritual good that can be opposed to or at least distinguished from other particular spiritual goods, as happens among communities in the order of history.

17.3.5   History as Transcendental Order of Being

What is in question here is the understanding of the order of history as an order of beings, or as the higher order of a universe that opens beyond the order of nature. Insofar as this order still includes individuals that are the product of nature in some sense and continue to interact with other beings of nature, it has roots and principles in nature. Some of its parts at least remain material and act as material beings. But insofar as these same individuals constitute a new kind of whole, a spiritual whole or a true community in being, through mutual recognition, they enter into a new kind of order, a spiritual order of being, which transcends the order of nature in two senses. First, it transcends it in the sense that history introduces an order of being for our consideration that is not to be found in the order of nature as such. But second, it does so only by extending the transcendental order that we have already found in nature, the order of the diversity of species from the lowest to the highest, into a realm that the order of nature can no longer encompass but that human reason can still determine through its own consideration as well as its own initiative.

In this order that opens up beyond the order of nature, we can still discern a certain diversity of particular spirits, each of which entails a certain absoluteness relative to the individual humans that make it up. These are the spirits of the various communities that we can discern in history, our own along with that of others. Even if we do not insist on working out any hierarchy among these diverse spirits, as is frequently done within the modern developmental spirit, which distinguishes between more primitive spirits and more advanced spirits, as it usually considers itself the most advanced, we have to see that each spirit is a determinate whole unto itself in the order of history, to be taken as something absolute in itself, at least relative to the individuals that make it up and to any individual of mere nature. In this way we come to a different understanding of the order of being according to different forms of spirit that are to be related to one another absolutely above any order of nature as given.

The question of the truth of being and of the good to be sought thus opens up into a new dimension of spirit that cannot occur in a consideration of mere nature, into a communion in being through intelligence and will that is not limited to any individual existence, and that, once it comes to encompass humanity as a whole rather than just particular communities, is not limited to any particular human form of spirit.

At this point we come to understand not just the question of history as a whole, but also the question of something to be understood beyond nature altogether and also possibly beyond history itself. For even if we do stand at the summit of history, as Hegel and modern thought likes to suggest in all sorts of ways, there is still the question of how we are constituted in our very being, not just in our determination as natural or as historical, but in the very order of being, which encompasses both of these determinations into the single universal order of being as being.

PART SIX

THE SUMMIT OF BEING

Introduction: Raising the Ultimate Question

≈

$\mathbf{W}$ ITH OUR CONCEPTION of the universe as a communication in being among many and diverse beings, we might think that we have
come to the end of our inquiry into being as being. But is this truly the end
of metaphysics? Does our knowledge of the universe as a totality of determinate beings in interaction with one another really bring our inquiry to an
end, or is there a further question to be asked about a cause that has yet to
be disclosed?

So far we have raised the question of causes only with reference to particular beings that come to be and cease to be. In beginning our inquiry into
causes, we saw that the question of causes first arises with reference to particular differences of being and to becoming in being. While we did not
equate becoming and particular differences with being in the full sense of
the term, we began our inquiry there because that is the being we know
best in the direct exercise of judgment, especially if we take human being as
our primary analogate of being.

What this gives us to understand, however, is the ontological constitution
only of particular beings, which includes a particular act of being as well as a
particular essence, and the particular extrinsic causes that account for the
coming to be of such particular beings. What about being in its commonality, that is, being as common to all particular things or as the concrete universal? Has that been accounted for yet? Can it be accounted for by any particular cause, if such a particular cause always undergoes being itself as part of
the universe, no less than its effects? Does it not take a universal cause of being simply as being to account for being in its commonality? If so, how is
such a universal cause of being as being to be understood?

In raising this question about a universal cause of being we enter into a
very different kind of perplexity than anything we have seen heretofore. After raising the question of being as being initially in its most universal sense,
we were brought, by the differences understood in the analogy of being, to
consider being in its particularity as one being and another and as different

kinds of being, each with its own essential standing and its own act of being, and each active in influencing other beings as well as passive in undergoing the influence of other beings, all of them together forming a universal order. What we were thinking of originally in terms of being simply has now come to be understood as a totality of beings. How is it possible to now raise the question of a universal cause of being? What does it mean to raise such a question in the face of this totality of beings that we now take for granted or for what is actually the case?

We have seen with Parmenides that, apart from being, there is nothing, and from nothing nothing comes. In asking about a universal cause of being, we must be careful to understand the precise orientation of the question. Are we asking about something apart from being simply, which would be nothing and from which nothing comes, or are we asking about another being that would have to be distinguished entirely from any particular being we have come to know in this totality of beings we call the universe? If it is another being that we are asking about, can it be just another particular being that we could add on to the totality of particular beings we call the universe or is it a being of a totally different kind that cannot be understood as part of any universe, the one we know concretely or another one that would include the cause we are now inquiring about as one of its parts? Would the universal cause of being as being be just another part of the universe in addition to the parts we have so far considered or would it be something totally transcendent in its very being?

What we are asking about cannot be just another particular being, for that would make it just another one of the particular beings to be accounted for, another part of the universe to be accounted for, and not that which accounts for the universe as a whole. What we are asking about has to be understood as something totally different from any particular being we know in the universe and hence as transcending even the universe as a whole, for we are asking about the cause of the whole or of the totality of beings as given in experience.

Moreover, what we are inquiring into cannot be understood as something merely in potency, for that would require something else again to reduce it from potency to act, given the absolute priority of act over potency we have already demonstrated in section 16.5 with regard to becoming and being. What is in question here would have to be understood as a being totally in act, since it would have to be understood as an efficient cause of all that we know to be in act in the universe. In this sense it would have to be understood as the cause of the act of being in all particular beings. But as universal cause it would also have to be understood as cause of the order that constitutes the universe as horizon of being.

The universal cause of being would thus have to be understood as something distinct from all particular beings, and yet not as nothing. What would distinguish it from any particular being would not be some particularity, but precisely its universality as cause of everything there is. It would not be just one of many beings, but Cause of the many beings in their very being, so that metaphysics could use the name "Cause" as its proper name. This Cause, if we can speak of it as a *this* without making it a particular, could not be understood as one among many particular beings or as coming under the subject of metaphysics as we determined it from the beginning, for this subject has now come to be understood as the totality of diverse particular beings in action and interaction. It could only be understood as the Cause of all that is included in our subject, and not as a part of that subject, which still refers to being as experienced in the direct exercise of judgment.

As such a universal cause of being, however, it would have to be understood as entering into each one of the particular beings we know in experience. Unlike any particular cause, the universal Cause would not remain apart form its effect, but enter into its very being. Hence it would be difficult to distinguish it from each one of its particular effects, as the act of being is difficult to distinguish from the essence of any particular being. In fact, it would have to be present in each finite act of being but without being finite, since it would also be the cause of all other finite acts of being. It would have to be an infinite act.

The perplexity here is one of immanence and transcendence for something in act that is in something finite and yet is not limited by this being-in, as the act of being of a finite being is limited by being received in its determinate essence. How can something infinite be in the finite and yet transcend the finite? How can it be totally transcendent cause and yet immanent in the effect?

Finally, we might look at this perplexity that surrounds the question of a universal cause of being in relation to the way we have distinguished the differences of being according to different degrees of being, some higher, such as human being, some lower, such as a stone or anything else we might refer to as a mere thing. If there is a universal cause of being, it would have to be the first or the highest cause, and the Cause itself would have to be the first or the highest Being, the one in relation to which all others are measured as higher or lower.

It is in this sense that we speak of it here as the Summit of being. In terms of the properties of being, it would have to be thought of as most one, to the point of being utterly simple, most active, to the point of being creative in the most radical sense of the term, most true, to the point of being the source for all disclosedness in being, and most good, to the point of being that which all things desire or acquiesce in ultimately to the extent that they desire or acquiesce in anything. If we could understand the highest perfection of each of these properties of being without any of the limitations associated with particular beings, we could understand this Summit of being. But the perplexity remains, because each time or each way we try, we find ourselves on the side of particular beings having to work our way out toward a perfection of being we can barely glimpse because it surpasses the understanding we have of being in experience, the understanding that is proportionate only to particular being and not to any sort of universal being we are now inquiring into.

To work our way out of this perplexity, or at least to clarify in what the perplexity consists concerning this universal cause of being as an infinite act transcending the universe as well as all particular beings in it, or as the unique Summit of all being, we must enter into a higher level of reflection than the one we have followed up to now even in metaphysics. We saw how every exercise of judgment, direct as well as indirect, entails some reflection, but that metaphysics, or the science of being precisely as being, requires a special kind of reflection. It is this special reflection that has led us to our conclusions about the ontological structure of determinate beings and the universe in its natural and historical order.

This reflection, however, in its concrete reference, cannot take us any further than the bounds of the universe we have seen up to now. If we are to raise the question of a universal cause of being, we must move to a higher level of reflection with regard to the totality of being as we know it. We must entertain the thought of some other being that we do not know, but that we do know would not be a part of the universe as is any determinate being.

We can do this with the help of our concept of being, which can be extended by analogy in yet another way than the one we have followed up to now from human being as our primary analogate. Up to now we have extended our first conception of being from human being mainly downward, so to speak, to include lower forms of being such as the nonrational, the nonsentient, and the nonliving. Now we must see if this conception can be extended upward into higher degrees of being and ultimately into a highest degree of being with the help of the transcendental properties of being, whose analogy can and must also be extended upward.

More specifically, we must do this by extending our own metaphysical effort to understand being as being to the fullest degree possible, that is, by recognizing that, having said all that we have said about particular beings and the order of the universe, both natural and historical, there still remains a question about being or, more precisely, about the universal cause of being as being, to be dealt with, a question that may open into a question for religion and for which only religion may have an answer, but that still has to be dealt with in metaphysics. In fact, this connection of metaphysics with religion will have to be explored in metaphysics, since the universal cause of being as we have to think of it in metaphysics would have to be what is worshipped as God in religion.

Before we can even entertain such a question in the philosophy of being, however, we must show metaphysically that this question of the universal cause of being must be raised, just as we had to show, at the beginning of metaphysics itself, that the question of being as being must be raised. If we can show that the question must be raised, and if in addition we can show that an answer to the question in the affirmative must be given, namely, that there is a universal cause of being, who is God affirmed as Creator of all things, then metaphysics may have to give way to religion in speaking more amply of this Cause and how we have to relate to it for our complete good and the good of the universe.

In doing so, metaphysics will not abandon its autonomy as rational discourse about being. In fact, it will extend the scope of this discourse into a realm that transcends its proper subject of consideration, not in order to reduce it to the finite confines of this subject, but rather to open up this discourse to a contemplation of what surpasses it absolutely and simply. In this it will retain its own reflective or critical function in sorting out the way we can speak of this transcendent Cause. Even in relating to theology, it will not become onto-theological, especially if theology is understood as based on faith in a supernatural revelation from God. It will remain strictly a science of being as being, an ontology, without passing over into theology, where God himself becomes the subject of science, for, as we have already suggested the Cause we are inquiring into has to be understood as totally other than the universe or any determinate being that would be part of it.

Even if metaphysics succeeds in raising the question of God and demonstrating his existence, God cannot become part of the subject of metaphysics because of the way this existence has to be demonstrated from particular beings, which are the only ones included in our initial conception of being as being. At its own summit metaphysics itself becomes religious in a certain way, insofar as it acknowledges being as ultimately received from God, but in doing so it does not cease being itself, a science only of being as being and not of the Creator of being, nor "of God as he is in his eternal essence before the creation of nature and a finite spirit," as Hegel thought with reference to the content of his *Logic* (*WL* 31/50).

Before it can become religious even in this restricted sense, however, metaphysics must prove the necessity of raising the question about a universal cause of being and the necessity of answering the question in the affirmative. This is what we propose to do here first and foremost. After that we shall have something to say, not so much about God in himself, but rather about how creatures or, simply, beings relate to him as Creator.

CHAPTER 18

The Necessity of Total Transcendence

⟨⟪⟩

W E HAVE SPOKEN of transcendence in different ways in the course of this reflection. We have spoken of being as a transcendental concept and of the properties as equally transcendental concepts, in that all of these concepts cut across the different categories of being that can be distinguished in the predicamental order. In opposition to Kant we have argued that metaphysics begins in a transcendental reflection, not just on the structure of our knowing, which is prior to any object known in experience, but also on the structure of being itself, which is prior to our knowing as well as to any object known in the primordial equation where we first understand that knowing is of being.

We did this, however, without supposing, as Kant does, that metaphysics has to be about objects that would be beyond all possible experience. We have insisted rather that metaphysics follows from experience, as the particular sciences do, even though it begins properly in the reflection found in any exercise of judgment where being makes itself present to intelligence as act. In the course of our reflection we have referred only to being as it presents itself in experience or in the direct exercise of judgment.

Hence, up to now, even while insisting on a transcendental order of being or beings, we have remained with what we could call the "immanent order of being" as experienced. The substances we have learned to distinguish from other substances on the basis of their constitutive principles have been a part of this order. The extrinsic causes we also learned to distinguish from their effects in the communication of being have also been part of this immanent order of being.

Now, however, with the question of a universal cause of being, which would itself be something infinite and universal, we come to an understanding of transcendence that does take us beyond all possible experience, or beyond being as the horizon of our knowing, and beyond anything that could still be understood as finite or determinate in any way. Until now we have insisted that metaphysics had, as the subject of its consideration, the being we know in experience. But now the question arises as to whether there is something that would be beyond the horizon of experience, something whose existence could not be experienced as we might experience anything in the universe, but whose very existence would have to be demonstrated in some way that is somehow *a priori* as well as *a posteriori*. We come to this understanding of total transcendence now only because our inquiry into being as being has brought us to it with the question of a universal cause of being. Is there such a cause of being, which would have to be transcendent in this radical sense? Is there even a question about such a transcendent cause?

18.1   The Necessity of the Question Concerning Total Transcendence

Our first task in this final extension of our metaphysical reflection is to prove or demonstrate the necessity of doing so, that is, of raising the question of a totally transcendent universal cause of being, just as our first task at the beginning of metaphysics was to prove or demonstrate the necessity of raising the question of being as being over and above the question of any or all the particular sciences. We must do this not by attempting to leap out of metaphysics, but from within metaphysics and the historical lifeworld in which our discourse on being emerges. How do we go about proving the necessity of raising such a question about a totally transcendent universal cause of being? To answer this question we must begin by asking: How do we go about proving the necessity of raising any question? What kind of necessity is involved in questioning?

Questioning begins as an exercise of intelligence in experience. As we have seen frequently, there are questions for understanding and questions for reflection. While it is difficult, if not impossible, for an intelligent human being to put off all questioning for the whole of one's life, there is perhaps no particular question that one cannot put off at any given time. In this sense no particular question is ever strictly necessary for anyone at any given time, unless it comes up as part of a need or a desire to know in a given context.

The necessity we are speaking of, then, presupposes an initiative or an exercise of intelligence. It stems from a radical desire to know that, precisely, gives rise to questioning. Keeping in mind the distinction between questions for understanding and questions for reflection, and the relation between them in the actual exercise of judgment, we realize that questioning can take many directions in experience and lead to many different kinds of conclusions, whence a plurality of particular sciences, none of which seems strictly necessary to pursue but each of which does satisfy some desire or some necessity to know. With regard to metaphysics, however, we argued at the beginning for a certain necessity to raise the question of being as being over and above the question of any particular science on the supposition that all sciences have to do with being and that the particular sciences always deal with being only under one aspect or another, while none of them deals with being precisely as being.

In this way metaphysics not only distinguishes itself from all the particular sciences, but also proves itself to be a necessary form of questioning. In fact, one might say that metaphysics itself begins with the recognition of this necessity to question being as being, strange and mysterious as such a question might sound from the standpoint of any particular science. The being that is presupposed in all the particular sciences but never itself brought into question as being cannot be left out of questioning. It must ultimately come into question, if we are to pursue the intelligibility of being to the end. This is what metaphysics does in its own indirect way with reference to the direct ways of understanding being in accordance with the distinction we made in section 2.4.

Thus there is a certain necessity of the question of being, a necessity that has been our guideline up to now in this inquiry. Each step we have taken along the way could be said to have been required by this necessity, from the recognition of the analogy of being to its properties and its causes in the structure of finite being and in the communication among beings within the order of the universe. Having reached an understanding of the universe as a whole, the question now arises as to the intelligibility of the whole. Is it intelligible or sufficient unto itself and are the beings in it intelligible by themselves or at least as parts of the universe, or is there still the question of a cause of their very being as a universe to be raised?

That is the question that arises at the *end* of metaphysics as being presents itself in its articulation as a universe of many and diverse beings. Is it a question that we have to contend with or is it a question that begins only by abstracting from being, or from history and nature as given, as Marx argues at one point (Marx 1963, 166), so that it is only a perverted question that presupposes nonexistence rather than existence? Is it only an abstraction to be abandoned? If we begin by supposing that we do not exist or that nothing exists, then there is no necessity of any question to be dealt with since there is not even any question of anything.

But in asking about a universal cause of being are we supposing that nothing exists? Are we not rather supposing the contrary, namely, that we do exist and that the universe does exist, and are we not asking of these beings that are disclosed in our experience whether they have a cause of their very being? We have seen that these beings do have causes in their coming to be as particular beings and as parts of the universe? But does this exhaust the question of their being caused? Does it exhaust the question of the universe itself as a whole being caused?

Coming to be terminates in being or, more properly, in the be or the *act* of being of *what* has come to be. If we distinguish this *act* of being from its essence or from *what* has come to be, and if we focus on this *act* as a more positive aspect of being than the essence in its coming to be, is there not a question as to the cause of this *act* of being to be raised precisely insofar as it is distinct from its essence and its coming to be?

In a way, this question transcends the order of time and coming to be, as the question of the real distinction between the *act* of being and its essence in a finite being transcends the order of coming to be and ceasing to be, as we tried to show in section 14.1. It has to do with a relation of dependence on the part of a finite being, understood as a composite of essence and its *act* of being, with reference to some other being that can no longer be understood as composite or finite. As such, it has to do with an act that is finite by reason of the essence that limits it, as this finite act relates to an act that has to be thought of as pure or without the limitation of any potency (see section 14.3), that is, as infinite. If there is in finite being as such a relation of dependence on a universal cause of being, it is a relation of dependence on an infinite *act* of being that therefore appears as the cause of finite being as such, that is, of any finite *act* of being limited by its determinate essence.

But this infinite act would have to be a cause in a totally different sense than any efficient cause we can understand in the immanent order of the universe or in what we have also referred to as the predicamental order. It would have to be a totally transcendent cause belonging to a totally different order of being than anything we know in the universe. Because this relation between the finite being and the infinite act would be a dependence in being, we would have to say that the infinite act *is,* but we would have to recognize immediately that it is not in any way like a finite being. It could not be just another particular being among particular beings. Nor could it be the totality of all particular beings, which is still finite, even if we remain ignorant of the dimensions of this totality. It would be an infinite being and in this sense the universal cause of all beings in time and in the universe.

We are not yet affirming that there has to be such a totally transcendent being. We are only trying to articulate something of what is at issue in raising the question of a universal cause of being. It is a question that engages us in a path where the answer lies beyond anything we can understand in the universe, including the universe itself. It takes us into a realm of being whose very existence has to be demonstrated, because it appears to us, so to speak, only as a question to be raised at the end of metaphysics.

If we insist on this total transcendence of the being in question at this point, it is in order to make as clear as possible what has to be demonstrated in any proof for the existence of a totally transcendent being. For not every demonstration of such a being takes proper aim, especially when it aims only at some particular being, even if it is set off from the universe as a whole. The transcendence of the absolutely universal cause is not something that can be understood spatially or temporally. It is simply infinite in the most positive sense of this double negation, the negation of the negation implied in finitude. To think anything less is to misunderstand both the question and what has to be demonstrated.

Though it transcends the order of time and coming to be, however, the question does arise within this order. And it does so necessarily. We could think of the universe and our consciousness of it as a fact, as something given to us in experience. This fact includes all that there is and all that we are certain of as being. But as a fact, like all facts of experience, this consciousness of a world gives rise to questioning even as a whole. How is this whole of consciousness and world to be understood? How is it to be accounted for in its very existence? Can it be sufficiently accounted for in the way we have done up to now, in terms of immanent principles and causes, or is some other being, a totally transcendent being, necessary to account for this universal fact of being of which we have an absolute certainty? Even if we do not know the answer to the question, it does arise necessarily in the way being presents itself in our knowing. If we are concerned with the full intelligibility of this universal fact of being in the absolute certainty we have of it, since knowing is of being, can we rightly or rationally avoid or evade the question?

Another way to come at this necessity of the question that is perhaps more metaphysical would be to reflect further on the real distinction we have been led to recognize between the *act* of being and the essence of any finite being in the universe we experience. The *act* of being accounts for the actuality of everything that is. In fact, it is the actuality of everything that is.

But as distinct from its essence in any finite being, it raises the question of a certain *contingency* in the finite beings we can distinguish from one another and in the totality of them.

We first understand contingency in things that come to be and cease to be, with reference to which we first come to understand the distinction between being in potency and being in act. It is by distinguishing the subject of a change as matter or as being in potency from the form or the act of what comes to be that we understand coming to be, whether simply, as in the case of a substance, or only according to some aspect of a substance, as in the case of an accident. We also understand ceasing to be as the reverse of this. This first distinction of potency and act as matter and form thus accounts for the contingency of composite beings in the order of becoming.

In maintaining a further composition in finite beings as such between the *act* of being and essence as the potency limiting that act, apart from any consideration of coming to be or ceasing to be, we were extending this first understanding of contingency in becoming to the order of being as such. The finite essence as such has to be thought as being in potency in relation to its act and, even if this essence is thought of as unchanging or without matter, it still has to be thought of as being in potency and hence as contingent, precisely insofar as the finite *act* of being is really distinct from its essence or from *what* it is.

This second composition in the finite being, namely, of essence and its *act* of being, entails another kind of contingency than any in the order of becoming. It is a contingency in the order of being as such, but one that also calls for some elucidation in terms of an efficient cause. Just as we found it necessary to look for an extrinsic cause in the coming to be of a composite of matter and form, so also we find it necessary to look for something like an extrinsic cause in the very existence of a finite being as such, for it too is a composite of potency and act and as such it is contingent even if it does not come to be or cease to be. Is it contingent only in itself or is it contingent on some other act not contingent on any other act but absolutely necessary in itself as the cause of all finite contingent being?

The question of a transcendent cause of being thus arises necessarily from our understanding of a real distinction between the *act* of being and the essence in a finite being, if we keep in mind the aspect of potency that remains attached to the essence of a finite being in relation to its actuality. In this composition of essence and its *act* of being we find an opening to an ontological dependence on another being that would be a pure *act* of being and not just another composite of essence and its *act* of being. But this opening remains only a question for us at the moment. Can we find an answer to the question? Can we demonstrate that there is such another being, even if we cannot represent to ourselves *what* such a being would be, since our representation of being is always the representation of a composite being, as we saw in our logic of being (sections 3.1–2)? What sort of logic is required for such a demonstration?

18.2   The Necessary Logic for Arriving at Total Transcendence

The question before us is a unique question that does not occur in any other science and that does occur only at the end of metaphysics. Not only is it a question of something that does not immediately appear in our experience, but that might be made to appear under certain conditions. It is a question of something that, by definition, cannot appear as part of our experience.

Ordinarily we do not question about the existence of anything. We simply take things as given, as matters of fact, and we begin our questioning from what is given. Sometimes, in the particular sciences, for example, we take one object for granted and we hypothesize about another object to account for the object taken for granted. The hypothesized object is not immediately known to exist, so that its existence has to be demonstrated. But this is done by a process of verification where it is shown that the existence of the object still in question is a necessary condition for the existence of the object that is not in question. Thus a certain necessary connection between two objects, usually going from effect to cause, is used to demonstrate the existence of an object whose existence is not known immediately, a connection that is taken to be part of the immanent order of the universe. That requires a certain logic that we think of as characteristic of the scientific method.

This logic, however, is not sufficient in dealing with the question about the sort of being or cause we are now bringing into question. To be sure, we could think of this universal cause of being as a hypothesis to account for the existence of the universe as a whole, but there would be no way of testing or verifying such a hypothesis in the immanent order of the universe, as there is for hypothetical causes in the particular sciences. Nor can the universal cause of being as being be properly thought of as any object in the universe. If it is an object, which is something we might want to question even as we try to demonstrate its existence, it cannot be an object in the universe, which means that its existence cannot be verified by any scientific method based on observation of differences in the universe. Hence the absurdity of such naive statements that there is no god because it does not appear at the end of a telescope or a microscope. If there is a god, properly understood, it is something that cannot possibly appear in this way.

Hence also the falsity of any expectation of finding god in the universe as one might find a gardener in his garden (Wisdom and Flew). After all is said and done, the gardener falls within the immanent order of the garden or is an object in the garden, even if it is the object that explains the existence of the garden. It is not the universal cause of both the gardener and the garden, which is what we are asking about here, for the gardener is not the cause of what she has to work with in the garden and she cannot be cause of herself. If there is a universal cause of all being, it has to remain invisible and it has to be found in all things, whatever they are actually. It cannot appear as only one of them.

If we wish to dwell with the analogy of the garden and its gardener for a moment, we should think rather of the gardener as the universal cause of all that the garden produces and as transcending all of these products. If one looks for the gardener as one of these products, the gardener will remain invisible. We shall see only fruits, vegetables, and flowers, not a gardener. But if one understands them as the products of the gardener, one will find the gardener in all of them, as one finds the artist in any work of art. So it *has* to be with the universal cause of being as well. It cannot be any particular being among others. It has to be totally transcendent to the immediate or the immanent order of finite beings, or the universe, while it is somehow present in each of them as particular in being.

Our demonstration, then, must begin from what is given to us in experience. We must begin from being as it presents itself. In this sense, the demonstration has to be empirical and *a posteriori*. However, it has to be empirical and *a posteriori* in a special way, like metaphysics itself. While other sciences focus on some particular aspect of being and therefore inquire only into particular causes that can still be understood as parts of the universe, metaphysics focuses on being as being and inquires into its properties and its cause or causes precisely as being or as the universe of beings.

Because it follows from experience and because it starts from being as understood in the direct exercise of judgment, that is, from a being that is concrete and composite, metaphysics does not come immediately to this ultimate question of a cause of being as being. It does not immediately raise the question of an absolutely universal cause of being. It examines first the structure of the finite beings it starts from and the kind of communication that takes place among them. It is only in the end, when all things have been considered in their differences and in their intercommunication as a universe of beings, that the question of an absolutely universal cause or a transcendent universal cause of being comes clearly to the fore. And it is only from this universal consideration of being as being that the question can be properly understood.

Hence while the demonstration has to be empirical, in that all questioning begins from experience for us, it also has be quite metaphysical or aprioristic, so to speak, at least in the sense that it requires a very precise understanding as to what is at issue. Unless we first raise the question of being as being, we cannot in any way raise the question of a universal cause of being as being. But more importantly for us here, unless we have elaborated some metaphysical understanding of being as it is given to us through some rational discourse such as we have tried to reconstruct here, we cannot properly understand even the question regarding a transcendent universal cause of being, let alone a demonstration that there has to be such a cause.

Thus, our demonstration starts not just from being as given in our experience, but also from being as understood in its ontological structure and its communication through extrinsic causality among determinate beings in the universe. The question can be raised only at the end of a systematic understanding of the universe of beings and it can be answered only in terms that have already been elaborated metaphysically. Without some metaphysics to mediate the terms of the question there is no possibility of answering it.

In this sense our metaphysics of the immanent order of being or of the being that presents itself in the direct exercise of judgment has to be a part of the demonstration we still have to undertake. In other words, it is not just being as given directly in experience that we start from in this demonstration, but being as now understood metaphysically in its ontological structure and as a universe. It is from this that we must proceed in the further elaboration of a demonstration toward a transcendent universal cause of all determinate beings.

It is the failure to grasp this metaphysical component in any proper demonstration, even *a posteriori,* for the existence of a transcendent universal being that causes many to misunderstand what is at issue in most of the classical arguments for God's existence that have been proposed by authors who were, after all, metaphysicians and used their understanding of metaphysics in their argument. To say that the argument does not work without having understood the metaphysics in use may be more a reflection on one's own failure to grasp the metaphysical argument than on the validity of the argument itself. If a demonstration is understood as a syllogism making someone know *(syllogismus faciens scire),* or bringing someone to a conclusion, as Aristotle and Aquinas understood it, and if one wishes to demonstrate to another that there is a transcendent universal being, that is, if one wishes to bring this other to this conclusion in the other's own mind, one must first of all make sure that this other has some metaphysical understanding of the transcendental order of being in the universe, for without such an understanding there can be no demonstration of this conclusion.

Nor can there be any proper disapproval of such a conclusion without such metaphysical understanding; so that one would have to say that God does not exist, for that too would require some metaphysical understanding of the question. In other words, there cannot be any proper discussion of a conclusion about the existence of God except in a discourse that presupposes some metaphysical understanding of being. Even when one agrees to the conclusion that God exists, say, in faith, if there is no metaphysical understanding, it can only be a non sequitur open to all sorts of misunderstandings. Demonstrations of a transcendent universal being without some metaphysical understanding simply do not work and, what is worse, they can lead to all sorts of misconceptions or misunderstanding regarding the "being" in question.

Hence, Kant was quite right in recognizing an ontological component in any demonstration for the existence of a totally transcendent being, and not just in the so-called ontological argument. Without such a component there can be no understanding of what is to be demonstrated, even if the argument purports to be cosmological, teleological, or *a posteriori* in any way. In the end of any demonstration for the existence of such a being one still has to understand that what is at issue is not a being whose existence can be given in experience or discovered *a posteriori* in the direct exercise of judgment, but one whose existence can only be *a priori,* universal, and irreducible to anything like the determinate being or beings we know in the direct exercise of judgment. Kant erred only in failing to understand the full implication of this necessary ontological component in demonstrating the existence of a totally transcendent being.

Kant's approach to the question is through his understanding of such a being as the transcendental ideal of pure reason, the *Inbegriff* or the sum total of all possibilities, which is presupposed as an *a priori* condition in the principle of complete determination for every or each thing. "Presupposing this sum as an *a priori* condition, it [the principle of complete determination] proceeds to represent everything as deriving its own possibility from the share which it possesses in this sum of all possibilities" (*KrV* A572; B600). Thus, for Kant, the principle of complete determination for things, which concerns content and not merely logical form, contains a transcendental presupposition, which he takes to be "the matter for all possibility, which in turn is supposed to contain *a priori* the data for the particular possibility of each thing" (*KrV* A573; B601).

Though Kant speaks of a "highest being," he is thinking mainly of a "transcendental substrate that contains, as it were, the whole store of matter from which all possible predicates of things must be taken," a substrate that "cannot be anything else than the idea of an all of reality [*omnitudo realitatis*]" (*KrV* 575; B603). What this suggests is not so much a being in *act,* as one expects in reading of a highest being, but rather some being purely in potency such as prime matter. This is quite in keeping with the idea of a sum total of all possibilities, that is, of all potency, since, taken in abstraction from any form actualizing it, pure being in potency, which we have referred to as prime matter, can be understood as the substrate that contains the whole store of matter from which must be taken all possible predicates that would express the actual forms of particular things. If our understanding of matter as a principle of being for things in becoming is correct, this idea of a sum total of all possibilities makes a lot of sense, but it is hardly what one should think of as the highest being *in act.* It seems to refer rather to the opposite end of the order of being, to the lowest kind of being or to being only in potency, which is not nothing, but which is not being in *act.*

We have seen how Kant ignored the question of being as being from the very beginning of our discourse in section 1.2. We have seen also how he ignored the very conception of being as act, only to remain in a conception of possibility even when speaking of real predicates in synthesis with their subject. For him, *Sein,* or be, could not be a predicate, as he explained in his dismissal of the ontological argument, so that to say that anything is or exists is not to say anything more than what is already said in saying "anything," whatever the anything may be. For Kant the question of reality or objectivity plays itself out completely in the order of predicates that can be joined synthetically to subjects, without reference to any *act* of being. This is why, in his presentation of the ideal of pure reason, he can so easily pass from possibility to reality or from reality to mere possibility. The question of objectivity for Kant is a question of finding predicates that are not contained in the positing of a subject, and nothing more. It begins and ends in what we have called the order of essence, without reference to any distinct order of actual existents or *Daseiende.*

Kant is so caught up in this Suarezian conception of finite being, where no real distinction is recognized between the essence of a thing, or *what* the thing is, and its *act* of being, that the question of being can no longer occur except as the question of *what* a thing is in its essence or its properties. To raise the question of being as distinct from the question of *what* a thing is would be for him to raise the question of another thing or another essence and hence to call into question the adequacy of the knowledge we already have of the thing we begin by positing. The idea of an *act* of being distinct from its essence in a determinate being simply does not occur to Kant, as it still did to Suarez, even though Suarez denied the distinction as real, so that when Kant comes to articulate the idea of a sum total of all possibilities, he has to think of it as a substrate or a kind of matter from which possible predicates can be taken, as forms are educed from the potency of their matter. To say that such a substrate, apart from any composition with form, can only be an idea, without objective existence, is quite right, since, as we have seen repeatedly, what comes to be or exists objectively for us in the direct exercise of judgment is the composite of matter and form, or a totality of such composites, and never just the material principal alone or a form alone.

But when, at the end of a metaphysics of the *act* of being, we come to raise the question of a universal cause of being, we are no longer talking about such a substrate. We are talking rather about something that cannot be understood in any way as a substrate or as being in potency, but only as an *act,* indeed, as a higher act than any act we know of in the composition of determinate or finite beings. This follows from the real distinction we have seen between *what* a finite being is and its *act* of being. It is this distinction that enables us to think of the highest being as a being in act and not just as a transcendental substrate for the possibility of particular things, an idea that tends to confuse the highest with the lowest in the order of being.

To be sure, Kant does speak of his transcendental idea as if it were unlimited in its perfection and of things as sharing in this perfection in limited ways. "The possibility of that which includes in itself all reality . . . must be regarded as original. For all negations (which are the only predicates through which anything can be distinguished from the *ens realissimum*) are merely limitations of a greater, and ultimately of the highest, reality; they therefore presuppose this reality, and are, as regards their content, derived from it" (*KrV* A578; B606). But this reality, as high as it might be conceived to be, is for Kant still only a "common substratum, just as all figures are only possible as so many different modes of limiting infinite space."

Kant speaks of a summit of being, but he cannot think of it except as a lowest common denominator for things given in experience, a matter for the possibility of all objects of the senses that must be presupposed as a sum total *(Inbegriff),* "and it is upon the limitation of this whole that all possibility of empirical objects, their distinction from each other and their complete determination, can alone be based. . . . Consequently nothing is *for us,* unless it presupposes the sum total of all empirical reality as the condition of its possibility" (*KrV* A582; B610). But it would be an illusion for us to posit this principle or sum total of all empirical reality as anything more than an idea that Kant may speak of as being of outstanding preeminence, on the one hand, but which he conceives of as only an empirical principle of our concepts, on the other. What is in question for Kant is not "to be taken as signifying the objective relation of an actual object to other things, but of an *idea to concepts.* We are left entirely without knowledge as to the existence of such outstanding preeminence" (*KrV* A579; B607).

What is at issue for us here, however, is not so much the existence of such outstanding preeminence, but rather the way of conceiving it. If it is conceived only as a substrate that contains the whole store of matter from which all possible predicates of things must be taken, then not only is there no knowledge as to its existence; there cannot be any such existence. If we know anything of such a substrate, as we saw with regard to prime matter as being in potency, it is that it cannot exist by itself. It can be only as the constitutive principle of material composites, along with their forms, from which it is really distinct, at least in things that come to be and cease to be, and it can be known as real only in its analogy to particular forms.

This is not the way to go if we are going to raise the question of a highest or a totally transcendent being. The summit of being, if it exists as something other than the totality of all possible objects of experience, cannot be understood as a material sum total of experience. We must distinguish it as *being in act* from all being in potency. Only in this way can there be a proper demonstration of the existence of such a being. What Kant thought had to be demonstrated cannot be demonstrated because, even as a sum total, it was still only a substrate, only being in potency. The true question of existence with regard to an outstanding preeminence arises only with regard to a being that is pure act and not pure potency.

Nor must we be too quick to identify the existence of such a being with the existence of an individual or a particular being of the kind we know in experience. As an ideal of pure reason, the sum total of all possibility is not just an idea removed from objective reality for Kant, but an idea "*in individuo,* that is, a singular thing, determinable, or rather quite determined through the idea alone" (*KrV* A568; B596). In other words, the sum total of all possibility is a "concept that is completely determinate *a priori*. It thus becomes the concept of an individual object that is completely determined through the mere idea, and must therefore be called an *ideal* of pure reason" (*KrV* A574; B602). In fact, it is "the only proper ideal of which human reason is capable, for only in this one case is a concept of a thing, a concept that is in itself universal, thoroughly determined through itself and known as the representation of an Individual" (*KrV* A576; B604). That individual, of course, is supposedly the supreme or the highest reality, which we may proceed to hypostatise as a single, simple, all-sufficient, eternal original essence, as Kant admits, but for him this ideal is still only "the supreme and complete material condition of the possibility of all that exists, the condition to which all thought of objects, so far as their content is concerned, has to be brought back" (Ibid.).

Here we must ask: In what sense is this ideal of pure reason an individual? Is it an individual in the same sense as individual composites of matter and form that come to be and cease to be? To the extent that Kant maintains that this ideal is the material condition of possibility to which all thought of objects must be brought back, we might be inclined to think so, since, as we have seen, matter is the principle of individuation. But matter, as being only in potency, cannot be thought of as supreme and complete in itself. As a concept that is in itself universal, it is not determinable or determinate through itself, but only through another principle, which is form, the principle of determination.

The ideal of pure reason thus cannot be an individual in the sense of a thing that comes to be and ceases to be, which is determinable or determinate through a principle distinct from its principle of individuation, even though as the highest it can be said to be singled out. But then what kind of an "individual" can it be? How is it singled out or how is it determinable or determinate through itself as an idea so that it can be understood as an object in itself distinct from any determinate object given in experience? Is it only as the material condition of the possibility of all that exists? Is it even possible that such a material condition exist as an individual determinate only through itself?

This is a question that Kant does not clearly face up to, except to say that the sum total of all possibility is at the same time the supreme or the highest being. This is clearly an ontological leap, which for him is unjustified, given his propensity to speak of this sum total as a material condition with regard to the content of objects given in experience. But why must this sum total be understood as the highest reality if it is only a material condition or a substratum, albeit a "transcendental" one, for material objects?

To get to the ideal of pure reason as the summit of being, Kant must make another ontological leap than the one he recognizes, one that starts from the being of objects as beings *in act,* and not just from their being in potency, so that being itself, or the *act* of being, is understood as a perfection, the perfection of perfections, or the highest of determinations that is no longer individual or particular in itself, as for individual determinate beings, but simply universal in a way that can single the highest being out from any finite being as simply infinite, encompassing all perfection, the perfection of being as well as the perfection of any determination in a finite being.

Such an ontological leap might be justified, but not from the standpoint of a material condition for any object of experience. To make the ontological leap to a highest being presupposes a certain metaphysical understanding of the structure of finite being such as we find at the end of metaphysics, where the *act* of being is understood as really distinct from its essence or determination and where the question of a highest *act* of being can be raised without confusing it with the question of a material condition for all determinate beings that come to be and cease to be, as Kant does.

For, if we distinguish the *act* of being of a determinate being from its essence, we should no longer confuse that *act* with anything that is constitutive of the essence, least of all with the matter or the material condition that is, along with form, constitutive of the essence, when the essence is itself a composite of matter and form, as we have seen in the case of beings that come to be and cease to be. If there is a highest or most perfect kind of being, it can only be conceived in terms of an *act,* and not as a material condition, no matter how "transcendental," of the beings we know in experience.

Indeed, it can be conceived only as *pure act* of being, as we shall try to show, which is what precisely singles it out, so to speak, from any other being, which, as finite, always entails some composition between *its act* of being and an essence that limits that *act.* In other words, the idea of a highest being cannot be singled out from individual determinate beings as only another individual determinate being that comes to be and ceases to be, nor just as a transcendental material condition of such being. It has to be singled out as a *pure act* above and beyond all material conditions. The question, then, is to see whether we have to affirm the existence of such an *act* as part of the ultimate intelligibility of being.

The question of the existence of a totally transcendent being is thus intimately connected with the understanding of a distinction between the *act* of being and its essence in finite being. The distinction gives us a way of conceiving what Kant calls the "idea of pure reason" without falling into the vicious circle in which he finds himself when he examines the logic of any proof of the existence of a totally transcendent being. What this means is that, as we approach this question, we must allow for another kind of existence than that which Kant conceives only for individual or particular objects of experience. For even when he singles out the ideal of pure reason as a determinate object in itself, he continues to think of existence only in terms of individual determinate things as found in experience. Hence it is that, when the question of existence is raised, the ideal is always reduced to being just an idea of reason, without any content of its own, while content, which gives us knowledge of existence, is found only on the side of objects in experience. Analysis alone of this idea will not yield any kind of synthesis with existence for Kant, even though we always have this idea as the condition to which our conception of real objects has to be brought back.

With Kant, therefore, we have to think of every object of experience as conditioned and as necessarily relating to an unconditioned, but we cannot affirm that unconditioned as existing because we are reduced to thinking of existence as relating only to individual determinate objects, or to a transcendental substrate of such objects. We are thus left hanging in a state of unknowing between the conditioned and the condition, and every attempt to say that the condition or, more exactly, the unconditioned exists is always interpreted as bringing the unconditioned into the chain of conditioned objects, which once again begs the question of an unconditioned.

To get out of this vicious circle in which Kant finds himself, and to which he would condemn human reason, we must have some prior conception of being as *act* over and above mere possibility and we must understand that the *act* of being in itself is not necessarily limited as it is in the case of finite beings. Such a conception is surely *a priori* in relation to any particular object of experience, but it is a way of opening up the question of a totally transcendent being beyond all possible experience, without reducing the question of such an existence to one of pure immanence, where being is finite and always a composite of a determinate essence and an *act* of being. Without such a conception of the *act* of being as distinct from any finite essence, which we have seen has to be maintained for any finite being, we cannot properly understand what is at issue in any discussion of whether there is a totally transcendent being that singles itself out only by being universal and infinite, unlike any other being, which, as distinct from the infinite, can only be finite, as we have shown in explaining how an act is not limited except by a subjective potency that receives it (section 14.4.1). This unreceived act, of which there can only be one, is neither limited nor multiplied. It is simply infinite or the sum of all perfections we can think of in being.

18.3   Demonstrating the Existence of a Totally Transcendent Being

The question, then, is whether there is a being such that it is totally transcendent to any being we know in experience and to the entire order of beings in the universe. We have to think of such a being as a summit in being, in the sense that it would the highest in the order of being, an absolute Summit of being, and then we have to ask whether such a Summit would still be immanent to the order of beings we know in experience or whether it would be totally transcendent to any such order. Hence the extreme difficulty of the question we are asking, since we can only answer the question from within the immanent order of being. If we can say that there is such a being, it is only from within an order where it is not to be found in its proper actuality.

In order to answer this question we cannot go immediately to *what* such a being would be in its substance or its essence, so that from a mere consideration of this essence we could deduce its existence, as is done in merely *a priori* arguments that proceed from the idea of a most perfect being or a necessary being. It is not that such arguments are false. It may very well be that they are true, if the idea of a Summit of being is properly understood. But they remain at best problematic for us, because we have no understanding of *what* such an essence would be in itself. The only idea of it we can have from where we stand in the universe of beings is too abstract or detached from any sense of actuality to afford us any passage to affirming that it is. Even if we cannot think of a most perfect being or a necessary being except as one that exists, as different versions of the ontological argument have maintained, this does not mean that we can immediately conclude that it does exist, for there is nothing that we know as being in the direct exercise of judgment, where we first exercise judgment as to what exists and what does not, that warrants such a conclusion from just an idea. If we are to come to the conclusion that such a being exists, we must find the warrant for it in the being that we know exists from experience.

What we take to exist in the first and most basic sense of the term for us is what we experience in the direct exercise of judgment, including ourselves as well as other selves and other kinds of determinate being. But we never think of having to prove the existence of such beings, except when faced with some radical skeptical doubt. Even in the face of skeptical doubt, we do not strictly prove that anything exists. We only show that the doubter is already affirming what he is purportedly denying in the very act of expressing his doubt, for it is only with a sense that knowing is of being, where our entire metaphysical enterprise has its beginning, that we come to think of our "knowing" as perhaps not true or as doubtful, that is, as perhaps not "of being."

Doubt arises in our knowing most fundamentally, as it should, only with some prior reference to being or to something we take to exist. What we doubt is not that there is something to be understood, but rather our understanding of what is present to us as being in experience. In fact, we could say that there is some such doubt in any exercise of judgment, as we go from questions for understanding to questions for reflection. Once we have formulated a clear understanding of something, we ask ourselves whether this understanding of ours is true to the thing to be understood. But always, we take the thing, whatever it may be, to be existing as the subject about which we are questioning.

The only time we feel compelled to prove the existence of anything is when we can find no immediate evidence in our experience for its presence in being, but find reasons for affirming something on the basis of something else immediately evident in experience, as we do even in the particular sciences. Physicists argue to the existence of all sorts of things or quanta that we could not possibly experience directly in any way. And economists similarly argue to hidden causes for what they observe more directly in their statistics, even if it be such a mysterious power as an invisible hand in "the market" or the more visible hands that can be found manipulating strings in the market behind its back.

One can contest such particular affirmations of existence without denying one's own affirmation that there is knowing of being, because they are only reasoned conclusions to some existence. One may not only doubt the reasons given but also have other reasons for denying the conclusion to such an existence. The argument in any case always begins from some understanding that there is some being to be interpreted and accounted for and it proceeds from some understanding of that being that both contenders agree upon as a first evidence.

Hence having to prove the existence of anything in any science is always bound to be difficult, especially as we seem to be approaching what is most significant for the existence of what we start from as existing. We normally start from some existence and take it for granted, and what we take to exist in the most basic and fundamental sense for us are what we have spoken of as the determinate beings whose presence is immediately given in experience. If we assume that all our ideas about these beings are always right, we soon find out that they are not necessarily so, and that bright ideas alone, not even the brightest idea of them all, that of a most perfect or a necessary being, are not enough to assure the truth of any claim regarding existence based only on the idea.

This does not mean that we should reject all ideas out of hand, for sciences, particular as well as universal, are made up of such ideas. Nor does it mean that we should reject the brightest of them all. It means only that we cannot go directly from the idea as thought by us to actual existence. The best that we can do is use it as a heuristic means for raising questions about being and for exploring the causes of being, universal as well as particular, as we have been doing up to now in our metaphysical discourse.

But if we wish to argue for the existence of a universal cause of being, we must go one step further. We must start from what we take to be something in existence in the way that determinate being presents itself and proceed to ask if there is anything in this something that would point to the existence of such a cause, which is not and cannot be directly given in our experience, since we have to prove its existence. In the process we may discover not only that such a being does exist, whatever existence may mean in that case, but also a better idea of it that would enable us to understand why such a being has to exist. For if we do arrive at affirming an absolute Summit of being, we may come to a better understanding of why such a being is necessary not only from our standpoint in being but also in itself, even if we still cannot say *what* it is in its essence as we can say *what* determinate beings are in their essence. In other words, through the *a posteriori* proof we may come to see why the *a priori* proof remains as part of our understanding of what we have proven, even though in the end it may still be impossible to make the *a priori* proof work all by itself without the *a posteriori* proof.

What, then, do we have to start from in the direct exercise of judgment to prove the existence of an absolute Summit of being, if there is one? Apart from the ontological or *a priori* argument, which he rejected, of course, Kant distinguished between two different arguments *a posteriori:* the cosmological, which proceeded from a general experience of contingency in the world as a whole, and the physicotheological, which was based more upon observations of particular properties of the world disclosed to us by our senses (*KrV* A615; B633 & A620; B648). The difference between them, as Kant saw it, seems to have been that the cosmological argument barely made any reference to actual existence or experience in general before reverting back to the old ontological attempt to derive existence from the concept of a most perfect being, while the physicotheological dwelt longer on the order of causes and effects in the world in order to arrive at some highest cause for the universe as a whole, before once again reverting to the ontological argument in order to attribute to the first cause what we think of as proper to our ideal of the most perfect and necessary being. But we can rightly ask whether the two are really different arguments or whether they are not rather one and the same argument, one a more condensed version of the other, since both do claim to start from the experience of order in the universe in order to arrive at some highest being.

For his part, Aquinas speaks of five ways to prove the existence of God, all of them *a posteriori,* as he insists quite emphatically in opposition to his fellow theologian Anselm (*ST* I, 2, 1–3), each way laying out different elements of what can be found in the cosmological, the physicotheological, and even the ontological arguments as later thought of by Kant, in order to bring one who is asking whether a totally transcendent being exists to an affirmative conclusion. Here again we could ask whether these are really five different arguments or whether they are not just different versions of one and the same argument, the difference between Aquinas and Kant being that, while Kant thinks there can be no valid argument for affirming the existence of a highest, most perfect being, Aquinas thinks that he has at least one, based on a metaphysical understanding of the universe we experience as being. How can such a metaphysical understanding yield a proof for the existence of an absolute Summit of being?

We should bear in mind that the question before us now at the *end* of metaphysics is similar in some respects to the question that was before us at the *beginning* of metaphysics. At the beginning we had to focus our questioning on being as being in contradistinction from any one or all of the particular sciences, which always focus on being under some particular aspect or other. Our question had to do not with being as physical, or as living, or as a product of labor, but with being simply as being. Being, which is presupposed as being in every particular science, we argued, has to come into question at the point where all the particular sciences cease or converge in their determination. In other words, being must eventually be taken as the subject of a new science in its own right, namely, the science of being as being.

At the same time, however, we should bear in mind that the situation or the question at the *end* of metaphysics is no longer the same as it was at the beginning. We have come a long way in our metaphysical understanding of being and the question that remains before us is much more pointed than it was or could have been at the beginning. Having arrived at some understanding of both the intrinsic and the extrinsic causes of being within the universe, that is, intrinsic to each determinate being as well as extrinsic to the same determinate beings within the totality of what we experience as being, we now come to the question of a single universal cause of being for all of these beings in common, or as being, and for the universe that they constitute together through their action and interaction, since the universe itself can only be understood as the totality of beings we find present in our experience. We have to speak of this cause as a universal cause because it would be the cause of all that is, or all there is in our experience, and we have to understand it as a single cause because we understand it as the cause of a single universe, namely, the totality of all there is in our experience of being.

We raise this question now, at the *end* of metaphysics, already knowing something about the properties of being and the causes of determinate being, including final and efficient causes, at least within the immanent order of the universe. We do not have an exhaustive knowledge of all there is or all that presents itself as being in the universe of our experience, but we do have an understanding of how determinate beings are ontologically constituted in their individuality and particularity, and how there is communication of being among these many and diverse determinate types of being within the universe. And it is from this understanding of determinate causation among the diverse beings of the universe we know in experience that the question arises as to whether there is a first cause to be understood as operative over and above, or perhaps even within, all particular causes, for the action of the first cause may be such that it enters directly into the action and the being of each particular cause. The problem for us is to understand how the first cause does act in the action of particular or secondary causes, so that we may recognize its existence even from within the immanent order of the universe.

In demonstrating an answer to the question of whether there is a totally transcendent being such that it cannot be merely given in experience or understood as part of the universe of experience, one has to start from experience, as we have been doing for the whole of our metaphysical discourse. But we cannot proceed directly from experience, as we do in the particular sciences. We must proceed indirectly, as we have also been doing in the whole of this metaphysical discourse. We can focus on different aspects of being as given in experience, as Aquinas does in the first three ways he suggests, the one starting from beings we see in motion, the one starting from beings we understand as effects, and the one starting from beings understood as contingent. But we must then ask how they are moved, how they are effects, or how they are contingent. These are questions we have already asked in raising the question of the efficient cause in the communication of being. We have seen that what is moved has to be moved by a *moving cause* other than itself; that what is an effect in the proper sense of the term has to be the effect of a *cause other than itself;* and that what is contingent, in that it comes to be and ceases to be, has to depend on some other being that is not contingent, in other words, on *some necessary being* such as a universal cause that does not come to be and cease to be in the way that its particular or contingent effects do.

Recognition of such efficient causes that are higher or at least the equal of their effects in being is already an important step or middle term on the way to an answer to the question as to whether there is a totally transcendent being. It points in the direction of beings that are not only other than the ones we start from in experience, but also *higher* and *more necessary* in being than the beings we start from as moved, as effects, or as contingent. But it does not yet point in the direction of a totally transcendent cause. There are many ways of representing the kind of causation we are speaking about in the various particular sciences, about which there can be all sorts of agreement and disagreement, in physics as well as in biology or economics. To explore each order of movement from the moved to the mover tends to be an unending task. Each time we arrive at the mover that accounts for some movement in one thing or in one order of things, we discover that it too is moved and so we are driven to look for its mover, and so on and on.

In this sense, every particular science is a never ending quest for what might be an ulterior cause, because with every mover found there is always the discovery that it too is moved, which means that it too must be moved by another. Even when we have come to some conception of the universe as a whole, with a list of entities that make it up and a spatiotemporal structure to tie them all together, what the physicalist may refer to as the manifest universe, or the universe as presently known or categorized (Post 117), we may still be led to suppose some other universe to account for the motion of this manifest universe or at least to think of the manifest universe itself as "eternal," "immutable," "uncreated," "self-existent," "necessary," with respect to the more particular causes known in the particular sciences.

In a more indirect exercise of judgment, however, such as we have been exercising in metaphysics, we come to an understanding of the universe as a totality, both natural and historical, in which there is an order of effects and causes and of causes that are themselves caused by some other cause and so on. We have not gone into all the ramifications of this order, which can be studied in the diverse ways of particular sciences. But as metaphysicians, or as scientists of being as being, we must inquire into the universal direction of this order and ask whether there has to be a first cause that would be the cause of the order and of everything in it, without taking away from the action and the being of the things that make up the universe, including the intelligence and the willing of human beings.

This is a question that cannot be answered in any further pursuit of the particular sciences, but that can only be answered from a consideration of the entire movement as a whole as we already understand it in the direct exercise of judgment or in the diverse particular sciences. Can we understand this entire order of *per se* subordinated causes as real if we take every cause as somehow moved by another cause, so that we are left with an unending chain of caused and causing, or do we have to come finally to some first cause that is cause but not caused by any other, an *unmoved Mover* or an *uncaused Cause* that would then have to be understood as a Summit or as an absolutely First with regard to the entire order? If we assume that every thing that moves another is always only moved by another and so on and on, would we have any movement at all in the universe or would the thing we first take to be in motion actually be in motion as we take it to be?

It is difficult for us to think of such an order of *per se* subordinated causes in terms of the entire universe, because it is so complex and because there are still so many parts of it that we do not understand in any one of the particular sciences, let alone in the science of the whole. Let us consider a more simple case of such a *per se* order among things that are moved and things that actively move them, like that of a game of pool or even a single shot of pool where a player sinks the eight ball in the corner pocket of a pool table. If he does this as he must according to the rule, he must use a cue to hit the cue ball and use the cue ball to push the eight ball in the direction of the pocket. In this case the eight ball is moved by another, the cue ball, which is the moving cause of its motion. This moving cause, however, is itself moved by another, that is, by the cue, which is the moving cause of the cue ball's motion. The cue is in turn moved by the pool player. We could go on to ask if the pool player is moved as well and, if so, by what other, and so on.

If, however, we take this action of the pool player as a self-contained order of movement among four different things subordinated to one another in this movement as a whole, namely, the eight ball, which is taken here as only moved and not as moving something else, the cue ball and the cue, both of which are seen as both moved and moving something else, and the pool player artfully using the cue in such a way as to get the cue ball to push the eight ball into corner pocket, and if we assume it to be an extremely difficult shot exhibiting the pool player's championship caliber as the originator of this motion, we are then thinking of the pool player as the first cause in this order of moved and moving causes, not only for one single shot but also for all the shots he makes as part of a game or on the way to a championship.

Let us then ask if there would be any of these motions among the different things we have distinguished as moved and moving, respectively, if there were not the initial moving of the pool player, who is the first mover in all his shots but who is himself unmoved in relation to the way that the cue, the cue ball, or the eight ball are moved. If there were only a chain of things moved by other things, like the eight ball is moved by the cue ball or the cue ball by the cue, without a first mover like the pool player, who is quite a different kind of mover than either the cue or the cue ball, there would be no movement at all in the eight ball caused by the cue ball, whose movement is in turn caused by the cue.

Thus from the existence of the movements on the pool table we can conclude to the existence of the pool player as the *first cause* of these subordinated movements in the one shot sinking the eight ball. If every mover were only an intermediate in the series of movements, if there were no first, which stands above the series as somehow unmoved, there would be no movement at all. From the standpoint of this series of *per se* subordinated moving causes, therefore, we have to conclude to the necessity of a first, unmoved mover, even though from another standpoint we might also think of the unmoved mover as affected by some desire to achieve some good or as moved by a coach.

This conclusion rests squarely on the understanding of two things in a series of subordinated movements: first, that whatever is moved is moved by another, so that in every instance of something moved we have to think of something else moving it; and second, that in thinking of an other as the moving cause at any particular point in the series, we cannot assume that we could go on indefinitely, as if there were no first mover, for without a first mover of some kind there would be no movement to begin with in our experience, just as without the pool player there would be no movement of a ball on the pool table caused by an other ball or by a cue.

Thus, the first Mover we arrive at in the order of *per se* subordinated movement in the universe has to be other than anything in the movement and it must be unmoved, at least with respect to the movement in which it is the first cause. In other words, the first moving cause of a series of moving and moved causes cannot itself be just another moving cause in the series that is moved. If it is first, it has to be unmoved, uncaused, or absolutely necessary in itself, without having its necessity from anything else.

Coming to the existence of a first Cause in this way makes it difficult, if not impossible, for us to grasp *what* the first Cause is since we can only represent it from the standpoint of the series as such or some particular moved mover in the series, since every moving cause we know in the series is also moved by another. In other words, it is difficult to grasp what the pool player is from just the standpoint of the movements we observe on the pool table. But it is still possible to affirm the existence of the pool player as the necessary extrinsic cause of the movement on the table, as we do when we proclaim him champion, and it is necessary for us to affirm the existence of such a first mover, if we wish to come to the fullness of the truth about that movement or the effect we actually observe as existing. Having affirmed the existence of a first unmoved Mover, we are then left with the question of understanding *what* it is in itself or as other than the entire order of which it is the cause and as other than the beings in that order.

There are many instances of such series of subordinated movements in the order of nature. If we apply this understanding to the order of nature as a whole or to the universe as we know it through things moved by other things, we are led to the conclusion that there must be one thing, which is the mover of everything that we experience as moved, a thing that is itself unmoved, that is, one being that is not part of the entire movement of which it is the mover, nor of anything in it, since such a part, even when it is a mover, is still moved by something else caught up in the movement. Such a conclusion to an unmoved Mover is a leap beyond anything given or possible in experience or beyond the whole of what is given in this experience, and there is no guarantee that we can ever know *what* such an unmoved Mover is in itself, but the affirmation of such a necessary unmoved Mover or uncaused Cause is itself necessary from our very understanding of things moved and things moving in the universe understood as a series of subordinated things moved and moving.

Once we arrive at the affirmation of such an absolutely unmoved Mover or uncaused Cause, the temptation is to bring it back into the series, as only one more thing in the chain of causes and effects, as Kant did, when he maintained that the principle of causality is "applicable only in the sensible world," outside of which "it has no meaning whatsoever" (*KrV A600; B637*), and as physicalism still does in speaking of the first Cause as the spatiotemporal "sum of all the ultimate explainers plus anything else that has no explanation (even for an infinite intelligence)" (Post 136), as if these were still only parts of the physical universe, or of the "sum total of all the events, entities, and processes that explain but have no explanation, plus any that have no explanation and do not explain either" (Post 137). But we have to resist this temptation, which is contrary to the very conception of the Cause we have arrived at as first, uncaused, and absolutely necessary in itself.

It has been argued that the universe itself is this absolutely necessary being, on the grounds that it is the explanation for everything but is not itself explained by anything else, so that it is itself the first Cause or the uncaused Cause (Post 131–38). For the physicalist, who can think of being only in physical terms, this can be a convincing and conclusive argument, since nothing can be conceived beyond the physical universe in physicalist terms. If every being can only be a physical existent, then, to be sure, being can only be part of the physical universe. And every newly discovered existent can only be conceived as one more thing to add to one's conception of the universe in its necessity, one more thing that may remain unexplained, as the universe itself remains unexplained. Hence, according to the physicalist, the universe itself is not the sort of thing that can allow for anything that is not a part of it, "since by hypothesis every existent is a part of it" (Post 130). But is this hypothesis justified in nonreductionist terms and is the universe itself the only kind of necessary being we arrive at from our experience of contingency in the universe?

It is not enough to think of necessary being as only that which remains unexplained or unexplainable in a particular frame of reference such as that of physics, even if it be the being of the physical universe. Nor is it enough to think of that necessity within the universe of experience only in physical terms. One has to allow for different degrees of necessity in accordance with the different degrees of being that present themselves in experience through the analogy of being. Could we not argue for a certain kind of necessity in the order of life as part of the universe, that is, for a certain higher form of being that remains unexplained and unexplainable in biological as well as physical terms but that itself would explain or account for the living things that come to be and cease to be? And could not a similar case be made for the higher forms of life as well, such as sentient life and, beyond all these levels of being, rational life? All the beings that are contingent in these higher orders of being are not explained or explainable in merely physical terms, but they are explainable in terms of higher forms of being that are also part of the universe and its necessity.

Even if we include these higher forms of necessary being in the universe, along with those of physicalism, however, we still have not reached the kind of necessary being that is uncaused. For all of these different kinds of being are still only parts of the universe that can or may be explained or accounted for with reference to other parts of the universe or to the universe as a whole. Each order of necessity has its place in the order of the whole. In fact, even the universe itself as a whole, including what we do not know of it as well as what we do know, cannot be thought of as uncaused, for it is still made up of these parts, and as such it still has to be accounted for. Even if it is the ultimate frame of reference for the kind of explaining we can do within the universe, it is still something that remains ontologically *contingent* even in its necessity.

This is not to say that we can have an explanation for the entire universe of being similar to the explanations we may come up with for the different parts of the universe in which there is contingency, or that we can ultimately have an explanation for the universe as such. It is only to say that the universe itself cannot be the cause of its own necessity and that some other kind of necessity must be sought to account for its necessity, an absolutely first Necessity that is uncaused. It is in the absolutely necessary transcendent Being, which we can affirm and which we cannot adequately understand, that the mystery of the universe ultimately resides, and not in the universe itself, not even in what remains unknown to us of it.

All this has been argued from the standpoint of a *per se* subordinated order of causes in the universe. One could also argue for a similar idea of the existence of an absolutely First in the order of being more directly from our understanding of diverse degrees of being and goodness in experience, such as the diversity between living things and nonliving things, sentient things and nonsentient things, rational things and nonrational things. Some of these we understand as higher in being than others, once again according to some order of dignity in the analogy of being. In our discussion of this analogy we have insisted on human being not only as our primary analogate, but also as the highest kind of being given or present to us in experience. Our point was not to say that human being is absolutely the highest kind of being, but only the highest kind we know directly in experience, and that there are also lower kinds of being according to different degrees of being, each of them real, true, and good, or with its own dignity as a being in its own standing, however less this might be in comparison to the dignity of human being in its standing.

In fact, our understanding of being in its analogy allows us to conceive of beings of even higher dignity than human being with proportionately higher degrees of truth and goodness, such as totally immaterial substances or separate intelligences, of which we have no direct experience but whose existence is by no means inconceivable, unless we postulate that there can be only material substances, as materialism and perhaps physicalism would appear to do rather arbitrarily. In conceiving of such higher substances, we are not abandoning human being as the primary analogate of being in our experience. We are only taking off from this primary analogate, and our understanding of it as an intelligent being in its standing, to think of what an intelligent being, or a separate intelligence, would be if it did not have the limitations of being at the same time a material being, as human being does.

We do not have to suppose that there are such higher degrees of being as separate intellectual substances. But to the extent that we do think of different degrees of being, even within the ontological order of beings we know in experience, we do have to think of some highest or some Summit of being that is absolutely the highest and that is not part of the ontological order we start from. We cannot think of different degrees of being, or of higher and lower degrees, without reference to such a *highest* or *first* in the order of being. For different degrees are understood as higher or lower in relation to one another in an order of being only to the extent that some are understood as closer to a highest while others are understood as more distant from that same highest.

This is what Aquinas presents as the fourth way of proving the existence of the totally transcendent Being. The idea of a relation to a highest, as we first come to understand it, is expressed in spatial terms, so that what is highest is still represented as part of the order in which it is the highest. But in the ontological order of dignity that we are distinguishing here, this representation of the highest no longer holds. As highest in the order of being, the first cannot be like any of the different kinds of finite or determinate substances that are compared to one another in their different degrees of being. For, as highest, it is not in any way compared or related to any other. This follows from what we have said in section 14.4.2 about an unreceived act as neither limited nor multiplied. On the contrary, all others as composites are compared to it and found lesser in their determinacy, including the first next to or after the highest. The first or the highest in the ontological order of being has to be absolutely the Highest unto itself, absolutely Infinite, without comparison to any determinate being where there is a composition of an *act* of being that is received and thereby limited by a finite essence. As we saw in speaking of the composition of potency and act in determinate being as such in section 14.4, the first or the highest Being can only be an unreceived pure act that is infinite.

The argument here starts from the metaphysical judgment that there are different degrees of being or different degrees of dignity in being in the world we know directly in experience. In this sense it is *a posteriori*. It is based on our understanding of being in its substantial differences in this world. But it leads us to the affirmation of a Being that cannot be of this world as the basis for our judgment that some things are higher, or lower, than others in the order of beings as a whole. What each being is within the order of the universe, of course, depends on the form that constitutes it in its degree of being. But what each one is as higher or lower in dignity of being depends on yet another being, the absolutely Highest, in relation to which each is graded, so to speak, in its being, and upon which it depends for its very being in its own degree. For the absolutely Highest is not only the point of reference in our judgment about different degrees of dignity in being, but also the cause of being in all these differences. It has all priority in being, and upon it all other beings depend in their very being, since the cause is what has priority over the effect.

There is yet another way of proving the existence of a totally transcendent Being that depends less on any *per se* order of moving or efficient causes in the universe and more on finality in beings as they appear in our experience, especially in the beings that have no consciousness and hence do not act of themselves in view of an end. This is the way Aquinas referred to as the fifth and Kant found the most persuasive of all the *a posteriori* arguments. Evidence for this finality in nature does not have to suppose any kind of consciousness on the part of many beings we observe in nature. In fact, the argument works best especially with regard to those beings in which there is no consciousness out of which action in view of an end would come.

In this argument we do not have to ask what precisely is the end in view of which intellectual beings may act or in view of which the things without consciousness may act, as we did earlier, in section 15.2, in speaking of finality in nature. It is enough to see that they do have some direction in their action and to ask whence is this finality, if it is not from themselves. If we think of nature as a whole in this way, as we surely do when we inquire into the causes of certain determinate effects, we are led to affirm an intellectual being, which does act in view of an end, as the cause of these beings, the cause that orders them to certain determinate ends as it produces them in their nature. In other words, the discovery of intelligence in nature, at least in the sense of things acting in view of an end, leads us to the affirmation not of some kind of conscious intelligence in nature as such, but of an intelligence that produces them in and as nature.

This intelligence we have to think of as the first Cause of these beings of nature, since it produces them in their very nature, and again, since it is the first Cause, we have to think of it as the absolute Summit of being, the very Summit to which we refer in our judgment about different degrees of perfection in being, and as having already to be understood as intellectual.

Against this final version of the argument, the objection has been made that it does not require positing an absolute intelligence, since it proves the necessity only of an intelligence sufficient to account for the intelligibility or the rational finality in nature itself, which is determinate and finite as we know it, and does not exhaust all possible intelligibility. This is the objection of Kant, mentioned earlier at the beginning of this discussion of ways to prove the existence of an absolute summit of being, against any physicotheological argument, which, according to him, always requires the introduction of an ontological argument to conclude from a very intelligent being, one sufficient to account for the intelligibility of nature as a whole, to one that is absolutely intelligent or the sum of all intelligibility, goodness, and whatever other perfection there is in being (*KrV* A624; B652–A630; B658).

It is important to consider this objection at least with reference to this final version of the argument, where its strength seems most obvious, if not with reference to every version of the argument for the necessity of an absolute Summit of being, because it shows the difficulty of any argument going from what is relative to what is absolute, or from what is finite in its perfection to what is infinite in its perfection. It shows a keen sense of the radical difference between what we start from in our understanding and what we supposedly arrive at affirming, an absolute Summit that is not part of anything we understand. It is not just that our understanding is finite. What it is that we understand in being is also finite or determinate. How can it be grounds for affirming a Summit of being that is absolute and positively infinite?

Two things must be kept clearly in mind in answering this question. First, it is not the existence of an absolute Summit of being as such that we are trying to ground. The existence of such a being is not in need of any grounding. If there is such a being, it is itself the ground of everything else that is grounded. What has to be grounded is our affirmation that there is such a Being, which can then be understood only as the ground for everything else we say there is.

Second, it must be understood that we are arguing about a first Cause of the order of nature as a whole, which means that it is a universal Cause, one to which none of its particular effects can be proportionate, as in the case of particular causes. When we argue from effect to cause within the order of nature or of history, we usually proceed according to some proportion or similitude between a determinate effect and its particular cause, and we are entitled to affirm nothing more about the cause than what is proportionate to the effect. Kant's objection is quite valid in this respect. From a finite effect understood as finite we can arrive at no more than a finite cause. But it does not take an ontological leap to break out of this finitude in the case of the first and universal Cause of everything, since such a Cause can only be understood as infinite in relation to its finite effects or as not determined in the way that the effect is determinate.

To illustrate this kind of universal causality, let us go back to the example of our champion pool player. We know this champion to be the first cause in a series of subordinated moved and moving causes that displays great intelligence in conception and skill in execution. But as a champion, we do not think of this individual as capable of only one determinate shot, as if this shot alone would define the champion. If so, we would be unable to distinguish the champion from another who might sink the same shot out of beginner's luck, which usually runs out rather quickly and disappears. We think of the champion as one who has proven the caliber of a champion by a series of good shots, usually in competition with other players who have not made as good shots, and as one who can go on with more spectacular shots that we have not seen yet and that perhaps no one else could imagine, except possibly a better champion or a coach of champions.

In other words, we understand the champion as a universal cause in pool playing and as far from being determined by any particular shot taken. There is no single defining moment for such a cause. There are only many moments, each one different from the other and none of them defining for the cause. The champion is the universal cause not only of all the particular shots taken, but also of any number of other shots one might dream up beyond what we have seen. Thus in affirming an individual as a champion on the basis of a plurality of shots we have marveled at, we affirm a lot more than what we have seen in the realm of pool playing, without making an ontological leap and without knowing precisely all that we are affirming, since the champion could still astound us with shots we have yet to imagine.

The same thing might be said of an artist, who is recognized not only in a plurality of works of which the individual is understood to be the universal cause but also in the power to produce other works that are not determined by anything already given in experience. The recognized artist too is a universal cause whose existence is affirmed without knowing precisely all that lies in the artist's power. When we recognize the artist as the cause of a particular work, we may also recognize the same artist as the cause of other works as well, some of which we may already admire, and as one capable of more works that no one else could produce. And however we may conceive of the artist's inspiration, we do not think of it as limited by what is given in the materials one has to work with but rather as bringing a new order to these materials through intelligence and skill, head and hand.

The idea of a universal cause within nature does not in itself necessarily entail intelligence and skill, but in the case we are speaking of, that is, with regard to the finality we see in nature, it does entail intelligence and skill, as does any championship shot in pool or any work of consummate art. We do see what we take to be the effect of an intelligence in nature and from that we affirm the existence of an intelligence, which, as universal cause, is not confined in its particular effect, namely, the universe of nature and history, but rather transcends it in a way that includes all its perfections as well as more than anything we may be able to think of. Such transcendence of a universal intelligent Cause cannot be understood as merely that of a higher being than the determinate beings we know in nature, which would make it still just another determinate or finite being in the universe of determinate beings separate from other determinate or finite beings. It cannot be understood as just a higher champion in a world of pool players or as a higher intelligence in the art of creating worlds. It has to be understood as the Highest, as positively infinite in its perfection or as absolutely transcending all determinate or finite forms of being or perfection, just as the pool player transcends any particular orchestration of shots or the artist transcends any particular work of art or any portfolio of works.

Thus the argument from finality in nature grounds an affirmation that there is an intelligent universal Cause of the universe. But it does not ground any understanding of *what* that absolute Summit is in and of itself. This is what the ontological argument in Descartes or Spinoza seems to claim and what Kant himself seems to have been looking for in any proof for the existence of God, confined as he was to the idea or the order of particular causes. Such a claim, however, cannot be justified with regard to the affirmation of an absolutely first universal Cause. We should not be looking for an understanding of *what* the universal Cause is on the basis of effects that are only particular.

By definition, a universal Cause cannot be defined in terms of any of its particular effects, even if that be the universe of being as a whole. *What* we understand, at least up to a point, is only the effect, and not the cause. And when we affirm the Cause, we cannot affirm it as if we knew *what* it is in itself. We can affirm it only as transcending what we do understand, namely, any determinate being or the totality of all determinate beings. Moreover, we can affirm it only as infinitely more perfect than anything we do understand, without knowing precisely *what* it is we are affirming in its own perfection. There is no need for an ontological leap to affirm that there is such an intelligent universal Cause. On the contrary, understood properly, the argument shows that there cannot be an ontological argument of the kind Kant had in mind, since that would entail somehow knowing *what* the transcendent universal Cause is, and this we cannot know from any particular effect, even if it be the universe as a whole.

We find here a remarkable convergence in the thought of Aquinas, who proposes five ways to prove the existence of God, and of Kant, who objects to these ways on the grounds that they do not give us any certain knowledge of *what* is affirmed in the end. Both agree that we cannot know *what* it is that we have to affirm in the end of our inquiry into the causes of things. Even as a theologian, Aquinas insists that we cannot know what God is. We can only know what God is *not,* namely, that God is not like anything we know in the world, including ourselves, or even not like anything we could know in the world, for there are still many things about the world we do not know.

But whereas Kant takes occasion of this agnosticism with regard to *what* God is in his essence to deny all validity not only to the ontological proof for the existence of God, but also to any proof *a posteriori* as well as *a priori,* Aquinas still insists that we can demonstrate that God *is* without knowing *what* that is. Kant expects to know *what* a thing is in itself or according to what it is at the end of a demonstration and so denies that there can be a demonstration of the existence of God, just as he denies that we can know any noumenal object or *Ding an sich.* Aquinas, following the *Posterior Analytics* of Aristotle, distinguishes between two kinds of demonstration, one *a priori,* which proceeds from the definition of *what* a thing is and arrives at a property of the thing, and another *a posteriori,* which proceeds from effects and arrives at their cause, without knowing *what* the cause is in itself, but also without denying that we do know *what* the effects are "in themselves" or in their substance.

Such an *a posteriori* demonstration from effects to cause gives true knowledge of the conclusion that there is a totally transcendent Being and it does give rise to the *question* of *what* such a being is. But even after it is understood that this last question about *what* such a being is cannot be answered from where we stand in a metaphysics of determinate being, the truth of the conclusion to the demonstration as to its existence is not denied. In fact, it is understood not only that there has to be an unmoved Mover, an uncaused Cause, a Being necessary in and of itself, a highest or most perfect Being, and a first Intelligence governing the order of the universe, but also that there is no way of understanding *what* that being is in its own essence from where we stand in experience.

From this it might be argued that, if we do not and cannot know *what* such a being is in its essence, it makes no difference whether we say that it *is* or *is not,* since in either case we still do not know *what* we are talking about. But that would be a mistake on our part, even if we do not know *what* it is that we are affirming in its essence. For it is the affirmation itself, namely, that there is an absolute Summit of being, that is a moment of truth for us in our inquiry into the immediate and into the ultimate causes of being as we know it in the universe. In our search for causes we are driven from one cause to the next not just as a succession of things coming one after the other, but also as an order of causes that are themselves caused and that therefore do not exercise their causality independently of higher causes. With each new higher cause discovered we enter more deeply into the truth of being, for the cause always has priority in being over its effect. But we also know, in this understanding of subordinate causes, that there has to be a first Cause that is uncaused if there is to be any causation at all, for none of the caused causes can cause without the causation of that first uncaused Cause.

This is the ultimate moment of truth in our inquiry into being and its causes, which can always be enhanced by a better understanding of the always subordinate causes in the universe, since none of them can be the first or uncaused. But it is a moment that can be reached even before we have reached a perfect understanding of how everything works or conspires in the universe. In fact, it is a moment that has to be reached even before we reach any such perfection of understanding, since it is the truth of this Summit of being which sets us on our way in the inquiry into the causes of being, just as it is itself the uncaused Cause of all other causes, which are therefore understood as caused and subordinate to the first One. The entire argument hinges on this necessity for a first, to account for all the rest, and through this necessity we come to some understanding of the total transcendence of this absolute Summit of being, without understanding *what* it consists in.

18.4   The Total Transcendence of the Summit of Being

To speak of a Summit of being, however, is to speak of something that could still be understood as part of the immanent order of being from which we begin our investigation into being and its causes. In this sense we could speak of the human being or the human spirit as the summit of the order of being we know immediately in experience. But it is not in this sense that we are speaking of the absolute Summit of being, for, as the un-moved Mover, the uncaused Cause, the Being necessary in and of itself, the highest or the first Being, or the supreme Intelligence, the absolute Summit of being cannot be part of what we take to be the immanent order of deter-minate being. This is implicit in the different ways we have used for affirm-ing that there is such an absolute Summit. It is what we shall refer to as the total transcendence of this Summit and, in conclusion of this argument for saying that there is such a Being that totally transcends the immanent order of being, it is important to bring out in what way it is totally transcendent and why it has be understood as such.

We should note, to begin with, that there is something quite paradoxical in saying such a thing, for it is being said from within an immanent order about something that is totally transcendent to this order. It is an affirmation of reason about something that totally transcends reason. Thus, we are speak-ing of a paradox in the Kierkegaardian sense of the term, but we are affirm-ing it in the name of reason itself, as the conclusion of our investigation into the causes of being. For at the *end* of metaphysics, where we find ourselves, we find ourselves having to affirm rationally something that cannot be total-ly taken in by reason, that is, something that reason has to point to, so to speak, but without being able to grasp it totally as it is in itself. This is the only thing of which it can be said that we cannot know strictly *what* it is in itself, but it is not a thing in the order of experience. In fact, it is not a thing at all, if by "thing" we understand any sort of determinate being. Even when we say that it is, we cannot say that it is a determinate being in accordance with our first conception of being, which, as we saw in section 3.1, signifies according to a mode of concretion and composition.

How can reason come to understand such an affirmation? In a way, as Hegel maintained against Kant and Jacobi in his early essay on *Faith and Knowledge* (GW 1802), reason cannot allow for anything beyond itself. Rea-son is either the power of understanding being as whole or it is the order of being itself as it presents itself to understanding. Our investigation into the causes of being is an exercise of reason itself in which reason discovers the order of being. Hence, at the *end* of metaphysics, where we come to some understanding of beings and their causes as a whole, it would seem that we are encompassing everything there is to be understood. And indeed we are, for what there is in the totality of our experience is the measure of reason itself and of what there is to be understood. Yet the thrust of reason does not end there. All the causes that we discover as part of the order of reason in the universe are themselves caused and therefore give rise to a further question about an uncaused Cause, which cannot be part of this order of reason but which is necessary to account for the order of reason itself as it discloses itself in the universe.

We can speak of this uncaused Cause as infinitely perfect, containing all the perfections of the beings we know in the universe in a supereminent way. This corresponds to what Hegel speaks of as the good infinite, as opposed to the bad infinite, which represents no more than an indefinite stringing out of individuals according to some form of $n + 1$. But the uncaused Cause is a good infinite that perhaps expresses more than what Hegel had in mind. For Hegel, the good infinite, which is a unity of the finite and the infinite, that is, of the infinite still understood as only opposed to the finite and therefore as still only finite, puts us in the realm of spirit, but it is not clear whether this spirit is truly the Spirit as uncaused Cause. If it is only the World Spirit, which is at the same time the human spirit, it is still part of the immanent order of being and hence not totally transcendent, as the uncaused Cause has to be.

In this respect Hegel's thought is at best ambiguous. While he seems to be a genuine theist in the eyes of most, he has also been interpreted as an atheist by some serious commentators like Kojève. Without going into the details of what precisely Hegel is affirming in his proof for the existence of God (*BDG* 1966), we would insist that the uncaused Cause we arrive at at the *end* of metaphysics cannot be understood as part of the immanent order of determinate being.

If this means that the uncaused Cause has to be understood as something *beyond* this order, *jenseits*—a word Hegel abhors when it comes to positing something beyond reason—then so be it. Reason itself requires that we do so. We have to talk about an uncaused Cause, which is not in the immanent order where causes are still caused. But *beyond* is not precisely the right word for what we mean when we speak of this uncaused Cause as totally transcendent. *Beyond* expresses a spatial metaphor. It suggests a space or a series of things and then something more, beyond or in addition to that, but still as an extension of the series. It remains caught in the movement of what Hegel speaks of as the bad infinite.

This is why we prefer the term *transcendent,* which is not so obviously spatial. But it must be understood as *total* transcendence when it comes to the uncaused Cause, something that Hegel does not seem to admit, since for him everything seems to be contained within a totality in which there is transcending but no reference to a totally *Transcendent.* How are we to understand this total transcendence with regard to the immanent order of determinate being?

The physicalist is hard put to understand it at all, because for him anything transcendent has to be taken in purely spatial or, at most, spatiotemporal terms. According to this view, the term "'beyond' expresses a spatial metaphor, or perhaps spatio-temporal" (Post 154). With reference to the universe, understood in purely physical terms, this means there can be nothing beyond the universe, because "by definition it is the spatio-temporal-sum or supremum of everything" (Ibid.). If there were something beyond what we take to be the universe, it would have to be something physical, for the physicalist, and it would have to be included in what we understand by the *universe.* We may be able to distinguish between the manifest universe and the universe as it presents itself in today's physics and the further universe there might be, which may present itself in tomorrow's physics, since physics is itself in a constant process of revision. But for the physicalist, the beyond of this revision can never yield anything more than a physical understanding when it comes to the universe. There can be no beyond the universe because every being always has to be understood as something physical and therefore literally as a part of the universe, manifest or yet to become manifest in physics.

In a nonreductive physicalism, there is some attempt to recognize other "faces of existence" than the purely physical, but this recognition of other faces never seems to affect the physicalist conception of the universe as such. The universe as a whole continues to be viewed only in physical terms. When, however, we recognize higher levels of being than the purely physical as part of the universe, we come to another understanding of transcendence and of something *beyond* the purely physical that is still within the universe.

Life is such a level of being, which cannot be defined in purely physical terms, even though it does have physical dimensions. It is not situated anywhere outside the manifest physical universe, as another physical entity we have yet to discover in physics might be, but it does *transcend* the purely physical from within the physical, no matter how physics may try to account for it in purely physical terms. It represents for Hegel the first instance of a truly infinite movement in contradistinction to mere force as the object of understanding (*PhG* 124–26/98–101).

The same may be said of reason itself, or spirit, in relation to mere life. It too transcends the merely vital, though from within the vital, even though vitalism may try to account for it in purely vitalistic terms. In each case we have an instance of transcendence, or a moving beyond, which is not spatially located outside what we take to be the physical universe, but which is nevertheless a difference or a higher kind of being that cannot be expressed in purely physical terms. And in each case we have an instance of something that is infinite and higher in being in comparison to what comes before it, as the champion is higher than any particular game or the artist than any particular work of art.

It is this understanding of the movement of transcendence in being from one degree to another that we must bring with us when we come to interpret the transcendence of the Summit of being, especially as this movement appears in the human being transcending every other kind of being in nature or in the *Lebenswelt*. It is the understanding that comes with the understanding of the champion, who transcends any particular shot taken. It is the understanding that comes with the artist, who transcends any particular work produced. Politically, it is the understanding that comes with the citizen, who transcends the part one plays in society as one who is free and spiritually equal to the whole. But when, at the end of metaphysics, we come to the absolute Summit of being, we must take this understanding of transcendence one step further to a complete reversal of perspective in relation to every determinate being we know, including human being and the universe as a whole. We must understand the Summit not only as transcendent to the order of lower beings, but as absolutely transcendent in itself, so that it is relative to nothing other than itself, and so that all other things, precisely as being, are relative to it.

At this point we come to an end of what is understood under what we spoke of as *ens commune,* or being in its commonality, in the beginning of metaphysics. Within this commonality we came to understand not only differences of being, but also a certain order of transcendence among the different kinds of being, in accordance with the analogy of being. With the affirmation of a totally transcendent universal Cause of being as we know it within the immanent order of the universe, we come to a certain limit in this commonality of being. On the one hand, we go beyond this limit in affirming that such a cause *is,* thus reaching beyond the limit, so to speak, to include it within the commonality of what we say *is.* Yet on the other hand, in saying that we cannot know *what* such a being *is,* we deny that there is anything *what*soever in common between the kind of determinate being we know and the Cause of all such determinate being, including the entire universe of determinate beings, unmanifest as well as manifest.

With the Summit of being as we have come to understand it, the analogy of being opens up into a positive infinity that is no longer proportionate to any finite being we know or, to speak more exactly, with which no finite being can be proportionate. With this analogy, we may still be able to spell out some names for this totally transcendent being, as Aquinas does in his *Summa Theologiae* (*ST* I, 13), but such names will always be predicated by way of double negation, that is, by way of negation of any proportion between finite beings of any kind and the infinite Being, as the idea of the positively infinite implies. As finite implies a negation, so the positively infinite implies a negation of this negation, even if we do not have the terms for saying *what* such an affirmation refers to except in a negative way, starting only from *what* we know first in experience.

The order of transcendence we have to refer to at the *end* of metaphysics cannot be properly understood according to *what* it is, since every order of transcendence we do understand is still an order of transcendence within the universe of being we know in experience, even if we place ourselves, as intellectual or self-conscious beings, at the summit of this universe. Indeed, to speak of this absolute Transcendence as an order is still to misrepresent it, for we cannot represent such a being in any way that we represent any other being, which is to say any being attained through our experience. The absolutely Transcendent is totally other than anything we know, a Being that is not determinate nor a *this* of any particular kind, but pure Being in act or pure Act of being that is its own essence. All of these expressions make sense in a metaphysics of the *act* of being, but ponder them as we may, we cannot arrive at an adequate understanding of *what* they are about.

To express this total transcendence of the absolute Summit of being more clearly, we can only go back to our first conception of being and try to think of a being that is pure be, without any mode of concretion and composition, or a being in which there is no distinction between the *act* of being and an essence that would limit it. We can only think of it as an Act of being that is infinite in and of itself. For such an act there is no essence other than the act itself, or the essence is itself the *act* of being, without distinction or confusion. We cannot properly think *what* such a being is in itself, since everything we think of as being, we think of always as a *this, something* that *is* according to a mode of concretion and composition.

This is not to say that to think of the absolute Summit of being as pure Act of being without any distinction of essence to limit that act is a meaningless expression. For, at the *end* of metaphysics, it can be an important expression for clarifying the ontological status of everything we do know in experience, as we shall see when we come to speak of being by participation. It is only to say that, with this clarification of our own ontological status and that of the entire universe, we still do not know *what* that Summit of being is in itself.

But even if we do not know *what* it is in itself, how do we know it still as totally transcendent? This is something we must know at the *end* of metaphysics in the same way we know the necessity of affirming the existence of such an absolute Summit of being. For each way used to arrive at affirming the existence of such a Being is also a way of elaborating a language for speaking about this Being, whether as pure unmoved Act of being at the summit of being, as absolutely necessary Being whose essence is to exist, as the Highest or the Summit of being who cannot be numbered among the determinate beings whose degree of being or finitude is measured in relation to the infinity of the Summit, or as the supreme Intelligence that totally transcends the order it produces in the world.

CHAPTER 19

Transcendence and Immanence

WITH THIS AFFIRMATION of the total transcendence of the Summit of being we come to the *end* of metaphysics understood as the science of being as being. We set out to explore not only what we mean by being but also what are its properties and causes. Through the analogy of being we came to understand how our conception of being is open to different degrees and to different causes of being in the world of movement. It is at the summit that we discovered a Being totally other than any we know in experience, the uncaused Cause of the being we do know, a Being that is not caused in any way whatsoever and so one that is totally transcendent, so much so that we hardly dare to call it a being, since for us a being is always understood as something quite determinate in our experience.

The only way we can characterize it as being is by saying that it is totally other than any determinate being we know, without thinking of this otherness as just another determination. Just as, at the *beginning* of metaphysics, we had to learn how to characterize the subject of this science of being precisely as being, without making it just another particular science among other particular sciences, like physics, biology, and economics, so also now, at the *end* of metaphysics, we must learn to characterize the Summit of being as a being, or as the Being par excellence, without making it into just another particular determinate being as distinct from other particular beings.

The difficulty here is one that Kant was not able to overcome in merely opposing the infinite to the finite, for, as Hegel showed (*WL* I, 125–40/137–50), in opposing the infinite to the finite he was only turning the infinite into something finite, something opposed to or limited by some other finite. This was only a false or a bad infinite, as Hegel called it, one that gave rise to an infinite regress in dialectic. The true or the good infinite is the one that encompasses both sides of the opposition in a higher unity, an infinite that encompasses the opposition between the finite and the infinite. For

Hegel, this true infinite is something that reason itself can encompass, since, unlike understanding *(Verstand)*, reason *(Vernunft)* is not fixed in any kind of opposition.

For reason, there is nothing beyond, as there is in a mere opposition of the understanding, because in speaking of a beyond reason is already encompassing this *beyond*, which is within reason and not beyond it. In this Hegel was quite right, for in thinking of anything as beyond something else, even if this something be the whole of what is finite, one is already thinking of two sides and of either side as caught up with its opposite through some infinite that is neither this side nor that side, neither here nor beyond, but simply all-encompassing. There is no going beyond this true infinite, since going beyond it is always still only reinventing it. Reason, in its own infinite movement, is always already beyond any attempt to set any limits beyond which it cannot go.

But is this true infinite of Hegel the totally transcendent Summit of being we speak of at the end of metaphysics? If it were, would we be justified in speaking of an *end* of metaphysics? For Hegel there is no end to metaphysics, or to the philosophy of absolute spirit, or to philosophy simply. There is always a going further, to encompass more in its infinite movement. There is no way of setting a limit, because reason is always already beyond that limit in its encompassing movement. What we have demonstrated, however, at the end of metaphysics, is the existence of, or rather the necessity of affirming, a Being that totally transcends anything reason can encompass in its grasp.

To affirm such a being as part of what has to be understood rationally is, in a way, to encompass it in the infinite movement of reason itself. The totally Transcendent is thus, in a way, immanent to the movement of a rational discourse that is prepared to go to the end of its exigencies. It is present, so to speak, as the first and final Cause in being's own disclosing of itself for the process of reasoning to discover. But even as present or immanent in this way, the Summit of being can be understood only as that which is totally transcendent, or as that which cannot be understood in any immanent fashion, not even if it be in the infinite movement of reason. For in its infinite movement reason itself is led to affirm this total transcendence of the Summit of being and to confess its own total inadequacy in speaking about *what* this being is in its essence.

This acknowledgment of inadequacy at the end of metaphysics opens the way for a certain religious dimension in what we have spoken of hitherto only in terms of a science of being as being. This science, as rational discourse about being as being, has come to the necessity of affirming something, some Being, which by its own admission reason cannot adequately encompass even in its infinite movement. It is forced, so to speak, by its own effort to account for everything or to understand everything through causes, into an attitude of pure expectation in the face of a Cause that is totally uncaused.

This uncaused Cause is the source of all there is in our experience of being, from which our investigation always has its beginning. It is distinguished from all there is in our experience, by reason itself, only as the Source of all there is. To attain this uncaused Cause in any way we must leave behind everything that we start from in our experience, everything that is caused as well as causing, something that we cannot properly do rationally, since what there is in experience is the ground for our rational affirmation that there is something else, and, in a *total reversal of perspective,* we must come to understand everything as coming from this something else. This is the moment in which science gives way to religion, or reason gives way to faith or to trust in an Other who is totally other, at the end of metaphysics.

In his effort to distinguish this movement from anything else in philosophy, especially Hegelian philosophy, Kierkegaard insists on paradox or on the absurd in this moment, as something distinct from anything that can be grasped in rational discourse. But Kierkegaard characterizes the absurd as a presence of the universal in the individual, or of the eternal in the temporal, or as a restoration of the individual and the temporal in an infinite value of being that transcends anything that can be grasped by reason in its universal validity. Without denying the importance of characterizing the immanence of the transcendent in this way, here we shall insist more on the necessity of reason itself for going along with such a characterization of the actual being we start from in our experience and we shall speak more of the mystery that lies at the heart of this actual being. This we shall do not in order to add mystery to our experience of being, but rather to open reason itself to the fullness of light that comes with the actuality of being.

In order to do this we shall look once again at the being we start from in our investigation into being as being, but now we shall examine it in the light of the *reversal of perspective* that comes with the affirmation of an uncaused Cause and an unmoved Mover as the universal Cause of all there is. In this light we shall come to understand what there is in our experience not just as actual being, but as being by *participation* in its very actuality. From this we shall be led to inquire into the source of these actual beings, not just in their coming to be, as we have already done, but in their very ontological dependence as actual beings, in what we shall speak of as *creation,* which is a coming to be or an emanation of being of a totally different kind than anything we have been able to understand in the immanent order of our universe. Finally, we shall speak of the necessity of the *supernatural,* recognizing that we can say nothing of the content of this necessity except insofar as it manifests itself in what we take to be the natural and the historical order in this world.

In all of this we shall be brief because metaphysics is at its end in this discourse about the Transcendent, or rather about how the immanent relates to the Transcendent, and it must recognize that it must give way to another kind of discourse that may speak more properly from the standpoint, so to speak, of the Transcendent itself.

19.1   Being by Participation

Naturally speaking, we take being as that which presents itself in its actuality. This is what we take to be the subject of our consideration from the beginning in metaphysics, that from which our discourse on being as being develops, and that to which our first conception of being is tied. It is with reference to actual being as it discloses itself in experience that metaphysics gets under way.

In experience, however, being discloses itself as *this* or *that,* and as being of one kind or another. In accordance with this way of disclosure for being, we argued for a real distinction of principles not only between matter and form for things that come to be, but also between essence and an *act* of being for any finite being as such. In and of itself the *act* of being has to be understood as infinite, but as it presents itself in any finite being it is limited by the essence of which it is the *act* of being. It is in this way that we come to understand that there are different degrees of being according to different kinds of essence for being or different ways of standing in being. Each standing is a limitation in being with its own *act* of being limited by this standing. At least so it is for the many and different kinds of being in which being discloses itself as an immediate presencing.

When we come to the absolute Summit of being, however, we can no longer understand being in this way. To be sure, we cannot understand *what* this Being is in itself or *what* it is according to its own necessity, but we can understand it in a negative way, by setting it apart from the way we understand the composition of finite being. As the universal and infinite Cause of all finite being we do know, it cannot be understood as a composite of essence with its *act* of being, for that would be to think of it as just a finite

being like any other from which we begin in our exploration. As the unmoved Mover and the uncaused Cause it has to be thought of as *pure Act,*
without any passive potency whatsoever, and this act can only be thought of
as pure Act of being, without limitation and without composition of any
kind.

If we continue to speak of an essence with reference to the standing of
this Summit in being, then we must speak of it as identically the very *act* of
being itself, infinite and not in composition with any essence other than its
own self as pure act, the pure Act of being, which is unique in relation to
any finite being as the very Summit of all being. It is the Being whose very
essence is to be by reason of its own absolute necessity to be. This necessity
is not a constraint or a limitation on its freedom, as it would be for a finite
being, but is rather identical with its freedom to be totally all that it is.
Though we cannot think of this identity except through the complexity of
some composition between essence and existence, as we do for any finite
being of experience, we have to affirm it as utterly simple in its identity,
without reference to anything outside itself, and without any composition
of any kind, whether between substance and accident, between form and
matter, or between essence and *act* of being.

In fact, we should not even think of this Being as a particular being apart
from other particular beings, let alone as gendered in any way. That too
would be to turn It into something finite. What sets It apart from particular
beings is that, as being, It is not particular, either as a *this* or *that* or as one
kind or another. The only thing to set It apart, so to speak, is that It is positively infinite. As infinite It cannot be contained in any finite being and,
more significantly, It has to be thought of as somehow containing all finite
being, though not as the universe contains all finite being, since the universe
itself is not pure Act of being but only the combination or the coming together of all finite beings. The infinite pure Act of being has to contain all finite beings as being somehow in all of them, but without being a part of
them or numbered among them. If we think of It as gendered in any way, it
is because we think of It as somehow personal, with intelligence and will as
positive infinite perfections without any real distinction between them, and
our way of signifying such a personal Being betrays the inevitable particularization of our speech as either male or female in signifying anything personal. In using the neuter to avoid this particularization of gender when referring to the infinite pure Act of being, however, we are not escaping from all
particularization in our speech. In fact, we may be getting into a worse kind
of particularization, that of merely impersonal thinghood, which is even fur-

ther removed from what we have to think of as the Highest or the Summit of being. To indicate that this particularization in our speech has to be overcome as well, we use capitals for any noun or pronoun that refers to this supreme Being in Itself by way of suggesting that It is highly or supremely personal even in its Universality.

The ultimate metaphysical task, then, with reference to the pure Act that is the Summit of being, is not so much to try to think of how It is separate from finite being in its total transcendence, but rather to think of how finite being is other than infinite Being without being outside of It. If the pure Act of being is infinite, there can be nothing outside of it. The distinction between finite and infinite must take place within the infinite, which means that finite being, from which we begin in our exploration of being as being, must be understood as somehow being within the Infinite.

In this sense the understanding of uncaused Cause as an extrinsic cause breaks down, when we understand it as pure Act of being that can only be infinite. This efficient and final cause cannot be understood as purely extrinsic to its effects, as other in the way that finite efficient and final causes are extrinsic to their effects or separate from them in the order of the universe. It can only be intrinsic to its effects, that is, even more intrinsic to these effects than these effects are to themselves. *Intimior intimo meo,* in accordance with the phrase of Augustine: more intimate to me as the primary analogate of being than I am to myself in my own standing in being, for as an effect in its own standing, the finite being has something of the pure Act of being, its own *act* of being limited by its own standing.

At this point, at the end of metaphysics, it is the Platonic notion of participation that suggests itself as the most profound way of expressing what we have taken to be the most actual kind of being from the beginning. Our inquiry has been into being understood as actual in the concrete, with human being as our primary analogate. This inquiry has led us to the affirmation of a higher being still, an absolute Summit of being that is pure Act of being. What we have taken to be actual from the beginning, we must take to be actual only by *participation* in an act, an *esse commune* that is actual in all beings by participation. This does not make the being of experience any less actual than we have taken it to be from the beginning. It only situates this actuality in its more universal and infinite context of actuality, namely, that of the infinite pure Act of being.

But if we are to speak of the being of experience as being by participation, how are we to speak of the being who is the uncaused Cause of this being? Because this Cause is totally other than any being we know in expe-

rience, we might be tempted to speak of it as nonbeing or at least leave behind all language of being in speaking of it. But this would be contrary to
the very discourse that has led us to affirm this uncaused Cause of being as
being. For, if we have properly demonstrated that there is a totally transcendent uncaused Cause of all there is in experience, it is no longer a matter of
indifference to understand this cause as either being or not being. Even if we
cannot in any way say *what* It is, we have to say *that* It is, and we can no
longer say that It is not. To say that It is is true, given our demonstration. And
to say that It is not is false. This is to speak of It in terms of being even as we
say that It is not like any finite being we know.

What enables us to speak in this way is the analogy of being itself. To be
sure, when we come to the Summit of being, this analogy comes to its limit.
The real composition of diverse finite essences with their respective acts of
being enables us to speak of many different degrees of being even as it discloses itself in our experience. At the Summit, of course, we pass beyond the
scope of this experience, but we do not leave the intelligibility of being behind. We pass into a totally other realm of intelligibility where there is still
the question of understanding *what* being is there. Though we cannot in any
way say *what* that being is, and though we may recognize that even the question "*what?*" as distinct from the question "*whether?*" may not make any sense
with regard to this Summit of being, we still have to say that It *is* in some
way that surpasses all other ways of being, which is to introduce some notion of essence in our speech about this totally transcendent Being. The
problem is to do this without reducing this infinite Being to the measure of
any finite being in our understanding, as essence has been shown to be the
measure of the *act* of being received in a finite being (section 14.4).

We have already seen how this can be done, if we take the very Act of being to be the essence of this supreme Being, so that there can be no real distinction between the two in this Being. To be sure, in our understanding
there is still a distinction between the essence and the *act* of being, since that
is the way we still conceive being starting from our experience. But for the
Being that we affirm at the end of metaphysics we deny that the distinction
can be real, unlike what it has to be for any finite being.

It is important to note, however, that this denial is the denial of a denial, a
negation of all finitude for the Being in question, setting this Being off from
all other beings as the first and only being who is pure Act. Earlier we encountered the problem of speaking of finite beings as real and distinct from
this infinite Being without being outside of It and we spoke of them as being by *participation*. Here, in relation to this expression with regard to caused

beings, we have to speak of the uncaused Cause as being or as existing by its own essence, which cannot be said of any caused being. In this way we reiterate something that we can understand as the conclusion of the way of proving the necessity of a totally transcendent Summit of being from the contingency of beings given in experience, namely, that It has to be absolutely necessary, for a being whose very essence it is to *be* cannot not be. The Being that *is* through its own essence cannot not be.

Having said this, however, we cannot forget that being by participation still has to be distinguished in reality from this Being by essence, since only the essence at the Summit of being can be the pure Act of being or the absolutely necessary Being. What distinguishes being by *participation* from Being by essence is that the being by participation can only be a part of all that the Being by essence is in itself. It is a part, however, not as only a piece or a segment of what would be called one being as a whole, nor as a finite being along with other finite beings in the universe taken as a whole, but only as having in its own finite standing what the pure Act of being has in its own infinite way. This allows for each being, the finite as well as the Infinite, to have a standing of its own in being, but without erecting a limit of separation, as if there could be something between being by participation and Being by essence. It also allows for the Infinite to be more intimate to the finite than the finite itself, though without confusion or mixture between the two, since only the pure Act of being can be infinite and the finite can only be as a composite of an *act* of being limited by its essence or its standing in being.

The point is not to keep the Transcendent separate from the immanent but to understand the Transcendent as radically constitutive of the immanent in its very being. The finite is thus understood as having its very own standing in being through its *act* of being, which is by definition and composition finite, but only in radical dependence on the pure, unparticipated, and hence infinite Act of being. This idea of participation in the *act* of being understood as *esse commune* in the universe of beings allows not only for each finite being to have a standing of its own in being according to its essence, but also for each one to be *active* in its own original way as part of nature or history in the universe.

Moreover, it allows for a wide diversity of beings according to different degrees of participation in both being and action. This is an important consideration for the understanding of being by participation, which is perhaps not entirely clear in an overly simplified Platonic understanding of participation. In such an understanding, participation is understood mainly in terms of a plurality of individuals of the same kind each participating in one and the same form, without reference to the diversity and the order of the forms themselves. This simplified understanding allows for participation in a univocal sense, so to speak, where the plurality of individuals is understood as participating in one and the same genus or category of being. But it does not allow for participation in the full analogous sense of being, which entails a wide diversity of being according to form as well as pluralities of individuals within the diverse forms.

When we think of being by participation, we must not think of being as if it were a single genus in which all beings participate equally or univocally, but rather as a rich diversity in which the highest Being discloses its richness through a diversity of forms, from the human down to the inanimate. This rich diversity of being by participation, which includes the free initiative of human beings, is important for appreciating the surpassing richness of the Being by essence, which is not a supreme genus of being but a totally transcendent pure Act of being.

19.2   Creation

This brings us to the question of how being by participation relates to Being by essence. For it is important to understand not only how the diversity of finite beings can have a standing of its own in being according to a diversity of essences that each limit their *act* of being diversely, but also how each finite being, or the totality of all finite beings, still relates to the pure infinite Act of being. This brings us back to an idea we alluded to earlier, in connection with coming to be, but which we then said could not be properly discussed until we had come to some understanding of a first universal Cause of being. This is the idea of *creation,* which has to do with the causing of being precisely as being or, more exactly, with the radical ontological dependence of all finite being on the infinite Being.

We alluded to this idea earlier in speaking of coming to be and the Parmenidean axiom that from nothing nothing comes, which could be understood as denying the idea of creation from nothing (sections 12.1–2). At the time we were dealing with the question of coming to be and we saw how a distinction had to be made between coming to be from matter as being in potency and not simply from nothing or privation. Matter is not nothing, but as being in potency it is that from which something comes to be in *act.* This is the way we saw Aristotle get around Parmenides' axiom in order to allow for coming to be and ceasing to be in being. Coming to be is not from nothing, but from matter. But we also pointed out that this way of getting around Parmenides did not have to do directly with the question of *creation from nothing,* but rather with coming to be simply from the nothingness of the composite that comes to be. *Creation from nothing* in the strict sense of the term is another question with which we were not then prepared to deal. Now finally, at the end of metaphysics, we are in a better position to deal with it.

How is the idea of creation to be understood properly as a matter of causation, not just in becoming, but in being precisely as being or as a matter of strict ontological dependence on the first universal Cause of being? In contrast to the axiom of Parmenides, we have to say that creation is somehow a coming to be *from nothing.* The universal Cause of being as being is the cause of everything in being, including the matter or the being in potency *from* which anything comes to be, though not of Itself, as Spinoza would have it, since It is uncaused. But at the same time we have to ask in what sense creation is a coming to be, if what is created is also something that comes to be and ceases to be. For Parmenides the axiom meant that there could be no coming to be, since coming to be for him would be either from nothing or from being and in either case there was a contradiction, the fundamental contradiction between being and not-being. As we saw, Aristotle introduced a third term to get around this contradiction, namely, that of being in potency, which is neither actual being nor simply nonbeing, but something positive in between, something that can become one thing or another, depending on the form that comes to be actualized in it, as we saw in section 12.1.

This is why Aristotle was led to posit three principles of becoming: two principles that are *per se* or constitutive of the being, namely, being in potency, or matter, and its actual form, and a third principle that is *per accidens,* namely, privation, insofar as matter is in potency to a form or to forms other than the one currently actualizing it. In this way he was able to both agree with the axiom of Parmenides and allow for coming to be by distinguishing between coming-to-be-from *per se* and coming-to-be-from *per accidens.* Speaking absolutely or abstractly, it is still true that from nothing nothing comes. What comes to be does not come to be *per se* from nothing nor from actual being. It comes to be *per se* from being in potency or from matter as a principle of being. On the other hand, it does come to be from nothing, or from privation, but only *per accidens,* that is, only insofar as the matter that is now actualized by this form was previously actualized in another individual by another form, which entailed the absence or the privation of its present actual form. What comes to be does not come to be from nonbeing absolutely, but rather from the nonbeing of itself—*ex nihilo sui*—as it comes to be from the potency of its matter that was at one time a potency actualized by another form.

In this sense there is something that does come from nothing, but only if we take that something to be an individual that *was not* before, something that Parmenides did not allow for in his conception of being. But the individual does not come to be *from* nothing absolutely. It comes to be *from the nonbeing of itself,* which was a privation in the potency of the matter from which the individual comes to be.

All this is said about an order of being in which there are individuals that do come to be as composites of matter and form. Would it be said, however, about an order of being in which there is no composition of matter and form, but only pure forms, or no coming to be and ceasing to be, even though there might be some composition of matter and form?

We do not have to suppose here that there is such an order of determinate beings higher than human being other than the universal uncaused Cause, the affirmation of whose existence we have demonstrated to be necessary. But if we try to think of beings such as pure forms without matter or even composites of form and matter in which the form totally exhausts the potency of its matter, so that there is no privation to make them subject to change or coming to be and ceasing to be, as Aristotle did for the heavenly bodies, we shall find that for such beings there can be no coming to be or ceasing to be, or at least no way of understanding how they can come to be or cease to be, since there would be in them no being in potency such as we find in individuals that do come to be and cease to be. In fact, such beings could not be strictly thought of as individuals of a species, since each one would be a species unto itself. Nevertheless, for such beings could there not still be a question of creation, apart from all coming to be and ceasing to be, and could we not still speak of a radical ontological dependence upon the absolutely first and universal Cause of being?

We raise this question about finite beings that would not come to be or cease to be not in order to speculate on their existence, if there are any, but rather in order to focus more clearly on the question that still remains about being as such even after the question of coming-to-be-from has been settled for individual composites of matter and form. Is there still something *from* which pure forms or incorruptible composites would *be,* even as necessary beings apart from any coming to be? If we say there is, are we not simply falling back into treating these pure forms as things that only come to be? But if we say that there is not something *from* which they come to *be,* what else is there to say, if not what is meant by *creation* in the strict metaphysical sense of a radical ontological dependence upon the universal Cause of being as being which we have to speak of as the *Source,* or the *Whence,* on which all finite beings depend, though not as the origin or as that *from* which we think of material things as coming to be.

It is impossible for us to represent or to understand *creation* except as a coming to be, given our way of understand being from things that come to be and cease to be. This is why we have to think of it as a coming to be from nothing in some sense, something that can already be said of any individual that comes to be as coming to be from the nothing of itself—*ex nihilo sui.* But to speak less improperly of *creation* in the radical ontological sense we must go one step further and speak of a coming to be of an individual not just from the nothing of itself, but also from the nothing of any subject of change—*ex nihilo sui et subjecti.* When something comes to be simply from the nothing of itself, it is still coming to be *per se* from a subject of change or from the potency of some matter. To think of something properly as *created* in being we have to think of it as *not* from any subject of change whatever, or rather we must think of the *subject* itself or being in potency as itself created along with its form as part of the composite that comes to be (see *ST* I, 42, 2). In the creation of being there is nothing presupposed except the act of the Creator itself as absolute Source, the act that has to be presupposed for any finite being as a composite of essence and its *act* of being, even where there is no coming to be or ceasing to be but only the necessary being of a pure determinate form without matter.

At this point it should become clear that we are no longer talking about "coming to be" in the ordinary sense or in any immediate sense of the term. To speak of "coming to be" without a *subject* of change is no longer to speak of a change as we understand it in becoming. In fact, *creation* can be thought of without reference to any thought of coming to be or of what we can speak of as contingency or the potency to not be as well as to be, but only with reference to the absolute necessity of a totally transcendent Summit of being. A finite being, even if it is *necessary* by reason of its determinate form or essence, so that it has no contingency to not being, is still a created being. There is *creation* not only of things that come to be and cease to be, but also of any being, no matter how necessary or eternal it may be in its essence, if it is a finite or determinate being.

In other words, to be created does not depend strictly on coming to be. It is not a matter of contingency in the sense of a potency to not be as well as to be. It is rather a matter of a strict ontological dependence on the first uni-

versal Cause of being for any being other than this uncaused Cause, whether
necessary or contingent in its own ontological constitution.

Thus, in saying that *creation* is a coming to be from the nothing of itself
and *of any subject of change,* we are still not going against the rationale of Parmenides' axiom. In appealing to a subject as being in potency to get around
the contradiction expressed in the axiom, Aristotle was speaking only of being in process or of coming to be. He was not speaking of *creation* as we are
trying to speak of it here. In speaking of *creation* here we mean a dependence
in being such that what is thought of as being, whether it is thought of as
contingent, that is, as subject to coming to be and ceasing to be, as most beings that disclose themselves in our experience appear to do, or whether it is
thought of as necessary, as perhaps some other kinds of beings such as pure
or separate forms might be, has to be thought of in either case as depending
ontologically in its very being from the first uncaused Cause.

It is important to keep in mind that we can say this not from the standpoint of the Creator, which, whatever It may be, simply surpasses our understanding, but only from the standpoint of what is caused, where being discloses itself. In this disclosure it is understood not only as finite but also as a
composite of *what* it is and its *act* of being. And it is in this composition that
it is understood as ontologically dependent on an infinite Act that is the
Summit of all being, as we have shown in section 14.4. Through this composition of its essence with its *act* of being, in which the essence limits as it receives its *act* of being, the created being is distinguished as a being both from
the infinite Act of being and from every other finite being that is similarly
composed according to its own essence and similarly dependent on the one
infinite Act of being at the summit, in relation to which all finite beings in
their diversity are understood as being radically or ontologically dependent.

In thinking of the *act* of being of any finite essence as received, we might
also think of it as given by the Creator. For, as Aquinas says, creation terminates in the *esse* or the *act* of being of creatures. But this does not give us any
purchase on the act of creation itself as it flows from the Creator. It is said
only from the standpoint of an act as received, that is, as limited by its
essence, an essence that cannot be understood as given or even as concretely
possible without its *act* of being.

The thought of merely possible essences or merely possible worlds does
not properly enter the thought of *creation* as a radical ontological dependence. To be sure, if we think of the Creator as acting through intelligence
and will, as we must, we might entertain the thought that It might have *cre-*

ated other essences and other worlds. But that is already an unjustifiable transgression beyond the metaphysical thought of *creation*. It presupposes that we can adopt the viewpoint of the Creator in creating, as we sometimes adopt the viewpoint of an artist in producing his work of art. But, as Aquinas also says (*Pot* 3, 14, ad 6), creation in the strict sense of the term is an art to which we have no direct access. Our only access to it is in the term or in the result of the art or of the act, namely, in the universe of beings in act from which we begin in our metaphysical reflection on being as being.

In a metaphysics of being as given in the concrete, even with the thought of *creation,* there can be no proper thought of "possible worlds" or "the best possible world," since such a "thought" is not only purely abstract, and hence removed from being in *act,* but also presupposes that we can rise to the standpoint of the Creator. As we have argued, this is something we simply cannot do. We cannot penetrate into the thought of the One who is about to create the world, as Hegel claims at the beginning of his *Logic* or as Leibniz presupposes in arguing that the most perfect being had to produce "the best possible world." If we reflect upon it carefully, the very idea of a "most perfect world" does not make any metaphysical sense, for it presupposes some kind of necessary proportion between what can only be something finite, any created world, and an infinite Act, whereas the difference, if we can call it that, between the Infinite act and anything finite can only be infinite.

For a metaphysics of the concrete, there is ultimately only the thought of the actual world, which is the best there is in our experience and which gives us the best, if not the only, access to the thought of *creation* as radical ontological dependence on the Creator. We know *creation* only from what is actually created, and not from what might have been from the standpoint of our finite understanding or even our infinite reason, which is still tied to our understanding of *what* is given or *what* discloses itself as being in experience.

To clarify this metaphysical understanding of *creation* further, two more questions should be asked, one concerning prime matter or being in potency as such, the other concerning the freedom or necessity of creation itself as an act of the Creator. Concerning matter as being in potency, we must keep in mind that it does not come to be or cease to be in the strict sense, though it is the principle of coming to be. What comes to be or ceases to be properly is the individual composite of form and matter. And it comes to be from matter that previously was only in potency to the form under which it comes to be or the form of this individual that has come to be. Indeed, in the matter of this individual there remains some potency to other forms as well, so that it too can or will eventually cease to be. Can it be said that prime matter so understood, or mere being in potency, which is not nothing, is itself created even though it does not strictly come to be or cease to be and appears to be perpetual as being in potency?

This is not to ask whether pure being in potency can be created apart from being in *act*. That would make no sense, since being in potency is understood concretely as being only in its composition with some act. In distinguishing prime matter from substantial form in material substance, we did not say that it could exist by itself any more than we said it could come to be or cease to be as such. Prime matter "exists" or is only as a constitutive principle, along with its form, of an individual that has come to be, the individual whose essence is not only a composite of form and matter but is also in composition with its *act* of being. To ask whether pure being in potency is created is to ask whether pure being in potency, or prime matter, as distinct from form in an individual essence, still comes under *creation,* or is it something that is presupposed by creation as it is by the demiurge in Plato's *Timaeus?*

This question brings us back to the classical expression for *creation* that we saw earlier in terms of coming to be from nothing. The expression states quite precisely that *creation* is the production of something in being from the nothingness of itself and of any subject of change whatsoever. We can understand how an individual comes into being through the agency of an art or through the agency of another being of the same kind in nature. But this kind of production always presupposes some matter or some being in potency. When we say that creation is the production in being of something from the nothingness of any subject whatsoever, we are transcending this kind of production. We are speaking of a production that has to include the very potency or matter *from* which what is created is also coming to be, if the thing produced is a being that comes to be and ceases to be. We are talking about the production of any finite being, even where there is no contingency to not being as well as being but only necessity that attaches to a determinate form as such.

The relation of creation or radical ontological dependence does not merely transcend the relation of coming to be abstractly. It also includes it. This can be understood not from the standpoint of the Creator, which remains inaccessible to us even here, but from the standpoint of the ontological constitution of the created being. *Creation,* as we saw, terminates in the *act* of being of a creature. This act, however, is not some abstract act that would be infinite by itself. As received in *what* is or is created, for here we must understand being simply as being created, the *act* of being is limited by its essence.

If the essence, or the form, is further limited by being received in a subject that is principle of individuation as well as principle of becoming, as we argued with regard to beings that come to be and cease to be, then the *act* of being of such a being is further limited to such individuation and becoming. In being thus received, however, the *act* of being does not presuppose matter as the principle of individuation and becoming without having been created, since nothing *is* actually except by its *act* of being. The *act* of being simply includes being-in-process as part of the essence that receives it and that it actualizes. Being in potency is not anything by itself, but only in composition with something that actualizes it. What is actually is being and, if actual being is in process, the process itself as essential to *what* is comes under being and hence under the act of *creation*. In actualizing a form that requires matter for its proper individuation, the *act* of being is at the same time actualizing the matter in process.

There is nothing in the universe of determinate beings that does not come under *creation* or this radical ontological dependence in being. This follows from the understanding that the order of being encompasses the order of becoming, whereas the order of becoming cannot encompass the order of being, even if every being that discloses itself in experience is in becoming.

To try to think of this radical relation of ontological dependence as distinct from the relation of any dependence on prime matter or on an efficient cause in the immanent order of the universe can be very confusing. To do so we must distinguish the order of being clearly from the order of becoming, even if everything in the universe is understood as being in a process of becoming. Such a process cannot be understood without some understanding of prime matter or being in potency as principle of becoming. But this does not account for the *act* of being of the individual essence that has come to be. It only accounts for the coming to be of *what* this act actualizes in being.

What there is in the end, or even in its coming to be, is still the *actuality* of the being in process or at the end of its process. This actuality is distinct from the essence in process and it encompasses the essence in process in its own act. In the concrete order of being with other determinate beings, at least some are in process, while others may not be, even though they are finite. Finitude in being does not necessarily imply process in the strict sense of coming to be and ceasing to be. If we think of a finite being apart from any coming to be or ceasing to be, we still have to think of this being as ontologically dependent on the pure infinite Act of being.

Though a consideration of finite being apart from any coming to be or ceasing to be may be altogether too abstract for us, it does have the advantage of helping us focus on the relation of *creation* as radical ontological dependence in being without having to include the other relation of coming to be and ceasing to be. Needless to say, such finite beings would have to be thought of as somehow incorruptible or eternal, since they include no principle of coming to be or ceasing to be in their constitution, but as finite and composite they would still have to be thought of as created or ontologically dependent on the pure infinite Act of being at the Summit of being.

Concerning the question of freedom or necessity of creation itself as an act of the Creator, we must also say that there can be no necessity, on the part of the Creator, to create at all or to create one thing rather than another or one universe rather than another. Such a necessity would presuppose either an imperfection on the part of the first, absolutely infinite Act or some kind of necessary connection between some finite being and the infinite Act of being, both conditions which cannot be justified rationally with reference to the Creator who is *Being by essence.*

Be itself is the ultimate perfection that contains all other perfections. The *act* of being, as we saw in section 14.2, is the perfection of perfections in actuality. The absolutely infinite and pure Act of being, who is Being by essence, can only be thought of as absolutely perfect in Itself, even though we cannot fathom *what* It is in Itself. In other words, the pure Act of being, in Its infinite perfection, cannot need anything apart from Itself, unlike even the most perfect finite being we might think of, who can still be wanting of something by reason of its limiting composition of an *act* with some potency and who, precisely as finite, is also limited by the presence of other finite beings. It is not *what* any other finite being is, which is no less lacking some perfection. The pure Act of being is not lacking in any perfection, so that it would not have to perfect itself by creating, as Hegel's World Spirit has to perfect itself through history or Whitehead's highest actuality has to perfect itself through a process.

Nor can any finite being have any necessary binding relation on the Creator, for in its finitude it can never do anything more than fall short of the infinite Act of being which is by its own essence. Not only is the finite being not necessary for what is the radical Source of its being. It is also not sufficient in any way to return to that Source. It falls short of the true Infinite in both directions, so to speak, either as coming from or as returning to, even though we have to think of it as both coming from and returning to the Infinite, since everything that comes to be, whether from the potency of some subject or from nothing, has an inclination to return to its Source or to somehow become like It, as the infant, that is, one who cannot yet speak, has an inclination to become an adult, that is, one who can reproduce its own word as well as another of its own kind.

If there is any necessity in creation, it can only be on the part of the creature, which depends ontologically on the totally free act of the Creator in its very being. Such necessity, however, does not in any way determine the absolutely prior act of creation. It results from this act and it follows upon the form that is created. It presupposes a certain intention or a certain will to create, not just generally, but to create *this* being in *this* world, which is created with its perfection and imperfection still to be perfected through the interaction of its parts. It is a necessity that follows from this supposition *(necessitas ex suppositione)* and that it is for us to discover through our critical reflection on being as it is given to us in experience.

Free on the part of the Creator, creation entails necessity on the part of the creature that is determined as either one kind of being or another and as this individual or that. It is in relation to these determinate beings that we come to understand what necessity there is in creation understood as being in the concrete. It is from this creation, where being discloses itself as determinate, that we come to understand even the principles of reason itself, including the most fundamental principle from which necessity flows to all other principles, namely, that we cannot both affirm and deny the same thing simultaneously, for in understanding one finite or determinate being we understand that it cannot at the same time be another finite or determinate being (*Ver* 5, 2, ad 7). It is from this initial division among finite or created beings that our inquiry into being as being begins.

Thus, the more we think about creation, the more we come to understand that we cannot understand it from the standpoint of the act itself of the Creator. Rational metaphysical discourse on being as being leads us *to* It from the standpoint of finite and therefore created being, but It cannot lead us *into* It. Whatever we can say about it is from the standpoint of the gifted and never from the standpoint of the Giver. In saying, however, that creation is a free act on the part of the Creator, we are implying that it is somehow an act of intelligence and will. We cannot fathom the wisdom from which this act follows. The wisdom *whence* flows the universe of being we know in experience remains hidden from us in itself. We can only understand what is disclosed of It in what is effected by It or by what flows from It.

Nor can we enter into what we have to think of as the deliberation that must have gone into this act, for that too would be to presuppose that we are fathoming the absolutely transcendent wisdom of the Creator. Hence, even in saying that the Creator chose this universe rather than another, we cannot enter into what reasons It might have had for this choice. We only know the reasons that appear in the universe concretely, namely, the beings actually created. Nor can we argue that the perfectly wise and good Creator must have chosen the best possible world, since there can be no such thing as "the best possible world" from the standpoint of an absolutely first and pure Act of being that is being by its own essence, where other beings are only by participation, that is, by reason of some limitation and imperfection. We can only say that the Creator creates out of a totally gratuitous love for what is created, so gratuitous that before creation there is nothing there to love and after creation or rather through creation there is the call back to its Source as to its End.

19.3   The True Mystery of Being

It is not contrary to reason to speak of mystery in being. In fact, it is necessary to speak of mystery when we come to the end of reason's power to investigate. Many have spoken of the mystery of being and the mystery of the universe, including physicalists who deny any necessity to affirm a Creator (Post 128–31) or humanists who find human being and the universe self-sufficient (Munitz 1965). But they have spoken of mystery only as pertaining to the universe or to existence as a whole, as if reason did not have access to the intelligibility of these ultimate dimensions of being as it presents itself in experience. We have argued that, even in these ultimate dimensions, being is not strictly mysterious, inasmuch as reason still has access to this totality of being. But there is still good reason for speaking of mystery in being, on the condition that we locate the mystery, so to speak, where it belongs, in the Creator rather than in what is created.

To speak of mystery in a properly metaphysical sense, it is not enough to speak of where our knowledge ends or where our ignorance continues in any particular sphere of being. Such a divide may be found in any particular science and it does not denote any mystery in the metaphysical sense of the term. It denotes more a sense of wonder peculiar to a particular science that gives rise to further rational inquiry into the subject of that science. And though there is wonder about what the answer to our questions might be, there is no anticipation that these answers will surpass our capacity to understand.

Not so with the true sense of mystery that comes at the end of metaphysics. To be sure, there is still a certain line of demarcation between what we have understood of being and what we have yet to understand. But the two sides of the line are no longer proportionate to one another. It is no longer a *beyond* in which "the other side" is still somehow like "this side." In fact, it is not another side at all, since that would only make it another finite side opposed to this finite side. In this we must agree with Hegel when he argues that the true infinite is not beyond reason in its infinite movement. We cannot agree with him, however, when he claims to take hold of this infinite in absolute knowing or in the *Science of Logic.* Far from understanding being "prior to creation," as Hegel claims, this logic is still only a logic of finite being locked in a dialectic of opposition wherein the true Infinite or the pure Act of being cannot be absorbed.

Hegel's *Logic* begins with an opposition between pure be *(das reine Sein)* and pure not-be *(das reine nicht-Sein),* which are then understood as the same. Try as it will, reason in this logic never gets beyond this basic opposition of the principle of contradiction which, as we have just shown with regard to the fundamental opposition between affirmation and negation, presupposes *creation.* It only sinks immediately into becoming and into the opposition between determinate beings, where the logic of the infinite is understood only in relation to the opposition or the determinacy among finite beings (*WL* I, Bk I, sect. I, ch. 2). It never rises above this opposition, except in an Idea that in the end is still understood only in relation to this opposition, just as absolute knowing is understood as only relative to the phenomenological movement through which it arises. Far from resolving or dissolving the mystery of the Creator, Hegel's *Logic* only leaves us gaping into it at the summit where *being by participation,* in which opposition is first found, hangs from *Being by essence,* where there is no real distinction and no opposition of any kind, not even that between being and not being.

This follows from our understanding of the necessity to affirm a totally transcendent universal first Cause of being as being and the idea of *creation* that follows from it, since in coming to this affirmation we come to understand that we cannot possibly understand what we have yet to understand in affirming a Creator. What we understand properly of being is still only *what* is given to us to understand in experience and not *what* the Giver is of this gift. This is clear from what we have said about *creation* in the strict metaphysical sense of a radically ontological dependence in being. What there is on the other side of this affirmation, so to speak, is something that we not only do not understand but that we also cannot possibly understand, no matter how far into the infinite our reason might reach. In this way we come to understand that the science of being as being has ultimately to resolve itself into a mystery, the mystery of the Creator Itself, Who is affirmed to be in its act of creating and not just in the infinite rationality of any finite being, which is understood only as ontologically dependent in its very being on this infinite pure Act of being.

With this understanding of creation as a radically ontological dependence on a Creator whose essence we cannot encompass in our reason, we come also to a better understanding of the way in which the science of being as being, or ontology, can resolve itself into a theology, if we take our idea of the Creator to refer to what is also referred to as God *(theos)* in religion. We have argued against calling this science a theology from the beginning, since the subject of its investigation is not God but being as being or being as given in experience. As we now understand it better than we could at the beginning, this being is created being and can only be created being, even though at the end of our inquiry we come to the necessity of affirming a totally transcendent uncreated Being as the mysterious Source of this being. To be sure, this final affirmation has some theological ramifications, insofar as it refers to the same Being as what religion refers to as God. But this reference does not change our ontology into any sort of positive theology, which would presuppose that we somehow know *what* the Creator is in Itself.

Aristotle did allow for this name of theology for the science whose subject he thought had to be determined in terms of being precisely as being. This is something he could do more readily than we can, since for him anything above nature here below was somehow divine, including the heavenly bodies *(Metaph* 1026a 17–18). For us, however, who have come to a more clear idea of creation and the Creator, this overlapping of terms cannot be accepted so readily, when we focus properly on what is the subject of our science and what would be the subject of theology as a science, in the strict sense of a rational investigation. Strictly speaking, the subject of theology, or of a science of God, would have to be God as God or as Creator. This would presuppose that we can know *what* God is as we know *what* finite being is in our experience. But as we have shown with regard to the Creator as the infinite pure Act of being, we cannot know *what* God is in any way, at least not in the way we come to know *what* beings are in our experience.

If there were to be a science of God in the strict sense of the term, it would have to presuppose a knowledge of God that is totally other than anything we can have in metaphysics or philosophy, a knowledge in which God as God would be the subject of consideration and in which there would still be room for rational investigation. In other words, this would be a theology based on divine revelation to human beings, where God, who is the only one to know *what* It is in Itself or in all that It does, reveals something of Itself to a being who still has to investigate, by rational means, what is meant in the revelation. This is the way Aquinas, for example, understands his enterprise of theology as distinct from philosophy or from the science of being as being, which somehow refers to everything even though it cannot understand *what* God is as God (*ST* I, 1, 1, ad 1; Blanchette 1976). Quite remarkably, this theology can still use philosophy in its reasoning on what is revealed, as Aquinas does extensively, to make what is revealed more manifest in human knowing (*ST* I, 1, 4, ad 2). But it does not transform philosophy into theology, given the radical, not to say infinite, difference between the subjects of the two sciences that philosophy itself, as well as theology, has to affirm. Philosophy remains only an ontology, and not a theology, even though at its summit it is open to some theology and can be used in an investigative theology such as that of Aquinas based on Articles of Faith.

But does this openness of ontology at its summit to theology allow us to speak of it as an onto-theology in the modern sense of the term, that is, as Heidegger uses it with reference to Kant and Hegel? It is Kant who first uses the term onto-theology with reference to what he calls physicotheological proofs for the existence of God (*KrV* A632; B660). While denying the validity of such proofs, he still thinks they can be of some use in determining *what* God is as God, once the existence of God can be proved on other grounds or at least postulated on the grounds that such an Idea is necessary from the standpoint of pure practical reason. Thus, in spite of his agnosticism with regard to God in the realm of pure speculative reason, both as to *whether* God is and as to *what* God is, Kant still reasons as if some determination of *what* God is as God can be arrived at on the basis of what we know about being as given in experience. This is the idea of an ontotheology, which Hegel is more than willing to take over, not only to reinstate the ontological argument by turning the idea around into one of theo-ontology, but also by proceeding as if everything, spirit as well as nature, could be derived from his *Science of Logic,* bypassing the entire question of the total transcendence of the Creator in relation to the totality of creation or of finite beings.

If this is what is meant by modern onto-theology, then clearly the ontology that we have reconstructed is not an onto-theology, since it is contrary to what we have had to say about the impossibility of our knowing *what* God is in Itself from where we stand at the end of this science. Heidegger was quite right in rejecting this modern ontology as irrelevant to the question of be or being, but he was not right in thinking that all ontology or metaphysics is reducible to such onto-theology. In this he was still too sub-servient to the rationalist supposition of Kant's own approach to the ques-tion of being as expressed in the idea of an onto-theology. Such an idea has to be rejected at the *end* of metaphysics as well as at the *beginning.*

It is not just that human being is the clearing in which being discloses it-self. What discloses itself is the being that we understand according to *what* it is in its own standing or essence. In raising the question of being as being, as mysterious as this may seem to any of the particular sciences, we do not en-ter immediately into the mystery of being, as the Heideggerian deconstruc-tion of finite being would perhaps have us think. We enter rather into what can be understood of finite being, its properties, and its causes. It is the anal-ogy of being itself that opens the way for this understanding, the way we have tried to follow it in this rational discourse on being as being. To the ex-tent that we have come to some understanding of being as being according to its principles and causes, we have penetrated what appears as mystery from the standpoint of particular sciences and what is for Heidegger the true question of being, the question of be as be (*Sein als Sein*) which is pre-supposed but left unasked in what Heidegger thinks of as the question of being as being (*Seiende als Seiende*).

But in raising the question of a totally transcendent Summit of being and in affirming the necessity of such a Being, we have indicated or signified more truly where the mystery of being lies most properly, in that which re-mains unasked *(im Fraglosen),* even in the question of finite be as be. We have come to the necessity of a question that must be asked at the end of meta-physics, namely, *what* is this totally transcendent Being in Itself, but which cannot be answered from the standpoint of metaphysics, since from this standpoint we can only express being according to a mode of composition while recognizing that the totally transcendent Being cannot be a composite of any kind. At the end of metaphysics we can only encounter the impene-trable mystery of being as such, which is the Source of being as being pre-cisely in its actuality, but we cannot enter into it. This is where the analogy of being leads us and where it ultimately leaves us, in the recognition and the necessary affirmation of a Being that is totally transcendent in relation to any being that discloses itself in experience.

But if metaphysics ends with this affirmation of a Being that cannot be known according to what It is, is there not some sense in which ontology does ultimately resolve itself into a theology? Yes, but if not a positive theol-ogy or any sort of onto-theology, what kind of theology? Given what we have said of the impossibility of our knowing *what* the totally transcendent

Being is in Itself, it can only be a negative theology, a *via negativa,* which tries to say *not what* God is or *how* God is, but rather *what* God is *not* or *how* God is *not,* as Aquinas puts it (*ST* I, 3). This is no mean theology, when it is informed by all that we know of finite being and, through it, of the *act* of being. It is, for example, the theology that Aquinas develops at some length when he tries to speak of the attributes of God, such as God's simplicity, perfection, goodness, infinity, immutability, eternity, or unity, starting always from what we know about composite, imperfect, finite, mutable, temporal, and multiple being. This negative theology opens us to a broader under- standing of *what* we are as finite beings, creatures of God, but it also leaves untouched the essence of God as God or of the uncaused Cause, which is the ultimate mystery of being.

The mystery, it should be carefully noted, is not impenetrable because it is too dark, but rather because there is too much light in it for us to see clearly in the clearing where being discloses itself. Plato and Aristotle both spoke of how the brilliance of the divine origin of being strikes our intelli- gence as the bright light of day strikes the eyes of bats (*Soph* 254 A–B & *Metaph* 993b 7–11). It is we who remain in the dark with regard to *what* this first Cause of being is in Itself, even though the slight glimpse we have that it is is the highest beacon of light we have from being. This beacon is the mystery in which the light of being bathes and basks. And it is in the light of finite being that we come to God as a Light that is beyond all light for us. In order to say less improperly in what this mysterious Light consists we must leave the positive way of analogy, going from effect to cause, and recognize that we are entering into a depth of being that we cannot fathom but that must be expressed as a negation of all negation.

In this way metaphysics can open the way for a certain negative theology in which what is said makes no pretense of expressing *what* the Creator is, knows, or even wills, except as it is made manifest in actually created being. But this theology has no positive content other than that expressed in the affirmation that there is a Creator. It must not stand in the way of entering into the mystery of creation itself or of whatever else the Creator might will. This is rather a way that must be opened up systematically and hence necessarily at the end of metaphysics to whatever comes from the Giver of being and of ultimate meaning in being, a way that cannot be opened up unless we affirm the necessity of this totally transcendent *Being.*

Here we come up against what is perhaps the final objection to meta- physics in the name of some negative theology, where it is claimed that we must learn to speak about God without being (Marion 1991), because supposedly metaphysics leaves us only with an idol and not with the true God. An idol, according to this view, is something that closes off vision or understanding and keeps it from going beyond itself, unlike an icon, which opens a way beyond itself (Marion 7–24). But this view of metaphysics is based on an inadequate view of the science of being as being, the modern essentialist view of being which has come to an end in Nietzsche and Heidegger with proclamations of the death of God and nihilism.

Without trying to defend this inadequate view of metaphysics, which has been rightly deconstructed, we must defend or reconstruct a less inadequate view that is necessary for understanding any theology or discourse about God. It is not enough to reject the idolatry that may follow from the modern essentialist conception of being. It is also important to reject the atheism that is sometimes thought to follow from this rejection of idolatry or superstition, because otherwise we are left without any way of speaking positively about God as *Being* and not nothing. This is important for the truth of religion itself as well as for the truth of metaphysics.

There is no need to go back over the various ways in which the argument for the necessity of a totally transcendent Summit of being has been made. The short way of expressing the conclusion to that argument in religious terms is to say: God *is*. It is important to note, however, that what is affirmed at the summit is not a cap that would close finite being in upon itself. That would be to idolize finite being, which is what we find not just in superstition but also in nihilism or any sort of self-sufficiency in finitude. There is superstition or idolatry on either side as long as the question of a relation to the truly infinite *Being* has not been recognized. What is affirmed at the end of metaphysics is not a barrier, but an opening into what we can only speak of as something totally Transcendent. And it is an essential part of the argument to conclude with this opening as well as with affirming that God is, for that is in the very nature of this affirmation that concludes our rational discourse on being as being.

In the end we do not merely affirm that there is something, a being like any other being we know. That could be just another composite finite being. We affirm an infinite, absolutely simple, pure Act of being. Nor do we affirm It according to our way of knowing or signifying It, which still entails some composition and finitude. For, as we saw from the beginning, we always signify being according to a mode of concretion and composition. This is true even when we speak of God as a "being."

When we affirm the necessity of a totally transcendent Summit of being, however, we do not affirm the mode of this signifying. We only affirm whatever there is that is as totally transcendent at the summit, without knowing precisely *what* that is, but knowing at least that It *is,* though not according to the mode of our signifying or the mode of any finite being we do know according to our mode of signifying. In fact, we affirm that we cannot possibly know *what* that Being is in Itself or make an idol of It, for that would be contrary to what we know in the final conclusion, which, paradoxically, cannot include *what* it concludes to.

Having said this about our way of signifying being and its total inadequacy in expressing *what* God is as God, however, we cannot then turn around and say that it makes no difference whether we say that God is or that God is not, because, as it is said, in either case we still do not know *what* we are talking about. The truth of the proposition that God is in metaphysics is still an important truth for religion. It is a way into the truth of religion. For, if we say that God is not, then there is no way into that truth. This is a matter not just of common sense, but of metaphysical and theological sense as well.

If we say that God is dead, there is nothing left to do but dispose of the corpse. If we say that there is no God, there is nothing more to be said about the matter. If we wish to say anything about God, we must begin by saying that, whatever God is in God's infinite transcendence, God *is.* In doing so we invoke not only the analogy of different degrees of being, to get to the idea of a *highest* Being, but also the principle of noncontradiction with regard to the Summit of being. Having formulated the necessity of such a Being, we cannot both affirm and deny that It is. If the affirmation is true, then the negation must be false. Nor is it enough to say that what is being affirmed or denied in a particular case is only an idol, and not God. In religion at least, and in a metaphysics of the *act* of being, we still have to say that God *is* and acknowledge the ultimate falsity of atheism.

Nor does saying that God *is* lock us into any particular conception that would be idolatrous or superstitious. What we affirm in the end is a necessity that opens directly into the transcendent and in affirming this transcendent as *Being* we do not affirm It as being in any way composite or finite or determinate. The simple affirmation that God, taken as totally transcendent Summit of being, *is,* breaks through and out of every possible limitation by a double negation that rides on the conception of being as *act.*

The *act* of being is always understood as limited when it is in composition with or received in a finite essence. In this way it is also diversified and multiplied, as we come to know it in the world of finite beings. But if we try to understand the *act* of being as pure Act apart from any composition with a finite essence, we have to understand it as unlimited, unique, and transcen-

dent at the summit of diversified being. This is not a definition that expresses *what* God is as God, or at least it is not a definition that we can properly
understand, since the only being we can properly understand is a finite being. But it is an idea that enables us to discern the difference between the
truth of the proposition that God *is* from its contradictory. Without this understanding with regard to the infinite Act of being, which is by Its own
essence, we would have no way of getting beyond the threshold of finite being into the true mystery of Being. With it we can speak truthfully about the
God who *is*. Without it we run the risk not only of falling into nihilism or
atheism, but also of turning any revelation of the divine in the world of experience, even every "icon," including the Word of God made flesh, into an
idol, which is anything but God.

19.4 The Necessity of the Supernatural

In speaking of the true mystery of being, however, we are speaking of a
truth that is no longer merely metaphysical but rather more properly religious. This entails a discourse that totally transcends that of metaphysics. We
have already referred to this religious dimension of truth in speaking of theology. Though we have come to the end of metaphysics, we cannot end it
without saying something more about this religious dimension of truth, especially in terms of its necessity at the end of metaphysics. How can we do
this without transgressing beyond the discourse open to metaphysics into a
discourse that, by its own definition as well as that of religion, metaphysics
cannot enter into?

Let us think back to the notion of theology we have already referred to as
the science that would have God as the *subject* of its consideration. We have
argued that metaphysics, by itself as the science of being as being, cannot
give rise to any kind of positive theology of this kind, since that would have
to presuppose that it can give us an account of *what* God is as God, which, as
we have also argued, metaphysics cannot do. We have also argued that there
can be no onto-theology in any strict sense of the term, much less a theo-
ontology in the Hegelian sense of the term, since that would entail a radical
misunderstanding of *creation* as a fundamental ontological dependence in finite being precisely as being and, even more so, a misunderstanding of the
pure infinite Act of being as the Source of being.

The only kind of theology that is possible at the end of metaphysics is a
negative theology, because that does not claim to say anything about *what*
God is as God but only what God is *not,* from the standpoint of created and
finite being. Can we say that such a theology is truly a discourse about God

or is it still only a discourse about the creature? Is there a natural theology, as some like to speak about it, at the end of metaphysics or is all theology ultimately supernatural, that is, discourse based on something more than a metaphysics of being, coming directly from a supernatural revelation of God?

To the extent that we insist on the need for a negative theology at the end of metaphysics, we must say that there can be some natural theology at the end of metaphysics. In fact, such a theology is important not just for metaphysics itself, but even for any kind of positive or supernatural theology based on Articles of Faith. The first thing we must know about God is, "God is." Now it is true that one may know that God *is* by revelation or by faith in the word of another. But is that really knowing as we understand knowing in metaphysics and is it knowing enough to keep us from turning *what* we know by faith into an idol? Or do we need a demonstration that God is to keep us from turning our religious discourse into superstition or idolatry? Can we affirm the total transcendence of God without a demonstration such as the one we have proposed? Is there not room, even a need, for the elaboration of some rational argument within a discourse about the supernatural revelation?

It is not enough just to affirm that God is at the *beginning* of a theology. It is also important to understand *what* it is that we are affirming, or rather what it is that we are *not* affirming, and this cannot be done without a proper demonstration, which concludes not only that God *is* positively but also that we cannot know *what* that is except in a negative way. Hence the necessity of a negative theology at the end of metaphysics that can be called natural, in that it can be demonstrated rationally, but that opens systematically into the supernatural, in that it demonstrates that *what* we are affirming cannot be known by human reasoning alone. If there is a true discourse about God other than this negative theology at the end of metaphysics, it is not one in which reason alone can discern. Yet it is one in which rational discourse can serve in the search for some understanding of what is known or affirmed only by faith in a supernatural.

This is where we can understand what is profoundly wrong or inadequate with the Hegelian claim that philosophy supersedes religion or theology. If there is a God, whose existence can only be demonstrated *a posteriori* from created being, without the possibility of understanding *what* It is in Itself, as we have argued, philosophy cannot supersede religion, much less replace theology as the highest form of knowing. At the Summit of being, philosophy or metaphysics must declare its unknowing, not because something lies beyond the infinite movement of reason, but because reason itself in its infinite movement cannot close in upon itself, much less upon the true Infinite. It falls short of what is affirmed at the end of metaphysics and it knows that it does so. It knows therefore that, if there is any content in the truth of religion, it cannot be reduced to the form of philosophy, and that if a theology can be positively articulated from the truth of this religious content, it will not be reducible to the truth of philosophy.

In other words, against the Hegelian claim of absolute knowing in the science of logic, metaphysics must insist upon a positive content of religion that enables theology to supersede philosophy when it comes to speaking about God, both in Itself and in the world. Hegel's philosophical interpretation of Christianity is thus not true to Christian religion, but a reduction of it to something created, to a purely human self-actualization. This is why it has been interpreted both as an atheism and as a philosophy of religion, though it ends up as no more than a philosophy of human spirit hypostatized as World Spirit. If God, or the divine, is understood as totally immanent to the historical movement of reason, and one wishes to insist on a conception of God as totally transcendent, then one can interpret Hegel's immanentism as a kind of atheism, albeit a post-Christian atheism (Gillis 1995). This is not, however, a true view of Christian religion, because it fails to recognize the radical transcendence of God as understood through the idea of *creation* as a radical ontological dependence in being at the Summit, not just as this transcendence is in Godself but also as God appears in history, where the Incarnation of the Creator remains even more of a mystery than the mystery of the Creator as Creator.

In the face of the totally transcendent Summit of being affirmed at the end of metaphysics, then, the situation of reason remains totally paradoxical, as Kierkegaard would say. It must affirm that something *is* and that it cannot know *what* this something is, even if God appears in history. It cannot go beyond its affirmation that God is, even though it can still *ask what* God is without knowing how to answer that question except in a negative way.

This is not just a matter of fact, but, much more importantly, a matter of necessity for reason itself. What we conclude to at the end of metaphysics is not so much the existence of God as such, for that too would be a claim to know *what* God is, since we have to say that God's existence is God's very essence. Rather it is the simple necessity to affirm that God *is.* This is a necessity of reason itself. But it is a necessity that reaches beyond the power of reason itself to understand. It is a necessity to affirm that there is something absolutely supernatural about the Creator-God that reason cannot attain or discern but that must be understood as necessary for reason itself, even though it cannot be attained, much less produced, by reason.

It is this necessity that is the most paradoxical for reason. For, on the one hand, it is affirmed most rationally, or at the summit of rationality, and yet, on the other hand, it is affirmed as radically transcendent, as a total *reversal of reason* itself with regard to the Transcendent. At the Summit of being reason turns itself around and comes to accept its own necessity as coming from the Creator. In creation there is not just the totally free act of creating. There is also the reception of a necessity to be and to act on the part of the creature, the necessity that reason discerns in the *form* of what is given in experience, with its own standing and with its own initiative in being, including the form of reason itself.

Thus in affirming the necessity of a supernatural, reason is affirming the necessity of something quite strange or foreign to reason, something that it may not be able to justify from the standpoint of reason as such but that reason might still have to accept as necessary from its own standpoint, if some higher supernatural gift is proffered gratuitously by the Creator. For just as creation itself, which is gratuitous from the side of the Creator, gives rise to a necessity in being for reason, so also a further gift from this Giver of all being that would transcend all power of reason would also give rise to a similar necessity for reason itself that it would have to either accept or reject freely.

This follows not from any understanding of *what* such a supernatural gift might be, nor even from any understanding of the very possibility of such a gift, for that would still presuppose that we have direct access to the mystery that offers such an added gift, let alone the mystery of creation itself. If we have no purchase on the art of creation as such, except as it makes itself manifest in created being, much less do we have any purchase on the art of superabundant giving over and above the universe as we know it through the natural power of reason to investigate on its own. It follows only from the necessity of a total transcendence, with all its ramifications, which we affirm at the end of metaphysics, where the power of reason itself to investigate comes to its end.

It is necessary to affirm the Creator. It is necessary to affirm that the Creator creates freely and gratuitously, since prior to creation there is nothing apart from the Creator, nothing to which God is bound except to Godself. It is necessary to affirm that what is created has whatever necessity there is in it from the Creator and that reason accepts this necessity as ultimately from the Creator. It is necessary to affirm that, if a further gift is given even more gratuitously than the initial or the initiating creation, or than what is already understood of finite being, then it too will have to be received as a necessity by reason itself. What we have in the relation of *creation* is a categorical necessity, that is, one that follows from reason's own understanding of finite beings as created. What we have in the relation of a *supernatural giving* from the Creator is a hypothetical necessity, one that depends on whether a further gift is given that reason alone cannot discern. Such a necessity regarding the supernatural gift, however, would be no less rational than the necessity reason can discern in the initial gift of nature itself.

It should be noted that this understanding of necessity is not based on any understanding of God as necessary being. God is necessary, but not necessitated by anything outside of God. God is necessitated, so to speak, only by God's own intending to create the universe with its beings, some of which we understand as necessary and some of which we understand as contingent. We can speak of God as necessitated in this way because we take the nature of things to be a manifestation of the abiding Will to create. But God is not necessitated to any other gift by this Will to create finite being as we understand it rationally. If there is more given or offered, it is by a still more gratuitous Will and an even greater manifestation of love than is found in the original and originating gift of creation. The understanding of necessity, which we say is necessary here, is based only on the understanding of creaturehood as it relates to the Creator in whatever is given, natural or supernatural.

It is this understanding of concrete necessity in being that would make it possible, even necessary, for philosophy or metaphysics to mediate in the understanding of a positive theology based on a supernatural revelation. For not only is the affirmation of a totally transcendent Summit of being necessary to keep such a revelation from collapsing into a mere idol or superstition. It is also necessary for articulating at least the negative side of this theology and for making more manifest to human knowing the truth of what has been revealed by way of what may be called an analogy of faith. The necessity we are speaking of does not in any way bridge the distance between finite being and the infinite Act of being, but it does tie the truth of philosophy, especially with regard to the Creator, to the truth of a theology based on a further revelation from the Creator than the one already accessible through created finite being as such in a way that expands the human understanding of faith, taken as a higher principle for understanding than reason alone.

Thus, part of the necessity that is affirmed at the end of metaphysics is that, if there is a revelation in being over and above what is known about being as being from the totality of finite beings, it is not to be taken in blindly or mindlessly. It must also be inquired into critically for understanding, as great theologians have always done. It is not for metaphysics, of course, to say how it is to be used in a positive theology based on revelation, since that depends more on the truth of revelation, which metaphysics cannot fathom, than on the truth of philosophy. But it is for metaphysics to say that the way to such a supernatural truth must be kept systematically open by affirming the necessity of a totally transcendent Summit of being and by exploring all the ramifications that this necessity might imply. In this way, without crossing over into the proper realm of religion, which supersedes philosophy, metaphysics might be understood as ending in what might called a religious expectation, without ceasing to be strictly a metaphysics of being as being, for such an expectation is a necessity of its very conclusion, which is neither unscientific nor a postscript, as Kierkegaard would have it, but part of its essential truth and knowing.

Reference List

Aquinas, St. Thomas. See List of Abbreviations.

Aristotle. See List of Abbreviations.

Ayer, A. J. 1952. *Language, Truth and Logic*. York: Dover. (Originally published in 1936.)

Barrow, J. D., and F. S. Tipler. 1986. *The Anthropic Cosmological Principle*. New York: Oxford University Press.

Blanchette, Oliva. 1974. "Language, the Primordial Labor of History: A Critique of Critical Social Theory in Habermas." *Critical and Social Philosophy* 1, 325–82.

———. 1976. "Philosophy and Theology in Aquinas." *Science et Esprit* 28, 23–53.

———. 1981. "The Philosophical Beginning." *Thought* 56, 251–62.

———. 1983. "The Idea of History in Karl Marx." *Studies in Soviet Thought* 26, 89–122.

———. 1991. "Are There Two Questions of Being?" *Review of Metaphysics* 45, 259–87.

———. 1992. *The Perfection of the Universe According to Aquinas: A Teleological Cosmology*. University Park: Pennsylvania State University Press.

———. 1999. "Suarez and the Latent Essentialism of Heidegger's Fundamental Ontology." *Review of Metaphysics* 53, 3–19.

Blondel, Maurice. 1893. *L'Action: Essai d'une critique de la vie et d'une science de la pratique*. Paris: Alcan; reprinted, Presses Universitaires de France, 1950. *Action (1893)*. Translated by Oliva Blanchette. South Bend, Ind.: University of Notre Dame Press, 1984.

Bunge, Mario. 1963. *Causality: The Place of the Causal Principle in Modern Science*. Cleveland, Ohio: Meridian Books.

Chroust, Anton-Herman. 1961. "The Origin of 'Metaphysics.'" *Review of Metaphysics* 4, 601–16.

Courtine, Jean-François. 1990. *Suarez et le système de la métaphysique*. Paris: Presses Universitaires de France.

Flew, Anthony. 1955. *New Essays in Philosophical Theology*. Edited by A. Flew and A. MacIntyre. New York: Macmillan.

Gibson, William. 1963. *The Miracle Worker: A Play in Three Acts*. New York: Bantam Books.

Gillis, Hugh. 1995. "Anthropology, Dialectic and Atheism in Kojève's Thought." *Graduate Philosophy Journal* 18, 85–107.

Gilson, Etienne. 1952. *Being and Some Philosophers*. Toronto: Pontifical Institute of Mediaeval Studies.

Gracia, Jorge J. E. (Ed.). 1994. *Individuation in Scholasticism: The Later Middle Ages and the Counter-Reformation, 1150–1650*. Albany: State University of New York Press.

Hegel, G. W. F. See List of Abbreviations.

Heidegger, Martin. See List of Abbreviations.

Kahn, Charles H. 1973. *The Verb "Be" in Ancient Greek*. Dordrecht, The Netherlands: Reidel.

Kant, Immanuel. See List of Abbreviations.

Lonergan, Bernard. 1958. *Insight: A Study of Human Understanding*. New York: Philosophical Library.

Marion, Jean-Luc. 1991. *God without Being.* Translated by T. A. Carlson. Chicago: University of Chicago Press.

Marx, Karl. 1906. *Capital.* New York: Modern Library.

_____. 1963. *Economic and Philosophical Manuscripts.* In *Early Writings,* pp. 61–219. Translated by T. Bottomore. New York: McGraw-Hill.

_____. 1904. "Preface" to *A Contribution to the Critique of Political Economy.* Translated by N. I. Stone. Chicago: Kerr. (Originally published in 1859.)

_____. 1967. *The German Ideology.* In *Writings of the Young Marx on Philosophy and Society,* pp. 403–73. Edited and translated by Loyd D. Easton and Kurt H. Guddat. Garden City, N.Y.: Anchor Books/Doubleday.

Merleau-Ponty, Maurice. 1945. *Phénoménologie de la perception.* Paris: Gallimard. English translation, *Phenomenology of Perception.* Translated by Colin Smith. London: Routledge, 1962.

Munitz, Milton. 1965. *The Mystery of Existence.* New York: Appleton-Century-Crofts.

Plato. See List of Abbreviations.

Portmann, Adolph. 1990a. *Essays in Philosophical Zoology: The Living Form and the Seeing Eye.* Translated by R. B. Carter. Lewiston, N.Y.: Mellen.

_____. 1990b. *A Zoologist Looks at Humankind.* Translated by Judith Shaefer. New York: Columbia University Press.

Post, John F. 1987. *The Faces of Existence: An Essay in Nonreductive Metaphysics.* Ithaca, N.Y.: Cornell University Press.

Reiner, Hans. 1954 "Die Entstehung und ursprungliche Bedeutung des Namens' Metaphysik." *Zeitschrift für philosophische Forschung* 8, 210–37.

Rosen, Stanley. 1993. *The Question of Being: A Reversal of Heidegger.* New Haven, Conn./London: Yale University Press.

Spinoza, Benedict de. See List of Abbreviations.

Schurmann, Reiner. 1987. *Heidegger on Being and Acting: From Principles to Anarchy.* Translated by C.-M. Gros. Bloomington: Indiana University Press.

Strawson, P. F. 1959. *Individuals: An Essay in Descriptive Metaphysics.* London: Routledge.

Suarez, Francisco. See List of Abbreviations.

Swartz, Norman. 1991. "Negative Theories: Qualities and Relations as Individuator." In *Beyond Experience: Metaphysical Theories and Philosophical Constraints,* pp. 284–311. Toronto: University of Toronto Press.

Sweeney, Leo. 1964. *A Metaphysics of Authentic Existentialism.* Englewood Cliffs, N.J.: Prentice-Hall.

Teilhard de Chardin, Pierre. 1959. *The Phenomenon of Man.* New York: Harper & Row.

Whitehead, Alfred N. 1929. *Process and Reality: An Essay in Cosmology.* New York: Macmillan.

Wisdom, John. 1951. *Logic and Language.* Vol. 1. Oxford, U.K.: Blackwell.

Wolff, Christian. See List of Abbreviations.

Index of Names

Analytical Index

Philosophy of Being: A Reconstructive Essay in Metaphysics was designed and composed in Bembo by Kachergis Book Design of Pittsboro, North Carolina. It was printed on 60-pound Sebago Eggshell and bound by Maple-Vail, Binghamton, New York.